546-92

READINGS
IN
LABOR ECONOMICS

Edited by

FRANCIS S. DOODY

Associate Professor of Economics
Boston University
College of Business Administration

1950

ADDISON-WESLEY PRESS, INC.

CAMBRIDGE 42, MASS.

38409

CONTENTS

MINIMUM WAGES

CAUSES OF STRIKES

EXTENT AND NATURE OF COLLECTIVE BARGAINING

INDUSTRY-WIDE BARGAINING

UNION SECURITY

PREFACE

This book is intended primarily as a supplement for collegiate courses in labor. It consists principally of outstanding articles selected from leading economic journals. The editor has not hesitated to include controversial papers, but he has excluded the more difficult articles that might well be found in a group of readings for the professional economist. The articles from economic journals have been supplemented by descriptive material from the *Monthly Labor Review* and by a few thought-provoking papers that were written originally for lay consumption. All articles are reprinted in their entirety in order to preclude misrepresentation.

As a group, the papers represent the recent tendency to emphasize "labor economics" rather than "labor problems." Also apparent here is the growing recognition of collective bargaining as a subject of special importance in the whole field of labor. The volume should prove useful in courses in labor economics, wage practices and policies, collective bargaining, and economic aspects of labor law.

The postwar years have seen the appearance of several volumes of readings in the whole area of economics. Changing educational conditions are partly responsible. Large enrollments and limited library facilities present major problems to the teacher. Obviously he cannot tell a class of fifty or a hundred students to read an article when only one or two copies of the journal are available in the library. Volumes of carefully selected articles seem to be the best solution.

Should the demand warrant, revisions of this volume are contemplated in order to keep its contents timely. The editor would appreciate suggestions concerning possible inclusions.

Advances in printing technique permit photographic reproduction of many articles from the original journals. This helps to reduce the selling price — an important consideration in supplementary texts — and also may give the student the visual "feel" of the original journal.

The editor is grateful to Professor Charles A. Myers of the Massachusetts Institute of Technology and Professor James W. Kelley of Boston University for providing him with copies of their reading lists. The final selection of materials was the editor's responsibility.

Finally, gratitude of the highest order is due to the authors and original publishers of the articles for their generous permission to reprint them. Detailed acknowledgments are made in the text.

F. S. D.

Scituate Center, Mass.
December 1949

The Theory of Labor Organization

The Theory of Union Growth, by Horace B. Davis, Quarterly Journal of Economics, Vol. LV, August, 1941, pp. 611–637.

THE THEORY OF UNION GROWTH[1]

SUMMARY

I. Conditions favorable to union growth: unions as defensive organizations, 611; the "prosperity theory," 614; union growth and price movements, 617. — Preliminary formulation of a theory of union growth, 619. — II. Booms in union growth, 620. — The influence of wars, 622. — Inertia, 623. — Employer opposition, 624. — The "welfare" approach, 625. — III. The importance of leadership, 625. — IV. The influence of industrialization, 628. — V. Conclusion: expansion of the preliminary theory of union growth, 632.

I. CONDITIONS FAVORABLE TO UNION GROWTH

A union movement requires statesmanship and attention to the lessons of the past if it is to reach the greatest possible development. Many an organization campaign has been launched with high hopes only to peter out ingloriously within a few months, because the conditions were not favorable; many a discontented working force has remained unorganized, because the leaders of the appropriate union or unions neglected to approach it for organization at the propitious time; and many a union movement has been completely superseded or smashed, because the leaders paid too little attention to underlying economic trends and were content to continue a policy which had shown results in the past. The present article aims to make a preliminary answer to the vital question: What are the conditions, economic and other, which are favorable for the expansion of unionism?

Most unions seem to have come into being originally as defensive organizations, to preserve a standard already enjoyed. The boss announces a wage cut, or a lengthening of the working day, or an increase in the working load, and after quitting time little knots of men gather to vent their anger. Then somebody suggests organization, and a local union is born. It takes some major grievance to stir the average wage earner to action that may jeopardize his job. "Fear of a fall in the standard of living has always been the strength of labor agitation. The cautious man who will take no risk to add to his wages will fight the hardest to maintain them."[2] And without the support and active coöperation

1. Research assistance by Edith R. Levine.
2. E. Welbourne, The Miners' Unions of Northumberland and Durham, Cambridge, England, 1923, p. 61.

1

of the "cautious man" no union can hope to get established on a solid basis.

Many examples can be given of union movements that originated for purposes of defense. The embryonic French unions were known as "résistances" — an appropriate name for organizations which grew with economic crises.[3] In the United States, organization among the woodworkers was caused in the decade of the 1830's by "the attempt to prevent a reduction of wages and thereby to maintain a standard of living."[4] The reductions of wages resulting from the panic of 1857 brought into being the original union of iron workers.[5] The first dramatic event in the labor history of South Africa was the strike of the miners of Kimberley in 1884. Their grievance was the indignity of being searched for stolen diamonds.[6] In countries, colonies, and districts, moreover, where the union movement is only now becoming established, the essentially defensive nature of primitive unionism continues to come out clearly. Thus in the South of the United States, it was the worsening of the conditions of the sharecroppers that led to the formation of the first Sharecroppers' Union in Alabama, in 1931;[7] the first wave of union organization to spread over the British West Indies — in 1937–38 — was set off by riots due to unemployment, in the Barbados.

Removal of the grievance frequently causes the collapse of an incipient union. Thus the first union of steamboat engineers on the Great Lakes, formed to resist a reduction of wages in 1854, was permitted to lapse some three years later, after wages had been satisfactorily adjusted.[8] The early molders' unions had their rise in special grievances and for the first twenty years of organization they were stormy-weather affairs which disappeared with

3. Paul Louis, Histoire du Mouvement Syndical en France, Paris, 1920, p. 87. The *résistances* flourished during the period 1830–48, after which the modern trade union or *syndicat* began to take shape.

4. F. S. Deibler, The Amalgamated Wood Workers International Union of America, Madison, 1912, p. 44.

5. Jesse S. Robinson, The Amalgamated Association of Iron, Steel and Tin Workers, Baltimore, 1920, p. 11.

6. E. Gitsam and J. F. Trembath, A First Account of Labour Organization in South Africa, Durban, 1926, p. 15.

7. Katharine DuPre Lumpkin, The South in Progress, New York, 1940, p. 127.

8. H. E. Hoagland, Wage Bargaining on the Vessels of the Great Lakes, Urbana, 1917, p. 32.

the sunshine of prosperous years.[9] In England the same experience was often repeated. The miners of ˙Northumberland and Durham organized originally in a depression. After 1844 times got better; but "though high wages and steady work helped to silence the complaints of the men, the feeble remnants of the union survived the prosperity."[1] Even after this union grew strong enough to have an annual agreement, or "bond," the membership used regularly to decline after the signing of the bond in April.[2]

A period of declining business brings attacks on labor's standards and may thus cause the formation of a certain number of unions. The services which an established union may render to its members in time of depression are by no means unimportant. These include maintenance of wage and working standards, furnishing information about job openings,[3] and in some countries (but not in the United States to any extent) the payment of out-of-work benefit. Even unemployed members try hard to maintain good standing in a union having such services. In other unions, however, continued membership during these periods depends on loyalty to the union movement as such, and the unskilled especially are likely to drop away in large numbers.[4] Thus the general

9. Frank T. Stockton, The International Molders Union of North America, Baltimore, 1921, p. 16.

1. Welbourne, op. cit., p. 107.

2. Ibid., p. 147. The character of unionism is often misunderstood. Professor Commons omits the defensive function of the Labor Movement altogether from the definition with which he opens his article on that subject in the Encyclopaedia of the Social Sciences. Sometimes such oversight is deliberate. Employers like to paint the picture of an "outside agitator" (the union organizer) who injects himself into the happy family and disrupts it. They leave out, of course, their own aggressions which predisposed the employees to listen to a union organizer. Union leaders have stressed in their propaganda the gains which the unions have been able to make for their members, because this appeal is more dramatic than a recital of the injustices which unionism has prevented.

Marx, on the other hand, was fully aware that trade unions originate as defensive organizations. In Value, Price and Profit he wrote: "In all the cases I have considered, and they account for ninety-nine out of one hundred, you have seen that a struggle for a rise of wages follows only in the track of previous changes, and is the necessary offspring of previous changes . . . ; in one word, as reactions of labour against the previous action of capital." — Selected Works of Karl Marx (New York, International Publishers), Vol. I, p. 331. Cf. also The Poverty of Philosophy, in Marxist Library, XXVI, p. 145; and "Manifesto of the Communist Party," Selected Works, Vol. I, p. 215.

3. The chief resource of the British unionist in his search for jobs is his trade union, says Dr. Bakke. — E. Wight Bakke, The Unemployed Man: A Social Study, London, 1933, p. 137.

4. Ibid., p. 72.

rule is that union membership declines in a period of declining business.[5]

Union movements that begin during a period of revival[6] have a better chance of success than movements that begin when business is entering a depression. Payment of union initiation fees and dues is not so serious a problem.[7] When labor is fully employed and business men have plenty of orders ahead, workers have less fear of being discriminated against for joining unions, since a man who loses his job is likely to find another one. These circumstances, of course, are important for established unions as well as for those which are just starting, and a period of improving business is usually a period of increasing union membership.

Thus it has been rather hastily assumed by many students that union growth is positively correlated with prosperity, rising when business is good and falling when business is bad. There is inadequate statistical basis for such an idea. We have been able to compare the movement of union membership with a condition of "prosperity" in 61 cases, covering four major countries (England, France, Germany and the United States) in the period since 1890. (Table I.) We find that in approximately two-thirds of the cases (68 per cent) in which the year was classified as one of prosperity there were marked rises (more than three per cent)[8] in union membership, but in nearly 25 per cent of such cases union membership declined. Business recession and depression were accompanied by falling union membership in 25 cases, but there were also no less than 14 years of "poor" business which saw sharp increases in union membership.

5. There are some exceptions to this rule which will be noted presently.

6. Such movements may also be regarded as defensive, in the sense that prices tend to rise faster than money wage rates during these periods.

7. When unions are powerful and control many jobs, new applicants for membership may join even before they have a job; they have something to gain thereby when they can establish job contacts through other union men or the rare but not unknown pro-union employer. This type of new applicant is very seldom met with when the economic power of the union is weak. Cf. E. W. Bakke, The Unemployed Worker: A Study of the Task of Making a Living Without a Job, Yale University Press, 1940, p. 213. On the psychological obstacles which unemployment offers to the continued payment of union dues, etc., see ibid., Chap. xiv, and E. W. Bakke, Citizens Without Work, Yale University Press, 1940, passim.

8. A rise in membership of less than 3 per cent is not considered significant, because the secular trend of union membership was upward in all four countries during the period covered.

TABLE I

TRADE UNION MEMBERSHIP AND BUSINESS CONDITIONS
ENGLAND, FRANCE, GERMANY, AND THE UNITED STATES SINCE 1890*

No. of Years of —	Total	Number of Years in Which —		
		Membership Rose Sharply (more than 3%)	Membership Rose Slightly (less than 3%)	Membership Fell
Total	130	72	16	42
Business Recession and Depression	49	14	10	25
Business Revival	20	16	2	2
Business Prosperity	61	42	4	15

*England, 1891–1925; France, 1890–1914, 1917–1919, and 1921–1925; Germany, 1890–1925; United States, 1897–1936.

Our statistical findings are subject to certain reservations. The source which we have used for business conditions is Thorp and Mitchell's Business Annals (pp. 75–87), which has the advantage of having followed a uniform method for the four countries in question. But any source which undertakes to define the conditions existing in any year as a whole must overlook a certain number of minor fluctuations within the year. This difficulty applies also to the figure for union membership, which sometimes fluctuates markedly within quite short periods of time.[9] In the case of the unions the difficulty is perhaps not too serious, since most of the figures on union membership are collected each year at the same time — in the United States, when the A. F. of L. holds its annual convention, usually in the summer or fall.

Our figures on union membership, including all the unions except company unions, are not fully reliable in an absolute sense.

9. Wolman reports that he wrote several letters to the office of the United Textile Workers of America within a few years requesting figures on union membership. Thus he obtained three different figures for the year 1933. One was 150,000, the second 55,000, and the third approximately 250,000! Part of this variation was caused by the fact that the membership of the union actually did fluctuate very greatly within the year. Leo Wolman, Ebb and Flow in Trade Unionism, New York, 1936, p. 6.

Some unions pad their membership figures in order to obtain greater prestige and influence, a tendency which is only partly checked by the payment of per capita dues to a central union federation such as the A. F. of L.[1] Moreover, the definition of a union member varies from union to union, and from time to time within the same union. Is a member who has been excused from payment of dues because of unemployment to be considered a paid-up member? In the early years of the German Mine Workers Federation many miners subscribed to the union journal and acted with the union in time of crisis, but refrained from joining the organization, presumably because they felt sure they would be victimized. The Federation listed these non-member subscribers along with the members in some compilations.[2]

Dr. Leo Wolman, a firm believer in the "prosperity" theory of union growth, is driven to a series of specious and unconvincing arguments to explain why the period of "Coolidge prosperity" (1923–29) did not draw workers to the A. F. of L., and why the total reported union membership in the United States was actually lower at the end of this period than at the beginning.[3] In textiles, we are told, and in the clothing and mining industries, union membership failed to increase because these industries were depressed in spite of the general prosperity; while "in most classes of industry, the very prosperity of the period and the generally high standards of wages and employment acted, apparently, to retard rather than to accelerate the pace of union growth."[4] Thus, according to Wolman, union membership failed to increase in the depressed industries because they were depressed, and in the prosperous industries because of their prosperity! In similar perplexity Mr. G. D. H. Cole bemoans the fact that the British workers did not join the unions in the business boom of 1937–39, when, according to him, they should have done so. There has been, he says, "a collapse of organization among the less skilled workers, over a period when the conditions for recruitment ought to have been favorable."[5]

1. Estimates of the membership of the C.I.O. in 1939–40 ranged from one million to four millions.

2. Otto Hué, Die Bergarbeiter, Stuttgart, 1913, II, pp. 488, 736.

3. Wolman, op. cit., p. 16. Cf. also W. Z. Foster, From Bryan to Stalin, New York, 1937, p. 193 n.

4. Wolman, op. cit., p. 162.

5. G. D. H. Cole, British Trade Unionism Today, London, 1939, pp. 520–521.

The "prosperity" theory in its naïve form disregards not only the defensive character of many union organization movements and the importance of the market demand for labor, but also the highly important factor of prices.[6] We have been able to compare the movement of union membership with the movement of prices 146 times. (Table II.)[7] Of the 53 cases in which prices rose markedly (more than three per cent) within the preceding year, union membership increased markedly in 41, or 77 per cent, and fell in only eight. Sharply falling prices were accompanied by a drop in union membership two and one-half times as often as by an appreciable rise in membership. The evidence seems to indicate that changes in union membership correlate more closely with sharp changes in prices than with "prosperity."[8]

There are several reasons why we would expect a marked rise to stimulate union growth. In the first place, increases in wage rates tend to lag behind price rises, so that fully employed workers must organize if they are to avoid a drop in their standard of living. To that extent, as we have already noted, unionization moves in times of rising prices are defensive movements. In the second place, a period of rapidly rising prices is nearly (but not quite) always a period of increasing production and decreasing unemployment, so that the favorable factors of prosperity all apply. But when the rise in prices is accompanied with a falling off of production and employment, as was the case during the last stages of the inflation after the First World War in Germany and France, it may be accompanied also by a decline in union membership, and this in fact is what occurred in both these instances. Finally, a period of rising prices is a favorable time for employers to pass along

6. Price movements are strongly emphasized by Professor J. R. Commons and his associates in their History of Labour in the United States, New York, 1918, as the major cause of waves of trade union organization. (See I, pp. 347, 350, 396, 488, 582; also II, 5, 15, and 17–18.) They do not sufficiently distinguish between rises in price and improvement in business. Hoxie emphasizes the importance of price changes. (See R. F. Hoxie, Trade Unionism in the United States, 2d ed., New York, 1924, pp. 81–87.) Professor Catlin, after considering both the price theory and the "prosperity" theory, leans to the former. (W. B. Catlin, The Labor Problem in the United States and Great Britain, rev. ed., New York, 1935, pp. 365–366.) The Webbs, on the other hand, emphasize business conditions. (S. and B. Webb, The History of Trade Unionism, London, 1920, passim.)

7. The data on which this table is based are given in the Appendix.

8. A notable exception was the great swing to unionism in the United States during the years 1884–86, which took place during a period of slowly falling prices.

TABLE II

TRADE UNION MEMBERSHIP AND PRICES
ENGLAND, FRANCE, GERMANY, AND THE UNITED STATES SINCE 1890*

No. of Years in Which —	Total	Number of Years in Which —		
		Membership Rose Sharply (more than 3%)	Membership Rose Slightly (less than 3%)	Membership Fell
Total	146	78	16	52
Prices Rose	53	41	4	8
Prices Changed Slightly (not over 3 per cent)	63	30	7	26
Prices Fell	30	7	5	18

*England, 1892–1934; France, 1890–1914 and 1917–1925; Germany, 1891–1920 and 1924–1930; United States, 1897–1934.

increases in cost to the customer in the form of higher prices, and to that extent the antagonism between capital and labor decreases in intensity. In the sectors of industry where excessive competition is a bar to unionization, as for example in the building of small homes and in small-scale industry generally, excessive competition then tends to give way and moderate competition, a condition more favorable to unionization, takes its place.[9]

Rising prices correlate more closely with union growth than does the prosperity phase of the business cycle partly because prices affect all workers, while the cycle is much more violent in some industries than in others.[1] The printing unions, the railroad service brotherhoods, and unions in service trades such as those of teachers and actors, or in industries producing directly for consumption, such as the apparel and food industries, are compara-

9. Cf. Solomon Blum, Labor Economics, New York, 1926, p. 380.
1. Professor Cassel goes so far as to say that the business (trade) cycle is a cycle of production in the heavy industries: ". . . The movements of the trade cycle are merely expressions of the fluctuations in the production of fixed capital. . . ." — Gustav Cassel, The Theory of Social Economy, 2d ed., tr. Barron, New York, 1932, p. 559.

tively little affected by the cyclical ups-and-downs of business, and while they are considerably influenced by progress or recession in the rest of the labor movement, they show a capacity to grow throughout a minor depression which at times surprises their own leaders.[2] A recent illustration is that of the American Federation of Teachers, which had grown only to 15,000 members by the summer of 1938, then doubled its membership in one year, though business as a whole was by no means booming.[3] Union developments in any country must be interpreted in the light of the composition of that country's working force.[4]

In our discussion thus far we have confined ourselves to major price changes. Gradual changes, however, if cumulative, may have a cumulative effect. Thus it seems probable that the gradual rise in prices in England and the United States during the period 1903-10, though it did not produce any marked growth in unionism at the time, was a factor in the very noticeable "labor unrest" of the period and in the subsequent tremendous expansion of unionism during the First World War.

The "prosperity" theory and the price theory of union growth are both too simple.[5] Our theory of union growth in its preliminary form is as follows: *Under conditions of "liberal capitalism," when labor has major new grievances and an improving position in the labor market, unions tend to grow. When labor has no major new grievances or when its position in the labor market is not improving, conditions for organization are not especially favorable; and when labor is economically weak or losing ground in the labor market,*

2. On the Typographical Union in 1858 (depression year) see George A. Tracy, History of the Typographical Union, Indianapolis, 1913, p. 170; on 1908, another depression year, see ibid., p. 913. The Order of Railway Conductors increased its membership in each of the four years 1893-97, a period of major depression. (E. C. Robbins, The Order of Railway Conductors, New York, 1914, p. 23.) The Actors' Equity Association showed a steady increase in paid-up membership during the summer of 1921, a depression year. (Paul F. Gemmill, "Collective Bargaining by Actors," Bulletin 402 of U. S. Bureau of Labor Statistics, Washington, 1926, p. 16.)

3. Of course the influence on the teachers of the preceding boom in the labor movement as a whole cannot be disregarded.

4. Hence it is only in countries as large as the four chosen for our analysis that such a study is possible at all. In several smaller countries, the statistics are more complete, but the economic life of those countries is dominated by the fortunes of one or a few industries.

5. If prosperity were always a period of rising prices, as some descriptions of the business cycle imply, these two theories would, of course, come to the same thing. But prosperity and rising prices do not always go together.

though grievances exist and give rise to organization movements, these movements are not likely to result in a general increase in union membership, which tends to decline.

The best index of labor's economic power is no doubt employment. Unfortunately employment indexes are still so limited in scope that a conclusive test of our theory is not possible. A partial test, however, is available. The period of the business cycle when labor is most apt to have grievances and to be gaining in economic power is the period of revival from depression. Revival is likely to be accompanied by rising prices and increasing employment, while labor has major grievances that have accumulated during the depression. We have examined twenty cases of revival from depression, and in sixteen of them, or eighty per cent, union membership increased markedly, while in only two of them did it decline. (See Table I, *supra*.)

The fact that revival is a more favorable time for union growth than "prosperity" illustrates an important point in the theory of union growth. *The direction of the movement of the indexes is more important than their absolute level.* Thus in the summer of 1933 prices and employment in the United States were "low," but increasing, and labor had an unprecedented accumulation of major grievances. A great wave of unionism swept the country.[6]

II. Booms in Union Growth

Our theory is still incomplete unless it can offer some explanation of those occasional booms which sweep into the unions hundreds of thousands of previously unorganized workers.[7] The significance of such periods is hardly lessened by the fact that

6. For a different explanation of the organization wave of 1933 and after, see Wolman, op. cit., pp. 43–44.

7. The traditional "theory" of booms and declines in unionism makes them coincide with changes in the business cycle and is thus essentially the same as the "prosperity" theory of union growth, which we have already criticized. The Gompers "law of the growth of labor" was formulated in 1904 as follows: "From the formation of the first *bona fide* trade union movement in modern times, it has grown with each era of industrial activity and receded to some degree with each industrial depression, but with each recurring revival in industry the degree of growth has been greater, and with each recurring period of depression it has receded to a lesser degree than its immediate predecessors." — Report of the Proceedings of the Twenty-Fourth Annual Convention of the American Federation of Labor, 1904, p. 15, quoted in The American Federation of Labor: History, Policies and Prospects, by Lewis L. Lorwin (Brookings Institution, 1933), p. 233 n. The idea that there are wave move-

many of the newly organized drop away soon after, perhaps without even paying any dues at all.[8] A wave of unionism may sweep into the movement workers in trades where the conditions are at the time unfavorable for unionization, and yet the union so formed may strike firm roots.[9] Furthermore, the effect on the public, including that part of it which has no sympathy, actual or potential, for the union movement, has to be remembered. Just as the workers in a militantly led strike sometimes keep on fighting when their cause appears hopelessly lost, and thus demonstrate to the world that the working class has unsuspected reserves of endurance and solidarity, so a wave of organization reminds the employers that they have to do with a whole class and not with a few agitators or with an aristocracy of labor alone.

In the early stages of the union movement, when an unfavorable economic conjuncture leads to the complete breakup of many unions, the wave movement is apt to be violent. An established union movement continues to show waves but they are less violent. Since 1890 the membership in the long established union movements of the United Kingdom and the United States has fluctuated less violently than that in the comparatively new unions of Germany and France.

In the United States peaks of union organization booms may be noted in 1837, 1854 or 1857, 1872 (in New York City), 1886, 1903, 1920, and 1937.[1] The seventeen-year interval since 1886 is

ments in unionism was common currency before 1886. Cf. also Zwing's slightly more dialectic statement: "The social process proceeds not in a straight line, but in wave movements, in crests and troughs, but still with the tendency to permanent upward development." — Karl Zwing, Soziologie der Gewerkschaftsbewegung, Jena, 1927, p. 7. Neither Gompers nor Zwing contemplated a condition where the secular trend of factory employment and population in general would cease to be upward.

8. Nobody knows exactly how many workers joined the Knights of Labor in 1886, partly because before they could become stabilized many members dropped away again. — Commons and associates, op. cit., II, p. 370.

9. Cf. Paul S. Taylor, The Sailors Union of the Pacific, New York, 1923, p. 46.

1. The Lynds, writing on the "Middletown" of 1924, compared the tepid sentiment which they found there for the A. F. of L. with newspaper descriptions of Gompers' visit to the same town in 1897, when he apparently was accorded an enthusiastic reception. Thus they thought that they had discovered a secular trend toward decline in sympathy for unionism. (R. S. and H. M. Lynd, Middletown: A Study in American Culture, New York, 1929, pp. 78–79.) Their conclusion would, of course, have been different if they had been able to compare Gompers' visit of 1897 with (say) a mass meeting addressed by John L. Lewis in 1936. The coming of the CIO to "Middletown"

rather striking,[2] but it is probably a coincidence. There does not seem to have been any regularity in the recurrent spurts and lags of the German and French union movements in the modern period. In England there have been four great periods of growth in the union movement: 1833–34, 1871–74, 1888–92, and 1916–20.[3] Geoffrey Drage, writing in 1905, thought he could discern a wave of growth culminating in 1854, and concluded, "Trade unionism has shown its greatest vigor at intervals of twenty years."[4] But according to the Webbs, the period from 1852 to 1858 is almost a blank in union history.[5] Growth in union membership took place, but there was nothing that could be described as a boom. Thus Drage's generalization for the early period must be rejected.

The effect of war on unionism may be anything from abolition of the unions to a major boom. In the period of "liberal" capitalism, a short war unaccompanied by general mobilization has frequently been a stimulus to business and to the union movement. The great advance of the A.F. of L. at the end of the 1890's was, according to Lorwin, stimulated by the Spanish-American War.[6] When the outbreak of war is accompanied by general mobilization and the adoption of drastic decrees for the regimentation of labor, the immediate effect on unionism is catastrophic. The Franco-German War of 1870–71, which lasted a very short time, had a disastrous effect on the young German unions,[7] and was scarcely less serious for the French unions of the time. Similarly the outbreak of war in 1914 was followed by a big decline in the membership of the German unions, which was not recouped until two years later.

In England and the United States, where the call to the colors was more gradual, there was no marked falling off in membership at any time during the First World War. The later stages of that

is partially foreshadowed in Middletown in Transition, by the same authors (New York, 1937).

   2. The author, after studying the chart of A. F. of L. membership, was impressed, as many students must have been before, by the regularly recurring seventeen-year peaks. He wrote an article in 1929 predicting that 1937 would see a new high in union organization, and sent the article to a labor paper. The editor returned it with the remark that eight years was "too long for the boys to wait."

   3. Webb, op. cit., passim.

   4. Geoffrey Drage, Trade Unions, London, 1905, p. 5.

   5. Webb, op. cit., p. 224.

   6. Lorwin, op. cit., p. 58.

   7. S. Nestripke, Die Deutschen Gewerkschaften, I, Stuttgart, 1925, p. 80.

war brought a steep rise in prices everywhere and the greatest boom in unionism that the world has yet seen.[8] The later effect of the war, however, was in a number of countries just the reverse of the immediate effect. The social regime had been so weakened that it sought desperate means to stabilize itself and hit on abolition of the unions as one means.

The other great booms in unionism have followed, at least in England and the United States, after a more or less protracted depression.[9] We have already noted that revival from depression seems, on the record, to be the most favorable time in the business cycle for growth in union membership. The intensity of the boom in unionism is presumably related to the sufferings of labor in the preceding depression.[1] When all working standards have gone by the board, and men have picked up jobs where and how they could, for whatever money they could get, and when this condition has continued for years, the average cautious wage-earner is willing to take a risk for the sake of reëstablishing his standard of living. The women of the wage-earning class have learned the lesson too; sometimes they drive the men into the unions. Who does not remember how Gottlieb in Hauptmann's The Weavers, and Jim in Odets' Waiting for Lefty were shamed into action by their womenfolk? As a matter of fact, the risk, as pointed out above, is not so great; the employer too has had his lean years and is willing to make concessions to the unions rather than risk a strike.

Both in war-time and in peace-time, changes in the direction of union growth are featured by considerable inertia. It takes a major grievance to get labor on the move, and a major setback to stop it. A period of growth, once well under way, tends to continue with accelerating speed as long as conditions remain even moderately favorable; there have been numerous cases where the unions continued to grow throughout a minor depression, as for example in the United States during 1883–84. The peak of a union boom

8. Cf. International Labor Office, The Growth of Trade Unionism During the Ten Years 1910–1919, Geneva, 1921, p. 2. Concerning the effect of the First World War on American labor see further below.

9. Cf. Drage, loc. cit. In the United States, the "roaring forties" were followed by the union boom of 1849–57; the depression of the 1870's was followed by the boom which culminated in 1886; the depression of the middle nineties was followed by the union boom that culminated in 1903; and the depression of 1929–32 was followed by the union boom of 1933–37.

1. But we would not imply that the intensity of the union boom is necessarily proportional to the severity of the preceding depression.

tends to occur after the peak of a business boom, even allowing for the fact that there is a certain lag in reporting union membership figures.[2] When the idea once gets around that the union is winning concessions and that joining is safe, the stage is set for a big rush to the banner of unionism. This idea seems to have penetrated the ranks of the semiskilled and unskilled in the United States during 1886 and in England during 1889–90.

Typically, the reaction of employers to a boom in unionism has been one of belligerency. In England, when the employers had had time to get their breath after the first great sweep to unionism in 1834, they counter-attacked and presented in a concerted way the "document" (yellow-dog contract). The same story was repeated after 1852, with the result in each case that labor was intimidated and many unions were broken up. In the United States, employers who had been ready to put their trust in arbitration in 1900 were swung into the "open-shop" drive in 1903. A similar "open-shop" movement of employers developed in 1921.[3] Each time, the effort of the employers was to push home an advantage which the turn of the business cycle had given them. The great growth in labor's power and influence in 1918–20, coming on the heels of the union boom during the First World War, gave rise to a violent reaction on the part of British employers. It became a common saying among them that there was going to be "a finish fight with labor." The fight did not materialize at the time, but in 1926 the organized employers saw their chance and drove labor into its ill-fated General Strike.[4]

Employer support of Fascism in Italy and National Socialism in Germany may be considered another example of organized resistance to the growing power of labor, resistance whose intensity was definitely related to the extent of labor's power during the preceding union boom. In these instances the employers' purpose of smashing the union movement was realized. Some have concluded that labor should have refrained from pressing its demands during the period of its relative economic power, for fear that such insistence would stimulate a later reaction. This reasoning seems to us fallacious. The Social-Democratic Party leaders and the

2. The business recession of 1903 in the United States did not reflect itself in a decline of union membership until 1905.

3. See Savel Zimand, The Open Shop Drive, New York, 1921.

4. See W. H. Crook, The General Strike, Chapel Hill, 1931, Chap. ix-xi.

unions under their influence in Germany did much in the Weimar
period (1919–31) to avoid antagonizing the employers, but their
organizations, and also the "Christian" unions which had been on
the whole much less militant, were abolished just the same by
Hitler. The causes of Fascism are deep-seated and appeals to the
good sportsmanship of the Fascists plainly do not meet the case.
Labor can never afford to trust the good sportsmanship of employers as a class.

The "welfare" approach, which had been adopted by individual employers already before the First World War, principally in
Germany but also in other countries, was much advertised in the
United States from 1923 to 1929. The purpose was partly to keep
labor contented and cut down labor turnover, which had been a
serious problem in the period 1916–20; and partly to head off unionism. The number of firms practicing "welfare" was never large
and the extent to which labor benefited from such practices has
been much exaggerated. Nevertheless, as we have seen, the union
movement was checked for the time being.[5]

III. The Importance of Leadership

The periods which were really favorable for the growth of
unionism have occurred seldom and have lasted a relatively very
short time. Thus the question what type of leadership was in
command of the union movement has in practice been of decisive
importance. Reactionary leadership has thwarted organized labor's
progress and progressive leadership has carried it to unanticipated
victories. Similarly in periods of defense and decline, a courageous
and determined leadership can halt a backward movement and
even initiate an advance, while defeatist leadership can toss away
gains and even lead to the collapse of a whole union movement.

A striking example of differences in leadership is furnished by
the last two union booms in the United States. The first took
place during the First World War. Perhaps never before or since

5. Slichter notes that the membership of the A. F. of L. unions in manufacturing was cut nearly in half between 1920 and 1923, and decreased further
by eighteen per cent between 1923 and 1926. However, he attributes this result
not primarily to "welfare" but rather to the eleven per cent increase in the real
earnings (per hour?) of factory workers between 1920 and 1926. Further, he
very justly refuses to be much impressed by the lack of growth under the circumstances. Sumner H. Slichter, "The Current Labor Policies of American
Industries," this JOURNAL, May, 1929, pp. 426–428.

have the opportunities for trade union organization been so good. The membership of the unions did rise to new heights and some industries were penetrated for the first time; but these gains were made in spite of, rather than because of, the top leadership of the A.F. of L.[6] Foster has described how the organization campaigns in packing and steel in 1917–19 were initiated by himself as a rank-and-file member and minor official of the A.F. of L., whose Executive Council actually sabotaged both campaigns.[7] In Foster's opinion, "had there been a progressive trade union leadership in control at the time . . . every important basic industry in the country could have been organized."[8] Actually the great steel strike of 1919 was lost, the union in the packing industry was broken up (largely through the folly and shortsightedness of the A.F. of L. craft union leaders), and the union boom spent itself without having realized more than a fraction of its potentialities.

The organization of the basic industries which has been carried out in recent years by the CIO depended primarily on the factor of leadership. The policies of the A.F. of L. were the same as in 1916–20 and the results could easily have been the same. The promising union movement in rubber, for example, did actually reach a peak and start a decline under A.F. of L. leadership, a decline from which it was rescued just in time by the militant leadership of the CIO. The Lewis group raised huge amounts of money and sent organizers from outside to aid the struggling workers who by themselves could hardly have matched the concentrated power of the large employers. Even with the aid of this powerful leadership the workers in the more important basic industries did not become fully organized. The achievements of the CIO leadership appear all the more remarkable because America has furnished so many examples of corruption and stagnation in union leadership.[9] However, the experience of the First World War with its lost opportunities may have had something to do with the aggressive and successful policies of the CIO. People do sometimes learn the lessons of history.

6. ". . . Reactionary policies . . . cost the A. F. of L. . . . 5,000,000 to 10,000,000 possible members during the war time." — William Z. Foster, From Bryan to Stalin, New York, 1937, p. 112. Cf. Lorwin, op. cit., p. 161.

7. W. Z. Foster, The Great Steel Strike and Its Lessons, New York, 1920, and From Bryan to Stalin, Chap. viii and ix.

8. Communicated.

9. Cf. Hoxie, op. cit., Chap. vii; Harold Seidman, Labor Czars, New York, 1938; and W. Z. Foster, Misleaders of Labor, New York, 1927.

Great Britain also has furnished examples of a trade-union leadership which failed to rise to the occasion of a union boom.[1] The wave of unionism in 1888–92 swept many of the old leaders out of office. Similarly, in 1916–20, a number of the old leaders resigned or were removed,[2] but the change was by no means complete. Subsequently the greatest defensive battle in the history of British unionism — the General Strike of 1926 — was called off without gains, and the British labor movement settled down to a long period of stagnation and retrogression.[3] From 1937 to 1941 we find a new wave of criticism against the inactivity of British trade-union officials.[4]

The examples already cited indicate pretty plainly that a mere analysis of economic conditions does not suffice for an adequate understanding of the ups-and-downs of unionism. It cannot be assumed that when the existing leadership fails a new leadership will arise and do the job that the incumbents are leaving undone. Indeed Foster, who has done more than any other one man to lay bare the shortcomings of the A.F. of L. bureaucracy, is almost equally critical of the Socialist Party's failure to enter the field of union organizing during the First World War. Had it done so, he believes, it could have signed up one or two million workers under its own banner, outside the A.F. of L. Instead, it confined itself to verbal propaganda of a somewhat sectarian nature.[5]

1. Cf. letter of F. Engels to Bebel, October 28, 1885, in which Engels says that the old unions "cling to their traditional superstition, which does them nothing but harm themselves, instead of getting quit of the rubbish and thus doubling their members and their power. . . ." — Karl Marx and Friedrich Engels Correspondence, 1846–1895, in Marxist Library, XXIX (New York, 1935), p. 442.

2. On the building trades, see R. W. Postgate, The Builders' History, London, 1923, pp. 434–435.

3. On the timidity of the union leadership in the 1926 General Strike see John Pepper, The General Strike and the General Betrayal, Chicago, 1926, and especially articles by J. H. Thomas in Answers (London, January–March, 1927).

4. Harold J. Laski wrote in 1937: " . . . Trade-union leaders refuse to take advantage of the present boom. . . . In almost every big union militant members are penalized, unofficial strikes vigorously suppressed, and too zealous strikers, like some in the Transport Workers' Union and the Electrical Trades Union, are actually expelled. The leaders, in fact, have assured the government and the employers that they need not expect difficulties from the trade unions in completing the armament program." — The Nation (New York), October 2, 1937, p. 343.

5. Daily Worker, February 27, 1940.

The old leaders do not give way to a new leadership without a struggle,

Class-conscious leaders make the best organizers. They are harder to bluff, harder to bribe, and harder to fool. Similarly class-conscious workers join unions more readily and stick to them better than workers who are only "wage conscious," to use Hoxie's phrase.[6] The newly organized worker is apt to be politically conservative, but he will stick obstinately to the leadership which has won him economic concessions, even though this leadership presents demands which are politically rather advanced. For example, leaders of the "outlaw" union movement in Germany during the First World War were able to advance in conjunction with the economic demands (largely defensive, to meet the rising cost of living) certain highly important political demands (no forcible annexations, no punitive indemnities). The Russian workers, accustomed before 1914 to the militant leadership of the Bolsheviks in the economic as well as the political field, sought the guidance of the Bolsheviks during the war in the struggle to maintain real-wage rates and shorten hours, and eventually helped them to establish a new government. One is reminded of Saul, who went out to seek an ass and found a kingdom. The leaders of the German union movement, overwhelmingly Social-Democratic in their politics, saw the political future less clearly, and failed to make sweeping advances on the political field. National Socialism eventually came to Germany. Who will question that the difference in the political orientation of the union leadership had everything to do with the different developments in the two countries?

IV. The Influence of Industrialization

The direct influence of industrialization on union growth is only partly favorable. Indeed, factory workers have organized

either in England (see previous footnote) or in the United States. It has been charged that the A. F. of L. leaders did not wish to see the unions expand into new industries during the First World War, because the new element might have voted the old leaders out of office. — W. Z. Foster, "An Open Letter to John Fitzpatrick," in Labor Herald, January, 1924, p. 6, and From Bryan to Stalin, pp. 129–130.

6. The German Metalworkers Federation had greater success in penetrating the heavy industry in the period before the World War than the corresponding American union. The author has set forth elsewhere his reasons for believing that this result flowed largely from the greater attention paid by the German union to political education on a class-conscious basis. See "International Differences in the Labor Movement: The Iron and Steel Industry" (in German), Weltwirtschaftliches Archiv, xxxviii, Heft I (July, 1933), pp. 237–263

somewhat later than the workers in the hand trades. In the United States, "few of the workers in trade-unions prior to 1827 had been affected by the Industrial Revolution. . . . The carpenters, ship-wrights, shoemakers, and tailors, among whom the early trade-union activities had most commonly been carried on, were engaged in pursuits which were not yet affected by the machine and the factory system."[7] In part, no doubt, this circumstance is due to the fact that the economic power of the factory operative whose skill the machine has taken over tends to be less than that of the pre-machine craftsman.[8]

Moderate competition between employers, a favorable condition for the growth of unions, is characteristic of the early phases of industrialization, when the scale of production is still not very large.[9] Moderate competition is better for the unions than cut-throat competition, because employers bear down on labor when their own economic position is very difficult.[1] The "lumpers" in the building trades (small sub-contractors who purchase no materials), the "buck-eye" shoe manufacturers, and the small industrialists generally, who today suffer from the competition of larger, more favorably situated establishments, beat down labor standards by a variety of stratagems; they are a perennial headache to the unionists.

The growth of large-scale production poses a new set of problems to a labor movement which developed institutions suited to production on a small or moderate scale. Economic power is concentrated in the hands of a few large employers, who can use it with telling effect against labor, especially when labor's organizations are small and divided. Collaboration between employers has become routinized through the practice of price control. The influence of large employers and finance capital on the government is now dominant; the industrialists and bankers have replaced the

7. Labor Problems in America, by Emanuel Stein, Jerome Davis, and others (New York, 1940), p. 145.
8. On the small proportion of factory workers organized even today see Wolman, op. cit., pp. 122–123.
9. Cf. Blum, loc. cit. — Marx, in a work which antedates the Communist Manifesto, had pointed out in a characteristic paradox that "the more modern industry and competition develop, the more there are elements which call forth and strengthen combination." — The Poverty of Philosophy, in Marxist Library, XXVI, p. 143.
1. The term "cut-throat competition" was formerly used to describe the price wars between large competing units, especially the railroads. It is used here in the modern sense of excessive competition between quite small units.

landed interest as the major economic power, with the commercial interest still important; but the commercial interest is now itself a major employer of labor. The practice of concerted employer restriction of output, even in times of prosperity, and the development of chronic overcapacity mean that strikes are less apt to be immediately successful, except under specially favorable conditions.

Pressure from labor brings about the passage of an increasing number of measures setting minimum standards for labor and introducing partial security in the face of increasing basic instability. The unions have had little directly to do with the passage of certain of these laws, but they have become increasingly interested both in the new protective laws and in the improvement and enforcement of the old. Laws are even adopted for the protection of the unions and of collective bargaining. It becomes inevitable that labor should have some kind of organization which shall be at least nominally its own.[2] Under these circumstances the political activities of the unions become of increasing importance. In a sense, union activity is basically political anyway, since the alternative to unionism (as A.F. of L. leaders have always insisted) is slavery; and slavery, whether economic or other, represents a political status.

Governmental encouragement may become a major factor in promoting union growth. The classic example is the Soviet Union, but the unions of Soviet Russia are excluded from the present discussion because their status is unique and their functions quite different from those of unions in capitalist countries. In capitalist countries, the influence of government as such in promoting unionism has often been overestimated. In England it was thought for many years that the repeal of the Combination Laws in 1825 was what set off the wave of union organization which followed immediately, but it is now believed that the real cause was the sudden revival of business and the resulting favorable economic conditions, which stimulated successful organization. It might seem that the assumption of power by a Labor

2. Outright suppression of unionism takes the form today more usually of the establishment of some kind of state-controlled unions, comparable with company unions. This type of state-controlled union has been widely copied since Mussolini introduced the first in Italy in 1925. Neither the "corporations" of Portugal nor the *sindicatos* of contemporary Brazil can be considered *bona fide* unions within our definitions.

government would be a peculiarly favorable time for the growth of unions, and in France during 1935 the establishment of the Popular Front government was indeed a factor in the tremendous upswing in union membership which took place. Yet there does not seem to have been any great influx of members into the British unions after the first Labor government took office there in 1923.[3] In Australia, also, it is hard to trace any chronological correlation between the rise and fall of the several Labor governments and the rise and fall of unionism. In the United States, some students have attempted to account for the growth of unionism between 1933 and 1937 on the basis of "government legislation on behalf of labor, especially the National Industrial Recovery Act and the National Labor Relations Act;"[4] but the growth of the unions continued after the NIRA was declared unconstitutional and slowed down soon after the National Labor Relations Act was held constitutional. It has been said that the pro-labor attitude of the second Wilson administration (1917–21) was largely responsible for the growth of unionism in 1917–20. This view, however, not only disregards the fact that neither Wilson administration was basically pro-labor; it fails to explain why the growth was so slow during the first Wilson administration, and fails to mention that the Wilson administration fought labor after the war, e.g. in the 1919 coal strike.

In countries such as the United States it is sometimes hard to tell whether unions grow because the government is "pro-labor" or whether the government is "pro-labor" because unionism is on the march. Without at all underestimating the influence of a comparatively sympathetic government administration (thousands of workers in northern New Jersey, for example, joined the unions in 1937–38 after receiving leaflets headed "The President wants you to organize"), we may feel that the "pro-labor" government is a result rather than a cause of the upswing in unionism.[5] Or

3. To be sure, this was a minority government. But defenders of the "ministerialist" point of view generally argue that any government including labor representatives will stimulate union growth. Jaurès, for example, made this argument in 1904. — Samuel Bernstein, "Jean Jaurès and the Problem of War," in Science and Society, IV, No. 3 (Summer, 1940), p. 145.

4. Speech by Dr. Leo Wolman to a meeting of Trade Association Executives in New York City, October 21, 1937; see New York Times, October 22, 1937, p. 42.

5. The Franklin D. Roosevelt administration in its most progressive phase should be rated "pro-labor" only by courtesy, or by comparison with

both may be the result of a third factor. The "accumulation of grievances" during the crisis of 1929–33 was mentioned as helping to explain the dimensions of the subsequent union boom. The same accumulation of grievances undoubtedly caused the labor sweep for Roosevelt in 1932.

V. Conclusion

In view of the considerations developed in the three preceding sections, the preliminary theory presented at the end of Section I may now be expanded as follows:

(1) Union growth proceeds by waves which are not closely synchronized with those of the business cycle. These waves indicate that there is considerable inertia in the movement of union membership. A major wave of growth, if not brought on by a war, will nearly always be found to have been preceded by an accumulation of wage-earners' grievances, as during a major depression, while the accumulation of employer resistances during a wave of growth is a factor in the ensuing period of absolute or relative decline.

(2) Leadership can account for the success or failure of a strike, for the growth or decline of a union, and even for the success or failure of a whole union movement. The quality of the leadership in a particular critical situation may have a determining influence on the subsequent development of unionism.

(3) The early growth of industrialism is featured by a comparatively small but growing scale of production, moderate competition, and in practice a "hands-off" attitude on the part of the government. This condition, with capitalism in its expanding phase, is favorable for the growth of unionism.

(4) The later development of industrialism is featured by rapid technical displacement of labor and transference of skill to the machine, increasingly close relations between industry and government, and crises which are deeper and more prolonged. This condition, with capitalism in its phase of decline, is a condition of crisis for unionism. It is a period when the government is not able to disregard unionism and when the unions must willy-nilly assume a positive attitude toward government. The leaders who seek to

previous administrations. At the height of the union boom the President declined to condemn the lawbreaking Republic Steel Corporation, and tried to have John L. Lewis call off the General Motors sit-down strike.

make labor class-conscious will be violently attacked during this period of crisis. Yet a failure of labor to assert itself when conditions for organization are favorable may leave labor in a desperate position when conditions change. To maintain and improve labor's position economically is the traditional task of the unions. Today, not only the growth but even the existence of the unions has become in large measure a political problem.

HORACE B. DAVIS.

SIMMONS COLLEGE.

Wages and Productivity

Factors Affecting the Trend of Real Wages, by Alvin H. Hansen, American Economic Review, Vol. XV, No. 1, March, 1925, pp. 27–42

Union Wage and Hour Policies and Employment, by Waldo E. Fisher, American Economic Review, Vol. XXX, No. 2, June, 1940, pp. 290–299

Union Participation in High Productivity, by William Gomberg, Annals of the American Academy of Political and Social Science, Vol. 248, November, 1946, pp. 70–75

FACTORS AFFECTING THE TREND
OF REAL WAGES[1]

It is the purpose of this paper to take a long-run view of the course of real wages, and to consider the leading factors affecting the wage trend together with the major fluctuations about this trend.

I

Chart 1 shows a comparison of two wage curves. Curve A was constructed by joining together several series.[2] The data are for daily wages from 1840 to 1890, for full-time weekly earnings from 1890 to 1914 and for actual weekly earnings from 1914 to 1923. Curve B is an average of the index numbers of the weekly wages of laborers and artisans compiled by the department of statistics of the Russell

[1] Previous articles on the trend of real wages appearing in the REVIEW are as follows: I. M. Rubinow, "The Recent Trend of Real Wages" (Dec., 1914, pp. 793-817); F. W. Jones, "Real Wages in Recent Years" (June, 1917, pp. 319-330); Paul H. Douglas and Frances Lamberson, "The Movement of Real Wages, 1890-1918" (Sept., 1921, pp. 409-426).

[2] Curve A consists of the following series: (a) From 1840 to 1860 and again from 1880 to 1890 the Falkner index was used. It is a simple average of 61 series beginning with 1840 and 543 series in the latter period. These series cover from nine to twenty-one industries; the cotton, woolen, and metal industries are heavily represented (see pp. 172-4 Senate Report no. 1394). I have used Falkner's simple average index in preference to his weighted average. In this connection see Mitchell's criticism of the method of weighting used (p. 172 in *Gold, Prices and Wages*). Falkner's simple average index indicates a smaller increase in wages than his weighted index; it is the more conservative of the two, but it is not all that is to be desired. (b) From 1860 to 1880 Wesley Mitchell's weighted average index, more scientifically constructed than the Falkner index, was used. Mitchell's method, applied to the other periods covered by the Aldrich report, would no doubt yield a more accurate index, but the labor involved is great, and it is not likely that the results would be nearly as significant as for the period of great price and wage fluctuations in the sixties and seventies. (See Mitchell: *Gold, Prices and Wages*, p. 120.) (c) From 1890 to 1914 the index constructed by Douglas and Lamberson (AM. ECON. REV., Sept., 1921, pp. 409-426) is used. It is a simple average for ten industries. The general reliability of this index for the period in question can be checked by comparing it with the weighted index for forty-one industries computed by the Bureau of Labor for 1890 to 1907 (see *Bulletin of the Bureau of Labor*, July, 1908, p. 7) and with the index computed by W. I. King for the period 1890 to 1912 (see *Wealth and Income of the People of the United States*, p. 203). These indices are all for manufacturing and mechanical industries. King also presents a weighted index of manufacturing, agriculture, mining and railroading. This general index shows a greater rise in money wages from 1890 to 1912 than the manufacturing-wage index, due to the sharper upward trend of wages in agriculture and mining. (d) From 1914 to 1923 a weighted index of the average weekly earnings in the two states, New York and Wisconsin, was constructed, the weights used being 5 and 1 respectively, corresponding roughly to the relative number of wage-earners employed in manufacturing in the two states. For weekly-earnings data see *New York Industrial Bulletin* and the *Wisconsin Labor Market*.

CHART 1

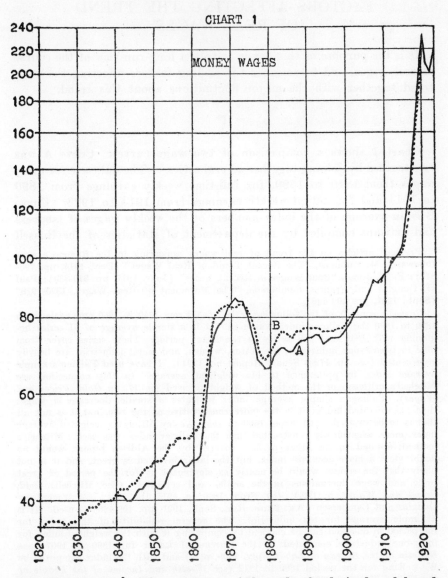

Sage Foundation.[3] The curves are independently derived and based on somewhat different data, yet the correspondence is remarkably close, giving reasonable assurance that either curve gives at least the general trend of money wages with substantial accuracy.

Daily and weekly wages are used in preference to hourly rates or earnings since the latter obviously do not give a correct index of the

[3]Dr. Ralph G. Hurlin kindly supplied the figures. The data came largely from governmental sources including Massachusetts reports, the Weeks and Falkner reports, and the bulletins of the Bureau of Labor Statistics.

trend of the money income received from wages. If, for example, there had been a decline in the hours worked it might appear from the hourly earnings as though there had been a gain both in leisure and wages, when in fact it might well be that the income from wages was no larger than before. By using daily or weekly wages it is possible to differentiate more clearly the gains or losses in leisure from the gains or losses in the wage income.

But daily and weekly wages give a correct picture of the trend of the wage income only on condition that the *trend of unemployment* remains approximately the same. This assumption can neither be proved nor disproved by existing information. A comparison will be made later, however, between the trend of real wages measured by daily and weekly wages and the trend of real wages measured by annual earnings.

It is not possible to get a thoroughly reliable index of the cost of living prior to 1913. We have the retail prices of food as far back as 1890. Beyond this we have to rely on wholesale prices. But we can at least do much better than simply take the general wholesale price level. In so far as it is impossible to get retail prices we shall at least be much nearer the truth as to changes in the cost of living if we construct an index for food, clothing, fuel, light, and house furnishings weighted roughly according to the expenditures of workingmen's families. An interesting example of this method is the index recently constructed by Professor N. J. Silberling for Great Britain in the period 1779 to 1850.[4]

Using the data described in the footnote below[5] I have constructed a

[4] *Cf.* the Supplement to the *Review of Economic Statistics* for October, 1923. Mr. Silberling gives a weight of 42 to foods, 8 to clothing, 4 to fuel (coal) and 2 to light (tallow). The commodities in the food group with their weights are as follows: wheat (15); mutton (6); beef (6); butter (5); oats (3); sugar (3); tea (2); coffee (1); tobacco (1). The commodities in the clothing group are: wool (3); cotton (3); flax (1); leather (1).

[5] This series was constructed in the following manner:

(a) For the period 1820 to 1840 a weighted index number was constructed consisting of the following series: foods, clothing, fuel (coal) and light (candles). The weights are roughly similar to those used for the period 1840 to 1860 (see below). The food group consists of the following commodities: flour (15), beef (16), pork (7), butter (11), sugar (6), coffee (5), cheese (1), fruit (3), fish (1), lard (2), molasses (1), tea (2). The weights (given in parenthesis) are roughly according to the expenditures of 232 families as given on page 62 of Senate Report no. 1394, part 1. The clothing group consists of cotton sheetings (3), wool (3), leather (1). I have used Mr. Silberling's weights for this group.

(b) For the period 1840 to 1890 the Falkner weighted cost-of-living index was used. The series consists of a weighted index of food (41.0), clothing (15.3), fuel and light (5.9), house furnishings (2.5), and miscellaneous (3.8). The food group consists of beans, bread, butter, coffee, cheese, eggs, fish, flour, fruit, lard, corn meal, bacon, beef, ham, lamb, mutton, pork, milk, molasses, rice, salt, spices, sugar, tallow, and potatoes weighted according to expenditures (Senate Report no. 1394, p. 62). The clothing group consists of women's dress goods, silks, linen goods, hosiery, underwear, cotton textiles, cassimeres, suitings, checks, overcoatings, flan-

cost-of-living index for the period 1820-1923. The index numbers
are given in table II. In table I a comparison of the index numbers
of foods, clothing, the cost of living,[6] and general wholesale prices[7] is
made by decades. It is clear that, during the first five decades particularly, the cost-of-living index was considerably below the general
price level relative to 1913. This can be accounted for by the low
price of foodstuffs in the early decades. On the other hand, clothing
prices were very high. In 1820 the index number for clothing stood at
215 while the index number for foods was only 56; the average figures
for the decade of the twenties were 171 and 54 respectively. Probably
the cost-of-living index would be lower in the early period than here
shown, if it had been possible to include rent.[8]

nels, blankets, leather, hides, boots and shoes. The weights used are according
to the expenditures of 232 families. Many of the commodities included in the
miscellaneous group do not logically belong in a cost-of-living index, but the
inclusion of this group does not vitiate the results appreciably since the whole
miscellaneous group was given a weight of only 3.8, against a total of 68.6. It
does not appear to have been commonly recognized that the Falkner weighted index
was intended to be a cost-of-living index. The system of weighting used may be
criticized from the standpoint of a general price index, but this it never purported
to be. The writer believes that this weighted index gives a reasonably accurate
picture of the wholesale prices of food, clothing, fuel and house furnishings. The
foods used are geniune food items and not the raw materials out of which the
finished product is made. In the clothing group, on the other hand, cloth rather
than clothing predominates. In the period in question, however, purchases of
cloth were more important than purchases of ready-made clothing. It is of course
impossible to say to what extent the wholesale prices of these things give a correct
picture of the movements of the cost of living. We know from Mitchell's studies
that the divergence between wholesale prices and retail prices was very considerable
during the period of the great price upheaval. The index here given exaggerates
the rise in the cost of living in this period. By the decade of the eighties, however,
it is probable that wholesale prices and retail prices had reached a fairly normal
adjustment. The cost-of-living index (wholesale prices) here presented for the
United States declined 3 per cent from the decade 1850-9 to the decade 1880-9.
The British cost-of-living index, given in terms of retail prices, declined 6 per cent
in the same period. On the other hand it is possible that the spread between
wholesale prices and retail prices has been growing wider. If this is so, the cost
of living was relatively lower in the early decades than the index shows.

[6]For the period 1860-1880 it is possible to get a more accurate picture of the movement of living costs by using Mitchell's index. Unfortunately it is not feasible
to join Mitchell's figures to the Falkner index, because in the extraordinary price
decline from 1865 to 1880 retail prices lagged behind wholesale prices. If the retail price series were joined to the wholesale price series before this maladjustment
had been fully rectified, it is obvious that the whole curve would be thrown out of
line.

[7]This series was constructed from the index of wholesale prices made by the
present writer for the period 1801-1840 (*Cf. Quart. Pub. Am. Stat. Assoc.*, December, 1915), Falkner's simple average index for 1840 to 1890, and the index of the
Bureau of Labor Statistics from 1890 to 1920.

[8]The difference would not be great if we may judge at all by the prices of
building materials. The index number for building materials for the decade of the
forties was 70 (1913 being 100).

TABLE I (1913 = 100)

Decade	Food	Clothing	Cost of living	General wholesale prices
1820–9	54	171	80	104
1830–9	60	161	83	108
1840–9	56	124	74	93
1850–9	71	122	86	94
1860–9	100	197	124	136
1870–9	90	135	102	109
1880–9	75	104	83	87
1890–9	68	83	72	73
1900–9	78	91	83	87
1913	100	100	100	100

By means of the cost-of-living index we may now make an estimate of the movement of real wages. Table II gives the index numbers.

The real-wage index here presented corresponds closely with estimates made for Great Britain. Table III gives the comparison by ten-year periods. Beginning with 1850 the British wages are given in terms of retail prices (house rent is included).

Table IV compares the real annual earnings (derived from the *Census of Manufactures*) with the daily and weekly index numbers. Except for the year 1869 the two series correspond quite closely. The general trend is unmistakably the same.

The curve for real wages is plotted in chart 2 on semi-logarithmic paper. The trend has been fitted to the data by the free-hand method. The marked decline in real wages appearing in the decade of the sixties is doubtless an exaggeration and therefore the trend was drawn so as to discount this decline. The trend here shown $[Y = b(1+r)^x]$ shows a uniform rate of increase unlike the linear trend $(y = m x + b)$ which indicates a diminishing rate of increase. The rate of increase in the trend as given is 1.04 per cent per annum. This trend is of course not to be taken too seriously. Certainly the latter portion of it will be considerably altered by the course of events during the next decade.

II

So far as the general trend is concerned, it is clear that the dominant factor is the increase in production. The production index[*] plotted in chart 2 has been reduced to a per capita basis by dividing the series by the index numbers of persons gainfully employed. It is an

[*]This curve was derived from an average of the indices of W. W. Stewart (Am. Econ. Rev., March, 1921, p. 68) and E. E. Day (*Review of Economic Statistics,* 1921, pp. 20, 37). The index has been extended back to 1880 by using W. I. King's series for this decade.

TABLE II (1913 = 100)

Year	Index of money wages[1]	Index of cost of living	Index of real wages[1]	Year	Index of money wages	Index of cost of living	Index of real wages
1820	36	88	41	1873	85	106	80
1821	36	84	43	1874	82	107	77
1822	37	86	43	1875	77	106	73
1823	37	82	45	1876	74	101	73
1824	37	76	49	1877	68	93	73
1825	37	78	47	1878	67	86	78
1826	37	74	50	1879	66	78	85
1827	36	77	47	1880	66	86	77
1828	37	76	49	1881	68	89	76
1829	37	78	47	1882	70	90	78
1830	37	72	51	1883	71	88	81
1831	38	75	51	1884	71	84	85
1832	38	77	49	1885	70	77	91
1833	39	75	52	1886	70	77	91
1834	39	69	57	1887	72	78	92
1835	39	81	48	1888	73	79	92
1836	40	92	43	1889	73	81	90
1837	40	97	41	1890	74	77	96
1838	40	96	42	1891	74	76	97
1839	40	96	42	1892	75	75	100
1840	41	80	51	1893	75	76	99
1841	41	81	51	1894	72	71	101
1842	41	74	55	1895	73	70	104
1843	40	69	58	1896	74	69	107
1844	40	70	57	1897	74	67	110
1845	41	72	57	1898	74	69	107
1846	42	78	54	1899	75	72	104
1847	42	78	54	1900	77	76	101
1848	43	73	59	1901	78	75	104
1849	43	69	62	1902	81	78	104
1850	43	73	59	1903	83	81	102
1851	42	81	52	1904	83	81	102
1852	42	80	53	1905	85	81	105
1853	43	86	50	1906	88	85	104
1854	45	86	52	1907	92	90	102
1855	46	90	51	1908	91	87	105
1856	46	92	50	1909	92	91	101
1857	47	94	50	1910	94	94	100
1858	46	93	49	1911	95	92	103
1859	46	85	54	1912	98	96	102
1860	47	82	57	1913	100	100	100
1861	47	77	61	1914[2]	102	102	100
1862	48	96	51	1915	104	104	100
1863	55	109	50	1916	118	111	106
1864	64	141	45	1917	134	131	102
1865	72	191	38	1918	168	159	106
1866	76	154	49	1919	193	183	105
1867	78	136	57	1920	232	208	112
1868	79	143	55	1921	207	182	114
1869	83	125	66	1922	201	168	120
1870	84	119	71	1923	220	171	129
1871	86	112	77				
1872	85	109	78				

[1]The index constructed by joining various series is used. See footnote 1 above.
[2]If we confine ourselves to New York and compare the weekly earnings in New

incorrect procedure to reduce such production indices as we have to a population basis. Much of our national production is not registered in these indices since they take no account of production which is not

TABLE III

Years	Real wages: Great Britain[1]	Real wages: United States
1790–9	37	
1800–9	41	
1810–9	41	
1820–9	47	46
1830–9	47	48
1840–9	49	56
1850–9	58	52
1860–9	63	53
1870–9	74	77
1880–9	84	85
1890–9	98	103
1900–9	102	103
1913	100	100

[1]*Cf.* Sir William Beveridge (*Economic Journal*, September, 1923, p. 462); G. H. Wood (*Journal of Royal Statistical Society*, March, 1909); and N. J. Silberling (*Review of Economic Statistics*, supplement, October, 1923). For Great Britain, agricultural wages are used from 1790 to 1850. Fragmentary data on industrial wage-earners indicate that the real wage index for this group ran about one eighth lower than for agricultural laborers relative to 1850. With increasing industrialization a relatively larger proportion of British wage-earners have been drawn from low-paid occupations into better-paid occupations. After 1850 the British index takes account of this. Probably this factor is of less importance in the United States since our manufacturing industries had to draw from the beginning from relatively high-priced labor, due to the abundance of free land.

TABLE IV

Years	Real annual earnings	Real wages (daily and weekly)
1849	62	62
1859	59	54
1869	42	66
1879	76	85
1889	95	90
1889	103	104
1904	104	102
1909	100	101
1914	100	100
1919	111	105

York State with the cost of living in New York City and Buffalo for identical months we get the following real wage index for 1914-1923:

1914 (Dec.)	100	1919 (June, Dec.)................101
1915 (Dec.)	104	1920 (June, Dec.)................108
1916 (Dec.)	103	1921 (May, Sept., Dec.).........112
1917 (Dec.)	 95	1922 (Mar., June, Sept., Dec.)..118
1918 (Dec.)	103	1923 (Mar., June, Sept., Dec.)..125

for the market. The farther back we go in our history the larger was the proportion of such production. Relatively more was produced for home consumption. The census data on occupations show that the proportion of the "gainfully employed" increased considerably up to 1910. This probably does not mean that a larger proportion were actually engaged in production in 1910 than formerly, but merely that the proportion producing for the market, i. e., "gainfully employed," was greater. If therefore any comparison is to be made

CHART 2

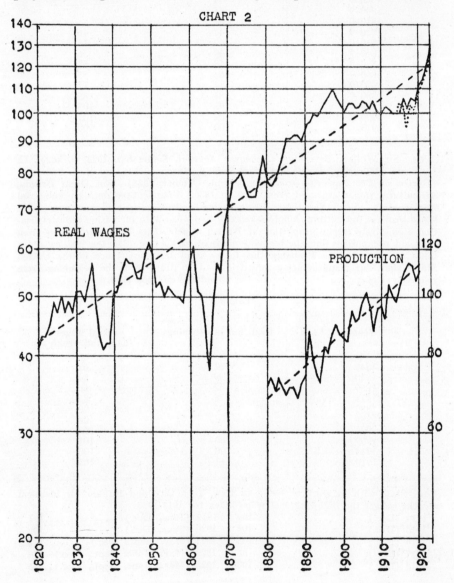

between real wages and production, it is clear that we should use production per person gainfully employed, and not production per capita. The difference between the two methods is considerable.

From the chart it is clear that the trend of real wages has not increased as rapidly as the trend of production per person gainfully employed. The real-wage trend shows an increase of 1.04 per cent (compounded) per annum, while the production trend indicates an increase of 1.29 per cent per annum.

On the basis of the marginal productivity theory of wages it is to be expected that real wages would not increase as rapidly as average production.[10] The trend of wages may be expected to follow the marginal product of labor, but not the average product. The confusion over this matter may perhaps be traced partly to the fact that many of the standard textbooks do not distinguish sharply between diminishing average productivity and diminishing marginal productivity. The return to any one factor depends, however, upon the marginal product of that factor and not upon the average product measured in terms of that factor.

Take an illustration from agriculture. So long as land is free,

[10]In the March, 1923, Supplement to the AMERICAN ECONOMIC REVIEW, Mr. George Soule takes the untenable position that real wages may logically be expected to increase in proportion to the increase in per capita production. In addition to the theoretical analysis, certain statistical errors appear in Mr. Soule's paper. His data show that the average per capita production increased 28 per cent for the 22-year period from 1899 to 1920, yet he concludes that the "average per capita increment to national production was slightly under 2 per cent a year," and that "real wages might have increased between 30 and 40 per cent for the period in question." The error here appears to be due to the fact that the per capita increase in the volume of manufacture was about 38 per cent. But manufacture tells but a part of the story. Food, the most important item in the workingman's budget, is dependent upon agricultural production.

Another serious error is made by Mr. Soule in splicing the index of real wages for New York state and Wisconsin on to the index of real wages based on annual earnings at the year 1914. The year 1914 was one of deep depression with an unusual amount of unemployment. *Annual earnings* were therefore far below normal in this year. I have estimated that the year 1914 was about 7 per cent below normal in production and employment (*Journal of American Statistical Association*, March, 1922). This conclusion is supported by the index of business conditions computed by the statistical department of the American Telephone and Telegraph Company as well as by the Index of Trade of the Harvard Committee on Economic Research. To join a weekly-earnings index to an annual-earnings index in a year in which annual earnings were about seven per cent below normal is clearly indefensible. Had the weekly-earnings index been joined to the annual-earnings index at the year 1919, a year closely comparable to Mr. Soule's base year, 1889, (see Am. T. & T. index) the index number for real wages would have stood much higher in 1922 than Mr. Soule has it. Moreover, Mr. Soule appears to have overlooked the fact that the census data on annual earnings prior to 1889 were for manufactures and hand industries, while after that date hand industries are omitted. The later figures are therefore not of the same order of magnitude. The data for 1899 give the figures both ways, and therefore it is perfectly possible to make the index numbers comparable.

cultivation will tend to become intensive up to the point at which the average product in terms of the variable factors of labor and capital is equal to the marginal product. So long as the marginal product is higher than the average product (which it is up to the point of diminishing average returns) every added application of variable factors will raise the average product. As soon as the marginal product falls below the previous average product, the application of that added increment becomes uneconomical. As long as land is free, the return to the variable factors depends upon the average product. Hence the most desirable degree of intensivity of cultivation will be that which brings the highest average returns. As soon as the land becomes scarce, however, cultivation is pushed beyond the point of highest average .returns, the marginal product falls below the average product, and the decline in the marginal product is of necessity more rapid than the decline in the average product. As soon as land becomes scarce the variable factors can command only the marginal product, the difference between the marginal product and the average product going to rent. Assume that the average product had declined five per cent below the point of highest average returns. It would not follow on the basis of the productivity analysis that the return to the variable factors should therefore fall only five per cent, for in that case no rent could be paid on land even though it had now become an economic factor in production and not merely as before a technical factor. Unquestionably the lag of real wages behind production from 1897 to 1915 was to some extent the result of the increasing scarcity of land.

The use of machinery has resulted in a much larger per capita product. But obviously wages could not increase *proportionally* or there would be nothing with which to pay interest. It is of course clear that, the more round-about or capitalistic the process of production becomes, the smaller of necessity must be the *share* of the total product going to labor. When an increase in production is due to a greater use of capital, real wages must of necessity lag behind the increase in production.

Suppose the increase in production were due to new inventions in machinery and equipment which, however, call for no additional capital outlay. The return to capital would rise with its increased productivity, but labor would make no gains until an increased supply of capital resulted from the high rate of return. This would lower the marginal productivity of capital and raise the marginal productivity of labor. Wages would rise, but not in proportion to the total product.

Finally consider the case of a larger total product due to increased labor efficiency. Let us say that labor doubled its output. If piece rates remained the same, wages would also double. This situation would, however, result in lower capital costs per unit of output since the capital costs would now be spread over a larger output. In other words, while labor costs remained constant, capital costs per unit of output would have decreased. Substitution of capital for labor would follow and wages would fall. Labor would therefore be unable to retain the entire gain in increased output.

Moreover, it may well be true that the increase in production consists predominantly of producers' goods rather than of consumers' goods. This no doubt indicates a greater quantity of consumers' goods for the future than could be possible without this larger supply of capital, but so long as the rate of increase in the production of capital equipment exceeds the rate of increase in the volume of production as a whole, real wages may be expected to lag well behind general production. E. E. Day's studies in national production indicate that the rate of increase in the volume of producers' goods is much greater than for consumers' goods. If however we take a weighted average of his food and textiles groups,[11] giving food the weight of 2 and textiles the weight of 1, we get a much closer correspondence between production and real wages. In this case we are forced to use per capita product, but in doing so it is certain that the production index shows a somewhat exaggerated increase, since more food and clothing were prepared for home consumption in 1899 than in 1919.

TABLE V

Years	Per capita production of food and textiles	Real wages
1900–04	93	103
1905–09	100	103
1910–14	97	101
1915–19	111	104

Increased productivity may moreover be expected to increase the real wages of the working class only on condition that this increased production comes within the field of the workingman's budget. If improvements result in lower cost and increased production of goods not purchased by workingmen, the real incomes of other classes are increased, but there may be no gain for the wage-earners. It is in such cases as this that the difference between value productivity and physical productivity becomes important. If the increase in physical product is general, no significance from the standpoint of the present discussion attaches to this distinction; but, if the increased physical pro-

[11] E. E. Day, *Quart. Pub. Am. Stat. Assoc.*, March, 1921, p. 557.

ductivity is limited to a few industries, it may well be that the increased physical product results in little or no increase in value product. It is the value product that concerns producers, while it is the physical product that is important to consumers. Hence, if the commodity in question is one in which labor is interested as producer only and not as consumer, he may quite conceivably gain nothing from increased physical productivity.

There is, however, one consideration which qualifies the above argument. If the increased production of the commodity in question draws labor from other less productive fields, we shall have a higher margin of production over the whole field of industry. Diversification raises the margin of production, just as variety raises the margin of consumption (if the psychologists have not robbed that concept of all meaning). In agriculture, for example, diversification not only helps to maintain land fertility, but also—and this is the point we wish to stress here—results in fuller utilization of various kinds of land adapted to the new uses, but not well adapted to the old. With increasing population, instead of going down on lower margins in the production of the old commodities, diversification makes it possible to spread out in new lines where the marginal product is higher. The same is true in other fields. Thus the automobile industry has undoubtedly raised wages, for it has given employment to labor at a higher level of value productivity and thus drawn labor from lower levels in other industries.[12]

Finally we have to consider the share of the national product going to the community as a whole. Much of the laborer's income does not appear in the pay envelop. An increasing proportion of the national income is being absorbed by the community as a whole and distributed not according to value principles, but according to the principles of equality or need. The wage-earners pay envelop may or may not be affected by these public expenditures, depending upon the manner in which the funds are raised. At any rate these are matters that cannot be overlooked in considering the relation between the movement of wages and national production. Moreover, workmen's compensation and other forms of social insurance do not appear in the pay envelop.

III

With the exception of the decade of the seventies, real wages move inversely with the general price level. In the burst of prosperity pre-

[12]If the rich were limited in their consumption to fancy foods and expensive clothing and housing, it is likely that the margin of production would be lower. The more varied the consumption the higher the margin of production will tend to be over the whole field of industry, including that covered by the wage-earners' budget.

ceding the panic of 1873 real wages rose, and in the deep and prolonged depression which followed, labor was so thoroughly deflated that the purchasing power of wages suffered a decline. With the exception of this decade real wages rise with falling prices and depression, and fall with rising prices and prosperity. On the other hand, the purchasing power of labor as a group rises with prosperity and falls with depression, due to increased employment in the first instance and widespread unemployment in the second. It is a common fallacy to suppose that the wage-earners' purchasing power will be high if his real-wage rates are high. High real-wage rates do not avail if one is out of a job.

This relationship between real wages and price fluctuations holds true of both the major and the minor movements. Five major price and wage movements are apparent. The tendency of real wages was upward from 1820 to 1849 while the trend of prices was downward. From 1849 to 1865 the general trend of prices was upward, and in this period real wages tended downward. From 1865 to 1897 the price trend was heavily downward while the real-wage movement was strongly upward. From 1897 to 1919 the general trend of prices was upward but real wages at first fell and then remained stationary. With the heavy fall in prices beginning with 1920, real wages rose sharply.

If we center our attention on the cyclical movements we shall notice a similar situation. In the price upheaval of the thirties culminating in the panic of 1837 the purchasing power of wages suffered a serious decline. With the rising prices leading to the panic of 1857 real wages again fell heavily. A further drop to still lower levels came with the price upheaval of the sixties. The seventies, the exception to the rule, brought the next period of declining real wages beginning with the panic of 1873 and culminating in 1877. The last sharp decline came from 1897 to 1900 when wages failed to respond to the unexpected upward turn in prices.

It is evident that price fluctuations have a powerful influence on the distribution of the national income. The marginal product of each factor is no doubt the *normal* rate of returns to each. But this normal distribution is constantly being upset not only by changes in the relative supply and efficiency of the various factors, but also by the redistribution of income accompanying price changes. If prices rise, the benefit accrues immediately to the entrepreneurial class. In time, however, competition among entrepreneurs compels them to bid up the prices paid for labor, land and capital until the surplus profits are absorbed. In the meantime, however, a fresh rise in prices has created a new margin of profits above costs. Entrepreneurs, naturally, do not pass on these gains to the other factors until compelled to do so by the pressure of competition. It is therefore inevitable that in rising-price periods wages and other costs should lag behind prices. Rising prices amount in fact to a redistribution of the national income in favor of the entrepreneurial class. It amounts to an enforced taxation of wage-earners, salaried persons, investors and landlords with long-term rent contracts.

In the period from 1897 to 1915 when real wages were falling in spite of an enormous increase in national production, business profits far outran the rise in the general price level. This shows itself, for example, in the rise in the stock market. From 1897 to 1913 railroad and industrial stocks advanced about 100 per cent. The classical doctrine that profits and wages correlate inversely is abundantly true when applied to the effect of price fluctuations on those distributive shares.

Moreover, this was a period in which huge corporate surpluses were being set aside out of profits. This meant a great addition to our capital equipment. Thus a large part of the increased national production was in the field of producers' goods, as Mr. Day's studies, previously alluded to, show. The capital equipment came immediately out of the savings of the corporations, but ultimately and in reality out of the enforced saving imposed by the rise in the price level upon wage-earners, salaried people, bond and mortgage holders, insurance policy holders, etc. Rising prices cause a gap between the marginal productivity of the various factors employed by the entrepreneur and the return that each receives. Indeed in such periods it is literally true that "labor does not receive the full value of its product."

On the other hand, labor gets more than its marginal product in falling-price periods. Prices may fall, but labor hangs tenaciously to a wage level once achieved and does not hesitate even to accept unemployment in preference to wage reductions. The employer in such periods is therefore hard put to it to reduce costs in some other way than by reducing wages. This he may do by eliminating waste, introducing improved processes and machinery and by better management.

Moreover, the marginal product of labor is higher in falling-price periods, due to the reduction in the labor force. Thus at least in part the high real wages are purchased at the price of an excessive volume of unemployment.

The low profits of falling-price periods result in a diminution in corporate surpluses and social saving. Probably the production of consumers' goods assumes a relatively greater importance. Thus industry in the falling-price period operates to a large extent on the capital accumulated in the previous period of rising prices. Falling prices hand back to the wage-earners (and fixed-income classes) the fruits of the property "stolen" from them by the preceding rising-price level. The "unearned" property acquired by entrepreneurs in the rising-price period is scaled down by bankruptcy, reörganization and reduction in capitalization in the period of falling prices. Labor now receives, as it were, the dividends that have been accumulating but which have remained unpaid in the rising-price period.

Labor gains, moreover, at the expense of farmers in periods of falling prices. Along with many movements of less importance, we have had, during the last century and a quarter, eight outstanding periods of severe decline in the purchasing power of farm products, beginning with each of the following dates: 1817, 1838, 1857, 1868, 1875, 1882, 1893, and 1919. These were all periods in which the general price level was falling heavily. What is the reason for this relationship? When general prices fall, industrial depression prevails, and the more precipitate the fall the more severe is the depression. When industry is depressed the market for farm products is poor for two reasons: first, because manufacturing consumes a large part of the raw material produced on farms—80 per cent of the raw material used in manufacture comes from farms—and, second, because the purchasing power of wage-earners, much of which is applied to farm products directly or indirectly, is low, due to the prevailing unemployment.

In spite of this restricted market, farmers continue to produce the normal supply of the raw materials of industry while other factors rigidly control the supply. In a period of depression, wage-earners do not go out on the program of selling all their labor at whatever price it will fetch. They prefer unemployment to a precipitate decline in wages. Entrepreneurs curtail production in the face of a falling market. This curtailment checks the extent of the decline in the selling price of manufactured goods. The farmers, however, totally unable to control supply, find themselves in the position of residual claimants. Throwing their commodity on the market in undiminished volume while other groups are controlling supply, they face an adverse purchasing-power ratio. It would be interesting to know how low wage rates would have fallen in 1921 if wage-earners had insisted on selling their full labor supply at whatever rates it might fetch.

It is sometimes argued that high wage rates in the depression period are favorable to farmers, for it is thought that the high rates will create a good market for farm products. But, unfortunately, high wage rates do not help an unemployed man to buy commodities. It is the widespread unemployment that causes low purchasing power, despite high wage rates in the depression period. Now labor is no doubt wise from a long-run point of view in resisting wage reductions at all costs, but it cannot be claimed that these high wage rates are favorable to farmers. Labor and the raw materials of farms constitute the chief prime costs of manufactures. They share in the value of the product according to the relative supply of each. If labor curtails its supply (chooses to remain unemployed rather than accept lower wages) while farmers throw the full supply of their commodity on the market, the share that goes to the farmer will be inordinately low. Thus we find that in each period of heavily falling prices the purchasing power of wages rises while the purchasing power of farm products falls.

The writer believes that the above factors account in the main for the phenomenal rise in real wages since 1919. Real wages are now 25 to 30 per cent above the pre-war level. No doubt restriction of immigration has contributed to the result, but it is easy to overestimate this obvious factor. The more fundamental factors discussed above have operated to produce similar results in many previous periods when there was no restriction on immigration. Certainly real wages would however not have risen as rapidly as they have, had our pre-war immigration continued. Moreover, an unprecedented flood of immigrants, such as we should probably have were there no restrictions, would certainly jeopardize the existing level of real wages.

ALVIN H. HANSEN.

University of Minnesota.

UNION WAGE AND HOUR POLICIES
AND EMPLOYMENT

There is no one wage and hour policy to which all unions subscribe. Generally speaking, unions like most employers sell their product at the best price and under the best conditions that they can obtain. What price they can command depends on many factors. In the short run if the industry is a profitable one, as for example petroleum refining and automobile manufacturing, and if the union has substantial bargaining power and its leadership is able and aggressive, relatively high wages and short hours of work may be attained. On the other hand, if the industry is faced with ruinous competition and overdevelopment, as for example in cotton and certain other textile industries, particularly if the scope of union organization is not industry-wide, the workers will have to content themselves with *relatively* low annual earnings and with relatively long hours.

Other factors which affect wage and hour levels are (1) the character of the demand for the product, that is, whether the demand is elastic or inelastic, (2) the proportion that labor costs constitute of the total cost of production, (3) the economic organization and financial structure of the industry, (4) competition from substitute products, (5) general business conditions, and (6) the relation of capacity to demand. Because of the operation of these factors, wage and hour levels and policies vary by regions, markets, industries, and often establishments.

In a number of industries, unions, like employers in numerous instances, have successfully maintained the price of their product during periods of drastic deflation. In the anthracite industry, for example, the union has not taken a single wage reduction since the Award of the Anthracite Strike Commission of 1903 and in the building and construction industry it is not uncommon for organized crafts to retain their nominal wage rates during periods of depression. In other industries, unions, like employers on numer-

41

ous occasions, have taken substantial cuts in the price of their product when faced with economic conditions which required such action. Witness the ten per cent reduction taken by the railroad workers in 1932 and the 60 per cent reduction accepted by the union in the full-fashioned hosiery industry during the years 1927 to 1932.

Some idea of the variations in wage and hour levels and policies is disclosed by an analysis of wage and hour data published by the Bureau of Labor Statistics for manufacturing industries. In 71 of the 87 industries at present included in the Bureau's survey, data were available for both 1933 and 1939. An analysis of these data for the months of May, 1933, and May, 1939, brings to light some interesting facts. During the six years beginning in May, 1933, the increases in hourly earnings ranged from 19.5 per cent in the book and job branch of the printing and publishing industry to 105.2 per cent in sawmills. Thirty-four industries, or about 48 per cent of the total, showed increases which amounted to 50 per cent or more. In fifteen industries the increases ranged from 60.0 to 69.9 and in five from 70.0 to 79.9 per cent.

The data for average weekly hours of work, not standard or maximum hours, also show wide variations. In 27 of the 71 industries, or 38.0 per cent of the total, average hours of work actually increased between 1933 and 1939. All but four of these industries, however, were durable goods industries whose volume of production undoubtedly had been greatly curtailed by the depression. Of the remaining 44 industries the reductions in average weekly hours below the May, 1933, level ranged from 1.0 to 33.1 per cent. In 22 industries reductions ranged from 0.1 to 9.9 per cent, in 15 from 10.0 to 19.9, in six from 20.0 to 29.9 per cent, and in one the increase was 33.1 per cent.

While economic conditions and union leadership have resulted in different wage and hour levels and the application of different wage and hour policies, it should be recognized that union leaders are in common agreement that workers must obtain a greater share of the national wealth and income. To attain this end many of them, notably since 1933, have strongly advocated the raising of the rates of pay as a means of increasing purchasing power and the reduction of hours of work to increase employment. In this they have been aided by federal legislation in recent years. It is not surprising, therefore, to find that in the 87 industries for which the Bureau of Labor Statistics compiles information, average hourly earnings between May, 1933, and May, 1939, have increased 53 per cent and weekly hours of work have been reduced 6.9 per cent below the abnormally low level that prevailed in May, 1933. How do the wage and hour levels of May, 1939, compare with those prevailing in May, 1929? According to the data published by the National Industrial Conference Board for 25 manufacturing industries or groups of industries, hourly earnings in May, 1939, were 21.6 per cent higher and weekly hours 24.9 per cent lower than their respective levels in May, 1929.

One wonders whether any other period in American history has witnessed such drastic changes in the rates of pay and weekly hours of work. The achievement is all the more impressive in that the cost of living between May, 1933, and May, 1939, increased only about 10 per cent. Unions, however, cannot go on reducing hours and raising wage rates indefinitely. At some point the union will have to shift its demands to other aspects of industrial relations.

What have been the economic consequences of these drastic revisions of wage and hour levels upon costs, prices, profits, mechanization, annual wages, and opportunity of employment? Do shorter hours of work make for fuller employment and do higher wage rates improve the standards of living of workers?

Some light can be thrown on the answers to these questions by an examination of recent developments in the bituminous coal industry.[1] In April, 1934, the operators and miners in the Appalachian fields signed wage contracts that provided for reductions in hours of work and for substantial wage increases. The terms of the wage contracts were embodied in the Coal Code and applied with modifications to outlying fields by the N.R.A. As a result, daily hours of work were reduced from eight to seven, weekly hours from 40 to 35, and rates of pay were increased about 22 per cent, the rate of increase varying by occupational groups and by fields.[2] The average hourly earnings of all employees equalled approximately 71 cents and daily earnings about $5.00 after the new agreement went into effect. It is with the effect of these adjustments that this paper is primarily concerned.

Effects of the April, 1934, Agreements on Costs, Sales Income, and Margins

The N.R.A. compiled cost and income data for fifteen months, November, 1933, to January, 1935, for approximately 1,000 mines located east of the Mississippi River. The combined production of these mines amounted to 61.7 per cent of the total output of the industry in 1934. The cost data that were compiled by the N.R.A. did not include interest payments on investments or taxes on income and unassigned acreage.

---

[1] For a more detailed discussion of developments in the bituminous coal industry see *Economic Consequences of the Seven-Hour Day and Wage Changes in the Bituminous Coal Industry,* by Waldo E. Fisher, University of Pennsylvania Press, 1939.

[2] Based on data published by the Bureau of Labor Statistics for bituminous coal mines in monthly issues of *Employment and Pay Rolls.* To compute the changes in hourly earnings resulting from the adjustments made in April, 1934, the author took the average hourly earnings for the four months preceding and the four months following the month of April.

To determine the effects of the April adjustments in hours and wages on costs it was necessary to select comparable months before and after April, 1934, that is, months in which the volume of production and the number of days worked were about the same. Such a procedure was necessary because per ton costs of coal rise with great rapidity as the number of tipple starts or days worked approaches zero and the production of coal is curtailed. The months selected for the pre-agreement period were December, 1933, and January, 1934, and those for the post-agreement period were December, 1934, and January, 1935. What effects did the seven-hour day and wage changes have upon costs and sales income?

Total reported costs increased 22.7 cents or 14.5 per cent; labor costs increased 16.8 cents or 18.5 per cent; costs of supplies, 2.9 cents or 12.6 per cent; and total producing costs 20.3 cents or 14.3 per cent. The fixed costs for which data were segregated on the cost reports—namely, administrative expenses, costs on a fixed lump-sum basis, mine supervisory and clerical costs, as well as mine office expenses and salaries and expenses of other employees distributed to the mine—showed an increase of one-half cent a ton. Mixed costs, that is, cost of supplies (including power purchased and mine fuel) and selling expenses, increased about five cents or 14.7 per cent, and direct costs, 17.6 cents or 17.9 per cent.

Sales income per ton was increased 29.5 cents or 18.3 per cent. In other words, the entire increase of 22.7 cents a ton in total reported costs was passed on to the consumers together with an additional charge of 6.8 cents a ton. In the selected two-month period following the wage and hour adjustments, operators' margins were 10.9 cents a ton. This figure should be compared with 4.1 cents a ton, the amount received during the selected two-month period before April, 1934. These margins, it should be noted, do not represent net earnings. The operating companies still had to pay interest on investments as well as taxes on income and in some cases on unassigned acreage.

The behavior of costs, sales income, and margins for the industry as a whole cannot be taken as representative of what happened to the individual coal fields. Actually the impact of the wage and hour adjustments upon the various fields showed great variations. This was to be expected because, while the reduction in hours was the same throughout the industry, the increases in the rates of pay were far from uniform. The increases in labor costs ranged from a low of 2.7 per cent in Indiana to a high of 28.4 in Alabama, Southern Tennessee, and Georgia. The increases for producing costs ranged from 2.8 to 23.6 per cent, for total reported costs from 3.9 to 22.1 per cent, and for sales income from 11.0 to 26.3 per cent.

The operators in most of the districts, however, were able to improve definitely their financial position as far as margins were concerned, but the extent to which this was done differed greatly in the various fields. Only three fields were unable to pass the total increase in costs on to the consumers. Although most of the operators were able to improve their financial position, it should not be assumed that the margins were too high. Data for measuring profits and losses were not available.

In passing, it should be pointed out that the wage and hour revisions did not improve the competitive situation within the industry. In the case of both labor and total costs the spread between low and high costs was greater after the April adjustments than that which had prevailed prior to April, 1934. The coal mines in Indiana and Illinois definitely improved their competitive standing in the industry.

Some Other Economic Consequences

The effects of the seven-hour day and wage changes upon costs, sales income, and operators' margins, although of major importance in any discussion of wage and hour policies, are incidental to the particular aspect of the problem under consideration at this session. Let us, therefore, examine the effects of the April adjustments on employment, annual income, and related factors.

The months and years immediately following the wage and hour revisions were characterized by a marked improvement in production, employment, and other business indicators. Much of the gain occurring in these years must be attributed to the general forces of recovery that followed in the wake of one of the worst depressions in American history. To determine the net effects of the wage and hour revisions on employment, annual per capita income of full-time employees, and total payrolls, it was necessary to remove the cyclical influences that were at work during these years. This was accomplished by the use of such common denominators as millions of tons and 200-days worked.

The introduction of the seven-hour day and the accompanying increases in the rates of pay was immediately followed by a 10.0 per cent drop in output per man per day. To meet their market requirements during the twelve months beginning with April, 1934, the operators added more men to their payrolls and increased the number of days their mines worked. As a result man-days per million tons produced increased 8.1 per cent. Per capita income of full-time employees per 200-days of work rose 14.9 per cent, and the total wage bill per million tons produced increased between 31 and 35 per cent.

Faced with substantially higher labor costs (18.5 per cent above the level prevailing during the selected months prior to the April agreements) as well as a 10 per cent reduction in employee productivity, and finding themselves in a somewhat better financial position, the operators placed heavy orders for mechanical loading equipment. In 1935, the proportion of the total output of deep mines that was mechanically loaded—which incidentally had remained practically stationary for the three preceding years —rose 10.7 per cent. By 1937 the proportion of the total output of deep mines that was contributed by this type of equipment stood at 20.2 per cent as compared with 12.3 per cent in 1933—an increase of 64.2 per cent.

With the extension of mechanical loading the output per man per day rose steadily. By 1937 it was only 1.9 per cent below the 1933 level. As the output per man per day rose, the opportunity of employment was reduced. By 1937, man-days per million tons were only 1.4 per cent above the 1933 level. Money per capita income, responding to two additional wage increases—one of approximately eight per cent in 1935 and another of about twelve per cent in 1937—continued to rise. By 1937, money per capita income of full-time employees per 200-days of work was 35.8 per cent and real per capita income 22.0 per cent higher than their respective levels in 1933.

What about the total wage bill? Did it continue to rise? The replacement of men with capital—although extraordinarily rapid during these years— did not begin to offset increases in the rates of pay which during the years 1934 to 1937 amounted to about 74 per cent. As a result, by 1937, nominal payrolls per million tons produced were 45.9 per cent and real payrolls 31.2 per cent above their respective 1933 levels.

To summarize, in the bituminous coal industry the immediate effects (within a period of nine to twelve months) of the seven-hour day and substantial increases in hourly or piece rates were:

1. Increases in all major cost items, but especially in labor costs, selling expenses, supplies, and total reported costs.
2. Increases in average sales income per ton that were greater than those required to absorb the additions to the cost of production. It should be noted that the increase in sales income was made possible by the power granted to the Code Authority to regulate prices under the supervision of the federal government.
3. Increases in operators' margins that placed all but three of the reporting fields east of the Mississippi River in a better financial position.
4. A material reduction in output per man per day.
5. A substantial increase in man-days worked per million tons of coal mined.
6. A substantial increase in the per capita income of full-time wage-earners per 200-days worked.
7. A very material increase in the total wage bill per million tons mined.

The economic consequences of the 1934 agreement plus additional wage increases in 1935 and 1937 over a period of three years, 1935 to 1937 inclusive, may be summarized as follows:

1. A sharp increase in the introduction of mechanical loading devices. It should be pointed out that it is impossible to say how much of the very rapid rise in

mechanical loading was due to wage and hour adjustments and how much to other factors such as the improved financial position of the industry and a more optimistic attitude among operators.

2. A steady increase in the output per man per day.
3. A loss in most of the gains in employment as measured by man-days per million tons produced.
4. Further material increases in both per capita income of full-time wage-earners per 200-days worked and in the total wage bill per million tons of coal produced.

Generalizations on the basis of these findings for the bituminous coal industry should be drawn with caution. In the first place, labor costs constitute an extremely high proportion of the total cost of mining coal—approximately 65 per cent. For this reason increases in labor costs should tend to raise prices to a greater extent in bituminous coal than in industries with a relatively low labor cost.

Second, much of the work done by coal miners involves heavy physical effort. One would expect a reduction of hours from eight to seven to reduce the output per man per day less for work of this character (because of the element of fatigue) than for work which is less strenuous.

In the third place, because it was possible in the bituminous coal industry to substitute instrumental capital for labor, the operators were able to overcome in part the loss in employee productivity and to reduce the number of men necessary to mine a given tonnage. This procedure could not have been utilized had the work been of such a nature that men could not be replaced with machines, or had the substitution of labor by machines and labor-saving devices practically been completed.

In the fourth place, the fact that many mines had been operating at substantial losses for a considerable time as well as the opportunity to regulate coal prices under the supervision of the federal government enabled the operators to pass on to the public an amount which was greater than the actual increase in costs. Under different circumstances in this decentralized, overexpanded industry such a procedure would not have been possible.

In the fifth place, the bituminous coal industry is greatly overdeveloped. As a result, when the output per man per day declined, the operators had the choice of working their mines more days per year or adding more men to the payrolls of the industry. In the absence of excess capacity and reduced working schedules, the introduction of the seven-hour day when accompanied by a decrease in employee productivity would require, in the initial stages at least, substantial additions to payrolls, assuming of course the same or increased demand for the product.

In the sixth place, the demand for bituminous coal in the short run is relatively inelastic and therefore the increased costs could be passed along to the consumers without an immediate effect on the volume of coal sold.

The result might well have been different if the demand were elastic.

Last, the wage and hour adjustments were made on the upswing of the business cycle which made it possible for the increased costs to be absorbed with less difficulty than would otherwise have been the case.

The economic consequences of the seven-hour day and substantial increases in hourly and piece rates in the bituminous coal industry were those which the orthodox economist would have predicted, except its effect on annual earnings. Even in this instance, were the demand for coal more elastic, his contention might well have been substantiated. It may still be borne out over a longer period of time if the higher coal prices caused by the shorter work-day and substantial wage changes result, as the operators maintain they will, in the more efficient utilization of bituminous coal or in the further growth of substitute fuels.

Up to this point our analysis has been confined to an examination of the net effects of the seven-hour day and wage changes since 1933. What light does a comparison of employment and earnings in 1937 with those in 1929 throw on our problem? For such a comparison, it is desirable to choose two periods showing the same level of production. Since identical levels, however, are not available, use was made of February, and March, months in which the 1937 production was about seven per cent above that of 1929.

Although hourly earnings of all wage-earners in 1937 were 20.2 per cent above those paid in 1929, the money wage bill was 11.0 per cent below. The real wage bill, however, was 5.5 per cent above the level prevailing in 1929. It is disturbing to discover that despite a reduction in standard daily hours from eight to seven and weekly hours from 48 to 35, the number of wage-earners employed by the industry was still 1.2 per cent less than the number at work in comparable months in 1929. Thus a 20.2 per cent increase in hourly earnings was accompanied by a loss of 11 per cent in money payrolls but by a 5.5 per cent increase in real payrolls because cost of living was still below the 1929 level. Moreover, a 16.0 per cent decrease in weekly hours of work failed to maintain a level of employment equal to that which existed in 1929 when production was about 7 per cent under the level prevailing in 1937.

Hourly Earnings, Payrolls, and Employment in Manufacturing Industries

What happened to hourly earnings, payrolls, and employment opportunity in manufacturing industries? Because manufacturing production in October, 1939, was about 2.0 per cent above the level of October, 1929, a comparison of the data on employment and payrolls for these two periods should be of interest. Hourly earnings in 1939 were 22.1 per cent above those paid in 1929. Nominal payrolls were 9.8 per cent below while real payrolls were 8.4 per cent above those paid out in 1929. Hours per week in 1939 were

20.9 per cent below 1929 and the number of wage-earners on manufacturing payrolls was 3.9 per cent less than those employed in 1929.[3]

We see, then, notwithstanding very substantial increases in hourly earnings, that the average nominal payrolls in 87 manufacturing industries as well as bituminous coal are still below, while real payrolls are from 6 to 8 per cent higher than, their respective levels in 1929. Moreover, despite substantial reductions in weekly hours, the number of wage-earners at work in these industries is slightly less than the number employed in 1929. Do these represent the accomplishments of almost seven years of feverish activity on the part of organized labor and the federal government to increase purchasing power by raising the price of labor and to increase employment by shortening the hours of work? This limited analysis does not give a completely satisfying appraisal of union wage and hour policies but it does suggest that over-emphasis on shorter hours and higher wage rates may not be the way to raise the standards of living of wage-earners in American industries.

The ardent proponents of the purchasing power and shorter hour theories will argue: "Well! We are not surprised. This is what we should have expected considering technological developments during these years." To this contention one can only say: "Under what conditions does the replacement of men and women with instrumental capital take place more rapidly—when wage and hour levels are related to changes in productivity that follow the gradual introduction of machinery, or when they are drastically revised in a few years in the hope of immediately attaining desirable objectives which may not be capable of realization in the short run?"

Of especial significance to us in the United States is the following comparison of recent developments in Great Britain and the United States that was published in *The Economist* (London) of July 1, 1939.

Between 1929 and 1938 the average hourly earnings of American workers (according to the figures of the National Industrial Conference Board) increased by 23 per cent. Relatively to the movement of average wholesale prices, the increase was no less than 49 per cent. But payrolls—the total amount of money paid out in wages—fell, according to the official index, by 18½ per cent in the same period. To place two figures in juxtaposition is not to prove that the one is the cause of the other. But it is at least suggestive that, while wage-rates in

---

[3] The percentages that wages (not including salaries) constituted of the total income paid out by manufacturing industries for the years 1929 to 1937 are presented below:

1929	1930	1931	1932	1933	1934	1935	1936	1937
59.9	54.6	53.3	53.3	58.0	60.2	61.0	58.4	58.7

It will be observed that in all years except 1934 and 1935 the wage earners' share of the total manufacturing income was less than in 1929. It is also important to note that total manufacturing income in 1937—the last year for which data are available—was still 13.3 per cent below the 1929 level. Robert R. Nathan, *Income in the United States, 1929-37*, U. S. Department of Commerce.

Great Britain rose over the same period by less than a third of the American increase, British payrolls (so far as they can be calculated) increased by 20 per cent instead of the American fall of almost the same proportion—and this in the country which is the more "mature" of the two.

I close this discussion of union wage and hour policies and their relation to employment opportunity with three questions:

1. What is organized labor's objective? To secure high wage rates, shorter hours of work, and perhaps higher annual earnings for a restricted number of employees in a given industry, or to improve the economic well-being of all employees in the industry?
2. If organized labor is concerned with the improvement of the economic status of all employees, have not its leaders in many instances been too much concerned with high wage rates and short hours and too little with total payrolls and maximum employment opportunity?
3. Will not continued emphasis on wage and hour levels occasion an even more rapid replacement of labor by machines and therefore aggravate rather than improve the unemployment situation?

WALDO E. FISHER

UNION PARTICIPATION IN HIGH PRODUCTIVITY

By William Gomberg

THE public's interest in the administration of a labor contract may be found in the answers to the following two questions: (1) Does the contract provide adequate methods to secure labor peace during the life of the contract, thus assuring continuous production and a free flow of services and commodities? (2) Under what circumstances is it possible to make the union an active participant in high productivity techniques?

An investigation of the answer to question number one leads to an examination of the nature of industrial grievances and the interpretation placed by both labor and management on the subject matter at issue.

An understanding of work stoppages where a collective agreement exists calls for an investigation of the nature of grievances that arise under such contracts. In an attempt to standardize the approach to a resolution of these grievances, many manuals of grievance procedures have been developed.

The Legalistic Approach

Most of such manuals have laid emphasis in two areas: (1) the formal methods of recording and taking up grievances; that is, the formulation of methods of presentation and appeal in accordance with the hierarchy of authority; and (2) the separation of "fancied" grievances from "real" grievances; that is, the necessity for resolving disputes in accordance with the facts that are available.[1]

Although there has been an occasional reference to the necessity for what is called a human approach to the problem, the whole emphasis has been placed upon what Professor Selekman has called the legalistic approach to handling grievances.[2] Running like a red thread through all the recommendations is an emphasis on "securing the facts." This gives a pseudo-hard-boiled objective appearance to the solution of most .of these problems which unfortunately seldom matches reality.

A Fair Work Load

Among the workers' grievances, it would seem that arguments over a fair work load should lend themselves to a more objective treatment based on facts than perhaps the more emotional subjects like discharges due to infractions of discipline. To what extent do grievances over a fair work load lend themselves to an objective determination based on facts?

The question of what constitutes a fair day's work is one of the most potent sources of industrial disputes. Edwin A. Lahey, writing in the *Pittsburgh Press* about the acute Detroit labor situation immediately before its explosion into the General Motors strike of 1945–46, expressed the belief that behind most of the unrest on the local level (i.e., shop grievance level) were disputes over the measurement of a fair day's work.[3] An examination of the files of the National War Labor Board of World War II discloses case after

[1] See U. S. Department of Labor, Division of Labor Standards, *Settling Plant Grievances,* Bull. 60, 1943, and *The Foreman's Guide to Labor Relations,* Bull. 66, 1944, Washington: Government Printing Office.

[2] Benjamin M. Selekman, "Handling Shop Grievances," *Harvard Business Review,* Summer, 1945.

[3] Edwin A. Lahey, *Pittsburgh Press,* Sept. 25, 1945.

case in which disputes over work loads had resulted in work stoppages.[4]

Much of the trouble revolving around the setting of production standards stems from management's misinterpretation of some of the techniques of industrial engineering which are used to set production standards. A good example of this sort of misinterpretation may be found in the writing of Leland Hill and Charles R. Hook. In discussing the fixing of a wage incentive payment plan, they recommend the writing of the following clause:

When a bona fide new job is created, or when changes are made in equipment or method of processing which will result in a substantial change in job duties for those employees covered by this agreement, management may develop an appropriate rate by the regular procedure in effect in the company for its industrial engineering and industrial relations activities. The rate thus developed shall be the rate for the job, subject to the following provisions:

The union delegate representing the employee or employee to be affected shall be informed by the management concerning such rates. Should the union delegate allege that the rate as determined by the management is improper, the union may regard the matter as a problem, and may present the problem to management as provided in section nine of this agreement provided, however, that problems arising under this paragraph *may not* be carried beyond step three of section nine hereof (nonarbitration).[5]

[4] E.g., Case No. 111-16460-D, Lockheed Corp. v. International Association of Machinists; Case No. 111-3692-G, G. F. Richter Mfg. Co. v. United Electrical, Radio and Machine Workers Union; Case No. 111-8458-D, Allis-Chalmers Mfg. Co. v. United Automobile Workers Union; Case No. 83068-D, Curtiss-Wright Corp. v. United Automobile Workers Union; and Case No. 111-1073-D, Timken-Detroit Axle Co. v. United Automobile Workers Union; *War Labor Reports,* Washington: Bureau of National Affairs.

[5] Leland H. Hill and Charles R. Hook, Jr., *Management at the Bargaining Table* (New York: McGraw-Hill Book Co., 1945), p. 225.

The assumptions behind this denial of the resolution of a grievance around the production standard by resort to arbitration are, first, that the setting of rates is a management prerogative; and second, that the setting of a production standard is something that is based on facts and only facts.[6] It therefore follows, of course, that production standards based on such austere facts cannot be changed by negotiation.

The position taken by the management generally is that it will negotiate base rates with the union. If the system of wage payment is measured day work, management reserves the right to fix the work load expected. If the system of wage payment is some incentive payment plan, management reserves to itself the right to fix the production standard underlying the incentive earning opportunity.

The trade union, in turn, takes the position that it is concerned with the amount of work expected from its membership under measured day work and with the earning opportunities afforded its membership under a wage incentive plan.

Management attempts to justify its position by maintaining that the facts disclosed by the time study provide the sole basis for fixing the production standard.

THE TIME STUDY

The usefulness of the time study in settling a grievance depends primarily on what the margin of error of the time-study technique is. If the margin of error of this technique exceeds substantially the usual increment or decrement to or from a pay roll that results from collective bargaining negotiations, it follows at once that the technique is exceedingly limited in its usefulness as a means of resolving work load disputes.

[6] See J. Keith Louden, *Wage Incentives* (New York: J. Wiley and Sons, 1944), pp. 161-62.

An exhaustive study by Leng [7] of the accuracy of the decimal minute stop watch, the instrument used in time study, indicates some amazing results. The data used here are from Leng, but the writer should be held responsible for any of the conclusions drawn.

The pertinent parts of Mr. Leng's experiment follow: A calibrated synchronous motor was set up to drive an endless loop of film. At fixed intervals a sticker was pasted over the frame of the film. Readings were taken on the stop watch as the pasted frames bypassed a fixed pointer. In this manner a calibrated time interval with definitely fixed end points was being measured by a number of observers. These end points were much more definite and exact than those which the average time-study practitioner is compelled to choose in actual industrial operations.

The observers were made up of nine men whose time-study experience varied from six months to ten years. Their competence was vouched for by Professor Robert K. Morrow of the New York University School of Engineering. Twenty readings were recorded for each observer, making a total of 180 readings on the stop watch.

Yet the deviation of the observed arithmetic mean from the true reading varied from a low of 3.30 per cent for readings of 0.10 minute to a high of 12.6 per cent for a reading of 0.025 minute. When we realize that the permissible percentage error for the entire time study is restricted to plus or minus 5 per cent, the size of the collective bargaining increment or decrement, it seems that this is indeed a large percentage to use up on the most objective part of time study, the actual measurement of the time elapsed.

[7] Richard B. Leng, "Observational Error and Economy in Time Study," unpublished M.A. thesis, Department of Administrative Engineering, New York University, 1941.

What is even more interesting than the percentage deviation from the true readings is the coefficient of variation for each of these samples. If we assume that the stop-watch readings are distributed normally—indeed an optimistic assumption for stop-watch readings—then plus or minus three times the coefficient of variation will indicate the possible deviation of any individual reading from the true value in terms of the percentage of the arithmetic mean in 997 cases out of 1,000. Thus the stop-watch readings indicated a tripled coefficient of variation, varying from a high of 89.1 per cent for a true mean of .025 minute to a low of 33.4 per cent for .10 minute.

With such large sources of error in the readings themselves, we need but add the residual errors of the less objective parts of time study, such as the allowances for personal fatigue and the application of the rating or leveling factor, to conclude that the facts in the situation, that is the time-study facts, are completely inconclusive in an effort to settle a grievance as objective as one over the work load.

EMOTIONAL GRIEVANCES AND THE CLINICAL APPROACH

A survey of other typical grievances that are likely to arise under the collective agreement includes complaints against discipline, objections to a particular supervisor, and disciplinary layoffs.[8] All the complaints that arise under these headings are fraught with symptoms of emotional maladjustment on either side. Having already seen how difficult it is to gather facts under the most objective circumstances, is it reasonable for us to suppose that the very legal establishment of the exact facts according to the rules of evidence will actually establish industrial peace?

[8] U. S. Department of Labor, *Settling Plant Grievances, op. cit.,* pp. 2–4.

It is for these reasons that the students of industrial relations, such as Selekman of Harvard, after re-examining the legalistic approach to the handling of shop grievances, recommend the substitution of the clinical approach.[9]

The clinical approach frankly recognizes the emotional content of grievances and accepts these emotions as facts that are every bit as important as the legalistic facts involved. That is perhaps why, despite all strictures against logrolling in the official manuals describing how to handle grievances, practical business agents and workers' representatives have sensed that if you want to live with a person, it is necessary to permit him to "save face" on occasion. Thus, of a number of grievances that require settlement, the practical business agent concentrates on the most important ones and may sacrifice some of the lesser complaints even where they are justified. It is part of his discovery of an empirical means of living with management. I do not doubt that the same is true on the other side. Under such circumstances it can be readily seen why it is so difficult to lay down general rules or principles for the settlement of grievances: so much depends upon the temperament and emotional make-up of the people who are doing the negotiating.

It is too early yet to draw any general conclusions about how to handle grievances, and until more information is available it may be well to remember simply that pseudo facts may occasionally be as misleading as outright falsehoods.

WORKERS' OPPOSITION TO TECHNOLOGICAL ADVANCE

A clear understanding of what is involved in the emotional content of workers' gripes in the factory assists in determining under what circumstances

[9] Selekman, *op. cit.*, p. 471.

unions can become active participants in high productivity techniques, or at least the circumstances under which unions will interpose no obstacles to the introduction of improved technological procedures.

Management thinking in the Hill-Hook tradition denies the working force any voice in the introduction of new techniques into the manufacturing process of the industry. This, it maintains, is purely a management function and responsibility.

On the other hand, the union whose membership sees its skills made obsolete over night and its entire apprenticeship investment dissipated at once is not likely to be guided completely by the rules of clear, detached logic. It is much more likely to be tempted to emulate those members of management who likewise seek to protect an obsolete investment, even if it requires antisocial activity.

The usual pleas of academicians about the long-run benefits of technological progress to public, labor, and management will fall on deaf ears for two reasons: (1) It is by no means certain that the immediate working group will participate in these benefits, even in the long run; and (2) practically all workers live in the short run, they marry in the short run, they bring up their children in the short run, and they either starve or prosper in the short run between birth and the grave. Democratically conducted unions are the organs of expression of these short-run human beings.

WORKERS' ACCEPTANCE OF TECHNOLOGICAL ADVANCE

Yet it has been possible to secure the active co-operation of the trade union in the application of high productivity techniques to certain industries.

Industries like the garment trades, where the classic pattern of the atomistic market is most closely approximated, are in a constant state of shift and flux. The industry is highly portable, requires little fixed capital, and approximates most closely the ideal competitive condition of free entry of new entrepreneurs. Because of this constant state of flux that results in the constant opening of new factories, requiring union organization, it is possible to persuade the garment workers that it is to their interest to keep union factories in a good competitive position. Under the circumstances, less worker resistance to technical labor-saving innovations is encountered in the garment industry than in more stable or less fluid industries.

Thus the acceptance of advanced manufacturing techniques does not flow from any exaggerated sense of making a social contribution, but from the very fundamental consideration of competitive survival.

On the other hand, workers' organizations in the more stable industries, like the railroads, merely reflect in their so-called "make-work" policies the policies of the carriers themselves when they band together to protect their old investment by agreeing to restrict the introduction of more modern equipment.

SOLUTION OUTSIDE OF INDUSTRIAL RELATIONS

Problems such as these can no more be solved by the grievance machinery of industrial relations than can the monopoly problem be solved by antitrust legislation. The remedies for technological obstructions such as those described lie outside the field of industrial relations. Occasionally, public-spirited humanitarians recommend that individual firms key their technological displacements to the normal labor turnover. This presupposes a control over competitive costs which few firms have. Under the circumstances, the problem

offered by these displacements calls for political remedies as distasteful as the word "political" has become to most people. These political measures, related to unemployment insurance and restraining program, plus the assurance of a perpetually expanding economy, contain the answer to these problems, rather than the field of industrial relations per se.

The grievance that arises in connection with technological problems is merely a symptom of a weakness much more deep-seated than an industrial relations failure. Once the fundamental problem of worker security against unemployment has been solved, and increases in man-hour productivity mean something more than merely a shorter work season, it will become possible to use the clinical approach in industrial relations to gain unrestricted acceptance of technological improvements. This approach can be used to overcome the emotional disturbances that arise from upsetting the stability of the worker's customary working habits, provided he is assured that his fundamental security is not threatened.

PUBLIC RESPONSIBILITY

Thus, many of these stoppages that interfere with the public interest may be traced directly back to the public failure to assume some of its social obligations.

It may be emphasized that the public itself is made up of agricultural workers, industrial workers, and managerial members, among other groups. This can bear repeating because many newspaper editors, in their zeal to become the public spokesmen in assailing industrial disturbances, resort to the "plague on both your houses" technique, completely overlooking, first, the fact that the public is made up of diverse members of the same social classes involved in the conflict, with all the sympathies

and group loyalties that such a classification implies; and second, the fact that
the public itself has obligations as well
as rights.

For example, the miners' contempt
for the public interest merely reflects
the public callousness and indifference
to the problems of the miners. Though
they are employed in one of America's
most hazardous industries, very few
provisions have been made for the care
of those injured in the course of work.
Families deprived of their breadwinners

as the result of mine accidents become
public charges and the objects of
charity. Public reaction has confined
itself to public investigation. Miner
reaction to the public hardship under
the circumstances is, "So what?"

A public interest in and contribution
to the solution of some very fundamental economic problems, accompanied by
a sound clinical study of industrial relations by specialists, would enable the
real administration of the labor contract on behalf of the general public.

The Form of Wage Payments

INCENTIVE PAY IN AMERICAN INDUSTRY
1945–1946

JOSEPH M. SHERMAN[1]

About 30 per cent of the plant workers in manufacturing industries studied by the Bureau of Labor Statistics in 1945 and 1946 were paid on an incentive basis. Comparison with previous studies indicates that there has been little change in the extent of incentive payment in recent years. Among the major industry groups studied in 1945 and 1946, incentive methods were most widespread in the manufacture of apparel. In this industry a relatively high proportion of time is spent in handling as contrasted with machine operation. Consequently, control over output is exercised predominantly by the worker rather than the machine. This factor, together with the comparatively small danger of spoilage in most operations, makes the use of incentive payments highly advantageous.

Incentive systems were least common in industries such as industrial chemicals and tool and die jobbing shops. In the former, the speed of production is set to a large degree by the requirements of the manufacturing process and cannot be controlled by the worker, and in the latter, output is on a unit rather than a mass production basis and a high degree of precision is emphasized.

Information for the present summary was obtained by the Bureau of Labor Statistics in a comprehensive series of industry wage studies during 1945 and 1946. Altogether, 56 manufacturing industries, including 34,000 establishments with about 5½ million workers, and 8 nonmanufacturing industries, including 21,000 establishments with about 1½ million employees, were surveyed.[2] Together they are believed to provide a fairly representative sample of wage-payment practices in manufacturing as a whole, although the studies, which were made primarily to provide data on wages in individual industries, do not include such important industries as basic iron and steel, printing, rubber, and lumber.[3] Because of the limited number of industries studied, no generalizations are drawn for nonmanufacturing as a whole.

1. Formerly of the Bureau's Wage Analysis Branch.
2. Data were obtained in the Bureau's studies for about 46 percent of the plants, employing 58 percent of the workers, in these manufacturing industries and from about one-third of the establishments, with two-fifths of the workers, in the nonmanufacturing industries surveyed.
3. It should be borne in mind that the proportion of establishments studied varied among segments of the same industry and among industries. Larger proportions of large establishments and of establishments in large cities and in certain regions were included in order to permit presentation of separate wage data by region, city, and size of establishment. The effect of this varying coverage on the proportion of incentive workers was offset by weighting, so that each industry and each industry segment was given only its appropriate influence on the data; however, the proportion of establishments that are predominantly on an incentive basis has not been adjusted to compensate for differences in coverage.

Prevalence of Incentive Methods

Two-thirds of the workers in the apparel group were paid on an incentive basis and 85 per cent of the apparel establishments were predominantly incentive (table 1).[4] Incentive workers were numerically important in all apparel industries, varying from over two-fifths of the plant labor force in the manufacture of women's suits and coats and of knit underwear to four-fifths in work shirt manufacture (table 2).

The textile group, with nearly two-fifths of its workers on incentive systems, ranked next to apparel in the extent of incentive pay. Full-fashioned and seamless hosiery plants used such methods more extensively than any other textile industry studied. About 1 in 3 workers in the cotton, wool, and rayon textile industries were on incentive. In contrast, textile dyeing and finishing, with its small plants and with processes more closely allied to the chemical industries than to textile manufacture, paid only about a fifth of its workers under incentive systems.

About a fourth of the labor force in the metal-working industries, considered as a group, was paid on an incentive basis. Among these industries, copper alloying, rolling, and drawing ranked highest in prevalence of incentive methods, paying two-thirds of its workers in this manner. At the other extreme, tool and die jobbing shops paid all but 2 per cent of their workers on a time basis.

In the chemical industries, where speed of production is typically set by the requirements of the process rather than by the worker, time work was comparatively more important than in the other major industry groups shown in table 1. Only 3 per cent of the plant workers in industrial chemical production were paid on an incentive basis. Soap and glycerin manufacture had the highest proportion of incentive workers (18 per cent) in this industry group.

The extent of incentive payment varied widely among the remaining manufacturing industries studied. Whereas about three-fourths of the workers in the manufacture of cigars were paid in this manner, all but 6 per cent of the labor force of the cigarette industry, with its widespread use of automatic machinery, were time workers. Similarly, a third of the workers making corrugated and fiber boxes were on incentive, while the machine-paced pulp and paper industry reported less than a tenth of its workers on incentive work.

In New England chemical, textile, and apparel plants, incentive plans

4. The proportion of the labor force paid on an incentive basis was lower than the proportion of apparel establishments with incentive systems, since some workers, such as cutters and those in maintenance jobs, were paid on a time basis. However, because incentive pay is more common among larger establishments, the proportion of workers on incentive pay exceeds the proportion of establishments with incentive systems. Establishments paying at least a fourth of their plant workers under a piece-rate or bonus system were considered as predominantly incentive, but, in determining the proportion of workers paid on an incentive basis, workers in all establishments were included regardless of their predominant method of wage payment.

TABLE 1.—*Extent and type of incentive plans for plant workers in selected manufacturing and nonmanufacturing industry groups, 1945–46*

Item	Total plants studied[1]	Manufacturing				Nonmanufacturing					
		Apparel	Chemicals	Metalworking	Textiles	Automobile repair shops	Bituminous coal (underground)	Clothing stores	Department stores	Limited price variety stores	Power laundries
Percent of all employees studied paid on an incentive basis	30	65	7	25	39	37	22	34	28	3	14
Percent of establishments—											
With incentive systems for plant workers	34	85	6	17	70	58	61	72	64	6	14
Predominantly piece rate	29	82	2	11	67	51	60	15	9	[2]	10
Individual	28	81	2	10	66	51	58	15	9	[2]	8
Group	1	1	[2]	1	1	[2]	2	[2]			2
Predominantly bonus	5	3	4	6	3	7	1	57	55	6	4
Individual	3	2	2	4	3	7	1	56	55	6	3
Group	2	1	2	2	[2]	[2]		1	[2]	[2]	1
With no incentive system	66	15	94	83	30	42	39	28	36	94	86
Information not available	[2]	----		[2]	[2]			[2]		[2]	[2]
All establishments studied	100	100	100	100	100	100	100	100	100	100	100
Number of establishments studied	15,636	2,261	999	6,647	1,448	1,399	492	759	355	1,441	1,621

[1] Includes other manufacturing industries not shown separately.
[2] Less than 0.5 of 1 percent.

were somewhat less common than in most other regions. Among metal-working and other manufacturing industries, incentive payments were most common in the New England, Middle Atlantic, and Great Lakes States and least common in the Southwest, Mountain, and Pacific regions.[5]

Among nonmanufacturing industries, about one-third of the employees of clothing stores and department stores and nearly two-fifths of those in automobile repair shops were on incentive. About one-fifth of the underground bituminous coal miners were paid incentive rates, but none of the surface soft coal mines studied provided incentive pay. Few incentive workers were reported in the electric light and power and warehousing industries.

Regional variations in methods of wage payment were minor in automobile repair shops and clothing and department stores, compared with those in power laundries. In the latter industry, incentive methods of pay were most common in the Middle Atlantic and Border States. In variety stores incentive pay was important only in New England.

Incentive systems, especially individual piece-rate plans, rarely apply to all workers in an establishment. They cover workers engaged in direct production; maintenance, custodial, supervisory, and other workers whose output cannot readily be measured are usually paid on a time basis. Exceptions to this rule are found largely in establishments with group or other bonus systems, in which a certain proportion of the incentive pay of direct production workers is set aside for the indirect workers. Among production workers, those whose work must conform to exact specifications or whose output is not standardized are generally paid on a time basis, as are those whose work is machine-paced. In contrast, workers who control their own output and whose production can be measured and identified are frequently paid on an incentive basis, unless emphasis on speed can result in costly material losses. In retail trade, incentive systems are limited largely to clerks.

NATURE OF INCENTIVE PLANS

Among the manufacturing industries piece-rate plans, nearly all based on individual output, predominated. Such plans were reported by five-sixths of the plants with incentive systems. In the apparel and textile industries, 19 out of 20 incentive plans provided for individual piece rates. In contrast, nearly half of the comparatively small number of incentive

5. The regions used in this study include the following: *New England* — Connecticut, Maine, Massachusetts, New Hampshire, Rhode Island, and Vermont; *Middle Atlantic* — New Jersey, New York, and Pennsylvania; *Border States* — Delaware, District of Columbia, Kentucky, Maryland, Virginia, and West Virginia; *Southeast* — Alabama, Florida, Georgia, Mississippi, North Carolina, South Carolina, and Tennessee; *Great Lakes* — Illinois, Indiana, Michigan, Minnesota, Ohio, and Wisconsin; *Middle West* — Iowa, Kansas, Missouri, Nebraska, North Dakota, and South Dakota; *Southwest* — Arkansas, Louisiana, Oklahoma, and Texas; *Mountain* — Arizona, Colorado, Idaho, Montana, New Mexico, Utah, and Wyoming; *Pacific* — California, Nevada, Oregon, and Washington.

TABLE 2.—*Extent of incentive plans for plant workers in selected manufacturing industries, 1945–46*

Industry	Number of plants studied	Percentage of—	
		Plants with incentive systems	Workers on incentive pay
All manufacturing industries studied	15,636	34	30
Apparel			
Knit outerwear	253	64	67
Knit underwear	161	94	44
Men's and boys' dress shirts and nightwear	220	88	74
Overalls and industrial garments	132	86	70
Women's and misses' dresses	976	92	69
Women's and misses' suits and coats	305	67	44
Work pants, cotton	155	89	67
Work shirts	59	88	80
Chemicals			
Drugs and medicines	258	7	11
Industrial chemicals	255	4	3
Paints and varnishes	291	4	6
Perfumes and cosmetics	121	6	9
Soap and glycerin	74	18	18
Metalworking [1]			
Aircraft engines and engine parts	201	23	20
Communication equipment	115	15	16
Copper alloying, rolling, and drawing	37	59	66
Electric generating and distribution equipment	267	28	([2])
Electroplating, plating, and polishing	252	9	7
Fabricated structural steel	324	4	7
Foundries, ferrous	646	28	29
Foundries, nonferrous	350	20	20
Iron and steel forgings	168	57	34
Machine tool accessories	156	13	19
Machine tools	181	21	29
Machinery	2,034	14	23
Oil burners, hot-water and steam-heating apparatus	68	41	25
Power boilers and associated products	271	5	6
Radios, radio equipment (except tubes), and phonographs	277	18	24
Sheet metal	385	5	10
Small arms	72	40	36
Stoves and ranges	164	52	39
Tanks	10	10	3
Tool and die jobbing shops	623	3	2
Textiles			
Cotton textiles	346	75	35
Hosiery, full-fashioned	187	98	73
Hosiery, seamless	206	95	68
Rayon and silk textiles	237	65	35
Textile dyeing and finishing	193	19	22
Woolen and worsted textiles	279	65	34
Other manufacturing industries			
Bakeries	1,320	1	([3])
Chewing and smoking tobacco	31	39	21
Cigarettes	18	28	6
Cigars	198	98	73
Corrugated and fiber boxes	171	43	33
Fiber cans and tubes	52	27	23
Folding paper boxes	188	16	21
Footwear (except house slippers and rubber footwear)	347	89	69
Jewelry, costume	94	17	22
Jewelry, precious	123	8	14
Paperboard	111	12	9
Pulp and paper	208	6	9
Set-up boxes	286	24	19
Structural clay products	331	34	26
Wood furniture, other than upholstered	514	25	19
Wood furniture, upholstered	289	43	33

[1] Includes data for automobiles.
[2] Information not presented because of sample limitations.
[3] Less than 0.5 of 1 percent.

plans in the chemical industry group provided group bonus payments for above-standard production since frequently the output of individual workers cannot be readily identified or measured.

In retail trade, incentive plans were mainly of the individual bonus type, with commissions paid in addition to salary, although some retail clerks are paid on a straight commission basis. PM's ("push money") paid during special sales, or other commissions for selling slow-moving items, may constitute additional payment. Individual piece-rate plans were the predominant type of incentive reported in power laundries, underground soft coal mines, and automobile repair shops. In the latter establishments, workers typically receive a certain percentage of the labor charge on the repair work that they perform.

EARNINGS VARY WITH METHOD OF WAGE PAYMENT

Generally, incentive workers receive higher earnings than do time workers in comparable jobs, although the size of differential is not consistent from industry to industry. The earnings advantage of incentive workers ranged from less than 5 percent to at least 40 percent in the individual manufacturing industries studied in 1945–46; in many of the industries the difference was between 15 and 25 percent.

Among the four major manufacturing industry groups presented in table 1, the largest differential appeared in the apparel industries where incentive workers earned from a fifth to two-fifths more than time workers. In the metalworking industries, incentive workers most commonly received from a fourth to a fifth more than time workers, whereas in the textile industries the differentials were typically between a sixth and a tenth. The chemical industries, in which incentive pay is relatively unimportant, showed no consistent pattern of differences between time and incentive earnings, although in several of these industries the difference was small. Among the nonmanufacturing industries in which incentive pay was most important — automobile repair shops and clothing and department stores — the differential amounted to about a third.

PREMIUM PAY PROVISIONS
IN SELECTED UNION AGREEMENTS[1]

Most union agreements in effect in the second half of 1946 — 85 percent of those studied — provided overtime pay at the rate of time and a half for all work in excess of 8 hours a day or 40 hours a week.[2] Exceptions to this general rule were found in the West Coast longshore and in women's clothing industries. In flat glass, men's clothing, and leather products it was not uncommon to find an established workday of less than 8 hours and workweek under 40 hours, with the premium rate, however, starting after 8 or 40 hours.

Almost half the agreements, covering over 750,000 workers in the sample, had provisions requiring penalty rates for work performed on Saturday as such; and about 60 percent, covering a similar proportion of workers, required penalty rates for Sunday work as such. In these agreements, more than 80 percent of the workers who received premium pay for Saturday or Sunday as such were paid time and a half for Saturday work and double time for Sunday work, irrespective of the number of hours previously worked during the week.

About a fourth of the agreements, covering approximately 40 percent of the workers in the sample, specified time and a half for work on the sixth consecutive day. About 30 percent, covering about 25 percent of the workers, specified a premium rate for work on the seventh consecutive day; half of these workers received time and a half for work on the seventh day and the other half, double time.

More than four-fifths of all workers in the sample received premium pay for production work on holidays. Of these, two-thirds were paid double time, and a third, time and a half. Six holidays were most frequently specified.

Three out of every four workers in the sample were under agreements which required a differential for work on shifts other than the first or regular day shift. Workers on the third shift generally were paid a higher differential than those on the second shift.

1. Prepared by the staff of the Collective Bargaining Division in the Bureau's Industrial Relations Branch.

2. This analysis is based on a selection of 437 union agreements which were in effect in the latter half of 1946, covering slightly over 2 million workers in the following 31 manufacturing and nonmanufacturing industries: Aircraft; alloying, rolling, and drawing of nonferrous metals; aluminum; automobiles; canning and preserving; chemicals; cigars; concrete, gypsum, and plaster products; cotton textiles; electrical machinery; flat glass; glassware, pressed or blown; iron and steel and their products; leather products; leather tanning; longshoring; meat packing; men's clothing; nonelectrical machinery; paper; petroleum refining; pottery; rubber; shipbuilding; shoes; smelting and refining of nonferrous metals; structural clay products; sugar; tobacco and cigarettes; trucking (general pick-up and delivery); and women's clothing.

Executive Order 9240

Prior to World War II, most union agreements provided premium rates for Saturday and Sunday work, as well as for holidays. Two basic reasons accounted for the existence of special rates for work on these days: The principle that holiday work, as such, deserved special reward; and the deterrent effect of premium rates on the extension of work over the week-end holidays.

During the war, however, as plants normally on a 1-shift basis converted to 24-hour, 7-day operations, most of the usual premium pay provisions for Saturday, Sunday, and holiday work were altered by Executive Order 9240, which was in effect from October 1, 1942, to August 21, 1945. This order provided that no premium wage or extra compensation was to be paid for work on Saturday or Sunday, as such, on work relating to the prosecution of the war; that time and a half was permissible but not obligatory for work performed on the sixth day worked in the regularly scheduled workweek, or for work over 40 hours a week, or 8 hours a day, where otherwise required by law or by contract; that double time was to be paid for work on the seventh day worked in the regularly scheduled workweek; and that time and a half, but no more, was required for work on the six holidays enumerated in the order, premium pay or extra compensation having been prohibited for any other holidays.

Of the 437 agreements included in this study, all of which were in effect on July 1, 1946 (almost a year after the end of the war and the revocation of Executive Order 9240), approximately 60 percent had reinstated the provisions requiring premium rates for Sunday work as such, and about 50 percent, the clauses for Saturday work as such.

Weekly or Daily Work Schedules

Agreements covering most of the workers in the sample required that time and a half was to be paid for hours of work which exceed 40 a week. In the shipbuilding industry on the West Coast and in ship repair on the Gulf Coast, however, the zone standard agreements[3] provided for double time after 40 hours.

3. During 1941, labor and management in the shipbuilding industry voluntarily agreed to cooperate with the Government in establishing standards in the industry, through the Shipbuilding Stabilization Committee (composed of representatives of labor and management in the shipbuilding industry and of the procurement agencies of the Government — Maritime Commission, Navy and War Departments). Four zone agreements (Pacific, Atlantic, Gulf Coast, and Great Lakes) were negotiated and went into effect between April and October 1941, to continue for the duration of the national emergency. These zone agreements covered certain basic conditions of employment: Basic hourly wage rates for standard skilled mechanics, hours of employment and overtime rates, a clear definition of shift premiums, provision for apprentice training, and provisions for employee health and safety. Individual collective-bargaining agreements entered into between shipbuilding management and labor incorporated the provisions of the zone standards.

The change to prewar practices in overtime payments became effective October 6, 1945, as the result of a national referendum held in August of that year, on instruction of the Shipbuilding Stabilization Committee. See Report of the Shipbuilding Stabilization Committee, in Annual Report of the Secretary of Labor, June 30, 1946 (Washington, 1947).

Most of the agreements which required a premium rate for work beyond a scheduled workweek under 40 hours were in the West Coast longshore industry and in women's clothing. The West Coast longshore agreements stipulated an amount almost equivalent to time and a half after 30 hours of work a week, averaged over 4 weeks. In women's clothing, many agreements required time and a half after 35 or 37½ hours of work, and some prohibited overtime altogether.

In men's clothing, the association agreements for the principal manufacturing areas established a 36-hour week, and one agreement required time and a half thereafter. The agreement with the New York Clothing Manufacturers' Exchange contained no mention of overtime work. The Philadelphia and Boston association agreements permitted 4 hours' overtime beyond the scheduled 36-hour week at the regular rates. Agreements in other areas with individual manufacturers in some cases established a 40-hour week, with time and a half thereafter.

A number of trucking agreements provided a premium rate for time worked beyond a schedule of 48 to 54 hours.

Agreements affecting more than 4 out of 5 workers in the sample required that time and a half was to be paid for all work in excess of 8 hours a day. About half of the men's clothing agreements studied, which covered about a third of the industry's workers in the sample, required time and a half after 8 hours. In other agreements in this industry, overtime work beyond 8 hours was prohibited. About two-thirds of the workers in the trucking industry sample received time and a half after 8 hours. Double time after 8 hours was provided for in the Zone Standard Agreements of the West Coast shipbuilding industry and of ship repair on the Gulf Coast, and also in an agreement in iron and steel products. In the Alaska salmon industry, which paid its workers on a monthly basis, and occasionally in trucking, the premium rate for work over 8 hours was a fixed sum an hour.

Only 11 agreements, covering less than 5,000 workers, provided for a workday of more than 8 hours. Eight trucking agreements required time and a half after 9 hours, and the remainder (2 trucking and 1 cigar manufacturing agreement) required similar overtime after 10 hours.

A premium rate for work beyond a day of less than 8 hours was found principally in the West Coast longshore industry and in women's clothing. In the former, the premium rate applied to work after 6 hours. In the latter industry, some agreements stipulated time and a half after 7 or 7½ hours, others required a premium rate after 8 hours, and still others prohibited overtime. One trucking agreement provided for time and a half after 6⅔ hours of work for men on a 6-day week schedule.

In 3 industries it was not uncommon to have an established workday of less than 8 hours and workweek under 40 hours with the premium rate starting after 8 or 40 hours. For example, agreements with the two major producers in the flat glass industry established a normal 36-hour week and provided for time and a half after 8 hours a day or 40 hours a week. Similar arrangements were found in some of the men's clothing agreements. In leather products, agreements affecting a substantial number of workers provided for a 7½-hour day and a 37½-hour week, with the premium rate starting after 8 hours a day or 40 hours a week. Two agreements in petroleum refining, which covered 2 plants of a single company, established a schedule of 40 hours a week or 72 hours in any "predetermined" 2-week period, with time and a half after 8 hours a day or 40 hours a week.

Twenty-four agreements covering less than 5 percent of the workers in the sample stipulated time and a half for the first 2, 3, or 4 hours of overtime work and double time thereafter. This provision was most common in aircraft, appearing in 7 of the 21 agreements studied in this industry and affecting about 25,000 workers. In the aircraft sample, 2 agreements required double time after 10 hours and 3 after 12 hours, in 1 day; another required double time after 2 hours of overtime, and the seventh, after 3 hours of overtime.

In lieu of a higher premium rate, or in some cases in addition to it, some agreements provided that an employee who worked a specified number of hours overtime was to receive a meal at the employer's expense or payment for his meal period, or both.

Premium Calendar Days

Slightly less than half of the agreements, which affected more than 750,000 workers (over a third in the sample) required that a premium rate was to be paid for production work on Saturday as such. Table 1 shows the proportion of workers in each of the industries analyzed who received this premium rate.

Over four-fifths of the workers who were paid a premium rate for Saturday work received time and a half; the others, double time. The majority of those paid the latter rate were in the West Coast shipbuilding industry or in ship repair on the Gulf Coast; some were in electrical machinery and a few other industries.

More than 260 of the agreements, covering about three-fifths of the total workers in the sample, required a premium rate for production work on Sunday. The proportion of production workers who received such payment is shown in table 2, by industry.

More than four-fifths of the production workers who received a premium rate for Sunday work were paid double time. Others were paid time and a half, or in a few cases, a fixed sum.

In the following industries most of the production workers in the sample who received a premium rate were paid time and a half: Aluminum; flat glass; glassware, pressed or blown; longshoring; paper; petroleum; pottery; smelting and refining of nonferrous metals; and structural clay products.

TABLE 1.—*Saturday work—Proportion of workers receiving premium pay, by industry*

Two-thirds or more	One-third and under two-thirds	Under one-third
Aircraft. Alloying, rolling, and drawing of nonferrous metals. Cotton textiles. Electrical machinery. Longshoring.[1] Nonelectrical machinery. Tobacco. Shipbuilding.	Leather tanning. Men's clothing. Shoes. Trucking.	Aluminum.[2] Automobiles. Canning and preserving. Chemicals. Cigars.[2] Concrete, gypsum, and plaster products.[2] Flat glass.[2] Glassware, pressed or blown.[3] Iron and steel. Leather products.[3] Meat packing. Paper. Petroleum. Pottery.[2] Rubber. Smelting and refining of nonferrous metals. Structural clay products.[2] Sugar.[2] Women's clothing.[3]

[1] In longshoring, a premium rate was required for work performed between 5 p. m. on Friday and 8 a. m. on Monday.
[2] None of the agreements in the sample for this industry required a premium rate for Saturday work.
[3] Work on Saturdays often was not performed; in some instances it was expressly prohibited.

TABLE 2.—*Sunday work—Proportion of workers receiving premium pay, by industry*

Two-thirds or more	One-third and under two-thirds	Under one-third
Aircraft. Alloying, rolling, and drawing of nonferrous metals. Aluminum. Automobiles. Cotton textiles. Electrical machinery. Flat glass. Glassware, pressed or blown. Longshoring. Meat packing. Nonelectrical machinery. Pottery. Rubber. Shipbuilding. Smelting and refining of nonferrous metals. Tobacco. Trucking.	Canning and preserving. Chemicals. Iron and steel. Leather tanning. Paper. Petroleum refining. Shoes. Structural clay products. Sugar.	Leather products.[1] Men's clothing.[1] Women's clothing.[1]

[1] Since production work generally is not performed on Sunday, the agreements usually contained no reference to premium rate of work on that day.

Double time was the prevailing rate for production work on Sunday in aircraft; alloying, rolling, and drawing of nonferrous metals; automobiles;

cotton textiles; electrical machinery; iron and steel products; meat packing; nonelectrical machinery; rubber; shipbuilding; shoes; tobacco; trucking. There were some workers in these industries, however, who were paid time and a half.

TABLE 3.—*Sixth consecutive day of work—Proportion of workers receiving premium pay, by industry*

Two-thirds or more	One-third and under two-thirds	Under one-third
Aluminum. Automobiles. Cigars. Flat glass.[1] Iron and steel. Leather tanning.	Chemicals. Structural clay products.	Aircraft. Alloying, rolling, and drawing of nonferrous metals. Canning and preserving. Cotton textiles. Electrical machinery. Glassware, pressed or blown.[2] Leather products.[2] Longshoring.[2] Meat packing.[2] Men's clothing.[2] Nonelectrical machinery. Paper. Petroleum refining. Pottery.[2] Rubber. Shipbuilding.[2] Shoes.[2] Smelting and refining of nonferrous metals. Sugar.[2] Tobacco.[2] Trucking. Women's clothing.

[1] When on a regularly scheduled day of 8 hours or more.
[2] No agreement in the sample in these industries contained a provision concerning the sixth day.

In chemicals, leather tanning, and sugar, about half of the workers in the sample who received a premium rate were paid time and a half, and the other half received double time. In canning and preserving, the Alaska salmon agreement provided that a fixed sum per hour was to be paid for work on an employee's day of rest. Before and after the fishing season the day of rest was Sunday; during the season it was Sunday or Monday.

Premium pay for production work on the worker's sixth consecutive day of work was provided in 105 agreements, covering nearly 800,000 workers. The rate in all cases was time and a half.

The proportion of workers who received premium pay for work performed on the sixth day worked in the regularly scheduled workweek is shown in table 3, by industry.

A premium rate for production work on an employee's seventh consecutive day of work was required in 126 agreements, affecting slightly more than 550,000 workers (about a fourth of the total in the sample). The number of workers who received double time and the number who received time and a half were approximately equal.

The proportion of workers who received a premium rate for the seventh consecutive day of production work is shown, by industry, in table 4.

TABLE 4.—*Seventh consecutive day of work—Proportion of workers receiving premium pay, by industry*

Two-thirds or more	One-third and under two-thirds	Under one-third
Aluminum. Cigars. Flat glass. Iron and steel. Leather tanning. Structural clay products.	Chemicals Paper. Petroleum refining. Smelting and refining of nonferrous metals.	Aircraft. Alloying, rolling, and drawing of nonferrous metals. Automobiles. Canning and preserving. Cotton textiles. Electrical machinery. Glassware, pressed or blown.[1] Leather products.[1] Longshoring.[1] Meat packing. Men's clothing. Nonelectrical machinery. Pottery.[1] Rubber. Shipbuilding.[1] Shoes.[1] Sugar. Tobacco. Trucking. Women's clothing.[1]

[1] Agreements in this industry contained no mention of the seventh day.

In petroleum refining, 6 agreements, which covered about 11,000 workers, required that a worker was to be paid time and a half "for work on his day off." In pressed and blown glassware, 1 agreement required time and a half for the 13th and 14th consecutive day of work, and 3 required time and a half for Sunday in a "6–1" system (6 days of work followed by 1 day of rest) or for the 13th and 14th day in a "12–2" system. These 4 agreements cover over 3,000 workers.

Holidays: More than 380 of the agreements, which covered more than four-fifths of all workers in the sample, specifically required that a premium rate was to be paid for production work on holidays. In men's clothing and women's clothing, work is rarely performed on holidays, and consequently premium-pay provisions were frequently absent from the agreements. Additional agreements scattered in several other industries had no holiday provisions. The absence of a holiday provision from an agreement, however, does not invariably mean that a premium rate is not paid.

Of the number of workers covered by the agreements sampled who received a premium rate for work on holidays, approximately a third were paid time and a half and two-thirds, double time. Seven agreements, covering about 7,000 workers, required that employees were to be paid their regular rate for certain holidays on which no work was generally done, and that either 2½ times the regular rate or triple time was to be paid if work was performed. Three of these agreements were in trucking, and 2 each in leather products and meat packing.

A majority of the workers of the sample were paid double time for holiday work in the following industries: Aircraft; alloying, rolling, and drawing of nonferrous metals; automobiles; electrical machinery; meat packing; nonelectrical machinery; pottery; rubber; shipbuilding; tobacco; and trucking. Time and a half was paid the majority of workers studied in aluminum; chemicals; cigars; cotton textiles; flat glass; iron and steel and their products; leather products; leather tanning; longshoring; paper; shoes; and structural clay products. Either time and a half or double time was paid to a substantial number of workers in canning and preserving; glassware, pressed or blown; petroleum refining; smelting and refining of nonferrous metals; and sugar.

The number of holidays for which a premium rate was required ranged from 3 to 11. Six days was most common; next, in order, were 7, 8, and 6½ days. Over 1.5 million workers were under agreements which specified either 6 or 6½ days. The 6 holidays most frequently mentioned were New Year's Day, Memorial Day, Fourth of July, Labor Day, Thanksgiving, and Christmas.

About 200,000 of the production workers in the sample (about 10 percent of all those covered) were under agreements which required pay for holidays not worked. Approximately three-fourths of these workers were paid for 6 or 6½ days; the number of holidays paid for but not worked in other agreements ranged from 1 to 8.

SHIFT DIFFERENTIALS[4]

Approximately three-fourths of the total number of workers in the sample were under agreements which required a differential for work on shifts other than the first or regular day shift. Many of the agreements which did not specify shift differentials were in industries such as men's and women's clothing, where only 1 shift was normally scheduled. Longshore agreements, as noted in a following section, made no reference to shifts but required a premium rate for work after specified hours.

Table 5 shows the proportion of workers who received shift differentials for work on shifts other than the first or regular day shift, by industry.

About 400,000 workers, or about a fifth of the sample, were under agreements which required a differential of 4 cents an hour for the second shift and of 6 cents for the third shift; about 120,000 workers were paid a differential of 5 cents for such shifts. Approximately 350,000 workers

4. For a study of shift differentials in manufacturing, 1945–46, see Monthly Labor Review, August 1947 (p. 183).

were covered by a differential of 5 percent for the second and of 7½ percent for the third shift; nearly 200,000 workers were paid a 10-percent differential for such shifts. Other differentials ranged from 2 cents an hour for night shifts to 18 percent (in 1 instance) for the third shift.

TABLE 5.—*Proportion of workers receiving shift differentials, by industry*

Two-thirds or more	One-third and under two-thirds	Under one-third
Aircraft. Alloying, rolling, and drawing of nonferrous metals. Aluminum. Automobiles. Cotton textiles. Electrical machinery. Flat glass. Iron and steel. Leather tanning. Meat packing. Petroleum. Pottery. Shipbuilding. Smelting and refining of nonferrous metals.	Paper. Rubber. Trucking.	Canning and preserving. Chemicals. Cigars.[1] Glassware, pressed or blown.[1] Leather products. Shoes.[1] Structural clay products. Sugar. Tobacco.[1]

[1] No references to shifts were contained in the agreements sampled in these industries.

In flat glass, when four 6-hour shifts were scheduled, all the agreements in the sample required a differential of 4 cents an hour for work performed between 6 p.m. and midnight, and of 6 cents for work between midnight and 6 a.m. For shifts other than daylight single shifts, a differential of 4 cents an hour was paid for work done between the hours of 4 p.m. and midnight, and of 6 cents for work done between midnight and 8 a.m. "Appropriate" differentials were paid for daylight single shifts, which began or ended after specified hours.

In the pottery industry, a 5-cent an hour differential was stipulated for work on the second and third 8-hour shifts when three 8-hour shifts were scheduled. When four 6-hour shifts were operated, this differential was specified for work between 6 p.m. and 6 a.m. Most of the agreements in the sample in petroleum refining required differentials of 4 and 6 cents an hour for the second and third shifts, respectively. In the Pacific Coast shipbuilding industry, a 10-percent differential and 8 hours' pay for 7½ hours of work were usually required for the second shift, and 15 percent and 8 hours' pay for 7 hours of work, for the third shift. In shipbuilding on the Atlantic Coast, a 7-percent differential for both the second and third shifts prevailed.

Leather tanning agreements generally required a 5-cent an hour differential for the second shift (except 1 agreement, requiring 4 cents) and from 5 to 10 cents for the third. The prevailing shift premium in meat packing was 5 cents an hour for work done between 6 p.m. and 6 a.m.

Most aluminum workers were paid a differential of 4 cents an hour for the second shift and 6 cents for the third. In smelting and refining of nonferrous metals and in alloying, rolling, and drawing of nonferrous metals, the second shift differential ranged from 4 to 6 cents or 5 percent; and the third, from 5 to 8 cents or 7½ percent. Agreements covering over 90 percent of the workers in the sample in iron and steel required 4 cents an hour for the second shift and 6 cents for the third. Other differentials in this industry ranged from 3 cents an hour to 12½ percent for the second shift, and from 5 cents to 12½ percent for the third.

Nearly 350,000 automobile workers in the sample were under agreements which required differentials of 5 percent and of 7½ percent for specified shifts. A differential of 7 cents an hour for the third shift only was most common in cotton textiles. Over 175,000 workers in the sample in electrical machinery were under agreements which require a differential of 10 percent for the second and third shifts.

In the aircraft industry, all agreements in the sample contained provisions for shift differentials. Three-fourths of these workers were under agreements which also prescribed a differential in hours for the third shift — 8 hours' pay for 6½ hours' work. About 35,000 aircraft workers were under agreements which specified a differential of 6 cents an hour for the second and third shifts, with 8 hours' pay for 6½ hours of work on the third. One agreement provided for a differential of 10 cents an hour for the second and third shifts, with 8 hours' pay for 6½ hours' work on the third shift. Another, without differential in hours, provided for a differential of 15 percent for the second and third shifts. The premium rate for overtime work in the aircraft industry usually began in the third shift after the scheduled hours of work, rather than after 8 hours a day or 40 hours a week.

In rubber, the shift differential most often specified was 3 cents an hour for work between 6 p.m. and 6 a.m. or, in a few cases, between 7 p.m. and 7 a.m.

OTHER PREMIUM PAYMENTS

It was a general practice in the longshore industry to require a premium rate, rather than a shift differential, for work performed before or after designated hours. All agreements in the sample in this industry required that work performed after 5 p.m. or before 8 a.m. on a weekday was to be paid for at a stated monetary rate, which was generally equivalent to time and a half of the regular rate. Some agreements in alloying, rolling, and drawing of nonferrous metals, automobiles, canning and preserving, cotton textiles, men's clothing, shipbuilding, smelting and refining of nonferrous metals, and tobacco specified that work outside an employee's regular shift was to be compensated at time and a half. Four agreements in trucking required that a premium rate was to be paid for work before or after certain hours.

Provisions regarding hazardous, dirty, or unpleasant work were common in longshoring, where premium rates, varying from 5 cents an hour to more than double the regular rates, were required for handling certain commodities or damaged cargoes. Six shipbuilding agreements stipulated premium rates ranging from 10 cents an hour to time and a half for "dirty" or other specified work, such as galvanized burning, spray painting, tank cleaning, or working with certain materials in closely confined space. Some of the agreements in the paper industry required workers who were called in while off duty for repair work and changing screens to be allowed 4 to 6 hours' pay for the job, or time and a half for actual hours worked, whichever was greater. A chemical agreement provided that men working 30 feet or more above the ground were to receive a 5-cent an hour premium.

Meal Periods

Three of the 4 longshore agreements in the sample required that a stipulated amount virtually equivalent to time and a half was to be paid for work performed during the noon lunch period; in the other agreement, the rate was double time. Work during meal periods other than the noon lunch period in this industry was usually compensated for at a higher rate than work during the noon period.

Two agreements in petroleum refining stipulated that an employee who was required to work during his regular meal period was to be paid time and a half for such work, with an equal period of time allowed for eating. Four agreements stipulated that a meal was to be provided by the employer to workers who had to work past their regular quitting time. Under 1 of these 4 agreements, day workers on a night shift were allowed a 20-minute paid lunch period; under another, the employer paid for a lunch costing not more than 75 cents for an employee who worked 2 hours beyond his quitting time. According to some of the petroleum agreements, certain workers were permitted to eat while on duty.

Three shipbuilding agreements required time and a half for work performed during an employee's meal period and another, double time. A fifth specified time and a half for work during meal periods on new construction work and double time on repair work.

Agreements covering three-fourths of the workers in the sample in meat packing required the payment of time and a half for work performed during a worker's lunch period. When overtime was worked, the second meal period of the employee, not to exceed 20 minutes, was generally paid for by the employer.

One rubber agreement allowed a paid lunch period, with the additional provision that employees were to produce a half-hour's extra output. Another provided that "employees engaged in jobs which are operated on 3 continuous 8-hour shifts, the nature of which requires a cessation of production for the purpose of eating, shall be paid 80 percent of their average straight-time hourly earnings for an assigned lunch period."

Two agreements in sugar required that time and a half be paid for work during the meal period.

Collective agreements in a number of industries provided that, during 3-shift operations, a fully or partly paid lunch period be allowed. Workers on continuous operations in some agreements were also permitted to eat while on duty. A number of agreements specified that an employee who worked more than 5, 6, or any other indicated number of hours without a meal period was to be paid a premium rate for additional work until a meal period was allowed, or was to be allowed a paid meal period, or both.

PAID VACATIONS AND SICK LEAVE IN INDUSTRY
1945–46[1]

About 3 out of 4 manufacturing establishments, by 1945–46, had formal paid vacation plans for plant workers after a year's service, and almost 9 out of 10 provided paid vacations for office workers with similar length of service. In contrast, formal plans for paid sick leave were uncommon both for plant and office workers. Typically, plant workers received a 1-week vacation with pay after a year's employment; office workers were allowed 2-week vacations in more than two-fifths of the establishments with vacation plans. Information available for the machinery industries indicated that after 5 years' service, 2-week vacations were most common for plant as well as for office workers.[2]

In contrast, paid vacations in 1937 were provided for plant workers by only 1 in 4 manufacturing establishments. Even at that time, however, about 8 out of 10 establishments granted vacations with pay to office and other salaried workers.[3] Although extension of paid vacation plans from office to plant workers began prior to World War II, rapid progress was made during the war years. Under wartime wage stabilization, the National War Labor Board developed a vacation policy under which virtually automatic approval was given to the voluntary introduction of paid vacations of specified duration.[4]

The interest in vacations as an objective of collective bargaining is reflected in the rapid increase in the number of agreements providing vacations. In 1940, only about 25 per cent of all workers under union agreement were entitled to paid vacations, as compared with 85 percent in 1944.[5]

METHOD AND COVERAGE

Data for 1945–46 were collected as part of the Bureau's general wage surveys of 56 manufacturing and 7 nonmanufacturing industries.[6] The manufacturing industries together employed about 5½ million workers, or

1. Prepared by Edyth M. Bunn of the Bureau's Wage Analysis Branch.
2. For further discussion of vacations in the machinery industries, see Wages in the Machinery Industries, October 1946, p. 317 of this issue.
3. Monthly Labor Review, August 1938, p. 269. The present study differs in coverage from the earlier survey, but it is believed that rough comparisons are warranted.
4. This automatic approval was limited to plans for 1 week of vacation after 1 year's employment and 2 weeks after 5 years. Further details regarding War Labor Board policies on vacation plans will be available in the forthcoming Termination Report of the National War Labor Board.
5. See Paid-Vacation Provisions in Union Agreements, November 1944, Monthly Labor Review, February 1945, p. 299.
6. The manufacturing industries studied are listed in table 2; the nonmanufacturing industries appear in table 1.

more than a third of the entire manufacturing labor force of the country, and contained more than 34,000 establishments. The nonmanufacturing industries included 19,000 establishments having 1,300,000 employees.[7]

Although it is believed that the coverage of manufacturing industries is sufficiently large and representative to provide a rough picture of vacation and sick-leave practices for manufacturing as a whole, it should be borne in mind that the individual studies were made primarily to provide data for individual industries.[8] Such important segments of manufacturing as basic iron and steel, lumber, printing, meat packing, and the rubber industries were not studied. Coverage of nonmanufacturing was limited to a few industries, so that no generalizations could be drawn for nonmanufacturing as a whole.

This article is intended to provide only a general picture of the prevalence of formal vacation and sick-leave plans and the amount of vacation provided after 1 year's service. It does not attempt to cover differing vacation provisions for workers who had been employed longer than a year.

Arrangements whereby workers were given vacations or paid wages during illness at the discretion of their employer or supervisor were not studied; these informal arrangements are particularly important with respect to sick leave.

Formal Paid Vacation Practices

Formal vacation plans tended to be most common in industries characterized by large operating units and high wage rates and, within the individual industries, were most frequently provided in large unionized establishments.

Manufacturing Industries: Among the major manufacturing industry groups for which data are available, the chemical industries provided vacations most commonly after 1 year's service and also tended to furnish the longest vacations (table 1). Although the metalworking industry group granted vacations somewhat less frequently than other industry groups, there was considerable variation among the separate industries within this group (table 2). The apparel trades,[9] although ranking rela-

7. For the basis of this study, 15,500 manufacturing establishments employing slightly above 3 million workers and 6,400 nonmanufacturing establishments having 600,000 employees were actually surveyed. Establishments with less than 8 workers were omitted, except in a few industries where small establishments accounted for a substantial proportion of the industry's employment.

8. No attempt, moreover, has been made in the summary of paid vacations and sick-leave practices, presented in terms of number of establishments, to compensate for differences among industries in the proportion of establishments studied or for differences in coverage between segments of the same industry. As the individual industry surveys were made primarily to obtain wage-rate information, a larger proportion of large establishments and establishments in large cities and in certain regions were included in order to permit presentation of separate wage data by region, city, and size of establishment.

9. Union agreements in the women's coat and suit and dress industries, particularly in the New England and Middle Atlantic regions, frequently provided that employers contribute a portion of the pay roll for a health and vacation fund. This fund was distributed among the workers according to a predetermined plan, which varied in details in the different markets.

TABLE 1.—*Length of paid vacations after 1 year's service in selected manufacturing and nonmanufacturing industry groups 1945–46*

Length of vacation	All industries studied [1]	Manufacturing				Nonmanufacturing						
		Apparel	Chemicals	Metal-working	Textiles	Automobile repair shops	Clothing stores	Department stores	Electric light and power	Limited price variety stores	Power laundries	Ware-housing
Plant workers												
Establishments studied:												
Number	15,567	2,258	999	6,605	1,447	1,397	754	355	130	1,439	1,620	723
Percent	100	100	100	100	100	100	100	100	100	100	100	100
Percent of establishments with paid vacations after 1 year's service	73	81	92	68	75	76	94	97	98	95	45	73
Less than 1 week	2	1	1	4	1	[2]	[2]	[2]		1	1	
1 week	65	63	70	61	73	67	67	79	46	87	43	67
Over 1 week but under 2 weeks	[2]	[2]	[2]	[2]	[2]	[2]	[2]	1		1	[2]	[2]
2 weeks	4	2	20	3	1	9	26	17	52	6	[2]	6
Over 2 weeks	[2]	[2]	[2]	[2]			1	[2]				
Other [3]	2	15										
Percent of establishments with no paid vacations after 1 year's service	27	19	8	32	25	24	6	3	2	5	55	27
Office workers												
Establishments studied:												
Number	12,880	1,451	932	5,915	1,241	[4]	588	341	125	1,063	1,206	668
Percent	100	100	100	100	100	[4]	100	100	100	100	100	100
Percent of establishments with paid vacations after 1 year's service	87	83	95	86	88	[4]	94	97	100	98	69	89
Less than 1 week	1	1	1	1	[2]	[4]	[2]	[2]		1	1	
1 week	47	56	38	42	55	[4]	64	78	38	88	60	46
Over 1 week but under 2 weeks	1	1	1	1	[2]	[4]	[2]	1		1	[2]	2
2 weeks	38	26	56	42	33	[4]	29	18	62	8	8	41
Over 2 weeks	[2]	[2]	[2]	[2]	[2]	[4]	1	[2]		[2]	[2]	[2]
Percent of establishments with no paid vacations after 1 year's service	13	17	5	14	12	[4]	6	3		2	31	11

[1] Includes other manufacturing industries not shown separately (see table 2.)
[2] Less than 5/100 of 1 percent.
[3] Establishments (in women's and misses' dresses and coats and suits) operating under union agreements which provide for a health-vacation fund into which employers pay a determined percent of their pay roll and from which vacation payments are distributed. Also includes firms providing vacations to begin in 1947.
[4] No coverage.

TABLE 2.—*Extent of paid vacation plans for plant workers after 1 year's service in selected manufacturing industries, 1945–46*

Industry group	Pay-roll period studied	Number of establishments studied	Percent of establishments having paid vacation plans after 1 year's service
All manufacturing industries studied ----	Jan. 1945–July 1946	15,567	73
Apparel----		2,258	81
Knit outerwear----	July 1946	252	81
Knit underwear----	July 1946	161	90
Men's and boys' dress shirts and nightwear.	Apr. 1945	220	77
Overalls and industrial garments---	Apr. 1945	132	64
Women's and misses' dresses---	Apr. 1945	975	83
Women's and misses' suits and coats--	July 1946	305	95
Work pants, cotton---	Apr. 1945	154	56
Work shirts---	Apr. 1945	59	54
Chemicals----		999	92
Chemicals, industrial---	Jan. 1946	255	92
Drugs and medicines---	July 1946	258	93
Paints and varnishes---	July 1946	291	94
Perfumes and cosmetics---	July 1946	121	91
Soap and glycerin---	July 1946	74	85
Metalworking----	Jan. 1945	6,605	68
Aircraft engines---	Jan. 1945	199	77
Communication equipment--	Jan. 1945	46	78
Copper alloying, rolling, and drawing.	Spring–summer 1946.	37	97
Electric generating and distribution equipment.	Jan. 1945	265	85
Electroplating---	Jan. 1945	252	52
Fabricated structural steel---	Jan. 1945	323	63
Foundries, ferrous---	Jan. 1945	642	68
Foundries, nonferrous---	Jan. 1945	346	68
Iron and steel forgings---	Jan. 1945	167	77
Machine-tool accessories---	Jan. 1945	156	75
Machine tools---	Jan. 1945	181	82
Machinery (miscellaneous)---	Jan. 1945	2,013	69
Motor vehicles---	Jan. 1945	115	78
Metalworking—Continued			
Oil-burners, hot-water and steam-heating apparatus.	July 1946	68	87
Power boilers---	Jan. 1945	270	65
Radios---	Jan. 1945	277	78
Sheet-metal work---	Jan. 1945	384	28
Small arms---	Jan. 1945	72	86
Stoves and ranges---	July 1946	163	83
Tanks---	Jan. 1945	10	100
Tool and die jobbing (shops)---	Jan. 1945	619	66
Textiles----		1,447	75
Cotton textiles---	Apr. 1946	346	76
Hosiery, full-fashioned---	Jan. 1946	187	67
Hosiery, seamless---	Jan. 1946	205	59
Rayon and silk textiles---	July 1946	237	89
Textile dyeing and finishing---	July 1946	193	88
Woolen and worsted textiles---	Apr. 1946	279	83
Other industries----		4,258	------
Bakeries---	July 1945	1,309	81
Cigarettes---	Jan. 1946	18	78
Cigars---	Jan. 1946	197	52
Corrugated-fiber boxes---	Oct. 1945	170	88
Costume jewelry---	Jan. 1946	94	76
Fiber cans and tubes---	Oct. 1945	52	75
Folding boxes---	Oct. 1945	187	76
Footwear---	Oct. 1945	345	86
Paper and pulp---	Oct. 1945	208	88
Paperboard---	Oct. 1945	111	86
Precious jewelry---	Jan. 1946	123	89
Set-up boxes---	Oct. 1945	283	62
Smoking, chewing, and snuff tobacco.	Jan. 1946	31	77
Structural clay products---	Oct. 1945	328	45
Upholstered furniture---	Oct. 1945	288	56
Wood furniture---	Oct. 1945	514	57

tively high in paid vacations for plant workers, provided somewhat shorter vacations for office employees than did the other industries studied. Considering individual industries outside these major industry groups, the cigar, set-up box, structural-clay product, and furniture industries fell below the all-manufacturing average for formal vacation arrangements (table 2).[10]

Nonmanufacturing Industries: Of the nonmanufacturing industries for which data were available, almost all department, clothing, and limited-price variety stores and electric light and power systems provided vacations for both plant and office workers after 1 year's service. On the other hand, less than half of the power laundries and under three-fourths of the warehousing establishments reported such plans for plant workers; 7 out of 10 power laundries provided paid vacations for their office employees. In 9 out of 10 warehouse establishments, office workers were granted vacations after 1 year (table 1).

Electric light and power was the only industry in which a 2-week vacation period after a year's service was more common than 1 week for plant workers. Among office workers, the 2-week period was more frequent than 1 week in the chemical industries, as well as in the electric utility industry; in the metalworking industries it was of equal importance with the 1-week vacation.

Regional Vacation Practices: The Southeastern and Southwestern regions[11] lagged behind other areas in paid-vacation practices in most manufacturing industries; the Pacific region ranked highest in the proportion of such plans. New England clothing and department stores granted 2-week vacations more frequently than 1-week periods; stores elsewhere generally followed the custom of 1-week vacations in effect in both manufacturing and nonmanufacturing industries. Although vacations were more common for office employees than for plant workers in almost all industries studied, this pattern was not found in every region, apparently because office workers were sometimes given vacations on an informal basis.

10. The size of the interindustry differences in vacation provisions presented in the tables of this article was affected by the fact that the periods studied varied among industries (from January 1945 to July 1946), and that paid vacation plans were being extended during this period. The changes during the interval, however, were apparently not large enough to alter the relative position of the industries discussed in the text.

An example of the increase in vacation plans is provided by the machinery industries, which were studied in both January 1945 and October 1946. The proportion of machinery establishments having vacation plans for plant workers increased from 70 to more than 80 percent between the two periods, but there was no marked increase in the length of the vacation period provided.

11. For definition of regions, see Wages in the Machinery Industries, October 1946, p. 317 of this issue.

Sick Leave

Formal plans for paid sick leave for plant workers were found in less than 3 percent of the manufacturing establishments studied, although more than 8 percent granted sick leave to office workers. Chemical establishments led other manufacturing industries in formal sick-leave plans and also differed from other establishments in providing such leave more frequently for plant than for office workers. Sick leave was granted more frequently in the nonmanufacturing industries studied than in manufacturing. More than a half of the electric light and power systems regularly paid their workers for time lost while sick, and a third of all retail stores studied had plans in operation in 1945 and 1946. In view of the low incidence of formal sick leave plans in most industries, no tabulations are presented.

Wage Differentials

Regional Wage Differentials: 1907–1946, by Joseph W. Bloch, Monthly Labor Review, Vol. 66, No. 4, April, 1948, pp. 371–377

Wage Differences in Local Labor Markets, by Lloyd G. Reynolds, American Economic Review, Vol. XXXVI, No. 3, June, 1946, pp. 366–375

Wages and the Movement of Factory Labor, by W. Rupert Maclaurin and Charles A. Myers, Quarterly Journal of Economics, Vol. LVII, February, 1943, pp. 241–264

REGIONAL WAGE DIFFERENTIALS: 1907–46

LONG-TERM MOVEMENT OF MANUFACTURING WAGES IN THE SOUTH, THE FAR WEST, THE MIDDLE WEST, AND THE NORTHEAST

JOSEPH W. BLOCH[1]

Few aspects of United States wage structure have aroused more public interest or have created more difficult problems for employers and trade-unions than the existence of regional or area wage differentials. Large groups of workers performing similar tasks in the same industry receive different rates of pay from city to city and from region to region. Bricklayers in Chicago are paid more than bricklayers in Milwaukee; women attaching pockets to overalls in factories situated in the Northeast earn more per hour than women doing the same kind of work in southern plants.

In most of the widely dispersed industries, regional or area differentials have long constituted an important issue in collective bargaining and wage administration, but in few instances have uniform pay scales been achieved. A number of reasons, such as differences in technique, equipment, or product, are usually emphasized in explaining why men doing the same work are paid different rates in one region as compared with another. To some extent, however, the persistence of a particular wage differential is nourished by the persistence of all differentials. For example, southern furniture workers earn less than those in the North partly because such differentials also exist in other industries.

From a study of average hourly earnings[2] for manufacturing occupations in 1907, 1919, 1931–32, and 1945–46, the Bureau of Labor Statistics concluded that relative wage uniformity among regions was further advanced in 1945–46 than in 1931–32 and 1907, but that the percentage differential between the high- and low-wage regions was about the same in 1945–46 as in 1919.

After 1907, manufacturing establishments in the Far West maintained the highest average level of wage rates in the country; in the South the lowest wages were paid for work of the same character as that performed elsewhere. From a comparison of each region with the Northeast, it appears that the level of occupational wages was about 51 percent higher,

1. Of the Bureau's Division of Wage Analysis.

A more detailed discussion and additional data will be contained in a forthcoming mimeographed report.

This article is the second dealing with regional or area wage differentials. The earlier one appeared in the October 1946 issue of the Monthly Labor Review (p. 511).

2. "Occupational earnings" and "job" or "wage rates" are used interchangeably in this article. The difference between earnings and rates, strictly defined, is of little significance in the context of this study.

on the average, in the Far West than in the South in 1907. By 1919, this
spread had been reduced to approximately 32 percent by reason of the
loss in position of the Far West. The over-all differential widened after
1919 as the South lost ground, and in 1931–32 the spread between the
Far West and the South amounted to 53 percent. Later improvement in
the position of the South accounts for the reduction in the Far West-South
differential to about 35 percent by 1945–46.

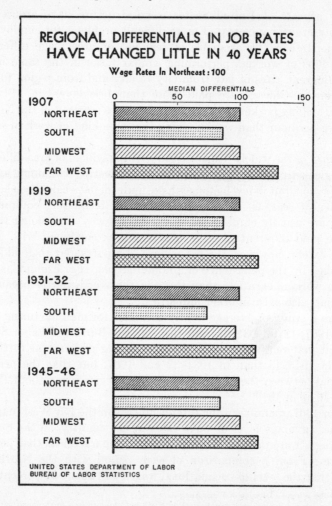

However, largely because hourly wages were higher in 1945–46 than
ever before, the cents-per-hour differences among regional manufacturing
wages were larger in 1945–46 than in the three earlier periods.

As a result of the study of the changing status of each region it was possible to evaluate the overall movement of geographic wage differentials. The major conclusions are:

(1) Percentagewise, geographic wage differentials narrowed between 1932 and 1945–46 in manufacturing, in building and printing trades, and in farming. The data for the years prior to 1932, however, do not support the conclusion that this narrowing of differentials was a consequence of long-term pressure.

(2) In terms of cents-per-hour, wage differences among regions and cities tend to correspond with the level of money earnings. Thus, geographic wage differentials, in money, were generally greater in 1945–46 than at any previous period.

(3) It is significant that this study did not show a more profound modification of regional wage differentials. Over the 40-year-period, the changes in manufacturing wage differentials among regions had, on balance, no far-reaching effect. For example, there was no significant change in the ranking of the four regions studied — the Far West remained the high-wage region, the South the low-wage region, and the Middle West and the Northeast were in the middle at about the same level. Moreover, except for the decline in the position of the Far West between 1907 and 1919 and the loss and subsequent gain in the South between 1919 and 1945–46, the size of the differentials between regions was extraordinarily persistent.

The practice of establishing job rates with relation to prevailing wage levels in the immediate locality appears to be deeply rooted in the Nation's wage-determination methods. Thus, in the absence of stronger counter-forces regional differentials tend to be self-perpetuating. This dependence upon local conditions in the determination of wages contrasts sharply with the pricing policies of industrial establishments competing in regional or national markets. Localization, which was dominant in early American industry, has persisted longer in wage setting than in price setting. It is a question whether regional differentials in the prices of essential commodities purchased by wage earners vary with or are as substantial as regional differentials in wage rates. A study of this relationship would throw considerable light on the regional wage problem.

BACKGROUND OF STUDY

Those persons dealing with differentials prevailing within their own plants or industries must take account of the status of all differentials. However, to evaluate the present status of regional wage differentials it is important to know what trends are in operation. The purpose of this study was to measure, insofar as available data permit, the long-range movement of regional differentials — both absolute and relative[3] — in manufacturing wage rates as a whole rather than in terms of specific industries.

More specifically, the major trends in regional wage differentials are measured in terms of occupational wage rates, differentiated by industry and sex of workers. For each period covered, the hourly earnings of workers of roughly equivalent skill levels, doing essentially the same type of work in the same industries, are compared. Being limited to similar employments, such a comparison is not significantly influenced by regional differences in industrial make-up, nor by inter-regional shifts in industry or labor, nor by the differences among regions in the composition of the labor force for a given industry (e.g., the ratio of skilled to unskilled and of men to women).[4]

This analysis is limited to four periods for which the Bureau collected occupational wage data covering a large and diversified group of industries — 1907, 1919, 1931–32, and 1945–46.[5] These periods have the advantage of being spaced rather evenly, and represent severe depression as well as postwar peaks. Of course, the data covering four such periods cannot form a connected series, but they indicate long-range movement and identify those intervals in which significant changes in regional differentials took place.

The procedures employed in selecting, combining, and integrating the available data are important features of a study of this nature. Briefly, in order to obtain a statistical measure of regional differentials that is not affected by differences among regions in the importance of each industry and occupation, the following method was employed: In each of the four

3. It is important to distinguish between the two forms in whicn differentials might be expressed: One is absolute in terms of cents-per-hour, and the other is relative, in the form of an index, ratio, or percentage. Although at any given time the absolute differential has meaning if interpreted within the framework of existing standards its significance changes with money wage levels. For example, the 10-cent difference between average earnings, of 20 and 30 cents looms large as labor cost and buying power when compared with the difference between 80- and 90-cent averages. For the most part, therefore, this study is based upon relative differentials.

4. A comparison of occupational wage rates is one of many possible measurements of regional differences. This approach throws little light, except by very broad inference, upon changes in total earnings and the relative well-being of all workers in each region. Moreover, in some industries there are characteristic regional differences in technique and equipment, quality of product, method of wage payment, and productivity; hence differentials in occupational earnings cannot be taken as indications of equivalent differences in labor cost. In particular industries, these factors go far towards explaining regional wage differentials, but in the composite picture of regional differentials presented here the effects of these factors are partly offset by others.

5. The industries covered during each period were diversified enough to be considered as an approximate representation of all manufacturing industries. The data for these periods consist of average hourly earnings for selected occupations, by region, industry, and sex of workers. The regional alignment that appeared to have most significance in terms of historical differentials and that could be applied to the data for all four periods was as follows:

Northeast (including New England and Middle Atlantic States).
Middle West (including Great Lakes and other Midwestern States).
South (including Southeast and Southwest States).
Far West (including Mountain and Pacific States).

periods covered, average hourly earnings for each occupational group in the South, Far West, and Middle West were converted to percentages of the earnings for corresponding groups in the Northeast. The median percentage was then selected as the best indication of the average differential between each region and the Northeast. This method was used in the calculation of differentials for all occupations, occupations in which men were engaged, occupations in which women were engaged, and those of the male occupations that could be classified as skilled. Although comparison with the Northeast results from use of this method, it also gives an approximation of the relationships between occupational earnings in each region and those in all other regions. For example, if in one period occupational earnings in the Far West were, on the average, 110 percent of corresponding earnings in the Northeast, and in the South 90 percent of earnings in the Northeast, the advantage of the Far West over the South can be assumed to be about 22 percent (i.e., 110 ÷ 90).

POSITION OF THE SOUTH

The status of occupational earnings in the South relative to the rest of the country, or usually to the North, has long been considered the core of the regional wage problem. The persistence of lower wage levels in the South has, among other things, influenced the pattern of industry location and labor migration.[6] During recent years, the wage gap between the South and other regions has narrowed; yet over the 40 years covered by this study the relative wage position of the South showed no progressive improvement that might be attributable to long-term forces affecting the industry and the population of the South. Notwithstanding gains in recent years, the percentage gap between manufacturing job rates in the South and in other regions was as wide in 1945–46 as in 1919. In relation to the industrially dominant Northeast and Northwest, the wage position of the South was the same at the end as at the beginning of the 40 years.[7]

Regions as broadly defined as the South and the Northeast include varying industry and area wage levels. Therefore, a job-for-job comparison between the two regions, cutting across industry lines, exhibits a wide range of differentials. Thus, for each southern occupational group in which earnings were less than 75 percent of the Northeast average in 1907 there was one for which hourly earnings were higher in the South than in the northern region. In 1945–46, a similar situation prevailed. However, the wide and uneven distribution of differentials between the two regions that was characteristic in 1907 and 1919 had developed into a rather

6. See Bureau of Labor Statistics Bulletin No. 898, Labor in the South, 1947, especially chapters 1 and 2.

7. In farm wage rates, the differential against the South had increased between 1907 and 1946. Even in terms of union rates for skilled building and printing trades, southern cities were not in their most advantageous positions at the end of the 1907–46 period.

symmetrical pattern by 1946. Of course, this cannot be attributed to changes in the South alone. Similar tendencies were noted in other regional comparisons presented in this article.

On the whole, the southern wage level for all jobs covered was no closer to that of the Northeast in 1945–46 than it had been in 1907 and 1919 (see chart). The considerable improvement in the position of the South relative to the Northeast which took place between 1931–32 and 1945–46 merely reduced the differential to that prevailing during the two early periods. In both 1907 and 1919 southern occupational rates were, on the average, slightly more than 85 percent of corresponding Northeast rates; in 1931–32, the median.relationship dropped to 74 percent; but between 1932 and 1945–46, southern wage rates increased proportionately more than Northeast rates and the ratio again became 85 percent.

The widening of differentials between the South and the Northeast between 1919 and 1931–32 and the narrowing between 1932 and 1945–46 are highly significant as indicators of the forces that tend to narrow regional differentials.[8] The widening of the gap between the two regions during the earlier period probably is related to the 1930–32 depression. However, as the accompanying chart illustrates, the Northeast, Far West, and Middle West maintained fairly stable relationships to one another through 1919, 1931–32, and 1945–46; hence there is reason to believe that the conditions that made for the changing status of the South were peculiar to that region.

The reasons for the improvement in the position of manufacturing wages in the South between 1931–32 and 1945–46 are more readily apparent than those for the earlier loss. Because of the relatively low wages paid in the South, this region was undoubtedly affected to a greater proportionate extent than others by the NRA codes, the Fair Labor Standards Act, and other Federal wage legislation; by the spread of unionization; and by the full employment of the war years. Whether or not the spread between the South and the Northeast continues to narrow, the 1945–46 position of the South relative to the Northeast reflected no progressive improvement over the 40 years covered, such as might be attributable to the working of long-term forces.[9]

In general, the over-all tendencies described above apply also to skilled male jobs, to semiskilled and unskilled male jobs, and, with slight modification, to all female jobs studied. The wage position of skilled men in the South relative to that of similarly skilled men in the Northeast was

8. In terms of wage rates paid to farm labor, the differential between the South and the rest of the country also widened between 1919 and 1932 and narrowed between 1932 and 1945–46.

9. Moreover, over this 40-year period, there appeared to be no long-run constant improvement in the relative position of union rates for skilled building and printing workers in southern cities such as might be attributable to general economic forces affecting the region as a whole. Rather, the various movements of southern cities toward and away from the average level and from each other might be explained best in terms of local and short-run factors.

substantially better than that for the semiskilled and unskilled (combined) in all four periods. In 1907 and 1919 (see table), the southern skilled group earned approximately 95 percent of northeastern rates, on the average, as contrasted with 88 percent for all male jobs and somewhat less than this amount considering only the semiskilled and unskilled male jobs. The increased differentials of 1931–32 brought the skilled in the South down to 83 percent of Northeast levels; for the less skilled the loss was even greater. The recovery of both groups in the South between 1932 and 1945–46 failed by narrow margins to bring them to the relative positions they held in 1919. Thus, in 1945–46 all southern male occupational groups were paid about 84 percent of corresponding job earnings in the Northeast. However, skilled groups in the South were within 10 percent of Northeast wage levels.

Median regional differences in occupational wage rates in manufacturing industries, by skill and sex, selected periods

[Wage rates for corresponding occupations in the Northeast=100]

Occupational category and period	Median relation to Northeast (in percent)		
	South	Middle West	Far West
All occupations:			
1907	86	100	130
1919	87	97	115
1931–32	74	97	113
1945–46	85	101	115
Men's occupations:			
1907	88	100	131
1919	88	98	117
1931–32	74	97	114
1945–46	84	102	115
Men's skilled occupations:			
1907	93	99	131
1919	95	98	(¹)
1931–32	83	96	(¹)
1945–46	91	101	113
Women's occupations:			
1907	(¹)	(¹)	(¹)
1919	81	92	(¹)
1931–32	73	(¹)	(¹)
1945–46	87	98	114

¹ Number of occupations covered too small to justify selection of median.

Skilled workers were consistently in a more favorable position than other groups in the South, but the range of differentials between southern and northeastern skilled occupations was quite wide. In all periods, a substantial proportion of southern skilled groups earned less than 80 percent of the rates for similar workers in the northern region. This variation reveals that the acquisition of a skilled status did not, in itself, assure the southern worker a wage equal or close to that received by like workers in other regions.

The median relationships also indicate that the percentage wage advantage of the skilled over the semiskilled and unskilled was greater in the South than in the Northeast (and other regions) in all periods. Moreover, the wider spread between the pay of skilled and unskilled in the South was due to the fact that the wage standards of the low-skilled occupations in the South, as a group, were further below those of low skilled in other regions than were those of the skilled.

In contrast with the situation of men workers, the wage position of women in the South relative to the Northeast appeared to be substantially better in 1945–46 than during the earlier periods studied. In 1919, occupational earnings of women in the South were, on the average, about 81 percent of corresponding earnings in the Northeast, as compared with 88 percent for men's jobs. Women's occupations were affected less than men's by the subsequent widening of differentials, and, in 1931–32, were at about the same level, that is, approximately 73 percent of northern wage levels. The 1945–46 data indicated that the women's group in the South was paid 87 percent of comparable rates in the Northeast — a somewhat better position than that of men's occupations (84 percent).

In the abstract, the changes in the position of the South might have resulted from the changing status of the Northeast and not from the changing status of the South relative to the country as a whole. For example, the differentials between the South and the Northeast might have decreased between 1932 and 1945–46 as a consequence of a smaller increase in wages in the latter region as against the rest of the country or of other factors affecting the Northeast region alone. However, the data for the Middle West and the Far West, discussed later in this article, show little change in relationships between each of these regions and the Northeast in the three later periods, and thus support the following conclusion: In the main, the widening of differentials between the South and the Northeast between 1919 and 1931–32 was caused by the South losing ground to the rest of the country in terms of occupational wages for men, and the subsequent reduction of differentials between 1931–32 and 1945–46 resulted from an improvement in the position of the South relative to other regions. The fragmentary data for women's occupations present an inconclusive picture.

POSITION OF THE FAR WEST

The Far West, and particularly the Pacific Coast, has long been a high-wage region and, in 1907, was in a particularly favorable wage position. By 1946, the relative wage status of the Far West was appreciably lower.[10]

10. A loss in relative status over this period, particularly in the early part, was also experienced by Far West cities with respect to union rates for skilled building and printing occupations, and by the Mountain States with respect to farm wage rates. In contrast, the Pacific States showed a rather steady advance in farm wage status over this period.

Probably continuing a tendency that had been set in motion earlier, it appears that the major decline in the position of the Far West took place between 1907 and the early 1920's.

Manufacturing wages in the Far West were substantially above those in the Northeast in all four periods studied. In 1907, about a fifth of the Far West occupational groups covered had hourly earnings as much as 50 percent or more above those of like groups in the Northeast; only a negligible number were at a wage disadvantage. Between 1907 and 1945–46 the differentials were reduced; in the recent period only about 6 percent of the occupations in the Far West showed 50 percent or more pay than in the Northeast and the proportion of jobs for which wage rates were lower in the Far West than in the Northeast was slightly above 10 percent. Occupational differentials for 1945–46 had quite a wide range, but approximately 44 percent of the Far West occupational groups showed wages from 5 to 20 percent more than those received in the Northeast.

As the chart illustrates, the Far West at least since 1919 has not held the substantial wage advantage it had over the Northeast and the Middle West in 1907. The average wage differential of the Far West over the Northeast amounted to 30 percent in 1907. By 1919, the spread had been reduced to 15 percent, and was maintained at approximately that level during 1931–32 and 1945–46. This evidence of a long-term stability in the Far West manufacturing wage differential is inconclusive insofar as short-run changes might be concerned. It does, however, bear out the conclusion that the growth of industry and the heavy in-migration of population that have characterized the development of the Far West during the past three decades apparently have not created a strong impetus towards the equalization of wage rates as between the Far West and the Northeast and Middle West.

In men's occupations alone, much the same showing was made. Among these occupations, the number classified as skilled was not sufficient in 1919 and 1931–32 to provide reliable averages, but the medians for skilled men in 1907 and 1945–46 differed only slightly from those shown for all men's occupations. Thus, the loss of wage advantage between 1907 and 1919, and the relative stability thereafter, can be attributed to the different skill levels in roughly the same measure.

In 1945–46, the only period for which the number of women's occupations covered in the Far West was sufficient to make possible a comparison with other regions, the wage position of women in the Far West relative to similarly employed women in the Northeast was about as favorable as that for men. The average differential between the Far West and the Middle West was slightly larger for women than for men; compared with the South the opposite was true.

Position of the Middle West

The job-for-job comparison between the two great industrial regions, the Middle West and the Northeast, revealed a wide range of wage differentials. However, in each period covered the proportion of occupations in which earnings were greater in the Northeast than in the Middle West was approximately the same as the proportion in which earnings were less. The median differential (3 percent at its highest) did not disclose an appreciable gap between the wage levels of the Middle West and the Northeast in any period. Average relationships between manufacturing wage rates in the Middle West and the Northeast remained comparatively stable throughout the four periods covered by this study.

The Middle West-Northeast differentials for men's occupations and for the skilled group of occupations, considered separately, were about the same as for all occupations, as the table shows. The slight difference between the median differentials for the skilled occupations and for all men's occupations, in favor of the latter, indicates that the unskilled and semiskilled in the Middle West generally held a slight advantage over the skilled in wage status relative to the Northeast. It also indicates that the wage spread between the skilled and other groups was slightly smaller in the Middle West than in the Northeast. Although women in the Middle West showed an improvement in wage status relative to the Northeast in 1945–46 as against 1919, in both periods women's occupations held less favorable positions than men's in relation to wage rates for similar jobs in the Northeast.

Broadly, the average wage differentials between the Middle West and the South and Far West took much the same course over the periods covered as those between the two latter regions and the Northeast. Compared with the Far West and the South, the Middle West showed a gain in status between 1907 and 1945–46 — a considerable narrowing of differentials with respect to the high-wage Far West region and a slight widening of the spread over the low-wage southern region.

Position of the Northeast

To evaluate the effect of the changes on the position of the Northeast, the main points already presented are recast below in such a way as to emphasize the region's relative status.

Between the 1907 and the 1945–46 periods, the Northeast advanced in relation to the Far West, but its status relative to the South and Middle West remained about the same. The wage advantage of the Northeast over the South increased substantially between 1919 and 1931–32 and decreased to about the same extent between 1931–32 and 1945–46, thus bringing the Northeast-South differential to the 1907 and 1919 level. The Northeast-Far West average differential, which favored the latter region throughout the 40 years covered, narrowed markedly between 1907 and 1919. The magnitude of the differential in 1945–46 was substantially smaller than in 1907 but was about the same as in 1919. Compared with the Middle West, the Northeast tended to gain slightly in relative status between 1907 and 1919 but experienced an offsetting loss between 1932 and 1945–46. Between 1932 and 1945–46, the Northeast lost ground to each of the other regions — only a superficial loss relative to the Middle West and Far West but a considerable loss relative to the South. This movement reversed the trend that operated between 1907 and 1932.[11]

The differentials between the Northeast and other regions with respect to men's occupations and the skilled groups among these occupations followed much the same course as that described for all occupations. However, in 1945–46, women factory workers in the Northeast did not hold the same favorable wage advantage over similarly employed workers in the South and Middle West that they held in 1919. This loss in relative status for women in the Northeast was not matched by an equivalent loss for men.

11. The pattern of gain in status followed by a loss marked the trend in wage differentials between the two northeastern farm regions and the country as a whole. The New England and Middle Atlantic farm regions improved their relative wage positions considerably between 1919 and 1932, but lost ground almost as drastically between 1932 and 1945–46. The standing of both regions was somewhat better in 1946 than in 1919 and 1910.

WAGE DIFFERENCES IN LOCAL LABOR MARKETS

By Lloyd G. Reynolds

The perfect labor market usually assumed in discussions of wages tends toward an equilibrium position in which workers of equal ability working equally hard at identical jobs under uniform conditions would receive equal wage rates. While actual labor markets are obviously far from perfect, one is still inclined to believe that some such tendency toward wage equalization is operative.

It is always somewhat disturbing, therefore, to observe the great variety of rates for apparently comparable jobs which prevails in actual labor markets. The National War Labor Board has during the past several years collected the rates paid by different firms for certain "key occupations" in a large number of industrial areas. Inspection of these data indicates that the highest rate in an area is usually at least 50 per cent and frequently 100 per cent above the lowest rate for workers classified under the same job title.

These differences in rates are of course not necessarily significant for wage theory. Their significance could be determined only by correcting for all the conditions assumed equal in the theoretical problem. First, the workers whose earnings are being compared may not be of equal ability or may not be working equally hard. This could readily account for differences in piece-rate earnings, and even under time rates, inter-firm wage differences might be offset by differences in the level of ability or effort required by various firms. Second, jobs called by the same name may not be the same jobs and the workers doing them may not be interchangeable. Terms such as "machinist," "welder," and even "common laborer" are notoriously unreliable indicators of job content.

Third, even if one could find two jobs requiring performance of exactly the same operations, these jobs might differ in almost numberless other respects. Among these are the extent of "fringe" wage payments—bonuses, paid vacations, paid holidays, pension systems, free medical care, etc.—the shift involved and the shift differential if any, the expected regularity of work, the length of the work day and week, the extent to which the worker is protected against layoffs by seniority or other rules, the opportunity for advancement, physical conditions of work, the congeniality of fellow-workers and supervisors, the quality of personnel management in the company, and the presence or absence of a union. Competition in a perfect labor market is supposed to equalize, not money rates of wages, but the total attractiveness of the same job in different plants. The conclusions of theory could be tested, therefore, only if it were possible to measure the total attractiveness of a job by reducing each of the factors enumerated above to a cents-per-hour equivalent and totaling.[1] Comparison of the totals would indicate the presence or absence of what may be termed "true" wage differences, to distinguish them from mere differences in base rates of pay.

Since no study of this sort has ever been made, it is not possible to assert categorically that "true" wage differences exist, still less that they are as large as the apparent differences in base rates.[2] Moreover, in order to be theoretically interesting, wage differences must have persisted sufficiently long for workers to learn about them and have reasonable opportunity to move to the more desirable jobs. This means that measurements must probably be extended over a period of at least a decade.[3]

The writer is of the opinion that "true" wage differences are of significant size in actual labor markets, and that they do not diminish appreciably with the passage of time. Whether this is so, however, can be discovered only by further research. The object here is simply to develop hypotheses capable of explaining the appearance and persistence of wage differences and capable, therefore, of serving as guides to investigation.

I

It is necessary first to distinguish between conditions which might make different firms willing to pay different wage rates, and conditions which would permit the continued payment of different rates. In other words, one must distinguish between *positive* factors operating on the demand side of the market and *permissive* factors operating on the supply side.

It is not difficult to construct conditions of labor supply which would permit the persistence of wage differences. If full employment is assumed, a forward-rising supply-curve of labor may be posited on any of several

[1] A worker makes an implicit calculation of total job attractiveness every time he decides to change or not to change his job. And workers might be able to provide an investigator with rough quantitative estimates of the importance they attach to various job characteristics: 10 years' seniority = 7 cents per hour, pleasant supervisor = 4 cents per hour, and so on. The main analytical difficulty is that some job attributes, notably things like security, would probably be valued very differently by different workers. It would not be legitimate to average out different workers' ratings of the same job to arrive at a score for it; for the fact that different workers react differently toward the same constellation of job characteristics is the important thing.

[2] Charles A. Myers and W. Rupert Maclaurin, after careful observation of a New England industrial community for several years, expressed the opinion that differences in wage rates in this area were not accompanied by offsetting differences in other job characteristics: "The low-wage firms generally did not compensate for their poorer rates by providing better working conditions, welfare plans, or good 'informal relations.'" (*The Movement of Factory Workers* [New York, Wiley, 1944], p. 73.)

[3] Strictly speaking, even a demonstration that substantial wage differences had persisted unchanged for ten, twenty, or more years would not refute the possibility that a tendency toward wage equalization had been operative *at each moment of time* within that period. The market might at each moment of time be tending toward an equilibrium position of equal wage rates; yet because of the continual intervention of dynamic changes, involving changes also in the appropriate equilibrium position, the observed wage differences might not decrease and might even increase.

grounds,[4] of which the most realistic are probably (a) differences in workers' preference for specified combinations of wages and conditions, analogous to differences in consumer preference; (b) attachment of workers to a familiar workplace and work-group; (c) attachment of workers to a familiar place of residence. These last two factors may be considered as operating independently of the intrinsic attractiveness of the job, and would produce a forward-rising supply curve even if all jobs in the market were equally attractive. If all firms in the market have sloped supply curves, there is obviously no reason why different wage rates should not continue indefinitely.

A different and in some ways more interesting model may be constructed under conditions of unemployment. Suppose that layoffs have been made in such a way that a considerable proportion of the unemployed are more efficient than the least efficient of the employed. Suppose further that any firm which wishes to expand its work force will hire unemployed workers rather than workers already employed by other firms. Suppose finally that the alternative to employment is relief at a level below the workers' conception of a tolerable wage.

Under these conditions the supply curve of labor to each firm would look somewhat as follows: starting from a point representing the firm's present wage rate and employment, the curve would run horizontally to the right for at least a considerable distance and possibly all the way to the point of full employment. Viewed from the other direction, it would run vertically downward to a level which would provoke the workers to quit work in a body, and would then become horizontal. This level will be referred to hereafter as the "minimum wage" of the firm. In this sort of labor market each firm would clearly have wide latitude in choosing a wage rate and wage differences, once established, could persist indefinitely.

While these supply conditions will *permit* wage differences to exist, the conditions which will actually *produce* wage differences must be sought on the demand side of the labor market. The remainder of the paper will be devoted to exploring these demand conditions. In order, first, to isolate the effect of different types of competitive situation in product markets, let us assume (a) that each firm knows the location of its "minimum wage," and that the minima of all firms are the same; (b) that the supply of factors other than labor is perfectly elastic to each firm; (c) that the local labor market under consideration is completely isolated from all other labor markets. The effect of removing these restrictions will be considered in the next section; it is obvious that the result will in each case be to render wage differences more likely. We shall assume throughout that union organization is absent. It will also be assumed that only one occupation exists in the market and that differences in individual efficiency either do not exist or are taken into account through the use of efficiency units.

The average and marginal net value productivity of labor for any firm in

[4] This does not mean that only a rising supply curve can be derived under full employment; horizontal, vertical, "kinked," and zigzag curves may also be derived from various combinations of assumptions. The argument of this and the two following paragraphs is much more fully developed in my article on "The Supply of Labor to the Firm," *Quart. Jour. Econ.,* Vol. LX, No. 3 (May, 1946).

the market may be represented, as in the figure below, by curves of the type *ANP* and *MNP*, while *OA* represents the minimum wage. It is possible to introduce discontinuities into the marginal productivity curve by assuming similar discontinuities in the firm's marginal revenue curve.[5] The results which can be obtained in this way, however, are probably of rather short-run

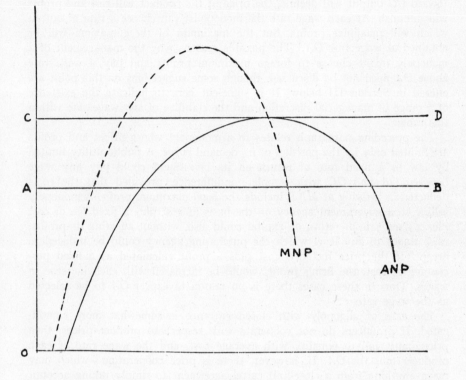

significance, and results derived from a continuous marginal productivity curve can be taken as approximately correct over considerable periods of time.

It is clear that the figure does not represent an equilibrium position for any firm in an industry to which entrance is open, whether the situation is one of pure competition, monopolistic competition, or oligopoly. If new firms can enter at wage rate *OA*, then *ANP* and *MNP* will be forced down

[5] For example, vertical discontinuities in *MNP* may be obtained by assuming that prices are not varied continuously with changes in cost—for example, that prices are never changed by less than 5 per cent, or that prices are set only in certain "brackets" or "price lines," or that prices are changed only at fixed intervals of time. Horizontal discontinuities can be introduced by assuming that the demand curve for the product is itself discontinuous and that marginal cost is constant over the relevant range; if a horizontal section of the marginal productivity curve happened to coincide with a horizontal supply curve of labor, the equilibrium employment of the firm would be indeterminate over this range. These complications will be ignored here.

until AB becomes tangent to ANP. Thus even if a firm had established a wage rate above OA while profits in the industry were temporarily high, it would not be able to maintain this wage rate but would be forced back to OA.[6]

If, however, the firm in question is a monopoly, in the technical sense, it will be free to pay any wage rate between OA and OC. As the wage rises toward OC output will decline, the price of the product will rise and profits will diminish. At each wage rate the monopolist can choose a rate of output which will maximize profits, but the maximum of these maxima will be obtained at wage rate OA.[7] The possible reasons why the management of a monopoly might choose to forego maximum profits and pay a wage rate above OA need not be discussed, though some suggestions on this point are offered in Section III below. It is sufficient here to indicate the existence of a range of managerial discretion and the stability of any wage rate within this range.

The preceding paragraph relates to a monopoly whose prices and profits are limited only by the position of its demand curve. A public utility limited by law to a fixed rate of return on its investment could pay any wage between OA and OC with complete indifference, provided that the costs deducted in arriving at MNP include the legal maximum profit. A monopoly selling to a government agency on the basis of cost plus a fixed fee or cost plus a fixed rate of return on capital could also, without affecting its profits, raise wages to any level which the purchasing agency could be induced to accept. If the price included cost plus a profit calculated as a fixed percentage of cost, the firm's profits would be increased with each increase in wages. Thus in these cases there is no reason to expect OA to be selected as the wage rate.

The case of oligopoly with closed entrance is somewhat more complicated. If producers do not coöperate with respect to product prices, then prices must fall to equality with average cost, and the wage rate of each producer must be OA. If, however, there is price coöperation—which may mean anything from a close-knit cartel agreement to simply taking account of the probable reaction of other firms in the industry to a price change— the resulting price, demand conditions permitting, will be somewhat above average cost. Each firm will then have something of the monopolist's latitude with respect to wage rates: it can pay anything between OA and the wage which would just reduce its profits to normal. The freedom of each producer is qualified, however, by the necessity of maintaining cordial relations with

[6] A wage higher than OA can be established permanently if, while the industry is out of equilibrium and profits are above normal, a union enters the industry and enforces a wage greater than OA from all firms, at the same time preventing any new firm from entering the industry at a lower wage. But this amounts to saying that the minimum wage OA has now been raised by trade union action and does not constitute an exception to the statement just made.

[7] If profits were introduced into the figure as a third dimension, MNP would resemble the backbone of a mountain range sloping downward on either side and also running downward as one goes from AB toward CD. MNP is a locus of profit maxima, and the greatest of these maxima will occur at its intersection with AB.

other producers. If most firms in the industry choose to pay wages considerably above *OA*, then a firm which pays only *OA* may be suspected of undermining the price agreement and pressure may be put on it to come up to the general industry level. One would, therefore, expect a certain clustering of wage rates rather than an even distribution over the possible range. The oligopolists may even agree to pay the same wage as a means of buttressing the price agreement. If they seek also to maximize their profits, the agreed wage will be *OA;* but other motives may dictate selection of a higher wage.

Under the conditions assumed, then, the wages of firms operating under conditions of pure competition, monopolistic competition, or oligopoly with either free entrance or uncontrolled prices, will tend toward equality at *OA*. Monopolies and members of oligopoly groups with closed entrance and controlled prices will also pay *OA* if they wish to maximize profits; if they are willing to accept a lower level of profits, however, they can choose to pay wages above *OA* by amounts varying with the position of their demand curves. Firms whose prices are set by government acting either as purchaser or regulator are still more likely to pay wages above *OA*. Thus, in any labor market containing firms of these latter types, one would expect to find some dispersion of wage rates for comparable work.

II

Let us now consider the consequences of removing some of the assumptions made in the previous section. Suppose, first, that a firm in a competitive industry is able, because of imperfections in the market for a factor other than labor, to purchase that factor more cheaply than its competitors.[8] Suppose further that this advantage is not open to would-be entrants to the industry. Then part or all of the surplus income accruing to the advantageously-situated firm may, at the discretion of management, be transferred to labor through higher wages. Thus even firms subject to pure or monopolistic competition in product markets may have something of the monopolist's latitude with respect to wage rates.

Second, suppose that the labor market under consideration is only one of many, and that these markets have differing "minimum wages." This implies that movements of labor and capital are not sufficiently rapid to eliminate inter-area wage differences within the period of time taken into account. Now suppose the firms in a competitive industry are distributed among these markets in such a way that their minimum wages form a statistical array resembling the so-called "bulk-line cost curve." Then the price of the product will tend to settle at a level sufficient to cover the minimum wage of a firm at, say, the ninth quartile of the array. If costs other than wages are uniform throughout the industry, all firms below the ninth quartile will have some latitude with respect to wage rates. Each of these firms can pay anything between the minimum wage in its own area and the

[8] This may mean purchase of a higher quality of a factor at the standard price rather than payment of a lower price for the same quality. It seems likely, for example, that especially able managers will receive less than their full contribution to production, particularly in a situation in which individual income-tax rates are high.

minimum wage of the "marginal" firm; the lower the minium wage in a particular area, the wider the range of discretion of firms in that area. This situation is stable, of course, only if there are obstacles to new firms entering the industry in the areas with the lowest minimum wages; otherwise, the industry would become concentrated increasingly in those areas, and dispersion of wage rates arising from geographical dispersion of the industry would disappear. If one brings into the picture not one industry but a large number of industries, each with a somewhat different geographical distribution, then it is clear that each labor market in the economy may have its own pattern of inter-firm wage differences, which will not be reproduced exactly in any other market.

The individual firm is caught between the area and the industry. Conditions within the area, particularly the wage levels of other firms, determine the minimum which it must pay. The wage rates of other firms in the industry, *ceteris paribus*, will determine the maximum which it can afford to pay. If the latter figure is less than the former, the firm will in time be forced out of operation; but if it is greater, the firm can be guided by the wage level either of the industry or the area. Developments in the industry may lead the firm to make wage changes independently of any developments in the local labor market. Indeed, for firms in competitive industries which are geographically dispersed, it appears that the industry is normally the dynamic influence in bringing about wage changes, while the influence of the local labor market is merely passive or permissive.

Third, let us admit the possibility that different firms in the same labor market may have different minimum wages. One reason for this is that wage differences which have persisted for some time become customary and workers tend to presume that they should continue. A wage rate which would be accepted if paid by a traditionally low-wage firm may provoke a revolt if adopted suddenly by a high-wage firm. Each firm thus has its own minimum wage which is related to its present and previous actual wage rates. These minima lie one above the other like steps on an escalator. The relative ranking of the various firms doubtless changes gradually over long periods of time, but at any one time it is rather firmly fixed in the minds of both workers and employers.[9] Any attempt by one firm to drop its wage rate below the minimum expected of it, or to retain the same wage rate when the wage escalator is moving upward, will cause serious labor unrest.

This circumstance helps to explain not only why wage differences persist but also why they may widen with the passage of time. Once a set of differentials has become customary, a management gains no credit with its workers by merely doing what is expected of it. It can add fresh luster to its reputation for generosity only by *increasing* its wage differential over other firms. But this new differential will in time become customary, and so on.

---

[9] Witness the large number of cases in which a firm requests the War Labor Board to approve a wage increase in order to enable it to maintain or restore its "historical position" in the area wage structure. Such requests are uniformly refused, and must be refused under the wage stabilization policy. There can be no doubt, however, that this refusal frequently works severe hardship on the firms involved.

The differentials presently existing in most United States labor markets are clearly too large to have been attained in one jump, and can only be understood as the outcome of some such historical process. Investigation might reveal a long-run tendency for local wage-structures to open out like the ribs of a fan, the higher-wage firms increasing their advantage in successive jumps, each of which gradually becomes conventionalized.

Under the assumptions of Section I, one would expect to find in any locality a "prevailing rate" of wages, from which only monopolies or quasi-monopolies could deviate. When the three assumptions just discussed are relaxed, however, the likelihood of a "prevailing rate" is removed. There is now no reason why each firm in the market should not have a different wage rate. Moreover, there is no longer any reason to expect a clear relation between a firm's wage level and the type of product market in which it deals. The effect of differing types of product market, while still present, is mingled with the effect of conditions influencing each firm's cost position in its own industry—notably the wage levels of other areas in which rival producers are located, and the cost of factors other than labor to this firm as compared with others. Added to these factors affecting each firm's ability to pay are differences in managerial judgment concerning the wisdom of paying as much as one can. The actual wage structure of an area reflects the composite effect of these influences. The effect of each can be gauged only approximately and only through studies which reach beyond the area concerned to the cost-price structure of each industry represented in it.

With these considerations in mind, it is possible to suggest one or two reasons why a firm may choose to pay a higher wage than it has to at the moment. The firm is likely to be uncertain about the precise location of its wage minimum, particularly under dynamic conditions in which the minimum may change very frequently. If it can afford to do so, it is likely to "play safe" by paying somewhat more than its estimate of the minimum. Different firms may thus be at differing distances above their wage minima because of differences in the accuracy of their estimates and also because of differences in the safety margin which they feel able to afford.

The degree of uncertainty is increased if one takes into account a factor hitherto excluded from the discussion, *viz.*, variations in individual efficiency. A reduction in wage rates will lead to a less than proportionate reduction in wage cost per efficiency unit of labor; for efficiency will fall both through a lowering of the grade of labor which the firm can recruit and through a reduction in the efficiency of those already employed. The wage level which would actually yield minimum cost per efficiency unit could perhaps be determined by successive wage reductions. But since such experimentation is dangerous, it may not be undertaken unless the pressure of competition compels it, and the firm may continue at a level of wage costs somewhat above what is strictly necessary.

A monopoly or a closed oligopoly group may pay more than the minimum wage in order to render the industry less attractive to potential competitors. It has frequently been pointed out that a monopolist may for this reason charge a price below that which would maximize profits. But profits can be held at a moderate level by paying high wages instead of by charging low prices. Provided potential competitors take the wage level of established firms as an indication of what they would have to pay to secure labor, this technique may be highly effective.

Payment of a relatively high wage may also simplify the problems of personnel management by facilitating recruiting of labor, stabilizing the working force, stimulating efficiency, improving labor coöperation with management, and so on. Maximizing profits is hard work. Some sacrifice of profits in order to make the job of management easier may be perfectly "economic" action from the standpoint of the managers, though not from the standpoint of the owners.

III

The argument has been directed toward explaining the long-run persistence of differences in wage *levels* within a local labor market. But it is also relevant to the problem of how wage *changes* occur and how changes in one labor market are transmitted to others. Under usual assumptions about labor market structure one would expect that, during a cyclical upswing, wages would rise in an area *only* when full employment had been reached. The area would then begin to draw labor from other areas and, as full employment was reached in more and more areas, wage increases would become general throughout the economy. During periods of cyclical decline this process would be thrown into reverse. In either case, local labor markets would be linked together primarily by inter-area movements of labor, and the rapidity with which wage changes were transmitted throughout the system would depend on the rapidity of this movement.

This sort of model, however, does not explain the fact that wage rates frequently rise in an area while heavy unemployment still exists,[10] and that wage impulses are transmitted within and between labor markets much more rapidly than could be explained by actual or even potential movement of labor. These facts can perhaps be more nearly explained by the considerations set forth above. Suppose that the leading firm of a "controlled oligopoly," located in labor market A, raises wages—perhaps as prelude to or aftermath of a price increase. The wage increase is followed by another member of the industry, located in labor market B. This action will raise the estimates which other firms in area B make of their own minimum wage; as demand conditions permit, some of them will make increases to maintain their "historical position" in the wage structure. Thus the whole "escalator" of minimum wages in the area moves upward, carrying actual wage rates along with it. But the firms in area B have competitors in areas C, D, etc., some of whom will be influenced by the wage changes in B, and so on. A sym-

---

[10] Indeed, statistics of average hourly earnings by industry indicate that wage rates tend to rise first and fall last in industries in which cyclical unemployment is greatest. See the discussion of this point in John T. Dunlop, *Wage Determination Under Trade Unions* (New York, Macmillan, 1944) pp. 130-43. It would be interesting to make a similar analysis on an area basis, but wage statistics are not now organized in such a way as to permit this.

metrical explanation can be offered for the transmission of wage decreases.[11]

Thus, through industry linkages, a wage change in one area may be transmitted rapidly to distant and apparently unrelated areas. This need not involve any actual or even threatened movement of labor between areas. Inter-area movement of labor appears indeed to perform, not its traditional function of equalizing wage rates, but the quite different function of equalizing unemployment ratios in different areas. During recession and depression labor mobility declines greatly and, because of differences in the cyclical variability of different industries, unemployment piles up more rapidly in some areas than in others. As recovery gets under way, movement sets in once more toward areas in which the unemployment ratio is relatively low.[12] But the areas in which unemployment is low are not necessarily those in which wage rates are high.

IV

The wide gap between the accepted models of the labor market and the actual behavior of wage rates and employment has inhibited systematic research in this field. This paper has attempted to advance hypotheses around which the wealth of data available in any local labor market may profitably be organized. It has been suggested that attention should be concentrated primarily on the supply conditions of labor to the individual firm, the characteristics of the product market in which each firm deals and its cost position relative to other firms in its industry, the considerations influencing the exercise of managerial discretion with respect to wage rates, and the way in which changes are transmitted among firms and labor market areas. It is important also to make accurate measurements of wage rates, appropriately defined, and to extend these measurements over as long a period as possible.

[11] The only important difference in the two cases is that the firm initiating a wage decrease is likely to be a member of a competitive industry. Dunlop's observation that "declines in product prices and not unemployment constitute the effective downward pressure on wage structures" (*op. cit.*, p. 146) is entirely consistent with what has been said here.

[12] See on this point the studies of the Oxford Institute for Economic Research, reported in *Oxford Economic Papers*, October, 1938, and September, 1940.

WAGES AND THE MOVEMENT OF FACTORY LABOR

SUMMARY

Method of investigation, 242. — Movement between factories, 245. — Effect of inter-factory movement on wages, 248. — Persistence of wage differentials: factors affecting wage practices, 254; non-competitive hiring practices, 257. — Lack of competition among workers, 259; influence of family and friends, 260; absence of effective vocational guidance, 261; weakness of financial incentives, 261. — Summary, 262.

Economic analysis of the influence of labor movement in equalizing wage rates for comparable jobs has been based on a common-sense interpretation of how the labor market might be expected to operate. A clear statement of the economist's interpretation of the tendency toward wage equalization is given by Hicks in The Theory of Wages:

> The movement of labour from place to place is insufficient to iron out local differences in wages. But the movement does occur, and recent researches are indicating more and more clearly that differences in net economic advantages, chiefly differences in wages, are the main causes of migration. . . . Even in a position of equilibrium, some local differences indeed would probably persist. . . . The conditions of equilibrium postulate no more than that the "net advantages" of employment in different places must be equal for labour of equal efficiency.[2]

Labor market investigations, both in England and in the United States, have been focussed largely on the transfer of unemployed workers to other regions and the experience of workers "after the layoff." The effect of movement or lack of movement on the existence of wage differentials within and between regions has been given scant attention.[3] The process of equalization is admittedly not rapid; it may in certain cases be extremely slow. Further analysis, based on observational studies, is therefore important.

1. This is part of a larger investigation undertaken by members of the Industrial Relations Section of the Massachusetts Institute of Technology.
2. J. R. Hicks, The Theory of Wages (London, 1932), pp. 76 and 74.
3. A few studies have been made of movement within particular labor markets. Among these are Gladys L. Palmer's "The Mobility of Weavers in Three Textile Centers," this JOURNAL, May, 1941, pp. 460–485; Anne Bezanson, Miriam Hussey, Joseph H. Willits and Leda F. White's Four Years of Labor Mobility: A Study of Labor Turnover in a Group of Selected Plants in Philadelphia, 1921–24 (Supplement to Vol. CXIX, Annals of the American Academy of Political and Social Science, Philadelphia, May, 1925); Anne

This article is based on a study of a New England labor market during the pre-war years of 1937, 1938 and 1939, and a re-examination of the same market in 1942. Attention was focussed on the amount of movement between firms and the effect of movement or lack of movement on equalization of wage rates for comparable jobs.

METHOD OF INVESTIGATION

Two adjacent, medium-sized Massachusetts cities were chosen for this study. They contained a considerable number of different industries,[4] and were the trading centers of a substantial farming area. They were sufficiently distant from any other important towns to form a distinct and compact labor market. In 1940 their combined population was approximately 64,000. In these two cities, manufacturing industries accounted for over half of the total employment, according to the 1930 Census. This was not a high-wage region, and unionism did not become an important factor in wage determination until 1941–42. The community was also characterized by considerable home ownership and important racial and religious influences. For example, it was a strong Catholic region in which the parish ties were very important. The community had large numbers of French Canadian, Italian and Finnish, as well as Anglo-Saxon workers. The foreign groups were quite cohesive and tended to live in certain districts with others of their nationality.

The method followed in this investigation was to call on all the manufacturing concerns in the community which had more than fifty employees. Permission was requested at the interview to visit the plant and have the principal operations explained. On making these visits and at subsequent interviews we recorded our impressions of the executives, the nature of the supervision provided, working conditions, the labor relations atmosphere of the plant, and the firm's awareness of its labor turnover; and we tried to get some general information on the competitive position of the com-

Bezanson's "The Advantages of Labor Turnover," this JOURNAL, May, 1928, pp. 450–464. These studies, however, do not discuss the effect of movement on wage differentials.

4. The city dominated by one industry is apparently not the typical industrial community in Massachusetts. A study of thirty-one Massachusetts cities and towns, made by Professor Dwight L. Palmer of Massachusetts Institute of Technology for the National Resources Planning Board, showed that for 1938 in two-thirds of these cities no one industry employed more than 60 per cent of the factory wage-earners, and in many cities the dominant industry was considerably less important than this.

pany, its past history and development, and profit and loss record. Visits were also arranged with the mayor, the manager of the public employment service, bank officials, the Chamber of Commerce, the principals of the various public and parochial schools, etc. After many visits and discussions, we gradually acquired a better understanding of the general reputation and characteristics of the various companies in the community.

When we had become sufficiently well acquainted with a manufacturing concern, we asked permission to inspect the company's wage and employment records. These records showed wage rates, hours worked, and weekly and annual earnings. They varied in the extent to which complete information was given concerning previous employment history and other personnel facts. By photographing on microfilm, earnings and employment records were obtained for all the employees from 1937 to 1939 in 37 firms. These firms employed 75 per cent of all industrial workers in the community, as shown in Table I.

TABLE I
COVERAGE OF THE SAMPLE
Number of Firms and Number of Employees in Sample
Compared with All Firms, Grouped by Industries
(November, 1938)[1]

Industry	NUMBER OF FIRMS			AVERAGE NUMBER OF EMPLOYEES		
	All	Sample	Per Cent	All	Sample	Per Cent
Plastics..................	20	5	25	2,922	2,400	82
Metal Products..........	14	3	21	1,989	750	38
Textiles.................	8	7	88	1,935	1,915	99
Paper Manufacturing.....	5	5	100	1,723	1,723	100
Apparel.................	7	2	29	1,378	1,050	76
Furniture...............	12	2	17	912	535	59
Shoes and Leather Products	4	3	75	800	650	81
Machinery..............	11	4	36	404	255	63
Public Utilities..........	3	2	67	231	225	97
Converted Paper Products	6	3	50	230	150	65
Food Products...........	9	1	11	205	100	49
Miscel. Manufacturing....	21	0	00	267	0	00
Total...............	120	37	31	12,996	9,753	75

[1] Employment estimates, provided by the local Chamber of Commerce, are approximate only. These estimates were used in this comparison, rather than the figures from our microfilm records, in order that data for firms in the sample would be comparable with data for all industries in the community. There were no important discrepancies between the Chamber of Commerce estimates and our microfilm records.

In returning to the community in 1942, we obtained information concerning the employment and wage-rate changes that had occurred since 1939. Records were not photographed again, but an examination was made of the inward and outward movement of workers and the sources of labor supply.

The period of the study (1937–42) covered one complete cycle of employment in this labor market[5] (Chart I). At the beginning

CHART I

Trend of Employment, 1925–1942

(1925–1927 = 100)

— Employment in one city

— — Employment in the United States

•••••• Estimated

Source: Average number of wage earners in manufacturing for one city only; figures are not available for the other. From the Annual Report (1941) of the Massachusetts Department of Labor and Industries. Employment data for the United States: U. S. Department of Commerce, Bureau of Foreign and Domestic Commerce, *Survey of Current Business*, 1940, Supplement, p. 31 and February 1941, p. 59.

of the period in 1937 this market had largely recovered from the great depression, and was experiencing some shortages of skilled labor but no general labor shortage. Employment in the concerns

5. Detailed figures (Chart I) were available only for the larger of the two cities, but the trend of employment in the adjoining city was generally comparable.

in the sample and in the community declined slightly less than total United States factory employment during 1937–38. Recovery in 1939 was distinct, but less marked than for the United States as a whole. The lack of complete recovery in 1939 can be attributed to the shutdown of a small textile mill and the partial closing of one of the large branches of a nationally owned plastics concern.

By 1942 employment was reaching an all-time high, and serious shortages of skilled workers had developed. However, the expanding factories were not experiencing an acute shortage of unskilled and semi-skilled help. Some workers were being laid off by industries forced to curtail operations by shortage of materials and War Production Board orders. New labor was being attracted from domestic service, retail trade, restaurants and the surrounding rural area by the prospect of higher rates paid to factory workers. As a consequence, the community was regarded as an area of "labor surplus" in relation to many other New England labor markets in mid-1942.

MOVEMENT BETWEEN FACTORIES

An examination of the employment records of the 37 firms from 1937–39 showed that there was very high labor turnover. A total of 15,800 different workers was employed at one time or another during 1937–39 by these firms, although peak employment at any one time was less than 9,800. Only 4,600 workers were employed steadily without moving during the three years.

Of the 11,200 workers who either were laid off or left voluntarily, about 1,500 moved to another one of the 37 firms in the sample. This meant that in proportion to the total movement in and out of employment and between jobs only a small amount took place between the principal factories in the community. Following separation from a job in one of the 37 firms, the most common employment experience for a worker was to find odd jobs in retail trade, on a farm, driving a truck, etc., rather than to get work in another factory in this community. Factory jobs were the most sought after, but when a lay-off came many employees did not have another such opportunity until they were called back to their previous work.

A detailed examination of the experience of the 1,539 workers in our sample who found other factory jobs showed that they made

2,451 moves during 1937–39. About 70 per cent of these moves were "forced" because of lay-offs or discharges.[6] The remaining 30 per cent were voluntary changes, resulting primarily from dissatisfaction with wages, hours, or working conditions, or from the prospect of a better job elsewhere. At no time during the three-year period were voluntary movements greater than forced movements.[7]

In the 1942 labor market, forced movements were still predominant. A number of firms in civilian industries, such as paper, plastics and furniture, had curtailed their operations as a consequence of shortage of materials or orders by the War Production Board. Laid-off employees sought, and frequently found, employment in expanding war plants, such as metal products and machinery companies. Voluntary movement, on the other hand, was still not large, although it was increasing.

Some of the low-wage companies had experienced considerable turnover under war-time labor market conditions. "It's tough," explained an official of a women's shoe firm, "because defense plants are hiring more, and our people are anxious to get into work which pays better anyhow." Workers were also leaving jobs in the plastics, converted paper products and apparel companies, which ranked with shoes as low-wage firms in 1937–39 and continued to pay relatively less than other industries in 1942.

Other firms, however, were able to hold their workers, despite the attraction of employment in expanding war plants. A few specific examples may help to visualize the situation. One small cotton textile firm, which had no losses to other firms during 1937–39, continued to enjoy a favored position in 1942 because most of its workers were older, long-service people who lived in the neighborhood around the mill. A furniture firm, which also had a machine shop, explained why it could pay less than the war plants and still keep its labor:

6. Professor Slichter's term "forced movement" seems preferable to "involuntary," because it aptly describes the character of movement resulting from lay-offs and discharges. Sumner H. Slichter, "The Impact of Social Security Legislation upon Mobility and Enterprise," American Econ. Rev. (Supplement), March, 1940, p. 43.

7. Woytinsky states that ". . . after the beginning of 1930 about 75 per cent of all terminations of employment in manufacturing industries were initiated by employers." W. S. Woytinsky, Three Aspects of Labor Dynamics (Washington, Social Science Research Council, 1942), p. 4.

We haven't lost a machinist, because they get steady work and they work only during the regular daytime hours. Many of them are oldtimers and they realize that if they went elsewhere they might have to take the night shift or stand for some other inconvenience.

A similar explanation for low turnover was given by the manager of a woolen textile mill:

Many of our people would rather work 40 hours a week for the paychecks they get now than have to put in a lot of overtime and sometimes work seven days a week as they would have to in the metal plant next door. Furthermore, our people are not looking just at the present; they are looking to the future too. They realize that before this war they were getting steady work and we were running 24 hours a day. So they want to hang on to a steady job and will do it as long as they do get some pay increases from time to time. Then don't forget, "Once a textile worker, always a textile worker."[8]

Detailed information concerning the nature of the inter-factory movement which took place from 1937 to 1939 is shown in Table II.

TABLE II

TOTAL MOVEMENT OF WORKERS (VOLUNTARY AND FORCED)
IN RELATION TO WAGE LEVELS

(Number of Moves between Groups of Firms, 1937–39)[1]
Wage Level for Semi-Skilled Workers[2]

To	From Very High (4 Firms)	Moderately High (6 Firms)	Medium (8 Firms)	Low (10 Firms)	Very Low (9 Firms)	Total (37 Firms)
Very High.......	3	16	9	27	8	63
Moderately High..	4	6	12	29	17	68
Medium.........	0	9	41	62	67	179
Low............	7	8	72	305	396	788
Very Low........	2	7	87	391	866	1,353
Total.........	16	46	221	814	1,354	2,451

[1] A total of 1,539 workers made the 2,451 moves, 70 per cent of which were forced and 30 per cent voluntary.
[2] Information on the approximate hourly rates or, if piece rates were paid, the straight time average hourly earnings for semi-skilled workers (such as assemblers or machine-operators), was supplied by each firm. An attempt was made to choose semi-skilled operations that were fairly comparable.

8. Cf. Reëmployment of Philadelphia Hosiery Workers after Shutdowns: "This study illustrates the tenacity with which skilled textile workers seek work in the labor market of the industry to which they have usually been attached and also their sense of attachment to particular mills. A union hosiery worker considers he has a certain equity in a particular job in a particular mill and may delay seeking work elsewhere if a shutdown is accompanied by rumors of reopening." Gladys L. Palmer and Constance Williams, Works Progress Administration, National Research Project and Industrial Research Department, University of Pennsylvania (Philadelphia, 1939), p. 46.

The amount of movement in the direction of the higher-wage firms was very small during this period. There was a strong tendency for clustering of movement among firms situated within a comparatively short distance of each other. Within these neighborhood clusters of firms, the greatest total movement occurred among the seasonal industries,[9] which were also the low-wage industries. While we had no detailed data with which to analyze these same tendencies in 1942, it was clear that the greatest movement still occurred between neighboring firms, and particularly between non-war and war plants in the same neighborhood. Most of the workers lost by a shoe firm in 1942, for example, went to a nearby cotton yarn mill which was working on war orders. Among the applicants for employment at a large munitions plant there were more workers from another shoe firm in the neighborhood than from any other company.

EFFECT OF INTER-FACTORY MOVEMENT ON WAGES

Most of the inter-factory movement that took place from 1937 to 1939 resulted from lay-offs, as has already been pointed out. About 30 per cent of the moves, however, were voluntary. The relationship between this voluntary movement and the wage level of the various firms in the sample is indicated in Chart II. It is clear from this chart that there was a tendency for voluntary movement to be in the direction of the high-wage firms, although, as was shown in Table II, the amount of such upward movement was very small, since most of the movement was forced and took place in the low-wage, seasonal industries. The wage-level comparison between firms, shown in Chart II, is based on an analysis of semi-skilled jobs requiring comparable intelligence and training in the various mills.[1] In spite of the differences in the kind of work that was done in the various plants in the community, a considerable number of jobs were comparable in all the plants.

While there was some voluntary movement in the direction of the high-wage firms, the relative ranking of high- and low-wage

9. Except for reasons of convenience of location, the interviews with workers in seasonal industries gave no evidence that they wanted to stay in those industries. Four-fifths of the persons interviewed said that they wanted full-time work, which they were not getting in the seasonal industries.

1. Unskilled and semi-skilled women constituted a relatively large part of the labor supply of the seasonal industries. In contrast, the labor forces in the non-seasonal industries were more largely male and semi-skilled and skilled.

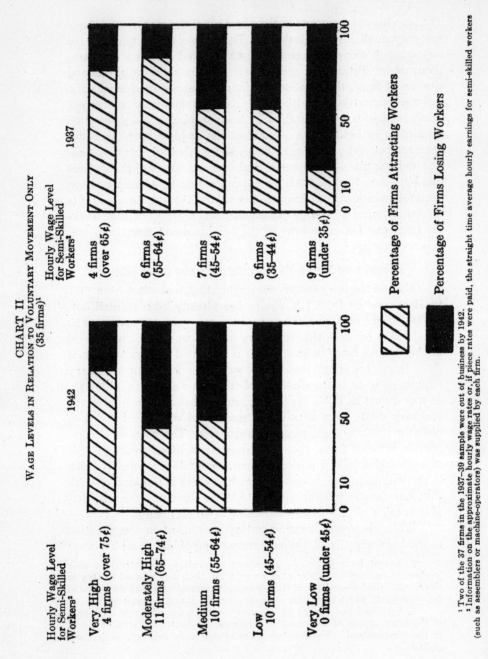

CHART II

WAGE LEVELS IN RELATION TO VOLUNTARY MOVEMENT ONLY
(35 firms)[1]

Hourly Wage Level
for Semi-Skilled
Workers[2]

1942

Hourly Wage Level
for Semi-Skilled
Workers[2]

1937

Very High
4 firms (over 75¢)

Moderately High
11 firms (65–74¢)

Medium
10 firms (55–64¢)

Low
10 firms (45–54¢)

Very Low
0 firms (under 45¢)

4 firms
(over 65¢)

6 firms
(55–64¢)

7 firms
(45–54¢)

9 firms
(35–44¢)

9 firms
(under 35¢)

Percentage of Firms Attracting Workers

Percentage of Firms Losing Workers

[1] Two of the 37 firms in the 1937–39 sample were out of business by 1942.
[2] Information on the approximate hourly wage rates or, if piece rates were paid, the straight time average hourly earnings for semi-skilled workers (such as assemblers or machine-operators) was supplied by each firm.

companies was *not significantly altered* from 1937 to 1942. A somewhat larger proportion of the medium- and low-wage concerns cut wages in the 1938 recession (Table III), but these cuts were later restored. In 1942 the nine very "low-wage" firms, which had paid semi-skilled workers less than 35 cents an hour in 1937, remained low relative to the others. However, their rates of pay for semi-skilled workers had now been raised to a level between 45 cents and 54 cents. Some of these firms made increases because higher minimum rates were ordered under the federal wage-hour legislation. Although these orders usually affected unskilled rates only, semi-skilled rates were raised at the same time to maintain the approximate differentials, in cents per hour, within the company. Other increases were caused by union organization drives, which resulted in the unionization of many of the low-wage firms for the first time in 1941–42.

Chart II shows that there was a corresponding upward movement in the wage levels of many of the better-paying firms. These firms made general wage increases during 1941 and 1942, partly through negotiations with established (or, in a few cases, new) unions, but more frequently on their own initiative. Undoubtedly the desire to attract and hold labor was a factor in these increases. The usual explanation, however, was that these firms thought their employees "were entitled" to an increase because other firms were raising wages, because the cost of living had risen, or because the firm was making money and could afford to be generous. There was no evidence that the voluntary movement of workers toward these high-wage firms had the effect of preventing further advances in wages.

The result of these increases by higher-wage firms was that the ranking of all firms in the wage structure of the community remained much the same from 1937 to 1942, although the spread between high- and low-wage firms was narrowed slightly. Other than the increases at the bottom of the scale, which were due more to unionization and minimum wage orders than to voluntary movement, there were only five significant changes in the relative standing of firms. Two small metal-working plants failed to make increases in line with those made generally in the community, and they were losing younger workers and trainees as a consequence.[2] A larger

2. The director of one of the local vocational schools was particularly disturbed about the failure of some local machine shops to pay starting rates

machinery firm likewise had not raised wages as rapidly as others; but because of the great amount of overtime work offered, it experienced few losses of personnel. On the other hand, a large metal-products firm and a converted paper products company, both of which had considerable war work, increased their wage levels by greater amounts than the others in the group. In both, the possible loss of workers was a less important explanation than the fact that the companies were making money and wished to avoid being unionized.

While the relative standing of firms in the community's wage structure remained approximately the same from 1937 to 1942, we found a somewhat more distinct relation between wage rate levels and voluntary movement in the 1942 labor market. This contrast is brought out in Chart II. All of the low-wage firms were losing workers in 1942, while only four-fifths were losing workers in 1937. Similarly, more of the medium-wage firms experienced losses in 1942. There were no differences, however, in the experiences of the very high-wage firms between 1937 and 1942.[3]

Chart III shows that the voluntary movement in 1942 was caused by the attraction of higher wages rather than by expansion or contraction of employment in the various groups of firms. For example, two-fifths of the low-wage firms were expanding, but all were losing workers through voluntary movement to other firms.

The persistence of wage differentials for jobs requiring comparable skill and training was not due to compensating differences in working conditions or in other perquisites, such as welfare plans. Generally the companies with superior working conditions were *also* those which paid relatively higher wages and had more comprehensive welfare programs for their employees (see Table III),

It was our impression, furthermore, that in the period studied the low-paying concerns did not suffer nearly so much in inferior workmanship as might have been expected. As will be pointed out later, during most of this period the opportunity to get a job in a

that would attract graduates of the school. "They'll be sorry and will adjust their rates too late," he said. "Some of our employers are just short-sighted. They are thinking about next Friday, not next January. Then next January they'll want us to furnish trainees and there just won't be any."

3. The contrary experience in the "moderately high" wage group is explained by the fact that four of the six firms losing workers in 1942 were paper manufacturing firms whose employment was declining because of lack of orders.

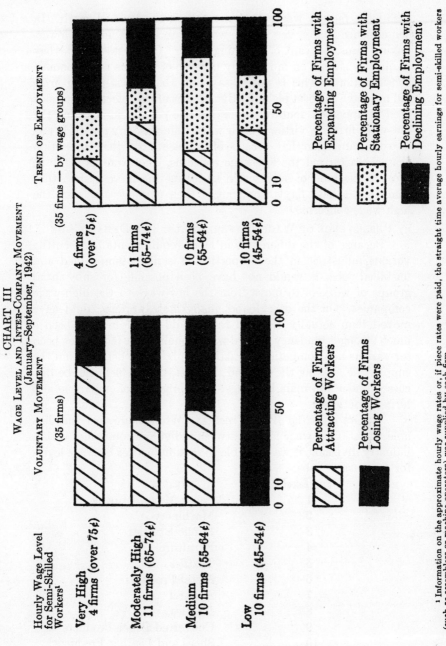

CHART III

WAGE LEVEL AND INTER-COMPANY MOVEMENT
(January–September, 1942)

VOLUNTARY MOVEMENT
(35 firms)

TREND OF EMPLOYMENT
(35 firms — by wage groups)

Hourly Wage Level
for Semi-Skilled
Workers[1]

Very High
4 firms (over 75¢)

Moderately High
11 firms (65–74¢)

Medium
10 firms (55–64¢)

Low
10 firms (45–54¢)

4 firms
(over 75¢)

11 firms
(65–74¢)

10 firms
(55–64¢)

10 firms
(45–54¢)

Percentage of Firms
Attracting Workers

Percentage of Firms
Losing Workers

Percentage of Firms with
Expanding Employment

Percentage of Firms with
Stationary Employment

Percentage of Firms with
Declining Employment

[1] Information on the approximate hourly wage rates or, if piece rates were paid, the straight time average hourly earnings for semi-skilled workers (such as assemblers or machine-operators) was supplied by each firm.

high-wage factory was not open to all on the basis of merit. In consequence many very good workers took jobs in the lower-paying firms for want of anything better. Once established, they frequently stayed on indefinitely because of various non-economic considerations. This is not to say that the highest-paying firms did not have the best picking. But in view of the selection methods used, it appeared doubtful to us that the penalty imposed on the low-wage firms by virtue of their wage scale was very great. It was also our impression that, because of the keenness of the competition that characterized the low-wage concerns, they were as likely to provide the kind of supervision and wage incentive system that would get a hard day's work out of their employees as were the high-wage concerns.

PERSISTENCE OF WAGE DIFFERENTIALS: THE DEMAND SIDE

Because of the differences in labor requirements between the various industries in the proportion of skilled, semi-skilled and unskilled jobs, it would not have been possible for substantial groups of workers to move from the low-wage to the high-wage companies. On the other hand, many more workers could have moved than actually did, and there could therefore have been a much stronger tendency toward wage equalization had it not been for various non-competitive practices on both the demand and the supply side. Taking the demand side first, the problem can be discussed under two main headings: wage practices of employers and hiring practices.

Factors Affecting Wage Practices. While there was considerable variation in wage levels between individual companies within industry divisions, it was possible to rank industries by wage levels for comparable jobs:

Wage Level	Industry
1	Paper Manufacturing
2	Machinery
3	Public Utilities
4	Furniture
5	Textiles
6	Metal Products
7	Apparel
8	Plastics
9	Converted Paper Products
10	Shoes and Leather Products

TABLE III

Welfare Programs, Working Conditions, and Wage Cuts in Firms in the Various Wage Level Groups, 1937–39; and Unionization, 1937–42

Hourly Wage Level for Semi-Skilled Workers	Total Firms	Welfare Programs			Working Conditions			Wage Cuts			Unionization (1937–42)			
		None	Isolated	Comprehensive	Below Average	Average	Above Average	Individual Changes Only	One General Cut	No Cuts	Not Unionized 1937–39	Unionized 1937–39	Not Unionized until 1941	Unionized until 1941
Very High (Over 65¢)	4	0	1	3	0	0	4	0	2	2	1	2	2	1
Moderately High (55–64¢)	6	1	3	2	0	2	4	1	0	5	4	2	2	0
Medium (45–54¢)	8	6	1	1	0	6	2	1	4	3	3	3	3	2
Low (35–44¢)	10	4	4	2	0	7	3	4	2	4	4	1	1	5
Very Low (under 35¢)	9	6	3	0	3	6	0	6	0	3	5	0	0	4

In analyzing this ranking, it was our conclusion that there was a distinct correlation between the wage-rate level and the degree of competition in the various industries. To substantiate this point will require some explanation of the nature of the industries in this community.

Near the bottom of the wage scale were the plastics, converted paper products and shoe and leather products industries. The plastics industry employed more workers than any other, the principal products being plastic novelties such as inexpensive combs, sun goggles, necklaces, hairpins and toilet ware. Price competition was very keen in these products.

The largest company in the shoe and leather group manufactured women's inexpensive shoes, another smaller concern produced boys' shoes, and a third manufactured women's pocketbooks and handbags. When asked in 1942 why he did not pay higher wages, an officer of the largest shoe company replied, "We have a low-priced commodity which requires about as much labor as a better-grade shoe, and you know a $2.00 shoe can't stand the gaff on wages that an $8.00 shoe can." The president of a paper box firm held a similar view: "We don't get much for our stuff and we can't afford to pay as good wages as some of the other firms in town."

The apparel industry maintained a somewhat higher scale because the principal company specialized in a well-known, nationally advertised product which was not sold on a price basis. The largest metal-products firm manufactured a line of inexpensive hardware which was quite keenly competitive with that of firms in other regions, though not so much so as in the plastics industry. Four of the seven textile firms manufactured woolens and three cotton textiles. The products of three of these textile companies were sufficiently differentiated so that competition was not serious. The products of the furniture industry were a well-known line of baby carriages and children's furniture, and special-order wooden radio cabinets.

At the top of the wage scale, paper manufacturing and machinery were the industries with the largest capital investment and the lowest proportion of wages to total cost. The paper companies were competitive, but to some extent they sold differentiated products and price competition was not cutthroat. Three of the four machinery companies in the sample were operating largely on special order and selling high-priced "quality" machines, which in the period studied were not very keenly competitive because they were in such great demand. Two of the firms had contracts from 1937–39 arising from foreign armament expansion.

It may be pointed out, parenthetically, that in this community the most competitive industries happened also to be the most seasonal ones. The lower wage level of the seasonal industries does not bear out the principle suggested by Marshall that "in those occupations in which employment is irregular, the pay must be high in proportion to the work done."[4]

Within industries such as paper manufacturing, plastics, textiles, etc., the larger companies tended to pay higher wages than the smaller concerns.[5] This was probably because the larger companies also had a greater capacity to pay. Our impression was that the high-wage concerns maintained the wages they paid partly because of a conception in their minds as to what constituted a "fair wage" and partly because of the belief that it "paid to be above the local market." We found no evidence of any careful analysis having been made as to whether a high-wage policy was financially worth-while to a company.

The low-wage concerns tended to justify their wage level to themselves and others on the basis of inability to pay more, because of the keenness of competition. No analyses were made either of turnover or of the quality of the workmen they were obtaining at the wage rate offered, nor was any desire expressed to find answers to these questions by developing more effective personnel procedures. "The textile industry can't afford the overhead of a personnel manager," declared the president of a textile mill with nearly a thousand employees. His "hunch" may very well have been correct. He had, however, made no attempt to determine

4. Alfred Marshall, *Principles of Economics*, 8th edition (London, 1930), p. 555.

5. The tendency of wages to vary directly with the size of the company is summarized by Jacob Perlman as follows: "For a long time, it has been generally understood that the larger companies paid higher wages than the smaller firms. This is confirmed by a number of recent surveys. Moreover, it appears that the differences in hourly earnings by size of company are fairly well pronounced, which means that this factor deserves greater consideration than has been given to it in the past." Jacob Perlman, "Extent and Causes of Differences in Hourly Earnings," Jour. of American Stat. Assoc., March, 1940, pp. 7–9. This tendency is not found in all industries, however. See T. N. E. C., Monog. No. 13, "Hourly Earnings of Employees in Large and Small Enterprises," by Jacob Perlman, 1940, p. 11.

what the turnover in his company was and how much might have
been saved by changing some of its personnel practices.

Non-Competitive Hiring Practices. There was relatively little active competition among employers for labor, because of a gentlemen's
agreement between a considerable number of the firms not to hire
labor away from each other. By 1942 this agreement was confined
largely to plants with war work, but among these its influence in
reducing voluntary movement and preventing wholesale wage
changes was significant. When a new machinery firm entered the
community early in 1942, rumors spread that it would pay the
high starting rates which were characteristic of its plants located
in other communities. Pressure was therefore brought on the company by the Chamber of Commerce, with the result that it agreed
to bring its starting rate down "into line." As one local machinery
company executive said, the company "is coöperating now. They
realized that a wage-rate war here would benefit nobody."

There was very little "pirating" of workers in this community,
except from a few non-war plants. One explanation was the absence
of an acute labor shortage, except for certain types of skilled workers. More important, however, was the fact that open competition
for employed labor on a wage-rate basis had long been frowned
upon, and customs and traditions deeply ingrained in the community's industrial structure were not easily abandoned. Employers felt that shortages should be met by recruiting labor from non-
industrial employment, from laid-off workers, or from outside
regions, rather than from other factory jobs in the community. In
the words of the local manager of the United States Employment
Service, "This is not a bidding market, because most of the firms
are closely held or are family-owned."[6]

Despite this tradition, labor shortages forced some firms to
make modifications in the agreement. A few of the war plants
would not hire any applicant who said he was actually employed
elsewhere on war work, but they did not hesitate to hire without

6. The principal breaches in the "gentlemen's agreement" in 1942
occurred when "outside" managements entered the town. In the two cases
of this that occurred, the initial hiring practices were later modified to conform
to community standards.

There were, of course, a few individualists who, as in 1937–39, did not
observe the agreement in any way. They were like the manager of a woolen
textile mill who said in 1942, "When I hire a worker, I don't bother to look
up his past history."

further investigation a worker who said he had quit his job. One of the woolen mills had stopped using the Employment Service as a source of new labor, because

They will not refer a man if he is already employed on defense work somewhere else. But if you put an ad in the paper, even though it says no one should apply who is in a defense job, you will get more applicants. They will say that they are not on defense work, but everyone knows that they are and no one blames them for leaving for better jobs in our plant.

In addition to this "gentlemen's agreement," other hiring practices of employers accentuated the difficulties of free movement of labor. Hiring by the majority of the firms in the community was done by foremen rather than through a centralized personnel department, although this situation was being improved in 1942. Employment tests were virtually non-existent. Favoritism and undue emphasis on friendship and relatives are likely to be considerably more prevalent when the foreman hires than if hiring is done centrally. We found one firm in the community, a public utility, which had a fixed rule against hiring relatives. This was the only company with such a rule, and it did very little hiring during the period studied.

Prior to the war expansion, it was difficult to get employment except through introduction by a friend or relative. Only one or two of the lowest-paying companies were inclined to take anybody who turned up at the gate, if there happened to be an opening at that moment. The streams of movement, therefore, were directed largely on the basis of the social contacts of the prospective workers. This meant that there was a strong tendency for young workers to go into the same firms in which other members of their family or friends were working and in which they were assured of an entree.

Another restrictive hiring practice was the aversion of some companies to workers who had been employed for a considerable time in the low-wage industries. These workers were thought to be "unreliable" or "not a high type of worker." Difficulties were anticipated and experienced in training them to factory methods in a different industry. As a result of these difficulties and prejudices, the higher-wage concerns frequently preferred to recruit "unspoiled" new help from the high schools. In a number of cases it was discovered, under the pressure of war-time conditions, that some of the poorer-paid seasonal workers made excellent recruits.

Employer and union emphasis on length of service in lay-offs and rehiring was also a factor which kept many of the longer-service workers in the low-wage industries from competing for higher-wage openings in other plants. As a result, the workers who moved voluntarily tended to be young, short-service workers. Those with longer service hesitated to move to war jobs with higher pay, because they feared insecurity after the war. On the same basis companies were reluctant to hire away a long-service employee from any concern that was likely to survive the war.

Lack of Competition among Workers. The problem of explaining the special characteristics of the supply side of the labor market which clearly distinguish it from other types of markets has troubled economists for some time. Cairnes, impressed by the vertical barriers to the movement of workers from unskilled to skilled jobs and from the artisan class to jobs requiring professional skill, advanced the doctrine of "non-competing groups."[7] This early attempt at an analysis did not go beyond a very broad and ill-defined classification. To make Cairnes's concept more useful, it needs to be tested to determine the extent to which actual barriers exist between various occupations and what effect this has on earnings differentials.[8]

The empirical material presented in this article is confined to unskilled, semi-skilled and skilled workers in one labor market. As such it includes only two of Cairnes's groups — the unskilled and the skilled worker. With universal free education up to sixteen in the United States, the simple barrier that Cairnes observed between the unskilled and the skilled has been greatly reduced. Many unskilled workers who obtained employment in a good industrial firm in the community studied could progress to a highly skilled position over a period of years. This was true in the paper industry, for example, where a machine tender, who is the highest-skilled

7. J. E. Cairnes, Some Leading Principles of Political Economy (London, 1874), p. 72.

8. See E. S. Mason, "The position of the theory of non-competing groups in English value theory is, as has been said, ill-defined and somewhat ambiguous. It rests upon no statistical analysis, or very little, and in the matter of grouping almost anyone's guess is as good as that of anyone else . . . to be used as an actual tool in the analysis of a problem . . . we must have more than a guess about the mobility or immobility of different groups of labor." Edward S. Mason, "The Doctrine of Comparative Cost," this JOURNAL, November, 1926, p. 80. For a discussion of Cairnes's meaning see also H. J. Davenport, "Non-Competing Groups," this JOURNAL, November, 1925, pp. 52–81.

worker in the mill, does not always rise through formal apprenticeship but frequently works up to his position from an unskilled job.

While there were undoubtedly some barriers to vertical movement between unskilled and skilled jobs in this community, the most important barriers appeared to be horizontal — the lack of opportunity to move from one industry to another and the absence of effective competition among all workers for job openings. The reasons for this lack of competition are of substantial importance in explaining the persistence of wage differentials for comparable jobs.

Influence of Family and Friends. It has already been pointed out that we found a strong tendency for clustering of movement among firms situated within a comparatively short distance of each other.[9] This occurred despite the fact that there were sometimes considerably more promising opportunities in other sections of the community further removed from the workers' homes.

One explanation for this narrow range of movement is undoubtedly the fact that workers knew more about openings in nearby plants. The word got round quickly in the neighborhood when a particular company needed additional workers. In all our interviews, both in 1937–39 and in 1942, the influence of friends and relatives in locating jobs was brought out clearly. For example, an officer of one of the leather goods companies said:

> Most of our new employees drift in on the recommendation of friends and family members who are already at work here. Nearly everybody who applies has friends in the place.

Among the seasonal industries a family wage system involving the pooling of earnings frequently prevailed.[1] In these industries there was a strong tendency for occupations to be transmitted from father to son. This applied not only to broad occupational groups but to particular factories. Both sons and daughters frequently went to work at sixteen in the same company as their parents.

9. Cf. a report by G. C. Allen on an English survey in the West Midlands, in which he writes, "A distance of only a few miles separates the centers of high unemployment or low wage rates from those with superior standards in these respects . . . It is evident then that even today the mobility of workers (including new entrants into industry) may be restricted by what appears to be an insignificant barrier of distance." G. C. Allen, Economic Journal, June, 1930, p. 246.

1. For a brief discussion of this, see Charles A. Myers and W. Rupert Maclaurin, "After Unemployment Benefits Are Exhausted," this JOURNAL, February, 1942, p. 238.

Transportation expenses and inconveniences also discouraged some movement to jobs in more distant parts of the community. Secondary family workers, particularly wives, preferred to work near their home so that they could return at noon in order to prepare lunch for children. Many working wives kept house while supplementing the family income, and they could do so more easily if home and plant were close together.

Absence of Effective Vocational Guidance. The importance of family and friends in directing the streams of worker movement in this community was not counteracted by other associational influences. The public high schools and the Catholic schools offered very little vocational guidance. From 1937 to 1939 there was little coördination between the school system and the factories of the community. The schools were run largely on classical lines. No attempt was made to present to the students the various alternatives open to them for work in the community. By 1942 some vocational training was offered for the metal trades, but the student still got a job largely without seeking or being given advice at the school.

The public Employment Service was also quite ineffective in directing the stream of workers entering the labor market from 1937–39. At that time the Employment Service knew comparatively little about the various companies in the town in terms of their wage policies, general personnel practices and lay-off records. Moreover, the principal employers were not using the service to any extent. This situation was much improved by 1942. The Employment Service was being used more, and its staff had learned a great deal about the job opportunities in the town. It was probably still true, however, that the majority of workers considering a change or entering the labor market for the first time applied for jobs on their own, rather than utilizing the Employment Service.

Weakness of Financial Incentives. Another reason why substantial differentials continued to exist between firms in this labor market was the apathetic attitude which some workers showed toward change. Frequently, in the lower-wage concerns, there were large groups of employees who had become sufficiently habituated to their working environment so that they were not interested in moving to another concern that paid better wages for comparable types of work.

For example, we got the impression from several different

sources that employees living in one of the large French-Canadian districts manifested less of the money-conscious, restless ambition that is characteristic of many American workers. In the fall of 1942, in one of the low-paying, non-defense factories in this district, the employees refused to work overtime. They maintained that a forty-hour week was long enough, and that they wanted the rest of their time for themselves and their families. There was no evidence that these workers were not efficient during the hours when they were at work. What they wanted to protect was their way of life. A number of the workers from this region of the town did not appear to be ambitious to rise to foremen's positions, nor did they wish to change environmental conditions with which they were familiar and reasonably satisfied for an unfamiliar working environment in which the pay was higher. And yet the French-Canadian employees in general were regarded in the community as excellent workers. They were reported to be much better workers than they were high-school students, and they characteristically left school early to go to work.

SUMMARY

Our findings suggest that the theory of wages as presented in economic literature must be modified to take more adequate account of the barriers to movement which exist within a labor market.[2] It should be remembered, of course, that the importance of these barriers undoubtedly varies in different regions. But we have no reason to suspect that this community was not typical of a great many small American manufacturing cities in the period from 1937 to 1942.

The principal barriers to inter-factory movement found in this study may be summarized as follows:

A. Demand Side

    (1) The existence of a "gentlemen's agreement" among many of the factories not to hire labor away from each other.

    (2) The prevalent practice of hiring primarily relatives and friends of present workers. The absence of effective cen-

2. To do this requires further development of what Hans Neisser calls the science of "economic biology," which in an all-embracing economic-sociological approach tries to "evaluate the strength of all forces working in the society." Hans Neisser, " 'Permanent' Technological Unemployment," *American Econ. Rev.*, March, 1942, p. 71.

tralized hiring methods which would ensure employment on the basis of merit.

(3) The prejudice against hiring older employees who had worked for a considerable period in some of the lower-paying industries, and the real difficulty of re-training the less adaptable of such workers to work on new types of machines. The preference for "unspoiled" new workers from the high schools.

B. Supply Side

(1) The tendency of workers to seek and accept jobs in their immediate neighborhood, often through the influence of employed friends or relatives.

(2) The absence of effective vocational guidance or advice on the part of the school system which would widen the workers' horizon and choice.

(3) The reluctance of many workers to risk their seniority position by moving.

(4) The weakness of financial incentives for movement as opposed to accustomed and friendly environmental conditions.

These barriers were so effective that, except under extreme boom conditions, the amount of movement in the direction of the high-wage concerns was distinctly limited. The absence of a greater threat of movement considerably weakened the economic pressure on the low-wage firms to bring their wage levels into line. In addition, entirely apart from the question of movement, many of the high-wage concerns were reluctant to take advantage of periods of unemployment by cutting wages. This appeared to be caused partly by the fear of labor resentment, which would reduce morale and output even though not affecting movement, and partly by unwillingness to cut workers' incomes as long as the company had the capacity to pay the existing scale of wages.

Further classification and analysis of the relation between wages and movement in other types of labor markets and for other types of workers should be helpful. It would be valuable to know, for example, in various labor markets the extent to which the freedom of movement that exists in certain trades,[3] such as machin-

3. Miss Bezanson found among upholstery weavers "a considerable knowledge on the part of workmen of conditions and working opportunity in

ists, tends toward equalizing efficiency earnings for the groups of workers who do not move. In so far as companies try to maintain a more or less proportional wage relationship between their skilled trades and other jobs in the factory, this movement would tend toward general equalization. But we do not know the facts. How long can a worker stay in industries such as textiles, shoes, and plastics before he becomes so specialized that he finds it very difficult to be employed in higher-wage industries? In what types of labor markets do the strength of geographical proximity and the influence of friends and relatives in getting a job make it possible for lower-wage concerns to continue to obtain an adequate and effective supply of new labor more or less indefinitely?

We need, furthermore, to understand and analyze the various social systems to which workers belong, including the influence of the family and the school, and the kind of social organization developed by some employers, which succeed in tying workers to particular firms regardless of wage differentials.

Our study suggests that horizontal barriers to movement make the gravitational process toward the higher paying jobs very slow. Further standardization of wages may, therefore, be brought about more by "interference" from the State and by the spread of collective dealing, both on the part of management and unions, than by any tendency toward equality of efficiency earnings resulting from the flow of labor into the most favorable channels.

W. RUPERT MACLAURIN.
CHARLES A. MYERS.

MASSACHUSETTS INSTITUTE OF TECHNOLOGY

the trade. How far this knowledge is due to the specialized skill of the occupation, the organization of the craft or the moderate size of the industry is uncertain." "The Advantages of Labor Turnover," this JOURNAL, May, 1928, p. 464.

See also Gladys Palmer, "The Mobility of Weavers in Three Textile Centers," this JOURNAL, May, 1941, pp. 460 ff; and Bezanson, Hussey, Willits and White: "Within the highly skilled trades it is probably true that some of the skilled men have a very high turnover in the first ten or fifteen years following apprenticeship. . . . In a study of Philadelphia tool makers, based on the histories of workmen, the Industrial Research Department has found not only a large number of changes on the part of expert workmen, but a consistent reiteration of the belief that such changes were essential in developing the highest degree of skill." "Four Years of Labor Mobility" (Supplement to Vol. CXIX, Annals of the American Academy of Political and Social Science, Philadelphia, May, 1925).

Minimum Wages

The Economics of Minimum Wage Legislation, by George J. Stigler, American Economic Review, Vol. XXXVI, No. 3, June, 1946, pp. 358–365

Some Effects of a Minimum Wage upon the Economy as a Whole, by Weir M. Brown, American Economic Review, Vol. XXX, No. 1, Pt. I, March, 1940, pp. 98–107

Geographical Aspects of a Minimum Wage, by John V. Van Sickle, Harvard Business Review, Vol. XXIV, No. 3, Spring, 1946, pp. 277–294

THE ECONOMICS OF
MINIMUM WAGE LEGISLATION

By George J. Stigler

The minimum wage provisions of the Fair Labor Standards act of 1938 have been repealed by inflation. Many voices are now taking up the cry for a higher minimum, say, of 60 to 75 cents per hour.

Economists have not been very outspoken on this type of legislation. It is my fundamental thesis that they can and should be outspoken, and singularly agreed. The popular objective of minimum wage legislation—the elimination of extreme poverty—is not seriously debatable. The important questions are rather (1) Does such legislation diminish poverty? (2) Are there efficient alternatives? The answers are, if I am not mistaken, unusually definite for questions of economic policy. If this is so, these answers should be given.

Some readers will probably know my answers already ("no" and "yes," respectively); it is distressing how often one can guess the answer given to an economic question merely by knowing who asks it. But my personal answers are unimportant; the arguments on which they rest, which are important, will be presented under four heads:

1. Effects of a legal minimum wage on the allocation of resources.
2. Effects on aggregate employment.
3. Effects on family income.
4. Alternative policies to combat poverty.

1. *The Allocation of Resources*

The effects of minimum wages may in principle differ between industries in which employers do and do not have control over the wage rates they pay for labor of given skill and application. The two possibilities will be discussed in turn.

Competitive Wage Determination

Each worker receives the value of his marginal product under competition. If a minimum wage is effective, it must therefore have one of two effects: first, workers whose services are worth less than the minimum wage are discharged (and thus forced into unregulated fields of employment, or into unemployment or retirement from the labor force); or, second, the productivity of low-efficiency workers is increased.

The former result, discharge of less efficient workers, will be larger the more the value of their services falls short of the legal minimum, the more elastic the demand for the product, and the greater the possibility of substituting other productive services (including efficient labor) for the inefficient workers' services. The discharged workers will, at best, move to unregulated jobs where they will secure lower returns. Unless inefficient workers' productivity rises, therefore, the minimum wage reduces aggregate output, perhaps raises the earnings of those previously a trifle below the minimum, and reduces the earnings of those substantially below the minimum. These are undoubtedly the main allocational effects of a minimum wage in a competitive industry.

The second and offsetting result, the increase of labor productivity, might come about in one of two ways: the laborers may work harder; or the entrepreneurs may use different production techniques. The threat of unemployment may force the inefficient laborers to work harder (the inducement of higher earnings had previously been available, and failed), but this is not very probable. These workers were already driven by the sharp spurs of poverty, and for many the intensity of effort must be increased beyond hope (up to 50 or more per cent) to avoid discharge.

The introduction of new techniques by the entrepreneurs is the more common source of increased labor productivity. Here again there are two possibilities.

First, techniques which were previously unprofitable are now rendered profitable by the increased cost of labor. Costs of production rise because of the minimum wage, but they rise by less than they would if other resources could not be substituted for the labor. Employment will fall for two reasons: output falls; and a given output is secured with less labor. Commonly the new techniques require different (and hence superior) labor, so many inefficient workers are discharged. This process is only a spelling-out of the main competitive effect.

Second, entrepreneurs may be shocked out of lethargy to adopt techniques which were previously profitable or to discover new techniques. This "shock" theory is at present lacking in empirical evidence but not in popularity.

There are several reasons for believing that the "shock" theory is particularly inappropriate to the industries paying low wages. All of the large manufacturing industry categories which in 1939 paid relatively low wages (measured by the payroll of wage-earners divided by their average number) are listed in Table I. A study of this table suggests two generalizations: (1) the low-wage industries are competitive, and (2) the ratio of wages to total-processing-cost-plus-profit is higher than in high-wage industries. The competitive nature of these industries argues that the entrepreneurs are not easy-going traditionalists: vigorous competition in national markets does not attract or tolerate such men. The relatively high labor costs reveal that inducements to wage-economy are already strong. These considerations both work strongly against the shock theory in low-wage manufacturing industries in 1939.[1] Since these industries were on the whole much less affected by the

---

[1] The current extensive and confident uses made of labor productivity indexes seem to me inappropiate to their ambiguity and inaccuracy. For those who are less skeptical, I may add that for the period 1929 to 1937, output per worker can be approximated for 9 of the industries in Table I (using data from S. Fabricant's *Employment in Manufacturing,* 1899-1939 [New York, Nat. Bur. of Econ. Research, 1942]). In 6 of the 9 industries the increase in labor productivity equalled or exceeded that of all manufacturing.

war than other manufacturing industries, they will probably be present in the post-war list of low-wage industries. The low-wage industries in trade and services display the same characteristics and support the same adverse conclusion with respect to the shock theory.[2]

TABLE I.—EMPLOYMENT, AVERAGE ANNUAL EARNINGS OF FULL-TIME WAGE-EARNERS, AND PERCENTAGE WAGES FORM OF VALUE-ADDED, IN LOW-WAGE MANUFACTURING INDUSTRIES, 1939

Industry	Employment	Average Earnings	Wages as Percent of Value Added
Men's and boys' furnishings	166,945	$632	52.2
Canned and preserved foods	134,471	660	28.0
Cigars	50,897	673	42.0
Cotton manufactures	409,317	715	51.1
Fertilizer	18,744	730	24.0
Wood containers	45,070	735	47.2
Women's accessories	58,952	740	41.3
Misc. fabricated textiles	49,242	746	36.2
Misc. apparel	38,288	769	45.5
Rayon and silk manufactures	119,821	779	54.4
Animal and vegetable oils	21,678	781	25.1
Costume jewelry, etc.	25,256	782	43.5
Sawmills, etc.	265,185	810	52.0
Leather products	280,411	847	50.9
All Manufacturing		1,153	36.8

Source: *Census of Manufactures, 1939.*

Employer Wage Determination

If an employer has a significant degree of control over the wage rate he pays for a given quality of labor, a skillfully-set minimum wage may increase his employment and wage rate and, because the wage is brought closer to the value of the marginal product, at the same time increase aggregate output. The effect may be elucidated with the hypothetical data in Table II. If the entrepreneur is left alone, he will set a wage of $20 and employ 50 men; a minimum wage of $24 will increase employment to 70 men.

This arithmetic is quite valid, but it is not very relevant to the question of a national minimum wage. The minimum wage which achieves these desirable ends has several requisites:

1. It must be chosen correctly: too high a wage (over $28 in our example) will decrease employment. The accounting records describe, very imperfectly, existing employment and wages; the optimum minimum wage can be set only if the demand and supply schedules are known over a considerable range. At present there is no tolerably accurate method

[2] We should perhaps also notice that, even if the shock theory were of general applicability, the maintenance or increase of employment would require also (1) that demand be elastic, and (2) low-efficiency workers continue to be used with the improved techniques.

of deriving these schedules, and one is entitled to doubt that a legislative mandate is all that is necessary to bring forth such a method.

2. The optimum wage varies with occupation (and, within an occupation, with the quality of worker).
3. The optimum wage varies among firms (and plants).
4. The optimum wage varies, often rapidly, through time.

TABLE II.—HYPOTHETICAL DATA ILLUSTRATING EMPLOYER
WAGE DETERMINATION

Number of Workers	Wage Rate	Marginal Cost of a Worker	Value of the Marginal Product[a]
10	$12		$36
20	14	$16	34
30	16	20	32
40	18	24	30
50	20	28	28
60	22	32	26
70	24	36	24

[a] Or marginal value product, if this is less.

A uniform national minimum wage, infrequently changed, is wholly unsuited to these diversities of conditions.[3]

We may sum up: the legal minimum wage will reduce aggregate output, and it will decrease the earnings of workers who had previously been receiving materially less than the minimum.

2. *Aggregate Employment*

Although no precise estimate of the effects of a minimum wage upon aggregate employment is possible, we may nevertheless form some notion of the direction of these effects. The higher the minimum wage, the greater will be the number of covered workers who are discharged. The current proposals would probably affect a twentieth to a tenth of all covered workers, so possibly several hundred thousand workers would be discharged. Whatever the number (which no one knows), the direct unemployment is substantial and certain; and it fairly establishes the presumption that the net effects of the minimum wage on aggregate employment are adverse.

This presumption is strengthened by the existing state of aggregate money demand. There is no prospective inadequacy of money demand in the next year or two—indeed, the danger is that it is excessive. If the minimum wage were to increase the relative share of wage-earners and, hence, the propensity to consume—which requires the uncertain assumption that the demand for inefficient labor is inelastic—the increment of consumer demand will be

[3] One can go much farther: even administratively established minima, varying with firm and time, would be impossibly difficult to devise and revise, and their effects on private investment would be extremely adverse.

unnecessary, and perhaps unwelcome.[4] (Conversely, the direct unemployment resulting from the wage law would diminish faster in a period of high employment.)

It is sufficient for the present argument that no large increase in employment will be induced by the legislation. Actually, there is a presumption that a minimum wage will have adverse effects upon aggregate employment.

3. *Wage Rates and Family Income*

The manipulation of individual prices is neither an efficient nor an equitable device for changing the distribution of personal income. This is a well-known dictum that has received much documentation in analyses of our agricultural programs. The relevance of the dictum to minimum wage legislation is easily demonstrated.

One cannot expect a close relationship between the level of hourly wage rates and the amount of family income. Yet family income and needs are the fundamental factors in the problem of poverty. The major sources of discrepancy may be catalogued.

First, the hourly rates are effective only for those who receive them, and it was shown in Section 1 that the least productive workers are forced into uncovered occupations or into unemployment.

Second, hourly earnings and annual earnings are not closely related. The seasonality of the industry, the extent of overtime, the amount of absenteeism, and the shift of workers among industries, are obvious examples of factors which reduce the correlation between hourly earnings and annual earnings.

Third, family earnings are the sum of earnings of all workers in the family, and the dispersion of number of workers is considerable. The

TABLE III —PERCENTAGE DISTRIBUTION OF WAGE-EARNER FAMILIES BY
NUMBER OF EARNERS: MINNESOTA, 1939

Family Income	One Earner	Two Earners	Three Earners	Four or more Earners
$250–$500	94.5	4.6	.7	.2
500– 750	92.4	7.1	.3	.2
750–1000	86.7	10.7	1.5	1.1
1000–1250	88.5	10.4	1.1	.1

Source: *Minnesota Incomes, 1938–39*, Vol. II (St. Paul, Minnesota Resources Commission, 1942), p. 152.

summary in Table III for low income wage-earner families in Minnesota in 1939, shows that in the $250-$500 income class one-twentieth of the families had more than one earner and in the higher income classes the fraction rose to one-eighth.

[4] This line of argument implies that a minimum wage is more likely to have beneficial effects in depression (if the demand for the relevant labor is inelastic), but it does not imply that the beneficial effects are likely.

Fourth, although wages are, of course, the chief component of the income of low-wage families, they are by no means the only component. It is indicated in Table IV that a tenth of the wage-earner families had cash investment income, a quarter had entrepreneural income, and a quarter owned their homes.

TABLE IV.—COMPOSITION OF INCOME OF WAGE-EARNER FAMILIES:
MINNESOTA, 1939

Income Class	Total	Wages and Salaries	Income		Investment Income	
			Entre-preneural Income	Room and Board	Cash	Total
1. *Percentage of Families Receiving Income*						
$250–$500		99.9	26.5	1.3	12.3	28.2
500– 750		100.0	25.2	1.7	10.1	24.2
750–1000		100.0	21.4	2.7	9.4	31.2
1000–1250		100.0	18.4	3.0	10.4	22.8
2. *Average Amount*						
250– 500	$ 387	$ 308		–$ 9	$64	
500– 750	631	560		62	82	
750–1000	865	766		53	82	
1000–1250	1124	1032		91	96	

Source: *Minnesota Incomes, 1938–39*, Vol. I (St. Paul, Minnesota Resources Commission, 1942), p. 42; Vol. II, p. 200.

All of these steps lead us only to family income; the leap must still be made to family needs. It is argued in the next section that family composition is the best criterion of need, and whether this be accepted or not, it is clearly an important criterion. The great variation in family size among wage-earner families is strongly emphasized by the illustrative data in Table V; an income adequate for one size is either too large or too small for at least half the families in that income class.

The connection between hourly wages and the standard of living of the family is thus remote and fuzzy. Unless the minimum wage varies with the amount of employment, number of earners, non-wage income, family size, and many other factors, it will be an inept device for combatting poverty even for those who succeed in retaining employment. And if the minimum wages varies with all of these factors, it will be an insane device.

4. *The Problem of Poverty*

Minimum wage legislation commonly has two stated objectives: the reduction of employer control of wages; and the abolition of poverty. The former and much lesser purpose may better be achieved by removing the condition of labor immobility which gives rise to employer control. Labor immobility would be reduced substantially by public provision of comprehensive information on employment conditions in various areas and industries. The immobility would be further reduced by supplying vocational training and loans to cover moving costs. But employer wage control is not the important problem; let us turn to the elimination of poverty.

Incomes of the poor cannot be increased without impairing incentives. Skillful policies will, for a given increase in the incomes of the poor, impair incentives less than clumsy policies. But the more completely poverty is eliminated, given the level of intelligence with which this is done, the greater will be the impairment of incentives. This is a price we must pay, just as impairment of incentives is a price we have willingly paid to reduce the inequality of income by progressive income and estate taxes. Society must determine, through its legislators, what minimum income (or addition to income) should be guaranteed to each family. We shall assume that this difficult decision has been made.

TABLE V.—PERCENTAGE DISTRIBUTION OF WAGE-EARNER FAMILIES BY NUMBER OF PERSONS: CHICAGO AND ATLANTA, 1936

Income Class	Number of Persons in Family			
	2	3 or 4	5 or 6	7 or more
1. *Chicago*				
$ 0–$250	39.6	43.6	14.9	2.0
250– 500	35.3	45.8	17.6	1.3
500– 750	31.8	53.7	13.0	1.6
750–1000	29.0	56.5	12.4	2.1
2. *Atlanta*				
0– 250	30.	55.	15.	0.
250– 500	20.1	48.1	16.5	5.3
500– 750	22.6	46.9	24.4	6.2
750–1000	21.6	48.1	23.5	6.7

Sources: *Family Income in Chicago, 1935–36* (Bur. of Lab. Stat. bull. no. 642 [Washington, Supt. Docs., 194]),Vol. I, p. 117; *Family Income in the Southeastern Region* (Bur. of Lab. Stat., bull. no. 647 [Washington, Supt. Docs., 194]), Vol. I, p. 148.

One principle is fundamental in the amelioration of poverty: those who are equally in need should be helped equally. If this principle is to be achieved, there must be an objective criterion of need; equality can never be achieved when many cases are judged (by many people) "on their merits." We are driven almost inexorably to family size and composition as this criterion of need. It is obviously imperfect; the sickly require more medical care than the healthy.[5] But it is vastly easier to accord special treatment to certain families for a few items like medical care than to accord special treatment to every family for the sum of all items of expenditure.

It is a corollary of this position that assistance should not be based upon occupation. The poor farmer, the poor shopkeeper, and the poor miner are

[5] One could argue that rural families should receive less help, to offset the lower prices at which food and housing are procured. The group is of sufficient size and perhaps sufficiently identifiable to justify separate treatment. But there are grounds other than political expediency for rejecting this proposal.

on an equal footing. There may be administrative justification (although I doubt it) for treating the farmer separately from the urban dweller, but there is no defense in equity for helping the one and neglecting the other. To render the assistance by manipulating prices is in any case objectionable: we help the rich farmer more than the poor, and give widely differing amounts of help to the poor farmer from year to year.

The principle of equity thus involves the granting of assistance to the poor with regard to their need (measured by family composition) but without regard to their occupation. There is a possible choice between grants in kind and in money. The latter commends itself strongly: it gives full play to the enormous variety of tastes and it is administratively much simpler. Yet it raises a problem which will be noticed shortly.

Even if these general observations be accepted, the structure of administration is of grave importance, and I do not pretend to have explored this field. There is great attractiveness in the proposal that we extend the personal income tax to the lowest income brackets with negative rates in these brackets. Such a scheme could achieve equality of treatment with what appears to be a (large) minimum of administrative machinery. If the negative rates are appropriately graduated, we may still retain some measure of incentive for a family to increase its income. We should no doubt encounter many perplexing difficulties in carrying out this plan, but they are problems which could not be avoided, even though they might be ignored, by a less direct attack on poverty.

One final point: We seek to abolish poverty in good part because it leads to undernourishment. In this connection, dietary appraisals show that in any income class, no matter how low, a portion of the families secure adequate diets, and in any income class, as high as the studies go, a portion do not. The proportion of ill-fed, to be sure, declines substantially as income rises, but it does not disappear. We cannot possibly afford to abolish malnutrition, or mal-housing, or mal-education, only by increasing incomes.

Either of two inferences may be drawn. The program of increasing income must be supplemented by a program of education—in diet, in housing, in education! Or the assistance to the poor should be given in kind, expertly chosen. The latter approach is administratively very complex, but quicker and in direct expenditure vastly more economical. These factors affect our choice, but a thought should be given also to the two societies to which they lead.

SOME EFFECTS OF A MINIMUM WAGE
UPON THE ECONOMY AS A WHOLE

Most books and articles dealing with the subject of minimum wages are descriptive or argumentative works concerned chiefly with some specific legislative act.[1] In addition to works of these types there are several in which some attempt is made to give a theoretical explanation, of more or less general applicability, of the economic effects of minimum wages.[2] There is neither space nor necessity for detailed criticism of this literature, and it will suffice to indicate the reasons for believing that further study of the subject is necessary:

(1) Until very recent years, almost all theoretical discussions of wages and employment have been founded, consciously or otherwise, upon assumed conditions of perfect competition and full employment. The use of this hypothesis is entirely valid, provided its implications are thoroughly understood and the limitations they impose squarely faced. But failure to distinguish clearly between this analytical model and the real world has too often led writers to content themselves with making casual statements about the effect of minimum wages upon "cost" and equally uncomprehensive declarations about the consequences of changes in cost.[3] It seems

[1] The following are illustrative of these types: Rudolf Broda, "Minimum Wage Legislation in Various Countries," Bulletin 467, U.S. Bureau of Labor Statistics; Dorothy W. Douglas, "American Minimum Wage Laws at Work," *Am. Econ. Rev.*, Dec., 1919; Frankfurter-Dewson-Commons, "State Minimum Wage Laws in Practice" (National Consumers League pamphlet); Helen Fisher Hohman, *Development of Social Insurance and Minimum Wage Legislation in Great Britain* (New York, Houghton, 1933); Victor P. Morris, *Oregon's Experience with Minimum Wage Legislation* (New York, Columbia Univ. Press, 1930).

[2] See, *e.g.*, A. C. Pigou, *Economics of Welfare*, part iii, chapters 15-20; Sidney Webb, "The Economic Theory of a Legal Minimum Wage," *Jour. Pol. Econ.*, Dec., 1912; H. R. Seager, "The Theory of the Minimum Wage," *Am. Labor Legislation Rev.*, Feb., 1913; J. B. Clark, "The Minimum Wage," *Atlantic Mo.*, Sept., 1913; Pigou, "The Trade Boards and the Cave Committee," *Econ. Jour.*, Sept., 1922; Pigou, "A Minimum Wage for Agriculture," in his *Essays in Applied Economics*.

[3] These faults have characterized both advocates and opponents of minimum wage regulation. *Cf.* H. R. Seager, *op. cit.*, and J. B. Clark, *op. cit.*

desirable, therefore, to discover what results can be accomplished by utilizing a different model.

Furthermore, earlier analyses frequently neglected to differentiate between the effects of a wage change upon one firm and its effects upon the whole system, an error which usually resulted in their overlooking the relationship between wages and effective demand.

(2) Recent writings on employment, by correcting these particular faults, have given new and better direction to employment theory and to the theory of wages.[4] Like some of the publications of earlier writers, however, they are usually restricted in scope: (a) they analyze only generalized changes in wages, *i.e.,* changes in all wage rates; (b) they consider mainly the effects of such changes upon the economy as a whole; (c) in general, they do not deal with long-run[5] results.

The time seems propitious, therefore, for a reëxamination of the economic effects of a legal minimum wage.[6] Such a study logically divides itself into three sections, dealing, respectively, with the repercussions of various forms of minimum wages upon individual firms, upon single industries, and upon an entire system. Each of these sets of repercussions calls for and amply repays careful study, and one of them cannot be dissociated completely from the others. Yet it is manifestly impossible to undertake more than one of these lines of inquiry within the short space of one article. In consequence, the present paper will be confined to the examination of that aspect of minimum-wage regulation in which most interest and controversy lie: the effects of a general minimum wage upon the economy as a whole.

I

Before elaborating our own analysis of the effects of a legal uniform wage minimum, it will be well to give a brief résumé of another and quite different explanation of the consequences of this type of regulation. The argument runs as follows: The imposition of a minimum rate of pay will raise the expenses of production. Since entrepreneurs are obliged to equate marginal cost and price, they are faced with the alternatives of reducing out-

---

[4] See, for example, R. F. Harrod, "Professor Pigou's Theory of Unemployment," *Econ. Jour.,* March, 1934; J. M. Keynes, *The General Theory of Employment, Interest, and Money,* esp. chapters 3 and 19; Joan Robinson, "The Long-Period Theory of Employment," *Essays in the Theory of Employment;* P. M. Sweezy, A. P. Lerner, and others (round-table on "Wage Policies" at Fiftieth Annual Meeting of Am. Econ. Assoc.), *Am. Econ. Rev. Suppl.,* March, 1938; etc.

[5] But a beginning in this direction has been made by Mrs. Robinson in "The Long-Period Theory of Employment," published in her *Essays in the Theory of Employment.*

[6] The following paper, being an abstract, generalized study, unrelated to any actual law or administrative system, makes no pretense of providing a ready answer to the current question. However, the methods employed and problems raised may possibly suggest the points toward which further research might profitably be directed.

It will be noted that the discussion is limited to minimum-wage regulation and that control of hours of work is not considered.

put to the point at which the new cost curve crosses the price line or of raising price. Which of the two courses will be chosen will depend upon the elasticity of the demand.[7] But the results of either course will be deleterious, for in one case unemployment will be created, and in the other case prices will rise. Legal minimum wages, except in rare cases of extreme exploitation, are therefore inimical to the interests of workers and of society at large.[8]

If a price rise were the only possible result of increasing the costs of some producers; and if the price rise were the only significant economic change related to the imposition of the minimum wage, there could be little doubt that employment would be reduced. The fact that recent writings on employment have given prominence to certain factors which do not enter into the Mill-Clark treatment may indicate, however, that the earlier expositors had overlooked several complexities.

II

Wage legislation which contemplates the establishment, by public authority, of a minimum rate of pay for the entire economic system will have many and various repercussions, and it is necessary to select for analysis here only those of primary importance. Consequently, attention will be confined to the effects of a minimum wage upon employment, output, and prices. The basic assumptions hypothesized throughout the discussion must be made clear. The system under consideration will be a non-collectivist exchange economy which is either entirely "closed" or is virtually free from international influences. Existence of imperfections in the markets for commodities and for agents of production will be recognized, and the system will be assumed to be operating at less than full employment.[9] The question

[7] The elasticity of the demand curve of the *industry,* presumably, since under the conditions necessarily (though tacitly) assumed by this explanation the firm's demand curve must be perfectly elastic.

[8] A concise statement of this point of view, which is still widely held, was formulated some years ago by J. B. Clark: "Practical tests of the proposed policy are now in progress . . . and the results of these trials will be carefully watched; but a few things can be asserted in advance as necessarily true. We can be sure, without further testing, that raising the prices of goods will in the absence of counteracting influences, reduce sales; and that raising the rate of wages will, of itself and in the absence of any new demand for labor, lessen the number of workers employed." ("The Minimum Wage," *Atlantic Mo.,* Sept., 1913, pp. 289-90.) *Cf.* J. S. Mill, *Principles of Political Economy,* Ashley ed., p. 362.

[9] The assumptions above enumerated have many significant implications with regard to the individual firm and individual industry, and it is necessary to bear them in mind in studying the effects of a minimum wage upon the whole economy. The more important of these implications are indicated briefly:

(1) When the markets for the agents of production are imperfect, the several firms are likely—even within one industry—to vary not only in their technical coefficients but also in the prices they pay for each of the agents. A given minimum wage will thus affect some producers' costs and leave others' untouched; and, of the former number, there may be wide variation in the manner in which their marginal cost curves shift. (2) When the markets for commodities are imperfect, an individual firm has discretion as to how to meet

to be answered, then, is what are the principal consequences of setting a blanket, uniform minimum wage in all industries?

1. *Effects upon employment.* Adoption of a general minimum wage will increase the money incomes[10] of a number of employed wage-earners, the amount of the increase and the number of workmen affected depending at the outset upon the level at which the minimum is fixed and upon entrepreneurial responses to the regulation. Additions to the incomes of those who formerly stood at the bottom of the income structure might conceivably be used by them to increase consumption, increase saving, or both. But it is most reasonable to believe that virtually the whole of the increment will be spent. Whatever the ultimate result, the *initial* increase in the incomes received by workers covered by the wage order represents a transfer from other income receivers in the system, possibly from entrepreneurs. Since the latter are customarily persons of higher-than-average incomes, it is probable that their former incomes were more than sufficient to satisfy their desires for consumable goods and services and that the excess was saved. If this be true, the most plausible supposition is that any reduction in entrepreneurs' incomes will be met chiefly by reductions in their savings.[11] It is clear, then, that one initial result of the application of the minimum-wage order may be an alteration in the division of a given money income; and that this altered distribution is likely to be accompanied by an increase in the proportion of the total money income which is devoted to consumption.

An increase in the economy's propensity to consume, *ceteris paribus*, would of necessity raise the level of employment, since it is only in this way that the new demand for consumption goods could be satisfied. A wage increase might thus not only alter proportionate shares in the money income but bring about an increase in the real income of the economy. Such an eventuality might benefit not only the recipients of the minimum wage but

---

such a change in cost. Instead of the familiar price-output adjustment of perfect competition, the producer may accept a lower return, cut some other cost, "differentiate" his product, etc. (3) The adjustment of the "industry" to a given minimum wage depends upon how the cost structures of the component firms are affected and upon the courses adopted in response to these changes in cost. Thus there is no single pattern of adjustment which will be followed in every industry; and there is no simple explanation of the adjustment in any industry.

[10] The implications of this fact can be ignored in studying the individual firm or industry, but they are fundamental to the treatment of the effects on the economy.

[11] The reader will recognize, of course, that the persons whose relative savings are reduced are not necessarily the employers in the firms affected by the minimum wage, even in the short period. For example, many "sweated" trades are characterized by circumstances which result in exceptionally low prices for consumers but only meager returns for many employers and employees alike. But in these cases the principle is not altered: the essence of this initial phenomenon is a transfer to the persons at the bottom of the income scale from persons and groups of persons higher up in the scale; *i.e.,* from persons with higher average saving/consumption ratios. It may come wholly from a few entrepreneurs or be spread in very small amounts over a large number of consumers.

other wage-earners and even entrepreneurs as well. If an increase in the propensity to consume were the only consequence, the ultimate results of the minimum wage would therefore be to raise the level of employment, to augment the total real income of the economy, and to effect a redistribution in the relative shares with little or no decrease, in the long run, in the entrepreneurs' absolute share.

But "other things" are not likely to be equal, and the net influences of the minimum wage upon the marginal efficiency of capital and the rate of interest are not clear. At the outset, there may be some reluctance on the part of entrepreneurs to make investments out of reduced incomes. It must be remembered that the "marginal efficiency" of capital is the *anticipated* marginal productivity of capital, and if entrepreneurs' expectations are gloomy they will have a temporarily depressing influence on investment. It is also true that because of the alteration in the relative shares described above, the consumers' goods industries will benefit more, initially, than will the investment goods industries. On the other hand, there are also several features of the new situation which act favorably upon investment. First, the stimulation received by the consumers' goods industries from the heightened propensity to consume will itself increase, in all probability, the amount of capital required by the consumption goods industries.[12] Second, in so far as the investment goods industries are trades in which the ratio of capital to labor is high, the wage rise is likely to increase the investment attractiveness of these "more capitalistic" industries. Third, promulgation of a minimum wage may promote the desire to replace men by machines, and, where this substitution is possible, the increased use of machines will benefit the capital goods industries.[13]

The reduction in the proportion of the total income which is saved was noted above, but whether there would, in the long period, be a reduction in the absolute amount of money saving is uncertain. If the quantum of saving were diminished and the marginal efficiency of capital increased, on balance, by the establishment of the minimum wage, the rate of interest

[12] A great part of the demand for capital goods is derived from the demand for consumption goods, and a rise in the latter must therefore be beneficial to the former. Mr. Hicks overlooks this fact when he says that, although a wage increase will reduce unemployment in the consumption goods trades, this favorable result "will be directly set off by more unemployment in the heavy industries" (*The Theory of Wages,* p. 194).

[13] It is interesting to observe that, historically, the industries to which minimum wages have directly applied have been consumers' goods industries. This is probably attributable to the fact that the chief motivation of most minimum-wage laws has been the "living-wage" principle, and capital goods industries have generally not been major offenders against this standard. But, upon different bases, almost any industry might conceivably be regulated. It is therefore theoretically possible, though practically improbable, that a minimum wage might be applied to an investment goods industry. If so, and if the result were to raise the price of capital goods to any considerable extent, the adverse effect on investment might, in this special case, outweigh the favorable influence.

would tend to rise, and *vice versa*.[14] The importance of the rate of interest in determining the level of employment, however, is open to question.[15] Certainly the other two factors are more significant.

If there is an increase in employment which is accompanied by a decline in the numbers of the unemployed, there will be a consequent reduction in the volume of expenditures from public funds for the support of the unemployed. What effect this change will have will depend upon what fiscal policy the government employs to meet it.[16] If income taxes are decreased or the sale of government bonds diminished, the volume of money saving will doubtless increase; and the increase in saving will be greater if bond sales are reduced than if taxes are lowered. But a reduced expenditure for public poor relief may not induce fiscal authorities to lower governmental receipts. If there is no appreciable change in the burden of public relief, the problem of fiscal policy does not arise, of course.

2. Effects upon output. In the preceding paragraphs our attention was confined to the influences exerted by a uniform minimum wage upon *total* employment in the system. If the wage regulation should raise the level of employment, it follows that the total output would be thereby increased, though in the short run the operation of diminishing returns might prevent an increase fully proportional to the rise in employment. Whether or not the total volume of employment and output is changed, it might be well to inquire what, if any, changes may be expected in the *composition* of total employment and total output.

A wage increase sometimes sets up a tendency, in the opinion of Mr. Hicks,[17] for capital funds to shift out of industries in which large amounts of labor are utilized and into those industries which employ a smaller ratio of labor to capital. There appear to be several factors whose operation will tend to minimize that movement, however: (a) Any shifts in demand for particular products occurring as a result of the wage change will probably benefit industries in which the labor-capital ratio is high as well as those in which it may be low. (b) The initial cost involved in entering a business using a large quantity of capital is greater than the average cost of entering industry in general. (c) The usual impediments to the rapid movement of capital—reluctance to sacrifice a sunk investment, etc.—will be present. It

---

[14] This is the result which traditional interest theories would predict. Since the volume of saving and the marginal efficiency of capital play only minor rôles in Keynes's theory of interest, the changes here described would probably be regarded by Keynesians as unlikely to have much effect upon the rate of interest.

[15] *Cf.* J. F. Ebersole, "The Influence of Interest Rates upon Entrepreneurial Decisions," *Am. Econ. Rev. Suppl.*, March, 1938, pp. 74-75.

[16] A similar problem of relief financing is treated by Mrs. Robinson in "Certain Proposed Remedies for Unemployment," *Essays in the Theory of Employment*, pp. 64-66.

[17] *The Theory of Wages*, pp. 187-189.

seems probable that any "shifting-out of capital" will be gradual and of small magnitude.

In its effects on the supply of labor in various industries, a uniform minimum-wage law will differ from a generalized wage advance. In the first place, an upward revision of all wage rates might not alter appreciably the relative attractiveness of various jobs. But a minimum wage of the type here considered would initially and directly change only the wages of the occupations formerly receiving the lowest remuneration. Although its ultimate effect on total employment might benefit other workers also, such a wage regulation might nevertheless attract some workers from other occupations. Second, the minimum wage would be less likely to draw *new* workers into the labor market than a rise in all wage rates. Third, it is probable that either type of wage change would be accompanied by the withdrawal of some workers[18] from the labor market (*e.g.*, some wives would no longer have to work if their husbands' incomes were raised), though this movement would be more marked in the event of a minimum-wage order. Any shift of laborers to the regulated industries would be of limited significance, since the usual effect of an over-supply would be precluded by the existence of the law. It is also improbable that the transfer would be large enough to change wages or employment in the industries from which workers shifted.

Another change in the composition and location of total employment and output may be introduced by a geographical movement of firms. Although important, this subject cannot be discussed in the present paper, for the questions involved are more properly classified and more easily handled in the study of the effects of wage regulation upon the industry.

3. Effects upon prices. It has been seen that a general minimum-wage order may result in small rises in the prices of some commodities, and it is important to give further examination here to the nature of the price changes and to their effects upon various portions of the economy. Restricting our attention for the moment to instances of price rises, we may say that firms which raise prices will simply lose business to firms (in the same or other industries) which do not raise prices—if we assume with Clark that total demand is unaltered. The results in the system as a whole would then resemble those which may be found—upon an analogous but in that case more appropriate assumption with respect to total demand—to be experienced by the industry. But if the imposition of the minimum wage should produce no diminution in total consumption and employment, the results are not so simple. It is impossible, of course, to predict *a priori* the exact disposition of the income in such a case, but two factors to which allusion has already been made may be significant. It has been observed that, historically, both specific and general minimum-wage laws have applied to con-

[18] This is a point which Professor Douglas greatly stresses. See *The Theory of Wages,* pp. 313-314.

sumption industries, and it is therefore in these industries that any price rises are likely to occur. But the increase in total effective demand, being caused by the elevation of the propensity to consume, is also concentrated on the consumers' goods industries. It is therefore not too much to say that some of the very industries in which demand curves are raised perceptibly may be ones in which some firms have advanced prices. To the extent that this is true, the disturbances of readjustment will be minimized.

It is a commonplace that rises in prices do not fall upon all members of economic society in the same fashion and with the same force. Furthermore, any changes in money prices attributable to a minimum wage are less significant than changes, if any, in real income. It is equally familiar that a rise in the level of employment, with given organization, equipment, and techniques, is accompanied by a reduction in the short period of the average real income per head. The long-run effect, however, is not easy to predict. Let us examine how the real incomes of particular groups would be affected:

a. Real wages of workers covered by the regulation. It seems highly probable, at first glance, that the wage increase of workers affected by the minimum would be real as well as monetary. The introduction of a highly formalized analysis may be unnecessary, but the examination of one hypothetical situation will prove useful at this point. Let it be assumed that a uniform minimum-wage law has been enacted. Let it be assumed also that all firms which feel the incidence of the regulation had previously been paying the same wage; that technical coefficients are the same for each of these firms; and that the curves of average and marginal costs, respectively, of each firm are identical with the average and marginal cost curves of each other firm so affected. Suppose, finally, that each firm makes its adjustment wholly through price and output.

If the expenditures of the workers in the firms under consideration were restricted to purchases of the product of their own firms (or of products whose prices were raised in precisely the same degree) the problem of measuring the change in their real wages would be easy:

$$\frac{old\ wage}{old\ price} = old\ real\ wage, \qquad \frac{new\ wage}{new\ price} = new\ real\ wage,$$

$$and\quad \frac{new\ real\ wage}{old\ real\ wage} = index\ of\ real\ wages\ on\ the\ old\ base.$$

The above case, in which all of the workers' expenditures are on products whose prices are uniformly affected by the minimum, represents the smallest rise in real wages from a given change in money wages. The upper limit is the case in which workers spend *no* part of their incomes upon goods whose prices have advanced. In this event, the old price = new price (*ceteris paribus*), and the percentage rise in real wages is equal to the percentage rise in money wages. The actual rise in the real wage of workers employed in the regulated industries, then, will lie somewhere between the limits here delineated.

b. Real wages of other wage earners. Workers whose wages are already equal to or higher than the minimum legally adopted are not directly benefited by the kind of legislation considered in this section. If it be assumed that a few prices are raised by any amount whatsoever, the real wages of such workers will be lowered by an amount measured by the change in a hypothetical index of the prices entering into their budgets. More accurately, this is the result indicated if only the price changes are considered. But there are several factors whose operations are likely to limit or even entirely offset this apparent reduction in real wages. The multitudinous wage rates existing throughout the economy are often thought of collectively and referred to as the wage "structure." The image suggested by such a metaphor is that of an edifice with internal stresses and with interdependent parts the position of which may be changed if the thrusts are altered. It is interesting to inquire what influences the establishment of a minimum rate of pay throughout the economy may exert upon other wage rates. First, any increase in total employment arising from the heightened propensity to consume means an increase in the number of employed "labor-units" (however defined), and for individual workmen this is likely to mean more regular employment. Second, the rise in the level of employment will strengthen the bargaining position of all laborers, and those not covered by the minimum law may be able to secure an upward revision in their own wages by usual trade-union methods. These features of the situation will counteract, to a greater or less degree, the effect of price rises; but their existence depends upon whether employment is raised. It should be observed, third, that it is possible that some prices will actually fall. Some of the industries which experience an increase in demand as consumption patterns shift may offer economies to a large-scale operation. Expansion of these industries may lower somewhat the prices of their products.

Real wages of workers other than those embraced in the minimum-wage legislation evidently will be somewhat lowered in the short run if prices rise. But it is possible that in the long run the influences of the enlarged effective demand upon the regularity of employment, the bargaining position of the trade unions, and the attainment of more economical scales of operation may reduce, if not entirely counterbalance, the effect of price changes upon real wages.

c. Real income of entrepreneurs and rentiers. It has been observed above that, so far as its effect upon saving and consumption is concerned, a minimum-wage law would certainly lower the relative share of the social income going to the entrepreneurial class but might not lower, in the long period, its absolute share. Any price advances which may occur will affect rentiers adversely, of course.

In summary of the price discussion, though price advances may follow the establishment of a minimum wage, the real income of the class covered by the legislation will be increased. Whether the real income of other members of society will be altered is difficult to foretell, the result depending upon the extent of the price changes and upon whether or not the level of employment is maintained.[19]

Summary

Generalized, catholic conclusions as to the effects of a blanket minimum wage upon the whole economy are extremely difficult to formulate. As we have seen, there are many points at which the economy might feel the influence of the regulation, and unfortunately the manner in which one sector may be affected usually depends in large measure upon how others are affected. Obviously, the most important single (economic) question is whether the total volume of employment will, on balance, be maintained, diminished, or increased. This outcome depends, in turn, upon whether the increase in effective demand flowing from the heightened propensity to consume is equal to, less than, or greater than the decrease in demand caused by price rises or a flagging of investment. In any actual situation, a number of factors should be considered, such as the amount selected as the minimum rate, the phase of the trade cycle, the kind and number of businesses likely to be affected, etc.

It seems probable that adoption of a wage which would raise considerably the incomes of those who formerly had been receiving the very lowest incomes and which would bring the wage scales of all firms into some rough conformity with the marginal productivity of the system would be likely to be followed by more consequences favorable to the maintenance of the level of employment than unfavorable. And it is possible that in some circumstances there might even be some increase in employment.[20]

On the other hand, however, there undoubtedly exists at a given time a zone beyond which the wage could not be set without producing more adverse effects on employment than beneficial ones. The various unfavorable reactions on entrepreneurial expectations which might be produced by a large increase in wages serve to limit the heights at which the minimum wage might be set in a non-collectivist economy.

WEIR M. BROWN

---

[19] It is well to remember that the conclusions here and at certain other points in this section would have to be modified if the assumption of a closed system were relaxed. If there should be large changes in prices, for example, some adverse effects might be felt in an open system which do not arise here.

[20] See the remarks by A. P. Lerner at the round-table on "Wage Policies," *Am. Econ. Rev. Suppl.*, March, 1938, pp. 157-158.

GEOGRAPHICAL ASPECTS OF A MINIMUM WAGE

By JOHN V. VAN SICKLE

WITH proposals now before the two Houses of Congress to amend the Fair Labor Standards Act, it is time to reconsider the whole minimum wage question. There are many facets to this problem, but the present discussion will be focused primarily on the question of the desirability of imposing a *uniform* minimum wage throughout the length and breadth of a country as large and as diversified as the United States.

In this article, after tracing the history and operation of the present minimum wage law in this country, we shall examine some of the general economic principles involved in the uniform minimum wage. We shall then illustrate these principles by applying them to one specific area of the United States, the South; the effect of a uniform minimum wage on the industrialization of the South is one of the most serious issues to be faced by all proponents of a uniform minimum wage. Last of all, a solution to the whole problem will be presented; for it is the author's opinion, not that minimum wages as such are undesirable, but that they must be adjusted to the economic characteristics of our varying geographical regions.

Operation of the Present Act

The Fair Labor Standards Act, passed on October 24, 1938, imposed a minimum wage on all concerns whose products or services enter into interstate commerce. Agriculture, domestic service, and certain other activities were expressly exempted; and, for constitutional reasons, no attempt was made to cover firms in intrastate commerce. With these exceptions, the minimum wage applies equally to large and small concerns, to concerns located in New York City and concerns located in the smallest hamlets in the most rural parts of Mississippi.

The minimum wage rate was set by the act at 25 cents an hour for the first year, 30 cents for the following six years, and 40 cents thereafter, i.e., from October 24, 1945. The maximum normal work-week for those industries whose

145

rates were covered by the act was set at 44 hours for the first year, 42 hours for the second year, and 40 hours thereafter, with time and a half to be paid for work in excess of the prevailing maximum hours.

The administrator of the act was authorized to increase the minimum rate in any industry to any level between the starting minimum of 25 cents and the final minimum of 40 cents *before* the date set for the 40-cent rate (October 24, 1945), upon the recommendation of tripartite industry committees, and upon evidence that the higher minimum would not cause serious unemployment, and with due regard for the conditions of competition, such as transportation, living, and production costs, wage agreements for work of like character reached through collective bargaining, and absence of competitive advantage. On the other hand, the administrator might authorize minimum rates set as low as 30 cents an hour even after the 40-cent rate had gone into effect if it could be shown that the 40-cent minimum would cause "substantial curtailment of employment" in a particular industry. No exceptions could be made, however, solely on the basis of regional differences.

Amendments now before Congress would raise the minimum rate to 65 cents for one year, to 70 cents for the next year, and to 75 cents thereafter. Before we can determine the wisdom of these proposed amendments, it will be well to review briefly the evolution of the act so far.

Administration of the Act. The administrator of the act was from the beginning under pressure from organized labor in all parts of the country, and from plants and public opinion in high-wage areas, to advance rates to the 40-cent level as rapidly as possible. The industry committees supported the effort, as was to be expected in view of the fact that the administrator determined the personnel of the committees and was authorized to discharge a committee and appoint a new one if he was dissatisfied with its findings. Even before Pearl Harbor many industry rates had already been advanced to the 40-cent level. Moreover, through the Public Purchase Act the administrator was able to exert a further and powerful upward pressure on wage rates in general. This particular act provided that private firms could be excluded from bidding on federal contracts involving more than $10,000, upon an administrative finding that they paid:

. . . less than the minimum wages as determined by the Secretary of Labor to be the prevailing minimum wages for persons employed on similar work or in the particular or similar industries or groups of industries currently operating in the *locality* in which the materials, supplies, articles or equipment are to be manufactured or finished under said contract. [Italics supplied.]

Through a tortured interpretation of the "locality" restriction [1] the administrator frequently set minima appreciably higher than those required of plants under the Fair Labor Standards Act, despite the fact that the industry committees had presumably certified that the rates they recommended were the highest that could be set without causing serious unemployment.

Conditions Changed by the War. After Pearl Harbor the American econ-

[1] See "Regionalism: A Tool of Economic Analysis," by the writer in the *American Economic Review*, Vol. XXXV, No. 2. (May, 1945), pp. 356–358.

omy operated under forced draft. The most pressing problem confronting the government in the labor field was no longer that of raising wages but rather that of preventing them from rising to inordinate heights through the competitive bidding of labor-hungry businesses. Almost overnight the 40-cent minimum became virtually universal in businesses in interstate commerce. Businesses operating on war account were authorized by the revived War Labor Board to pay entrance rates well above this level when that was necessary for the successful prosecution of the war. For a time it looked as though a vicious spiral of rising wages and rising prices might engulf the country.

To prevent such a situation the government was soon forced to abandon one of the basic assumptions underlying the Fair Labor Standards Act, namely, that the minimum wage in an industry should be the same all over the country. It was apparent that the application of this doctrine would make it necessary to raise wages substantially and unnecessarily in many communities. Accordingly, the Stabilization Act of October 2, 1942, was passed. This act required the War Labor Board to stabilize wages "as far as practicable on the basis of the levels which existed on September 15, 1942." Exceptions were authorized, notably to permit increases in straight-time rates up to 15% above the level prevailing on January 1, 1941, to compensate for the rise in the cost of living in the case of workers who had not shared in the general increase in wages (the Little Steel formula). Thereafter wage differentials which had been established and stabilized were not to be disturbed. They were, according to a War Labor Board statement of November 6, 1942,

to be regarded as "normal to American industry."

On May 12, 1943, the Economic Stabilization Director further elaborated the wartime theory regarding geographical wage differentials in a directive in which he authorized the War Labor Board to establish by occupational groups and *labor market areas* "wage rate brackets embracing all those various rates found to be sound and tested going rates." Moreover, the War Labor Board was not to authorize wage increases above the minimum of the going rates within the brackets, "except in rare and unusual cases."

As the war proceeded, the pressures on wages and prices steadily increased. Some elasticity in the wage field was contrived through what were known as "fringe adjustments": portal-to-portal pay, holidays with pay, rate adjustments for afternoon and night shifts, and so forth. In some areas Regional War Labor Boards were authorized to permit increases in minimum rates to 50 cents an hour on the ground that rates below that level were "substandard" within the meaning of President Roosevelt's "hold-the-line" order of April 8, 1943 (Executive Order 9328). In November, 1944, a Senate Committee on substandard wages held lengthy hearings on the so-called Pepper Resolution (Con. Res. 48) to authorize the War Labor Board to allow wage increases up to 65 cents on the ground that rates less than 65 cents were to be regarded as substandard. The resolution was not passed by Congress, presumably because of lack of Administration support. Inflation was still regarded as a serious threat.

Proposed Amendments. With the coming of peace, however, the official position shifted. The Administration, while recognizing that inflation was still a possibility, appeared to regard deflation, through a drastic cut in wages, as a still greater threat. Accordingly, bills sponsored by the Administration were introduced into the two Houses to amend the Fair Labor Standards Act (S. 1349 and H.R. 4130). The amendments extend the scope of the law to certain industries hitherto exempt and, as already mentioned, raise the minimum hourly wage to 65 cents 120 days after the passage of the act, to 70 cents the following year, and to 75 cents thereafter.

The industry committees are instructed to recommend at any time, and the administrator of the act is authorized to impose upon any industry, a minimum wage not in excess of 75 cents upon evidence that the higher rate will not substantially curtail employment. Moreover, the industry committees are instructed to define reasonable job classifications for each industry and subdivision thereof and to recommend minimum rates for each job classification above the unskilled level; and the administrator is authorized to impose these rates after due notice to interested parties and an opportunity to be heard, "if he finds that the recommendations are made in accordance with the law and are supported by the evidence adduced at the hearings." The authority of the administrator to permit industry rates lower than the normal minimum where necessary to prevent substantial unemployment is withdrawn.

If these amendments are passed, the Fair Labor Standards Act ceases to be simply a minimum wage law. A government official is in effect authorized to determine the entire scale of wage

remuneration in an industry and not merely the entrance rate for unskilled labor. Here is a striking confirmation of Mr. Henry Hazlett's contention, in his discussion of the original Full Employment Bill of 1945,[2] that the Administration and its Congressional supporters are profoundly distrustful of the workability of the private enterprise system. It would also appear that they are distrustful of collective bargaining as a means of establishing appropriate job classifications and rates of remuneration for workers above the unskilled level.

In the remainder of this paper, it will be argued that the Fair Labor Standards Act in its present formulation, in addition to being an expression of the Administration's distrust of the private enterprise system, will in fact contribute to making the system unworkable. Because the practical defects of the act are the consequences of the faulty theoretical foundations on which it rests, it will be necessary to begin with a consideration of the arguments most frequently advanced by the proponents of the act.

Before entering into the details of the argument, however, the writer wants to make it plain that he is not opposed to the principle of a minimum wage. He believes, and will attempt to show in a final section of this paper, that a law could be passed which would be entirely consistent with the requirements of a vigorous and responsible private enterprise system.

Fallacies Underlying the Act

The Fair Labor Standards Act in its present formulation rests on three faulty arguments, which can be set forth in proposition form as follows:

[2] Henry Hazlett, *The Full Employment Bill: An Analysis*, National Economic Problems Series No. 415 (New York, American Enterprise Association, 1945) p. 7.

I. A fair wage is one which provides unskilled workers with a minimum standard of living necessary for health, efficiency, and general well-being.

There is no doubt that the *concept* of a minimum wage is useful — an idea in the public mind that a certain wage provides the minimum standard of living. It establishes a goal. It provides something worth striving for. Those below the "minimum" seek to reach it, while those above it strive to preserve their lead over their less fortunate fellows. In a free and progressive society the goal of yesterday becomes the accomplishment of today. Private capitalism, driven by our discontents and our aspirations, forges ahead — as it must to survive. The goal of yesterday is reached because business succeeds in equipping the labor force with ever better and more ample tools and backing it with more and better know-how. Labor productivity rises all along the line until that of the unskilled reaches the point where it is worth the "minimum." As the old goal is approached, a new and higher one is set and the process goes on.

The government can of course hasten the process by providing expanded and improved health and educational facilities, and by seeing to it that monopoly practices are kept at a low point. The supply of unskilled laborers can be reduced and their wages increased by training and equipping the more qualified among them and helping them to get access to better paying jobs. Wages in higher job classifications may have to be reduced somewhat to make places for these workers from below, but this is a constructive and socially desirable method of reducing inequalities. It increases total production. It results in a larger

pie from which the better paid may expect to get as much or more than before, even though they are obliged to take a proportionately smaller cut than before. Meantime, the accumulation of capital and the progress of the industrial arts make the more equal apportionment of an expanding national product socially and politically acceptable.

Yet this is at best a roundabout method of raising standards. It requires time, patience, and an environment favorable to risk taking. Patience in particular is necessary because there are always large numbers of workers, in the absolute sense, whose productivity is below the "minimum" which public opinion has momentarily settled upon; and this will always be so in a society in which less than complete equality of rewards exists.

Danger of Imposing a Minimum Prematurely. To impose a minimum prematurely and rigidly, however, is the surest way of denying to the lowest paid groups the realization of their dream. What they gain by a high minimum, set by fiat, does not come from an increase in production; it has to come from those whose productivity is already above the minimum. And if it is taken from the few at the very top of the income pyramid, pioneering investment will be reduced. Financial risk taking which, over the years, could have raised the national product to new and substantially higher levels will be retarded or prevented.

Moreover, in a society based on private enterprise the lowest paid groups are the greatest losers from an excessively high minimum wage, because no private employer will or can hire a man for more than he is worth. A legislated minimum which violates the relationship between wages and productivity reduces private employment. In and of itself, any minimum wage makes for some private unemployment. A people who wish to preserve a vigorous, expanding, and responsible private enterprise system cannot afford deliberately to legislate in favor of high unemployment.

II. *The cost of the minimum budget necessary to health, efficiency, and general well-being is approximately equal all over the country. Hence common labor rates should be approximately the same all over the country.*

This proposition disregards the relationship of wage rates to productivity previously discussed and in addition ignores the causes and functions of geographical differences in wage rates.

The causes: In a country as vast as ours there is great geographical variation in natural endowments (soils, minerals, climate, and so forth), in rates of population growth, in the supply and rate of formation of capital, in the quantity and quality of business leadership. This variation results in large differences in the amount of equipment back of workers in different parts of the country and hence large differences in their productivity. To impose a high and uniform minimum wage is to deny local opportunities for useful private employment to large numbers of workers, particularly those in smaller plants, in rural areas, and in smaller cities and towns.

The functions: In a private enterprise society, geographical wage differentials set in motion geographical movements of labor and capital which tend to equalize wages and interest rates throughout the country and to narrow or eliminate gross differences in levels of living. The lower wage rates which are characteristic of the more rural and less industrialized

parts of the country induce some of the labor there (where natural rates of population growth are highest) to migrate to the great metropolitan centers of high wages, abundant capital, and low or negative natural rates of population growth. Meantime, the somewhat larger profit margins made possible by the abundance of unskilled labor in the more rural areas induce outside capital to move in. Sometimes this movement of capital involves the shift of an existing industry out of high-wage areas. Very often, however, it means that a new industry opened up by technological advance develops first or at least predominantly in the more rural areas. This two-way movement of labor and capital exercises a powerful leverage on wage rates and levels of living generally in low-income areas, and promotes a wholesome decentralization of economic activities.

While this two-way movement of labor and capital sometimes produces painful results, the over-all effect is beneficial. The draining off of surplus workers from farms is greatly facilitated. Soil conservation and improved farm management are promoted by growing local markets. Rising levels of living in the more rural and less-developed parts of the country provide expanding markets for the very types of industries that predominate in the highly industrialized and high-wage areas. Interstate exchange of goods and services is promoted, thereby reducing the necessity of massive interstate movements of people.

Effects of Equalization by Fiat. The beneficial effects to be expected from respecting geographical wage differentials can be further illustrated by considering the consequences that will follow if they are prematurely eliminated or excessively narrowed by government edict. Any excessive and premature narrowing of the gap puts pressure on labor to move to existing centers of industrial concentration instead of encouraging capital and new saving to seek out areas of surplus population. It promotes centralization instead of decentralization — an excessive urbanism, on the one hand, and an excessive agrarianism, on the other. It distorts the locational pattern of industry, favoring big business in big cities at the expense of small business in smaller communities. It increases frictional unemployment and concentrates it precisely where the need for job opportunities is greatest. It promotes monopoly. It forces upon localities, states, and whole regions costs which they should not have to bear. It thus offends the very principle of our federal form of government.

It sets in motion a mass movement of men and women from low-wage areas which will seriously strain the economic, political, and social institutions in the high-wage areas. Strong pressures will arise in favor of excluding these impoverished migrants. During the "great depression" of the 1930's California found ways and means of doing this very thing. There is no need of elaborating on the strain such measures place on our form of government.

In addition to these social, economic, and political defects, the imposition of a high and uniform minimum wage diminishes the prospects of a further lowering of American protective barriers against foreign competitors. If the American people decide that it is unethical and uneconomical to ask workers in the wealthy industrial states to compete with fellow Americans on the basis of wage differentials, they will hardly be willing to ask American labor to compete in the home market with the laborers of impoverished Europe, not to mention those of India and the Far East. If we apply a fallacious fair wage test to products moving in interstate trade, it is difficult to believe that we will do otherwise when it comes to international trade. Yet upon our success in promoting freer international trading may well depend the peace and prosperity, and perhaps the very existence, of civilization.

Finally, the present proposal is unsound from the point of view of the nation's *military security*. Our military authorities are seriously concerned over the location of essential industries in a few large centers, in view of recent developments in offensive weapons like atomic bombs and rockets. Our most competent scientists tell us that no adequate defense against these new and terrible weapons has yet been found and that it may not be possible to devise one. Until we are surer than we can be at present that World War II was the last war, we should hesitate to adopt measures that increase our vulnerability. The very survival of nations in the dangerous years ahead may depend upon their ability to so scatter their productive resources that no sneak attack can seriously cripple them. Yet the measure here under discussion deliberately legislates an even greater centralization of industry than now exists. And, as was pointed out in the preceding paragraph, being inspired by a protectionist spirit, by a fear of competition, it reduces the prospects of a durable peace.

III. A high minimum wage will increase the purchasing power of workers and thereby create markets for volume production and full employment.

This argument has been repeatedly advanced in connection with the current proposal to raise the minimum wage to 65 cents an hour. It rests on the assumption that the volume of employment is more dependent upon the level of general purchasing power than upon wage rates. There is certainly an important element of truth in this new approach to the problem of employment. There is no denying, for example, that if wages all across the board sag and if employers have reason to believe that wage contracts closed at a later date will be more favorable than those closed today, there will be a delay in making long-term commitments; this delay will increase unemployment of labor and capital, with heavy losses in wages, interest rates, and profits; all will suffer. A general deflation of wages, therefore, may well prove an illusory method of solving the employment problem.

Unfortunately, the doctrine can be easily abused. It has been abused in connection with the proposal here under consideration. Properly understood, the doctrine provides no justification for wage distortions. There is such a thing as having some wages too high and some wages too low. What is needed is balanced production and a balanced wage structure. Balance can only be maintained by continuous small adjustments. Flexibility of wages and mobility of labor and capital are essential. One task of the government is to promote balance by assisting the more versatile and more gifted workers in low-wage paying industries and in low-wage paying areas to shift into jobs and into places with higher rates of pay. Unusually high wages should always be regarded as an evidence of a relative scarcity of labor of particular kinds or of labor generally in particular places.

Their social justification is that they will attract additional workers and that in the process they will be brought down to normal. Otherwise, few if any additional workers can be employed. An unnecessarily high and rigid wage rate restricts employment.

It must be emphasized: the volume of employment in a particular industry or in a particular area is related to the wage rate. In a free enterprise system some slight fall in high wage rates will facilitate needed transfers of labor and capital and will simultaneously firm up wages and profits elsewhere. It will tend also to reduce the duration of structural unemployment. If our industrial system is kept reasonably flexible, wage flexibility downward as well as upward will actually increase the total wage component in the national income and thus contribute to the maintenance of consumer purchasing power. Moreover, it is only through the lowering of wages which are too high that the raising of wages which are too low can be accomplished without inflation and without price controls.

The Act is Deflationary. In any event, the effect of the amendment here under consideration will be to destroy purchasing power and employment, unless Congress supplements it with additonal action. Here are the reasons:

The law applies only to activities whose products and services enter into interstate trade. In general, these affected businesses pay substantially higher wages than do farm employers and the operators of local businesses serving intrastate markets. The imposition of the 65–75 cent minimum will force many of these higher wage paying businesses to curtail employment. The displaced workers will be forced back into the uncovered segments of the economy in their areas or be obliged to migrate to the high-wage areas where it will be impossible to absorb them unless wage rates there are lowered. In either event there will be a large rise in the number of the unemployed while readjustments are taking place, the readjustments will be needlessly prolonged, and afterwards the total income going to the workers of the country will be less than before, and the resources of the country will be less effectively used. The law, in and of itself, destroys purchasing power.

The Congress, however, will not be able to stop at this point. Not only will it have a moral responsibility for helping those who have suffered as a result of the enactment of this amendment, but public opinion has come to expect that the Federal Government can and will do whatever is necessary to prevent massive unemployment. The much-discussed Full Employment Bill of 1945 is ample evidence of the growing belief in the responsibilities which the government should assume. It might be well, therefore, to consider the relationship of the Fair Labor Standards Act to the Full Employment Bill.

Relation of Act to Full Employment Bill. The Full Employment Bill states that "all Americans able to work and seeking work have the right to useful, remunerative, regular, and full-time employment" and that it is the government's responsibility to see to it that employment opportunities exist for them. The key word in this declaration of policy is the adjective "remunerative." The logical standard for the government to use in deciding whether or not a job is remunerative would be the standard set in the Fair Labor Standards Act, or the even higher wage that the administrator of the act may impose by virtue of the authority conferred upon him under the Public Purchase Act.

When the President makes his estimate, at the beginning of the year, of the size of the labor force and the aggregate volume of investment and expenditure required to produce the "volume of the gross national product, at the expected level of prices, as will be necessary to provide employment opportunities for such labor force," as he is required to do under the terms of the bill, he will inevitably find himself compelled to certify that prospective investment and expenditure will be substantially less than investment and expenditure needed for full and remunerative employment.

That conclusion follows, in the writer's opinion, from the fact that the experts who advise the President will have to accept the definition of remunerative rates contained in the Fair Labor Standards Act, while their estimate of prospective investment and expenditure will necessarily be based upon the lower rates of remuneration actually prevailing in agriculture and in the host of plants in industry and commerce and in the public services. The President will thus be forced to certify to the existence of a huge prospective deficiency in the National Budget even though the economy is in fact operating at a high level of employment.

It will thereupon be incumbent upon him to set forth a general program "for encouraging such increased non-federal investment and expenditure, particularly investment and expenditure which will promote increased employment opportunities by private enterprise, as will prevent such deficiency to the greatest possible extent. The President shall also include in such Budget such recommendations for legislation relating to such program as he may deem necessary or desirable. . . ."

The writer believes that neither the President nor his experts could possibly recommend nonspending measures that would enable public and private enterprise to provide employment for all at the required level of remuneration (i.e., with no job paying less than 65 cents an hour, "including the self-employed in industry and agriculture") throughout the ensuing fiscal period. The terms of reference impose upon the President and his advisers the obligation to recommend an enormous expansion of public spending, and the provisions of the bill make it obligatory upon the government to see to it that at the very least the wage provisions of the Fair Labor Standards Act shall be observed regardless of whether the activity is interstate or intrastate. Thus, the Full Employment Bill would become the means for freeing the Fair Labor Standards Act from its present constitutional limitations and for extending federal control of wages into every nook and corner of the country.

Surely the Federal Government would be forced to go to great lengths in carrying out its responsibilities under the provisions of the Full Employment Bill if it is obliged simultaneously to observe the wage provisions of the Fair Labor Standards Act. To overcome the deflationary effects of the latter act would require a perfectly enormous expenditure of public funds.

Inevitability of Deficit Financing. If the large public works programs which the government will be obliged to authorize for all areas affected by unemployment are financed by taxation or from real savings, the people in high-income areas will have to provide the bulk of the funds, and no new purchasing power will be created. Congress will be under pressure, therefore, to finance the programs by borrowing from the banks. This would be true enough even without the influence of the Full Employment Bill.

The public programs themselves will effectually discourage the migration of the displaced workers to the congested high-wage areas. Meantime the reductions in the output coming from the plants in low-wage areas will result in a rise in product prices, a rise in profit margins in high-wage areas, and, if the workers there are well organized, a rise in wages. This rise in wages will cause geographical differentials to emerge once more, and Congress will again be asked to raise the minimum wage. As the wage spiral develops, Congress may expect still more insistent demands than at present, from industry and labor for additional protection against low-wage competition from abroad, and from American agriculture for more generous price supports in order that it may provide not only for its own prolific population but also for those displaced from industry. In brief, the minimum wage law, and the companion measures which are practically certain to accompany it, point directly toward national self-sufficiency, inflation, and increasing sectional tensions within the United States and between the United States and foreign nations.

Now that we have examined some of the general economic principles affecting a uniform minimum wage, let us look more closely at the effect of such a wage on a specific geographical area of the United States.

Impact Upon the South

The Fair Labor Standards Act is directed against the industrially emerging South. The 1938 debates in Congress amply support this assertion. The current public discussion leads to the same conclusion. Advocates of raising the minimum always cite the deplorable conditions in the South.

The explanation for the South's poverty is that it is long on labor, particularly unskilled labor, relative to the supply of natural resources, capital equipment, local savings, and technical skills. The natural resources base is, in the absolute sense, large and reasonably varied. Some of these resources are of first-rate quality. But the most important of them all, the soil, is of mediocre quality. The single state of Iowa has more Grade A agricultural land than the entire South east of the Mississippi. (Yet the average Iowa farm is much larger than the average farm in the Southeast, and the number of persons dependent thereon is appreciably smaller.) Moreover, the soils of the South have been badly damaged by decades of misuse. About half the nation's 150 million acres of badly eroded land are in the South.

Under these circumstances it is, for the time being, inevitable that southern farm incomes should be very much lower than farm incomes in other parts of the country. The region's disadvantage is further increased by the heavy dependence of its population on this mediocre and abused soil, and by the exceptionally high rate of natural increase in the South's farm population. In brief, low farm incomes in the South are primarily responsible for the relatively low level of living in this region.

[3] Dr. Mordecai Ezekiel, "Agriculture and Industry in the Postwar South," *The South: Amer-*

The greater the emphasis on agriculture, the lower is the position of a state as measured by per capita income. In the table in EXHIBIT I this relationship is brought out clearly.

EXHIBIT I. WORKERS ENGAGED IN FARMING AND AVERAGE INCOME PER PERSON, 1940

State	Percentage of Workers Engaged in Farming	Average Annual Income per Capita of Population
Mississippi	59%	$205
Arkansas	53	257
Alabama	40	266
South Carolina	40	289
Kentucky	37	313
Georgia	36	317
Tennessee	34	319
North Carolina	34	320
Oklahoma	33	360
Louisiana	34	365
West Virginia	16	409
Texas	30	419
Virginia	25	447
Florida	20	472

Source: Quoted from Dr. Mordecai Ezekiel, "Agriculture and Industry in the Postwar South," *The South: America's Opportunity Number One.* (Atlanta, Southern Regional Council, 1945.)

Much has been done and more can and will be done to improve southern farming, but a satisfactory solution will not be reached until the region's farm population has been substantially reduced. Dr. Ezekiel of the Department of Agriculture has recently estimated that the proportion of the South's working population engaged in farming, forestry, and fishing should be reduced from the 1940 figure of 34.7% to 17.7%; i.e., virtually cut in half. He thinks that this could be done in a ten-year period. It would involve an absolute reduction in numbers from the 4,356,000 of 1940 to 2,820,000, a cut of a million and a half, and in addition the entire net natural increase would have to be drawn off.[3] The imminence of the mechanical

ica's Opportunity Number One (Atlanta, Southern Regional Council, 1945).

cotton picker and the flame weeder may well require an early upward revision of the estimated population surplus on southern farms. In any event, the needed shiftover runs into millions.

Migration not the Solution. The magnitude of this shift makes it quite unrealistic to look primarily to migration. Some migration is of course desirable and will certainly continue in the future as in the past. Some 1,700,000 persons left 11 southeastern states in the single decade of the 1920's. But migration on this scale is a form of social erosion which has already carried away *human* top soil badly needed by the South. Migration will no more solve the South's income problem than it will that of India or China. What the South needs is more industry, and the service and recreational facilities that develop in parallel with industry. Federal measures, to be helpful, should assist the southern people to use more effectively their nonfarm resources.

The South's Potentialities. The South possesses inadequately developed nonfarm resources which should make it possible to improve conditions materially. Iron, coal, and limestone, the indispensables for industrial development, plus asbestos, asphalt, barite, bauxite, clays, feldspar, fluorspar, gypsum, lead, marble, mercury, phosphate rock, pyrites, salt, sand and gravel, silica, sulphur, and zinc — all these are to be found in the South in relative abundance. The extent to which they are economic assets depends, however, on whether in combination with labor and capital they can be profitably developed. The higher the minimum

wage that must be paid to common labor, the larger the proportion of these resources that must be regarded as, for the time being, submarginal. It is ironical that the Fair Labor Standards Act, with its express exemption of agriculture, authorizes and indeed compels the people of the South to rely on one of their poorest resources, and reduces the opportunity to shift their efforts to the exploitation of these other resources until such time as unskilled laborers can be paid two or three times as much as they can earn on southern farms.

Until the passage of the Fair Labor Standards Act the prospects for the South were bright. Industrialization had been going on at a reasonably satisfactory rate for several decades. Professor Spengler of Duke University made a study of the shift in wage jobs in manufacturing by regions for the period 1899 to 1937. He found that the southeastern region (Virginia, the two Carolinas, Florida, Georgia, Alabama, and Tennessee) had increased its percentage of the nation's wage jobs from 6.2% to 11.5% while every other region, with one exception, had lost ground. The exception was the Louisiana–Texas region, which had increased its percentage by only 0.1%. His conclusion was that "a considerable proportion of such future manufacturing as takes place in the United States will take place in . . . the Southeast." [4]

This development occurred because the Federal Government and organized groups generally allowed economic forces to operate without serious interferences. The South was able to overcome the handicap of mediocre soils, scant local capital, thin local markets for industrial products, and lack of skilled

[4] J. J. Spengler, "Regional Differences and the Future of Manufacturing in America," *Southern* *Economic Journal,* Vol. VII, No. 4 (April, 1941), p. 488.

labor and managerial talents through its abundance of willing and trainable unskilled labor.

Interregional Repercussions. New England can testify to the fact that this development of the South has been hard to take. It is not surprising, therefore, that public opinion outside the South came to the conclusion that the rate of growth in the South was forcing adjustment in the more industrialized parts of the country at too rapid a rate. The imposition of a nation-wide minimum wage applicable to southern industries competing in national markets was urged as a means of slowing down the South's industrialization. Its purpose was to provide internal protection for the industrialized regions just as high tariffs provided protection from foreign competition.

Despite the generous expressions of concern for the South, the political forces behind the law were, and still are, protectionist. The status quo is to be preserved. Except for agricultural foods, fibers, and raw materials, the South is to be permitted to provide goods and services for the national market only to the extent that it can pay wages comparable to those paid in other parts of the country. Before World War II few of its nonagricultural industries could meet this test, despite the fact that they could pay substantially more than agriculture — and despite the fact that they did pay in wages a larger proportion of their value added by manufacturing than did the industries in other parts of the country.

The South's Wage-Paying Ability. Value added provides one of the best methods of determining the "ability to pay" of southern industry. The term as used by the Bureau of the Census means the balance after cost of raw materials, fuel, power, supplies, and so forth, is deducted from value of product. Out of it must come wages, salaries, taxes, capital costs such as interest and amortization, profits, and sundry minor costs. The relationship between wages and value added for selected years is shown in EXHIBIT II.

EXHIBIT II. NUMBER OF WORKERS (AVERAGE FOR YEAR), WAGES PAID PER AVERAGE WORKER, AND VALUE ADDED PER AVERAGE WORKER, IN MANUFACTURING, SOUTHEASTERN REGION AND UNITED STATES, 1929–1939

Year	Average Number of Wage Earners	Wages Paid per Average Wage Earner	Value Added per Average Wage Earner	Ratio of Wages to Value Added
	Southeastern Region			
1929	838,891	$ 784	$2,074	37.8
1931	642,143	675	1,829	36.9
1933	685,850	559	1,447	38.6
1935	769,866	635	1,511	42.0
1937	901,434	732	1,813	40.4
1939	902,755	732	1,948	37.6
	United States			
1929	8,380,536	1,301	3,668	35.5
1931	6,163,144	1,085	3,018	36.0
1933	5,787,611	869	2,420	35.9
1935	7,203,794	1,015	2,575	39.4
1937	8,569,231	1,180	2,938	40.2
1939	7,886,567	1,153	3,130	36.8

Source: Table VII in National Resources Planning Board Report, *Regional Planning* (Washington, D. C., U. S. Government Printing Office, 1942), Part XI, p. 130; based upon data from *Census of Manufactures*.

The average value added by manufacture for the Southeast in 1939 was $1,948 per wage earner; the average for the United States, including the Southeast, was $3,130 per wage earner. The differential is 34.6%, and the South therefore has that much less with which to pay fixed charges such as taxes and interest, which cannot be reduced, and wages, salaries, and profits. The value added by manufacture in the Middle West and Far West was more than 40% greater than in the Southeast.

Has the war changed the situation? We shall not know for some time to come. It is known, however, that the surplus of labor on southern farms was drastically reduced. The poorer the farming area, the greater the exodus. It is to be hoped that the migrants from these poorer areas will not return to their old homes. Doubtless many will not return to the South at all, but many will; and the South will need expanding nonfarm opportunities to provide for them. Can the South's industries provide the needed employment if a 65–75 cent minimum is imposed upon them? The answer is clearly "no." Most of the South's existing industries still do not pay anything like 65 cents an hour for unskilled categories, as the situation in Tennessee, one of the higher wage paying states, clearly demonstrates.

During the first quarter of 1945, for example, there were only six industry groups in Tennessee in which no employees received average hourly earnings of less than 65 cents. These were metal mining, ordnance, aircraft, shipbuilding, nonferrous metals, machinery other than electrical, and automobiles. These were either highly unionized industries or war industries working on a cost-plus basis. They employed 40,410 persons or 14.5% of those covered by unemployment compensation. The remaining 85% worked in industries paying a substantial proportion of their employees less than 65 cents an hour. As can be seen from the table in EXHIBIT III, 43% of the workers in the apparel industry were earning less than 50 cents an hour, 93% less than 65 cents; in textiles the corresponding figures were 27% and 92%; for manufacturing as a whole 42% received less than 65 cents an hour. To increase the minimum wage to 65 cents

would require a step-up of all rates above the minimum.

Most of Tennessee's industries, and most of the industries in the other southern states as well, cannot possibly absorb any such wage increases at prevailing prices. And until the output of the low-wage plants declines, there will be no force making for a rise in product prices. The plants in the big cities in

EXHIBIT III. EMPLOYMENT IN SAMPLE ESTABLISHMENTS CLASSIFIED BY AVERAGE HOURLY EARNINGS AND INDUSTRY, TENNESSEE, FIRST QUARTER 1945

		Percentage Employees Receiving Average Hourly Earning Less Than	
Industry Group	Total Employment Covered by Sample	50 cents	65 cents
Coal mining	6,273	0.0%	10.8%
Nonmetallic mining	2,029	0.0	100.0
Food	20,289	9.3	48.1
Tobacco	1,785	45.6	45.6
Textiles	34,698	27.5	91.9
Apparel	19,319	42.9	92.9
Lumber	12,778	23.9	68.1
Furniture	11,889	45.4	83.5
Paper	4,450	0.0	35.3
Printing	5,414	0.0	100.0
Chemicals	38,386	0.7	8.6
Rubber	7,810	0.0	15.6
Leather	8,485	0.0	57.3
Stone, Clay & Glass	5,743	11.1	50.5
Iron & Steel	18,883	4.4	26.9
Elec. Machinery	3,456	0.0	15.5
Miscellaneous Mfg.	2,471	76.6	100.0
Total Mfg.	266,506	12.5	41.7

Source: Preliminary Study, Research and Statistical Section, Tennessee Department of Employment Security.

the highly industrialized parts of the country will be little if any affected; competitive conditions have already imposed the 65-cent minimum on them. Hence most plants in the South, as well as many smaller concerns in the more rural parts of the industrialized North, will be obliged to reduce their present scale of operations or close down entirely.

Some Supporting Evidence. It is true that the administrator of the act and the economists of the now combined Wages and Hours and Public Contracts Division of the Labor Department deny that the South has been adversely affected, but the evidence they submit is unconvincing because it is fragmentary or because it fails to allow for the effects of the war. In general, it can be said that the war-induced rise in wages reduced to the vanishing point the significance of the 40-cent minimum even in the South. Evidence of the regional repercussions must therefore be sought in the developments prior to 1941.

In the seamless hosiery industry, for example, employment as a whole increased by 10.1% during the first nine months of 1939 as compared with the corresponding months of 1938; in the small low-wage plants it declined by 7.3%. The introduction of labor-saving machinery was stimulated, and inefficient workers were discharged. Most significant of all, employment in northern mills in 1940 was 4.9% above that in 1939, while it was 5.5% lower in the South. The southward trend of the industry had been reversed.

In the cottonseed industry a pronounced tendency to concentration in larger plants in larger centers occurred during the first two years of the act.

In the lumber industry the act stimulated mechanization which lent itself better to conditions in the Far West than it did to those in the South, where there are numerous small and scattered stands of lumber. As long as this lumber does not move into interstate channels, the law does not apply; but this naturally hurts the larger concerns and has given rise to a demand that the law be amended to bring intrastate workers

within its scope if the goods and services produced by them affect interstate commerce. Even without such an amendment coverage had been greatly extended by administrative ruling. Thus a small lumber mill selling exclusively and deliberately within a state was declared to be liable if the owner "intends, hopes or has reason to believe" that his product will eventually move in interstate commerce.[5] More recently, mills have been declared liable to the higher standards of the Walsh-Healey Act, despite the fact that the concerns were doing no business with the government, on the ground that their products were used by concerns that were doing business with the government.

Any socially minded person who is able to distinguish between slogans and facts cannot fail to be disturbed by the misguided humanitarianism which animates so many of the supporters of the Fair Labor Standards Act. The latter would do well to read and ponder a brief essay on "The American Interest in the Colonial Problem," by Professor Jacob Viner of the University of Chicago, which appeared recently in a little book entitled *The United States in a Multinational Economy*.[6] Its relevance to the problem confronting the South is striking. It is to be hoped that they will not miss one particular passage. Apropos of outside efforts at laying down minimum standards with respect to working conditions, wages, social security, and the like, Professor Viner remarks that such efforts "are not always unselfish or even non-selfish." He goes on:

It can rarely be certain, and it is often doubtful, that minimum requirements

[5] John F. Moloney, "Some Effects of the Federal Fair Labor Standards Act upon Southern Industry," *Southern Economic Journal*, Vol. 9, No. 1 (July, 1942).

[6] Studies in American Foreign Relations, No. 4 (New York, Council on American Foreign Relations, 1945).

with respect to such matters will serve to raise rather than to lower the economic productivity of the area to which such standards are applied. In fact, proposals for their application, when made from outside the area, at times have the appearance at least of having as their real objective the reduction of the competitive power of such areas insofar as it results from low wages and poor working conditions. The authorities in the areas, with this in mind, will tend in such cases either to refuse in general to accept the standards, or to demand nullifying special provisions for their areas, or to refrain from enforcing them, even though they have gone through the motions of formally accepting them. Or they may unwisely try to enforce them too quickly or too rigorously with unfortunate results for the people on whose behalf they were supposedly introduced.

A Bill of Particulars

We are now in a position to sum up. A high and uniform minimum wage in a country like the United States is unsound socially, economically, and politically. It is inspired by the same spirit of protectionism that helped to disintegrate the international order so painfully built up during the nineteenth century and to bring on two world wars in a single generation. It promotes centralization at the very time that rapid decentralization has become a national imperative. The present proposal to raise the minimum wage to 65–75 cents an hour is objectionable on at least eleven counts. Its enforcement will:

(1) Lower levels of living throughout the country.
(2) Widen existing geographical differentials in wages and levels of living.
(3) Obstruct commerce and the free flow of commerce between the states.
(4) Promote big business at the expense of small business.
(5) Promote monopoly at the expense of free competitive enterprise.

(6) Promote deficit-financed public investment at the expense of private investment, private enterprise, and stable prices.
(7) Reduce private employment and deny to many Americans able to work and seeking work the opportunity for private jobs in their home communities.
(8) Prevent full and effective utilization of the nation's resources.
(9) Reduce real farm income with a consequent demand for ever-increasing farm subsidies.
(10) Reduce international trade and thereby increase the likelihood of war.
(11) Promote centralization at the expense of small communities and perhaps at the expense of national survival in the event of another war.

A Way Out

Before suggesting a way to get the American economy out of the strait jacket into which we are attempting to force it, the writer wishes to state once again that he is not opposed to a minimum wage law and that the above analysis is not to be interpreted as a blanket rejection of the principle of a social minimum.

There is certainly some minimum in a wealthy country below which a family should not be allowed to sink, even though the breadwinner or breadwinners may not be worth it to a private employer. If a minimum wage law helps identify submarginal individuals and groups, the over-all effect may be beneficial. It opens the way for an intelligent diagnosis of the causes for their low productivity and hence for a constructive solution of the underlying problem. A minimum wage is thus a means to an end. Yet, in and of itself, it will cause some unemployment; and unless society is prepared to provide for those thus legislated out of the labor market, their fate may be worse than before. A minimum wage is not a humanitarian measure unless it is supplemented by relief and rehabilitation. Since even a wealthy country cannot afford to support large numbers in idleness or through unneeded public works, the minimum should be related to locally prevailing conditions.

A Suggested Amendment. Ideally, the law should recognize regions as did the WPA program. Originally, four regions were recognized under that program, and dollars-per-month earnings within each region were set by size of community. Communities were classified into five groups: counties with 100,000 population or over; counties with population between 50,000 and 99,999; counties with population between 25,000 and 49,999; counties with population between 5,000 and 24,999; counties with population under 5,000. For counties of the largest size the permitted earnings per month ranged from $55 in Region I, which was made up of the wealthier industrial states, to $30 in Region IV, into which most of the southern states fell. Thus a differential of $25 was recognized. Expressed as a percentage of wages in the high-wage region, the law recognized a differential of over 45%. Large differentials by size of community were also recognized within each region. The maximum differential in Region I in-May, 1935, was $15. Monthly earnings varied from $55 in the largest communities to $40 in the most rural communities. The differential here was around 27%. In Region IV the corresponding permitted dollar earnings per month ranged from $30 in the largest communities to $19 in the smallest. The differential thus exceeded 36%.

Despite the popular opposition, this structure was sound both from the economic and from the social point of view. The Fair Labor Standards Act should be amended to incorporate the same principle. State per capita incomes provide the basis for classifying the states into economic regions. A minimum should be set in each region beginning with the most rural communities and at such a level as not to cause any substantial unemployment; and then step-ups by size of community should be recognized. It is not suggested that the minimum should be set at the absolute lowest wage figure found in an area; it might well be fixed at approximately the wage rate representing the top of the lowest fourth of wage rates found in each community-class. This rate would tend to squeeze out some of the less efficient employers or else force them to discover ways and means of improving their methods.

It is obvious that the recognition of regions of the sort suggested in the preceding paragraph raises difficult issues of a political nature. A tolerable compromise might be to recognize differentials only by size of community. This solution would still involve a differential burden upon the agrarian Southeast which would slow down somewhat but not stop its industrial development.

There is something to be said for such a slowing down, provided it be not serious. The extremely low levels of earnings in southern agriculture would make it possible, if all wage floors were withdrawn, for American capital and know-how to come into the South and secure labor at rates so much below those prevailing in areas where the labor market is tighter and the capital supply more abundant as to cause serious disorganization and unemployment and social suffering in these wealthier areas. The development of the South may proceed on more wholesome lines if it does not proceed too rapidly. It gives the South time to prepare itself politically and emotionally for the new way of life that industrialization involves.

Meantime, the wealthier areas of existing industrial concentration would have more time to provide alternative opportunities for the labor and capital attached to those industries which would naturally tend to gravitate toward the South. Thus, some narrowing of regional wage differentials through government pressures can be defended on broad general grounds in precisely the same way that moderate and stable tariff rates can be defended.

The periodic upward manipulation by government fiat of wage rates in the agrarian South, however, will have the same disastrous effect upon the South's ability to secure and service outside capital as does the periodic raising of tariff rates against the products of poor countries, which have managed to gain access to American capital. The motivation in both cases is protectionist. For the Federal Government to squeeze wage differentials to the vanishing point, at this stage in the South's industrial development, is comparable to the levying of prohibitive tariffs upon products coming from abroad. Just as prohibitive tariffs make the world as a whole poorer and more warlike, so the fiat elimination of geographical wage differentials will make the American economy as a whole poorer, politically and socially more unstable, and more charged with sectional animosities.

This author contends, therefore, that for the long-run advantage, not only of the South but of the country as a whole, the principle of a *uniform* minimum wage should be abandoned. Rather than adopt the proposed amendments to the Fair Labor Standards Act, this country should pass a law setting minimum wage rates for different-size communities. Such a law would recognize economic characteristics of varying geographical regions of the United States. Such a law would be in keeping with the needs of a vigorous and responsible private enterprise system.

Causes of Strikes

Economic Changes and Industrial Unrest in the United States, by Dale Yoder, Journal of Political Economy, Vol. XLVIII, No. 2, April, 1940, pp. 222–237

Strikes Under the Wagner Act, by John V. Spielmans, Journal of Political Economy, Vol. XLIX, No. 5, October, 1941, pp. 722–731

ECONOMIC CHANGES AND INDUSTRIAL UNREST IN THE UNITED STATES

By DALE YODER
University of Minnesota

NUMEROUS hypotheses have been advanced to explain time-to-time fluctuations in industrial unrest in the United States, and efforts have been made to relate such changes to a variety of economic conditions that are regarded as proximate or indirect causes. It has been argued, for instance, that usual evidences of industrial unrest, particularly strikes, reflect fairly accurately the growth of population and the increased numbers of gainfully employed or of industrial wage-earners in the nation. Again, various relationships between business activity, the alternate periods of expansion and contraction in the trade cycle, and numbers of industrial disputes and of workers involved in them have been described. Similarly, current manifestations of industrial unrest are said to reflect the movements of retail or wholesale prices, costs of living, and real wages; and these more or less interrelated conditions are regarded as exerting significant influences on industrial unrest. A number of studies have sought to appraise these alleged relationships and to evaluate the influence of such economic changes on levels of industrial unrest.[1]

In these and other similar studies data describing the frequency of strikes and the time-to-time changes in the numbers of workers who participate in them have been generally accepted as the most satisfactory nation-wide current measures of industrial unrest. It is true, of course, that other evidences of such unrest may be noted. There are, for instance, sample data of labor turnover and of migration, but they describe conditions featuring only limited groups of workers. They may or may not accurately represent the condition of gainfully employed wage-earners as a whole. Strike statistics, on the contrary, are not samples but are inclusive compilations, and they are broadly

[1] See A. H. Hansen, "Cycles of Strikes," *American Economic Review*, XI (December, 1921), 616–21; Paul H. Douglas, "An Analysis of Strike Statistics, 1881–1921," *Journal of the American Statistical Association*, XVIII (September, 1923), 866–77; H. M. Douty, "The Trend of Industrial Disputes, 1922–1930," *Journal of the American Statistical Association*, XXVII (June, 1932), 168–72; John I. Griffin, *Strikes: A Study in Quantitative Economics* (New York, 1939).

representative with respect to industries, occupations, and geographical sections. For these reasons they are distinctly preferable to other quantitative evidence of industrial unrest.

Analysis of the possible positive or negative covariation that may feature these measures of industrial unrest and the various economic conditions assumed to be correlated with them has recently been facilitated by publication of a comprehensive compilation of all nation-wide strike statistics in the files of the Bureau of Labor Statistics for the entire period since collection was first undertaken in 1881.[2] The reports thus summarized, together with revised figures for 1937, reveal annual numbers of strikes for forty-nine years (there being an interval of eight years, from 1906 through 1913, in which no nation-wide compilation was made), and they list numbers of workers involved in strikes for forty-seven years (there being an interval of ten years, from 1906 through 1915, in which no reliable data on this point were collected on a nation-wide basis). These two series, reduced to the form of relatives, are shown in Figure 1, in which they are compared with a number of other series that are frequently assumed to be related to the rise and fall in levels of industrial unrest.[3]

The recent Bureau of Labor Statistics Bulletin No. 651 also reports on numbers of strikes beginning in each month from January, 1915, to the end of 1936, as well as on numbers of workers involved in strikes in each month from January, 1927, to the close of the period. Further, since February, 1927, data are available as to the number of strikes "in progress" in each month, numbers of workers involved in

[2] Florence Peterson, *Strikes in the United States, 1880–1936* (Bureau of Labor Statistics Bull. 651 [Washington, 1938]).

[3] Index numbers of strikes and of workers involved have as their base the average number per year for the three years 1927, 1928, and 1929. No explanation is made by the Bureau of Labor Statistics for the selection of these base years. For strikes the annual average in the base years is 744; for numbers of workers involved in strikes it is 310,907.

Sources of other series included in Figure 1 are as follows: numbers of trade-unionists, from Leo Wolman, *The Growth of American Trade Unions, 1880–1923* (New York, 1924) and *Ebb and Flow in Trade Unionism* (New York, 1936); index of business activity is that of Col. Leonard P. Ayres, of the Cleveland Trust Company; real-wage index from A. H. Hansen, as described in "Some Factors Affecting the Trend of Real Wages," *American Economic Review*, X (March, 1925), 27–48 (it has been extrapolated for recent years by linking with the data provided by the National Industrial Conference Board); general price-level index, from Carl Snyder, as described in his "The Measure of the General Price Level," *Review of Economic Statistics*, X (1928), 40–52.

these strikes, and numbers of man-days idleness occasioned by such strikes in each month.

It will be apparent that, for long-term comparisons, dependence must be be placed on the series describing numbers of strikes beginning

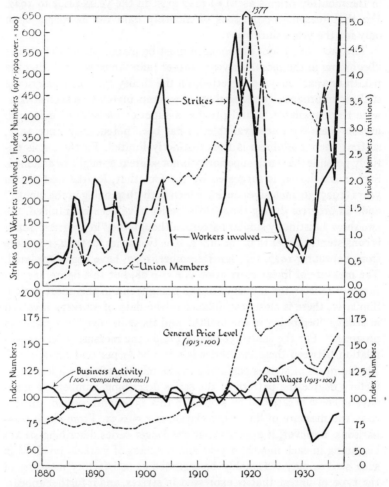

FIG. 1.—Index numbers of strikes, workers involved, and associated economic changes in the United States, 1880–1937. For sources of data see footnote 3 in text.

in each year and numbers of workers involved in these strikes, since these are the only series that extend into the pre-war period. Of the two long series, that describing the number of strikes is available for two years for which no data on numbers of workers involved can be secured. For a much shorter period numbers of strikes beginning in each month are available. Reports of such monthly data begin in 1916, but the Bureau estimates that an error of as much as 10 per cent in the monthly origins ascribed may exist in the years prior to 1927. For that reason, comparisons of monthly data can be relied upon only for the years since 1927.

The fact that major dependence must be placed on data of strikes "beginning in the month or year" rather than "in progress during the month or year" may be regretted, on the theory that data describing strikes "in progress" and numbers of workers involved in such strikes, were they available, would provide a superior measure of industrial unrest. Such data are available, as has been noted, only since 1927, so that their usefulness is thus distinctly limited. Further, it is entirely possible that their superiority is not so great as might be assumed. Such a conclusion is suggested by the fact that, for the first eleven years (1927–36, inclusive) during which both "beginning in the month" and "in progress during the month" series have been maintained, the two show a distinctly similar pattern, although the "in progress" series is consistently larger than the other. The two series for the 131 months from February, 1927, through December, 1937, have been correlated. The measure of linear correlation is $r = 0.98$, but this figure unquestionably reflects the influence of the rising trend in this short period. Similarly, there is close resemblance in the data of workers involved in strikes "beginning in the month" and those involved in strikes "in progress." For the same 131-month period the measure of linear correlation between these two series is $r = 0.88$ (1 per cent limit: 0.20). The numbers of strikes beginning in the month reflect to a less satisfactory degree the pattern of the series describing numbers of man-days idleness occasioned by strikes in this 131-month period. In this case, the measure of linear correlation is $r = 0.54$. From these comparisons, however, it appears that the longer series describing strikes beginning in each month or year and numbers of workers involved in such strikes may reasonably be regarded as satisfactory measures of the type of unrest that is expressed in strikes, and it further appears that these series reflect fairly closely the possibly superior evidence available over the shorter period from the "in progress" series.

The two long series—those representing numbers of strikes beginning in each year and numbers of workers involved in them—follow a somewhat similar course, as may be observed in Figure 1. They have closely related highs, such as those of 1916–19 and of 1937, and they show similar depressions in the years from 1881 to 1886 and from 1927 through 1932. For the forty-seven years for which annual data are available in both series their correlation is measurable as $r = 0.63$ (1 per cent limit: 0.38). Major movements, as is indicated by this measure and may be noted in Figure 1, are generally parallel, although individual year-to-year fluctuations are not closely co-ordinated. Reporting of numbers of strikes is, however, probably more accurate than is that describing numbers of workers involved, so that the former series may represent a generally more dependable index than the latter.

It has been suggested that numbers of strikes and strikers should be adjusted to take account of an expanding population and of increasing numbers of gainfully employed. In effect, such a deflation tends to translate the crude data of strikes and workers involved into adjusted rates or ratios. It has been further suggested that an even more appropriate deflation would adjust these data for changing numbers of "industrial wage-earners," thus eliminating from the category of gainfully employed a number of groups, including agricultural workers, self-employed, domestics, professional classes, and others, whose members seldom participate in industrial disputes.[4] Suggestion has also been made that deflation should take into account the growth of trade-union membership, since labor organization is obviously involved in the majority of strikes. Brief attention may well be given, at this point, to these suggestions.

As a preliminary test of the propriety of such deflation, consideration may be directed to the comparative rates of increase in numbers of strikes, of workers involved, of gainfully employed, and of industrial wage-earners. Actual enumerations of gainfully employed and industrial wage-earners are available in only four years in which numbers of strikes and of workers involved are known (1890, 1900, 1920, and 1930). However, no serious error is introduced by linear interpolation between census enumerations or by simple, least-squares linear trends fitted to the census data. Hence, for a primary comparison, linear trends were fitted to the data of these series, and, although such trends do not appear particularly appropriate for the data of strikes and strikers, least-squares linear trends of these series also were calculated.

[4] The definition of "industrial wage-earners" here and hereafter used is that described by A. H. Hansen in his "Industrial Classes in the United States in 1920," *Journal of the American Statistical Association*, XVII (December, 1922), 79–82.

Each of these trends was then reduced to the form of relatives with the initial year, 1881, as a base.[5]

The comparative rates of increase, as suggested by this method of analysis, are evident from Figure 2, where the four trends thus calculated are plotted. In the fifty-seven-year period strikes, measured in terms of their trend, increased by 43 per cent—from 1,390 in 1881 to 1,977 in 1937.[6] Workers involved, as represented by the trend of this series, increased by 286 per cent—from 277,906 to 1,071,353. Gain-

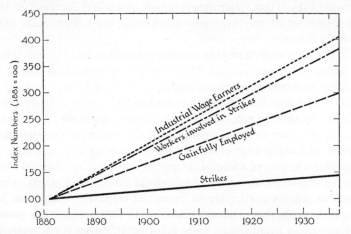

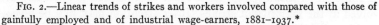

FIG. 2.—Linear trends of strikes and workers involved compared with those of gainfully employed and of industrial wage-earners, 1881–1937.*

* Trend equations are stated in footnote 5 in text.

fully employed increased by 198 per cent of the base level—from 17,899,798 in 1881 to 53,287,222 in 1937. Numbers of industrial wage-earners increased, in this period, by 304 per cent—from 5,326,139 to 21,531,796. It appears from these comparisons that adjustment of the numbers of workers involved in strikes for numbers of industrial wage-earners may have some justification as a means of eliminating one

---

[5] All trends were fitted by the method of least squares. The four trend equations may be summarized as follows: for strikes, $T = 1,390.18 + 10.476x$ (origin, 1881); for workers involved, $T = 277,905.6 + 14,168.7x$ (origin, 1881); for gainfully employed, $T = 33,065,836.5 + 631,918.3x$ (origin, 1905); for industrial wage-earners, $T = 12,271,421 + 289,386.7x$ (origin, 1905).

[6] The linear trend of strikes fitted by Griffin (*op. cit.*) shows an increase of 53 per cent over this period. The difference arises from the fact that he has, by reference to data collected in a few states, interpolated for the years for which no nation-wide data are available.

fairly constant factor in the explanation of changing levels of workers involved in strikes. There is, however, little similarity in the growth of gainfully employed and either numbers of strikes or numbers of workers involved. Numbers of strikes have increased at a much slower rate than that of any of the other series. That they have not kept pace with numbers of workers involved is presumably explained in part by the growing size of industrial units and consequent concentration of employees as well as by the changing nature of labor organizations. These explanations are supported by the increasing average size of strikes over this extensive period.[7] The gradual development of facilities for mediation and conciliation may also be noteworthy in explaining the rate of increase in numbers of strikes.

Such a simple comparison suggests that changing levels of strikes and of workers involved in them cannot be explained merely in terms of population growth and the concomitant shifting of age and occupational groups in the population, and it raises serious question as to the value of adjusting strike data for many of these changes. That conclusion is further supported by analysis in terms of annual numbers of strikes and strikers per thousand gainfully employed or industrial wage-earners. Ratios of this sort have been calculated for each year for which strike data are available, and annual averages for five-year periods from 1881 to 1937 are summarized in Table 1. For convenience, the ratios of strikes have been expressed in terms of thousands of gainfully employed and industrial wage-earners, while those of workers involved are expressed in terms of millions of gainfully employed and industrial wage-earners. In addition to annual averages for these five-year periods, annual averages for the years from 1881 through 1905 are compared with those for the years from 1916 through 1937.

The table indicates clearly the wide range of these ratios, apparent even in these five-year periods. It reflects, also, the growing proportions of industrial wage-earners among the gainfully employed. Thus, for instance, the percentage increase in workers involved per thousand gainfully employed from the 1881–1905 period to the 1916–37 period is 59, while that of workers involved per thousand industrial wage-earners is only 38.5. Ratios of strikes per million gainfully employed compared with those per million industrial wage-earners show the same effect. Comparison of annual averages for the two long periods indicates that strike rates per million gainfully employed decreased by 24.5 per cent. Meanwhile, strike rates per million industrial wage-

[7] Peterson, *op. cit.*, p. 48.

earners decreased by 35.2 per cent. The difference in these declines is
solely attributable to the growing proportions of industrial wage-
earners. Certainly, little in the way of consistency from period to
period or over long periods of time characterizes any of these rates,
so that changes either in numbers of gainfully employed or in numbers
of industrial wage-earners cannot be said to offer great assistance in
explaining the varying numbers of strikes or of workers involved in
them.

TABLE 1

RATIOS OF STRIKES AND WORKERS INVOLVED TO GAINFULLY
EMPLOYED AND INDUSTRIAL WAGE-EARNERS
YEARLY AVERAGES FOR STATED PERIODS

Period	Workers Involved per Thousand Gainfully Employed	Workers Involved per Thousand Industrial Wage-Earners	Strikes per Million Gainfully Employed	Strikes per Million Industrial Wage-Earners
1881–1885.........	9.2	29.7	27.5	88.9
1886–1890.........	16.7	51.1	63.0	191.7
1891–1895.........	14.4	41.6	56.7	164.4
1896–1900.........	13.4	37.3	48.5	134.7
1901–1905.........	18.6	50.3	91.7	249.4
1916–1920.........	48.8	80.3	85.7	220.6
1921–1925.........	25.9	52.5	34.4	87.7
1926–1930.........	6.1	15.3	16.5	41.4
1931–1935.........	17.3	43.0	28.3	70.4
1936–1937.........	24.9	61.8	65.1	64.4
1881–1905.........	14.4	42.0	57.5	169.8
1916–1937.........	22.9	58.2	43.4	110.0

That there is some similarity in the patterns of strikes, strikers, and
union membership is apparent from Figure 1. That would be expected,
of course, for it is clear that organization plays an important part in
most strikes. On the other hand, however, it is notable that numbers
of strikes and strikers show rates of growth distinctly different from
that of union members. Increases in numbers of unionists cannot be
appropriately described by any linear function; they more closely resemble a growth curve. Thus, the average union membership in the
five-year period ending in 1935 was approximately 3,395,000, as compared with an average of 153,600 in the five years beginning in 1881.
If this early period is represented by a relative of 100, the later period

has an index of approximately 2,210. If annual average numbers of strikes are similarly compared, the later period has a relative of 274, while the similar relative for numbers of workers involved is about 500.

It can be said, however, that strikes generally tend to increase in numbers or to continue on high levels in broad periods of expanding labor organization. It may be noted from Figure 1, for instance, that periods of notable increase in numbers of unionists include 1882–86, 1896–1904, 1909–13, 1916–20, and 1933–37. Strikes showed significant increases in the first and second of these periods; there are no nation-wide data of strikes for the third; they continued on a high level in the fourth; and they increased sharply in the last. On the other hand, recessions in unionism show less similarity to changes in numbers of strikes. There were marked reductions in numbers of unionists in 1887–91 and in 1921–32. In the first of these periods numbers of strikes increased. In the second, strikes declined sharply and remained at a very low level. That there is no consistent year-to-year covariation in these movements is also indicated by the measure of linear correlation for annual data of the two series (strikes and union members), $r = -0.02$—an obviously insignificant figure. A similar conclusion is suggested by correlation of numbers of unionists with numbers of workers involved in strikes. In spite of the evident similarity in broad periods of expansion in both series, the measure of linear correlation is $r = 0.38$ (1 per cent limit: 0.38).

Most common among economic conditions believed to be related to numbers of strikes and strikers is what is generally described as business activity. Conclusions as to the precise nature of this relationship vary widely,[8] but probably that most frequently mentioned describes cycles in strikes paralleling the similar cycles in business. Thus, it is said that strikes increase as business expands and that numbers of strikes decline when business recedes or is inactive. Sometimes this covariation is explained as resulting from the fact that real wages may fall in periods of business expansion, because wage rates lag behind prices in the upward movement, and employment (in terms of working hours) fails to expand sufficiently rapidly to overcome this discrepancy.

The data now available facilitate direct long-term comparisons of

[8] See, e.g., Hansen, "Cycle of Strikes," *op. cit.;* Paul H. Douglas, Curtice N. Hitchcock, and Willard E. Atkins, *The Worker in Modern Economic Society* (Chicago, 1925), pp. 619–20; Solomon Blum, *Labor Economics* (New York, 1925), p. 392; Carroll R. Daugherty, *Labor Problems in American Industry* (Boston, 1933), p. 359.

numbers of strikes and strikers with changes in business activity and accompanying fluctuations in real wages and in prices. Data representing all these conditions have been included in Figure 1, so that patterns of year-to-year change may be graphically compared.

A preliminary consideration of the extent to which fluctuations in numbers of strikes resemble those of business activity may well consider the usual seasonal patterns of these two series. In Figure 3

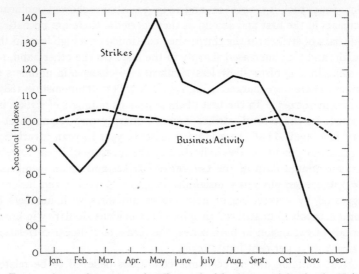

FIG. 3.—Seasonal patterns of strikes and of business activity in the United States.*

* Indexes of seasonality n business activity from Simon Kuznets, *Seasonal Variations in Industry and Trade* (New York, 1933); indexes of seasonality in strikes from Dale Yoder, "Seasonality in Strikes," *Journal of the American Statistical Association*, XXXIII (December, 1938), 687–93.

Kuznets' seasonal relatives of business activity are paralleled by seasonal indexes of strikes. The latter have been calculated by the ratio-to-moving-average method from the data of strikes beginning in each month of the ten-year period from January, 1927, through December, 1936.[9]

A certain superficial similarity of pattern may be observed. December, for example, is the low month in both series, and both strikes and business activity decline in November and December. But there

[9] Indexes of seasonality in business activity from Simon Kuznets, *Seasonal Variations in Industry and Trade* (New York, 1933); indexes of seasonality in strikes from Dale Yoder, "Seasonality in Strikes," *Journal of the American Statistical Association*, XXXIII (December, 1938), 687–93.

is an increase in strikes in summer months in contrast to the usual summer decline in business. Normally, business activity expands in the spring before strikes become numerous, and it experiences a late summer and fall pickup that is not reflected in numbers of strikes. A simple ranking coefficient of correlation for the items of the two series may be found as $r_r = -0.05$—a measure so low as to speak clearly for their haphazard covariation.

Attention may next be directed to a comparison of long-time changes in these series. Figure 1 shows annual indexes of business activity (their base is a computed normal), which may be compared directly with index numbers of strikes and strikers based on 1881 = 100, also included in the figure. Prevailing levels of strikes in each year as well as notable changes featuring particular years should probably be compared with levels of business activity and with changes in business activity from immediately preceding years. This process of comparison is difficult, however, for no simple relationship is apparent. To aid in the discovery of possible relationships, Table 2 has been prepared. There, four groups of years have been selected as representing various phases in the movement of strikes. In the first group years marked by sharp increases in numbers of strikes are included, while the second group represents years of marked declines in numbers of strikes. The third and fourth groups include years of high levels of strikes and years of low levels, respectively. For each year in these groups two measures of business activity were considered. First, the index of business activity was described as a deviation above or below normal. Second, the percentage change from the preceding year was noted. The years included in each of the four groups are listed in the footnotes to the table.

Results of the comparisons thus effected are not conclusive, but certain differences among the various groups of years stand out fairly clearly. Thus, for instance, when the first two groups of years (those in which numbers of strikes showed sharp increases or sharp declines) are compared, averages indicate that years in which strikes increased sharply have been featured by only a slight negative deviation from the normal of business activity (-0.75), while those in which strikes declined sharply averaged 2.42 points below that normal. Even more notable is the contrast in percentage changes in business activity from immediately preceding years. The group marked by sharp increases in strikes shows an average rise of 5.8 per cent in business activity, as contrasted with an average decline of 2.73 per cent for the years in which strikes were reduced abruptly.

When periods characterized by high and low levels of strikes are compared, it appears that the prevailing condition of business as well as its fluctuations may be reflected in industrial unrest. For the nine-

TABLE 2

NUMBERS OF STRIKES COMPARED WITH BUSINESS ACTIVITY
REAL WAGES, AND THE GENERAL PRICE LEVEL
IN SELECTED YEARS

	YEARS CHARACTERIZED BY—			
	Sharp Increases in Strikes* (I)	Sharp Decreases in Strikes† (II)	High Levels of Strikes‡ (III)	Low Levels of Strikes§ (IV)
Business Activity: Average deviation from normal..................	−0.75	−2.42	+0.89	−2.86
Business Activity: Average percentage change from preceding year.....	+5.80	−2.73	−0.30	−1.70
Real Wages: Average percentage change from preceding year.....	+2.70	+1.63	+1.80	+1.45
General Price Level: Average percentage change from preceding year.....	+6.20	−0.79	+3.56	−1.04

* Years selected as representing sharp increases in strikes include 1886, 1890, 1899, 1901, 1916, 1917, 1933, 1937.

† Years selected as representing sharp decreases in strikes include 1888, 1892, 1896, 1904, 1905, 1918, 1921, 1922, 1924, 1926, 1927, 1930.

‡ Years selected as representing high levels of strikes include 1886, 1887, 1890, 1891, 1899, 1900, 1901, 1902, 1903, 1904, 1905, 1916, 1917, 1918, 1919, 1920, 1921, 1936, 1937.

§ Years selected as representing low levels of strikes include 1881, 1882, 1883, 1884, 1885, 1888, 1896, 1897, 1898, 1914, 1915, 1922, 1923, 1924, 1925, 1926, 1927, 1928, 1929, 1930, 1931, 1932.

teen years selected as representing high levels of strikes, business activity averaged 0.89 points above the computed normal. For the twenty-two years representing low levels of strikes, business activity averaged 2.86 points below normal. Comparison of these two groups of years on the basis of percentage changes from preceding years is less impressive, probably because the periods selected as representing high and low levels frequently included numerous consecutive years,

so that variation was typically small. High-level years are characterized by an average change of −0.3 per cent, as contrasted with an
average change of −1.7 per cent for low-level years. Thus strikes appear to remain on high levels when business is holding its ground or
declining only slightly, and they remain at low levels when business
is receding.

This analysis would appear to justify the conclusion that, while business conditions are reflected in strikes, there is no simple pattern of
covariation. Strikes appear generally to increase when business is expanding rapidly from unusually low levels. They decrease when business is declining or when it holds on somewhat subnormal levels.
They are numerous in years when business is fairly steady and good,
and they are less frequent when business is receding and is notably
poor. No simple covariation such as might be measured by linear correlation is observable. For the forty-nine years for which numbers of
strikes are available, the linear measure of correlation between annual
data of strikes and indexes of business activity is $r = 0.11$ (1 per cent
limit: 0.36). If monthly data are correlated, the measure for the 276
months from 1915 through 1937 is $r = 0.16$ (1 per cent limit: 0.15).
From these calculations it is apparent that no significant covariation
in month-to-month or year-to-year fluctuations can be depended upon.

These results are not appreciably changed if numbers of workers
involved in strikes are substituted for numbers of strikes in these
comparisons. For instance, the measure of correlation for annual numbers of workers involved and business activity for the forty-seven-
year period for which these data are available is $r = -0.14$.[10]

The data represented by Figure 1 also permit similar comparisons
of changes in numbers of strikes and strikers with fluctuations in real
wages and in the price level. These series are, of course, not entirely
unrelated to business activity. Some similarity in their patterns, especially in the years since 1930, is apparent in the figure. It may be
noted, however, that there is greater resemblance between the series
representing the general price level and that of real wages than between either of these and the indexes of business activity. The chart
also evidences numerous divergences among all these series, and this
characteristic is apparent in measures of their intercorrelation. For
the correlation of real wages and the general price level, the measure

---

[10] Numerous experiments in lagging one of the series disclosed no such adjustment that provided a significant coefficient of correlation.

is $r = 0.79$ (1 per cent limit: 0.34). For that of business activity and real wages it is $r = -0.34$; for business activity and the general price level it is $r = -0.22$.

Data of real wages and of prices have been subjected to analysis similar to that applied to indexes of business activity and described in preceding paragraphs, and the results of this analysis have been included in the lower portion of Table 2. Items of the two series were expressed as percentage changes from preceding years, since it is these changes that are generally regarded as of major significance and because there is no computed normal with which to compare them. Results of the analysis may be summarized briefly, although they are fairly evident in the table. Years of marked increases in strikes show the highest average percentage increase in real wages, appreciably higher than do the years in which strikes declined sharply. At the same time the first group of years is featured by a notable average increase of 6.2 per cent in the price level, while the years of sharp declines in strikes have an average decrease of 0.79 per cent in prices. Somewhat similarly, high-level strike periods show an average increase in real wages (1.8 per cent) and an average increase in prices of 3.56 per cent, while years representing low levels of strikes show a slightly smaller increase in real wages (1.45 per cent) and an average decline in prices of 1.04 per cent. The data thus provide some support for Hansen's conclusions as to the covariation of strikes and prices.

As a further check on similarities and differences in these series, both real-wage indexes and those of the general price level have been correlated with annual data of strikes. For real wages and strikes the measure of linear correlation is $r = 0.15$ (1 per cent limit: 0.34). For real wages and numbers of workers involved in strikes the measure is $r = 0.22$. When monthly data of real wages and strikes are correlated for the 132 months from January, 1927, through December, 1937, $r = 0.47$ (1 per cent limit: 0.20). It is possible that the data of the recent period are distinctly more inclusive and reliable, and this covariation may well be investigated further as data accumulate.

As in the case of real wages and strikes, the measure of linear correlation provides little significant evidence of covariation in strikes and prices. While distinctive periods, as far as strikes are concerned, appear to be featured by fairly consistent price tendencies, correlation of annual indexes of prices with numbers of strikes discloses an insignificant measure. For the forty-nine years $r = 0.18$ (1 per cent limit:

0.36). It is apparent, therefore, that the tendencies observed in the averaging process employed in the calculations upon which Table 2 is based are not such as can be verified by the usual measure of linear correlation.

It must be recognized that the conclusions suggested by the comparisons made in preceding pages are of varying reliability, some being quite positive, others equally negative, and many highly tentative. It is clear, for instance, that strikes have not increased in the same proportions as have the gainfully employed, nor has their rate of increase closely approximated that of industrial wage-earners. Numbers of workers involved in strikes, however, have increased in proportions somewhat similar to those of industrial wage-earners. Numbers of union members have increased far more rapidly than either strikes or strikers. There is, however, a tendency for strikes to show marked increases in numbers in periods when labor organization is expanding rapidly, and there is a less persistent tendency for strikes to decline as union membership is reduced.

Numbers of strikes and workers involved unquestionably reflect the influence of changes in business activity. There is, however, no simple parallelism. Only a slight superficial similarity characterizes seasonal patterns. In longer periods there is evidence of a tendency for strikes to increase in periods of sharp expansion in business activity and a less clear-cut tendency for strikes to decline abruptly when business is receding. High-level years of strikes show little average change in business activity from year to year, but low-level strike periods are, on the average, years of declining business and those in which activity is below normal. The pattern of fluctuations in strikes is, therefore, different from that of the usual trade cycle. Typically, strikes increase in the early part of the recovery phase of the trade cycle. When business levels off in the the prosperity phase, numbers of strikes decline. When business recession begins, they may show further declines, and they tend to remain at low levels during the depression phase.

No simple relationship between strikes and real wages is apparent from the analysis presented here, although allowance should be made for the major limitation of all real-wage indexes, i.e., the fact that they refer only to changes in the purchasing power of employed workers and do not make adequate allowance for the highly important influence of unemployment on family incomes. Available data, however, appear to show that years characterized by sharp increases in strikes are those in which real wages have increased most abruptly, while years of low strike levels are those in which real wages advanced least. It is evident from Table 2, however, that the differences between the various periods described there are not great. Reflections of changing prices are somewhat more significant. Strikes appear to increase sharply in years characterized by rapid price advances or to remain at high levels in such years. They decline when prices are fairly constant or receding slightly. Years of increasing prices are likely to be featured by relatively high levels of strikes, while low levels of strikes are characteristic of years in which prices are falling. None of these relationships is highly consistent, however. They are evident only in comparisons of averages for distinctive strike periods.

STRIKES UNDER THE WAGNER ACT

By JOHN V. SPIELMANS

Washington, D. C.

HOW is the Wagner Act affecting strikes? Is it advancing or hindering the cause of industrial peace? The question is frequently raised but apparently not easily answered, even by specialists. Thus, when Chairman Smith of the House Committee investigating the National Labor Relations Board pointed out that there had been more strikes between 1935 and 1939 than in any period since 1921, Chairman Madden of the N.L.R.B. answered that fewer workers were involved in the 1938 strikes than in any year since 1932 and that fewer man-hours were lost in the two years (1938 and 1939) following the validation of the Wagner Act in 1937 than in the two preceding years (1936 and 1937).[1]

There are, no doubt, many ways of combining and comparing strike figures so as to obtain, in perfectly good faith, one result or its opposite, unless a definite method of comparison is first agreed upon: e.g., to use the number of strikes as a measure of the number of disputes arising in a given period; the number of workers involved as an indicator of the extent and hence of the industrial importance of the disputes; and the number of man-hours as a measure of the losses resulting both to industry and to the workers (or perhaps also as an indicator of the effectiveness of the existing machinery for settlement of disputes).

But even if one were to make a more uniform approach and trace consistently the number of strikes, of workers involved, and of man-hours lost since the operation of the Wagner Act in comparison to the preceding period, but little light would be shed thereby on the effect of the Wagner Act. For—this is our contention—it is only certain well-defined kinds of strikes which the Wagner Act can and may be expected to diminish; others which, through no fault of the Act, it may for the time being tend to increase; and, finally, many others which cannot reasonably be associated with effects of the Wagner Act at all. Unless these various kinds of strikes are studied separately instead of being lumped together in strike totals, nothing much can be achieved

[1] *Hearing before the Special House Committee Investigating the Activities of the N.L.R.B.*, January 31, 1940; reported in the *New York Times*, February 1, 1940.

in the way of discovering what may safely be interpreted as the influence of the Wagner Act.

Now, the Wagner Act, as also the several similar state labor relations acts sometimes referred to as "Little Wagner Acts,"[2] outlaw as "unfair labor practices," interference with the workers' right to organize and refusal to bargain collectively; and they provide labor relations boards to adjudicate disputes over these rights. Where, therefore, a Wagner act takes effect, employers ought gradually to cease to interfere with the workers' right to organize and come to bargain with them collectively, and labor ought to submit disputes over alleged unfair labor practices more and more to the labor relations boards instead of going on strike over them. For both these reasons ever fewer strikes ought to occur over the right to organize and bargain collectively in industries under the jurisdiction of a labor relations act—federal or state. That is, the immediate peace-promoting influence of these acts must be sought in the reduction of strikes over "Wagner Act issues" in "Wagner Act industries"—let us call them briefly, even though somewhat paradoxically, "Wagner Act strikes"—not, however, of strikes over other issues or in other industries.

Or is this taking too narrow a view? Should one not expect that with the growth of collective bargaining, the promotion of which is, after all, the chief purpose of the Wagner Act, disputes over wages and hours, or perhaps all kinds of disputes, will come to be settled more and more through negotiations in connection with agreements, and that, therefore, all other strikes ought to diminish as well? Could one not, in fact, point to the Railroad Labor Act[3] as having indeed succeeded in reducing all kinds of railroad strikes almost to the vanishing point?

To answer this last argument first: the peace-promoting powers of the Railroad Labor Act are very different from those of the Wagner Act. It not merely guarantees labor's right to organize and bargain collectively, but in addition it provides the most complete and effective machinery for the adjustment of all kinds of labor disputes in the railroad industries: mandatory joint boards of carriers and workers' representatives, culminating in the National Railroad Adjustment Board to settle all grievances and quasi-judicial disputes arising under existing

---

[2] *Massachusetts Laws of 1937*, c. 436; *New York Laws of 1937*, c. 443; *Pennsylvania Laws of 1937*, No. 294, amended by Act 162 (1939); *Wisconsin Statutes*, c. 111, State Labor Relations Act of 1937, amended by Employment Peace Act of 1939; *Utah Laws of 1937*, c. 55.

[3] H.R. 9861, Public No. 442 (73d Cong., 1934).

agreements, and the National Mediation Board with broad powers to intervene and assist in the settlement of disputes over the terms of new agreements.[4] The Wagner Act, on the other hand, applying as it does to all kinds of private industries otherwise largely removed from governmental control, merely guarantees labor's right to organize and bargain collectively but does not provide any adjustment machinery for the smooth and uninterrupted functioning of industry under this setup. Only the private adjustment machinery provided in agreements or the purely voluntary federal or state conciliation service are, in general, available for this purpose.[5]

Left to the interested parties, however, collective bargaining may well lead to strikes of far larger proportions than are apt to occur in a nonorganized state of industry. In fact, strike figures for some countries with reputedly well-functioning trade-unionism, such as Sweden and Denmark, show that in those countries the man-days per worker lost through strikes have for years been greater than in the United States, where trade-unionism was still fighting for recognition.[6] Hence, strikes over wages and hours and other specific working conditions, against which the Wagner Act has no provisions whatever, and which, per se, might increase with the growth of collective bargaining while otherwise fluctuating with the fluctuating fortunes of industry, cannot be expected to diminish in consequence of the Wagner Act.

Besides, there are strikes which are likely to increase, not really because of the Wagner Act, but because of its limited scope—namely, strikes over the right to organize and bargain collectively in industries outside the jurisdiction of "Wagner acts"—federal or state—where la-

[4] *Ibid.*, secs. 3 and 5.

[5] In recent years a number of states have passed new mediation laws with certain compulsory features: In New York and Pennsylvania the respective boards and commissions may proffer mediation on their own initiative and hold public hearings with power to subpoena witnesses but with no power of compulsion as regards the disputing parties (Act on Mediation of Labor Disputes, *Laws of New York, 1937*, c. 594, par. 753; Pennsylvania Labor Mediation Act, *Laws of Pennsylvania, 1937*, No. 177, sec. 7). In Minnesota and Michigan notices of intention to strike or lockout must be given to the respective mediation boards, and no strike or lockout may be resorted to within a fixed period after such notice, during which the board is to investigate and attempt settlement of the dispute: five days in Michigan, ten days in Minnesota, and thirty days in both states for industries affected with a public interest (Minnesota Labor Relations Act, 1939, secs. 6 and 7; Michigan Labor Mediation Act [Public Act No. 176 (1939)], sec. 17.454[9–13]).

[6] According to figures calculated from *I.L.O.* (Yearbook of Labor Statistics, Geneva, 1938), Tables III and XXIX.

bor is likely to demand this right with added insistence because it is guaranteed in the majority of other industries but not in their own industry.

For all these reasons an insight into the effect of the Wagner acts on strikes can be gained only by tracing separately the trends of the various kinds of strikes classified both with regard to issues and to Wagner Act jurisdiction.

With this purpose in view we turn to the strike statistics of the United States Bureau of Labor Statistics, the most complete and most authoritative source available.[7] Here we find analyzed month by month all strikes of which the Bureau obtains knowledge, classified: by industries; by states; by industrial groups relative to states; by major issues; by duration; by methods of settlement; by results; and by results relative to issues.

We begin with the classification of strike issues. Of these there are listed three main groups: wages and hours; union organization; and miscellaneous (comprising partly intraunion, i.e., jurisdictional and rival union disputes, sympathy strikes, and a large class of perhaps more truly miscellaneous character called "others"). For a first rough orientation let us glance at the trends of these several classes of strikes during the last fifteen years.[8]

Figure 1 shows unmistakably a great wave of strikes of all kinds, but in particular of strikes over union organization, beginning to rise about 1933, reaching a threatening peak in 1937, and, while falling off sharply in 1938, on the whole still fluctuating well above the former level.

It would be idle not to connect this great strike wave causally with the New Deal, with its promise and far-flung legislative efforts to lend support to labor in its struggle against poverty and insecurity, following the harrowing years of the depression. But it would be rash to interpret this strike wave at once as a proof of the unhappy effects of the Wagner Act.

We turn next to the further analysis of the organization strikes,

[7] *Monthly Labor Review*, monthly reports on industrial disputes.

[8] Here and in the following graphs only the number of strikes per year is shown, not the number of workers involved and of man-hours lost. For, as regards the question under consideration, the number of instances in which, Wagner acts notwithstanding, disputes over the right to organize lead to strikes seems of prime importance. The figures up to 1936 are taken from *U.S. Bureau of Labor Statistics, Bull. 651, Strikes in the United States, 1880–1936*, p. 39, Table 18; p. 61, Table 28. The figures for 1937–39 are taken from the annual strike summaries in the *Monthly Labor Review*, May issues, 1938–40.

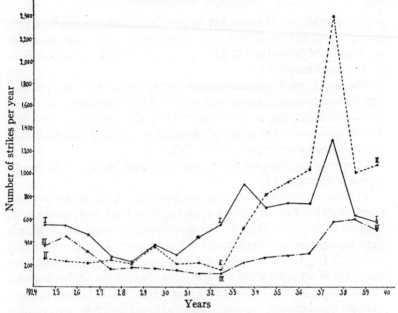

FIG. 1.—Strikes by issues, 1924–39: *I*, wages and hours; *II*, union organization; and *III*, "miscellaneous."

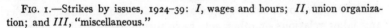

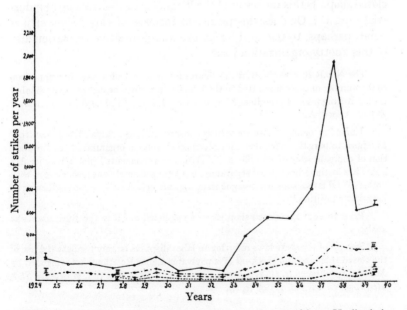

FIG. 2.—Organization strikes by issues, 1924–39: *I*, recognition; *II*, discrimination; *III*, closed shop; *IV*, "others."

which include the "Wagner Act strikes," although not nearly all organization strikes are Wagner Act strikes (as has sometimes been presumed, of late, following a line of argumentation used by the N.L.R.B. in its annual reports).[9]

The issues listed separately under union organization are: recognition (in isolation and coupled with wage and hour demands), the closed shop, discrimination, and "others."[10] Of these, only recognition and discrimination refer to "unfair labor practices" under Wagner acts, but not the closed shop or presumably "others."

By separating these several organization issues we obtain the results shown in Figure 2.

This reveals several interesting developments. First, strikes over the closed shop have about trebled since the New Deal, and, most likely, because of the New Deal.[11] The governmental guaranty of labor's right to organize and bargain collectively under the "majority rule," first according to section 7A of the National Recovery Act and later under the Wagner acts, has apparently intensified the further demand of the unions for the closed union shop. For—so the unions argue—workers who benefit by union contracts should be made to pay union dues. Disputes over this issue, however, not being adjudicable under any labor relations or other act, have meant more strikes over the closed shop. Is this the result of the Wagner acts' "stirring up of industrial unrest"? Or does this persistent increase of closed-shop strikes point, perhaps, to the need for an eventual legislative regulation also of this knotty organization issue?[12]

[9] The N.L.R.B. uses the Bureau's figures for organization strikes in comparison to the number of cases submitted to the Board to measure the degree to which labor is substituting resort to the Board for strikes (*N.L.R.B.*, *Third* [and *Fourth*] *Annual Report*, Appen. A).

[10] Under "recognition" are apparently subsumed all such "unfair labor practices" as refusal to bargain collectively, interference with union organization, and promotion of company-controlled unions. "Violation of agreements" (not a Wagner Act issue) has at times been listed separately, but later seemingly has been merged with "others." Of late a somewhat vague issue appears occasionally—"strengthening of bargaining position."

[11] Prior to 1927 the closed-shop issue is not listed at all in the Bureau's strike analysis.

[12] Several of the state laws referring to labor disputes largely regulate the use of the closed shop and the check-off (Pennsylvania Labor Relations Act, amended by Act 162, 1939, sec. 6 [c, f]; Wisconsin Employment Relations Act, *Wisconsin Statutes, 1939*, c. 111, sec. 111.06 [c, i]).

Strikes over antiunion discrimination, on the other hand, do not show a similar increase. After a marked rise under the N.R.A. these strikes have, on the whole, fallen off since 1935 without even taking part in the tidal wave of 1937. This, it is true, cannot at once be taken to mean that the old, ruggedly individualistic custom of firing and blacklisting workers for union activity is fast disappearing, for the reports of the various labor relations boards, national and state, show year after year thousands of complaints over discrimination. But together these two facts show that labor is defending itself against discrimination largely through the quasi-judicial machinery of the labor relations boards, where available, rather than through strikes, an undeniably fortunate effect of the Wagner acts, both for labor and for industry.

But what can one say about the tumultuous wave of recognition strikes which remains after the other organization issues have been deducted? An initial strong increase of such strikes was, of course, to be expected, especially as long as the constitutional and jurisdictional standing of the N.L.R.A. was doubtful, and the machinery of the N.L.R.B., operating uncertainly and under great friction, was as yet unfamiliar to labor. But why should not these strikes, the very kind which the Wagner Act was designed to render unnecessary, finally subside, five years after the passing and three years after the validation of the act? For, the sharp decline in 1938 notwithstanding, the level of recognition strikes is seen still to be about three to four times higher than before the New Deal.[13]

As a matter of fact, we have not yet carried our analysis far enough. For the strike figures used above refer to all industries, whether covered by labor relations acts or not. In industries outside Wagner Act jurisdiction, however, strikes over union recognition are a very different matter. As pointed out before, such strikes may well be expected to increase, simply because the guaranty of the right to organize in most industries can hardly fail to intensify this demand also in the remaining industries where Congress could not, and the state legislatures would not, guarantee the same right.

Hence, if the Bureau's figures for recognition strikes were broken up

[13] Nor must it be forgotten that, in addition to the disputes over union recognition resulting in strikes, there are thousands of others every year submitted to labor relations boards, so that the number of instances in which employers, at least allegedly, refuse to recognize the unions is several times larger than the number of strikes over this issue.

by industries within and without Wagner Act jurisdiction, two distinct
trends might appear: a falling trend for industries under labor relations
acts, which trend, if sufficiently marked, would be the desired proof
that the Wagner acts are achieving the effect on industrial relations for
which they were designed; and a rising trend for industries without
benefit of labor relations acts, which trend, in our opinion, would reveal
nothing so much as the need for more "Little Wagner Acts." If, on the
other hand, it were to show that the recognition strikes in Wagner Act
industries have failed to diminish, this would be proof that, to say the
least, industry is slow in complying with the law of the land and that,
unless the expected decrease in these strikes takes place in the near
future, the Wagner acts' effect as pacifiers of industry must as yet be
regarded as negative.

Accordingly, we turn to the Bureau's strike analysis by industries.
Following the several jurisdictional decisions of the Supreme Court, the
Bureau has grouped industries into those falling under the jurisdiction
of the N.L.R.A. and those falling wholly or partly outside it. And
while this classification puts industries under "Little Wagner Acts," so
to speak, on the wrong side of the fence, it might yet serve our purpose
well enough.

But, unfortunately, the strike classification by industries does not
separate strike issues. It lumps together strikes over union recognition
with wage-hour strikes, with strikes over the closed shop, over jurisdictional and rival union, and over a host of "miscellaneous" and "other"
disputes. What then can we do to distil out of these figures the effect
which we are trying to discover—the comparison between recognition
strikes in industries within and without Wagner Act jurisdiction?

The N.L.R.B. has tried to make this comparison by using the strike
totals as given.[14] On first thought one might accept this procedure as
logical. For—it might be said—as regards other than Wagner Act issues no difference in strike trends is to be expected for industries within
and without Wagner Act jurisdiction; hence, what differences are found
may be ascribed to the influence of the Wagner Act. The figures so
obtained[15] are shown in Figure 3.

[14] M. Weiss, "Savings Resulting from the Effective Operation of the National
Labor Relations Act in 1938 as Compared to the Cost of Its Operation," *N.L.R.B.
Report*, June 15, 1939.

[15] By summation of industries within and without the jurisdiction of the N.L.R.B.
from the annual strike summaries, *Monthly Labor Review*, May issues, 1936–40.
(The above-mentioned *Report* of the N.L.R.B. compares the figures for 1937 and
1938 only.)

The N.L.R.B. has made much of the relatively steeper decrease from 1937 to 1938 in the number and extent of strikes in industries under the N.L.R.A. which (without mentioning the corresponding steeper increase from 1936 to 1937) it has proclaimed as revealing the beneficial effect of the validated Wagner Act.[16] A little scrutiny of the industries involved, however, raises grave doubt as to the conclusiveness of the whole argument. Thus, according to the Bureau's strike analysis by industries, one of the chief contributors to the 1937 strikes in intrastate industries is the building and construction industry, long strongly unionized and with a well-established tradition of collective bargaining, where Wagner Act issues can hardly play any role but where the strikes concern wages and hours. Altogether, any large wage movement, any large closed-shop movement, in any industry within or without Wagner Act jurisdiction, may completely alter the relative trends of all strikes in the two classes of industries—wherefore the whole method of comparison seems of little value.

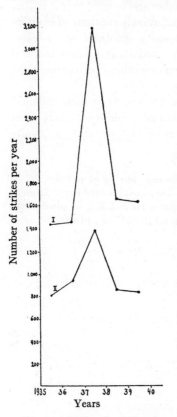

Fig. 3.—Strikes in industries within and without Wagner Act jurisdiction, 1935-39: *I*, within; *II*, without.

What is, therefore, needed to bare the effect of the Wagner acts on strikes is an additional cross-classification in the strike analysis of the Bureau of Labor Statistics, separating strikes classified by issues into those within and without jurisdiction of a "Wagner Act"—federal or state. Only such cross-classification can reveal whether and to what extent strikes over the right to organize and bargain collectively are

[16] Weiss, *op. cit.*, p. 4, Table A. The figures arrived at are these: Between 1937 and 1938 the number of strikes in industries under the N.L.R.A. fell by 48 per cent; the number of workers involved by 66 per cent; that of man-days idle by 71 per cent. For industries outside the N.L.R.A. the number of strikes fell by 29 per cent; that of

diminishing where they clearly ought to diminish: namely, in industries where a labor relations act has laid down the law in the matter and where labor relations boards stand ready to adjudicate such disputes as arise. And it would show separately whether and to what extent strikes over the right to organize and bargain collectively continue or even increase where they have very good reason to continue or increase: namely, in industries left without labor relations acts where labor, if faced with stubborn employers, can often do nothing better than fight for its right to organize through strikes.

Without the possibility of separating the trends of these different kinds of strikes there can only be obtained a blurred picture from which, so far at least, there cannot be read with certainty a definite influence of the Wagner Act on strikes.

---

workers involved by 52 per cent; that of man-days idle by 51 per cent. These figures have been widely quoted in the press. They are also cited in the *Minority Report of the Special House Committee Investigating the N.L.R.B.* as proof of the effectiveness of the Act (H.R. 1902, Part II, p. 43 [76th Cong., 3d sess.]).

Extent and Nature of Collective Bargaining

Extent of Collective Bargaining and Union Recognition, 1946, Monthly Labor Review, Vol. 64, No. 5, May, 1947, pp. 765–769

The Organized Business in America, by Neil Chamberlain, Journal of Political Economy, Vol. LII, No. 2, June, 1944, pp. 97–111

EXTENT OF COLLECTIVE BARGAINING
AND UNION RECOGNITION, 1946[1]

Union Agreement Coverage

APPROXIMATELY 14.8 million workers were employed under conditions determined by written collective-bargaining agreements in 1946, an increase of 1 million workers compared with 1945. The workers covered by agreement represent 48 percent of the 31 million [2] engaged in occupations in which the unions have been organizing and endeavoring to obtain written agreements. The percentage covered was the same in 1945, but fewer workers—approximately 29 million—were eligible for agreement coverage in that year. Nonmanufacturing industries accounted for much of the increase in employees eligible for agreement coverage.

About 7.9 million production workers in manufacturing were covered by union agreements in 1946 (69 percent of those employed) compared to 8 million (67 percent) a year earlier. In the nonmanufacturing industries 6.9 million workers, or 35 percent of the potentials were employed under union agreements. Part of the decrease in total coverage in the manufacturing industries can be accounted for by reduction in employment in such industries as aircraft and shipbuilding, in which a large proportion of the workers are covered by union agreement. In the nonmanufacturing industries the increase in the number of workers can be accounted for by higher employ-

---

[1] Prepared in the Bureau's Industrial Relations Branch with Philomena Marquardt in immediate charge of assembling the information.

For similar data for previous years, see Monthly Labor Review, April 1946, April 1945, April 1944, February 1943, May 1942, and March 1939.

[2] This estimate of 31 million includes all wage and salary workers except those in executive, managerial, and some professional positions, but excludes all self-employed, domestic workers, agricultural wage workers on farms employing less than 6 persons, Federal and State government employees, teachers, and elected or appointed officials in local governments.

It should be noted that the number of workers covered by union agreements is not the same as union membership. Except under closed- or union-shop conditions, agreements cover nonmembers as well as members employed within the given bargaining unit. On the other hand, some union members may be working in unorganized plants and many civil-service employees and teachers are members of unions but are not employed under the terms of bilateral written agreements.

ment in such industries as construction, in which the proportion of workers covered by collective bargaining is very high.

The extent of union agreement coverage in the various manufacturing and nonmanufacturing industries is shown in table 1.

TABLE 1.—*Proportion of wage earners under union agreements in 1946*

MANUFACTURING INDUSTRIES

80-100 percent	60-79 percent	40-59 percent	20-39 percent	1-19 percent
Agricultural equipment. Aircraft and parts. Aluminum. Automobiles and parts. Breweries. Carpets and rugs, wool. Cement. Clocks and watches. Clothing, men's. Clothing, women's. Electrical machinery. Furs and garments. Glass and glassware. Leather tanning. Meat packing. Newspaper printing and publishing. Nonferrous metals and products, except those listed. Rayon yarn. Rubber. Shipbuilding. Steel, basic Sugar.	Book and job printing and publishing. Coal products. Canning and preserving foods. Dyeing and finishing textiles. Gloves, leather. Machinery, except agricultural equipment and electrical machinery. Millinery and hats. Paper and pulp. Petroleum refining. Railroad equipment. Steel products. Tobacco. Woolen and worsted textiles.	Baking. Chemicals, excluding rayon yarn. Flour and other grain products. Furniture. Hosiery. Jewelry and silverware. Knit goods. Leather, luggage, handbags, novelties. Lumber. Paper products. Pottery, including chinaware. Shoes, cut stock and findings. Stone and clay products, except pottery.	Beverages, nonalcoholic. Confectionery products. Cotton textiles. Dairy products. Silk and rayon textiles.	(None.)

NONMANUFACTURING

80-100 percent	60-79 percent	40-59 percent	20-39 percent	1-19 percent
Actors and musicians. Airline pilots and mechanics. Bus and streetcar, local. Coal mining. Construction. Longshoring. Maritime. Metal mining. Motion-picture production. Railroads. Telegraph. Trucking, local and intercity.	Radio technicians. Theater-stage hands, motion-picture operators.	Bus lines, intercity. Light and power. Newspaper offices. Telephone.	Barber shops. Building servicing and maintenance. Cleaning and dyeing. Crude petroleum and natural gas. Fishing. Hotels and restaurants. Laundries. Nonmetallic mining and quarrying. Taxicabs.	Agriculture.[1] Beauty shops. Clerical and professional, excluding transportation, communication, theaters and newspapers. Retail and wholesale trade.

[1] Less than 1 percent.

Extent of Union Recognition by Types [3]

Approximately 4.8 million workers were covered by closed- and union-shop with preferential hiring provisions in 1946, compared to 4.25 millions in 1945. Union-shop clauses, without preference in

---

[3] For definitions of types of union recognition see footnote to table 3.

hiring, were specified for almost 2.6 million workers in 1946 and 2 million in 1945. The number of workers covered by maintenance-of-membership decreased from more than 3.9 millions in 1945 to 3.6 million in 1946.

Table 2 indicates the changes in the proportion of workers under each type of union recognition from 1941 through 1946. During the war there was a major shift from sole bargaining and bargaining for members only, to maintenance of membership. The 1946 figures indicate a change from the latter type, and to the union or closed shop.

Table 3 lists the industries in which at least half of the workers who are under agreement are covered by the type of union recognition specified.

A few industries (such as shipbuilding and iron and steel products) which were listed in the 1945 report do not appear in the present report because 50 percent of the workers in those industries are no longer covered by any type of recognition clause. Carpets and rugs and woolen and worsted were both listed under maintenance of membership in 1945 but in 1946 over half of the workers in those industries who were covered by union agreements were under union-shop provisions.

The most marked change has taken place in the automobile industry. In 1945 over half of the covered workers were under maintenance-of-membership provisions; in 1946 a little over 10 percent had such provisions, while a third were covered by union-shop requirements, a fourth by sole-bargaining arrangements, and another fourth by maintenance-of-union-dues requirements.

TABLE 2.—*Changes in union recognition in the United States, 1941–46*

Item	1941	1942	1943	1944	1945	1946
Eligibile for union-agreement coverage:						
Number (in millions)	[1] 35	31	32	30. 25	29	31. 2
Percentage under agreement	30	40	45	47	48	48
	Percentage distribution [2]					
Workers under agreements providing for—						
Closed shop	} 40	45	{ 30	28	30	33
Union shop			20	18	15	17
Maintenance of membership	([3])	15	20	27	29	25
Preferential hiring	([3])	5	2	2	3	3
Other [4]	([3])	35	28	25	23	22
Total		100	100	100	100	100

[1] This figure is not comparable with the number listed as eligible for other years since it includes all salaried workers and all government employees. The figure which would be comparable is 31 million.
[2] Percentages not strictly comparable, year by year, because of slight changes in volume of employment during the period.
[3] No data.
[4] No membership or hiring requirements are mentioned in these agreements, which have clauses specify-ing sole bargaining, maintenance of union dues, and bargaining for members only.

TABLE 3.—*Industries with 50 percent or more of the workers under agreement covered by specified types of clauses* [1]

MANUFACTURING INDUSTRIES

Closed or union shop with preferential hiring	Union shop	Maintenance of membership	Preferential hiring	Sole bargaining
Baking. Breweries. Canning and preserving foods. Clothing, men's. Clothing, women's. Dyeing and finishing textiles. Gloves, leather. Glass containers. Hosiery. Printing and publishing. Shoes, cut stock and findings.	Carpets and rugs, wool. Flat glass. Knit goods. Paper and allied products. Sugar, beet. Woolen and worsted textiles.	Aircraft and parts. Cigarettes and tobacco. Chemicals. Cotton textiles. Electrical machinery. Machinery, except electrical. Meat packing. Nonferrous metals. Petroleum refining. Rubber. Steel, basic.	Pottery.	Cement. Sugar, cane.

NONMANUFACTURING INDUSTRIES

Construction. Trucking and warehousing.	Coal mining.	Crude petroleum and natural gas. Metal mining. Public utilities, electric light and power, water and gas. Telegraph.	Longshoring. Maritime.	Railroads. Telephone.

[1] Definitions of the various types of union recognition are as follows:

Closed shop.—All employees under the closed-shop agreement must be members of the union at the time of hiring and must remain members in good standing during their period of employment.

Hiring through the union, unless it is unable to supply the required number of workers within a given period, is required under most of the closed-shop agreements and those employees who are hired through other procedures must join the union before they start to work.

Union shop.—Workers employed under a union-shop agreement need not be union members when hired, but they must join the union within a specified time, usually 30 to 60 days, and remain members during the period of employment.

Union shop with preferential hiring.—When the union-shop agreements specify that union members shall be given preference in hiring or that the hiring shall be done through the union, the effect is very much the same as the closed-shop agreement.

Modified union shop.—In some cases the union shop is modified so that those who were employed before the union shop was established are not required to become union members.

Maintenance of membership.—This type of union security requires that all employees who are members of the union a specified time after the agreement is signed, and all who later join the union, must remain members in good standing for the duration of the agreement. Following the pattern of the maintenance-of-membership clauses established by the National War Labor Board, most of the agreements with this type of union-security clause provide for a 15-day period during which members may withdraw from the union if they do not wish to remain members during the life of the agreement.

Maintenance of union dues.—During 1946 a few agreements covering workers employed by large companies which had specified maintenance of membership in 1945 were modified to provide sole bargaining with the check-off of union dues for all union members,.as a condition of employment. Clauses of this type (which specify this form of irrevocable check-off) are found in agreements negotiated with the General Motors Corp., the Goodrich Tire and Rubber Co., Akron, the International Harvester Co., East Moline, Ill., the Western Electric Co., and Yale & Towne.

Preferential hiring.—No union membership is required under this type of clause but union members must be hired if available. When the union cannot supply workers, the employer may hire nonmembers and they are not required to join the union as a condition of employment.

Sole bargaining.—Under some agreements no requirement for union membership or for hiring through the union is specified. The union is the sole bargaining agent for all employees and negotiates the agreement covering all workers in the bargaining unit whether they are members of the union or not.

Members only.—A few agreements stipulate that the union shall act as bargaining agent for its members only, and the agreement does not cover other workers.

Check-Off Arrangements

Approximately 6 million workers (41 percent of all those under union agreements) were covered by some form of check-off provisions in 1946. This is an increase of nearly three-quarters of a million from the 1945 total. Automatic deduction of dues was specified for a little over half of these workers while the others specified check-off of union dues only for employees who give the employer an individual written authorization. Some of these may be withdrawn at any time; others remain in effect for the life of the agreement.

In the manufacturing industries 4.7 million workers (61 percent) had their dues checked off compared to 4 million (about 50 percent) in 1945. The number of nonmanufacturing workers covered by check-off arrangements remained at about 1.3 million for 1946, but this was not quite 20 percent of the workers under agreement; in 1945, with only 13.8 million under agreement, the same number of workers covered brought the proportion to 24 percent.

Changes in check-off arrangements from 1942 through 1946, given in table 4, show a gradual increase in the number of workers covered by such provisions. Table 5 lists the industries which have at least half of the workers under agreement covered by one type of check-off. A few industries listed for 1945, such as chemicals, steel products, and men's clothing, no longer have 50 percent of the covered workers under a single type of check-off.

TABLE 4.—*Changes in check-off arrangements in the United States 1941–46*

Item	1941	1942	1943	1944	1945	1946
Number under agreement (in millions)	10.3	12.5	13.8	14.3	13.8	14.8
	Percentage distribution [1]					
Workers under agreements providing for—						
Automatic check-off	[2]	12	18	21	23	24
Voluntary check-off	[2]	8	14	20	16	17
No check-off	[2]	80	68	59	61	59
Total		100	100	100	100	100

[1] Percentages not strictly comparable, year by year, because of slight changes in volume of employment during the period.   [2] No data.

TABLE 5.—*Industries with 50 percent or more of workers under agreement covered by specified type of check-off*

Manufacturing		Nonmanufacturing	
Voluntary check-off	Automatic check-off	Voluntary check-off	Automatic check-off
Cement. Clocks and watches. Glass, flat. Petroleum and coal products. Sugar, cane. Textiles, except carpets and rugs (woolen) and hosiery.	Aircraft engines. Aluminum. Automobiles. Carpets and rugs (wool). Cigarettes and tobacco. Electrical machinery. Hosiery. Leather, except gloves and shoes. Meat packing and slaughtering. Nonferrous smelting and refining. Rubber tires and tubes. Steel, basic. Sugar, beet.	Crude petroleum and natural gas products. Telephone.	Coal mining. Iron mining. Telegraph.

THE ORGANIZED BUSINESS IN AMERICA

By Neil Chamberlain[1]

THE political and economic significances of the collective bargaining process stem from its setting in the larger problem of organized groups within society.

Regardless of one's acceptance or rejection of the pluralistic theory of the state, the importance of organized autonomous groups is not to be questioned. They exercise the functions of government over their own constituencies, composing their own laws, administering them through their own agents, and interpreting them through their own judicial authorities. They treat and war with other infrastate organizations, as well as with the state itself. Society in the United States today is rich with these associational forms; and the American people are faced not infrequently with the problem of resolving conflicts in loyalty arising out of their citizenship in a multiplicity of governments, of both group and state varieties.[2]

This study deals with two of the most important of such autonomous associations—the labor union and the business enterprise, with particular reference to the corporation in the latter group. These two collectivities, governments in themselves, engage in a process which has become known as "collective bargaining"—a process undefined in the laws which encourage it and ill-defined in the minds of those concerned with it. In its crudest form it consists of little more than an acceptance by two group-governments of a means of live and let live. In its most refined form it is the mutual embrace by two group-governments of the whole field of operating a business.

In any form the process of collective bargaining results in the establishment of a type of autonomous association or infrastate government, which may be called "the organized business." This government is peculiar in that it is the result of the collaboration of two lesser autonomous group-governments—the organized owners and the organized workers.

[1] Since the preparation of this article, the author has been on active duty with the United States Naval Reserve. In accordance with Art. 113 (2) of the 1920 (revised) *United States Navy Regulations*, it is here noted that the opinions or assertions contained herein are the private ones of the writer and are not to be construed as official or necessarily reflecting the views of the Navy Department or the naval service at large.

[2] Cf. Harold Laski, *Authority in the Modern State* (New Haven, 1919), p. 325; also James J. Robbins and Gunnar Heckscher, "The Constitutional Theory of Autonomous Groups," *Journal of Politics*, III (1941), 11–12, 15.

In a society in which collective bargaining prevails, neither the legal corporation nor the labor union possesses any functional significance in the absence of collaboration with the other. So long as collective bargaining is accepted, the corporation is a useless component of the economy in the absence of a working agreement with its workers,[3] while the labor union comes into being expressly for the purpose of treating with the employer of its members.

From the collaboration of the corporation and the union results the organized business, whose function is production. A collapse of collective bargaining relations does not necessarily entail a breakdown in the union or in the legal corporation, but it does involve a breakdown in the government of the organized business.[4] In a society in which collective bargaining prevails, then, the smooth operation of its procedures is necessary to the continuity of the organized businesses, whose function is production.

Thus collective bargaining is a species of functional self-government[5] which allows the constituent members—owners and workers—of a business or industry to determine the terms of their relationship. It constitutes, at the same time, a method of self-determination by a business or industry of the conditions of employment and a recognition that a business cannot be considered simply as the property of a ruling class of stockholders and management but is the concern of all the groups which comprise it. To the extent that government has intervened in collective bargaining conferences by imposing a settlement upon the conferees or by bringing the moral force of public opinion to bear upon them to oblige their acceptance of terms which, left to themselves, they would not have accepted, the industrial *self*-government implicit in collective bargaining is obscured. Moreover, the frequent breakdowns of this species of functional self-government evidenced in appeals to outside agencies to assist in composing differences among the representatives of the business or industry blur the picture by suggesting not a single self-regulating government, but two governments with conflicting interests.[6]

Despite such *ad hoc* state interventions in the collective bargaining process, it is no mere euphemism to declare that collective bargaining constitutes functional self-government. Perhaps the most conclusive proof of this fact is provided by the spread of a form of collective bargaining which has demonstrated its feasibility as an instrument for the joint determination by the constituents of a business or industry, and by them solely, of the terms of their relationship. This procedural form is the impartial machinery now established in many important industries. It would be difficult to overstate the significance of this movement toward the founding by the bargaining parties of the office of impartial chairman or umpire as the regulator of their relations. In a sense the president and su-

[3] It is only with the abandonment of collective bargaining that the corporation may assert complete control over the terms of its relationship with its employees and regain functional independence.

[4] It is true that the operation of the business may continue in such a case, but only upon the abandonment of collective bargaining—that is, it may continue, though not as an *organized* business.

[5] Cf. James J. Robbins, *The Politics of Labor Relations in Sweden* (Chapel Hill, 1942), p. 9.

[6] As has been noted, two lesser group-governments—the corporation and the union—are indeed involved, and the interests of one frequently do conflict with the interests of the other. The important consideration, however, is that they have their primary interest in common—the continuity of the organized business or industry which they have united to establish and from which each derives its functional significance.

preme court of their government, the impartial chairman is delegated the power to enforce the agreement and to determine all questions arising under it during its lifetime. In a further sense a legislative council, the impartial chairman is also frequently given the authority to determine all issues in dispute not covered by the agreement which arise during the lifetime of the agreement.[7] Thus, so long as there is an agreement in effect, the business or industry over which the impartial chairman rules has made provision for the complete self-determination of all questions concerning the governance of its labor relations. It has established a government which, *within the legal framework of the society of its origin,* successfully exercises complete autonomy.

This is not to suggest that industrial self-government occurs only in those businesses or industries which have organized their collective bargaining relationships around a jointly established impartial authority. This form of collective bargaining merely demonstrates most conclusively the autonomy possible in the field of industrial relations. Collective bargaining, even in the absence of such machinery, provides a mecha-

nism for the joint determination of conditions of employment without any necessary intervention by the state.[8] Without the functioning of an impartial authority, however, greater opportunity for a breach of relations exists and, as a result, greater incentive for state interference. As the consequences of a breakdown in industrial government become more far-reaching in an increasingly complex economy, it is quite possible that the constituents of industrial governments—the bargaining parties—will more and more turn to the use of impartial machinery as an effective means of preserving their autonomy.

To this point we have been concerned with collective bargaining as industrial self-government *in the field of labor relations.* While this is its popularly conceived function, to confine its application to labor relations in the narrow sense of the determination of job conditions would be to obscure the much vaster significance of the bargaining process. Collective bargaining is beginning to emerge not only as a method of control by the workers over their job conditions but as a mechanism for the joint control by the bargaining parties of the business or industry as a totality.

Collective bargaining in the sense in which it has customarily been used—the joint determination of wages, hours, and job conditions—involved a modification of the prerogatives of owners and management. No longer was the board of directors free to distribute profits as it saw

---

[7] There has also been a noticeable tendency on the part of the bargaining parties to call in the impartial chairman as mediator and consultant in the negotiation of superseding agreements. So much has this been the case that an official of the New York State Board of Mediation has said that where impartial machinery has been set up there is almost invariably a continuing self-determination of the conditions of employment, unbroken by intervention of governmental authorities at times of contract negotiations. As a result, this board has actively encouraged the establishment of impartial machinery wherever the organization of the industry and the financial ability of the bargaining parties have made this possible, recognizing that, as such industrial governments become more widespread, the area of operation of the board of mediation becomes reduced. Functional self-government replaces state intervention.

[8] Thus in the bargaining relations between the International Molders Union and the Manufacturers Protective and Development Association, and between the National Brotherhood of Operative Potters and the United States Potters Association, the fullest degree of autonomy in the determination of terms of relationship has been enjoyed, although no impartial machinery has been set up. The relationships have been such as to provide no occasion for interference by the state.

fit: organized workers insisted upon their right to be heard with respect to the distribution of profits.[9] No longer was management at liberty to hire and fire at its discretion: seniority rights and union security provisions, such as the preferential, union, or closed shop, modified its authority. This removal from the field of ownership-management prerogatives of certain broad areas of discretion has been approved in law.[10] It is now recognized that where organized workers seek joint determination of wages, hours, and working conditions, unilateral determination of these matters by management is barred. It has nót been generally recognized, however, that incursions into the field of management authority have not ceased at this point. Collective bargaining has provided a mechanism by which workers can extend their control into all phases of managerial "prerogatives." Such penetration by unions into fields once considered of sole concern to management is now in progress in many in-

dustries. Throughout the economy, at one time or another, in one place or another, there is hardly any field of managerial discretion which has been left untouched. In view of this development, the significance of such a phrase as "the inherent rights of management"[11] may be questioned.

The concept of "the prerogatives of management" continues to play an important part in industrial relations, however. One would expect that representatives of the managerial class would themselves cherish the concept, as they have. It has been used to deny organized workers the right to bargain with respect to certain issues, such as managerial salaries and depreciation policies,[12] or to deny arbitration upon such issues.[13]

[9] Although profits are legally the property of the owners of the business, they are in reality regarded as a proper subject for bargaining by the union, so that it becomes difficult to distinguish between what might be considered as bargaining for wages and what might equally be considered as bargaining for profit-participation. Note the following comment of the executive president of a large corporation in 1940 negotiations: ". . . . And then I just wondered whether you boys—and I don't mean to imply that you didn't go at this seriously, but I wonder if you have any conception of the vast amount of money that you have cut up and as to this new spread—that's one thing. If, on the other hand, you just have a misconception that this is some golden cheese that we are going to cut up now and whack it up, no matter what the amount is, I don't see where we are going to get anywhere at all. If that is the conception, we have a very bewildering situation. We might expect our customers to say, 'Whenever you are making a profit, you must immediately reduce the price of glass,' and whenever we are making a profit you immediately ask us to increase the cost of labor. When you get those two things together, there is no profit."

[10] In the National Labor Relations Act (49 Stat. 449); see Secs. 1, 7, and 8(5).

[11] Cf. Wayne L. Morse, "The Scope of Arbitration in Labor Disputes," *Papers Presented at the Fourth Annual Stanford Industrial Relations Conference* (Stanford University, 1941), p. 115: "There are certain rights which are not arbitrable, such as the inherent rights of management. . . . ."

[12] "There are certain problems which are definitely management's affair, responsibility for which management cannot duck. The test of a good [employee-representation] plan is that the employees recognize this, and trust management with such matters as selection and promotion of employees, and determination of executives' salaries, reserves and surplus" (from the record of the April 20 conference, p. 6 in "Collective Bargaining," the mimeographed record of ten conferences conducted by the Bureau of Personnel Administration in 1935).

[13] In "Authority and Responsibility in Industrial Management," an address before the University of Virginia's Institute of Public Affairs on July 14, 1934 (15 pp., mimeographed), S. M. DuBrul, now the director of the labor economics section, personnel staff, of General Motors Corporation, declared: ". . . . In any case in which any compromise would mean serious injury to the true long-term interests of the institution and the purpose for which it was created, no Management can be excused, if it voluntarily submits the issues to any form of arbitration which involves an irrevocable agreement to abide by the decisions of another party or agency. Suppose, for example, that the Management of a company in a given industry, employing a specialized kind of highly skilled workmen, was presented with a demand for a reduction in hours which would

Union representatives have been forbidden access to company books for fear of provoking attacks upon certain management policies now considered reserved to its sole discretion.[14] It has been said in support of this view that management delegates but does not share responsibility;[15] and part of the opposition to the

collective bargaining movement has been charged to the fear of management that its responsibility would thereby be diluted and its prerogatives endangered.[16] To management, *"joint* management" has remained a specter.[17]

Opposition from the managerial class to the invasion of its "prerogatives" by organized workers has found occasional support in the courts, where justices in a few instances have adopted the same approach by regarding labor legislation as a threat to management's preroga-

so reduce the supply of skilled labor that before sufficient additional workers could be obtained and trained the business as an institution would be irreparably injured. The Management, of course, should attempt to compromise at some point which would not produce this serious result. It should attempt to establish to the satisfaction of the men that the request was unreasonable. It should seek by all possible forms of mediation and conciliation to effect a settlement of this nature. But should all of these attempts fail, the submission of the matter to the unlimited, binding arbitration of an outside party would be dereliction and the investors would be fully warranted in discharging the Management forthwith.

"In principle, all questions of wages are essentially of this character, and only when the amount involved is not important and a settlement is essential in the best interests of the business can the matter be properly delegated without reservation to a third party for settlement. Furthermore, the decision to accept such outside arbitration can only be made by the Management itself, since it and it alone is accountable for the final results."

[14] Thus an attorney representing several companies in the Cincinnati area says he will willingly supply the union with a profit and loss statement but refuses to permit an inspection of the company's books, fearing argument over management salaries, capital investments, and similar issues, which he believes do not fall within the orbit of collective bargaining. Several other management representatives maintained in interviews that they did not want union conferees "prying into officials' salaries."

[15] Cf. DuBrul, *op. cit.*, p. 7: ". . . . In a business the Management is vested with certain powers sufficient to enable it to fulfill the functions involved in the conduct of the business. While it can delegate them, it is still responsible ultimately for the acts of those to whom it has delegated them." And on p. 8: "This precludes it from delegating authority to anyone whose interests may be in conflict with those of the owners of the business." Cf., too, the statement by the Chrysler Corporation in the 1939 strike, as expressed in a letter from the vice-president in charge of operations to the chairman of the Michigan Mediation Board: "Management cannot abdicate its responsibility for any aspect of this

business, whether it relates to labor, to engineering, to production or to selling. It cannot consent to 'sovietize' the plants" (*New York Times*, October 19, 1939).

[16] Cf. James H. Greene, *Organized Training in Business* (rev. ed.; New York, 1937), p. 206; and "National Industrial Conference, Washington, D.C.," *Monthly Labor Review*, IX (1919), 1348.

[17] Cf. the statement of one company representative in 1940 negotiations: ". . . . There are at least ten paragraphs in this proposal that to the men on this side of the table mean wide exploration into the realm of collective management. I know of no organization that has adventured into the field of collective management as you men have indicated here. Even the strongest organizations in the country recognize the rights of the management to run their business without first consulting the organization, and these ten paragraphs, at least, diverge widely from that field, and even make it an impossibility,—if I may use such a word at this time, to even consider such a paragraph. . . . ."

And somewhat later in the same conference:

UNION REPRESENTATIVE: "What's the difference between whether you hand them [service records and employment lists] to the local president or post them and have them copy them from the posted record?"

COMPANY REPRESENTATIVE: "There may not seem to be very much difference to you, Otto, and you may be honest about it, but to the company there seems to be quite a lot of difference. I don't know how to explain it, but there is a lot of difference. This may be minor in one respect, but after all, the company is not committing itself to a sort of joint management of its employees. They would still like to retain their right to shift around their employees as they see fit,—and subject to your criticism, if you don't like it, and as long as you can enter the office and ask for the records, as you know you can, the record of the man involved, why isn't that sufficient?"

tives[18] or by interpreting legislation as precluding union interest in certain managerial fields.[19] Somewhat more surprisingly, some labor leaders have renounced interest in fields of management discretion other than the traditional ones of wages, hours, and working conditions.[20]

[18] Cf. Justice McReynolds' dissent in *N.L.R.B.* v. *Jones and Laughlin*, 301 U.S. 103 (1937): "A private owner is deprived of power to manage his own property by freely selecting those to whom his manufacturing operations are to be entrusted."

[19] Thus in *Globe Cotton Mills* v. *N.L.R.B.*, 103 F. (2d), 91, 94 (C.C.A. 5), modifying 6 N.L.R.B. 461, the court held that the subject matter of collective bargaining did not extend to legislative policies, a matter which lay outside the purview of the rights of organized workers.

Note also the statement of Benedict Wolf, former secretary of the N.L.R.B., in "The Duty To Bargain Collectively," *Law and Contemporary Problems*, spring, 1938, p. 255: "There can be no doubt that the union may properly present demands with regard to matters directly affecting wages, hours and working conditions, and the employer would have no right to refuse to bargain regarding such demands. However, the union might have demands with reference to subjects which the employer could well claim were not properly within the scope of collective bargaining and his refusal to bargain in such a case might be justified. For instance, although the employees have a vital interest in the success of the business enterprise (since on this depend their wages and, in fact, their jobs), it is doubtful whether an employer will be under any duty to bargain with the union regarding the prices he fixes for his products, even though admittedly the prices fixed by the employer have an important effect on the success of the business. Although to salesmen working on a commission basis the amount of advertising done by an employer is undoubtedly important, the chances of an employer being penalized for refusal to bargain with regard to his advertising budget are slim. These matters are primarily management problems, and affect working conditions indirectly. There are few things with relation to the conduct of a business which do not have some effect on working conditions and it is difficult to conceive that an employer would be in duty bound to bargain with the representatives of his employees concerning all the details of running his business. The classic concept of management problems as differentiated from working conditions might well be used as the test in the determination of the employer's right to limit the scope of the bargaining process."

[20] See Samuel Gompers, "Collective Bargaining," *American Federationist*, XXVII (1920), 250: "Col-

The constitution of the Aluminum Workers of America acknowledges "management functions" which the union will not try to usurp.[21] The Brotherhood of Railroad Trainmen recognizes "matters that are strictly of managerial concern," interesting itself only in those fields which have "a material effect upon the welfare of the workers."[22] Trade agreements have specified areas of discretion

lective bargaining in industry does not imply that wage-earners shall assume control of industry, or responsibility for financial management. It proposes that the employees shall have the right to organize and deal with the employer through selected representatives as to wages and working conditions."

[21] From the Preamble: "The Aluminum Worker does not seek to usurp management's function. The Aluminum Worker does not ask for a place on the Board of Directors of the Aluminum Industry. He merely asks for his rights. . . . . The Aluminum Worker seeks a place at the conference table, together with management, when decisions are made which affect the food the Aluminum Worker, his wife and children shall eat; the extent of education his children may have, the kind and the amount of clothing they may wear. . . . ."

[22] From a letter of December 8, 1941, from A. F. Whitney, president of the Brotherhood of Railroad Trainmen: "I should be inclined to adopt the broad connotation of the phrase 'conditions of employment.' To me, this phrase means anything in an industry which affects in a material degree the welfare of the worker. However, this broad interpretation does not mean that our organization ever endeavors, or even wishes to endeavor, to exercise control in matters that are strictly of managerial concern. It is only when management policies have a material effect upon the welfare of the workers we represent that we propose to have a voice. Of course, this interpretation does not mean that our minds are closed or that we will remain silent, in the presence of extravagant managerial policies which in the end must adversely affect labor. Hence, we do not hesitate to point out and criticize the financial racketeering and appalling waste in the railroad industry, which, Senator Wheeler estimated in 1938, amounted to a million dollars a day. Our criticism of these policies does not mean that we propose to oust the management and conduct the policies for ourselves. It only means that our criticism is a defense mechanism against the claims of the railroads that the employes are 'racketeers,' or that the employes are selfish or are making unreasonable demands, or that the railroads cannot afford to give the employes fair wages and working conditions."

reserved entirely and solely to management.[23] It cannot be said, however, that the concept of "the prerogatives of management" has been accepted by the organized labor movement as a whole. Other union officials have expressed the view that "there are no management prerogatives."[24]

In this latter view that there are no special areas of business operation reserved to management discretion lies the truly revolutionary aspect of collective bargaining. Collective bargaining is not only "a step in the process of control";[25] it is the *mechanism* by which the workers may achieve control and exercise it jointly with management.[26] If joint management of business and industry by the workers' representatives and by the owners' representatives is revolutionary, then collective bargaining is revolutionary; for collective bargaining now gives promise of introducing a system of control of business and industry in which the workers are accorded the right to collaborate with owners and their representatives in determining business policies, methods of operation, and the distribution of the proceeds. The outlines of such an economic order are still vague and indistinct, but they can be observed. No longer can a system of collective control in the United States be considered only a revolutionary's dream; it is now in the first stages of realization.

The broad areas of managerial responsibility can be defined,[27] and among them there is not one in which labor unions have not at some time intervened. There is no necessity of urging this point too insistently. It must be acknowledged that certain areas have been left virtually untouched by labor, chiefly questions involving the financial methods to be employed for raising necessary capital,[28] the policy with respect to depreciation and reserves,[29] and the policy regarding

[23] Thus, note the agreement between the Ford Motor Company and the United Automobile Workers (1941), Sec. 13: "The Union recognizes other rights and responsibilities belonging solely to the Company, prominent among which but by no means wholly inclusive, are the rights to decide the number and location of plants, the machine and tool equipment, the products to be manufactured, the methods of manufacture, the schedules of production, the processes of manufacturing or assembling, together with all designing, engineering and the control of raw materials, semimanufactured and finished parts which may be incorporated into the products manufactured."

It is significant that managements have sought the inclusion of such protective clauses in their contracts, as though erecting defenses against an anticipated union offensive.

[24] See n. 53, below. When interviewed, one official of an important A. F. of L. international union expressed a belief that there must be a more explicit legal recognition of the right of unions to bargain on "management" matters. Cf. "Union-Management Cooperation," *Monthly Labor Review*, LII (1941), 1351-52: "Many union leaders are also insisting that organized labor be allowed increased participation and responsibility in the management of industry."

[25] R. F. Hoxie, *Trade Unionism in the United States* (New York, 1923), p. 275.

[26] See W. F. Ferger, "The Place of Collective Bargaining in Our Modern Industrial Life," *North Carolina Yearbook, 1929-1930* (Chapel Hill, 1930), p. 46.

[27] The list of fields of responsibility used here was adapted from a compilation prepared by Dr. F. F. Blachly, in his "Analyses for N.R.A., 1935." (Manuscript.)

[28] Though there have been loans by the union itself to the company, as by the United Mine Workers to the Rocky Mountain Fuel Company (see "Union-Management Cooperation," *Monthly Labor Review*, LII [1941], 1357). The Steel Workers Organizing Committee in one case assumed responsibility for negotiating a bank loan for an iron-fabricating concern recognized as a leader in its field. Other unions, such as the railroad brotherhoods, have made methods of financing a subject of conferences with management, without actually bargaining upon this subject.

[29] Note, however, that arbitration proceedings occurred in 1940 in New York City over several questions concerning a company's financial policies, the union contending, among other things, that the company's depreciation policy unfairly represented its earnings. This question was not settled by the

payment of dividends.[30] There has, however, been collective bargaining on questions involving the building or the extension or contraction of the plant or the industry,[31] the location of the plant or in-

dustry,[32] the co-ordination and integration of the work, the general organization of the plant,[33] the determination of

arbiter's decision, however, which turned upon whether present company depreciation policy was consistent with its policy in the past.

[30] Cf., however, the 1939 agreement between the S.W.O.C. and the Schwitzer-Cummins Company of Indianapolis, where the union agreed to payment of a 6 per cent dividend to stockholders before pressing for any wage increases. In wage bargaining the union is, of course, affecting dividend policy without bargaining directly upon that subject.

[31] As in 1941 negotiations between the Joint Board of the Dressmakers Union, I.L.G.W.U., and the five employers' associations in the New York area. In its printed proposal (Julius Hochman, *Industry Planning through Collective Bargaining* [New York, 1941], p. 36) the union declared: "Planned production can, of course, best be secured in plants that are large enough and have sufficient productive capacity to justify the expenditure necessary to effect these improvements and to supply the required services. It is for this reason, and in the interest not only of the workers, but of the manufacturers, jobbers and contractors as well, that the union urges a conscious effort on the part of all the factors of the industry to consolidate contracting shops into units that are large enough to make possible this type of good management.

"We suggest that the following are the minimum sizes of shops in the popular-price ranges, consistent with proper management: 50 machines in the $3.75 and $4.75 ranges; 60 machines in the $2.87 range; 80 machines in the $2.25 range; and 100 machines in the $1.37 range."

In its 1941 agreement (e.g., that with the National Dress Manufacturers Association, par. 12[9]) it is provided: "After the date of the execution of this agreement, a member of the Association who deals with or sends work to contractors shall not open an inside shop on his own premises or elsewhere, nor shall he enlarge his inside shop, wherever situated, if at the date of the execution of this agreement he maintained one, by employing a larger number of machine operators, unless with the consent and approval of the Administrative Board." A further provision (par. 12[10]) imposes the same restrictions upon contractors.

The 1941 agreement between the John B. Stetson Company and the United Hatters, Cap and Millinery Workers International Union provides for discussion between the company and union before discontinuance of "auxiliary departments providing services or goods incidental to hat manufacture."

[32] Cf. the 1941 agreement between the Associated Doll Manufacturers of New York and the Playthings and Novelty Workers Union: "No member of this association shall remove his factory, during the term of th.. agreement, outside of the five Boroughs which comprise the City of New York." And the *Collective Agreement between the National Dress Manufacturers Association and the Joint Board of the Dressmakers Union, I.L.G.W.U.* (1941) (par. 31): "No member of the Association shall, during the term of this agreement, move his shop or factory from its present location to any place beyond which the public carrier fare is more than 5¢."

[33] Perhaps the leading union in this field is the Steel Workers Union, which has sponsored a number of programs to streamline the production organization of companies with which it contracts, presenting these programs as a bargaining proposal or offering them as the outcome of the bargaining relationship.

Note Helen S. Hoeber, "Collective Bargaining by Amalgamated Clothing Workers," *Monthly Labor Review*, XLV (1937), 21: "The union took over other management functions [than the supply of an adequate and efficient working force] when it parried employer requests for lower costs through wage reductions by offering to reduce costs by improved efficiency. Union experts went into the shops, reorganized the flow of work, subdivided processes, established production standards under week work and later piece work, standardized styles, substituted machinery for hand labor, etc."

The International Printing Pressmen and Assistants' Union maintains an engineering department and has serviced more than five hundred newspapers in the United States, with intent to bring about improvement in quality with the best production speed, and to solve special problems.

The 1941 New York City dress industry conferences resulted in the establishment of an administrative board composed of representatives of both the union and the manufacturers' associations. One of the purposes of this board, as outlined by the union in its proposal (Hochman, *op. cit.*, p. 37), is "to study and develop a technique for closer cooperation between contractors and jobbers, and production men, for the purpose of making each jobber and his contractors an integrated unit for business planning and production."

See the *Report of the Officers and Executive Board of the American Federation of Hosiery Workers* (1941), p. 17, where Vice-President Hoffman spoke of the need for a "clean-up of internal department conditions," including "the practice of dividing out all work among all seamers irrespective of endage, style or construction."

the type of personnel,[34] the types of machinery and equipment,[35] the purchase of materials and supplies,[36] the nature and quality of the product or service to be produced,[37] the fixing of the price of

the product or service,[38] the quantity of production,[39] the advertising methods,[40] the sales and distribution policy,[41] and

---

[34] See Sumner H. Slichter, *Union Policies and Industrial Management* (Washington, 1941), chap. iii, "Control of Hiring," and chap. iv, "Control of Layoffs—Union Policies." Union concern with respect to personnel applies not only to workmen but to supervisory personnel as well. Cf. *In the Matter of Aladdin Industries*, 22 N.L.R.B., No. 101, where the union demanded discharge of a supervisor; and Hochman (*op. cit.*, p. 19), where he recounts how the union secured the discharge of one foreman and the hiring of a more efficient one; see also *In the Matter of Consumers' Research*, 2 N.L.R.B. 57.

[35] See Slichter, *op. cit.*, chaps. vii, viii, and ix, on union policies with respect to technological changes.

[36] Bargaining on this "management responsibility" usually takes the form of a limitation upon its right to purchase materials worked upon by non-union labor. For examples of such clauses in agreements see *Collective Bargaining Contracts* (Washington, 1941), pp. 394–95. The Steel Workers Union, however, has at times made representations with respect to the quality of raw materials going into the finished product.

[37] "Each day about 400 newspapers are examined at the [pressmen's] union headquarters for defects of appearance or workmanship. If a defect continues to appear, the company is informed and advised how to remedy the matter. Where necessary an engineering expert is sent to the plant" (from "Union Management Cooperation," *Monthly Labor Review*, LII [1941], 1356). See also Slichter, "Controlling the Quality of Work," *op. cit.*, pp. 177–79. Union control over company policy may sometimes be achieved outside the framework of the collective bargaining process a certain preliminary step to its inclusion within the bargaining process. Thus the Fifth Avenue Coach Company, in its *Study Relative to Demands Made by the Transport Workers Union of Greater New York* (New York, 1941), p. 32, charged: "The regulation of service is a matter which must remain wholly within the discretion of management. On the other hand, management is always ready to consider any and all grievances in respect to working conditions arising out of such regulation. However, there have been many cases in which drivers and conductors have told supervisors that they have received instructions from Transport Workers Union headquarters, some mentioning Mr. Kearns by name, that they were not to take on standees. There is a feeling, apparently growing among the personnel that, in

matters such as these, they are to look to the Union for instruction rather than to the officials of the Company."

[38] As in negotiations between the Journeymen Barbers and the Master Barbers. Cf., too, "Union-Management Cooperation," *Monthly Labor Review*, LII (1941), 1358: "In the men's clothing industry, the Amalgamated Clothing Workers . . . . has sent its technical experts into various plants to renovate managerial practices and advise employers on sales and price policies." In the abortive drive by the Anti-trust Division of the Department of Justice to prosecute unions indulging in "unquestionable violations of the Sherman Act," Assistant Attorney-General Thurman Arnold mentioned as one type of union activity he sought to eliminate, "unreasonable restraints designed to enforce illegally fixed prices. An example of this activity is found in the Chicago milk case, where a labor union is charged with combining with distributors and producers to prevent milk being brought into Chicago by persons who refuse to maintain illegal and fixed prices" (*New York Times*, November 20, 1939).

[39] See Slichter, *op. cit.*, pp. 166–76, respecting union limitations on output.

[40] The most common example of union intervention in this field involves the demand for the use of the union label. Thus the I.L.G.W.U. pledged $100,000 to a promotional campaign in the dress industry "on the condition that the tag and label on each dress bear the imprint of the International label, and that the promotional schemes include the union label" (Hochman, *op. cit.*, p. 25).

[41] Meyer Kestnbaum, "A Study in Management Prerogatives," *Harvard Business Review*, XIX (1940), 97 (speaking of the A.C.W. and the Hart Schaffner & Marx Co.): "The company contends that its labor costs are too high. The union alleges that the difficulty is not in labor costs but in manufacturing efficiency and merchandising skill. . . . . The concept that labor has the right to judge the skill with which management discharges its functions is one which represents a serious challenge to the accepted order of things in industry."

The suggestion that joint production planning gives the union a vital interest in merchandising methods is contained in the following statement of John P. O'Connell, as secretary and business agent of the United Textile Workers of America, Salem, Mass., in *Union-Management Cooperation at Naumkeag*, by F. Foster Smith, J. P. O'Connell, and Francis Goodell (A. F. of L. pamphlet [1930]), p. 13: "If there is not now the necessary sales planning to give assurance to the employees, this lack should be the policy as to extensions and improvements,[42] as well as general labor policies.[43]

Nor can such union intervention in management fields be readily dismissed with the comment that it has occurred only in isolated instances and only with respect to "sick" enterprises. While the dangers of extrapolation are great, there seem to be grounds for believing that if the strength and power of labor unions continue to expand in the future as in the past there will continue at the same time a slow but marked penetration by organized labor into the field of manage-

ment prerogatives. The growth of collective bargaining—the mechanism for worker control in industry—will itself facilitate this movement. In particular, its spread throughout the mass-production industries may be expected to result in agreements fully as startling and quite as significant as the acceptance by the Ford Motor Company of the union shop. The criticism of the ability and motives of private management which was stimulated by the depression of the 1930's and by the halting organization of the war-production program in the 1940's has provided an incentive for the leaders of organized labor to invade the field of industry planning.[44] The aura of inviolability once thought to surround—though never wholly effectively—the decisions of private business has been to a large extent dispelled by the reform programs of the New Deal administrations and supplanted by a theory of economic planning, a movement which has provided fertile soil for such union proposals as the industry-councils joint-management plan of the C.I.O.[45] Perhaps most important, there has been an increasing recognition by labor representatives of the impact of all management functions upon a company's wage structure, the traditional subject of collective bargaining. To implement criticism of management policies believed to have a deterrent effect upon a company's ability to pay wage increases or to sustain existing wages, unions have been establishing research departments for economic analysis and employing the services of industrial engineers. The spread

---

the major concern in order that the place of Pequot in the market may not be injured by the many powerful changing elements in the field of distribution—the increasing chain-store development, the general dissatisfaction with and review of present sales methods, the introduction of new basic fabric and intensive study of product design."

See also "Union-Management Cooperation," *Monthly Labor Review*, LII (1941), 1357–59, under "Comprehensive Programs for Improvement of Business."

The union may also exercise control over the sales and distribution policy by securing a ban on sales to nonunion companies. Note the following provision in the 1941 agreement between the Boston Coat and Suit Manufacturers Association and the I.L.G.W.U.: "If the Employer is doing part of his work or all of his work for jobbers or manufacturers or both, in this case the Employer agrees not to make any work for or sell garments to any jobber or manufacturer that does not have any contract with the Union."

[42] An excellent example of union intervention in this field is provided by the full-fashioned hosiery industry, where in 1936 the union accepted a cut in wages for its members upon the understanding that the employers would embark upon a "rehabilitation" program. Clauses providing for the effectuation of this program were written into the Supplementary Agreements. See also "Union-Management Co-operation," *Monthly Labor Review*, LII (1941), 1356.

[43] Involving the traditional subjects of collective bargaining, such as wages, hours, dismissals, overtime and emergency work, pay period, manner of wage payment, shifts, apprentices and learners, deductions from wages, membership in unions, methods of bargaining, seniority, stretch-outs, conditions of work, health, sanitation.

[44] As notably in the U.A.W. Reuther plan for rationalization of the automobile industry, and the S.W.O.C. plan for rationalization of the steel industry, as wartime measures.

[45] For an exposition of this plan by its originator, C.I.O. President Philip Murray, see *Steel Labor*, April 18, 1941.

of union training schools for the education of younger leaders encourages the use of the information which these research facilities provide.[46]

This penetration by organized labor into fields once considered of sole concern to management means that a self-government of business and industry is slowly emerging which encompasses not only the joint regulation of labor relations by the bargaining agents but also the joint regulation of the total business operation.[47] This process may extend

[46] The present importance of these research and training programs should not be overrated, since they are for the most part young and limited and still untried on any extensive scale and since the labor unions as yet have not demonstrated any marked ability in their effective use. They are, however, potentially of extreme significance.

[47] The managerial function requires authority, and the demands of business operation a flexible control. The collective bargaining relationship has thus far provided the only feasible means of integrating the union within the business structure and allowing management to exercise the authority necessary to the operation of an enterprise. It has done this by allowing the union a voice in the determination of the standards to be observed by management, but permitting management freedom of discretion within the framework of those standards—that is to say, by permitting management to exercise executive and administrative discretion within the bounds of the industrial legislation provided in the trade-agreement. In the terms of Commons' institutional economics, the bargaining transaction precedes the managerial transaction. This arrangement will prove workable in the long run, however, only in so far as both management and organized labor recognize the reciprocal obligation of a strict adherence to the terms of their agreement. Any subtle attempts on the part of management to undermine the authority of the union (which constitutes, in effect, a second board of directors), any failure on its part to recognize the right of the union to full information regarding the operation of the business, will inevitably create a feeling of suspicion among the workers, which may find expression in the form of illegal strikes or unwilling performance of job tasks. Similarly, any refusal by organized labor to permit management full discretion within the terms of the trade-agreement or any attempt on its part to extend its rights except through the proper procedural channels will provoke distrust by management and a greater reluctance to incorporate the irresponsible union within the business frame-

over a long period of years; it may be interrupted in the course of its development; but that at the present time it is on the way to realization seems fairly evident.

Concurrently with the two developments already noted—the rise of genuine self-government in business and the gradual incursion of organized labor into all fields of management discretion—a third development is also in process, the widening of the area of negotiations. This movement finds its most important expression in a trend toward industry-wide collective bargaining.[48] The incen-

work. If organized business wishes to retain the self-regulation and autonomy which it enjoys to a large degree, the bargaining parties must establish a form of self-government which will permit the peaceful solution of the increasing problems inevitably following in the wake of union penetration into all fields of management discretion.

In passing, it may be noted that in this extension of collective bargaining into all fields of activity of the enterprise lies the primary distinction between collective bargaining in private industry and collective bargaining in the government. While in the latter sphere organized workers may be given the right to collaborate with respect to working conditions, it is obviously impossible to accord them any rights with respect to the joint determination of broader fields of management—that is, government—determination.

[48] An interesting and valuable study might well be made of the trend from local to national or industrial bargaining. Cf. Selig Perlman, "Trade Agreements," *Encyclopedia of the Social Sciences*, XIV (1935), 667: "Historically the development has been from local agreements covering a single craft to those which, if not necessarily national in scope, are at least limited by the standards of the national or international unions." For a brief summary of this trend in the United States, consult David A. McCabe, *Notes on Collective Bargaining* (Princeton, 1939), pp. 4–31. (Mimeographed.) The same development was noted earlier in Great Britain. See J. R. Hicks, "Early History of Industrial Conciliation," *Economica*, X (1930), 25–39, esp. 25–26, where he notes three stages in the evolution of collective bargaining machinery, beginning with local negotiations, followed by "rudimentary forms of general negotiations used mainly as a court of appeals from the localities," and, lastly, national negotiations, which draw authority away from the localities, concentrating the agreement-making

tive to establish such industry-wide organization lies in the desire on the part of both the union and organized employers to eliminate any competitive advantage that the unorganized employers may hold, such as a cost differential arising from the payment of nonunion wages, which acts as a threat to the security of the union and the economic security of its members.[49] An additional motive from the union's viewpoint is that industry organization makes easier the securing of an advantage which even in a well-organized field would be detrimental to the competitive position of any individual employer were he alone to grant it.

With well-established industry-wide conferences, such as those found in the coal, flint-glass, bottle-manufacturing, and pottery industries, as the nucleus for this movement, there is an increasing tendency for local negotiations to expand into city-wide or regional negotiations and for such area negotiations to graduate into industry conferences. This has been true in recent years, for example, in the railroad, men's-clothing, and retail meat industries.[50] In other

industries, such as steel and flat glass, contract leadership prevails, with the result that the agreement negotiated between the union and the industry leader sets the pattern for the entire industry.[51] The formation of the C.I.O., with its emphasis upon the industrial form of organization, has provided an impetus to this movement.[52] It is not surprising to find

[50] The railway brotherhoods' negotiations, although initiated by systems, have been largely conducted on a national scale since 1932. The Amalgamated Clothing Workers undertook national negotiations in 1937. The National Association of Retail Meat Dealers and the Amalgamated Meat Cutters and Butcher Workmen now negotiate uniform conditions, except for wages, for thirty thousand retail meat dealers, whereas negotiations involving this union have in the past been most frequently on a city-wide basis.

Even if actual area or industry collective bargaining is not established, the trend toward these is evident in such union provisions as that terms negotiated with an employers' association must apply to all individual employers with whom the union contracts in a given area, or that unions while bargaining separately shall co-ordinate their bargaining efforts (cf. *Constitution of Wood, Wire and Metal Lathers' International Union* [1939], sec. 102). The unions' frequent insistence upon basing their wage demands on comparative wage data rather than upon the profit position of a company, indicates an industry-mindedness, as also does their demand that wage increases be based upon the profit position of an industry rather than the individual companies composing it (cf. *National Agreement by and between Full-fashioned Hosiery Manufacturers of America and American Federation of Full-fashioned Hosiery Workers* [1931–32], Art. H, sec. 6). Similarly, from the employers' side, even though bargaining be done individually, industry stands on specific issues may be made, as has been true in the American Newspaper Publishers' Association (*Report of the Special Standing Committee* [1938–39]): "The only point on which a united position has been taken by a majority of publishers was the agreement that the closed shop should be opposed in news and editorial departments."

[51] In the steel industry the Carnegie-Illinois contract sets the pattern, while in the flat-glass industry the jointly negotiated agreement with the Pittsburgh Plate Glass and Libbey-Owens-Ford companies performs the same function.

[52] The attitude of the C.I.O. unions is expressed in the industry-councils plan advanced by President Philip Murray. His position is stated in *Steel Labor*, April 18, 1941, p. 11: "Modern labor relations are an integral part of industry planning. Such rela-

power in the hands of national officials. Note *Report of the Commission on Industrial Relations in Great Britain* (U.S. Department of Labor, 1938), p. 4. The Whitley Councils plan did much to further collective bargaining by industries in Great Britain (see John B. Seymour, *The Whitley Councils Scheme* [London, 1932]). Though applied in the United States only in the form of sec. 7(b) of N.I.R.A., the extension of a collective agreement to apply to an entire industry has provided encouragement to genuine industrial negotiations (cf. Ludwig Hamburger, "The Extension of Collective Agreements To Cover Entire Trades and Industries," *International Labor Review*, XL [1939], 153–94).

In the United States, industry- or trade-wide collective bargaining has not been general (see "Collective Bargaining with Employers' Associations," *Monthly Labor Review*, XLIX [1939], 302–5). The trend in this direction is apparent, however.

[49] Cf. S. H. Slichter, "Changing Character of American Industrial Relations," *American Economic Review*, Suppl., March, 1939, p. 127, esp. n. 15.

a high C.I.O. official predicting that the future will see the spread of collective bargaining relationships in which local unions will negotiate with local plants and national unions or federated locals will negotiate with national companies, to reach agreements supplementing an industry-wide contract emanating from a joint industry council.[53]

If these three trends are correlated— the rise of self-government in business, the extension of union control into all fields of managerial discretion, and the expansion of the area of negotiations into industry-wide collective bargaining— there emerges the suggestion of a pattern of industrial organization resembling a loose system of industrial corporatism. The realization of such a system may be a slow process, its outlines may not be precisely drawn, and it is unlikely that it will be achieved by simultaneously equivalent progress in all industries. It is likely to find its first expression in the dress-manufacturing industry, largely concentrated in the greater New York area, an industry whose N.R.-A. code, the result of the collaboration of organized employers and organized workers,[54] provides the clearest example

of the form such a system is likely to assume in its earliest stages.[55] The men's-clothing industry likewise is well along the road to formation of some form of a total industrial organization, while the full-fashioned hosiery industry is being impeded in this development largely by the failure of the organized employers and the union to extend the coverage of the "national" agreement over the southern branch of the industry.[56] In the basic industries the movement is in progress in coal, steel, and glass. The concentration of the automobile and rubber industries, each dominated by a compactly located trinity of manufacturers, with strong and progressive industrial unions present in each, lends itself to a similar but perhaps somewhat later development. In the field of transportation the railroad industry shows signs of a movement in

---

tions encompassed in collective bargaining, are inevitably directed towards industry-wide agreements. The older collective bargaining relationships, as in the coal industry, are already carried on by joint conferences of the entire industry. A number of the industry problems are closely integrated with labor relations."

[53] Within each level of organization, says this official, the union must be conceded the right to bargain respecting all functions of management, including determination of the production policy, the sales policy, the price policy, and the financial policy. This bargain would result in a trade-agreement within the framework of which management would be free to operate (interview, October 7, 1941).

This hierarchical form of industrial organization frequently is found in Great Britain (*Report of the Commission on Industrial Relations in Great Britain*, p. 4) and in Sweden (*Report of the Commission on Industrial Relations in Sweden* [U.S. Department of Labor, 1938], pp. 4–5).

[54] L. L. Lorwin and A. Wubnig, *Labor Relations Boards* (Washington, 1935), p. 58.

[55] Code of Fair Competition, Dress Manufacturing Industry, effective November 11, 1933, as contained in Lewis Mayers (ed.), *A Handbook of NRA* (2d ed.; New York, 1934), pp. 537–49. That the spirit of collaboration did not pass with the demise of N.R.A. is indicated in the Preamble of the 1941 agreements in the New York City dress industry:

"WHEREAS, The parties hereto recognize that employers and workers alike have much to gain through cooperative effort in stabilizing the industry, in providing for its efficient management, in planning for improvement therein, in encouraging and effecting the modernization of production units, in establishing conditions that will tend to secure to the workers continuity of employment, a fair living wage, adequate annual earnings and fair conditions of labor, and in providing methods for an equitable and peaceful adjustment of all disputes which may arise between the parties hereto and their members so as to secure uninterrupted operation of work. . . ."

[56] One has only to examine the volumes of recorded decisions of the impartial chairman to appreciate the extent to which collaboration has been achieved in this industry and a mature form of constitutional government established. The annual reports of Alfred Hoffman, first vice-president and director of research of the American Federation of Hosiery Workers, indicate the detailed consideration which the union is giving to all phases of the economics of the industry.

the same direction; the maritime industry gives indication that it may follow;[57] and in truck transportation the area of negotiations is rapidly widening to secure the same result.[58]

That such a "corporative" system will actually arise in America is speculative. That it is now in the process of development seems less debatable. Some doubt of this development may be held by those who conceive industrial corporatism only in terms of systems which have had foreign roots. As a tool of fascism, it can't happen here, they will contend.

Should the budding organized industry of America ever blossom into full flower, however, we may expect that this *indigenous* plant will have its own characteristics, and we may find that it can be made a tool of the democratic as well as of the Fascist state. We cannot assume, but it may prove to be true, that the organized industry will open up a possibility of industrial democracy which will provide a concomitant to the political democracy of the state.[59]

In the light of this industrial evolutionary trend, the limited significance which frequently has been attached to collective bargaining must blush itself out of the picture. However, as Leon Duguit observed in 1913, the full implications of the collective labor agreement cannot be appreciated until a trade or industry is so effectively organized that it is "almost a legally organized body."[60] Thus, while the remarks below have partial applicability at the present time, their broader and deeper import awaits the possible consolidation of organized businesses into organized industries.

The rise of the organized enterprise in America has certain effects upon any system of government controls over businesses "affected with the public interest." Two are here noted. First, it now becomes evident that if such government controls are to be effective, they must operate not only upon the legal corporation, or only upon the legal corporation and the union as separate autonomous organizations, but upon the organized

---

[57] The aggressive National Maritime Union is now pressing for nation-wide collective bargaining (see *Report of National Officers to the National Maritime Union* [1941], pp. 44–45). The Maritime Federation of the Pacific is now co-ordinating the activities of most major maritime unions on the West Coast. For a discussion of the perfecting of self-government in the West Coast maritime industry see Paul Eliel, "Labor Peace in Pacific Ports," *Harvard Business Review*, XIX (1941), 429–37.

[58] Multistate negotiations have been established, the largest of which is the Midwest agreement, covering twelve interstate trucking lines (see "Collective Bargaining with Employers' Associations," *Monthly Labor Review*, XLIX [1939], p. 307). In the important New York City trucking industry, self-regulation has been furthered by establishment of an office of the impartial chairman. As to the ability of the powerful Teamsters Union to make its voice heard in spheres of management "discretion," see R. A. Lester, *Economics of Labor* (New York, 1941), p. 193.

[59] This is not intended as a prediction but rather as a speculation. The issues involved are too complex to be discussed here. It may be briefly noted, however, that, in so far as a greater number of members of an industry participate in the govern-

ment of that industry and in so far as the basis for economic policy formation is thus broadened, democratic purposes may be served by the organized industry. On the other hand, in the absence of a defined responsibility on the part of the leaders of the organized industry—responsibility to the general public, to the government, to the consumers, to the workers, and to the owners—the organized industry may prove a dictatorial device.

It is to be emphasized that the organized industry is not here presented as a tool either of democracy or of fascism. Under differing circumstances it may prove to be either. The only point being made —a point which it is not possible to argue within the space of this article—is that there is no reason to assume a priori that if organized industries arise in this country they are necessarily opposed in principle to the democratic state (see J. J. Robbins, *The Politics of Labor Relations in Sweden* [Chapel Hill, 1942], p. 5; Louis L. Jaffe, "Lawmaking by Private Groups," *Harvard Law Review*, XLI [1937], 201–53, esp. 212 and 253; C. P. Malick, *Labor Policy under Democracy* [Boulder, Colorado, 1939], p. 127).

[60] *Law in the Modern State* (1913), translated into English by Frida and Harold Laski (New York, 1919), p. 121.

enterprise, which alone is responsible for production. Since the organized enterprise is founded upon the collective bargaining relationship, any controls over "organized businesses affected with the public interest" must operate upon the bargaining relationship.[61]

Second, to the extent that the operation of an organized enterprise is deemed vital to the public interest, to the extent, therefore, that public controls are established to maintain the continuity of the bargaining relationship on which it rests —to that extent the traditional concept of freedom of, contract must be further modified; for under these circumstances the state is seeking to compel the continuity of industrial governments whose existence rests upon a contractual relationship. It is therefore seeking to deny freedom not to contract.

In the system of relative laissez faire by which much of our social thinking is still conditioned, freedom *not* to contract was considered concomitant with freedom to contract. However, freedom not to contract may have to be hedged when the contract is the basis of an industrial government charged with the public interest. More realistically, in a society in which autonomous groups—infrastate governments like organized enterprises— are permitted to exercise important public functions, it may prove difficult to accept their freedom *not* to govern as a

necessary corollary of their freedom to govern. Breakdowns in such important "governmental" spheres may prove intolerable. In this situation the negative solution of antistrike acts may be tried, but its success is likely to be limited. A more positive approach would seek to improve and assist the functions of these important public bodies in an effort to prevent any breakdown from emerging.

This discussion is by no means intended to exhaust the subject of the controls necessarily or desirably to be exercised by the state over group-governments operating within its framework. Only a few of the broader problems introduced by the developing system of organized industries have here been touched upon.

Nor is there any intent in the foregoing discussion to indorse or to condemn an industrial system modeled on the lines envisioned here. Open-mindedness is called for in evaluating the organized industry on the balance sheet of the democratic society. With proper controls, it may prove an asset. In the absence of proper controls, or with faulty regulation, it may prove a liability.

Four important relationships must be kept in mind in considering the regulatory requirements of a society of organized industries, if such a society should emerge in the United States: (1) the relationship of the individual to the group-government; (2) the relationship of the individual to the state; (3) the relationship of one group-government to other group-governments; and (4) the relationship of the group-government to the state. It is only upon an evaluation of the nature of these four relationships at a given historical moment that organized business in America may be properly appraised as a system of industrial government.

WASHINGTON, D.C.

[61] The nature of state intervention in the affairs of organized groups calls for thoughtful examination. If any large-scale curtailment of group autonomy is attempted, state domination may threaten democratic foundations. On the other hand, group autonomy cannot be permitted such scope that it may undermine the legitimate rights and interests of other groups or individuals. It is suggested here without amplification that in balancing these two important considerations, an emphasis on procedural requirements may help to provide a healthy solution. This is not to say, however, that standards of policy determination may not be found necessary in given situations.

Industry-Wide Bargaining

COLLECTIVE BARGAINING WITH ASSOCIATIONS AND GROUPS OF EMPLOYERS[1]

Most of the examples of industry-wide bargaining in the United States are the product of generations of experience, and as a rule the employer-union relations in these industries have been remarkably stable and peaceful. In the pressed or blown glassware industry, one of the branches of glass and glassware having national bargaining, no major strike throughout the industry has occurred since collective bargaining began with an employers' association in 1888. Similar conditions have prevailed in the pottery industry since 1922. The 1946 contract between the National Automatic Sprinkler and Fire Control Association and the United Association of Journeymen Plumbers and Steamfitters (AFL) is a revision of the original agreement of 1915; and the 1946 agreement between the Anthracite Coal Operators and the United Mine Workers of America (AFL) is a compilation of resolutions, revisions, rulings, and decisions dating back to 1903. Bargaining on an industry basis exists in the elevator installation and repair, installation of automatic sprinklers, pottery and related products, stove making, and wall-paper industries, and in coal mining.

Agreements covering all the employers in an industry within a geographic region are somewhat more numerous than those having application throughout an entire industry. Even more numerous are the instances in which associations or groups of employers are dealt with on a city-wide or metropolitan area basis. In this study, the existing extent and the areas of bargaining with associations and groups of employers are described. The most significant extension of this form of bargaining in recent years occurred during World War II in the shipbuilding industry. The Metal Trades Department of the American Federation of Labor negotiated a master agreement during 1941 with Pacific Coast shipyards organized by unions affiliated with the AFL. Prior to this time, joint agreements had been signed by these unions on the West Coast with employers in a single day. In other industries, since 1939, the practice only widened in those that had used this method of dealing for many years. The number of workers covered by these agreements increased somewhat as more of the Nation's industry became organized and was brought under agreement.

[1] Prepared by Roy M. Patterson and the staff of the Collective Bargaining Division of the Bureau's Industrial Relations Branch, under the general supervision of Harold S. Roberts, Chief. Special credit is also due for the contributions made by Abraham Weiss, Jesse Carpenter, and Philomena Marquardt.

However, the relative proportion covered in most industries did not change greatly.

Few of the examples of collective bargaining on an industry, geographic, or city basis occurred in the mass-production industries, although a single agreement in the automobile industry, for instance, may cover many more employees than an association agreement covering every employer in an industry or trade within the same city. In mass-production industries, trends are developing toward standardized conditions in large segments of industries through corporation-wide collective bargaining. The efforts of unions are directed first toward bringing all the plants of a given large corporation, regardless of geographic location, within the scope of a single agreement. An example is the corporation-wide bargaining between the Ford Motor Co. and the United Automobile, Aircraft and Agricultural Implement Workers of America (CIO). Notwithstanding the great number of workers affected, corporation-wide bargaining differs widely from multi—employer collective bargaining which is the subject of the present study.

Early in 1947, more than 4 million workers were covered by agreements negotiated between trade-unions and associations and groups of employers. These are about equally divided between manufacturing and nonmanufacturing industries. Approximately a fourth of all workers covered by union agreements in manufacturing and a third of such workers in nonmanufacturing are working under agreements negotiated with groups or associations of employers. The agreements were negotiated by one or more unions (1) with a formal or informal association of employers or (2) with informal multi-employer groups. In presenting the information on agreements, no attempt was made to distinguish between agreements with associations and with other multi-employer groups. Identical agreements signed by separate employers with the same union were included, if there appeared to have been negotiations with a group or committee of employers.

Worker Coverage of Group Bargaining

In table 1, the extent of association and employer-group bargaining is shown, based upon the percent of total workers under agreement in the respective industries.

TABLE 1.—*Percent of all workers under agreement who are covered by agreements with associations and groups of employers, by industry*

80–100 percent	60–79 percent	40–59 percent	20–39 percent
Clothing, men's Clothing, women's Coal mining Laundry and cleaning and dyeing Longshoring Maritime Shipbuilding and boatbuilding [1]	Baking Book and job printing and publishing Canning and preserving foods Construction Dyeing and finishing textiles Glass and glassware Malt liquors Pottery and related products Trucking and warehousing.	Building service and maintenance Leather products, other Newspaper and periodical printing and publishing	Beverages, nonalcoholic Hosiery Hotels and restaurants Jewelry and silverware Lumber Shoes, cut stock and findings Trade

0–19 percent			
Agricultural machinery and tractors [2] Aircraft and parts [2] Automobiles and parts [2] Bus and streetcar, local [2] Bus lines, intercity [2] Carpets and rugs, wool [2] Cement [2] Chemicals, excluding rayon and allied products [2] Clerical and professional, excluding transportation, communication, theaters, and newspapers Cotton textiles	Confectionery products Crude petroleum and natural gas [2] Dairy products Electrical machinery, equipment and appliances Flour and other grain products Furniture Knit goods, except hosiery Leather (tanned, curried and finished) Light and power [2] Machinery and machine tools	Meat packing Metal mining Motorcycles, bicycles, and parts [2] Newspaper offices Nonferrous metals and products, except jewelry and silverware Nonmetallic mining and quarrying Paper and pulp Paper products Petroleum and coal products, except refining [2] Petroleum refining [2]	Railroad equipment [2] Rayon and allied products [2] Rubber products [2] Silk and rayon textiles Steel, basic [2] Steel products Stone and clay products. other Sugar, beet and cane Telegraph service and maintenance [2] Telephone service and maintenance [2] Tobacco manufactures Woolen and worsted textiles

[1] During World War II most of the industry was covered by tripartite zone standard agreements, signed by representatives of unions, employers, and certain government agencies. The principal association agreement other than the zone standard agreements is between Pacific Coast Shipbuilders and the Metal Trades Department of the AFL, covering yards organized by AFL unions.   [2] Less than half of 1 percent.

Area Coverage of Group Bargaining

The industries are classified by area of bargaining in table 2.

TABLE 2.—*Area of bargaining with associations or groups of employers, by industry*

Bargaining on a national or industry-wide scale	Bargaining by geographic (regional) areas	Bargaining within a city, county, or metropolitan area
Coal mining Elevator installation and repair Glass and glassware Installation of automatic sprinklers Pottery and related products Stoves Wall paper	Canning and preserving foods [1] Dyeing and finishing textiles [1] Fishing Hosiery Leather (tanned, curried, and finished) [1] Longshoring [1] Lumber [1] Maritime Metal mining Nonferrous metals and products, except jewelry and silverware [1] Paper and pulp Shoes, cut stock and findings [1]	Baking Beverages, nonalcoholic Book and job printing and publishing Building service and maintenance Clothing, men's [2] Clothing, women's [2] Confectionery products Construction Cotton textiles Dairy products Furniture [2] Hotel and restaurant Jewelry and silverware Knit goods Laundry and cleaning and dyeing Leather products, other Malt liquors Meat packing Newspaper printing and publishing Paper products, except wall paper Silk and rayon textiles Steel products, except stoves [2] Tobacco Trade [2] Trucking and warehousing [2]

[1] There also is some bargaining on a city, county, and/or metropolitan area basis.
[2] There also is some bargaining on a regional and/or industry-wide basis.

Approach to Standardization of Working Conditions

One of the major efforts of labor unions in this country has been directed toward the standardization of working conditions throughout an industry or area, in order to lift substandard wages and to eliminate or reduce the factors of wages and hours in competitive costs. One of the ways the labor movement has sought to attain this objective has been by pressing for Federal or State legislation for the protection of certain groups of workers or to establish minimum standards applicable to all workers. Legislation has been sought especially for women and minors on the ground that the interests of society as a whole require that the health and welfare of these groups of workers be protected, and also because they often are in a weak bargaining position and might be used to lower the standards of all workers. Certain minimum standards of health, safety, and sanitation were established by legislation when large sections of the population felt a need for such, and the labor movement from time to time has favored legislative action as the most effective remedy for problems of health and safety. Under the Fair Labor Standards Act, minimum wage and hour standards have been established in much of American industry, thus raising the area of collective bargaining on these issues to higher levels.

Prior to World War II the approach to standardization of wages and working conditions through governmental action was secondary as far as American trade-unions are concerned. Organized labor in this country has directed its chief efforts toward standardization by means of collective bargaining. For this reason the labor movement generally has encouraged parallel organizations of employers for collective-bargaining purposes, in order to obtain extended coverage under one agreement. In some industries the employers also have favored the extension of uniform wages and working conditions by making the terms of a collective-bargaining agreement applicable to a large segment of an industry. When collective bargaining with groups or associations of employers has proved impracticable or impossible, some unions have utilized the technique of presenting identical agreements to the employers within an industry or competitive area. This latter method usually is practicable only in instances where there are a large number of small employers, particularly within a metropolitan area.

Although industry-wide trade associations have come to be a common characteristic of American business, the scope of employer groups or associations engaged in collective bargaining is generally much more limited. Within an industry, employers may be organized for purposes of collective bargaining on a city, regional or, in a few instances, nation-wide basis, or two or more such employer organizations may exist in the same area. As a rule, the unions work toward the extension of the collective-bargaining agreement to as wide a section of the industry as possible. In a number of cases the unions and employer organizations together have directed their efforts toward bringing unorganized sections of the industry within the scope of collective-bargaining agreements. A necessary corollary of dealing through employers' associations is a high degree of unionization among the employees.

During World War II, industry-wide production drives, settling of labor disputes by the National War Labor Board on the basis of industry or area practice, and the Government's wage stabilization policies all contributed to standardization of wages and working conditions throughout industries or areas. Directives of the National War Labor Board were influenced by precedent and prevailing practices in the industry or area and many agreements in the same industry came to have similar provisions on certain subjects. Frequently an order of the Board would affect several employers and the substance of the order would be incorporated into union agreements the employers might have negotiated, without regard to the existence of an employers' association. In the shipbuilding industry, in which a stabilization commission was established, tripartite "zone standard" agreements were negotiated, covering a limited number of subjects. The parties to the agreements were the Government itself and most of the employers and unions in the industry. The shipbuilding industry in the United States was divided into four zones, in each of which the "zone standards" determined practices with regard to those subjects covered by the agreements.

The attention directed to a few national associations with long records of collective bargaining should not be permitted to obscure thousands of employer organizations which have negotiated agreements on a regional or metropolitan basis and which affect hundreds of thousands of workers. These employer groups vary widely as to type, structure, procedure, and scope of activity. Some are temporary and highly informal, with no tangible evidences of permanent organization. Others have complex structures with elaborate constitutions and a staff of full-time employees. Between these extremes there are wide variations in organization, procedures, and functions.

Nation-Wide Collective Bargaining in the Coal Industry

In anthracite mining a single agreement is signed to cover the entire industry. In bituminous-coal mining, the union negotiated agreements with the operators in the Central Competitive Field (Ohio, Indiana, Illinois, and West Virginia) from 1898 until 1927. The agreement for this area set the pattern for negotiations in other areas between districts of the union and local associations of coal-mine operators. The interstate bargaining relationship in the Central Competitive Field collapsed in 1927 and was not reestablished until after the passage of the National Industrial Recovery Act. In 1934 an agreement was signed with the operators in the Appalachian Area which served, as the previous interstate agreement had, as a pattern which the remainder of the industry generally followed. Districts of the United Mine Workers of America negotiate agreements with parallel associations of employers, which follow the terms of the Appalachian agreement. In 1941 the northern and southern groups of operators in the Appalachian area signed separate agreements with the union, and unified negotiations were not reestablished until 1945. In that year, the first industry-wide agreement in bituminous-coal mining was negotiated.

Following the break-down of negotiations between the union and the operators in the spring of 1946, which led to a Nation-wide soft-coal strike, and the rejection by both the union and the operators of President Truman's May 16 arbitration proposal, the President on May 21 "authorized and directed" the Secretary of the Interior to take over the mines. On May 29 an agreement was signed by John L. Lewis, president of the union, and J. A. Krug, Coal Mines Administrator and Secretary of the Interior. The agreement covered all the wines which were seized.

National Bargaining on the Railroads

The traditional bargaining unit in railroad transportation is the individual railroad system. The workers are organized on the basis of craft, and agreements with the various systems are negotiated by each craft union or by "system federations" of shop craft unions. Although the regular working agreements continue to be signed by systems, on occasion certain specific questions of major importance, as wages, have been settled on a Nation-wide basis. Negotiations are generally conducted by the nonoperating unions (clerical, mainten-ance, and shop crafts) and by the operating unions (train and engine service) separately with representatives of the railroads selected on a regional basis.

Other Industry or Trade-Wide Bargaining

The American examples of trade-wide bargaining of longest status occur in the pottery and glassware industries. Since the early years of this century, an annual meeting has been held between the repre-sentatives of the United States Potters' Association and the National

Brotherhood of Operative Potters. The current agreement between these parties, for example, continues a provision for joint discharge committees first set up in 1913. Since 1888 the National Association of Manufacturers of Pressed and Blown Glassware, or its predecessor, has been meeting with the American Flint Glass Workers Union. The "Star Island Agreement" of 1903 established a grievance procedure which still is utilized in this industry. The Glass Bottle Blowers' Association of the United States and Canada signed its first national agreement in 1890 and currently has an agreement with the Glass Container Manufacturers' Institute which affects several thousand employees in the industry.

In each of these cases the bargaining agreements are confined chiefly to detailed piece-rate schedules, although a considerable body of "unwritten law" has developed to supplement the national agreement in governing employer-employee relations within a plant. Originally, the trade-wide bargaining was established to regulate the working conditions of highly skilled craftsmen within these industries. With the development of technological changes, one skilled occupation after another has been eliminated. As a result, the unions have extended their jurisdiction to include a major part of the workers in and around the plants and these skilled and semiskilled employees are now covered in the national agreements to the degree that they are unionized. In the glassware industry, however, there are some companies which have negotiated separate agreements. In the pottery industry virtually all of the vitreous and semivitreous branches of the industry are covered by the association agreement.

A different kind of bargaining relationship has been built up in the manufacture of flat glass. By far the major part of the production in this industry is centralized in two large producing companies. These companies, the Pittsburgh Plate Glass Co. and the Libby-Owens-Ford Glass Co., negotiate their agreements jointly, both with the Window Glass Cutters League (AFL) and the Federation of Glass, Ceramic and Silica Sand Workers (CIO), but each company signs separate, identical agreements. The two companies also collaborate in the administration of the agreement to insure uniform patterns of interpretation. Most of the other manufacturers are organized into the Fourcault Manufacturers' Association which negotiates the agreement with the unions.

There are a few other instances of industry-wide dealing, each of them originating from the efforts of a highly skilled craft to protect its conditions of employment. Among these are the Wall Paper Institute and the United Wall Paper Craftsmen and Workers of North America, covering wall paper printing; the National Automatic Sprinkler Association and the United Association of Journeymen

Plumbers and Steamfitters of the United States and Canada, covering sprinkler fitting; and the Manufacturers Protective and Development Association and the International Molders and Foundry Workers Union of North America, covering stove-molding and hot-water castings.

Employers engaged in the manufacture of paper-mill wire cloth sign similar agreements with the American Wire Weavers' Protective Association. Another instance of trade-wide bargaining occurs in the installation, repair, and maintenance of elevators. Although wage rates are negotiated locally, other working conditions are regulated by conferences between the National Elevator Manufacturing Industry, Inc., and the International Union of Elevator Constructors. A standard agreement is used in all localities, with the locally negotiated rates inserted as agreed upon.

The manufacture of wooden kegs and barrels should also be mentioned as an instance of national conferences between the employers and the union. The conferences, however, have resulted in no agreement on an industry scale and discussion of working conditions has been of far less importance than mutual discussion of trade-promotion plans.

Industry-Wide Bargaining in Mass-Production Industries

In the more recently organized, mass-production industries there are at present no examples of industry-wide collective bargaining resulting in a single union agreement covering the full range of employer-union relations. In a few such industries, however, certain bargaining relationships have come into existence which produce considerable uniformity in the agreements throughout an industry. In the rubber industry, for example, a wage-increase agreement was signed on March 2, 1946, by the four largest manufacturers, which affected a large proportion of the workers in the industry. This so-called "Big Four" agreement is limited in scope to a few subjects; it differs from the usual union agreement also in that it does not have the customary provisions relating to termination and renewal. The agreement provides: "This agreement shall finally dispose of all issues covered in these negotiations including all of the union's 7-point program for a period of 1 year except that during this 1-year period the general wage scale shall be subject to negotiation if conditions economically and in the industry warrant, but only on a four-company (Big Four) basis." If this joint relationship of the four corporations with the United Rubber, Cork, Linoleum and Plastic Workers of America is continued in the future, it may be possible to describe the collective bargaining in this industry as approaching industry-wide negotiations.

A degree of standardization has been achieved in the meat-packing industry through the medium of uniform expiration dates of the agreements with the principal packers. Certain agreements affecting a large number of workers negotiated by the United Packinghouse Workers of America (CIO) and by the Amalgamated Meat Cutters and Butcher Workmen of North America (AFL), covering various plants of the four largest corporations in the industry, have expired on the same day each year for several years.

Negotiation of Similar Agreements in the Steel Industry

In the basic steel industry in the United States there is no employers' association which engages in collective bargaining, yet a great deal of standardization in industrial relations has occurred in recent years. The industry is composed of two dominant groups of employers, one known as "Big Steel" and the other as "Little Steel." The first includes the United States Steel Corp. and its subsidiaries, and the second is made up of a number of independent companies. The Steel Workers Organizing Committee, now the United Steelworkers of America, first signed written agreements with the U. S. Steel Corp. in 1937 and since then, with a few exceptions, practically all of the basic steel industry has been brought under agreement. Even though there is no bargaining by employers' associations, the major provisions of agreements throughout the basic steel industry are similar. This degree of uniformity is occasioned by a number of factors, first among them probably being the predominant position of the United States Steel Corp. Agreements with this corporation tend to set the pattern for the rest of the industry. Also, by long-established practice the same wage adjustments generally are made throughout the industry at the same time. During World War II directives of the National War Labor Board, which generally were applicable to large sections of the industry, further encouraged the growth of uniform collective-bargaining practices. The United Steelworkers of America, the most important union in the industry, also tended to bring a degree of uniformity into the bargaining relationships and practices. Agreements with most of the employers in the basic steel industry will expire in February 1947, and negotiations are in process for new agreements. (Since this was written the parties have agreed to extend the agreements until April 30, 1947.)

Collective Bargaining by Geographic Areas

In the hosiery industry a bargaining relationship has existed between the Full-Fashioned Hosiery Manufacturers of America, Inc., and the American Federation of Hosiery Workers since 1927. The employers' association, originally covering only Philadelphia mills, now covers a major part of the northern section of the full-fashioned hosiery industry. Conferences occur annually, with occasional additional meetings on specific subjects. Under the agreement the joint relations are administered by a permanent impartial chairman.

In the textile industry there are association agreements between the Textile Workers' Union of America and associations of silk and rayon mills in a number of States. A joint arrangement of longer standing exists in the dyeing and finishing of textiles in nonintegrated mills. In cotton textiles in Massachusetts and in knit goods in Philadelphia and New York, many of the employers are members of associations which negotiate union agreements.

Maritime workers usually deal with employer organizations which represent the shipping operators on a given coast. Practically all the union agreements in the maritime industry are negotiated with associations or informal committees representing the employers. On the Pacific Coast the companies are organized into the Pacific American Shipowners Association. On the Atlantic and Gulf Coasts the most recent agreements were negotiated and signed by a Committee for Companies and Agents, Atlantic and Gulf Coasts, most of the members of which are also members of the American Merchant Marine Institute.

The Waterfront Employers of the Pacific Coast embraces employers of longshoremen along the entire West Coast; much of the work of the association, however, is carried on through affiliated local Waterfront Employers Associations in Seattle, Portland, San Francisco, and San Pedro (Los Angeles). The International Longshoremen's and Warehousemen's Union (CIO) negotiates a general cargo agreement with the coast-wide association, which signs "on behalf of" the four local organizations. Separate agreements covering dock workers and ship clerks are negotiated with each of the port associations. On the Atlantic Coast the International Longshoremen's Association. (AFL) as a rule, negotiates separate agreements with employer associations in each port.[2]

In the Pacific Northwest the pulp and paper industry, although dealing elsewhere on the basis of individual companies, is combined

[2] For some time there has been no formal federated organization of the unions in the maritime industry. For a few months during 1946, however, the CIO unions and an independent formed the committee for maritime unity for the purpose of joint negotiations with all employers simultaneously. The American Federation of Labor, also in 1946, established a Maritime Trades Department, composed of AFL unions in the industry. Most of the unlicensed personnel on the Atlantic Coast are represented by the National Maritime Union (CIO). On the West Coast these workers are represented principally by three unions, the Sailors' Union of the Pacific (AFL), the Pacific Coast Marine Firemen, Oilers, Watertenders and Wipers Association (independent), and the National Union of Marine Cooks and Stewards (CIO).

into the Pacific Coast Association of Pulp and Paper Manufacturers which deals with the two national unions in the field. The unions, representing different occupations in the industry, are the International Brotherhood of Papermakers and the International Brotherhood of Pulp, Sulphite, and Paper Mill Workers. The employers' organization is described in the agreement as follows: "This Pacific Coast Association of Pulp and Paper Manufacturers * * * of which the signatory company is a member, is an employer association of a majority of the pulp and paper manufacturing companies in the Pacific Coast area, comprising the States of Washington, Oregon, and California, and as bargaining agent with authority to bind its members by a majority vote of such mills, has met with a bargaining committee from the signatory union for a period of years, beginning in 1934 * * *." Notwithstanding this provision, each company signs a separate document with the local unions which represent its employees.

The lumber industry is one which is not yet well organized throughout the country but in which the dominant method of present dealing is through associations within the producing area. The Columbia Basin Loggers' Association and the Timber Producers' Association in Minnesota are examples of associations dealing with the union in this industry.

The fishing industry, particularly on the Pacific Coast where it is well organized, is an example of collective bargaining almost exclusively on an association basis. The employers, however, are organized into a number of separate associations, such as the Alaska Packers' Association and the Central Pacific Wholesale Fish Dealers' Association.

In retail trade, the National Association of Retail Meat Dealers, composed of affiliated State and local associations throughout the United States, negotiates with the Amalgamated Meat Cutters and Butcher Workmen of America. The national agreement between these parties, first negotiated in 1937, is confined to a statement of principles and policies of mutual interest to both parties, who agree to "give their aid and good offices to the execution of fair and reasonable contracts between local unions and affiliated associations in the various localities where the said unions and affiliated associations exist." The agreement further states that it is recognized "that local conditions require local treatment and that it is not practical or feasible to include in this agreement the matters of wages, hours, and conditions of employment." In the Midwest, the Central States Drivers' Council, an organ of the International Brotherhood of Teamsters, Chauffeurs, Warehousemen and Helpers of America (AFL) negotiates agreements with the Central States Area Employers Association Negotiating

Committee.   Collective bargaining in canning and preserving foods on the West Coast is largely on an association basis.

Most of the shipbuilding and boatbuilding industry on the West Coast is covered by a master agreement negotiated by the Metal Trades Department of the American Federation of Labor.   During the war, as previously noted, bargaining on major issues in this industry was on a tripartite basis, and wages and certain other questions were determined by the zone standards.   Issues not covered by the zone standards were settled in the ordinary processes of collective bargaining.   At the present time the zone standards are still in effect.

Bargaining in the Needle Trades Within Metropolitan Areas

Outstanding examples of stable bargaining relationships over a long period of time between employers' associations and unions are found in the needle trades.   In the men's and women's clothing, men's hats and millinery, and fur industries the earliest efforts of unions to organize were accompanied by efforts to combine into associations the employers within the producing area.   Bargaining has become established in these industries, with highly developed industrial relations machinery within each of the metropolitan areas which are important as producing centers.   These unions and employers' associations customarily make use of a permanent impartial chairman to administer the agreement and there are numerous examples of joint trade boards, stabilization commissions, and other similar bodies which deal on a day-to-day basis with the problems of the industry.

These industries all have the problem of "run-away" shops, which leave the unionized areas and, with the small capital investment required, are able to establish themselves in low-wage, semirural sections.   This has been a major reason for the unions' insistence upon dealing on an association basis, for it is through the combined pressure of both the union and the employer association that these "run-away" shops can be brought under control.   Another problem within these industries is the regulation of the jobber-contractor relationship.   Jobbers have taken advantage of both the extreme seasonal fluctuations and the small investment required in setting up a shop to encourage an oversupply of contractors.   Cut-throat competition among the contractors has been furthered by the frequent practice of establishing "fly by night" shops for the duration of a contract secured by underbidding regularly operating shops.   Both the owners of shops operating under union conditions and their workers have thus faced a constant threat to industrial stability.   Through collective bargaining, the oversupply of contractors has been dealt with and the jobber's responsibility for maintaining union conditions in his contract shops has been established. A large portion of the employer-union negotiations in the needle trades deal with these three-way problems, in addition to the usual wages, hours, and working conditions.

The employers within a given city are usually organized into more than one association within each of the needle trades. The basis of distinction is both the type of product and the classification of employers (i. e., jobbers, contractors, or inside manufacturers). The unions have frequently expressed a desire for more uniformity among the employers' organizations throughout the industry. Although a major part of the production in the country is covered by the New York City agreements alone, the unions have made repeated efforts over several decades to secure industry-wide dealing in the interests of national standardization. Thus far, however, only in men's clothing has there been a successful approach to industry-wide bargaining. For a number of years the Amalgamated Clothing Workers of America has negotiated major wage questions with the Clothing Manufacturers' Association of the United States and with the Shirt Industry.

Other City-Wide Bargaining

In many industries and trades characterized by numerous small establishments within a city, collective bargaining has been conducted with associations of employers within the city. In many cases the associations are formal organizations in which the association officers have the power to bind all members to the agreed terms of employment. In other cases the employers may unite informally and perhaps only for the duration of the bargaining conferences. In many instances the lack of a continuing employers' association makes no difference in the actual negotiation of the agreement, but complicates considerably the enforcement of the agreement.

In cases of city-wide bargaining the extent of coverage of the employers' association generally depends upon the strength of the union. It is common to find within a city an organized group of employers dealing with the union, while other employers within the same industry are organized into a separate association or have no organization. In some cases the union employers form an organized group within a trade association which also includes nonunion employers in the city.

There are probably 5,000 local or city employer associations throughout the country which deal with various unions. More of these are found in building construction than in any other single industry. Other examples, in which the predominant method of dealing is with city-wide associations, are brewing, retail trade, baking, printing and publishing, restaurants, trucking, and barber shops.

An important development is found in the electrical machinery industry, where the United Electrical, Radio and Machine Workers of America (CIO) recently negotiated an agreement with the Electronics Manufacturers' Association, representing 20 employers in the New York City area. This association was formed at the insistence of the employers, who are relatively small and who previously had signed separate agreements. The employers desire, through negotiating a single blanket agreement, to achieve a degree of uniformity in wage and working conditions in order to reduce these as competitive factors in costs.

Associations of Employers Across Industry Lines

Employer-group federations embracing all types of business within a city are largely a development of the last 10 years and are concentrated in the Far Western States. Leader in this field is the San Francisco Employers Council, formed in 1939, and which in April 1945 had 1,995 members, 919 of whom were affiliated through their various industry groups. The other members were individuals or independent companies. The objectives of the council, as stated in its articles of incorporation, are (1) to encourage the organization of autonomous employer groups and cooperation among these groups in matters relating to labor relations; (2) "to promote the recognition and exercise of the right of employers to bargain collectively"; and (3) upon request, "to assist its members and others in matters relating to the negotiation, execution and performance of fair labor contracts." The council negotiates or participates in negotiations of agreements between its members and the unions in the city, and performs various other services.

Of a similar character is the Industrial Conference Board of, Tacoma, Wash.—an over-all agency for a number of independent companies and 15 or 20 employers' associations each of which has one or more union agreements. Both the Reno Employers Council of Reno, Nev., and the Silver Bow Employers Association of Butte, Mont., participate in the negotiation of labor contracts for their various employer groups. In Sacramento, Calif., the Sacramento Valley Associated Industries is the unifying agency for a dozen or more associations covering such varied fields as bowling alleys, beverages, furniture warehouses, taxicabs, machine shops, liquor and tobacco dealers, retail foods, wholesale bakeries, draymen, druggists, tire dealers, and building owners. Each association has a union contract signed in its behalf by an individual, who serves both as executive secretary to the associations and as general manager of the Associated Industries.

PROBLEMS OF INDUSTRY-WIDE
OR REGIONAL TRADE AGREEMENTS

By DAVID A. McCABE

I shall confine my discussion to industry-wide agreements. Regional agreements, covering distinct geographical segments of the same industry but not connected through any "master agreement" for the industry as a whole, are not likely to be numerous enough or permanent enough to warrant the space necessary for treatment as a type separate from industry-wide agreements. They resemble industry-wide agreements much more than they do local bargaining in that they have to overcome the centrifugal forces of interlocality variation in living costs, transportation costs, and in the level of wages for "similar grades of labor in the locality." Once they have overcome the inertia of local differentiation, they tend to develop into industry-wide agreements, if the employers of the several regions are faced by the same national union. The boundaries of the several competitive regions are seldom either distinctly marked or fixed in time. The tendency is to bring the amount of the differentials allowed among the several regions under industry-wide control, if not to eliminate the differentials.

What are the prospects that the forces which had made industry-wide agreements in American industry so exceptional a decade ago will be overcome in the near future?[1] It would be hazardous to predict that industry-wide agreements will become general; yet there are good reasons for believing that in industries characterized by a wide area of production for the same market the trend of the quarter century before 1933 has been reversed and that industry-wide agreements will appear in a number of important industries.

We have to distinguish, of course, between the way and the will, between the technical difficulties and economic resistance. You will recall Professor Barnett's findings that national or regional agreements could not be expected to survive for long unless they were built around bargaining for wages and that this was not likely unless the wages were in the form of piece rates.[2] Here we encountered the technical difficulty, if not impossibility, in most industries, of fixing really standardized piece rates for the whole industry. Thus, industry-wide agreements seemed to

---

[1] I am not including transportation in this discussion. It presents some problems different from those in manufacturing or mining and to include it would make the paper too long.

[2] George E. Barnett, "National and District Systems of Collective Bargaining," *Quarterly Journal of Economics*, Vol. XXVI (1912), pp. 425-443.

be blocked by the technical difficulty of fixing uniform wages rates on a piecework basis.

In the light of changed conditions, we must now re-examine the possibilities. What degree of wage-rate control is necessary today for industry-wide bargaining and how difficult would it now be to attain it?

First of all, it would seem still to be necessary to control the ups and downs of the level of wages, of the percentage of general increases or decreases. I am referring to industries with wider than local areas of competition, not to such industries as the building industry, newspaper publishing, or local service industries. Without assuming too restricted an area of competition for these, it is obvious that it is much more limited for them than for most manufacturing industries. An industry-wide trade agreement covering the manufacture of structural steel, for example, would be difficult to maintain if some plants under the agreement were allowed to seize an important competitive advantage over others by securing a reduction in wages ahead of the others or delaying an increase that the others had already given. Whereas an industry-wide agreement in the construction industry, if one were possible, would not necessarily be wrecked by the fact that local wage rates were advanced or reduced in some localities without a similar change being made simultaneously in all the others.

The control of general percentage changes in the wage level does not require uniformity of wage rates, even where the area of competition is wide. What it does require is that the industry-wide joint conference shall control the geographical differentials. That may not be necessary at the outset but it is difficult to keep an agreement running on year after year while differentials are permitted to continue to which a considerable section of the industry objects and which are untouchable by the joint conference. In other words, the underlying basic wage rates in each locality as well as the general advances and decreases must be subject to the action of the joint conference. I am speaking, of course, of industries in which labor costs are an important part of the cost of production. And one gets the impression from the resistance offered in normal times to demands for wage increases that there are very few industries in which they are not.

The technical feasibility of this control is much greater when it is technically possible to fix piece rates for the work done under the industry-wide agreement. The piece rate shows the labor cost of the operation, as well as the earnings of the worker in terms of output. Where working conditions and facilities (for the workers) are uniform, uniformity of piece rates for a standardized product gives uniformity of labor cost and uniformity of earnings for skill and effort expended. And when differentials are allowed in piece rates for a standardized product under uniform working conditions and uniform facilities, the degree of discount allowed in the labor cost is clear. The control of labor costs by unitary control of the wage rates is thus technically feasible.

It is this clear expression of labor costs in the wage rate that made it easier to get unitary bargaining for wages over the competitive area when it was technically feasible to set piece rates. Where the minimum time-rate system prevailed, or such piece rates as were set were fixed locally for unstandardized products, the wage rate did not reveal the labor cost in terms of like or comparable products and there was not the same pressure for unitary control of wage rates over the competitive area. Generally, the pressure for unitary control was not strong enough to overcome the inertia of interlocality differentiation in time rates.

If the desire for industry-wide agreement on wages is strong enough, it should now be possible to surmount the technical difficulties in the way of reducing wage rates to labor costs where the fixing of standardized piece rates is not technically feasible. We have made enough progress in the techniques of fixing production standards to accompany basic time rates to be able to measure the relative labor costs of comparable products made in different plants. A good time-study group could give a substantially correct estimate of the difference in labor costs involved in the rates under discussion—good enough, at least, to settle the truth of a contention that a particular rate gives a substantial advantage in labor costs. If this can be done, it should be possible to get closely enough to the kind of control over labor costs and earnings that a standardized piece scale permits, to secure unitary bargaining on wages through the use of basic time rates.

I realize the difficulty of standardizing basic time rates in a large industry with job classifications varying from plant to plant. But a uniform job classification should not be necessary, any more than uniformity of process or uniformity of pattern. The objective is not uniformity of all time rates but the avoidance of competition based on lower labor costs due solely to lower wage rates, or at least the control of such competition. Obviously it is the total of the labor costs involved in the wages of the workers to whom the agreement applies that counts. Variations in classification are not disturbing unless they represent important differences in labor cost for the same grades of labor on the same or similar products under similar conditions. Undoubtedly, an industry-wide agreement would lead to a greater approach to uniformity in job classification, but such uniformity is not necessary to the establishment of an industry-wide agreement.

An agreement could well start with basic time rates for a few brackets, as minima, with provision for a joint committee, with expert assistance, to hear and act upon appeals concerning rates alleged to be unfairly competitive or to give too low earnings. Each plant could continue its job classification and basic rates and incentive system, if it has one, until its rates or standards were revised by the joint commission—if they were shown to need revision—to bring them into line with the labor costs standards of the remainder of the industry.

All of this sounds complicated, expensive, and a bit unreal. However, I believe it is technically possible if the industries want it enough. It does not appear today any more complicated and difficult, with today's techniques, than making an industry-wide uniform piece scale must have seemed a half-century ago in the glass and pottery industries.

The assurance to employers of protection against competition based on lower wages for the same operations has been the union's strongest argument with employers for unitary bargaining for piece rates over the competitive area. Uniformity has also been, for the most part, the union ideal in the fixing of piece rates. The unions have generally held that uniformity in piece rates not only benefits those who formerly received the lower rates but also supports the higher rates by removing downward pressure of competition based on lower rates and so strengthens the whole level for a subsequent advance, or against a threat of reduction in a downward turn of business. The same reasoning would doubtless be applied to basic time rates that represent equal outputs with similar conditions and facilities, if this relationship of equality in terms of output for the wage were once established. The union policy would tend to become substantially the same for time rates in output terms as it has been under piecework.

The kind of uniformity we are discussing is uniformity in labor costs for like operations with like facilities. It includes higher labor costs where the equipment or materials or other facilities are below standard for the worker. This is the usual union practice under a piecework scale. Nor need it exclude, any more than a uniform piece scale need exclude, lower labor costs where improved equipment is used which reduces the time needed to do the work. The uniformity would be in terms of basic hourly wages under given standards. And where these standards are maintained the labor cost should be substantially uniform.

Unitary bargaining for wages does not mean that no wage differentials for places or plants will be allowed within the agreement. It does not preclude differentials for outlying regions not in the main stream of competition or differences between areas that are practically set apart from each other as independent competitive units because of such controlling factors as relatively heavy transportation costs.

The case is otherwise, I think, with differentials to keep the employers enjoying the lower rates in competition with those required by the unitary agreement to pay higher rates. Such differentials are likely to be challenged by the higher-rate employers, and at times by the union on behalf of the lower-rate employees. The differentials will be brought repeatedly under fire and unless and until their justification is established they will constitute an element of instability and a threat to the continuation of the agreement system. If a differential can be clearly shown to mean lower labor costs to employers within the competitive area and lower earnings to the workers, it is not likely to be reconcilable for long with an industry-wide agreement.

I know that in the bituminous coal industry the so-called "principle of competitive equality" sanctioned lower tonnage rates for less favorably situated mines, with respect to transportation costs at least, as well as exemption in some degree from higher tonnage rates for abnormally difficult conditions for the miner. But the wage-rate problem in bituminous coal differs from that in manufacturing, not only because of the greater relative importance of the transportation costs that have to be absorbed by the employer, but also because many of the differences in physical conditions affecting the difficulty (for the miner) of getting out the coal are beyond the control of the employer. The practice of allowing differentials in the tonnage rate was well established before the second regional bargaining system was inaugurated. It is not at all clear now that it would not have been better to have made the fight for the principle of uniform tonnage rates for all employers with substantially the same physical conditions, with extra rates for abnormally difficult conditions. Certainly the experience with the tonnage differentials has not been such as to recommend a like policy in manufacturing. To be sure, with the miners' union it was not so much a matter of keeping the employers in business as of keeping them from becoming nonunion competitors. But—and this is a very important difference—the employer is no longer allowed to go nonunion unless his employees consent.

It is true that in a community industry the employees may choose to go nonunion rather than lose their jobs through the closing of the plant. However, if the union is willing to risk that, it will adhere to the principle of uniform wages for the same output with the same facilities and help the employer find the answer to the question of how to keep in competition. The union may choose this policy even if the decision costs it some of the weaker plants. For the union is under pressure from the members in the higher-rate places to put an end to competition at lower rates from other union plants, as well as under pressure from the union employers who are paying the higher rates. This pressure is likely to be heavy when business is falling off. Employers who may not object to the weaker competitors being allowed a discount from wages when there is plenty of business for all are likely to insist on being allowed to take advantage of their superior competitive ability under uniform wage standards when there is not enough business to go around.

It makes a difference, I think, in the determination of union policy whether the most troublesome competition for the weaker union establishments is coming from nonunion establishments or from union establishments. The union is less likely to refuse lower rates to the weaker establishments if the business lost by these plants is more liable to go to the nonunionists than to other union plants. The problem of uniformity is mixed in this case with the question of what level can be maintained in union plants in the face of the nonunion competition. The policy of accepting reductions only where and when it must and holding them off as long as possible in the more prosperous plants may appeal to the union as more expedient than accepting a lower uniform scale. It is difficult to see, however, how the union is going to be able to keep on exacting that ability-to-pay differential from the stronger union plants. As a permanent policy it does not seem to fit the case unless the union has some unusual kind of a permanent hold over the stronger union plants that it obviously cannot exercise over the weaker ones.

I am not attempting to tell unions whether their wage policy should be one of a uniform rate for the same output from all employers furnishing equal facilities, or one of charging each employer what the traffic will bear. The point of interest here is the effect of the wage-rate policy on the likelihood of industry-wide agreements. If the policy is one of uniformity in labor costs under the same facilities, experience seems to indicate that such a policy may reduce employer resistance to an industry-wide agreement. The other policy might appeal to some employers who would refuse to come in under the uniformity policy but it does not seem that it would be more conducive to an industry-wide agreement on wages than the policy of uniformity. If unions do not want uniform wages in terms of output, where substantially equal facilities are furnished, then we are not likely to see much extension of industry-wide agreements on wages. I think most of them do.

What of employer policy with respect to industry-wide agreements in industries characterized by competition over a wide area? Will they favor them or content themselves with a negative policy of opposing the exaction of higher rates from themselves than from their competitors or, as the case may be, opposing raising their own wages to what others are paying? It seems to me that in the face of a national union policy of uniformity, or of fixed differentials moving simultaneously, the employers may now favor industry-wide bargaining. As soon as they conclude that they cannot get rid of the union there is no longer the objection that an industry-wide agreement cements into the industry a union that otherwise might be got rid of. The old alternative of getting rid of collective bargaining altogether as a means of meeting competition rather than accepting the union as insurance against competition from other union producers based on lower wages, would be gone. Moreover, if the workers in the industry overwhelmingly want collective bargaining, the employer's fear of having to face strong nonunion competition "bound hand and foot by union restrictions" would also be gone. Indeed, the employers might prefer to meet the issue of "union restrictions" in industry-wide bargaining to having to accept the fact of restrictions in local bargaining without much chance to bargain about them. When it is no longer a choice between industry-wide bargaining and a fight for no union at all, with some chance to win, the employers may accept industry-wide bargaining.

Where competition is brisk and labor costs a comparatively large part of the cost of production the employers should be glad to get industry-wide bargaining. Otherwise they may have to fight a strong national union in isolated, individual-employer bargaining. If there is a ruling center of production, such as New York in the clothing industries, for example, it will not be isolated individual employer bargaining but group bargaining by the employers in the center, with the results controlling the pace for the industry as a whole. Even on that basis the union would seem to have an advantage over the employers. The ideal is bilateral industry-wide collective bargaining, not unilateral national collective action on the union side opposed to local collective action, if not individual employer action, on the other. Union domination of the industry with "employer representation" operating at the call of the union does not seem to be the perfect answer.

One of the most serious obstacles to industry-wide agreements in the past from the employer side has been the unwillingness of employers in the lower-wage localities to give up their differentials, coupled with the unwillingness of both the national union and the employers in the higher-wage localities to give open approval in a contract to their continuance. In part, the case for the differential has been based on the contention that the lower wages do not mean lower labor costs; that question could be settled, I believe, by investigation. Then there is the alleged justification of lower rates by lower living costs in the locality, or higher production costs or transportation costs. However, the tendency is now toward less geographical nonuniformity in wages in competitive industries. The operation of the Fair Labor Standards Act and the administration of the Walsh-Healey Act have been moving in that direction. The war will doubtless greatly expedite the movement. Resistance to industry-wide bargaining in order to preserve place differentials in wage rates will be greatly lessened, I believe, by the realization that they cannot be preserved intact even under local collective bargaining.

If the continuance of collective bargaining in an industry with a wide competitive area tends to lead to industry-wide bargaining, why has it not produced it in an industry like commercial printing, in which unionism is very old? This is a hard one to answer. The need is undoubtedly there. However, the wider market was added to a local market and the inertia of local bargaining has been hard to overcome, especially so inasmuch as the newspaper field, which has been the source and residence of the greater part of the union strength, is still local. Before the general spread of organization in recent years the printing trades were in some localities but union islands in a local sea of nonunionism and the pressure to conform to local wage standards was heavy upon them. Yet these are, I think, but causes of delay rather than explanations of a satisfactorily stabilized situation.

I do not wish to imply that the continuance of collective bargaining will in any industry of wide competition necessarily lead to industry-wide bargaining. I am dealing only with tendencies. Nor do I wish to imply that without industry-wide bargaining on wages, including the control of local differentials, if any, there will be no industry-wide bargaining. Furthermore, I do not say that there will be no national bargaining in local market industries. I hope that there will be. But it seems to me that its coming should be looked for first in the widely competitive industries. If it does not come there, why should we expect it in the local-market industries? It is significant that when the zone stabilization agreements of 1941 were made in the shipbuilding industry, then not very well organized, the employers were at least represented, whereas in the national stabilization agreement of 1941 for defense construction, the government dealt directly, and apparently exclusively, with the unions.

There are serious obstacles to be overcome on the labor side in some industries before collective bargaining on an industry-wide basis with the employers can be secured. I refer not merely to the existence of rival organizations in the same industry but to organizational segregation along occupational lines. Industry-wide bargaining separately with a number of different occupational groups is hard to attain. The prospects are much brighter when the bargaining is unitary in depth as well as geographical.

However, the war has brought about much more co-operation among separate national unions in the direction of bargaining unity. The trend may well be accelerated. Unity in bargaining does not necessarily require the merging or amalgamation of the unions concerned. Indeed, the same national union may be a party to several different industry-wide agreements, just as the same company may come under a distinct industry-wide agreement for each of several lines of product. But it does require that the unions act as a unit.

As to what we can expect from an extension of industry-wide agreements, one result is likely to be a synchronization of advances or decreases in wages throughout the industry. This should reduce the friction involved in changes in the money wage level. If the timing of the change is made uniform for all, there is no advantage to be gained in interlocality competition by holding back the increase or beating the others to the decrease. The friction is concentrated on the industry-wide issue, and though it may be intense for a time it is likely to be less in total volume than it would be if the issue were fought out separately in each locality. The disturbance in market conditions in the industry is also likely to be less.

It is probable that in the mass-production industries negotiations for wage advances or wage reductions involving a large number of workers will result in government intervention of one kind or another if the parties reach an apparent deadlock. It is much simpler and more in keeping with true collective bargaining to have the issue threshed out in an industry-wide conference than to attempt to dispose of it by "fact finding" or arbitration, in a so-called "key case." If the industry as a whole is to be expected to follow the decision in the key case, the industry as a whole should be in on the negotiations and on the submission of data and argument.

Thus, industry-wide bargaining will mean less flexibility in wage changes downward than we have had heretofore. We may look for that anyway, with strong national unionism and government intervention, even under local bargaining. It will also mean less flexibility in the upward swing than would come through local bargaining. It is harder for even a strong national union to get wage advances of uniform amount in all localities simultaneously than it is to bring about standardization or a "common rule" eventually, through local bargaining.

I have already expressed the conclusion that the extension of industry-wide bargaining will mean much greater geographical standardization of basic wage rates. That will also mean eventually a nearer approach to uniformity in labor costs. The employers with high labor costs at the standard time rates will have to improve their methods or drop out where labor costs are an important part of total costs. Lower wage rates will not be allowed as an offset to higher production costs of another kind. The tendency will be toward uniform rates in industry-wide agreements, just as uniformity of rates is an almost universal characteristic of local bargaining for the same industry. The employer with higher transportation costs will have to absorb them.

Does this mean that industry-wide bargaining will eliminate differentials in wages based on differences in living costs which merely equalize real wages? The tendency will be in that direction, I think. Industry-wide bargaining on piece rates recognized no cost-of-living differentials. The objective was not equality of real wages but equality of money earnings and equality of labor costs to the employer under standard facilities. Geographical differences in the cost of living are too controversial and too subject to change to offer an acceptable basis for stable differentials in an industry with a wide area of competition.

Will industry-wide agreements retard the introduction of laborsaving devices and so tend to get advances in wages out of price advances rather than through the reduction of costs?[3] There is, of course, that danger. But it is a danger that goes with any joint agreement covering the market, whether that be nation-wide or local. Such a system of bargaining can be used to make the buyers shoulder the cost of restrictions just as it can be used to make the buyers who continue to buy absorb a wage advance. However, as between industry-wide bargaining, on the one hand, and local bargaining where the market is local, on the other, the record, so far as I know it, is in favor of the industry-wide agreements.

As between industry-wide and local bargaining in an industry producing for a national market, there may be more slowing down of technological innovations under the former system. There may be a joining of union fears with fears on the part of employers (as competitors) of this new thing with the result of hamstringing it by restrictions or by the refusal of a reasonable wage rate readjustment for its use. On the other hand, the chances are as good that the employers' side will stand out for the right of any employer to introduce a change under guaranteed safeguards to the workers. These safeguards as to displacement and wages are not likely to be any more restrictive than those the strong locals would enforce under local bargaining. To be sure, the employers of the members of the weaker locals might force the change earlier and under less restrictive terms, but that result might be balanced by what would happen in the localities where the union is strong.

It must be remembered that we are comparing industry-wide bargaining with local bargaining, not with nonunionism. Under local bargaining there will be opposition to unrestricted technological change that threatens displacement of workers or reductions in wage rates for

[3] See Sumner Slichter, "The Economics of Collective Bargaining," in *Collective Bargaining Contracts*, p. 49; also his *Union Policies and Industrial Management*, p. 344.

the new way as compared with the old. Local collective bargaining, buttressed by strong national unionism, will mean an "administered" rate of technological change just as it will mean administered wage rates. Industry-wide bargaining is as likely, if not more likely, to produce a reasonable compromise as is local bargaining. My impression is that national officers usually take a more farsighted view of such problems than local leaders. Industry-wide agreements have inherited more restrictions from local bargaining, I think, than they have introduced. Moreover, there is more of the goldfish bowl about industry-wide bargaining. Public concern as to what is going on is likely to lead to consideration of public opinion or even of the prospect of governmental intervention, if not of the public interest directly for its own sake.

Finally, industry-wide bargaining should produce more union cooperation with employers. The "union" is ordinarily a national union, in ambition at least. The degree to which a national union can cooperate with an individual employer to the end of helping him to get business away from other union employers in the same industry must be limited. Industry-wide co-operation between the union and the employers offers greater possibilities. If we are to have anything like joint councils in industry, they may be expected to be more successful and enduring if they are grounded upon industry-wide collective bargaining. We may get "united action of management and labor" in an industry without a foundation of industry-wide bargaining in a great emergency. When the emergency has passed the parties are likely either to proceed to lay such a foundation or to go their separate ways.

Union Security

The Dilemma of the Closed Shop, by John V. Spielmans, Journal of Political Economy, Vol. LI, No. 2, April, 1943, pp. 113–134

Union Security and Its Implications, by Louis Stark, Annals of the American Academy of Political and Social Science, Vol. 248, November, 1946, pp. 62–69

THE DILEMMA OF THE CLOSED SHOP

By John V. Spielmans

THE issue of the so-called "closed shop" has of late become one of the liveliest on the economic front in the United States, giving rise to an ever growing number of disputes, and of peculiarly stubborn disputes at that.

In this article an attempt is made to analyze the nature of the issue, to confront arguments for and against it, to explore possibilities for a legislative settlement, and to survey the instances of actual and proposed closed-shop legislation in recent times.

I. SOME FACTS CONCERNING THE CLOSED SHOP

Under the term "closed shop" a considerable variety of arrangements is subsumed.

In its strictest form, which is the closed shop proper, the employer may hire only members of the union in question, sometimes being allowed to choose only from a list of available members submitted by the union, or, less stringently, to hire any union member he can get.

In its "inclusive" rather than "exclusive" form, more properly termed the "union shop," the employer is obliged to make it a condition of employment that any worker he hires must join the union, either at once or after a certain short, specified period, with the further understanding that he must dismiss any worker who, for one reason or another, has ceased to be in good standing with the union.

Further down the line of stringency stand the various forms of "preferential union shop" under which the employer is

to hire union members in preference but not to the exclusion of qualified nonmembers or under which he is to continue only certain jobs as union jobs. And, finally, there is the more defensive "union maintenance" or "union security" contract (of which much is heard these days) under which the employer is to require continued union membership as a condition of employment only for those employees who belonged to the union at the time the agreement was made or who join the union voluntarily during the life of the agreement.[1]

The common feature in all these arrangements is that it is the employer who, by making it a condition of employment, is responsible for union membership of the workers. A closed-shop contract is thus the exact opposite of the once popular but now outlawed "yellow-dog contract," under which the employer compelled the worker, as a condition of employment, not to join the union, except the company union, if any.

Closed-shop agreements[2] have been widely used in the United States, especially in certain industries.[3] It is, how-

[1] For a somewhat fuller account of the various forms of closed-shop agreements see "Closed Shop and Check Off in Union Agreements," *Monthly Labor Review*, October, 1939, pp. 830 ff.

[2] Here and throughout the following the term "closed shop" is used generically to signify any one of the various arrangements under which union membership is required as a condition of employment.

[3] In 1939 the Bureau of Labor Statistics reported that more than half of the seven thousand current union agreements on file with the Bureau contained provisions requiring that all employees be members of the union. At that time the Bureau estimated that about three million organized workers were un-

ever, only in recent times that the demand for the closed shop is being raised and insisted upon ever more widely and in ever more industries.[4]

The reason for this increase in closed-shop disputes, as also the reason for the

---

der closed-shop contracts (*Monthly Labor Review, loc. cit.*). According to the latest figures, the number of workers under closed-shop contracts during 1941 is estimated at four million (in addition to which are large numbers under "virtual" closed-shop conditions, notably the railroad employees and the longshoremen on the Pacific Coast). These four million under formal closed-shop agreements are said to represent 40 per cent of all workers under collective agreements. However, only 30 per cent of all employees (inclusive of clerical, technical, and professional) are at present under union agreement; therefore about 12 per cent of all wage-earners in the United States were under closed-shop agreements in 1941 (Florence Peterson, "Extent of Collective Bargaining," *Monthly Labor Review*, May, 1942, pp. 1066 ff.). Closed-shop conditions are most widespread in the coal-mining industry (which is now almost 100 per cent closed shop) in the clothing and printing industries, and among the organized construction workers. The signing of a closed-shop agreement by Henry Ford (June, 1941) marked a first breach in the solid anti-closed-shop front of the great mass-production industries.

[4] The strike statistics of the Bureau of Labor Statistics do not reveal the distribution of strike issues among industries. Taking all industries together, the percentage of closed-shop strikes has risen from an average of about 7 per cent per year for the years 1927–33 to an annual average of 12 per cent for the years 1934–40; that of workers involved from an average of about 2 per cent per year between 1927 and 1933 to about 12.5 per cent per year between 1934 and 1940 (calculated from annual strike statistics of the Bureau of Labor Statistics, *Monthly Labor Review*, May issues of the respective years). Senator Bridges, in a pamphlet on the present closed-shop drive, makes public a letter by Chester Wright, author of a "Washington Labor Letter" and "a close confidant of John L. Lewis": "A national drive to enforce the closed shop is under way; a drive for the closed shop in every industry and every plant is the immediate objective of organized labor wherever the issue can be forced without endangering past gains. . . . . That is the coming big labor issue in defense industries. It is the one on which strikes will hinge" (*Closed Shop Drive Threatens National Defense Program: Extensions of Remarks of Hon. Styles Bridges of New Hampshire in the Senate of the United States, September 29, 1941,* p. 4).

peculiar difficulty in settling them, seems fairly obvious. The demand for the closed shop, so the figures appear to say, has increased with the strengthening of the unions' position and the growth of collective bargaining under the protection, on the one side, and the compulsion, on the other, of the Wagner Act. But, while having surged up under the new labor law of the land, the closed shop as such has remained largely outside the law, being, on the whole, neither forbidden nor required by law. A closed-shop dispute, therefore, cannot be settled by adjudication by any labor board, since in the absence of a law there is no basis for adjudication. Nor is there, in general, any objective basis on which a closed-shop dispute can be impartially arbitrated—as is frequently the case in wage disputes—since it is the very principle involved which is controversial, with no consensus even of intelligent public opinion;[5] therefore an arbitrator in a closed-shop dispute could rarely do more than follow his own personal bias in the matter or else render his award on the ground of reasons of expediency applying only to the particular case but not to the issue as such.

For all these reasons the need for a legislative clarification of the national policy toward the issue is making itself more and more felt.[6] To prepare for the

[5] In fact, public opinion at large seems at present unfavorable to the closed shop. According to a Gallup poll taken in June, 1937, 59 per cent of the voters were opposed to the closed shop, 28 per cent in its favor, and 13 per cent undecided (that is, of those with an opinion on the subject, two-thirds were opposed to the closed shop). By October, 1941—apparently under the influence of public exasperation over strikes in defense industries, which in itself had of course nothing to do with the merits of the closed shop—77 per cent voted against, and only 13 per cent for, the closed shop, with 10 per cent undecided.

[6] This point was strongly urged by Dr. William Leiserson of the National Labor Relations Board in a lecture delivered at the College of the City of

discussion of that question, we shall first consider the arguments for and against the closed shop made by its advocates and opponents.

II. ARGUMENTS FOR AND AGAINST THE CLOSED SHOP

The basic argument for all-inclusive unionism may be said to be this: in a capitalistic society, where profit is the prime mover of industry, labor can win its fair share of the social product only through solidarity, that is, through organization. Under the prevailing condition of permanent oversupply of labor the fight for higher wages, shorter hours, for improved working conditions, and for increased security lies largely through labor's power to withhold itself from the jobs, that is, through strikes, actual or potential. For this fight solidarity, discipline, and funds are needed—funds which, coming from the masses of the workers, can become sufficiently large only if everyone contributes his share. Hence the selfish, shortsighted worker, unmindful of the needs of his class and of his own ultimate advantage, must, in justice to his class, be compelled to join the unions even against his own wishes. Such compulsion of the worker to contribute his share to the union is often likened to the unquestionably necessary compulsion of the individual to pay taxes to the government.[7]

Where collective bargaining through a union has become established—either through the union's own efforts or under the compulsion of the Wagner Act—the closed-shop argument takes on the simpler, more immediate formulation: that for workers who benefit by a union agreement it is only fair to pay their share to support the union.

A further strong reason for the unions to insist on the closed-shop clause in agreements is that collective-bargaining rights must be continually safeguarded, since otherwise they are easily lost again through the employer's hiring of non-union men, through members' dropping out of the union, or through the drives of rival unions.

Directly connected with this is another reason for closed-shop clauses and one which has greatly gained in importance in connection with the present schism in the American labor movement: a closed-shop agreement, namely, is one of the strongest weapons in rival union warfare through which a union can make it next to impossible for its rival to gain a foothold in the plant or industry.

Altogether, a closed-shop contract saves the unions their otherwise perpetually necessary organizational efforts and leaves them free to apply themselves to their more truly constructive tasks. From this point of view the closed shop may be desirable also for the employer. Matter-of-course union membership of all employees, namely, eliminates the continual disturbance of union agitation and membership drives. Moreover, with a closed shop securely established, an employer may enjoy greater stability also in other respects; for "a union relieved of the necessity of appealing to the workers through promise of better and better employment terms may be less likely to present ever new and perhaps unreasonable demands as to wages, hours, and working conditions."[8]

New York, on February 18, 1942 (published by the Bureau of National Affairs, Inc., Washington, D.C.).

[7] This often-heard argument was used only recently by Professor D. Lescohier of the University of Wisconsin in the University of Chicago Round Table broadcast, "Labor Policies in Wartime," February 8, 1942.

[8] These last two arguments are presented in the afore-mentioned article on the closed shop in the *Monthly Labor Review*, October, 1939, p. 830.

Coming next to the arguments against the closed shop, there is, first of all, the very general, very basic one: that for any man or woman to be forced, under penalty of losing their livelihood, to join and support a private organization is a flagrant violation of the basic rights of the individual in our democratic American society. In the language of congressional oratory: through the closed shop "the God-given, the constitutionally guaranteed right to earn a livelihood has been denied to hundreds of thousands of American citizens"; "the privilege of the unions to sell licenses to work" amounts to "taxing of American citizens by extra-legal organizations" and is "to be likened to the tribute-levying activities of the Barbary pirates which were supposed to have been ended by Perry";[9] that through their closed-shop contracts the unions "chain the workers to the oars of their galleys."[10]

Other arguments against the closed shop are directed not so much against the usurpation as such of compulsory powers by private organizations as against the malpractices and abuses of the organizations laying claim to such compulsory powers.

There are, first, the often unreasonable or even exorbitant initiation fees, dues, and assessments exacted by many unions.[11]

Second, there is the unlimited power of the unions to exclude or expel workers, which power, under closed-shop condi-

tions, means the power to deprive them of their jobs. (In fact, excessive initiation fees often constitute in themselves an effective principle of exclusion from jobs.)

Next there is, what is particularly objectionable in connection with the high contributions exacted, the failure on the part of many unions to account regularly for the funds collected from the members, together with the well-known fact that these funds are widely used for purposes having little if any bearing on the economic interests of the members, notably for political campaigns; or, worse, going simply into the pockets of the union bosses and their henchmen in the form of exorbitant salaries and expense accounts or otherwise.

In conjunction with these is the further fact—of late repeatedly brought into the open—that not infrequently union officers even in high positions, far from being bona fide labor leaders, are simply large-scale racketeers whose sole interest in the "union business" is their "profit," which they often find by playing labor and employers against each other; and that these racketeer bosses, even where known as such, are often hard to dislodge, because, having once wormed or battered their way into high union office, they perpetuate themselves in this position by preventing free and honest elections, or any elections whatever, through bribery and through outright terror against the opposition. And while anybody familiar with the facts will grant that many unions are free from at least the more flagrant and vicious of these abuses, still, these abuses are so widespread and so well known as to arouse keen resentment against the power of the unions, tainted as they are with corrupt practices, through closed-shop agreements to compel the support of all workers.

[9] Representative Clare Hoffman (Mich.) on the floor of the House, November 6, 1941, and September 19, 1941, respectively.

[10] Senator Styles Bridges (N.H.) on the floor of the Senate, September 19, 1941.

[11] In a letter written to President Roosevelt (March 14, 1941) Representative Howard Smith (Va.) claims that, according to information obtained by him, initiation fees ranged from $23 to $1,500 (letter placed into the *Congressional Record*, December 2, 1941).

In recent times one thing has added considerably to public resentment of the closed shop, namely, the charge that the federal government has aided and indorsed the closed shop by granting it in one form or another on many government construction works and through the "union-maintenance policy" of the National War Labor Board. The charge of fascism and naziism has repeatedly been made against such governmentally imposed compulsory unionism.[12]

A dilemma indeed thus seems to present itself in this issue of the closed shop: well established in some industries where trade-unionism has been functioning most successfully; unyieldingly insisted upon as necessary for effective unionism by most labor leaders; advocated as fair and just also by many well-informed intellectuals within and without the government; on the other hand, denounced as wholesale extortionism and tyranny unbecoming a democracy by many legislators and writers; unpopular also with the public at large; and with national policy uncertain and equivocal, seeming to favor it in deeds while disavowing it in words.

How, then, can one hope to find a common basis for a legislative settlement of this controversial issue?

III. A THEORY OF THE CLOSED SHOP

In searching for such a basis, we shall contemplate the issue some more in its broader socioeconomic aspects.

There we have, first, to realize that the parties involved are not merely the two traditional antagonists in labor disputes —labor and capital—but four, or more: (1) the unions (split into jealous rival factions and hence frequently forming two opposing parties), (2) the workers, (3) the employers, and (4) the government. The unions are trying to compel the workers to join by having the employers make union membership (more particularly membership in a particular union) a condition of employment; while the government, actually or potentially, sets the rules of the game.[13]

Now this question arises in our mind: why is it that the American labor unions —in contrast to unions in other countries with equally vigorous labor movements —are so insistent on applying the pressure method of the closed shop to assure themselves of the workers' membership? Apparently this must be, because without such pressure the workers do not readily join the unions, or, having joined, they easily drop out again if permitted to do so.

In former days this fact was quite generally blamed on the deterring effect of the ruthless antiunion policy of many employers and on the risks attending union membership in the form of loss of job and black-listing. Accordingly, the closed shop was and could be regarded as chiefly a device to protect and safeguard a union position once conquered against the employers' antiunion machinations.

---

[12] This view that the governmentally indorsed closed shop, if established, would constitute a Fascist form of organization was poignantly expressed by President Roosevelt in his letter to John L. Lewis (November 14, 1941) concerning the latter's insistence on the closed shop in the captive coal mines: "The government of the United States will not consider, nor will Congress pass legislation ordering a so-called closed shop. . . . . That would be too much like the Hitler methods towards labor."

[13] Where, as is frequently the case, the employer signs a closed-shop contract only under pressure from the union, the compulsion is more roundabout, for in that case the union compels the employer to compel the workers to join the union. And again where—as is lately said to be happening—the unions' demand for the closed shop is indorsed by an authoritative government agency, the path of compulsion is even more circuitous, for in that case (as has been pointed out repeatedly, e.g., by Mr. Westbrook Pegler) the unions compel the government to compel the employers to compel the workers to join the unions.

Seven years of Wagner Act operation, however, seem to reveal that the fear of the employer was not the only motive in the workers' reluctance toward the unions. Otherwise, safe and free to join under the effective protection of the Wagner Act, the workers should have flocked into the unions so generally as to render the coercive device of the closed-shop agreement rather less than more urgent.

. A number of reasons can, indeed, be given which in their entirety may well account for the reluctance of American workers toward union organization. There is, first, the cherished tradition of self-reliance and single-handed action of the American frontiersman. Next, there is the absence of a genuine class consciousness, notably of Marxian "proletarian" class consciousness, due, on the one side, to the high fluidity of classes in the new country and, on the other, to the heterogeneous backgrounds and standards of the many racial and national elements which constitute the American working class. Again there is, bred out of the essential optimism of the "American Dream" and thus closely related to the just-mentioned fluidity of classes, a certain short-viewed opportunism on the part of the workers, disposed to join a fight for an immediate goal only but uninterested in long-range aspects and in socioeconomic theories and ideologies, and thus indifferent or even áverse to sustained organized effort. Last but not least, there is the long record of widespread malpractice and violence on the part of many unions which through the years has built up an equally widespread antiunion resentment among large groups of workers.

Seen in this light the American labor movement appears, indeed, to have been waging a two-front war: on the one front it has battled against hostile employers trying to prevent unionization of their shops and industries; on the other it has struggled against the unwillingness among the workers to join. In the days before the Wagner Act the fight on the employers' front largely obscured the workers' front; that is, a universal desire on the part of ·the workers to organize, thwarted or held in check only by the employers' hostility was generally taken for granted. The new orientation of the national industrial policy under the Wagner Act, however, has changed this situation quite basically. For through this Act—to pursue the simile further—the federal government entered the fight on the side of the unions and, after some years of hard going, won the unions' battle on the employers' front. With the clamor of that battle subsiding, the workers' front as the unions' chief remaining line of fighting has moved into clearer view. The closed shop in particular, no longer seriously needed to combat employers' antiunion policies, has thus turned more and more into a weapon to coerce the workers into the unions—not against the will of the employers but against their own will.[14]

[14] The fact that the closed-shop issue has taken on a new and different meaning since the outlawing of antiunion policies on the part of the employers under the Wagner Act seems as yet little appreciated. Thus Florence Peterson, of the Bureau of Labor Statistics, in a recent article (*op. cit.*, p. 1069) comments as follows on the present increase in the "demand for greater union security by way of the union shop": "The expressed intent of the labor movement as a whole [is] to become established firmly and permanently in the industrial system. The leaders of organized labor, recalling the 'open shop' drives after the last war, which caused a collapse of unionization in many industries, were convinced that the fullest measure of security must be obtained to avoid a similar situation in the coming period of post-war readjustment." This argument completely disregards the reorientation of the national policy with regard to labor unions, which would seem to preclude any recurrence of the open-shop drives of the twenties.

In passing and enforcing the Wagner Act, the federal government clearly expressed the idea that it regarded trade-unions and collective bargaining as essential to the effective functioning of the American industrial system; so essential, indeed, that where the unions could not overcome the employers' resistance through the efforts of the labor leaders alone the government would lend its superior powers of compulsion against such employers. This coercion was felt to be in line with democratic ideals, the mere clearing-away of unfair money power, the "restoring of the equality of bargaining power."

But what about compulsion to be used against workers unwilling to join the unions? Totalitarian regimes, with their emphasis on the needs of the whole rather than the individual, have, without scruple, taken the step of governmentally requiring all workers to join the totalitarian equivalents of labor organizations. To a democracy such outright regimentation of the individual as well as of the unions is repugnant and unacceptable. However, there is the long-used method of the closed shop through which the unions, not the government, can effectively compel unwilling workers to join. By permitting, or even encouraging, the use of the closed shop, is the government violating democratic principles and ideals?

It seems to us that if national policy is actively in favor of representative organization of labor as essential to the stability and efficiency of our industrial society, and if workers remain reluctant toward union organization, that the good of society (which is also the good of the workers) might well require a certain pressure to be applied with government sanction to make the workers join their unions, just as it was found necessary to apply direct governmental pressure to make the employers recognize and bargain with the unions. Only in that case the government must, in justice to the workers as well as in the name of civic decency, assume responsibility for the reasonable and honest conduct of the unions which the workers are thus compelled to join.

For—and here we come to the root of much needless misunderstanding, a semantic misunderstanding, indeed—to favor and promote Trade-Unionism, that is, to promote organized bargaining for the wage-earners through representative organizations of the wage-earners, emphatically cannot be identical with favoring and promoting every actual American trade-union, international or local, A.F. of L. or C.I.O., just as they are among us here and now in the flesh, afflicted with all the weaknesses inherent in human nature and human organization in general, and additionally inherent in the militant organization of the masses, which, through their very size and extent, combined with the economic helplessness of their individual members, offer a most dangerously fertile ground for the most dangerously lucrative rackets.

The idea that governmental protection and sponsorship of the unions, and in particular, official tolerance or even indorsement of the closed-shop policy of such unions, implies the need for governmental responsibility—for the conduct of the unions has of late become widely recognized and advocated in the press, on the floor of both houses of Congress, and in many legislative bills designed to regulate the unions.

But so far this idea continues to be strongly resisted, chiefly by union leaders and by their unconditional supporters within and without the government (the latter perhaps partly under the influence of the just mentioned "semantic confusion"). Suspicious of all legislative regulation as equivalent to capitalistic repression and jealous of their tradition of independence, the unions continue to insist on their right as private organizations to manage their affairs as they see fit, free from "governmental meddling and regimentation."

This attitude of the unions, however, is by now a sheer anachronism, out of keeping with their actual status in our present social organization. For, having secured for themselves all the manifold governmental help and protection under the national and several state labor relations acts, the unions have truly ceased to be "private organizations" and have become quasi-public institutions instead.

Indeed, governmental labor relations boards, maintained by public taxes and with the coercive powers of the courts behind them, are operating to insure recognition of the unions by the employers for purposes of collective bargaining; to adjudicate complaints over nonrecognition and other discriminatory antiunion policies; to issue, and through the courts to enforce, orders against such practices; and to assess damages in the form of back-pay awards. More than that, these governmental boards officially assist labor to decide upon "representatives of its own choosing" by certifying majorities, by conducting governmentally regulated and governmentally supervised elections to determine a majority, and by prohibiting minority groups from bargaining separately with the employer. Still more, in case of labor's disagreement as to bargaining units (frequently engendered by conflicting A.F. of L. and C.I.O. diplomacy), these governmental boards have to determine for labor in what units it is to be represented—whether craft, plant, industrial units, employer units, or still others. To appreciate how very far from the status of "private organizations" the unions have moved under this Wagner Act machinery, one need only compare their situation to that of more truly private organizations—churches, political parties, scientific associations, Rotaries or Elks, or college fraternities—to whom the government certainly renders no similar assistance against external or internal difficulties.

The first step, therefore, toward a solution of the closed-shop problem would seem to be the clear recognition and candid admission on the part of all sincere advocates of trade-unionism in the United States that the governmental sponsorship of the unions under the Wagner Act requires as its counterpart a measure of governmental regulation of the unions that will safeguard the interests of the workers against union malpractices, where compelled through closed-shop agreements to join the unions.

The next question, then, would be in what respects and through what means such regulation could best be achieved. As to that, opinions would hardly differ widely.

First, to prevent arbitrary, undemocratic, or dishonest leadership, there should be a guaranty of regular and honest election of union officers, with safeguards for uncoerced nomination of candidates and uncoerced voting by secret ballot. To achieve this, it might be enough to expand the present functions of the labor relations boards, which now handle complaints against employers and elections of bargaining agents, so as to empower them to handle also complaints by union members against union officers concerning obstruction of regular elections, and, if necessary, to conduct and supervise such elections.

Second, unions should be required to give certified specific accounts at regular intervals showing the manner in which union funds were used.[15] Again, the labor relations boards could be empowered to handle complaints of members against officers who fail to give satisfactory accounts.

Such safeguarding of regular elections and accounting would go a long way toward removing public distrust against the "union racket." But it should not be enough to entitle a union to make closed-shop agreements. As to that, further safeguards are needed.

There is, first, the question of the contributions which a union exacts, notably in the form of initiation fees. Where union membership is voluntary (i.e., not required as a condition of employment), the question of contributions may perhaps be left to the unions, for the workers' self-interest would keep them from paying too high a price for the benefits of union membership, which tendency, according to time-honored economic laws, would presumably operate to keep fees and dues from becoming excessive. But where a worker is forced to pay what the union charges in order to obtain a job, the question of fees and dues should obviously not be left to the unions but, like rates charged by railroads or other public utilities of monopolistic character, should become a question of distinctly public concern.

Second, there is the question of the unions' powers over admission and expulsion of members. Where a union is a mere private benefit association, it should naturally be free to be as exclusive as it pleases. But where such an exclusive union makes closed-shop agreements, in debarring a man from union membership it debars him from a livelihood at his trade, which, again, is a matter of considerable public concern. Similar in its effects is the policy of the unions to expel or suspend a member for "breach of union discipline" or similar charges (e.g., for having worked Saturdays without overtime pay or for less than union wages or for having traded at a place declared as "unfair to organized labor" by some affiliated union). Under closed-shop conditions, under which the employer must discharge a man no longer in good standing with the union,[16] the union's power to penalize a man for "breach of union discipline" thus amounts to no less than firing him and putting him on a black list reaching as far as the closed-shop agreement or further. For an employer to fire and black-list a man for union activity is now an "unfair labor practice," with labor relations boards ready to reinstate him with back pay if found to have been unfairly dismissed. For a union to fire and black-list a man for "breach of union discipline" may be as unfair and certainly as disastrous for the man concerned.

It thus appears that where a union makes closed-shop agreements its powers to debar workers from membership must be limited so as to safeguard the workers against arbitrary or unfair denial of their right to work. The most natural way to achieve this would seem, first, to subject the union's general membership rules and

---

[15] On this point there seems to be considerable consensus. A recent Gallup poll (October 30, 1941) on the question: "Do you think labor unions should be required to make yearly public reports of the money collected and spent?" showed 87 per cent in favor, 6 per cent opposed, and 7 per cent with no opinion.

[16] Occasionally the closed-shop clause in agreements provides that the employer must be given a complete account of the case of the employee to be dismissed for loss of union standing or must be allowed some part in the decision to expel a member from the union (*Monthly Labor Review*, October, 1939, p. 831).

policies to the approval of labor relations boards and, second, to empower these boards to receive and investigate and take affirmative action upon complaints of workers who have lost their jobs through loss of union standing under a closed-shop agreement.

There remains an important question: granting the desirability of regulating the unions in some such manner as here suggested, would the proposed measures not be too cumbersome to administer and too difficult to enforce? Would it not require, most of all, too much unwelcome regimentation to promise success? We do not think so. On the contrary, we believe that all these several regulations of the unions here advocated—guaranties of regular elections and regular accounting and, for unions with closed-shop agreements, additional guaranties as to contributions and membership policies—could be enforced with a minimum of interference and compulsion. If, namely, a union objects to being so "meddled and interfered with" and insists on its rights as a private organization to run its own affairs, the answer would be very simple. Any union may remain as private as a country club or a sewing circle—free to elect or not to elect officers; free to charge what fees it pleases and to account or not to account for funds collected (provided the members are satisfied with such arrangement); free also to exclude anyone it likes to. Only, being thus strictly "private," such union would have no access to the special legal facilities of the publicly supported governmental labor relations boards to handle its complaints against employers' non-recognition, to conduct its elections of bargaining agents, or to settle its squabbles with rival unions over bargaining units and bargaining rights. Nor would such merely private unions be allowed to compel the workers' membership and to operate an unregulated job monopoly in the form of a closed-shop agreement.

This possibility of automatic self-enforcement of union regulation through the limitation of "Wagner Act status" to certain "Wagner Act standards" seems to indicate the inherent adequacy of the proposed measures.

IV. ENACTED AND PROPOSED LEGISLATION TO REGULATE THE CLOSED SHOP

We shall next discuss instances of enacted and proposed legislation in the United States directly or indirectly to regulate the use of the closed shop.

ENACTED LEGISLATION

First to be mentioned here is the clause in the Railroad Labor Act of 1934, according to which "no carrier, its officer or agent, shall require any person seeking employment to sign any contract or agreement to join or not to join a labor organization."[17] This law, which preceded the Wagner Act by one year, thus prohibited for the railroad industries what the Wagner Act was next to forbid for all "interstate" industries, namely, the "yellow-dog" and the company-union contract. But the Railroad Act forbade, in addition, the formal requirement of membership in any labor organization as a condition of employment, that is, the closed-shop agreement.

This prohibition of the formal closed shop notwithstanding, the railroad industries are, nevertheless, on a virtual closed-shop basis; that is, the employees join the unions almost without exception and as a matter of course, because among them this is regarded as the thing to do (a situation similar to that in the British and the Swedish trade-unions).

[17] Public No. 442 (73d Cong., 2d sess., 1934 [H.R. 9861]), sec. 2: "General Duties," Fifth.

From this it might appear that right here we have the best solution of the whole problem: prohibit the coercive "condition-of-employment" clause and put it up to the unions, fully protected in their rights by the Wagner Act, to make themselves so valuable to their members and to conduct themselves so fairly and honestly that the workers, likewise fully protected by the Wagner Act against old-time antiunion persecution, will want to joint the unions as a matter of course.

Such voluntary virtual closed shop instead of the coercive formal closed shop would, of course, be the ideal solution. Yet it must also be realized that many American industries are hardly ripe for this scheme. Labor relations in the railroad industries, long regulated through steadily improved legislation, stand indeed considerably above those in most other industries: collective bargaining firmly established, with the National Mediation Board at the ready disposal of the parties; adjudication of grievances by permanent quasi-judicial boards effectively operating; and strike procedure adequately and fairly regulated. In sharp contrast to this near-ideal situation, unionization and collective bargaining in many other industries even under the Wagner Act have remained precarious and fraught with friction and mutual distrust, with union methods in general and strike procedure in particular largely irregular and with the reluctance of the workers toward sustained, matter-of-course union membership unabated. Hence, as long as public policy is in favor of increasingly complete and representative unionization, a premature prohibition of the closed shop might indeed not be desirable because it likely might lead to deterioration of unionism in many industries.

Next to be considered are the restrictions placed upon the closed shop by the National Labor Relations Act. There is, first, the just-mentioned prohibition of the closed company-union shop under which employees were required, as a condition of employment, to join the employer-dominated employees' union.[18] But, contrary to widespread opinion, the Act places restrictions also on the use of closed-shop agreements with regular labor unions. On the one hand, it is true, the Act emphatically asserts that, while it is an unfair labor practice for an employer to encourage or discourage membership in any labor organization, "nothing in this Act . . . . or any code or agreement approved or prescribed thereunder, or in any other statute of the United States shall preclude an employer from making an agreement with a labor organization . . . . to require as a condition of employment membership therein." But, it goes on, "if such labor organization is representative of the employees as provided in sect. $9(a)$ in the appropriate collective bargaining unit covered by such agreement when made."[19]

The intention of the Act thus was obviously to restrict the privilege of closed-shop agreements to unions representing the majority of the employees in the bargaining unit or, also, to forbid closed-shop agreements with unions not representing a majority.[20] This restriction,

[18] Public No. 198 (74th Cong., 1st. sess., 1935 [S. 1958]), secs. 8(2) and 8(3).

[19] *Ibid.*, sec. 8(3).

[20] Senator Wagner, when speaking in the Senate for his bill, said: "The virulent propaganda to the effect that this bill encourages the closed shop is outrageous in view of the fact that in two respects it actually narrows the now existing law in regard to closed shop agreements: in the first place, while today an employer may sign a closed shop contract even with a minority group, the bill provides that he shall be allowed to negotiate such an agreement only with an organization which represents the ma-

however, becomes, of course, operative only where either the employer, a group of employees, or a rival union raises the question as to whether this condition is fulfilled.[21]

Quite recently the National Labor Relations Board has begun to proceed under this provision against closed-shop contracts where the represented majorities were alleged to have been unfairly engineered by the union and the employer jointly—a policy on the part of the Board which may lead far in the direction of stamping out other abuses of the closed shop as well.[22]

To the extent to which this restriction of closed-shop agreements to the majority bargaining agent is observed it might be expected to have a salutary effect against union abuses in general. For a union with a reputation for malpractices would presumably be unable to win an election and thus be debarred from collective bargaining and, a fortiori, from making a closed-shop agreement. In fact, however, the workers, in voting for a collective-bargaining agent, may often have little to choose between as far as union practices are concerned. Hence the restrictions which the Wagner Act places upon the closed shop seem so far to offer but little protection to the workers against excessive fees, lack of accounting for funds, and irregularities as to election of officers (implying danger of racketeering leadership).

Among the five states which in 1937 passed labor relations acts almost identical with the National Labor Relations Act,[23] two amended those acts soon after with a view to restrain unfair labor practices on the part of labor as well as on that of the employers and in particular as regards the use of the closed shop.[24]

According to the amended Wisconsin

---

jority of the employees in the appropriate collective bargaining unit covered by such an agreement. Secondly, the bill is extremely careful to forestall closed shop agreements with unions that are interfered with or dominated by the company" (*Congressional Record*, May 15, 1935, p. 7570).

[21] The above-cited article on the closed shop by the Bureau of Labor Statistics contains the statement: "It is, of course, possible for a union official and employer to agree that a closed shop shall be established without the employer's asking the proof that the union represents a majority of the employees" (*op. cit.*, p. 830). According to sec. 8(3) of the N.L.R.A., the employer, in so doing, would actually commit an "unfair labor practice," only with nobody making a complaint about it.

[22] In one case (H. Feinberg, New York wine merchant and the A.F. of L. Distillery, Rectifying and Wine Workers International Union) the employer had signed a closed-shop agreement with the union on the strength of some of his employees' having applied for membership in that union. After the contract was signed, the union refused membership to those same employees, whereupon the employer dismissed them in favor of union members. In another case (management of the Rutland Court apartment house in Washington, D.C., and the A.F. of L. Building Service Employees International Union) the employer, whose closed-shop contract with the union was about to expire, dismissed five employees who planned to join a rival C.I.O. union, hiring A.F. of L. union members in their stead, after which he renewed the closed-shop contract with that union as representing the majority of the employees. In both instances the Board set aside these closed-shop contracts as "fraud and conspiracy" and ordered reinstatement, with back pay, of the dismissed workers (October, 1942). A further case of considerable importance has arisen over the closed-shop policies

of three West Coast shipyards of Henry J. Kaiser. In these yards closed-shop contracts had been signed with a number of A.F. of L. unions at a time when the yards had a small number of employees only. These contracts have since been forced upon many thousands of new employees hired since the outbreak of the war, who had had no choice in electing the bargaining agent, and many of whom were members of rival C.I.O. unions. In enforcing his A.F. of L. closed-shop contracts, the employer went so far as to import A.F. of L. workers from the Atlantic Coast to replace hundreds of dismissed Pacific Coast C.I.O. members. This case is at present pending.

[23] Massachusetts, New York, Pennsylvania, Utah, and Wisconsin.

[24] Wisconsin Employment Peace Act, 1939 (Wis. Stat., c. 111); Pennsylvania Labor Relations Act as amended by *Laws of Pennsylvania*, Act No. 162 (1939).

act, an employer may sign a closed-shop agreement only where at least three-fourths of the employees in the bargaining unit have voted in its favor by secret ballot in a special referendum conducted by the Wisconsin Employment Relations Board. A closed-shop agreement signed without such referendum is to be declared invalid by the Wisconsin board.[25]

This provision is, of course, far more effective than that of the Wagner Act in protecting workers against an unwanted closed shop. Not only does it require a three-fourths rather than a simple majority but, more significantly, it completely separates the question of representation from that of the closed shop. Workers who may want a union as a bargaining agent, but who may not want to join the union or who are opposed to the closed shop in principle, may vote for the union in the election and against the closed shop in the referendum.[26]

[25] Wis. Stat., c. 111.06 (1) (c).

[26] The question of the validity of the Wisconsin closed-shop referendum has been raised variously. In the case of a manufacturing company whose employees had petitioned the Wisconsin Employment Relations Board for a closed-shop referendum, the union objected to the jurisdiction of the board on the ground that the company, being engaged in interstate commerce, was under the jurisdiction of the National Labor Relations Act, under which the duly elected bargaining agent is entitled to a closed-shop agreement without additional referendum. The board, while granting that the company was under the jurisdiction of the National Labor Relations Act, claimed that, nevertheless, the Wisconsin provision applied: "Both the National Act and the Wisconsin Act regulating labor relations saw fit to limit the right that employers formerly had to enter into all-union agreements. . . . . If Congress had granted to labor organizations any right which the State of Wisconsin was endeavoring to limit then there might be a question of a conflict in the administration of the Acts, and . . . . the Wisconsin Act would have to yield to the National Act. Where, however, rights previously existing were limited we see no reason why the State cannot limit them to a greater extent than Congress saw fit to do" (Wisconsin Employment Relations Board, Federal Labor Union 20741, and Island Woolen Co., Baraboo, Wis., Case No. 110, R-10).

Against the arrangement, however, it is to be said that it plays badly into the hands of the selfish, unsocially minded worker who is well enough satisfied to have the union obtain for him better wages and working conditions, paid vacations, protection of seniority rights, and protection against arbitrary dismissal, but who is unwilling to contribute his share toward the support of the union. As long as there are no sufficient direct checks on union abuses, it may be well to assure to the workers self-determination as a protection against closed-shop tyranny. As

Another case has led to an indirect upholding of the Wisconsin law by the United States Supreme Court. A milk-drivers' union in Milwaukee had struck and picketed as "unfair to organized labor" an employer who refused to sign a closed-shop agreement after the referendum among the employees had resulted in a rejection of the closed shop by the majority. The Wisconsin Employment Relations Board thereupon ordered the union to cease and desist from attempting to force the employer to make an "unlawful agreement" and from publicly asserting that the company's refusal to sign an unlawful agreement constituted an "unfair labor practice." This Board order was affirmed by the Milwaukee Circuit Court. The union, defying both Board order and court order, continued its picketing while also appealing to the Wisconsin Supreme Court, claiming that the order prohibiting peaceful picketing was repugnant to the constitutional guaranty of free speech. The Wisconsin Supreme Court upheld the decision of the lower court, declaring that picketing, whether peaceful or not, was unlawful where its object was to enforce an unlawful act. The union then appealed to the United States Supreme Court for review, which that Court refused (*Milk and Ice-cream Drivers and Dairy Employees Union Local No. 225* v. *Wisconsin Employment Relations Board* [62 S.C. 1033]).

A recent decision of the United States Circuit Court of Appeals on the Pacific Coast claimed that also under the National Labor Relations Act a union elected by a majority of employees as bargaining agent does not have the right to make closed-shop contracts unless additionally and specifically authorized to do so by the employees, "even if the plain words of the Wagner Act do not require it . . . . a consideration of many different objectives for which laborers may self-organize necessitates such a construction" (decision rendered by Judges Denham, Mathews, and Stephens, March 1, 1942). In our opinion this is a wholly unjustified construction of the Wagner Act.

an ultimate solution of the problem, however, this device seems of doubtful value.

Both Wisconsin and Pennsylvania limit the unions' closed-shop privileges in another important direction. In both states no all-union agreement may be made with an organization which "unreasonably" refuses membership to any employee of the employer. The Wisconsin act places further emphasis on this point by declaring that where this provision is found to have been violated the Wisconsin Employment Relations Board will declare the all-union agreement as terminated.[27]

Through these provisions one gross potential abuse of the closed shop is forestalled: a union which has won an election against a rival union may not next run its opponents out of the place by getting a closed-shop contract and at the same time refusing membership to the *persona non grata*'s in the defeated minority. A valuable beginning is thus made with clipping the power of the unions through closed-shop contracts to deprive a man of his livelihood by excluding him from union membership. But it is a beginning only, for the above provision protects only the men already employed but leaves in the cold the outsider who, for general or personal reasons, was refused membership[28] and also the man

who was expelled from the union for reasons judged only by the union or even only by the union bosses.

A recent Michigan law contains a closed-shop provision which, under proper construction, could furnish a further valuable method of protecting a defeated minority in a shop against victimization by the majority union. This provision states that an employer may enter into a closed-shop agreement with a labor organization "if it is the only organization established among his employees."[29] This provision might be construed so as to forbid closed-shop agreements where the employees belong to two or more rival unions; for example, an A.F. of L. union representing a majority would become the sole bargaining agent, but it could not force the C.I.O. members in the plant through a closed-shop clause to desert their own organization and join that of the "enemy," with loss of job as the alternative.

A provision of this kind seems of great interest; indeed, it embodies an important principle, namely, that a worker should contribute his reasonable share to an organization which fairly represents his economic interests might be granted as reasonable and socially desirable. But to which of several rival organizations he contributes his share seems immaterial from a social point of

---

[27] Wis. Stat., c. 111.06 (1) (c); *Laws of Pennsylvania*, Act No. 162, sec. 6(c). The recent decision of the National Labor Relations Board in the Feinberg case (see n. 22) takes a similar attitude under the less stringent closed-shop regulations of the National Labor Relations Act. The above provision in the Pennsylvania law contains the limitation "provided such employee was not employed in violation of any previously existing agreement with said labor organization."

[28] The Pennsylvania Labor Relations Act, it is true, excludes from among the "labor organizations" which are to come under the protection of the act any organization which, by explicit proscription or by practice, "denies a person or persons membership in its organization on account of race, creed, or

color" (*op.cit.*, sec. 3[f]). Under this provision a union which, e.g., admits only white men as members cannot enlist the aid of the Pennsylvania State Labor Relations Board to obtain recognition for collective bargaining from an unwilling employer or to have an unfairly dismissed member reinstated. On the other hand, nothing in this provision would seem to prevent such a union from making a closed-shop agreement with a willing employer or with one whom it can coerce through threat of strike to sign such an agreement, thereby excluding all nonwhites from jobs.

[29] Michigan Labor Mediation Act, No. 176 of the Public Acts of 1939, sec. 14.

view (much though it would interest the union organizers and bosses). Provisions of this kind, therefore, might have the desirable effect of preventing closed-shop agreements from being used as weapons in rival union warfare. This might not only eliminate much industrial disturbance and ill feeling among organized labor but might actually contribute toward the reunification of the labor movement, since the very possibility of obtaining a closed-shop agreement would then depend on the absence of rival unions among the employees.[30]

PROPOSED LEGISLATION

In addition to the various enacted measures discussed above, many others have been proposed in the form of bills introduced into Congress.[31] Among those referring directly to the closed-shop issue there is, at the present time most outstanding (because the bill was passed by the House), the provision in the Smith-Vinson Bill to "freeze" closed-shop conditions in defense industries:

Defense contractors [may not] encourage or discourage membership in any labor organization unless such discrimination is required under the terms of a previously entered valid closed shop contract, or by the terms of a voluntarily entered subsequent agreement with the same labor organization.[32]

[30] Of interest in this connection, as showing the presently prevailing official acceptance of the closed shop as a rival union weapon, is the following passage from a recent decision of the War Labor Board. In rejecting a C.I.O. demand for suspension of a closed-shop clause in an A.F. of L. contract, the W.L.B. decision said: "One of the characteristics of a closed shop contract is that it renders it very difficult for a rival union . . . . to gain control of collective bargaining rights in the industry. That is one of the chief reasons why both C.I.O. and A.F. of L. are desirous of obtaining a closed shop contract whenever they can secure one" (*In re Los Angeles Railroad Corp. and Los Angeles Motor Coach Co.*, February 19, 1942).

[31] No attempt has been made to study bills to this effect introduced into state legislatures.

[32] H.R. 4139 (77th Cong., 1st sess., 1941), sec. 5.

Violation of this provision (as well as of others designed to assure uninterrupted production) is to be penalized by liability for damages and by the loss to individuals and to organizations of their status under the National Labor Relations Act and of their claims to unemployment relief or other benefits under the Social Security Act.[33] This measure, according to which a closed shop may not be demanded where it has not previously been in use, could, of course, serve to prevent closed-shop strikes in war industries. But it would not be—and surely does not mean to be—a permanent solution of the closed-shop problem as such.

Another recent (unreported) bill, on the other hand, does attempt not merely to postpone but to solve the problem. Designated by its author, Representative Hoffman of Michigan, as "a bill to protect the right of American citizens to earn a livelihood and to restore to American citizens freedom from fear and equality under the law,"[34] this bill proposes uncompromisingly to make it unlawful for any employer, in particular also for any government or government agency, "to require or demand or to assist in demanding, either directly or indirectly, any American citizen that he or she pay to any organization any sum of money or anything of value as a condition precedent to obtaining work, or as a condition of remaining at work." Violations are to be punished by a fine, for each offense, of not more than a thousand dollars or by imprisonment of not more than one year or both.[35]

[33] *Ibid.*, sec. 7 (*b*), (*c*), (*d*), (*e*).

[34] H.R. 5696 (77th Cong., 1st sess., September 19, 1941).

[35] *Ibid.*, secs. 1, 2. Similar provisions were proposed in the Senate for a joint resolution to amend the Constitution by Senator O'Daniel, of Texas, on September 19, 1941.

This provision has the merit of being consistent and unequivocal. But—aside from not having a chance of being considered under the present setup—it might not be desirable even from a detached point of view. For, as pointed out above, because of the peculiarities of the American labor scene, an outright prohibition of the closed shop at the present time might, in poorly organized industries, be real harmful or even detrimental to the development of representative trade-unionism. Moreover, coercion in the form of violence and terror would be likely to replace the more civilized coercion of the closed-shop agreement.

Aside from these legislative proposals referring to the closed shop directly, there are many others to regulate the unions with a view to curbing abuses in conjunction with which—or even because of which—the closed shop is often felt as oppressive and odious.

Of special importance in this respect is, again, the Smith-Vinson Bill.[36] All the provisions of this bill, it should be noticed, refer only to unions with employees in defense industries.[37] To such unions the bill forbids, first of all, to have officers who are members of certain communistic and Nazi organizations, under penalty of losing their status under the National Labor Relations Act.[38] It further demands that such unions register with the N.L.R.B. and give, under oath, the following information: name and address of the union and all its officers; of the companies with which it deals; statements as to initiation fees, annual dues, and of assessments levied during the

[36] H.R. 4139 (77th Cong., 1st sess., 1941).

[37] Section I of the bill defines at great length the broad scope of the term "defense contract."

[38] *Ibid.*, sec. 1(A). The proscribed organizations are the Communist party of the United States, the Young Communists' League, the German-American Bund, and the Kyffhaeuser Bund.

past year; statements as to the limitations placed upon union membership; number of paid-up members; date of last election of officers; methods of election; the vote for and against each candidate for office; the date of the last detailed financial statement to the members and the methods of publication of such statement; copies of sworn, detailed, and intelligible financial statements; and copies of the constitution and bylaws. Failure to comply with these requirements is to disqualify the union to act as the representative of employees in collective bargaining "for such time as such failure continues."[39] In addition, the bill closely limits strike procedure in defense industries, prescribing postponement of strikes until mediation by the United States Conciliation Service has taken place and until strike ballots have been certified by the United States Secretary of Labor.[40]

From the point of view here adopted there is much to be welcomed in this bill, the idea, namely, that unions which wish to benefit by the governmental protection and sponsorship of the National Labor Relations Act should be required to give guaranty of reasonable, honest, and democratic procedure. But, on the other side, this bill, in our opinion, suffers from an unwholesome tying-together of war-emergency measures with measures having inherently nothing to do with the emergency. That uninterrupted production is of supreme importance for the nation at war is obvious and hence that effective curbs on strikes might become necessary as war measures, like many other temporary suspensions of civil rights, is plain. The same applies also to the ban on politically subversive elements in positions of union leaders. But that the unions, which under the National Labor Relations Act have become gov-

[39] *Ibid.*, secs. 8, 9, 10.   [40] *Ibid.*, sec. 3.

ernmentally sponsored, quasi-public institutions, should be required to give guaranty of being honest, democratic, bona fide representatives, and not profiteering exploiters of labor, is equally necessary in peacetime as in wartime and equally necessary in all industries, whether defense or not.

Regarded as peacetime measures, however, these various proposals to curb union abuses seem unnecessarily repressive. Thus, with regular elections and regular accounting made obligatory upon "registered" unions, it might be sufficient to place the N.L.R.B. at the ready disposal of union members having complaints against union officers instead of requiring the latter to report constantly on every phase of their activity. Also, as regards penalties for failure to give the required information, it seems unnecessarily repressive to debar nonregistered unions from all collective bargaining. It would seem enough, on the one hand, to prohibit closed-shop contracts with such unions and, on the other hand, to deny them access to the governmental labor relations boards for complaints over employers' nonrecognition or other unfair labor practices and for certification notably as against a rival union. The logic of facts would be likely to produce much better results than unpopular statutes.[41]

Of interest in this connection is another recent (unreported) bill, because it deals specifically and at length with the problem of regulating the unions but without direct bearing on the war emergency. It is called the "Unions Registration and Elections Act of 1941"[42] and

opens with a weighty introduction, "Findings of Facts and Declaration of Policy," phrased in obvious analogy to the corresponding part of the National Labor Relations Act:

The want of democratic standards in the election of officers of labor organizations, the want of standards in the accountability and reporting of funds, and the want of standards of procedure in strike balloting . . . . have led to abuses and practices which have burdened or obstructed interstate commerce or foreign commerce, and have interfered with national defense.

Protection by law of the exercise of the full rights of self-government by the members of labor organizations will tend to diminish the opportunities for corrupt and arbitrary leadership, for the perversion of labor organizations to purposes other than those for which they were formed.

It is hereby declared to be the policy of the United States to eliminate certain substantial obstructions to the free flow of commerce by encouraging and protecting the exercise of full self-government and democratic procedure by the members of labor organizations. . . . .[43]

These policies the bill plans to achieve through measures similar to those of the Smith-Vinson Bill: all labor organizations (not only those with members in defense industries) are to register with the N.L.R.B. and are to furnish exactly the same information required under the former bill, to which is added only the requirement that the constitution or by-laws must provide for determination, by secret vote of the members, of initiation fees, dues, and special assessments.[44] Failure to register and to furnish the required information is to disqualify a union as bargaining agent.[45] The bill again goes further than the Smith-Vinson Bill by providing for annual elections of union officers under the supervision of the N.L.R.B., in a way similar to the

---

[41] The difference between "registered" and "nonregistered" unions as to freedom from outside supervision, on the one side, and disqualification, on the other, would presumably develop to be similar to that between accredited and nonaccredited colleges.

[42] H.R. 6068 (Hoffman) (77th Cong., 1st sess., November 19, 1941).

[43] *Ibid.*, sec. 2.

[44] *Ibid.*, sec. 7.

[45] *Ibid.*, sec. 9.

present system of election of bargaining agents under that board.[46]

Finally, the bill lays down in great detail the procedure through which strikes are to be decided upon: the N.L.R.B., upon petitioning, is to investigate the dispute, take the necessary steps to assure full understanding of the issue by all parties involved, conduct a secret strike ballot, and certify a strike only if the majority of the employees of the particular employer to be struck declares in favor of it.[47]

This bill has the merit of focusing sharply and frankly on the union abuses it wants to curb rather than looking in the direction of the war emergency. As regards the measures through which it proposes to achieve regulation of the financial dealings, elections, and membership policies, it goes even further than the Smith-Vinson Bill in what appears to us as unnecessary supervision and regimentation. Most objectionable, however, seem the proposed regulations—to wit, meant not only for the emergency but for normal times—of strike procedure. Strike voting wherever it takes place should, of course, be honest and uncoerced. But whether every individual plant should under all circumstances decide as a separate unit for or against a strike in that plant is a wide-open question involving basic problems of union strategy. To legislate, in the name of democracy and civic decency, in favor of individual plants as the ultimate and independent strike units—provided a law to that effect could be enforced—would be a turning-back in the direction of the outlawed company unions through which an employer could always deal with his own employees only.

A number of other bills deal with qualification of union officers and members.

These measures, however, all born out of the national emergency, are intended not to protect workers against unfair exclusion from unions wielding closed-shop contracts but to protect industry against subversive elements in the unions. Most of these bills prohibit labor organizations to have officers, agents, or bargaining representatives who are not citizens of the United States or who are members of Communist, Nazi, or Fascist organizations.[48] Some bills go further and exclude "Communists, Bundists, and Nazis" not only from being officers or representatives but also from being members of the unions.[49] Another one wants to bar aliens from voting in labor organizations under fines up to a thousand dollars and imprisonment up to six months.[50]

CLOSED-SHOP POLICIES OF ADMINISTRATIVE EMERGENCY BOARDS

In addition to actual and proposed legislation to regulate the unions in general and the closed shop in particular, the policies of certain administrative emergency boards are of interest in this connection.

There is, first, the National War Labor Board (successor to the National Defense Mediation Board). This Board, having the urgent task of settling labor disputes in war industries as speedily as possible, naturally has to be more or less flexible as to general principles, dealing with each case as best it can on its particular merits. This applies especially to the closed-shop disputes which the Board is called

[46] Ibid., sec. 10.   [47] Ibid., sec. 11.

[48] E.g., S.J.R. 275 (Reynolds) (76th Cong., 2d sess., 1940); H.R. 8750 (Anderson) (76th Cong., 2d sess., 1940); H.R. 6154 (Landis) (77th Cong., 1st sess., 1941).

[49] H.R. 5030 (Ramsay) (77th Cong., 1st sess., 1941); H.R. 1842 (Ford) (77th Cong., 1st sess., 1941).

[50] H.R. 4406 (Woodruff) (77th Cong., 1st sess., 1941).

upon to decide.[51] In fact, the Board has emphatically disavowed any set policy regarding the closed-shop issue.[52]

Nevertheless, a definite principle has emerged from the Board's arbitral law-making in closed-shop cases—the principle, namely, of union maintenance or union security, according to which union members are required, as a condition of employment, to remain in good standing for the duration of the agreement, whereas nonunion workers are not required to join the union.[53]

At the principle of this compromise measure the Board seems to have arrived for two reasons: on the one hand, it regards stability of union status as a guaranty of stability of production; on the other, it grants the argument of the unions that the patriotic nonstrike policy, to which they pledged themselves at the outbreak of the war, is weakening their hold on and appeal to members and that therefore they should be protected against membership losses at least through a union-maintenance clause.[54] Consistent with this reasoning the Board has repeatedly denied union-maintenance contracts to unions which previous to

[51] In the case of the Bethlehem Steel West Coast Shipyards the National Defense Mediation Board ordered the company to sign a closed-shop clause because such a clause was contained in the master-agreement covering the whole industry, signed by thirty-eight shipyards and twenty unions, June, 1941. In the captive coal mines case, on the other hand, the Board refused to order the steel companies, controlling 10 per cent of the bituminous coal production, to conform to the closed-shop status prevailing in the other 90 per cent of the industry (November, 1941).

[52] "The National War Labor Board does not have an open shop policy, and does not have a closed shop policy. It examines thoroughly the facts and considers the circumstances and equities in each case, and attempts to arrive at a just decision" (from decision of the W.L.B. in the Federal Shipbuilding and Drydock case [April, 1942]).

[53] Federal Shipbuilding and Drydock case (April, 1942), International Harvester (April, 1942), Marshall Field & Co. (March, 1942), and others. The stringency of the union-maintenance order has varied almost from case to case, seemingly under the influence of the employer members of the Board (who dissented in all these union-maintenance decisions, insisting on voluntarism on the part of union members). Thus, in the Federal Shipbuilding case the order applied unconditionally to all employees who were union members at the time the agreement was made. In the International Harvester case it applied to all members "provided the majority of the members in good standing vote in its favor." Again in the Marshall Field case the order applied only to those among the employees "who after the consummation of this agreement individually and voluntarily certify in writing that they authorize union dues deductions and will, as a condition of employment, maintain their membership in good standing during the life of the contract." More recently (September, 1942) a split-panel recommendation of the W.L.B. has recommended the continua-

tion of an expiring closed-shop agreement rather than its replacement by a union-maintenance clause. The argument in favor of this recommendation by the public member of the panel, Dr. H. Shulman, of the Yale Law School, is noteworthy: "The maintenance of membership clause is a device for freezing the open shop during the emergency as far as Board orders are concerned, where the open shop prevailed before the emergency. Thus the unions are prevented from taking advantage of the crisis in order to achieve the union or closed shop and to threaten production for that purpose. It is entirely equitable that the theory be applied consistently by the adoption of the complementary notion that an employer should not be permitted to take advantage of the crisis in order to achieve the open shop in a plant which was theretofore union or closed shop, or to threaten production for that purpose." The principle truly advocated here, it seems to us, is that of freezing closed-shop conditions during the emergency, as advocated in the Smith-Vinson Bill. To designate, however, union maintenance as a "device to freeze the open shop" seems unduly one-sided and hence not helpful toward a fair application of the whole compromise device.

[54] "The experience of the War Labor Board has shown how strong, responsible union leadership can keep production rolling. . . . . An unstable membership contributes to an irresponsible leadership; too often members of unions do not maintain their membership because they resent the discipline of a responsible leadership (from the Federal Shipbuilding decision of the W.L.B.). Also: "The government of the United States is under a moral and equitable compulsion not to take advantage of the national [nonstrike] agreement which has disarmed this union of its only weapon" (*ibid.*).

their appeal to the Board had gone on strike over the issue.[55]

These union-maintenance decisions of the Board have been widely resented and criticized as establishing the governmentally ordered closed shop in disguise, and an illogical and unfair one at that, since the coercion applies only to union members, thus penalizing union membership.[56] Regarded, however, as what it doubtless is, namely, an emergency compromise, this principle may be as adequate as many another that could be devised, considering the embarrassement of the Board of having to rule authoritatively on an issue which Congress has up to now chosen not to tackle.

The dissatisfaction, however, stirred up over the governmentally ordered union-maintenance shop may well be expected to enhance the growing realization of the need for a legislative settlement of the whole closed-shop issue. In fact, the decisions and opinions of the W.L.B. in this matter, adapted from case to case to the situation, may furnish valuable material for an eventual attempt at such legislative settlement.[57]

Another federal agency which has recently come to grips with closed-shop problems is the President's Committee on Fair Employment Practices, which was established to prevent racial and religious discrimination in war industries.[58] Most of the committee's work consists in ascertaining facts as to employment practices, particularly as to the relative number of whites and Negroes employed in the various kinds of positions in a plant with war contracts, and to urge or order employers to desist from racial discrimination.

In the following case, however, a significant closed-shop situation was involved. The employer had a closed-shop contract with a plumbers' union under which only members of this union could be employed, while at the same time the union excluded Negroes from membership. The committee decided against the legality of this contract:

Said agreement as to that part which in effect prevents the employment of Negro plumbers on Defense projects solely on account of their race or color is hereby declared illegal, inoperative, unenforceable, undemocratic, and

---

[55] A. F. of L. Chemical Workers Union at the Monsanto Chemical Co. plant, Everett, Mass.; A.F. of L. Federal Union at the General Chemical Co., Buffalo, N.Y.; United Mine Workers at the General Chemical Co., Cleveland, Ohio.

[56] Montgomery Ward Co., Chicago and Elizabeth, N.J., actually refused to comply with the Board's order to sign a union-maintenance contract. Among the arguments of the president of the company in his letter to the Board were the following: that the order violates a fundamental principle of liberty; that it is economically unsound; that it is illegal, since Congress is the sole lawmaking authority; and that Congress had not empowered the W.L.B. to order "any employer to do any of the things it demands of Wards." He referred further to President Roosevelt's letter regarding the government's attitude toward the closed shop (quoted above in n. 12). The company later complied with the Board's order upon being directed to do so by the President in his capacity as "Commander-in-Chief in time of war."

[57] Of interest in this respect seems, e.g., the provision in the Federal Shipbuilding agreement, ac-

cording to which the obligations of members for maintaining the required union standing are limited to the regular monthly dues plus regularly imposed fines if any, that is, exclude extra assessments; likewise that the question regarding an employee's union standing is not left to the decision of the union but is to be "adjudicated by an arbiter appointed by the N.W.L.B." Such protection of the members against unfair union practices as the necessary correlate to the governmentally ordered union maintenance is also explicitly demanded in the dissenting opinion of the Board's employer-members in the Federal Shipbuilding case: "If this position is taken by a government agency and a national labor policy is thus established then Government must of necessity accept the responsibility of the supervision of that labor organization to which it forces an employee to pay dues, fees, and assessments."

[58] Executive Order 8802, June 25, 1941. In this order the President reaffirmed the policy of the United States that there shall be no discrimination in the employment of workers in defense industries or government because of race, creed, color, or national origin.

contrary to the national policy expressed in the President's Executive Order 8802.[59]

Unlike the union-maintenance principle of the W.L.B., the principle here applied has a significance going far beyond that of an emergency compromise. In fact, this ruling belongs closely with the Wisconsin and Pennsylvania laws,[60] under which closed-shop contracts may not be made with unions which "unreasonably" exclude employees of the employer from membership. Laws and rulings of this kind, so far limited in scope (the one applying only to employees of the employer, the other only to Negroes), will doubtless help to bring about a general recognition of the principle—emphasized above—that closed-shop contracts must be restricted to unions with regulated membership requirements.

V. CONCLUSIONS

This survey of enacted and proposed legislation and of administrative rulings shows clearly the acceptance of the following ideas: (1) that union methods and policies are subject to federal and state legislations; (2) that the N.L.R.B. —created to deal with labor's complaints against employers' unfair labor practices and to assist labor in determining its bargaining agents—could and should also be used to handle labor's complaints against the unions' unfair labor practices and to assist labor in the regulation of union procedure; and (3) that the very protection and assistance afforded under the Wagner Act by the government to the unions gives to the government an immediate power over the unions, namely, of withholding this protection from unions which refuse to give guaranty of

reasonable, democratic, and honest procedure. A comprehensive legislative plan, however, based on these ideas has so far not been adopted. As regards the closed shop as such, some beginnings have been made in federal and state legislation to restrict its use to the duly chosen representatives and to protect workers against victimization through closed-shop contracts by unions which exclude them from membership. Among legislative proposals, that to freeze the closed shop as also the union-maintenance policy of the W.L.B. are of emergency compromise character only, while the proposal to outlaw all closed-shop contracts seems out of line with actual needs and trends.

As to restraining union abuses, due to which the closed shop is so widely resented as oppressive, no legislation has been enacted so far. Among legislative proposals, it is true, measures are being vigorously advocated to insure regular election of union officers, regular accounting, and guaranties as to fees and membership requirements. But these proposals, in order to become more widely acceptable, seem to require some recasting: first, they should be frankly designed for the purpose they intend to achieve rather than trying to ride into enactment on the coattails of war-emergency measures; second, they should be clearly separated from strike legislation referring to controversial issues of legitimate union strategy; and, finally, they should strive to attain their ends by as little regimentation as possible.

All in all, we venture to suggest, the whole situation regarding union legislation would be greatly improved if the true friends of trade-unionism in Congress and in the legislatures would come to see and admit that certain regulations are needed in the best interest both of the workers and of sound unionism, and

---

[59] President's Committee on Fair Employment Practices, Negro Plumbers against the Chicago Journeymen Plumbers' Union Local 130, *Findings and Directions* (April 4, 1942).

[60] Wis Stat., c. 111; *Laws of Pennsylvania*, Act No. 162.

if they would make this matter their own cause rather than leaving it in the hands of the more unsympathetic critics of the unions. Indeed, it would seem only natural for the New Deal legislators, who launched the policy of governmental control of industrial relations, to continue their policy constructively in the same direction rather than to affect now a somewhat belated Manchesterism by indulging the unions' unreasonable claim to the combined blessings of governmental sponsorship and "freedom from governmental meddling."

Approached constructively in the spirit of bringing the intent of the Wagner Act to fuller fruition, the closed-shop issue should indeed prove quite amenable to a fair legislative solution. For, where regular elections and accounting are safeguarded, where unions with closed-shop contracts are restrained from exacting unreasonable contributions and from unfairly withholding membership, and where labor relations boards stand ready to handle complaints of workers against union officers on any of these points, there the closed shop can hardly be decried as a violation of a man's basic liberties. All social organization involves manifold restraints and obligations most of which constitute limitations of the freedom of the individual. Among these the—formal or moral—obligation of a man to contribute his fair share to the organization which quasi-officially represents his economic interests would seem a rather obvious and a very reasonable one.

WASHINGTON, D.C.

UNION SECURITY AND ITS IMPLICATIONS

By Louis Stark

UNION security in any of its phases is likely to be a thorny problem for a long time. Its implications go to the heart of employer-employee relations, to the question of intra-union democracy, and to the relations of government and unionism.

The broad sweep of unionism today is toward some form of the closed shop. That movement has been stimulated by government action, as will appear later. At the moment, one may perceive the force of the movement by a glance at a few figures.

According to the Bureau of Labor Statistics (Bulletin 829), approximately 10,500,000 of the 14,500,000 workers employed under collective contracts in January 1945 were covered by one of various types of union-status provisions, namely: closed shop, union shop, union preferential clauses, or maintenance of membership. In short, there were more than three times as many employees under union security provisions in January 1945 as were in the entire trade union movement in 1935.

VARIETIES OF UNION SECURITY

Union security may provide for the closed shop, the union shop, maintenance of membership, the preferential shop, or the exclusive bargaining shop.

A closed shop is one in which only union members may be hired and employees must remain members to retain employment.

Under the union shop, nonunion members may be hired but they must join the union after a certain time.

Where maintenance-of-membership provisions prevail, employees are not required to join the union, but if they do, they must remain in good standing as a condition of employment. Usually there is an "escape" clause in these contracts whereby employees have fifteen days to decide whether they wish to join, remain in, or leave the union before the contract becomes effective. If the employee withholds his union membership within this period, he cannot lose his job. If he is in the union after the "escape" period, his failure to keep up his dues may incur expulsion and loss of his job.

In preferential union shops, union members are given preference in hiring and layoffs. The employer is not called upon to discharge those who do not join the union.

The exclusive bargaining shop is one in which the union is recognized as the exclusive bargaining agent for all employees, whether they belong to the union or not.

The closed shop and the union shop are sometimes synonymous in current usage. Contracts seldom call for the closed shop, but usually provide for the union shop.

OPEN SHOP VERSUS CLOSED SHOP

The signal for a concentrated industrial attack on the closed shop came in 1892 when the Carnegie Steel Company abandoned its friendly relations with the Amalgamated Association of Iron, Steel and Tin Workers and opened a struggle for the "open shop." This movement compelled unions that had been working under verbal closed-shop or union-shop agreements to demand such provisions in writing. The resulting resistance led to employer demands for the open shop, sometimes labeled "The American Plan." Too frequently the "open shop" and "The American Plan" terms merely meant the "closed shop" to union labor.

When the United States entered World War I in 1917, the National War Labor Board, set up to further industrial peace, was embarrassed by the "open shop versus the closed shop" issue, but refused to decide it. While the Board encouraged collective bargaining, it also—inadvertently—gave an impetus to the Employee Representation Plan which became industry's mainstay against independent unionism until the National Labor Relations [Wagner] Act was passed by Congress in 1935.

Until the Wagner Act became law, the closed or union shop existed in various trades as a result of mutual agreement of employers and employees. It made no difference whether a union had an overwhelming majority of members in a plant or whether it had a small minority; if, for sufficiently valid reasons, the employer was agreeable to a union shop, he made a contract and that ended the matter. But the Wagner Act deprived a minority group of the right to make a valid closed-shop agreement. By so doing, the new law involved itself in what is apparently a contradiction.

CONTRADICTION IN THE WAGNER ACT

The theory of the act is opposed to the idea that employees should be forced to join a union not of their own choosing. Thus, Section 7, which contains the positive statement of employee rights, and constitutes the heart of the act, says:

Employees shall have the right of self-organization, to form, join, or assist labor organizations, to bargain collectively through representatives of their own choosing, and to engage in concerted activities, for the purpose of collective bargaining or other mutual aid or protection; . . . .

To protect these rights, the act established certain prohibitions on the employer. These, known as unfair labor practices, included the following, in Section 8(3):

It shall be an unfair labor practice for an employer. . . .

By discrimination in regard to hire or tenure of employment or any term or condition of employment to encourage or discourage membership in any labor organization. . . .

If the law had stopped there, obviously the closed-shop agreement would have been barred, since such a contract compels the employer to require that his employees join a specified union. But the law attached a proviso to Section 8(3) stating:

Nothing in this Act . . . shall preclude an employer from making an agreement with a labor organization . . . to require, as a condition of employment, membership therein, if such labor organization is the representative of the employees as provided in Section 9(a) in the appropriate collective bargaining unit, covered by such agreements when made.

Section 9(a) provides that representatives selected by the majority of employees shall be the exclusive representatives of all the employees.

This is where the apparent contradiction in the act developed. First, employees are given complete freedom to select and be represented by any union of their own choice. Next, the employer is told he cannot encourage (or discourage) membership in any labor organization. But then the exception is made, leaving the way open for the employer to encourage membership in a labor organization, and thus directly or indirectly prevent the employees from exercising their freedom of choice. In trying to solve this apparent contradiction the National Labor Relations Board has established the following principles:

Principles of NLRB

First, where there is a closed-shop contract, the employee must remain in good standing so far as his dues payments are concerned or else be subject to discharge. This is true at all times.

Second, if an employee becomes active in behalf of a rival union *at any time before the existing contract is nearing its termination date* (italics supplied), he is subject to suspension by the union and loss of his job.[1]

Third, any employee may exercise his right to select a different bargaining agent *toward the end* (italics supplied) of an existing closed-shop contract provided he remains in good standing as far as his dues are concerned. This principle was established originally in the case of Rutland Court Owners and was subsequently sustained by the Supreme Court in the *Wallace case.*

However, in recent months, the Board has attached a string to this last-named principle which may come close to destroying its practicability. In the *Diamond T Motor Car Company case* (No. 13–C–2414) the Board discovered that an employee had become active in behalf of a rival to the contracting closed-shop union *toward the end* (italics supplied) of the ·contract period. Although this was permitted under the *Rutland Court* and *Wallace cases* the Board upheld the legality of the discharge. The reason assigned was that the company was able to show that *it had no knowledge of the real cause of the man's suspension by the contracting union* (italics supplied).

In previous cases there was evidence that the company knew why the employees were suspended. In the *Diamond T case* the Board found that ignorance of this fact constituted a valid defense against a charge of committing an unfair labor practice.

[1] Southwest Portland Cement Co. Case No. 16–C–119.

Under current board theory, the burden of proof seems to be on the individual employee who tries to exercise the rights guaranteed him in Section 7 of the act. If he has not kept track of the legal rulings of the Board, which may and do change from time to time, and does not know that he must advise the proper managerial authority of the real reason for his suspension by the contracting union, he loses his job, his seniority, and his security. This would seem to be an unusually stringent requirement, and it is difficult to see where it will leave the closed-shop issue.

Origin of Maintenance of Membership

The closed-shop issue which was settled during World War I by not being settled (by maintaining the status quo) was a sore point before and during World War II. The unions, having made vast gains between the wars, were no longer content, when the emergency defense period opened in 1940, to maintain the status quo. The National Defense Mediation Board, predecessor of National War Labor Board for World War II, was besought to grant the closed shop, but did so in only one case. Before the Board wound up its work, however, it had opened a field for compromise between the closed shop and the status quo which was to be a big factor in the work of its successor, the National War Labor Board. That was the maintenance-of-membership provision which it had recommended in the *Federal Shipbuilding Corporation* and other cases.

When President Roosevelt called his labor-management conference after Pearl Harbor, the problem of union status arose, and on December 23, 1941, the President cut the Gordian knot by decreeing that the NWLB would settle "all disputes" whether over the closed shop or what not. The employer members had sought to obtain assent to a resolution stating that "the issue of the closed shop is not a proper subject for consideration. . . ." On this the conference deadlocked until the President acted in favor of the union contention. By this move, the problem of "union security" became one of the most contentious factors in the NWLB's proceedings.

On the one hand, public policy prevented the Board from granting the closed shop. (President Roosevelt had stated that the Government would not impose the closed shop.) On the other hand, the unions, having given up the right to strike during the war, pressed for some form of "security" even though it was something less than the closed shop.

The public members of the Board felt that a device that got the unions "over the hump" of recognition and moved toward greater responsibility would result in greater war matériel production, as it would tend to eliminate disputes over union membership and reduce turnover. In this way the maintenance-of-membership principle grew out of the Board's dilemma as between labor's demand for the closed shop on the one hand, and public policy and industry opposition on the other. It was frankly a compromise which did not suit either side, but as it developed, objection to it at times became less vocal by the employers, although toward the end they insisted on congressional disposition of the issue.

Since V–J Day the expectation of some labor and industry leaders have been fulfilled. There have been some costly strikes in which the security provision, inserted at NWLB direction, has been an important bone of contention. Among these strikes were General Motors, the Yale and Towne Manufacturing Company, International Harvester, and Western Electric.

MAINTENANCE OF DUES

The compromise worked out in these cases is typical of the tendency toward which the situation appears to be moving when stubborn strikes occur over this issue. Instead of requiring the employer to dismiss an employee who does not remain in good standing, the new clauses in some contracts provide for a checkoff of union dues. This means that even if an employee is ejected from a union during the life of an agreement, his dues continue to be deducted and the company is not required to dismiss him. This is maintenance of dues rather than maintenance of membership. It satisfies the employer because he will not have to dismiss a capable man who may have some difficulty with his union.

The maintenance-of-dues clause has been insisted upon particularly by the large oil companies and refineries which have established pension, health, and other employee benefit schemes. Under a union-shop or maintenance-of-membership provision, an employee's vested interest in these rights would be lost if he were separated from his union.

In its evolution, union security may take on new forms in the future. A long, bitter strike of CIO United Automobile Workers in the Windsor (Canada) plant of the Ford Motor Company was settled by arbitration in February 1946. The award, handed down by Mr. Justice I. C. Rand of the Supreme Court of Canada, ruling against the demand for the closed shop, provided for a checkoff compulsory on all employees within the bargaining unit, but did not insist that all employees be members of the union.

The union greeted this part of the decision with strong approval, on the ground that few workers in the plant would be willing to pay dues without availing themselves of the opportunity to participate in union activity.

Justice Rand proceeded from the premise that declarations of policy by Dominion and provincial legislatures maintained the social desirability of the organization of workers and of collective bargaining.

> The corollary . . . is that labor unions should become strong in order to carry on functions for which they are intended.
> . . . the employees as a whole become the beneficiaries of union action and I doubt if any circumstance provokes more resentment in a plant than this sharing of the fruits of unionist work and courage by the non-member.
> . . . I consider it entirely equitable then that all employees should be required to shoulder their portion of the burden of expense for administering the law of their employment, the union contract; that they must take the burden along with the benefit.

While the union regarded the checkoff section of the award as a progressive step, it was extremely skeptical of the section devoted to penalties imposed for unauthorized strikes.

RISING TREND OF UNION SECURITY

Obviously, employers would prefer maintenance of dues rather than of membership; but in many cases where they cannot avoid the latter, they prefer to link it with the checkoff. The reason is plain. If a man falls behind in his dues and is no longer in good standing in the union, he must be discharged under the usual union security provision.

It is significant that the National Industrial Conference Board, analyzing union security clauses in 212 contracts, finds that the checkoff of dues is becoming more prevalent. The checkoff was found in 90 contracts, membership maintenance in 91, the union shop in 47, the closed shop in 6, and preferential hiring in 13. These figures throw some light on the rising trend of some form of security clause in collective bargaining contracts.[2]

On May 19, 1946 the Bureau of Labor Statistics reported that "maintenance-of-membership clauses continue to figure conspicuously in collective bargaining agreements." It was stated:

> Of 224 agreements effective since January 1, 1946 covering approximately 655,000 workers, 40 now have maintenance clauses. Thirty-two of these were retained from previous agreements. The other eight had formerly provided merely that the union had sole bargaining rights for the employees, while the new contract provides for membership maintenance as well. . . . Ten additional agreements which continued maintenance-of-membership provisions last year do not have such clauses in their present contracts. Of these five have been strengthened from the point of view of the union to provide for a union shop, four provide for an irrevocable checkoff of the dues of union members in lieu of maintenance of membership, and one grants sole bargaining rights.

UNION MONOPOLY

In view of the current trends and tendencies toward some form of union security, it becomes pertinent to inquire into the possible future relationship of union security and the interest of (1) employer, (2) union membership, and (3) the public.

Unions ask for the union shop or some form of security (so they argue) because they can thus assure employers greater responsibility for discipline and production. The usual friction between union and nonunion members is avoided in shops where a form of security prevents employer discrimination, and the union, because it does not have to worry about retention of its membership, is in

[2] National Industrial Conference Board, *Trends in Collective Bargaining and Union Contracts*, Studies in Personnel Policy No. 71.

a position to offer constructive co-operation for production.

But while union security makes for a strong, disciplined union, it also makes for monopoly, and that carries with it dangers to production. A coal or steel workers union with a monopoly of employees may be the inevitable trend of the times. Assuming that this trend will continue in most basic and mass production industries, the time may come when instead of an aggregate membership of 14,000,000, we may see 25,000,000 or 35,000,000 employees enrolled in monolithic unions, each one capable of crippling the Nation or an important segment of it in the event of a strike.

The coal and steel strikes in the last three years are illustrations of the effects of modern monopolistic tendencies in unions. These tendencies sometimes go hand in hand with political decisions—leadership decisions. The top leaders may contribute toward a party campaign fund out of a union treasury, but the union members who are of a different political persuasion can do nothing about it. If the answer is, "the majority rules," it is fairly obvious that no member of an economic-purpose union entered upon a political compact when he joined the organization. On economic matters, the will of the majority carries. But how is the minority to be protected when political matters are brought into the union?

With some exceptions, employers are reluctant to grant any form of the closed shop. However, once it is won, they look to the union to enforce responsibility, to avoid slowdowns and unauthorized stoppages, and to discipline those who deviate from contract provisions. In many cases they prefer to deal with a labor organization led by a "strong" man rather than one where "rank-and-file" democracy prevails. This choice tends to place a

great deal of power in the hands of a single individual. Used capriciously or arbitrarily, this power may turn on the employer, forcing concessions felt to be uneconomic, or on the union member, resulting in expulsion and deprivation of a job or livelihood.

As to the first danger, that is no less likely under a closed shop with a "strong" leader than under any other form of arrangement, such as exclusive bargaining, where more democratic rank-and-file union control may normally be more prevalent. As to the second possibility, it is undeniable that abuse of authority may mean dictatorship by a single union officer or clique. Since the Government, as a result of the Wagner Act, has made possible the grant of this authority, it would seem to be no more than fair that some safeguards should be thrown around the enhanced power of the union officialdom. How that can be done without undue government interference in the internal affairs of unions is a difficult question to answer.

SAFEGUARDS AGAINST UNION POWER

A union member who feels that he has been unjustly expelled may, after exhausting his remedies inside the union, appeal to the courts. This is often quite impossible, for the individual does not have the time and the resources to fight such a long-drawn-out battle.

A voluntary approach to this problem is found in the proposal that an outside impartial agency be set up to pass upon alleged union abuses involving discrimination in membership and discriminatory expulsion. A contract between District 50, United Mine Workers of America and the Boston Consolidated Gas Company provides an arbitration board of three to review employees' appeals against suspension, expulsion, or exclusion; one arbiter is chosen by the union, one by the aggrieved member, and the third is selected jointly.

Unless unions themselves set up some form of impartial machinery to pass on these matters, the Government will do so. This may or may not be unwise, but it is probably inevitable unless labor acts on its own initiative.

Since the Government compels employers to bargain with anyone chosen by a majority in an appropriate unit, what protection will the employee (union or nonunion) have from arbitrary action of a dictator, especially if a closed-shop or security provision is set forth in the contract? One authority would grant power to the National Labor Relations Board to review inequitable restrictions on membership and disciplinary procedure in certain cases involving the closed shop. A verdict for the disciplined member would carry with it assessment of loss of wages, similar to the present practice when an employer is found to have discriminatorily discharged an employee for union activity.[3]

Public Aspects of Union Security

The internal actions of unions which have closed shops have important public aspects. Musical education, for example, is affected by the rules of the American Federation of Musicians; and the power of the federation, under its constitution, is vested in its president, James C. Petrillo, who, it so happens, can change the constitution at will. The International Typographical Union adopts "rules" from time to time and insists that these unilateral policies must be subscribed to by publishers without any bargaining. Building-trade unions have rules which limit production. The closed shop or union shop

[3] Joel Seidman, *Union Rights and Union Duties* (New York: Harcourt, Brace and Co., 1943), p. 208.

inevitably brings with it questions of public policy involving membership requirements such as discrimination due to sex or color. The interests of all parties require that the union shop shall not be synonymous with the closed union. All those eligible should be allowed to join, and the requirements should be as broad as possible. A closed shop and a closed union tend to monopoly.

It is sometimes asked why the closed shop is necessary in view of employee protection against discrimination guaranteed by the Wagner Act. The union answer is that despite the enormous growth of the labor movement, some employers are still unreconciled to unions and would, if they could, hamstring them.

The question of "Why the union shop?" becomes almost superfluous in light of the divided labor movement. The hard fact is that unions today are more anxious to win the closed or union shop or some form of union security than ever before, because they fear that if they do not do so, their rivals will encroach on what each union considers its preserves, or that raids by rival unions will whittle away their membership.

It is this fear that has involved the National Labor Relations Board so often in disputes among unions over rival jurisdictions and what is called "dual" unionism. The Wagner Act does not deal with problems of jurisdiction or dual unionism. It provides for elections where questions of representation exist. The act does not "hand over" employees to unions. It permits employees to choose their own representatives. Therefore, when unions seek to "turn over" members to other unions through "deals," recourse may be had by employees to the NLRB for domestic elections.

The closed shop in foremen's unions,

particularly those allied with production workers, is just another manifestation of the present-day tendency toward the bottlenecking of our entire industrial life. A strike of a small group of key workers may just as effectively cripple the Nation as a strike of a much bigger one.

Thus the closed shop, whether involving a small key union or a major industry, gives rise to questions that cannot be ignored. These questions must be discussed frankly by unions, employers, and government.

GOVERNMENT ENCOURAGEMENT

The Government encourages the spread of unionism but will not give its sanction to the closed shop, since it will not compel employees to join a union. Yet government encouragement leads directly to the spread of the closed shop and other union security provisions—a grant of vast power to union leaders.

What, then, is the answer to government encouragement of a kingdom within a kingdom?

Unless thoroughly democratic practices respecting membership and self-government are fostered within unions, the spread of the union shop will evoke demands for government regulation of one form or another. It will be difficult to draw up proposals for government control that do not interfere in some way with free collective bargaining. That may be a heavy price to pay for the union shop.

Problems and Trends in Collective Bargaining

The Seniority Problem in Mass Production Industries, by Frederick H. Harbison, American Economic Association, Papers and Proceedings, Vol. XXX, No. 1, March, 1940, pp. 223–225

Has Collective Bargaining Failed? by George W. Taylor, Annals of the American Academy of Political and Social Science, Vol. 248, November, 1946, pp. 154–160

The Economics of Wage-Dispute Settlement, by John T. Dunlop, Law and Contemporary Problems, Vol. XII, No. 2, Spring, 1947, pp. 281–296

Some Reflections on the "Labor Monopoly" Issue, by Richard A. Lester, Journal of Political Economy, Vol. LV, No. 6, December, 1947, pp. 513–536

The Changing Character of American Industrial Relations, by Sumner H. Slichter, American Economic Association, Papers and Proceedings, Vol. XXIX, No. 1, March, 1939, pp. 121–137

Are We Becoming a "Laboristic" State? by Sumner H. Slichter, New York Times Magazine Section. May 16, 1948

THE SENIORITY PROBLEM

IN MASS PRODUCTION INDUSTRIES

FREDERICK H. HARBISON: Labor unions, particularly those that have appeared in the mass production industries, have attempted to secure partial control over layoff, re-employment, and promotion policies by forcing employers to adhere to the seniority principle. Seniority is preference in employment based on length of service. In practice, seniority rights are modified by various competency and merit factors. The straight seniority clauses in labor agreements provide that length of service shall govern as long as the employees who are to be retained, rehired, or promoted are capable of performing available work according to minimum standards of quality and quantity. The flexible provisions, on the other hand, state that seniority shall govern only when the merit or competency factors are relatively equal.

Even under the best personnel management it is probably impossible to rate workers with sufficient accuracy to identify more than 15 per cent of any large group as distinctly superior or to identify more than 15 per cent of such a group as distinctly inferior. The less the precision in determining relative competencies of workers the more dominant the seniority principle may become. In practice, therefore, length of service is given major emphasis in determining layoffs and promotions even under the flexible type agreements.

The possible effects of the more widespread use of the seniority principle in employment relations in the mass production industries may be outlined briefly. First, one consequence of basing employment preference on length of service is an older working force. Senior employees will have job security at the expense of short-service workers who must bear the brunt of unemployment in periods of depression. Second, the continued application of the seniority principle may result in stagnation and consequent impaired efficiency of the working force. Third, the more competent workers may be discriminated against by any system that causes them to wait their turn for advancement on the basis of length of service. These arguments, however, are valid only if management has been and will be perfectly capable of determining relative competency among workers. To the degree that seniority displaces a haphazard and biased method of selecting workers for layoff and promotion, however, the efficiency of the working force as a whole may be increased rather than decreased. Furthermore, the longer experience, greater loyalty, and lower turnover of an older working force may offset the advantage of a more vigorous, yet less stable, group of employees. Indirectly, moreover, the imposition of seniority gives employers an inducement to establish higher work standards, to select new employees with greater care, and to train and maintain a working force with flexible skills and experience.

265

The danger of impaired efficiency comes not from a general application of the seniority principle but rather from the rigid enforcement of seniority in every individual case. Optimum efficiency might be maintained if a small minority of exceptional employees could be retained or promoted without regard to seniority. The difficulty lies not in the over-all recognition of the seniority principle, but rather in its too strict application in special cases.

Looking at the labor market as a whole a more general application of seniority may be beneficial. A seniority system tends to give permanent employment to older, long-service workers, and to create a "labor reserve" of more mobile younger workers. Yet the existence of an older working force puts a premium on hiring younger workers when new hiring is necessary. Thus, in general, the demand for new workers is focused upon the labor reserve of younger men, a condition which may, perhaps, facilitate the adjustment of supply and demand for new labor.

To a union struggling for complete recognition, control over layoff policies is important both as an organizing issue and as a protection from discrimination against union members. In the determination of merit or competency management has wide discretion over which a union can exert very little control. It is natural, therefore, that organized labor should attempt to limit management's control by forcing adherence to a clear-cut and definite formula based on length of service. In large measure the demand for rigid application of seniority is a defensive device which is of particular importance to unions whose recognition status is insecure.

Because of the difficulty of applying seniority by plants, departments, or occupational groups in such a manner as to satisfy the majority of workers, there are many indications that too rigid adherence to seniority is as troublesome to some union leaders as it is distasteful to management. Although attempts have been made to combine plant, department, and job seniority, no rigid system can be devised which will not discriminate in one way or another against particular groups of workmen. It is not surprising, therefore, that many unions have favored complete work-sharing instead of layoffs by seniority. It is significant, moreover, that several union officers have declared that there would be no necessity for rigid seniority rules in mass production industries under a preferential or union shop.

It is quite possible that the restrictions of rigid seniority might be largely alleviated through more complete acceptance of unions and joint determination of competency by union and management representatives. Some employers, who have signed labor agreements, are still combating outside labor unions. Many companies, furthermore, are developing merit or ability rating programs in order to implement what they think of as management prerogatives of determining competency without interference from union leaders. Both policies, it appears, are bound to force the unions to demand more rigid application of seniority to limit management's control over layoffs and promotions. When a struggling union is obliged to constantly demonstrate its value by offering job-conscious workers greater security, it cannot ask its members to rely on management discretion of relative competencies of employees. If unions are accorded some degree of joint control in judgment of competency, the basis for rigid seniority may disappear. On the other hand, the experience of the railroads has shown that if rigid seniority rules are once accepted by an employer, they tend to become a permanent feature of employment policy accepted by both sides in spite of the fact that more co-operative relations between management and the union may have developed in the meantime. The great danger of seniority rules, which have been developed as a defense measure to meet an organization problem, is that in their application they tend to become more detailed and all-inclusive, for workers learn to look upon seniority rights as vested interests. In the end, therefore, neither management nor the union has control of employment policies, for such policies become dependent on a law or formula rather than on the process of collective bargaining.

HAS COLLECTIVE BARGAINING FAILED?

By George W. Taylor

THE acceptance of free collective bargaining as the cornerstone of the national labor policy is based on the assumption that, by and large, once an "equality of bargaining power" has been established, the issues arising in labor relations can best be resolved by agreement between the parties of direct interest. The sufficiency of this policy as a safeguard of the varied interests of employees, employers, and consumers has been questioned ever since it was enunciated in the National Labor Relations Act. Significant exceptions have already been made to the basic concept that collective bargaining best preserves a balance between the conflicting interests.

The passage of minimum wage legislation to eliminate substandards of living,[1] for example, rested on a conclusion that the economic status of the lowest-paid employees could not be made dependent solely upon their bargaining power, even after the organization rights of these employees had been protected. During World War II, moreover, the Government determined that the resolution of the economic issues in labor relations could not be through unrestricted agreements between labor and management. They could disrupt economic stability and interfere with the control of inflationary forces. The wage stabilization program was developed and, over a period of more than three years, the economic issues of labor relations were closely regulated in accordance with governmental rules.

Nor has it yet been possible during the reconversion period for the Government to relinquish these responsibilities. The program to protect the consumer against rising prices has included a continuance of limitations upon wage increases. There have even been insistent demands for additional governmental action to "protect the consumer" by specific restrictions as to the way particular economic issues can be resolved in collective bargaining. Many objections have been voiced, for example, to the establishment of union funds for various purposes through a "tax" on production or pay roll. Concern has been expressed, too, over some agreements which have been worked out by a union and a management but which result in a relatively heavy cost to the consumer because of resulting high prices or limitations of supply. The Government's role in influencing and determining the economic issues of labor relations has become a leading one. It remains so despite the announced policy of re-establishing free collective bargaining at the earliest possible date. The question arises whether or not the role which has been thrust upon Government by economic crises and maladjustments can in fact be eliminated.

PROPER FUNCTIONS OF COLLECTIVE BARGAINING

Collective bargaining does not, of course, ensure economic stability. Some observers even go so far as to maintain that collective bargaining as it has been developed under the Wagner Act contributes to economic instability. In any event, the inequities and the hardships of deflationary and inflationary forces which will alternately plague the economy can be expected to induce varied programs for governmental ac-

[1] One of the purposes of minimum wage legislation was also to eliminate "cutthroat competition," based on differences in wages, from a number of industries.

tion to resolve pressing economic questions; and the demands for government action in these areas become more insistent as there develops a growing loss of confidence in the adequacy of free collective bargaining to meet the primary economic problems of this generation. These relate to the avoidance of mass industrial unemployment and to the production and consumption of a greater volume of goods than ever before. To some, the handwriting on the wall seems very clear. All economic roads need not lead to Washington, however, if collective bargaining could be developed as an effective substitute for work stoppages and as an institution geared to the objectives of economic progress. This possibility should not be lightly dismissed by anyone who appreciates the stakes which are involved.

It has become trite, perhaps, to observe that the big challenge faced by democracies is how to attain economic security without the loss of personal and political liberties. Trite or not, the observation calls for reiteration here especially since it has an important bearing on the place of collective bargaining in the field of labor relations.

Despite the crucial functions which have been assigned to collective bargaining, there has been relatively little thought and effort given to the constructive development of the process. So much attention has been directed to the issue as to whether or not collective bargaining should be established that only meager attention has been devoted to the development of collective bargaining itself. It is becoming more and more apparent, however, that the degree to which the Government will determine economic questions is closely related to the development of a collective bargaining capable of carrying out the functions which have been assigned to it.

What Leads to Government Action

The failures of collective bargaining to serve as an effective substitute for industrial warfare during the critical days of economic reconversion provide a pertinent illustration of how the interest of the consumer and the needs of the community can force the Government to occupy a prominent seat at the bargaining table. The greatest government pressure upon industrial relations has resulted from the Nation's demand for an uninterrupted flow of goods. Accumulated purchasing power is so vast that the pressure to get strikes terminated has tended to overshadow consumer concern about the cost of settlement. There is a growing realization, to be sure, that various forms of "feather-bedding" are an impediment to economic progress and that the relationship between wages and prices is a matter of concern to the consumer. In response to the consumer's interest in price control, a government program for economic stability has been devised; and because of the need for goods, the Government has had to take the initiative in terminating many strikes, sometimes by drastic measures. The Government finds itself, therefore, with a decisive voice in labor relations.

This is not a surprising or an unprecedented situation. The National Labor Relations Act itself was passed in part to reverse certain policies pursued by employers under so-called individual bargaining which caused economic instability. According to congressional finding, such policies contributed to deflationary wage and price movements and to the creation of mass unemployment. These were the outstanding economic problems of the 1930's. To meet them, the bargaining power of employees was increased by governmental protection of the right to organize, and collective bargaining was accepted as the national institution by which wages, hours, and working conditions were to be established and protected. To further the same objective, minimum wages were established by law, and many other government regulations were devised to regulate most of the segments of the Nation's economic life. The Government assumed heavy responsibilities concerning the economic issues of labor relations as a protection against deflationary movements.

The question now arises about the adequacy of the Wagner Act, and of related laws, in providing protection against collective bargaining practices which contribute to an inflationary movement through the addition of unreasonable increases to the cost of goods or through limitation of the supply of goods. These were not vital questions when the Wagner Act was passed. They are of great importance, however, in these days when a strenuous battle by the Government to control inflationary forces has already become a series of strategic retreats and could become a rout. These are urgent questions, moreover, to a generation which envisions the possibility of eliminating mass unemployment among industrial workers and of achieving an unprecedented production and consumption of consumer goods.

There are observers who believe the Government should now influence the resolution of economic issues not directly but by regulating unions and defining their collective bargaining responsibilities. These steps are urged as necessary to bring about an equality of bargaining power between unions and management and to make possible a labor relationship based on agreements instead of strikes. One strong argument for the Wagner Act was that, in the absence of government regulation of employers' activities, employees had a deficient bargaining power which ag-

gravated deflationary movements. It is now suggested that, in the absence of regulation of *their* activities, the unions possess an excess of bargaining power which contributes to inflationary movements.

The question of government policy about the economic issues of labor relations involves, therefore, the entire question of the adequacy of the labor policy adopted in the Wagner Act. This calls for a comprehensive appraisal of the employer's contention that direct government intervention in economic issues can be avoided by a limitation of the power of unions. The unions oppose any such reasoning. They insist that it is actually part of an antilabor drive to eliminate collective bargaining rather than to effectuate it. They would retain all of the status and protection achieved by them under the Wagner Act, on the ground that even this act cannot provide them with sufficient bargaining power to secure the minimum economic security to which workers are equitably entitled.

CONSUMER PROTECTION

In view of the wide divergence in thinking about the question outlined above, it is timely to ask: Can collective bargaining possibly be geared to the needs of the country for peaceful settlement of labor disputes and for more goods at lower prices? Are these impossible attributes to expect of such a democratic institution? It will be recalled that labor agreements are negotiated by thousands of separate transactions conducted under widely varying economic conditions and by negotiators with different philosophies and points of view. No all-pervading principles or responsibilities are recognized as compelling in the making of an agreement. Nor can it be expected that the terms of a labor agreement will be negotiated with the needs of the consumer given an overwhelming weight. It appears that our economic interests as consumers are dominant in every industry but our own. Negotiations are conducted, moreover, as an alternative to the exercise of powerful pressures which are available to either side to gain objectives irrespective of their economic soundness. Since a resort to industrial warfare usually involves grave consequences to both parties, self-interest is counted upon to induce a compromise of differences and the consummation of an agreement. What it takes to avoid the use of economic force, or to secure its withdrawal, is frequently a most potent force in arriving at settlements. "The lion's share to the lion" is a fact and not a theory in the disposition of many labor disputes. The development of collective bargaining as an institution for economic advancement is truly a formidable undertaking.

What is there in the system which provides protection to the consumer against unilateral dictation of terms by the management or by the union? or against an agreement between them which involves a heavy cost to the consumer? The consumer protection is presumably to derive, to some extent at least, from the "equality of bargaining power" which is mentioned in the Wagner Act and which is the subject of present controversy. Other checks and balances are available, even though they may be costly. Employees may secure high wage rates at which not to work if high prices drive consumers out of the market or to the use of substitute products. Restraints upon collective bargaining from exercise of the consumers' veto power, however, are not of much use in times like the present when goods are scarce and the demand for them so intense. It is rather anomalous that the cry for protection of the consumer against the terms of collective agreements is now raised when, we are told, the black markets are flourishing under extensive consumer patronage.

The seller's market will not last forever, and before long buyers will be concerned not merely with getting more goods at any price, but with an increasing supply of goods at lower prices. Does the present collective bargaining policy take this matter into account? When all price controls are finally eliminated and when all restraints on wage increases are removed, will collective bargaining be one of the forces for economic progress? Or, does it inevitably bring impediments and inconveniences which will be appraised, nevertheless, as a fair and reasonable price to pay for the retention of economic policy-making in private hands? Will an overwhelming need and demand for continued government regulation of economic policy-making be induced by the search for economic security? The answers which the future will give to these questions cannot fail to have a major bearing upon the way of life in the United States during the years to come.

DIRECTION OF NATIONAL LABOR POLICY

In the meantime, there are strong reasons why the government labor policy should center upon the conscious development of collective bargaining to the fullest possible extent as an institution capable of resolving economic issues with a minimum of work stoppages and in furtherance of the goals of economic progress. Such a policy would be an attempt to effectuate the idea that the Government should directly intervene in the economic issues of labor relations to a minimum extent. The eternal vigilance upon which personal liberties depend seems now to call for a defense of collective bargaining by a positive program to develop it into an institution capable of discharging difficult social responsibilities and minimizing the scope of government policy-making. The difficult road which is mapped out might understandably be dismissed as impractical or even idealistic. It is perhaps as idealistic as the concept of democracy.

There are some signs that lend encouragement to the proposed venture. Consider the way in which the present national labor policy has been developing. Congress did not adopt collective bargaining as the cornerstone of the national labor policy until 1935. The policy presupposed the organization of employees into unions. In 1935, however, only a small minority of industrial workers had organized. In most of the great mass production industries, permanent unions had not been established and collective bargaining with "outside" unions was virtually unknown.

The history of the American labor movement prior to 1935 centered primarily around the dispute about whether or not collective bargaining would be established. The major problems in labor relations since 1935 have primarily concerned organization for collective bargaining. Although the National Labor Relations Act provided detailed rules and regulations for carrying out this preliminary phase, collective bargaining itself was apparently conceived as a self-effectuating process. It has not been defined—and maybe it defies definition—nor has intensive consideration been given to procedures, objectives, and responsibilities which are related to the development of an institutional status for collective bargaining. A failure to expand this second phase of the national labor policy has often made it appear that the increased bargaining power provided to employees by the Wagner Act merely ensured bigger strikes between more evenly matched adversaries. If as much attention were given to the development of collective bargaining as was given by all hands to the tussle over organizing

for collective bargaining, constructive results could virtually be guaranteed.

DEVELOPMENT OF COLLECTIVE BARGAINING

A start on the constructive development of collective bargaining was made by the President's Labor-Management Conference of 1945. This was a highly significant meeting, even though it failed to arrive at any understanding about how strikes during the reconversion period could be eliminated. Despite this failure, the conferees did achieve successes in their long-run objective of building up collective bargaining as an agreement-making mechanism. The meeting stands out, moreover, as an example of a procedure which can be effectively utilized by labor and by industry as they take on the task of developing the process of collective bargaining. Agreements made in labor-management conferences, on national and local levels, have a potential which has been far from realized.

The conference of 1945, for example, arrived at a unanimous conclusion upon which procedures can be built to assist in the peaceful settlement of disputes over future agreements. It was agreed:

If direct negotiations and conciliation have not been successful, voluntary arbitration may be considered by the parties. However, before voluntary arbitration is agreed upon as a means of settling unsettled issues, the parties themselves should agree upon the precise issues, the terms of submission, and the principles or factors by which the arbitrator should be governed.

The statement might well be made stronger in later conferences. It would appear that the parties have a distinct obligation to explore every possibility by which voluntary arbitration might be used before they resort to industrial warfare. The objective of securing peaceful settlements could be furthered, moreover, by an agreement covering in greater detail the nature of the stipulation to arbitrate and the conditions under which the use of voluntary arbitration has been of value. The development of voluntary arbitration practices and procedures by labor and industry could become a program which could provide highly constructive results.

The Government also has an obligation to facilitate the development of collective bargaining. Provision of pertinent data and mediation services to negotiators has an obvious place in the government program. In building upon the conclusion of the labor-management conference referred to above, the Government should, moreover, provide a system of boards suited for voluntary arbitration in cases where labor and management determine to settle issues by this method. The mere availability of such boards would further the cause of industrial peace; their absence has often frustrated a desire to avoid strife.

The government program to develop collective bargaining might also include fact-finding boards. Despite every effort to reconcile differences, work stoppages are often inevitable. The reasons advanced by each party as to why an agreement is impossible are significant to the general public. Accountability to the public on this score would tend to discourage the avoidance of collective bargaining responsibilities by the parties. No delving into company records and no waiting period before striking need be involved. The purpose of such fact-finding procedures would be to high-light the public interest in collective bargaining and to encourage agreements by providing for the accountability of labor and management to the public about the manner in which they have discharged their obligations.

THE VOLUNTARY ELEMENT

The emphasis placed upon voluntarism in this discussion of how collective bargaining may be built up arises from a conviction that any restrictions upon the rights to strike and to lock out, which are necessary in the public interest, can soundly be provided only by agreement of the parties directly affected. Should it be concluded by the Government that restrictions must be imposed, the road will have been taken to personal sanctions and plant seizure methods which run counter to the democratic way of living and working together. Avoidance of such imposed "solutions" is worth a substantial price in inconvenience and travail. It is worth a sustained, intelligent effort to devise ways and means by which labor and management will be able to work out their own problems without government direction.

The events of recent months afford a stark preview of the way in which the national labor policy can evolve unless the constructive objectives of collective bargaining are voluntarily effectuated. When collective bargaining fails and crippling strikes occur in crucial industries, the Government has no choice but to take steps to terminate the work stoppages and to resolve the economic issues involved in them. The rights to strike and to lock out cannot be exercised in such a way as to jeopardize the transcendent right of the community to carry on its life and its work. Government intervention under the stress of dire emergency, however, has made the resolution of key labor disputes a matter of "crisis government." The disposition of the economic issues of labor relations has been undertaken on an opportunistic basis with political considerations always in the picture. It is questionable whether that approach properly serves the interests of labor, of management, or of the general public. Crisis government can also lead, moreover, to drastic measures which engender long-time conflicts.

Nevertheless, the Government has already had the responsibility, in this reconversion period, for designating the basic economic conditions of labor relations. Wage patterns have been determined by the Government for wide application without regard to the varying incidence upon high-labor-cost and low-labor-cost companies or industries. In some instances, the procedures of wage determination have approximated compulsory arbitration. Avoidance of these results is a part of the stake in a program for developing collective bargaining as an effective substitute for work stoppages.

Is Government Control Inevitable?

This discussion focuses attention upon the increasing tendency for the Government to resolve the major economic issues of labor relations. Is this an irresistible trend? During World War II and in the reconversion days, the need for controlling inflation and an attempt for controlling inflation and an attempt to check anticipated deflationary forces were the motivating factors in government intervention. Then, critical strikes kept the Government at the collective bargaining table with a decisive control over their settlement. Pressures for government action to facilitate economic progress and to provide economic security will undoubtedly persist. At a time when the trend is strongly in the direction of a centralized control of the economic issues of labor relations, the conscious development of collective bargaining could be undertaken with the object of providing a major bulwark in the defense of private control of these matters. Nor is success in this direction a foregone conclusion, even though great efforts are expended by labor, management, and the Government to develop collective bargaining as a more constructive institution. It would seem, however, that no one of these parties can afford to give up collective bargaining by default or supinely resign itself to the inevitability of government control of the economics of industry.

THE ECONOMICS OF WAGE-DISPUTE SETTLEMENT

By John T. Dunlop

"The science of political economy is essentially practical, and applicable to the common business of human life. There are few branches of human knowledge where false views may do more harm, or just views more good."[1] Ever since Malthus penned this high estimate of his chosen discipline there have been doubters and blasphemers.[2] While there have been notable advances in quantitative economics, the application of economic theory or principles to particular situations is a rudimentary craft. Serious economists have rarely been attracted to a practice, except in such a period as that of the recent war.

While the professional economist has tended to avoid the market place, participants in the world of affairs have borrowed liberally of economic ideas to rationalize their positions. As a consequence, never were economic clichés and slogans so widespread and so frequently utilized in public argument. It is doubtful if there is any greater real understanding of problems; there may be less. Mill's judgment of his day probably fits our own: "I do not perceive that in the mental training which has been received by the immense majority of the reading and thinking part of my countrymen . . . there is anything likely to render them much less accessible to the influence of imposture and charlatanry than there ever was."[3]

The debate over wage rates in the public press and in proceedings between management and labor organizations has popularized economic analysis. There has come into use a limited number of clichés or standard arguments which are employed by the side that regards them as most effective at the time in winning the case. Illustrative of these phrases are "comparable wages," "productivity," "cost of living," and "ability to pay." These slogans are not the distinctive trademark of any one side. Either party may use one of these arguments today and repudiate it tomorrow as a factor in wage determination under a different set of circumstances. Current wage argument is a "dreadful pudder o'er our heads."

[1] T. R. Malthus, The Principles of Political Economy (London School of Economics and Political Science Reprint, 1936) 9.

[2] For a recent discussion, see Elton Mayo, The Social Problems of an Industrial Civilization (1945) 34-56.

[3] John Stuart Mill, The Spirit of the Age (Chicago University Press 1942) 10-11.

The interest in arguments and slogans in wage negotiations has increased spectacularly in recent years with the growth of private arbitration, the participation of government in wage setting through the machinery of the Railway Labor Act, the wartime experience under the National War Labor Board, and the postwar vogue of fact-finding boards. The employment by management and labor organizations of technicians, such as lawyers, economists, statisticians, actuaries, industrial engineers, and publicists, who produce voluminous briefs and endless statistical appendices, has given wide currency to such wage-determining principles or slogans.

The subject of this paper might be developed along several entirely different lines. The emphasis might be placed on developing an explanation for wage determination under collective bargaining.[4] It has seemed more in keeping with the spirit of this symposium rather to appraise carefully and rigorously some of the more prominent arguments and slogans used in wage discussions. Much of the discussion will be devoted to exploring problems that arise in giving meaning to these standards and in translating them into definitely measurable guides to decisions in particular situations. The problems will be found to be stubborn and not always tractable. This emphasis is not, however, fundamentally defeatist with respect to the contribution of economics to wage dispute settlement. The identification of problems is the beginning of economic wisdom.

The orientation of the following pages is primarily on standards seriously proposed in particular cases. The discussion of the appropriate general level of wage rates for the economy as a whole has resort normally to a different group of criteria. The first four sections which follow organize the problems associated with the application of four standards for particular cases: "comparable wages," "productivity," "cost of living," and "ability to pay." A following section summarizes the fundamental problems raised by an examination of these standards. A brief sixth section is devoted to the criteria used in discussing the general level of wage rates. The final section appraises the distinctive contribution which the economist may make to the settlement of wage disputes.

I. Comparable Wage Rates

No argument is employed more frequently in wage discussions than that wage rates in one bargaining unit should be equalized with, or related by a particular differential to, wage rates in other "comparable" bargaining units. While other arguments are more decisive in the "key" wage bargains in basic industries affecting the general level of wage rates, the appeal to comparable rates is frequently employed in transmitting the impact of these critical decisions throughout the rest of the wage structure. The resort to this standard is also frequently the basis for the numerous changes in differentials that are made among occupations, plants, and industries each year.

[4] See John T. Dunlop, Wage Determination Under Trade Unions (1944) chaps. 2-6.

The principle that wage rates in one bargaining unit should be adjusted to the level of wage rates in comparable plants has an alluring simplicity. The economist indicates that in equilibrium the same wage rate will be paid in "a market" for a specified type of labor service. The slogan of "equal pay for equal work" commands wide support. However, for reasons which will now be surveyed, the illusion of simplicity vanishes in the attempt to give meaning to the concept of "comparable" wage rates in any particular dispute situation.

(1) The content of job classifications designated by the same job title varies widely among different employers. The range of duties assigned to a single worker has not been as standardized among plants as is widely assumed. The varying ages and types of equipment, the differing scales of operation between large and small plants, and the different techniques of various managers are factors making for different job contents among firms producing roughly similar goods. Various arrangements may be made, for instance, in machine operations for the cleaning, oiling and greasing of equipment. The flow of materials to a machine and the handling of processed parts and waste products permit different plans of organization. The extent of supervision and inspection in a job may also vary widely from one plant to another.

For instance, a study of the distribution of spinning-room duties in forty-seven cotton textile firms[5] divided the work of five customary job classifications—spinner, cleaner, oiler, sweeper and doffer—into twenty-five separate operations. No two of the mills divided these operations in the same way among the job classifications. Except for the operations of "creeling" and "piecing up," performed by the spinner in all cases, no operation was assigned to the same job classification in all mills. The total duties of the spinner varied from these two operations in one mill to as many as ten in another. The comparison of the wage rates by job classification among these various cotton textile mills under these circumstances requires temerity.

At the request of the United States Conciliation Service in particular disputes, the Bureau of Labor Statistics has made a number of surveys of occupational wage rates in comparable establishments. The most recent of these studies examines the differences between duties among the various firms studied. The ordinary occupational wage-rate survey of the Bureau of Labor Statistics[6] starts with a single description for a "standardized" job classification. As long as a common core of duties is performed, the wage-rate data are collected from a particular firm and compared with rates from other firms. The newer special studies for the Conciliation Service recognize that there are wide variations in the actual content of jobs which roughly fit the same job description. These inquiries uniformly reveal the same range of diversity in job content illustrated by the distribution of spinning-room duties.

(2) Comparability in wage rates is impaired by variations in the method of wage

[5] Presented as an exhibit before the National War Labor Board in the cotton textile cases decided Feb. 20, 1945, 21 War Lab. Rep. 793.

[6] *Wartime Wage Movements and Urban Wage-Rate Changes* (1944) 61 Mo. Lab. Rev. 684-704.

payment. Some workers and job classifications are remunerated on an hourly rate basis, others are on individual piece-rates or incentive rates, while still others are paid on group incentive plans. The content of job classifications may be identical, but the amount of services performed and purchased will ordinarily vary with the method of wage payment. Commission methods of wage payment add the further complexity of variations in the price structures of the products being sold. Among incentive systems there are substantial differences in the definitions of the "standard performance" and the extent of "incentive pull" for additional output. The provisions regarding minimum guarantees, including rates for machine breakdowns, poor materials, etc., and the method of calculating these guarantees—by day, by week, or other period—affect the meaning of inter-plant comparisons of wages.

(3) The influence of regularity of employment upon wage rates must be assessed in defining comparable wages. The level of rates for maintenance occupations with steady employment is frequently, although not always, below the rates for the same crafts engaged in seasonal construction work. While there are some important differences in job content, the regularity of employment is usually indicated as the principal reason for this difference. The difference between wages of mechanics in the repair shops of taxicab and truck companies and those of their fellow-craftsmen in commercial garages also reflects the factor of regularity of employment, although job content and methods of wage payment also differ. In fact, wage rates in "captive" departments of a company with relatively steady work opportunities are typically below those of the "outside" or "contract" firm with greater fluctuations in available work. Comparison of two groups of employees for wage-setting purposes will be complicated by the task of assessing the extent to which wage rates reflect differences in the regularity of employment.

(4) The terms and conditions of employment typically include not only the occupational rate but also other "money" conditions such as shift premiums, vacations and holidays with pay, sick leave, pensions, social and health insurance, paid lunch periods, Christmas bonuses, etc., to mention the more prominent terms.[7] The total contract of employment involves many other items that are less immediately "money" terms, such as union recognition, seniority, management rights and grievance machinery, and arbitration. In the bargaining process there is frequently give and take among the "money" terms. There is likely to be substitution among basic rate adjustments and shift premiums, vacations, and health insurance plans. There may even be important trades between the "money" items and other provisions of a contract. Comparison of wage rates under these circumstances may become particularly tenous.

(5) The geographical implications of "comparable wages" can be most perplexing. The concept of a "labor market" has no direct correspondence in geography.

---

[7] The Bureau of Labor Statistics now reports much data of this kind in connection with wage rate surveys on form OWR-17.

Specifying the labor market in accordance with the cost of transportation or the knowledge of job and wage opportunities does not yield precise results. The inclusion of suburbs and satellite communities can be as difficult as the grouping of larger towns and cities. The War Labor Board for the Boston Region was plagued throughout the war with the question whether to include Torrington (16 miles away) in the Waterbury, Connecticut labor market for metal trades occupations. The areas of uniformity of wage rates may vary widely among occupations even in the same industry: compare laborers and iron workers in the construction industry. The areas of uniformity have in general spread in recent years, although uniformity appears to be greater in periods of high employment than in loose labor markets. If the standard of comparable wages is to be employed we cannot escape the difficult task of defining the geographical limits of the appropriate labor market.

(6) The complications of "comparable" wage determination developed so far in this section relate to labor-market difficulties. They derive from relating the exact work performed by the wage earners in different bargaining units or from the influence of what are essentially labor-market influences on wage rates. There is another group of problems which must be faced in giving meaning to "comparable wage rates." These have their roots in the product market, or, more precisely, in the divergent competitive positions of the firms employing the wage earners.

Business enterprises are ordinarily regarded as clustering into industries, segments, or smaller groups among which product competition is relatively closer than with firms outside the group. But every business, outside the case of a few perfectly competitive markets, has its specialized market and clientele. The grouping of firms according to similarity of product-market conditions is a convention always subject to further subdivision. The definition of these clusters of "comparable" firms is probably as difficult as any issue in applying the wage standard discussed in this section.

The local transit industry includes primary and feeder-line companies; hotels are classified into first-line and several other classes; bakeries may be divided into large-scale operators and specialty shops. Are the larger or smaller units appropriate for comparison? The trucking firms in an area may be subdivided into over-the-road and local trucking enterprises. The latter may be classified in turn into product groups—oil, coal, grocery, department store, express, etc. Any one of these groups, such as oil, in turn could be further subdivided into: national distributors, local companies, home delivery, industrial uses, etc. While many of these groupings are associated with important differences in job content (type of equipment) and method of wage payment, competitive conditions among these various groups no doubt vary widely. The important question is to determine when these differences in competitive conditions are so significant as to warrant a separate wage determination regardless of labor-market influences.

The problem may be posed even more sharply by an instance in which labor-market influences are relatively more uniform than in the trucking case. An engine lathe operator may work for companies ordinarily classified in such groups as electrical machinery, textile machinery, machine tools, and shoe machinery. In determining the "comparable" wage rates, what grouping of firms should be selected?

There can be little doubt that wage rates do in fact vary by virtue of the influence of divergent product-market conditions. Maintenance workers, for instance, have rates that vary substantially through the range of industries even where job content is quite similar. The choice of groupings among firms presents the most difficult of problems.

The foregoing discussion of six groups of problems is adequate to divest the slogan or standard of "comparable wages" of any alluring simplicity. It is doubtful if there are any royal answers to these problems in principle or in measurement. The difficulties arising from the product market can be mitigated, however, if agreement is secured from the parties as to a list of comparable firms. This device has been frequently used by mediators.

II. PRODUCTIVITY

No argument is used with more conviction or sophistication than that wages should vary with changes in productivity. In the mid-Twenties the American Federation of Labor Convention adopted the policy that wage earners should share in rising productivity in the form of wage-rate increases. In recent days management, editorial writers,[8] economists, and some labor leaders have been preaching that increased productivity alone provides the basis for wage increases. These views have normally been associated with the conviction that wage rates have already outstripped productivity. As part of the mores or folklore of an industrial community there may be little objection to the slogan of productivity as a basis for increases in the general level of wage rates in the long run. As a guide or a rule of thumb in any particular negotiation, the principle has grave difficulties which may be briefly summarized.

(1) The rate of change in productivity in our economic system varies widely among the component segments. Within an industry the rate is normally quite different among firms. Even within a firm or plant the rate varies among departments, machines, and operations. The wage structure of a particular plant or department, if it were geared absolutely to changes in productivity, would soon become intolerable. Employees in continuous strip mills and on tin plate operations in the steel industry, for instance, would have had enormous wage increases in the past ten years in comparison with employees in other sectors of the industry. Under such circumstances the wage structure would bear very little relationship to skill, experience, or other factors typically taken into account in settling rate structures. Nor would

[8]See HENRY HAZLITT, ECONOMICS IN ONE LESSON (1946) c. XIX.

the wage structure bear any relationship to wages paid for comparable operations in other industries in steel centers. The exclusive adoption of the principle of adjusting wage structures according to changes in productivity would result within a very short time in an utterly chaotic wage structure within a single plant or industry.

In the same way, the adjustment of wage levels among industries exclusively by reference to this slogan would distort the wage structure of the country. Industries in which productivity increased rapidly would experience large wage increases, while in others in which productivity did not increase or actually declined (especially in extractive industries) wage rates would remain relatively unchanged. Either as a matter of allocation of resources or as a means to the maintenance of industrial peace, the absolute adoption of such a principle for determining the structure of wages among industries would be a catastrophe.

All this is not to say that changes in productivity do not have effects upon the structure of wages within plants or among industries.[9] It can be established, for instance, that wages in the past twenty-five years have increased more rapidly than the average in those industries in which employment and productivity have increased more rapidly than the average. Similarly, the wages have increased less rapidly than the average in those industries in which employment and productivity have either increased less rapidly than the average or actually declined. Despite all the publicity given to wage changes in the coal and railroad industries, wages in these relatively declining industries have increased less than in manufacturing firms. Between 1923 and July, 1946, average hourly earnings in manufacturing increased 109.4 per cent compared to 72.4 per cent for bituminous coal mining and 95.5 per cent for railroads. The simple fact appears to be that the wage structure over a period of time adjusts itself to changes in productivity in such fashion that wage rates increase most where productivity and employment have increased fastest, and wages increase less than the average where productivity and employment have increased less rapidly. However, a substantial part of the increase in productivity, where productivity is increasing fastest, is translated into price declines, increases in profits, and improvements in quality.

(2) The term "productivity" seems to have a fascination and rigor that impels many devotees to regard it as a formula for wage adjustments. The measurement of productivity presents, however, one of the most difficult problems of economic analysis, econometrics, and statistical measurement.[10] The customary measure of productivity is "output per man-hour," a measure secured by dividing a measure of product in physical units by a measure of man-hour inputs.[11]

In many industries the task of constructing an index of physical production is

[9] See Alvin H. Hansen, *Wages and Prices: The Basic Issue*, N. Y. Times Mag. Jan. 6, 1946, p. 9.

[10] For a more comprehensive survey of the statistical problems of measurement, see Nat. Bur. of Economic Research, Cost Behavior and Price Policy (1943) 142-169.

[11] For a current series, see *Productivity Changes Since 1939* (1946) 63 Mo. Lab. Rev. 893.

formidable, if not impossible. There may be many different products and their proportions in total output, or the "product-mix," may change frequently. While changes in quality and specifications will be particularly important in a job-order business, these factors are present to some extent in almost every case.[12]

(3) Between any two periods output per man-hour may vary as a result of a great many different factors, among which are the following: a change in the level of output, a change in the composition of production, changes in the average effectiveness of plant and equipment—as a result of scrapping obsolete facilities and bringing in new ones—increased effort and application on the part of the work-force, a change in the composition of the work-force, improvements in earlier stages of production as in the concerns which supply materials and parts, the substitution of other factors such as increases in wage rates, etc. These circumstances are hardly equally valid bases for an increase in wage rates in a particular plant or company.

In negotiations and public discussion little effort has been made to separate the effects of these factors influencing "productivity" in the sense of output per man-hour. The union may argue, on the basis of general knowledge of the industry, that productivity increases which have taken place provide a basis for wage increases. The Steel Workers Organizing Committee, as an illustration, argued in the *Little Steel* case in 1942 that "workers should receive an equitable share of the proceeds of increasing productive efficiency."[13] In addition to generally available output-per-man-hour data the union gave examples of man-hour savings through important technical changes. In a later case[14] the United Steelworkers of America supported its case by pointing in detail to new capacity, to the abandonment of obsolete facilities, to changes in the quality and composition of the labor force, and to the effects of further integration.

Evidence of changes in productivity is not readily transformed into cents-per-hour wage adjustments. In a number of industries, such as local transit and utilities, wage costs are to some extent a fixed cost, so that changes in output substantially influence output per man-hour. A higher wage rate in some industries·may induce more careful inspection or use of higher-quality materials. Such a change would be reflected in output per man-hour. As has been indicated, these various types of factors affecting output per man-hour are not equally valid grounds for a wage rate adjustment. Not only is the measurement of productivity changes difficult, but their interpretation for relevant wage negotiations is even more ambiguous.

(4) Depending upon the precise meaning given to the productivity argument, the problem of the relation of wage changes to declines in productivity may have to be faced. In the normal case, changes in productivity may be regarded as typically

---

[12] For an instance of the measurement of production in the steel industries, see *Steel Industry, Prices, Profits and Costs* (Office of Price Administration, August, 1944) 37-41a. This study is cited in PHILIP MURRAY, STEELWORKERS NEED A $2.00-A-DAY WAGE INCREASE (1946) 60-62.

[13] Brief submitted by the S. W. O. C. to a Panel of the National War Labor Board (1942) 75.

[14] MURRAY, *op. cit. supra* note 12, at 44-68.

in one direction. There are instances, however, in which performance per average unit of labor input may decline as a result of the exhaustion of a resource, the use of a less skilled labor force on the average, or as the result of less intensive application. Under these circumstances is there an argument for a wage decrease?

III. Cost-of-Living Index

The change in the cost-of-living index[15] has been used during some periods as a standard to determine changes in wage rates. The relative emphasis placed on the cost of living by management and labor organizations depends on whether living costs are rising or falling. The attention given to this influence in wage discussions is greatest during periods of pronounced changes in living costs. In a number of collective bargaining situations sliding scales[16] have been established to adjust wage rates automatically to changes in the cost-of-living index. The more typical case involves using the cost-of-living argument as one factor among many in negotiations or in other forms of wage fixing.

As an absolute principle of wage determination the cost of living has severe limitations:

(1) The cost-of-living index typically contains important components, such as food and rent, whose price movements are not necessarily good barometers of the change in other wage-determining factors. For reasons peculiar to agriculture and housing, these prices may be out of line relative to the general level of prices. If this be the case, there would be serious question as to the propriety of altering the general level of wage rates, or any rate, by the application of the cost-of-living standard. There have been periods, such as the Twenties, in which industrial prosperity has been associated with agricultural depression. To contend that this fact should be binding in industrial wage-rate determination is dubious, just as a temporary rise in the cost-of-living index arising from a disappointing harvest would hardly be regarded as an appropriate basis for an upward revision in wage-rate levels.

The absolute application of the cost-of-living standard would force practically uniform wage-rate adjustments in all cases. (Admittedly, there are minor geographical variations in rates of change in the cost-of-living index.) But there may be occasion for important variations in the rates of change in wages among firms and industries.

(2) Labor organizations have frequently indicated that application of the cost-of-living principle over any considerable period would result in a stationary real standard of living for wage earners. The gains of productivity in our system have nor-

---

[15] In 1945 the Bureau of Labor Statistics changed the name of its index to "Consumers' Price Index for Moderate-Income Families in Large Cities." This index ". . . measures average changes in retail prices of selected goods, rents, and services, weighted by quantities bought by families of wage earners and moderate-income workers in large cities in 1934-36. The items priced for the index constituted about 70 per cent of the expenditures of city families whose income averaged $1,524 in 1934-46."

[16] See Z. CLARK DICKINSON, COLLECTIVE WAGE DETERMINATION (1941) 117-158, esp. 132-135.

mally been translated in part into increases in wages and salaries. The rigid application of the slogan of cost of living would result in a stationary real wage rate.

(3) Mention may be made briefly of the difficulties of measuring the change in the cost of living. These problems have recently received widespread attention.[17] It is not always clear whether the proponents of the principle in collective bargaining are interested in measuring the *price* of a constant bundle of goods and services, or whether they are attempting to measure the change in average expenditures. The latter concept includes the effect of changes in income levels, the effects of administering price structure so as to make available particular price lines of commodities, and "forced" substitutions of the type necessitated by wartime conditions.

(4) The application of any cost-of-living principle to wage determination must surmount the difficult problem of an appropriate base period. If wages are to be adjusted to the changes in the cost of living, there must be some starting point. The unions normally would select the period of the last wage change, in cases of increasing cost of living, while employers would emphasize the point that some more representative period of real earnings should be selected.[18]

(5) Automatic adjustment of the general level of wage rates to the cost-of-living index is not always appropriate policy. There may be times of high employment and output in which such a policy would result in cumulative wage and price increases. High employment is always loaded with inflationary dangers, and wage rate adjustments at such periods must be approached with care to avoid unstabilizing consequences.

IV. Ability to Pay

The slogan of "ability to pay" has received particular attention in the course of postwar wage discussions in the public press and before fact-finding bodies. The argument is not new; probably it is as old as collective bargaining. In its simplest form the argument should be looked upon as a mere reflex of a wage demand. A union would not normally make a wage demand without at the same time stating that the demand could be met. There are, no doubt, some exceptions to this view, as in cases involving marginal concerns, but a union cannot make a demand with conviction unless it also implies that the company or industry can afford the wage increase. In much the same way, in the initial stages of bargaining the employer in rejecting the demand almost has to imply as a stratagem that it cannot be afforded. There are situations in which a company rejects a demand admitting that it can afford the requested adjustment, but these are not typical circumstances. On the most elemental plane, consequently, statements regarding ability to pay have been

---

[17] *Report of the President's Committee on the Cost of Living* (Office of Economic Stabilization, 1945). The various reports by labor and management representatives and by technical experts are appended.

[18] This issue was presented to the National War Labor Board in the *Little Steel Case*. The union sought to restore in 1942 the level of real wages as achieved on April 1, 1941, when a general wage increase of 10 cents an hour was placed in effect. See 1 War Lab. Rep. 324, 334-337.

typically mere concomitants or necessary adjuncts to the demand or rejection of the demand.

Any discussion of ability to pay in more serious terms in wage negotiations necessarily raises a host of conceptual and statistical problems regarding the meaning of the phrase in any particular case. Among the more prominent of these problems are the following:

(1) What is the period during which one is concerned with ability to pay? A firm may be able to pay a specific increase for a short period, but not for a longer one. A large part of the difficulties in the postwar period arose from the fact that the unions demanded immediate wage adjustments, while the view of many companies in the reconversion industries was that wage adjustments should be postponed until output had been raised to more nearly normal conditions. Here was a conflict concerning in part the period of time to be considered in decisions concerning ability to pay.

(2) How shall one estimate the effect of wage-rate changes on costs? This question involves the problem of labor productivity, which is dependent not alone on the efforts of wage earners but also on the flow of materials and supplies and the effectiveness of management organization. In estimating the effect of wage-rate changes on costs a decision must also be made on the allowance, if any, to be made for the indirect effects of the wage adjustment on materials, prices, purchased parts, and equipment.[19]

(3) The volume of production will no doubt materially affect ability of an enterprise to pay wages. This difficulty concerns not merely the level of production but also the way in which production may be distributed among different types of goods (broadly, the product-mix), particularly among high- and low-profit items.

(4) The character of competition in the markets in which the products must be sold will substantially affect the ability to pay wage increases. These circumstances will influence the extent to which wage adjustments may be translated into price increases and the effect of such adjustments upon volume of output.

(5) The rate of return on investment to which the company is regarded as entitled will create a problem in determining the ability to pay wages. The familiar complications that have arisen in the regulation of public utilities indicate that this is not a problem to be treated lightly. Differing views on rates of return and valuation will significantly influence the content of the ability-to-pay slogan.

(6) The ability to pay wage increases before and after income taxes will vary substantially. Which measure is appropriate? The handling of other tax issues, such as the carry-back adjustments, may present serious problems in defining ability to pay.

Several recent attempts have been made to apply the ordinary multiple-correla-

[19] For an illustration, see the discussion in the steel case of 1943-44, *Report of the Steel Panel*, 19 WAR LAB. REP. 580 (1944). Also see *Report of the Emergency Board* in the 1938 Railroad Case.

tion technique to the problem of determining the capacity of enterprises to pay wage increases.[20] The analysis of General Motors Corporation, for instance, determined the level of profits by these variables: the level of output, average hourly earnings, cost of materials, prices of the finished products sold by the company, and a productivity time trend. By solving for the values of these relationships to profits on the basis of average relationships for the period 1929-41, it is possible to estimate the level of profits with specified values for output, wage levels, prices, material costs and productivity (a function of time). The effects of wage-rate changes on profits may be estimated under designated conditions regarding prices, material costs, and output.

This type of analysis no doubt warrants further examination. At least it should contribute to a better understanding of the quantitative relations among production, prices, and costs. The method cannot, however, provide any automatic formula for measuring ability to pay. Its proponents have never claimed that it does. The problems summarized and enumerated above are not suddenly dissolved. The level of output for the future contract period remains dubious. There may be grounds to question whether productivity will be above or below levels predicted from any time trend.[21] The statistical technique does not eliminate these problems; it may present them in different form.

The correlation technique may present its results in the better-known form of a break-even chart, showing the level of output or the percentage of capacity operations at which the enterprise "breaks even." This point will vary with changes in the prices of the products of the firm, the wage rates, and the productivity of the enterprise. This simple device may provide a helpful basis for discussion in collective bargaining over the economic position of the enterprise. What level of output should an enterprise regard as normal for wage-setting purposes? The analysis may help to suggest that temporarily high or low levels of output are not satisfactory standards by which to fix wage rates expected to be maintained over relatively long periods.

As an absolute principle of wage determination[22] the ability-to-pay principle is widely recognized as having severe limitations. In such an extreme form it has probably never been proposed. Contrary to popular impression, the United Automobile Workers did not base their wage demand in the General Motors case on ability to pay. The Union's main case was that a 30 per cent increase—without price increases—was necessary to "prevent disastrous retreat from the national objective of adequate purchasing power in the peacetime economy." The Union then attempted

[20] *Purchasing Power for Prosperity, The Case of the General Motors Workers for Maintaining Take-Home Pay* (Presented by International Union, UAW-CIO G. M. Department, Walter P. Reuther Director, (1945)) 55-74.

[21] See General Motors Reply to UAW-CIO, Brief Submitted in Support of Wage Demand for 52 Hours Pay for 40 Hours Work (1945) 14-19.

[22] See F. R. FAIRCHILD, PROFITS AND THE ABILITY TO PAY (1946).

to show that the General Motors Corporation could pay such an increase without a price increase.[23]

The general adoption of the principle of determining wage rates absolutely in accordance with ability to pay would result in very unequal wage levels among different firms. It would be incompatible with many union progams for equalization of wage rates among firms in the same industry or locality. The principle would appropriate to wage earners the incentives which the more profitable firms would have to expand production and employment.

Just as unions have stressed that employers have the ability to pay wage increases in good times, so managements have emphasized inability to pay on other occasions. For instance, one of the major headings in the brief of a company resisting a demand for a wage rate increase stated: "The financial condition of the company with revenues at practically the lowest point in twenty years makes it impossible to increase wages already adequate and at the same time maintain the present standard of transportation service, retain the present number of employees, and continue to render unified service."[24] The ability-to-pay argument has been employed frequently by companies attempting to make a case for a lower wage scale than other companies in an industry or locality. By virtue of location, machinery, size, or temporary financial embarrassment, an enterprise may seek to secure special wage treatment on grounds of inability to pay.

There will be wide differences of judgment in any particular situation concerning the net effect of the factors defining and measuring ability to pay wages, differences not only between parties but also within any group of relatively disinterested observers.

V. FUNDAMENTAL PROBLEMS

The analysis of the slogans and principles of wage determination summarized in the four preceding sections indicates that there are fundamental limitations to the application of these principles to particular situations. These limitations must be faced with candor.

First, the range of possible wage rates which would follow from the various possible applications of each of the principles would generally be wider than normal variance between the parties in collective bargaining. The alternative meanings and measurements of each one of these standards are so diverse that the principle frequently can provide little help as an authoritative determination of wages. The same point may be made in alternative language: the differences between the parties are simply translated into alternative meanings and measurements of a particular wage slogan or standard. The range of disputed application of any of these principles is

---

[23] *Purchasing Power for Prosperity*, cited *supra* note 20, at 1, 21.

[24] Brief on Behalf of Pittsburgh R. Co., Arbitration between Pittsburgh R. Co. and Div. No. 85, Amalgamated Ass'n. of Street and Electric R. Employees of America (Hearings held from July 16 to August 18, 1934).

likely to be much wider than the normal range of disagreement between the parties.

Second, since all wage determination must be considered with reference to a prospective period, conflicting expections as to the future are certain to result in divergent applications of any set of wage principles. The point is not merely that the future in general is uncertain but that uncertainty exists in respect to the magnitude of specific factors—such as output, price, and productivity—vital to present wage determination.

Third, the application of wage slogans or principles is complicated by the fact that the parties frequently have conflicting and divergent basic objectives. These are particularly contentious when the "time horizons" of the parties are markedly different. The company may be interested in remaining in business over the long run while a union may be interested, by virtue of the political problems of leadership, in its position during the next year. Or the union may be interested in maximizing the position of union members during their lifetime without regard to new and younger employees. A further illustration of this basic conflict exists in a situation in which the management of a particular company may be interested in the continuation of its own position over a period of time, while the union may be concerned with the industry more broadly. Such conflicts in basic objectives are certain to yield divergent wage levels.

Fourth, even if any one of these standards could be applied in an unambiguous way, the problem would remain of choosing among these alternative standards or weighting the results they yield. No two of the principles would result in the identical wage-rate change in a specific situation.

These difficulties suggest a pessimistic conclusion as to the contribution which economics can make to the solution of wage disputes. There is no royal road to the application of economics to wage determination. There is no simple formula which may be simply applied to particular cases. The rigor of the classroom diagram blurs in the face of the complexities of collective bargaining when the rigid assumptions of the formal analysis have been removed. In fact there are no "economic" problems in the real world. There may be economic aspects of problems, but the real problems which require decision must be faced as entities. The more frankly and explicitly technical economists admit this fact, the greater the assistance they may eventually give in the solution of practical problems of wage determination in particular cases.

VI. Criteria for the General Level of Wage Rates

The slogans and clichés used in discussions of the general level of wage rates would require another major paper. Only some of the more prominent issues can be indicated. There is fairly general agreement among economists that the average increase in productivity constitutes the appropriate norm for the long-term movement of the general level of wage rates.[25] As average productivity increases, the

[25] Alvin H. Hansen, Economic Policy and Full Employment (1947), 152-160.

level of money wage rates and salaries should rise. The price level as a whole should remain relatively stable. These norms would roughly continue the actual relationships of the past century.

In order for the price level to remain constant, however, industries with greater than the average increases in productivity must decrease prices. In a day of extensively administered prices, these decreases may not be forthcoming. The pricing mechanism may have lost the flexibility requisite to this standard of wage setting. Moreover, the internal requirements of the labor movement may necessitate larger wage-rate increases than are possible under the productivity standard. Intense leadership rivalries may produce greater wage-rate increases, with a consequent rise in the price level.[26]

As a standard for setting the general level of wage rates, no slogan has received greater attention than purchasing power. While the cliché is used in particular cases, a separate section has not been devoted to it in the preceding discussion since no single wage bargain is so extensive as to permit a particular wage change to affect directly and appreciably the purchasing power expended on the products of the firms in negotiation. The standard of purchasing power must refer to the general level of wage rates.

The crudest form of the argument identifies wage-rate and purchasing-power changes. There is no need here to expand on the fact that the relation between changes in wage rates and the aggregate expenditures for consumption and investment in any period is not simple nor direct.

A more sophisticated form of the purchasing-power standard relates to the balance between wage rates and prices. The Nathan Report is cast in these terms.[27] The level of wage rates is regarded as too low at the existing level of prices to sustain high levels of employment. Decreases in the price level are regarded as unlikely. ". . . Businessmen show no signs of exercising such self-restraint in their natural search for profits as would bring about a decline in prices except in the face of a sharp reduction in demand."[28] The Nathan Report concludes that a substantial increase in the level of wage rates without corresponding price increases is required to sustain purchasing power and high-level employment.

The Nathan Report raises the fundamental question of the standards to be applied in appraising whether the levels of wages and prices are in balance.[29] If a lack of balance is determined, the issue must be faced whether wages or prices should be corrected. These questions cannot be answered by rote. Judgment as to appropriate policy must be based not only on the level of profits but also on the structure of wage rates and prices. (The Nathan Report fails to emphasize the necessity for corrections in the structure of prices. Prices for textiles and foods must be reduced.

[26] See John T. Dunlop, *American Wage Determination: The Trend and Its Significance,* a paper read before the Chamber of Commerce Institute on Wage Determination, Washington, D. C., January 11, 1947.

[27] ROBERT R. NATHAN AND OSCAR GOSS, A NATIONAL WAGE POLICY FOR 1947 (1946).

[28] *Id.* at 3.

[29] The analysis of the ability-to-pay standard in Section IV, above, provides a counterpart to this question in the case of a single negotiation.

They are out of line. A general wage-rate increase cannot improve the internal balance of the price structure.) Judgment as to appropriate wage-price policy must also be influenced by the level of interest rates.

An annual appraisal of the economic outlook, such as is provided in the Report of the Council of Economic Advisors, can promote a widespread understanding of the problems to be confronted in particular wage negotiations. A greater economic literacy among the rank and file of union members and business executives can improve the atmosphere in which specific wage conferences take place.

VII. The Contribution of Economic Analysis

The restraint of the previous sections follows not so much from modesty as from candor. It must not be concluded, however, that the economist has nothing relevant to say in the process of wage determination, whether it be collective bargaining, arbitration, or governmental wage-fixing. Economic analysis can make at least these distinctive contributions to the settlement of wage disputes:

(1) The parties or other wage fixers need to be reminded of the longer-run consequences of any decision. While no simple formula or standard may be available to fix a wage, the possible effects of any decision on the employer and the union involved need to be explored. Regardless of the standards used in setting wage rates or the objectives of the parties, economic analysis calls attention to the channels of effect of any wage decision on output, prices, and employment. It can serve as the conscience of the parties as to many of the less immediate effects of a wage rate decision.

(2) Economic analysis points to the impacts of wage rates in sectors of the economy outside the immediate decision. It is particularly concerned with the effects of wage changes on the total national income and the aggregate level of output and employment. "What is true of a firm or of a particular industry or of a set of industries need not be true of the economy as a whole. To draw attention continually to such relationships between the parts and the whole is probably the most distinctive function of the economist."[30]

The processes of wage-dispute settlement need to develop, as they are developing, specialized personnel within unions, employers' organizations, and public bodies who are skilled in the exercise of judgment in the intricate and complex business of wage determination. A person so skilled may profitably utilize the technical services provided by statisticians, lawyers, economists, actuaries, publicists, industrial engineers, and others; but the primary need is for the mature practitioner to exercise judgment.

Economic analysis purports to deal with one aspect of human behavior. Wage-setting must involve the totality of behavior. Any practitioner must develop the art of applying the tools of the technician in the light of all of the complexities, and frequently the perversities, of human behavior.

---

[30] Lerner, *The Relation of Wage Policies and Price Policies* (1939) XXIX Am. Econ. Rev., Proceedings 158.

SOME REFLECTIONS ON THE "LABOR MONOPOLY" ISSUE

By Richard A. Lester

ESPECIALLY during the last two years, the terms "labor monopoly" and "monopolistic unions" have been widely used in the newspapers, in congressional hearings, in periodicals, and in books. Unfortunately, those who employ the terms, although perhaps citing an example or two of what they have in mind, have not been prone to develop precise definitions or criteria for determining the existence and extent of such monopoly. It is not surprising, therefore, to find statements by economists that seem to be based on different conceptions of "labor monopoly," labor markets, and the nature of labor unions.

Unqualified application to labor markets of a term developed and refined with reference to product markets may be misleading. If practical and workable solutions are to be found for the problem of concentration of power and control in the field of labor, care must be taken to avoid superficial analogies that stimulate name-calling, obstruct real investigation, and cramp analysis within the confines of a preconceived pattern.

Part of the responsibility for the absence of adequate analysis and practical solutions of the problem of the concentration of power in the field of labor must rest with labor economists, including the author. Little has been offered in the way of cogent and well-grounded discussion of such matters as competition and monopoly in the labor market, limits to the area of collective action or the size of unions, checks on the concentration of power and control in organized labor, the operation of collective bargaining for wages in a full-employment economy, or the ultimate development of collective bargaining and the changes that it may effect in the character of our economy.

In the absence of such penetrating analysis by economists specializing in labor, we have, on the one hand, learned theorists spinning unrealistic abstractions and offering romantic remedies and, on the other hand, self-interest groups indiscriminately condemning union activities as "monopolistic" and pressing for the adoption of half-baked schemes that would be more injurious than beneficial to the common welfare.

The practical importance of a clear and analytical understanding of the problem is indicated by recent congressional hearings and sentiment. In the last Congress, as passed by the House of Representatives, the Hartley bill contained provisions forbidding "monopolistic strikes" and "monopolistic" collective bargaining (defined as involving two or more competing employers except where competing plants were less than fifty miles apart and together regularly employed a total of less than one hundred employees). The Senate defeated, by only a 44-to-43 vote, the Ball amendment to "reduce the concentration of bargaining power,"[1] which would have prevented the National Labor Relations Board from certifying national unions as bargaining agents and would have declared it an unfair labor practice for national unions to bring pressure to bear

[1] Senator Joseph H. Ball in the *Congressional Record*, XCIII (April 28, 1947), 4257; also contained in statement of purposes in S. 133 introduced by Senator Ball in the 80th Congress.

upon their locals to include or omit any particular terms or provisions in any collective-bargaining agreement.

The issue of the proper area of collective bargaining and action will undoubtedly be considered again in the 1948 and 1949 sessions of Congress. Indeed, the Taft-Hartley law provides that the Joint (Congressional) Committee on Labor-Management Relations, "shall conduct a thorough study and investigation of the entire field of labor-management relations, including," among seven matters specifically mentioned, "the methods and procedures for best carrying out the collective-bargaining process, with special attention to the effects of industry-wide or regional bargaining upon the national economy." The fourteen-man committee is to make its first report to Congress by March 15, 1948, and its final report not later than January 2, 1949.

In any study of the proper area and extent of collective action in labor matters, the first step should be to dispel some of the misconceptions and confusion that exist and to develop the analytical and factual considerations upon which answers should be based. Understanding is a prerequisite for intelligent, well-grounded proposals for improvement. Consequently, much of this paper is devoted to a discussion of fundamentals. The first four sections of the paper deal with (1) the nature of labor markets and how they differ from commodity markets, (2) the nature of unions and how they differ from business organizations, (3) various meanings of monopoly in the labor market, and (4) the relative level of wages under union and nonunion conditions and under collective bargaining on a national or regional basis. In the light of the data and analysis developed in these four sections, proposed reforms and restrictions are examined.

I. THE NATURE OF LABOR MARKETS

Labor markets differ significantly from commodity or security markets. Each buyer is distinguished from every other buyer and there are as many market places as there are buyers. In the absence of collective bargaining, the buyers quote the wage; research in labor economics generally supports the conclusion that it is normal and natural (in the absence of collective bargaining or employer collusion) for different employers (or even the same employer[2]) to continue indefinitely to pay diverse rates for the same grade of labor in the same locality under strictly comparable job conditions.[3] Adam Smith noted this phenomenon of multiple rates when he wrote: "The price of labour, it must be observed, cannot be ascertained very accurately anywhere, different prices being often paid at the same place and for the same sort of labour, not only according to the different abilities of the workmen, but according to the easiness or hardness of the masters."[4] It is, therefore, erroneous to talk of "pure competition in the labor market," or of "the wage which clears the market," or of "a free labor market [where] different wage rates for the same kind of labor could not long exist."[5]

[2] For such reasons as race, length of service, favoritism, etc.

[3] See Lloyd G. Reynolds, *Research in Wages: Report of a Conference Held on April 4–5, 1947* (Social Science Research Council, August, 1947), p. 27; see also my article, "Wage Diversity and Its Theoretical Implications," *Review of Economic Statistics*, XXVIII (August, 1946), 152–59.

[4] *The Wealth of Nations* (Everyman's ed.; 1931), p. 69; see also John W. Riegel, *Wage Determination* (1937), p. 8.

[5] Economists have insisted both that equal wage rates should be paid in the same locality for identical work regardless of the industry and that there should be a sufficient local differential to attract labor to, and maintain it in, expanding industries.

Not only is a quoted price (wage-fixing) characteristic of the labor market but, unlike commodity or security markets, a considerable degree of stability in wage relationships and in individual wage rates over time is essential for satisfactory employment and manufacturing operations. Perfect fluidity or flexibility in individual wage rates—with frequent upward and downward movements and numerous changes in occupational differentials within a plant—would have adverse effects upon labor efficiency. Such flexibility would be incomprehensible and upsetting to workers, creating all kinds of suspicions and ill will, stimulating undesirable insecurity for employees, and causing wages to be a constant source of friction and speculation.

In the labor market, competition does not establish a single rate for work of the same grade and quality. Real wage differentials exist and persist, in the absence of unions, because of differences in employer policies and because of the nature of the supply of labor.

Employers not only do not wish to vary their wage scales repeatedly but are prone to give general, across-the-board increases or decreases rather than to adjust each rate according to local demand and supply conditions for that occupation. They may not reduce individual rates or the whole scale when they can, or when other local employers are doing so, for fear of the psychological effects on their employees or for reasons of justice, fairness, or conscience. Indeed, the policies of employers toward labor are often in marked contrast to their policies in commodity markets. Many companies seek to lead in wage increases and to pay wages slightly above their competitors. They do not dismiss established employees to hire other labor that may be equivalent or better, even though such labor is offered to the company at wage rates well below the company's current scales. Formal systems of job evaluation, widely used in industry, have no real counterpart in commodity markets. Some multiplant companies pay the same wage scales regardless of the size of city or the region of the country in which their plants are located; others have uniform scales for each zone or region; while others (the majority) try to relate their scales either to those paid by certain other firms in the locality or to rates for the same industry in that area. Some companies tend to raise wages with each increase in the cost of living or to pay employees more per hour or per piece simply because they have been with the company a long time; other companies do not follow such policies. Differences in company wage policies, in employer evaluation of individual jobs, and in stress on various wage factors (including generosity), all contribute to the existence of a range of rates rather than a single rate for any grade of labor in a locality.

Competition also tends to establish real wage differentials because the supply of labor, especially unskilled labor, does not adjust to relative price changes as the supply of individual commodities tends to do. Lower real wages (at least above relief standards) tend to increase the supply of labor offered for sale by a family. Consequently, in the absence of unions, great diversity in wage rates for comparable work has existed in low-wage industries—such as garments and textiles—whose products are sold under market conditions closely approaching pure competition.

Without labor organization, employers tend to dominate the labor market. They establish the price, subject to limits and influenced perhaps by wage leadership. The employer pressure that has been brought to bear against individual companies (such as Ford, Owens-Illinois Glass, International Harvester, and American Telephone and Telegraph) not to upset local wage levels or bid away ("pirate") employees of other local companies is well known. Adam Smith explained the nature of common interest and action of employers when he wrote that they "are always and everywhere in a sort of tacit, but constant and uniform combination;" that "to violate this combination is everywhere a most unpopular action;" and that little is heard "of this combination, because it is the usual, and one may say, the natural state of things."[6]

The most extreme case of employer domination in the labor market is the buyer's monopoly which exists in company towns, where one company is the sole employer of labor in the "labor-market area." The situation may not be so different where most of the manufacturing labor in a community is employed by two or three large units, often the plants of multiplant companies employing from 25,000 to 350,000 workers. As indicated below, such companies may, through their wage and price policies, be able to stimulate intercommunity rivalry in the sale of labor, to curtail buyer competition in a local market, and largely to eliminate price competition in their product markets through delivered price quotations or other devices.

The Federal antitrust laws have never been applied to labor markets. Employers, as well as workers, have been free to combine and conspire as they might wish in the labor market, which is the only market where industrial firms are all buyers and in which it is practically impossible for sellers to become buyers when

[6] *Op. cit.*, p. 59.

prices fall. Nonapplication of the anti-monopoly laws in the labor market is recognition of the fact that, without unions, there are bound to be monopolistic elements in most labor markets and that there are essential differences between price-fixing and monopoly control in product markets and such phenomena as labor agreements, collective bargaining, and strikes by workers.

The nature of the labor market has been explained in such detail because some economists, who have not studied labor markets and employer labor policies, seem to consider employer control under nonunion conditions to be "unsubstantial," "transitory," and "infrequent."[7] They have tended to picture the alternatives as "monopolistic wage de-

[7] See Henry C. Simons, "Some Reflections on Syndicalism," *Journal of Political Economy*, LII (March, 1944), 7; and Fritz Machlup, "Monopolistic Wage Determination as a Part of the General Problem of Monopoly," in *Wage Determination and the Economics of Liberalism* (Chamber of Commerce of the United States, January 11, 1947), pp. 57–58, 80. Note especially such statements as: "Whatever lack there is in industry's competition for labor can be accounted for either by insufficiencies in the geographical or occupational mobility of labor, or by a lack of employment opportunities during periods of serious employment," and "I know of no evidence of employers' wage-fixing combinations in labor markets in which there were no unions; if there is such evidence, it has not been much publicized." For statements by labor economists emphasizing the practical importance of employer dominance or citing cases of concerted employer control in fixing wages see, e.g., Paul H. Douglas, "Wage Theory and Wage Policy," *International Labour Review*, XXXIX (March, 1939), 342; and Harry A. Millis, "The Union in Industry: Some Observations on the Theory of Collective Bargaining," *American Economic Review*, XXV (March, 1935), 6–7.

Economists familiar with employer wage policies during nonunion periods in such industries as steel, oil, or meat-packing or with employer control of labor markets in the South could readily supply "such evidence" to theorists who think in terms of "the competitive wage" as the normal and natural state of affairs when labor organization is absent; see also my *Economics of Labor* (1941), pp. 130–39.

termination" by unions or "free [competitive] pricing in labor markets" where unions are absent.[8]

II. THE NATURE OF LABOR UNIONS

Economists sometimes seem to overlook the fact that unions do not "sell labor," are not profit-making institutions, and are as much political as they are economic.

Monopolistic principles developed for business concerns cannot be applied directly to unions. Unlike companies, unions are not operated to make a profit. Their activities are not determined by comparisons of sales income and costs; their policies are not based on marginal sales revenue, marginal operating costs, or net returns. It is doubtful whether unions consistently attempt to maximize any monetary quantity.[9]

In fact, those who accuse unions of being big and strong monopolies often criticize them for not consistently pursuing monopolistic principles. In seeking and accepting uniform wage scales under national and regional collective bargaining, unions forego the monopolistic practice of charging all that the traffic will bear through discriminatory pricing. In denouncing arrangements for multiple employer bargaining (regional or national in application) as "monopolistic," the House Committee on Education and Labor complains that such arrangements "tend, in some cases, to reduce the resistance of employers to extravagant demands of the unions, and, in others, to holding down wages in plants where

greater efficiency than in others might, but for the group arrangements, result in better wages for the employees."[10] Holding down wages is condemned as "monopolistic practices" by unions!

In his famous article on labor monopoly, the late Henry Simons explains how, if he were a union leader, he would "gradually exterminate industry by excessive labor costs" and would "consistently demand wage rates which offered to existing firms no real net earnings."[11] Consistently following monopolistic theory, he would, through discriminatory pricing, charge all that the traffic would bear.

Unions, however, are political institutions, whose leaders are interested in maintaining their positions and in the growth and reputation of the organization, rather than merely in obtaining a maximum lifetime income for the present membership.[12] Unions seek not only to influence terms of employment but to obtain other goals such as security for the organization, protection of members against arbitrary action by management, and definite limits to the authoritarian system in industry. Consequently, union negotiators may swap a possible wage increase for "union security" or for certain provisions in the grievance procedure. And, for reasons of union security and convenience, union leaders may prefer multiple-employer bargaining, which strengthens the economic power of employers (reducing the relative power of the union) and which serves to eliminate the possibility of greater monetary gains

---

[8] See Simons, *op. cit.*, pp. 22–23; and Machlup, *op. cit.*, p. 80.

[9] For a more extended discussion of the differences between labor unions and business enterprises that appeared after this paper was prepared, see Arthur M. Ross, "The Trade Union as a Wage-Fixing Institution," *American Economic Review*, XXXVII (September, 1947), 566–88.

[10] *Labor-Management Relations Act, 1947* (House of Representatives, 80th Cong., 1st sess., Report No. 245 [April 11, 1947]), p. 36.

[11] *Op. cit.*, p. 8.

[12] See Sumner H. Slichter, *The Challenge of Industrial Relations: Trade Unions, Management, and the Public Interest* (Cornell University Press, 1947), pp. 129–30.

to the membership through "whipsaw-ing"—playing companies against one an-other by bargaining with or striking one at a time.

Most strikes do not occur and continue merely, or even mainly, to obtain the highest net money advantage to the strikers. Economists have pointed out that many strikes have not been in the economic interest of the strikers, citing cases, such as the General Motors strike in 1945–46, in which "a union imposes on its members a loss of earnings through strike that cannot be made up in less than eight years of work at the wage in-creases they won through the strike."[13] The psychological, political, and institu-tional factors in strikes are often much more important than purely monetary considerations. It is completely erroneous to assume that most strikes result be-cause union leaders have not correctly estimated the "employer's concession schedule" and the "resistance schedule" of the workers.[14] As part of a mass move-ment to emancipate and elevate laboring groups, unions seek to curtail the free-dom of management to take arbitrary ac-tion toward workers and hope, through written agreements, to gain some meas-ure of democratic self-determination in the workshop.

Union policies, practices, philosophies, and even objectives, have been too di-verse to permit any unitary explanation of the labor movement in this country. For example, restrictive policies and practices vary in character and extent with the union and the industry. Craft unions frequently have restricted en-trance to the trade, membership in the union, and introduction of labor-saving devices that reduce the demand for craft skill; those practices are not character-istic of industrial unions. As pure craft unions have been declining in relative im-portance or disappearing, such restrictive practices have been decreasing in general significance. "Make-work" restrictions, including the hiring of unnecessary labor, have also been confined chiefly to craft unions and local-market industries, like building, trucking, and amusements.

Restrictions of industrial unions in mass-production industries deal mainly with lay-off and promotion, method of payment, or the techniques of "scientific management." Insistence on seniority and equal treatment regardless of sex or race is to prevent favoritism or discrimi-nation by management. Industrial union policies with regard to methods of pay-ment and management techniques, how-ever, vary considerably. Some unions favor the piece-rate method; others op-pose it. Some favor certain formal incen-tive systems; others oppose all such sys-tems. Some co-operate with employers in establishing production standards or sys-tems of job evaluation; others refuse to participate, reserving the right to com-plain and oppose. Industrial unions may oppose increased tempo of operations or additional machine assignments; they may also oppose the setting of arbitrary production schedules or daily stints by workers.[15]

---

[13] Machlup, *op. cit.*, p. 50, n. 8.

[14] See J. R. Hicks, *The Theory of Wages*, chap. vii: "The Theory of Industrial Disputes," esp. pp. 141–42 and 146–47. Slichter (*op. cit.*, pp. 129–31) indicates how far actual practice is from theo-retical models of collective bargaining.

[15] For example, the 1945 agreements of the Fed-eration of Dyers, Finishers, Printers, and Bleachers of America (a department of the Textile Workers Union of America, C.I.O.) with employers in plain dyeing and machine printing and employers in lacquer and flock finishing, contained the follow-ing provision: "The Union agrees that every em-ployee shall perform a full day's work. The Union further agrees that the setting of arbitrary produc-tion schedules by workers is contrary to the principle of a full day's work and the Union further agrees

Whether unions serve to increase or decrease the net national product is a nice question. Professor Sumner Slichter has given considerable attention and study to the matter. In a chapter on "The Effect of Trade Unions on the Management of Business Enterprises" in his recent book, he points out that "many rules introduced into shops by collective bargaining [have] increased the net national product"[16] and concludes that "collective bargaining has stimulated more alert and dynamic management and better managerial practices more frequently than it has hampered management and interfered unduly with managerial discretion," so "that in most industries it . . . . yields a larger net output than would have resulted from individual bargaining."[17] Not only have restrictions on management's freedom sometimes increased, rather than reduced, total output, but increased wages in low-wage areas as a result of labor organization have frequently helped to increase labor productivity.

Like business organizations, unions in this country have been growing big, and with increasing size has come greater concentration of power and control at the top. National unions have expanded by extension of jurisdiction and organizing activity and by merger until a number of A.F. of L. and C.I.O. unions have from a half-million to a million members and extend over a number of important industries. A natural accompaniment of increased size and operations is concentration of effective power in the hands of top, paid officials. Numerous factors facilitate centralization of functions and authority in unions —growth in the size of companies and the area of competitive production, advantages of central pooling of benefit and strike funds, need for a bureaucracy of full-time officers for efficiency and responsibility in administration, headquarters control over paid organizers and official publications, and so forth.

With expanding union strength and concentration of control, the problem of the potential power of union officials over large sections of the nation's economy has become more and more serious, especially when that power is used for selfish or political purposes. Unions not only profess to be representative, democratic organizations but historically are part of a protest movement against autocracy in industry. Consequently, expansion of unions into industrial empires, subject to arbitrary exercise of central authority, raises the question of need for curbs to the area of control by a single union and to concentration of functions and power within unions.[18]

[18] For an analysis of the problem of concentration of control in unions by an official of the International Ladies' Garment Workers' Union, see Will Herberg, "Bureaucracy and Democracy in Labor Unions," *Antioch Review*, III (fall, 1943), esp. pp. 407–13.

Anthony Ramuglia, an organizer for the Textile Workers Union of America and for many years a member and officer of the Amalgamated Clothing Workers of America, has recently written regarding "Democracy in the Unions" as follows: "Most of our international unions operate on the level of the cities' political machines. We have in our unions the counterparts of the Hagues, Pendergasts, Vares, Penroses, etc. In many of our unions the democratic processes are as much a mockery as in the sectors of our nation just referred to. In some unions there is even no pretense of democracy. In others there is some finesse in the exercise of dictatorial powers. However, the whole movement is top heavy. The plague of concentrated powers is as general in the CIO as it is in the AFL" (*Labor and Nation*, III [July–August, 1947], 41).

that appropriate steps will be taken to eliminate any such condition." Some employers reported favorable results from this provision (see R. A. Lester and E. A. Robie, *Wages under National and Regional Collective Bargaining* [Princeton University: Industrial Relations Section, 1946], p. 66).

[16] *Op. cit.*, p. 34.   [17] *Ibid.*, pp. 69, 72–73.

III. MEANING OF "LABOR MONOPOLY"

Perusal of recent writings and statements indicates that the terms "labor monopoly" and "union monopoly" carry a variety of connotations and meanings. Some writers stress the purpose of unions as the controlling factor; some point to means (certain specified union activities or legislative policies) as the test; to others the economic effects are the criterion for judging the existence of "labor monopoly"; while still others emphasize personal power as the prime consideration.

On the basis of purpose alone, unions have been termed "monopolistic." For example, the Counsel of the National Association of Manufacturers asserts: "It must be recognized that labor unionism is, by its very nature, essentially monopolistic."[19] In much the same vein, Professor Charles O. Gregory has written: "Now labor unionism is a frankly monopolistic and anti-competitive institution, even if its major undertakings have been carried on and justified in the name of competition."[20] Professor Fritz Machlup has stated: "It is the chief purpose of a trade union to obtain monopolistic advantages for its members."[21] Such views would seem to make "labor monopoly" and labor union practically synonymous terms.[22]

In stressing union action and legislative provisions, some economists point to exclusive bargaining rights or to combined action as the essence of "labor monopoly." Thus, Professors Harley L. Lutz and Leo Wolman criticize as "monopoly" the certification of a union as exclusive bargaining agent under federal legislation.[23]

To other economists, the fact of combined action (and therefore collective bargaining or the strike per se) is "monopolistic," apparently regardless of purpose.[24] Presumably, therefore, the threat to strike, or its execution, to prevent discrimination in wages among employees by race or sex or to protest against arbitrary management action, say, in discharges or lay-offs would be as "monopolistic" as a strike for the closed shop.[25] To others, union activities or collective bargaining really become "monopolistic" when they cover jointly two or more employers,[26] and especially when the bargaining or strike includes a whole industry or a whole national union.[27]

"Industry-wide" bargaining per se is often condemned as "patently monopolistic" or "the essence of monopoly in labor relations."[28] Senator Irving M. Ives

[19] *Labor Relations Program, Hearings on S. 55 and S.J. Res. 22 before the Committee on Labor and Public Welfare* (U.S. Senate, 80th Cong., 1st sess. [March, 1947]), Part IV, p. 1807.

[20] *Labor and the Law* (1946), p. 418.

[21] *Op. cit.*, p. 54.

[22] Professor Jacob Viner refers to "labor monopolies, which is just another term for 'strong' trade unions" (see "The Role of Costs in a System of Economic Liberalism," *ibid.*, p. 24).

[23] See Lutz, "Wages, Profits and Prices," *Commercial and Financial Chronicle*, CLXIII (January 3, 1946), 43–44; and Wolman, *Hearings on S.55 and S.J. Res. 22*, Part I, p. 100.

[24] See John W. Scoville, *Labor Monopolies— OR Freedom* (Committee for Constitutional Government, Inc., 1946), pp. 20–23; and Hastings Lyon, *Dictatorship of the Proletariat in the United States: A Tract for the Times* (1943), pp. 20–23.

[25] Perhaps it is significant, however, that the closed shop is frequently condemned as "union monopoly" but that the same does not hold for seniority or rules regarding the handling of grievances.

[26] See *Hearings on S. 55 and S.J. Res. 22*, Part II, pp. 950, 957.

[27] *Ibid.*, Part I, pp. 115, 118, 484; and Part II, pp. 942, 1015.

[28] See, e.g., statement by Congressman Walter C. Ploeser in *Daily Report on Labor-Management Problems*, No. 138 (Washington: Bureau of National Affairs, Inc., July 6, 1947), p. A-8; and pre-

speaks of "the tendency toward monopoly which is apt to be present in nearly every type of industry-wide bargaining."[29] Senator Joseph H. Ball told the Senate in May, 1947: "I myself am convinced from my discussions with various employers although admittedly we did not have any evidence of it in the committee, that industry-wide bargaining is clearly monopolistic."[30] Uncertainty exists, however, as to what is meant by industry-wide bargaining, for that term is often mistakenly used to refer to unilateral nation-wide union action or to wage pattern-setting by negotiations with a few large concerns whose wage leadership the smaller companies are forced to follow. Senator Ball, for example, cited such a pattern-setting case in explaining why he thought industry-wide bargaining was "clearly monopolistic." Cases of real industry-wide bargaining are relatively rare if one means by the term that practically all the industry is represented in a single negotiation.[31]

Most frequently labor unions have been condemned as "monopolies" because of restrictive policies and practices that affect labor output, labor supply, and labor demand. Such policies, mentioned in the previous section, include restrictions on entrance to the job, on individual output, on use of labor-saving methods, on hours of work, and on management efficiency and discipline as well as other "make-work" restrictions, such as insistence on employment of unneeded labor.[32]

Earlier comment indicated some of the grounds for believing that, on balance, labor organization may result in a net increase in the national product through its beneficial effects on individual workers[33] and management. Also it was pointed out that most of the restrictive practices, and most of the really effective restriction, are to be found in craft unions, especially in local-market industries.

In connection with "restriction of labor supply," it is argued that "fixing monopolistic wage rates by contract" restricts the number of jobs available in the industries concerned and, consequently, the number of workers who find work in those industries.[34] To Henry Simons, workers, through unions, were "organized to price their services monopolistically," and so he could "see no way to avoid severely restrictive policies save by depriving them [unions] of control over wages, i.e., of bargaining power." Thus to him the issue was "simply whether wage rates should be determined competitively or monopolistically."[35] The same notion is expressed

---

pared statement of Charles E. Wilson, president of General Motors Corporation, in *Hearings on S. 55 and S.J. Res. 22*, Part I, pp. 484, 540; and John V. Van Sickle, *Industry-wide Collective Bargaining and the Public Interest* (American Enterprise Association, Inc., May, 1947), pp. 13–20.

[29] *Congressional Record*, XCIII (80th Cong., 1st sess. [May 7, 1947]), 4792, 4793.

[30] *Ibid.*, p. 5144.

[31] Railroads and men's clothing are perhaps the prime examples. Professor Van Sickle considers that industry-wide union organization in the bituminous coal industry has changed it from "one of the most competitive industries in the United States . . . . into a monopolistic enterprise . . . ." (*op. cit.*, p. 14).

[32] See, e.g., Viner, *op. cit.*, pp. 24–25; Machlup, *op. cit.*, p. 68; Wolman, *op. cit.*, p. 115; Lyon, *op. cit.*, pp. 81–82. Professor Lyon goes so far as to condemn the Fair Labor Standards Act and the Social Security Act as "monopolistic" because they serve to reduce the total hours of labor offered for sale (*op. cit.*, pp. 97, 101, 103, 107).

[33] The beneficial effects of labor organization on labor productivity in low-wage areas, such as sections of the South, deserve serious and systematic study. The importance of preventing the vicious circle of poverty breeding poverty is indicated by Professor Viner, *op. cit.*, pp. 28–29.

[34] See Machlup, *op. cit.*, p. 69.

[35] *Op. cit.*, pp. 25, 9, 23.

even more forcefully by John W. Scoville, former economist of the Chrysler
Corporation, as follows:

> General Motors must pay the market price
> for copper, for steel, and for labor. For if it pays
> less than the market price, it will be short of
> materials and be short of workmen. But the
> United Automobile Workers' Union is not will-
> ing that its members receive the market price
> of labor, for workers can secure the market price
> without any collective action.
>
> The purpose of the labor union monopoly is
> the same as the purpose of every other monopo-
> ly. The monopoly is formed to get a price above
> the market price.[36]

The preceding discussion of labor markets indicates how unrealistic and erroneous is such commodity-market reasoning
as applied to labor markets. Prior to labor organization in General Motors, the
company was the dominant or largest
employer in a number of the localities
where its plants were operating. General
Motors quoted the wage scales that it
would pay and enjoyed a significant
range of discretion in fixing and modifying such wage quotation. With real wage
differentials prevailing as a normal condition in the absence of employer co-
operation or union organization it is
fanciful to talk of *the* market price of
labor" in a labor-market area. Without
unions, labor markets are subject to employer "influence over price," which, by
commodity-market reasoning, is considered to be one of the two "essential criteria of monopolistic position"—the
other being "control of supply."[37]

The chimerical nature of *the* competitive wage" becomes evident when an attempt is made to set forth a definition or
criterion by which, in concrete cases, to
"answer the question whether a particu-

lar wage rate is or is not 'monopolistic.' "[38] Professors Simons and Machlup
both propose as the crucial test the existence or nonexistence of real wage differentials. If a wage differential exists so
that many qualified workers would prefer to be employed in an occupation,
firm, or industry but cannot obtain the
preferred employment for lack of job
openings, the wage rates are considered
to be "excessive" and "monopolistic."[39]
To quote Professor Machlup, "If many,
however, would like to shift but find that
no more workers are wanted at the places
which pay the better wage, then the better wage is not the result of a naturally
scarce supply but of monopolistic wage
determination."[40]

Judged by such a test, "monopolistic
wage determination" and "monopolistic
distortions in the wage structure" were
widely prevalent in industry prior to unionization. For example, companies like
Standard Oil of New Jersey, Goodyear
Tire and Rubber Company, Ford Motor
Company, International Harvester Company, and Botany Worsted Mills paid
wage scales 10–20 per cent above their
competitors during the 1920's. Many
qualified workers would have preferred
to work for those concerns but could not
do so with limits to the total number of
jobs available in such companies. The
same has been true for high-paying firms
in nonunion areas in the South. As previously explained, companies do not, in
the absence of unions or employer under-
standings, pay "equal wage rates for
identical work" in a locality. Economists
indicate their lack of understanding of
labor markets and policies when they assert that "different wage rates for the

---

[36] *Op. cit.*, p. 155.

[37] Machlup, *op. cit.*, p. 55. Actually, control
over price would seem to be the only essential
criterion.

[38] *Ibid.*, p. 70.

[39] See Simons, *op. cit.*, p. 14; and Machlup,
op. cit., pp. 69–71.

[40] *Op. cit.*, pp. 70–71.

same work in different industries ; . . . are economic foolishness."[41]

In the next section an attempt is made to compare union and nonunion wage scales in a number of industries and to compare wage levels under national bargaining with the general level of wages in industry. As the discussion there indicates, the statistics are not adequate for close comparisons or unqualified conclusions. However, they throw doubt on the contention that, through monopoly, labor organizations exact "excessively high" wages or that national bargaining necessarily results in higher levels of wages than local bargaining or unilateral employer determination.

Although it cannot be conclusively demonstrated by statistics, there can be little doubt that the spread of unionism since 1932 has tended to reduce the amount of "unjustified" differentials in wage rates (a) between occupations within a plant, (b) between plants in the same locality, (c) between manufacturing industries, and (d) between areas and regions. Union insistence on "equal pay for equal work" and the stimulus to job evaluation from labor organization—admittedly with some assistance from wartime scarcity of labor and War Labor Board policies—has resulted in the elimination of many intraplant and interplant "wage inequities." Consequently, the wage structure in American industry now is probably less "distorted" than it was in all nonunion industry during the 1920's. At least that is the opinion of a number of industrialists who are in a good position to make such a comparative judgment.

The application of a uniform wage scale throughout an industry, whether by industry-wide bargaining or union-wide enforcement of standards, has been called

"complete monopoly" and "monopoly pure and simple,"[42] on the grounds that such a wage scale is not adjusted to "the competitive wage level" in each locality and that it eliminates wage competition in the whole industry.

If uniformity in wage scales throughout the country is monopoly, then a number of multiplant firms—such as Ford and Libbey-Owens-Ford—were guilty of such monopoly prior to union organization in the 1930's, having for decades followed a policy of paying the same wage scale wherever their plants were located.[43] The same has been true for civil service jobs with the United States government.

The analogy to commodities is not usually carried over in this respect. For hundreds of industrial products, companies quote uniform delivered prices on a national basis so that purchasers pay the same price regardless of locality or region. Many other products carry uniform delivered prices by zone or region.[44]

[41] Machlup, *op. cit.*, pp. 65–66.

[42] See remarks of Senator Joseph H. Ball and Senator Robert A. Taft, *Hearings on S. 55 and S.J. Res. 22*, Part III, pp. 1191, 1578–79; see also Part II, p. 642.

[43] In reply to a questionnaire in the spring of 1945, six out of forty-eight interregional concerns—one in each of six industries—reported that they paid the same wage scales in their southern plants as in their northern or western plants. See the author's article, "Diversity in North-South Wage Differentials and in Wage Rates within the South," *Southern Economic Journal*, XII (January, 1946), 239.

[44] Products with uniform national or regional prices include branded items in such lines as rubber tires and tubes; drugs and cosmetics; household electrical equipment; advertised foods and groceries; cigarettes, cigars, and smoking tobacco; shoes; men's suits and furnishings; mattresses; some chemicals; national brands of prepared paints; plumbing fixtures; insulation board; many planing-mill products; wire; aluminum; some automobile parts; typewriters, calculating machines, and similar office equipment; business furniture; paper and newsprint; items of hardware like hand tools; turbines and switchgear; industrial motors and

Prices of such items have not varied with local demand and supply, with differences in freight costs from the producing plant, or with differences in local operating costs including retail delivery. Through various pricing devices, employers are able to achieve unity with regard to price and practically eliminate price competition.

It is no doubt advantageous to a multiplant company to follow a policy of geographic price uniformity in order to reduce price competition among sellers in its product markets, a policy of paying prevailing local wage scales in order to reduce price competition among buyers in local labor markets, and a policy of stimulating price competition on the seller's side of the labor market, especially intermarket rivalry. The policy of company adherence to local prevailing wage rates permits buyer co-operation to aid in local wage uniformity and to discourage competitive upbidding of local wage scales while encouraging intercommunity rivalry in the selling of labor. By quoting the price in both commodity and labor markets, manufacturing firms have often been able to take advantage of any monopolistic elements in their position in each market.

Critics argue that industry-wide uniformity in wage scales tends to curtail employment expansion in low-wage areas, citing such industries as the rub-

ber-tire and -tube industry.[45] Tires and tubes carrying the well-known brand names have a uniform price all over the United States, yet the cost of production of tires and tubes in southern plants apparently has, on the average, been lower than in northern plants, for the large companies report that wage rates for all comparable jobs have been 20–30 per cent below the rates in northern plants, and some companies also report that labor efficiency and actual labor output in their southern plants has equaled that in their northern plants.[46] Pricing on an f.o.b., plant-by-plant basis (cost plus reasonable profit) would, therefore, be the effective, competitive method of bringing about expansion in production and employment in the rubber-tire industry in the South. Uniform delivered prices with the producer absorbing the varying freight charges to all destinations and with cost and profits calculated on a company-wide basis may serve to confuse and conceal plant production-cost differences and to retard expansion in the South.

Actually, it is extremely difficult to argue that the price of labor should vary from locality to locality when the worker's tools or equipment, the materials he works on, and the products he makes all carry uniform prices regionally or nationally and when many of the goods he purchases (clothes, foods, household equipment, building supplies, etc.) likewise are sold at uniform prices geographically.

Especially is that the case when the

---

controllers; certain "catalogue items" of machinery; portable air compressors; food machinery; saws and saw tools; hydraulic lifts; chains, gears, and transmission machinery; water pumps; gasoline service pumps; and electric arc welding equipment; see, e.g., Saul Nelson and Walter G. Keim, *Price Behavior and Business Policy* (Temporary National Economic Committee, "Monograph No. 1" [Senate committee print] [Washington, 1940]), pp. 286–345; and Vernon A. Mund, "The 'Freight Allowed' Method of Price Quotation," *Quarterly Journal of Economics*, LIV (February, 1940), 232–45.

[45] See Van Sickle, *op. cit.*, pp. 11–12; see also Simons, *op. cit.*, pp. 10–12.

[46] See my articles, "Diversity in North-South Wage Differentials and in Wage Rates within the South," *Southern Economic Journal*, XII (January, 1946), 240; and "Effectiveness of Factory Labor: South-North Comparisons," *Journal of Political Economy*, LIV (February, 1946), 66.

reasons given by economists in support of South-North and other geographic wage differentials are found upon investigation to be weak half-truths and even to be, in some respects, erroneous. For example, Professor Simons writes: "Southern labor, on the whole, simply isn't worth much, to enterprisers or to the community"; "Climate, culture, poverty, and scarcity of complementary resources (especially capital) account for chronically low productivity."[47] Actually, interregional and intraregional wage structures, and the effects of elimination or reduction of wage differentials, are far more complex than such statements would imply. For example, the wage scales of many southern firms and some southern industries averaged as high as (or higher than) their northern counterparts prior to unionization in the South; wage differentials in single labor-market areas in the South are sometimes greater than real South-North industry differentials; and a majority of interregional manufacturing concerns and industrial engineers report labor efficiency and output as high (or higher) in their southern plants as in their northern plants. Additional factual data contradict other conventional assumptions of theorists, but space limitations permit only reference to the material.[48]

Much of the recent complaint against "labor monopoly" seems to be based on the trend toward concentration of economic power in the hands of the leaders of large national unions and the claim that, through "control over employees in great industries," they dictate the terms which must be met if such industries are to continue to operate.[49] Thus, employers and congressmen express alarm at the "monopolistic power" of "the top labor leader"; at "the heavy concentration of economic power and actual monopoly of the supply of labor in the hands of a few unions and their leaders"; at "the rank monopoly" involved in "the domination or dictation" from national headquarters; at "a great monopolistic union controlling the total labor supply in an industry"; and at some union leaders' "power to put great masses of people out of work."[50] It is Dr. Florence Peterson's opinion that "those who speak of union monopoly usually think in terms of a strongly entrenched clique of union officers who, because of compulsory membership requirements, are enabled to exercise despotic power over workers and employers alike."[51]

Increasing concentration of economic power in the hands of individual union officials or groups of officials, and the possibilities for arbitrary or imprudent use of such power, raise some real problems for a political democracy and a relatively free, market economy. Involved are such issues as the size and industrial jurisdiction of a national union, the distribution of power and functions within a national union, the extent and operation of the democratic process within the national union, and the possibilities of joint collusion under national or industry-wide bargaining.

In considerable measure, the problem is one of checks and balances rather than

---

[47] *Op. cit.*, pp. 10, 11.

[48] The summarizing article is "Southern Wage Differentials: Developments, Analysis, and Implications," *Southern Economic Journal*, XIII (April, 1947), 386–94.

[49] See statement of Professor Leo Wolman, *Hearings on S. 55 and S.J. Res. 22*, Part I, pp. 112, 115, 116; and Senator Joseph H. Ball, *Congressional Record*, XCIII (1947), 5145.

[50] See *Hearings on S. 55 and S.J. Res. 22*, Part II, pp. 684–85, 686, 935, 1016, 1068. Strictly speaking, a "monopoly of the supply of labor" is possible only in a slave economy.

[51] *Survey of Labor Economics* (1947), p. 640.

simply one of monopoly in the strict sense of that term. Merely to condemn as "monopoly" almost every well-established practice of trade-unions serves, therefore, to confuse, rather than to shed light on, the significant issues. Nor, in analyzing the problem, does it help to base one's reasoning on misleading and mistaken notions such as that wage-fixing and wage stability are economically undesirable, that all elements of monopoly can and should be eliminated from the labor market, or that unions seek to price labor so as to gain all possible monopoly advantage. Data in the next section seem to indicate that unions have not affected wage rates so much as is generally assumed or in the manner that reasoning on monopoly principles would lead one to believe.

IV. WAGE COMPARISONS

Statements concerning the effects of unions on wage scales and wage structures have often seemed somewhat contradictory. Some economists have contended that unions, by means of their bargaining power, have pushed wage scales too high in organized firms, occupations, and industries, thus causing "monopolistic distortions" in the wage structure. Other economists have pointed out that, in a number of industries, wage scales in unionized plants have averaged no higher than in nonunion plants; that hourly earnings or wage levels in unionized industries have not increased relative to nonunion industries over periods as long as four or five decades; and that during the last three or four decades wage scales and hourly earnings under national bargaining in manufacturing industries have not been higher, and have not increased more rapidly, than for manufacturing as a whole.

Adequate data are not at hand for de-

finitive conclusions as to the effects of unions and national bargaining on relative wage levels and wage structures. No statistical investigation specifically designed to ascertain such effects has been made, and statistics alone could not provide complete answers.

For comparative purposes, the available statistical material is deficient in a number of respects. Generally speaking, the larger firms and firms in larger cities are more likely to be organized. In some occupations, the union members are generally more skilled and better workers. On the other hand, hourly earnings data may be affected by the fact that incentive methods of payment probably prevail to a greater extent on nonunion jobs than on jobs subject to union agreement. Therefore, with the available statistics, it is difficult to obtain an approach to strict comparability in job, workers, size of firm, and method of payment. In addition, the United States Bureau of Labor Statistics' data on union and nonunion earnings are not broken down by length of organization of the firm, bargaining strength of the union, or area of bargaining. Nevertheless the figures are sufficient to demonstrate that the answers are not so simple and unequivocal as much of the literature implies.

The comparisons that follow are based on tabulations made by the author from data on average straight-time hourly earnings given separately by occupation or occupational grade and by sex in the surveys of single industries made by the Bureau of Labor Statistics in 1943, 1944, 1945, and 1946. The figures are either for a city or local labor-market area or for a region (with the country divided into nine regions). From 76 labor-market surveys by industry (dated in 1943 and 1944) which were at hand, the 22 in manufacturing that contained a breakdown for union and nonunion establishments were selected. Of 37 industry studies of occupational wage structure dated in 1945 and 1946, the 19 in manufacturing with a breakdown between union and nonunion establishments were chosen for analysis. A plant is classified as unionized if a union agreement or agreements cover a majority of the employees in that plant.

The first set of comparisons involves 10 surveys covering different industries in three southwestern, two midwestern, and three eastern cities. For the 10 surveys, there was an average per survey of 18 union establishments and 27 nonunion establishments. Of course, not all plants were represented for each occupation but averages were not given for less than 3 plants. Out of a total of 309 occupational comparisons, the occupational average for the nonunion plants in the city exceeded that for the union establishments in 51 cases and equaled the union average in 9 more. Five of the surveys contain no incentive payments in the hourly earnings averages. Of the total of 66 occupational comparisons in those 5 surveys, the average for the nonunion plants was higher in 18 instances and the same in 2, so that the nonunion average was higher in almost three-tenths of the cases. In the 4 surveys definitely stating that the union plants tended to be the larger ones, the nonunion average was higher in only 32 out of 217 comparisons (with 5 equal).

Wage surveys by the United States Bureau of Labor Statistics also permit comparisons between union and nonunion plants on the basis of wage rates or straight-time earnings for key metalworking occupations in each of twelve midwestern cities in 1943 and the first half of 1944.[52] Out of a total of 1793 oc-

cupational comparisons for the twelve cities, the average for nonunion establishments in the city was higher than the union-plant average in 590 instances and equal to it in 71 cases. In other words, local wage rates for specified metalworking occupations seem to have averaged higher for nonunion plants than for union plants in one-third of all the comparisons that were made.[53]

From B.L.S. studies of the wage structure in 37 industries in 1945 and 1946, comparisons can be made on a regional basis between straight-time earnings averages for union and nonunion plants in specified occupations in 19 manufacturing industries.[54] Each of the nine regions includes from three to seven states. Of 2296 occupational comparisons, the nonunion average was higher in 647, or three-tenths, of the cases and the same as the union-plant average in 90 instances. For the 19 industries, the nonunion-plant average ranged from two-thirds of the occupations in the manufacture of power boilers to only one-twelfth of the occupations in the soap and glycerin industry.

Such crude comparisons of occupational averages for nonunion and union

---

[52] The twelve cities are Chicago; Indianapolis; Milwaukee; Minneapolis; South Bend; Rockford and Springfield, Illinois; Fort Wayne and Evansville, Indiana; Green Bay and Racine-Kenosha, Wisconsin; and Joliet, Illinois; see *Wages in Seven Metalworking Centers (1943–1944)* and *Wages in Six Metalworking Centers, 1944* (U.S. Bureau of Labor Statistics, Region VI, n.d. and March, 1945).

[53] For individual cities, the ratio varied, since the nonunion average was higher in only one-eighth of the occupations in Fort Wayne and in almost three-fifths of the occupations in Evansville.

[54] Machine tools, machinery, electroplating and polishing, foundries, power boilers, cotton garments, structural clay products, radios, footwear, cigars, women's and misses' dresses, wood furniture, paperboard containers and boxes, pulp, paper and paperboard mills, copper alloying, rolling and drawing, jewelry, cotton textiles, and soap and glycerin (U.S. Bureau of Labor Statistics, "Industry Wage Studies Bulletins," Ser. 2).

plants seem to indicate that, locally or regionally, union wage rates average lower than nonunion rates for many occupations. It may be argued that even good cross-section comparisons as of a particular date are not too revealing either (1) because unions tend to set the wage pattern for nonunion plants as well as union establishments or (2) because the union plants may not have been organized long enough for the effects of union pressures to be fully reflected in relative wage levels. To shed some light on the latter contention, it is necessary to examine data permitting comparison between union and nonunion wages over considerable periods of time.

In his study of *Real Wages in the United States, 1890–1926*, Professor Paul H. Douglas develops annual indexes of "hourly earnings" for 7 "union" industries.[55] The basic data were the union wage rates in various cities collected annually by the United States Bureau of Labor Statistics. In addition, he calculated indexes of "hourly earnings" for 8 " 'payroll' manufacturing" industries. Unfortunately, the combined index for the "payroll" industries is not an index of nonunion earnings, including as it does men's clothing, boots and shoes, and hosiery, which were partially unionized during part of the period from 1890 to 1926.

One can, however, come close to making a comparison of union and nonunion rates or earnings for the same or similar industries by using two pairs of Professor Douglas' indexes: the indexes for union planing mills and for sawmills in general and the indexes for union metal trades and for iron and steel.[56] Between 1890 and 1920 the index for union planing mills and the index for sawmills in general both increased by about the same per-

centage (198 and 191 respectively) and moved fairly closely together throughout the three decades except for the war years (1917–19). From 1920 to 1926, however, the union index rose some 17 per cent, whereas the index for sawmills in general declined about 17 per cent. The indexes for the union foundries and machine shops and for the iron-and-steel industry both increased 180 per cent between 1890 and 1924 and were frequently close together during that period.[57]

Such data lend little support to the contention that unions follow the principles of "monopolistic pricing" by means of "excessive increases" in wage scales. From his statistical studies, Professor Douglas concluded that "since 1914 the wages in the nonunion manufacturing industries have risen at least as rapidly as have those in the union manufacturing industries," although he was of the opinion that unions undoubtedly were, in part, responsible for a more rapid increase in union than nonunion scales for some industrires during the early stages of labor organization in certain years prior to 1914.[58]

As indicated in the preceding section, multiple employer bargaining with a national union, especially if a single negotiation covers a large portion of an industry, has been condemned as "monopolistic wage fixing." In an effort to discover whether such bargaining has resulted in relatively high wage levels or in rapidly rising wage scales, an investigation was made of wages in 7 manufacturing industries having from ten to fifty-

---

[55] Pp. 77, 97.   [56] *Ibid.*, pp. 97, 102.

[57] Comparison of the 1928 figures with those for 1924 shows the union metal trades up 11 per cent compared with a rise of 3 per cent for iron and steel (see Paul H. Douglas and Florence T. Jennison, *The Movement of Money and Real Earnings in the United States, 1926–28* ["Studies in Business Administration" (University of Chicago, 1930), Vol. I, No. 3], pp. 32, 33).

[58] *Real Wages in the United States*, p. 562.

five years of experience with national and regional bargaining.[59]

In the pottery and the pressed and blown glassware industries the wage scales for skilled workers have, during the last forty-three and fifty-five years, respectively, been established in a single negotiation covering from 65 to 90 per cent of the industry.[60] The semiskilled and unskilled workers have been covered by such national bargaining during the last ten years in glassware and the last fourteen years in pottery. It is significant to note that, for the four or five decades of national bargaining, the average hourly earnings for skilled workers did not rise more rapidly than in manufacturing as a whole; that a number of wage reductions were negotiated averaging as much as 14 and 17 per cent each; and that a panel of the National War Labor Board found in 1944 that the hourly rates for skilled maintenance occupations and for unskilled labor in the glassware agreement were well below similar rates in neighboring industries, especially metal industries.[61]

The conclusions drawn from study of the 7 industries were that "generally speaking, wage and earning levels do not appear to have risen more rapidly under national and regional bargaining than for manufacturing as a whole" and that "levels of wages in the 7 industries taken as a group are not high; for some occupations or areas the rates are relatively high and for some comparatively low."[62] Most of the industries were, of course, subject to competition from outside the bargaining unit, from abroad, or from substitute products. That is not unusual, however, and such competition is not significant for 2 of the 7 industries.

Limitations of the data preclude sweeping generalizations about the effects of unions, or of national and industry-wide bargaining, upon wage scales and wage structures. The available material does not, however, support the assumption that unions act in the labor market as a monopolist would in a commodity market, or that more rivalry between unions would lead to lower rather than to higher wages. One reason that wage rates could remain relatively low for long periods of time under national bargaining in some manufacturing industries is that such bargaining arrangements increase the security of the union and its leaders. Under certain circumstances, industry-wide bargaining or union-wide action might, of course, result in relatively rapid wage increases and comparatively high wage scale. Especially is that likely to be true where rival union centers and dual unions exist, with competition between union officials for leadership, prestige, and personal position.

V. SOME PROPOSED REMEDIES

Suggested programs for curbing or eliminating "labor monopoly" vary with the authors' diagnosis of the difficulties to be remedied—their definition of "labor monopoly" and their conception of the labor market and of labor unions. Corrective proposals will differ radically depending on whether one envisages "labor monopoly" as exclusive labor representation, as union restrictive policies, as wage-fixing over wide areas, or as concentration of power and control.

Basically, one's concepts and objectives determine the character of his remedial proposals. An author who conceives of the labor market as essentially

---

[59] See Lester and Robie, *op. cit.*

[60] Statement includes only general ware in pottery.

[61] See Lester and Robie, *op. cit.*, pp. 16–18, 29; and *War Labor Reports* (Bureau of National Affairs, Inc., XXVIII, 1945), 60, 61.

[62] Lester and Robie, *op. cit.*, pp. 93, 94.

the same as a commodity market and the labor union as essentially analogous to a business enterprise producing and selling commodities will apply commodity-market reasoning to labor unions and attempt to make labor markets conform more closely to organized commodity or security markets. Assuming that labor unions are on all fours with business monopolies, he is likely to propose strict application of commodity-market principles and legislation (such as the anti-trust laws) to labor-union activities. On the other hand, one may conceive of the labor market as subject to its own peculiar principles and conditions, which normally and necessarily involve price-fixing and monopolistic elements, and view labor unions as political institutions, striving to survive, expand, and gain certain positions within a labor movement. Such a conceptual framework rejects the blanket borrowing of commodity-market programs intended to curtail monopoly or enforce competition and requires that any remedial programs be tailor-made for the labor market and labor unions.

The remainder of this paper will examine, first, recommended actions based on commodity-market reasoning and, then, some proposals designed especially for labor unions, which have been offered by congressmen and union officials. The discussion of each proposal must, because of space limitations, be rather brief.

One proposal, based on commodity-market reasoning, is that "competitive bidding" by labor unions be substituted for exclusive "monopoly of bargaining" granted under federal legislation to the union gaining majority representation. Professor Harley L. Lutz, for example, would have employers as free to bargain in the purchase of labor as they are in buying commodities, selecting the sup-

plier currently offering the best terms. On the assumption that unions are suppliers of labor, he would arrange it so that "an employer, having failed to reach an agreement with one group of workers as to wages or other matters of employment, [would] be free to invite some other group to enter into negotiations with a view to arriving at mutually agreeable terms. . . . ."[63] With slavery illegal, however, unions are not suppliers of labor in the sense that producers or merchants are suppliers of commodities.

Any such attempt to utilize "competitive bidding" between unions, with the employer free to choose among all offering unions, would stimulate interunion strife and strikes, with the recent evils of union rivalry increased many fold. Moreover, the proposal overlooks the essential differences between practices in labor and commodity markets and neglects the psychology of employees and employers. Workers value job security and employment stability; either seniority under the proposal would be meaningless and programs for employee advancement disrupted, or workers would have to shift from union to union at the will and interest of the employer. Companies value employee loyalty and employee knowledge of the company's jobs and policies. In encouraging frequent group turnover of labor, the proposal not only disregards company investment in employee training but also the other factors that cause employers to operate in the labor market differently than they do in purchasing and selling commodities.

A proposal that has won support by its superficial plausibility is that the anti-trust laws be applied to "labor monopolies" in the same way that they are utilized to curtail "industrial monop-

[63] *Ibid.*, pp. 43, 44.

olies."[64] Underlying such a recommendation is an assumption that it would be in the public interest to have labor markets conform as closely as possible to the pattern of organized commodity or security markets.

The proposal to subject labor markets and labor unions to the antitrust laws overlooks the fact that the market is not a satisfactory apparatus for solving many labor problems—the optimum hours of work, working conditions, child labor, job security, workers' grievances, and other human aspects of labor relations.[65] Employee and union rivalry and suits at law may be detrimental, rather than helpful, to labor productivity and labor relations. Labor and management are not competitors in the sense that producers of the same commodity are competitors; nor should unions be considered, or be forced, to be rivals in the manner of competing firms.

The antitrust laws do not define "monopoly" or "restraint of trade," nor does the Sherman Act set forth any definite criteria for determining their existence. Do unions restrain trade when they restrict employers by seniority rules, grievance procedures, definitions of normal working hours and holidays, and all the other nonwage provisions of the typical labor agreement? The restriction is not on consumers who, as pointed out above, may enjoy a larger output as a result of union restrictions on management. Do such practices as wage-fixing, domination of a labor market by a single employer, or agreement on labor-market policies by employers constitute "monopoly," which would subject employers to penal-

ties under the proposed extension of the antitrust laws? How would the extent of injury, for which treble damages can be collected under the Sherman Act, be calculated and assessed by the courts if collective bargaining and some of the provisions of typical labor agreements, including wage-fixing, were considered in violation of the antitrust laws? Presumably Senator Robert A. Taft had some of these questions in mind when he stated: "You would practically have to write an anti-trust law for labor, because I do not think the Sherman Act is really aimed at it, or that the wording is particularly suitable."[66]

The fact is that the antitrust laws and litigation under them have proved costly, ineffective, and ill-adapted for the determination and solution of monopoly problems. Court cases drag on for as long as ten years. Court victories usually are only moral victories; companies adjudged guilty can try other means, and generally there is no follow-up after the court decision. Through pricing and costing systems, common conventions, or other means of obtaining accord, firms in an industry can achieve unity of action with respect to price without any conversations or correspondence such as would be necessary in the case of labor because of the numbers involved and the characteristics of the labor market. For such reasons, the antitrust laws have proved to be impotent to prevent the growth of large industrial empires and increasing concentration of economic power in American industry.[67] Extension of the antitrust laws to labor markets, in

[64] See, e.g., Harold W. Metz and Meyer Jacobstein, *A National Labor Policy* (1947), pp. 91 and 159; *Hearings on S. 55 and S.J. Res. 22*, Part I, p. 541, and Part II, p. 686.

[65] For further discussion see my *Economics of Labor* (1941), pp. 39–45.

[66] *Hearings on S. 55 and S.J. Res. 22*, Part IV, p. 1793.

[67] For a good discussion of the weaknesses of our antitrust laws and machinery see Walton Hamilton and Irene Till, *Antitrust in Action* (Temporary National Economic Committee Monograph No. 16 [Washington, 1940]).

the face of their unsuccessful record in the field for which they were designed and in view of the essential differences between labor and commodity markets, would certainly not be sensible.

During the past year or two, a number of special limitations on labor unions have been recommended for congressional action. One type of proposal—embodied in the Hartley bill as passed in the House of Representatives in April, 1947, and also in the Ball bill (S. 133) considered by the Senate—would restrict collective bargaining to a single operating company or to one local labor-market area and would enforce independence of union policy and decision on a company or community basis.[68] Collective bargaining could encompass the employees of two or more employers only if the firms included had a combined total of no more than, say, one hundred employees and were all located in the same trade area or no more than fifty miles apart.

The stated objectives of such proposals are "to prevent monopolistic concentrations of bargaining power," to eliminate bargaining by national unions, to insure complete freedom of action by local unions, to secure more employer-employee participation in collective bargaining, and to forestall industry-wide shutdowns. Careful consideration indicates, however, that the proposed legislation is not well designed to achieve some of the avowed objectives and would not be in the public interest.

Since the restrictions are to be applied only to labor unions and not to employers or employer organizations, they seem patently unfair. One of the fundamental objectives of labor organization,

unity of action on wages over the whole area of competitive production of an article, is forbidden, but no corresponding restriction is proposed with respect to unity of action on the price of the article over the whole competitive area. If "employer" were substituted for labor organization in these proposals, such employer practices as exchange of wage information, use of a common consulting service, discussion at employer meetings, or even casual conversation or correspondence would presumably be considered illegal if they resulted in two or more companies (of any size or in separate communities) adopting any particular wage, hour, or other labor policy.

This type of recommendation is radical in the extent to which it would alter the character and structure of labor unions as they have existed here and abroad for as long as one hundred and fifty years. National unions would presumably become ineffectual federations, leaving the labor movement top-heavy with loose associations—some one hundred and sixty present national unions in addition to the existing duplicate sets of national, state, and local (A.F. of L. and C.I.O.) federations. Craft unions would be most severely affected, since they are organized by occupation rather than employer; even some existing craft and industrial locals would have to be divided.[69] Without a thoroughgoing breakup of industrial combinations and large companies, this sort of proposal seems neither logical nor defensible. There may be little more reason for unions to be cut up according to the odd conglomeration of activities in many of the multiplant companies than there would be for companies to be confined to

[68] In addition to congressional bills and discussion see, e.g., Raleigh W. Stone, "Trade Unionism in a Free Economy," *University of Chicago Law Review*, XIV (April, 1947), pp. 406–7.

[69] See Senator Wayne Morse's remarks in *Congressional Record*, XCIII (80th Cong., 1st sess. [May 7, 1947]), 4798.

the jurisdiction of individual national or local unions. A union limited to the operations of one employer or a few small employers in one community might be too small or distorted for economical and effective operation.

The consequences of such a proposal would not be what proponents indicate. It would foster union rivalry, instability in labor relations, and irresponsibility in organized labor. National unions generally are a restraining influence on local unions, because their officers are farther removed from the scene of conflict, have a broader and longer-run point of view, are more aware of the lessons of past experience, and are more interested in conserving strike funds and retaining their union jobs. To destroy the responsibility of the parent organization, to increase the number of independent unions in manufacturing by five hundred to a thousand times, and to have labor negotiations and changes in the terms of employment occurring in an industry all the time would serve to increase the confusion and turmoil, the labor unrest, the amount of industrial conflict, and the time lost from strikes. Also, compulsory independence of policy-determination would retard the spread of labor practices that the experience of one or more companies showed to be beneficial. In addition, there would be the unfavorable effects on labor relations resulting from the disruption of existing relationships and the bitterness engendered by dissolution of national unions and enforced segregation of the pieces.

It is not clear which of the various meanings of "labor monopoly" the proponents of this type of legislation have in mind as their target. Since the labor market is a local market, confining collective bargaining and policy determination to one "labor-market area" would

not necessarily prevent monopoly in that market, either on the demand or on the supply side. Limitation of the bargaining and collective action to an individual firm might seem to reduce the possibility of monopoly if the industry is not dominated by one or a few large firms and the number of firms is not decreasing. However, individual-firm bargaining favors the large company and may help to reduce the number of firms in existence. To prevent small companies in an industry from gaining the advantages of joint action in collective bargaining (except when they happen to be located in the same community) is to discourage the existence of small companies by exposing them both to pattern-setting in labor matters by the large concerns without consideration of the interest of the smaller firms and to the threat of strike action against one small company at a time. It has been to avoid such weak and unsatisfactory positions that many employers have resorted to multi-employer bargaining, which has been especially prevalent in industries characterized by a hundred or more small firms, with no one firm having as much as 5 per cent of the industry's total output, such as men's and ladies' clothing, women's hosiery, and cotton textiles.

Industry-wide shut-downs have often taken place in industries in the absence of multiple-employer bargaining and can readily occur through the spreading of a strike, regardless of the area included in a single negotiation. Indeed, the manufacturing industries subject to national and regional collective bargaining have been notably free from crippling strikes during the past decade, and some of them have had no authorized strikes since national or regional bargaining was instituted.

The proposal to compel local or company-wide independence of bargaining and union policy raises serious practical problems. The employer unit of organization is especially objectionable where employment is characteristically of short duration, as in the building and maritime industries and in some canning operations.

Even more difficult would be the problems of effective enforcement. To prevent national unions from playing any role in union policy formulation or determination and to compel independence of union policy by company or community, it would presumably be necessary to make it an "unfair labor practice" or illegal for national union officials to make statements on union policy or to print suggestions for union demands, if the granting or withholding of the use of the national union's support, insignia, funds, or favors were implied in any way. Therefore, enforcement would seem to require significant curtailments of freedom of speech and the press as well as a marked degree of government intervention in the internal affairs of unions. If national officials were trying to bring pressure upon an official or officials of an affiliated local in favor of some policy, the local officials would usually be the only ones directly cognizant of that fact. But they might hesitate to complain, for example, for fear that their progress within the union would be jeopardized thereby. Would the National Labor Relations Board or some other government agency attempt to prevent—for an *indefinite period* through an injunction or cease-and-desist order—the national union from withdrawing its charter to the local, or the national officials from discriminating against a complaining official in promotion? If so, how could the Board assure the complaining official that his opportunities to elective or ap-

pointive office in the national union were fully protected at all times? Such questions indicate the real practical difficulties facing any attempt to enforce decentralization of national unions and local autonomy within a political organization that is part of a labor movement, with its own loyalties, traditions, and codes of conduct.

Some union officials have urged enforced "union democracy" and "systematic decentralization of power and devolution of function," reducing the power of top officials of national unions by increasing rank-and-file control.[70] To attempt through legislative enactment and enforcement to control the operation of unions, or even the frequency and nature of elections to union office, would, however, involve governmental interference in the internal affairs of unions that could hardly be justified as an antimonopoly measure. To promote a broad outlook instead of narrow economic interests and stress on short-run advantages of single unions, Professor Sumner Slichter urges a shift of power and influence from national unions to the two great federations.[71] He does not, however, propose legislation for that purpose.

VI. SOME OBSERVATIONS

No doubt it would be desirable to reduce the power and control at the top of a number of large national unions and spread some of it both downward to the locals and upward to the national federations. With all the centralizing forces in our economy as well as within national unions, such a spread of power seems unlikely to occur on any scale, however, in

[70] See, e.g., Herberg, *op. cit.*, pp. 24, 25; *Hearings on S. 55 and S.J. Res. 22*, Part III, pp. 1596–97 and 1625.

[71] *Op. cit.*, pp. 175–76.

the absence of governmental influence directed to that purpose.

Certain provisions of the Labor Management Relations Act of 1947 are likely to reduce the possibility of unity of action and control by one national union over a whole industry. A larger number of national unions will undoubtedly be established in particular industries as a result of Section 9 (b) of the act, which favors the certification of separate craft units for collective bargaining within an industry, even though an industrial union now covers all the workers in individual plants. Section 8 (b) makes it an unfair labor practice for a union to "coerce an employer in the selection of his representatives" or to use the strike or boycott in order to force an employer to join any employer organization and also for a union "to refuse to bargain collectively with an employer." In other words, unions cannot force employers into multiple-employer bargaining, nor can a local union refuse to bargain in good faith at the company or plant level concerning an issue on which the national union has already adopted a policy. In a "national emergency" strike, provision is made in Section 209 for a secret ballot of the employees of each employer on their employer's last offer of settlement. Although the employer-by-employer vote is not binding, it may serve to break up unity of action within a national union and to encourage local variation in policy and practice. The ban on the closed shop and on discrimination in employment under the union shop if expulsion from the union occurs for any reason other than nonpayment of dues and initiation fees (Section 8 [a]), reduces the power and control of unions over individual members.

Perhaps the most serious curtailment of the power of national unions contained in the Labor Management Relations Act of 1947 is the provisions in Sections 8 and 303 making it both an "unfair labor practice" and "unlawful"

for any labor organization to engage in, or to induce or encourage the employees of any employer to engage in, a strike or a concerted refusal in the course of their employment to use, manufacture, process, transport, or otherwise handle or work on any goods, articles, materials, or commodities or to perform any service, where an object thereof is . . . . forcing . . . . any employer or other person to cease using, selling, handling, transporting, or otherwise dealing in the products of any other producer, processor, or manufacturer, or to cease doing business with any other person.

Any person, whether an employer or not, who is injured in his business or property by such a boycott or sympathetic strike may sue for damages in any federal district court. These "boycott" provisions of the act, together with the provision for damage suits against labor organizations for violation of labor agreements in Section 301, may make it difficult for a national union, under certain sets of circumstances, to take common action against two or more employers concurrently.[72]

There is no question that large unions, as well as large corporations, present a problem in a democratic country with a market economy and a federal form of government. Seven national unions have from half a million to a million members, or two to four times the number of employees of our largest corporations. Unions are not subject to the same technical and economic limitations to size that apply to business organizations.

Concentration of power and influence in national unions has both internal and

---

[72] The wisdom or merits of these and other provisions of the Taft-Hartley Act is not discussed in this paper because of limitations of space and subject matter.

external aspects. It affects the distribution of power and control within the labor movement. It may also affect the nation's economy through restrictive provisions written into agreements and through influence on wage scales. Preceding sections have indicated that restrictive practices probably have been declining in general importance to the economy and that there has been little evidence of excessively high wage scales under national and regional bargaining. Nevertheless the spread of the area of common organization and combined action both horizontally (to cover other materials, methods, or products) and vertically (to cover the various industries or stages of production) does present real possibilities for affecting not only the basis of competition in a single industry or craft but over a number of competitive materials and industries.

Multi-industry unions present a question of balance between the social interest in limiting size and power and the interest of unions in self-preservation and effective operation. Increased size may increase the strength and power of a national union and, through diversification, serve to spread its risks. Amalgamation of two national unions may be justified temporarily on the grounds that otherwise the weaker union could not survive or continue as an effective and responsible organization. Admittedly the union's survival as an effective instrument may require coverage of practically the whole area of competitive production (which may include as much as all of an industry). But the burden of proof would seem to rest on a national union for extension of its coverage beyond that point. When John L. Lewis states that the United Mine Workers of America has membership in the coal-mining industry and "approximately some 115 other in-

dustries,"[73] the question naturally arises whether, from a public point of view, that is not about one hundred and fifteen industries too many.

Some restriction on the industrial spread of the national union not only might help to preserve competition between different materials and product groups by forestalling the imposition of undue restrictions or inordinate wage scales on a whole group of industries by a single union but also should serve to reduce interunion rivalry within the labor movement and domination of the movement by a few individuals heading large national unions.

Any legislation to restrict union mergers and to curtail the industrial spread of national unions would need to be drafted in broad terms with latitude for intelligent and understanding administration.[74] Multi-industry unionism may be justified by temporary conditions within unions, by the nature of an industry including the area of competitive production and industrial spread of firms, by shifts in the structure of industry, by the degree of independence existing between departments or divisions of the union, or by other circumstances.

The immediate need is not for more hasty, "shot-gun" labor legislation but for more understanding and informed thought on the problem of union organization and the appropriate area of collective bargaining and union action. Already we suffer from a plethora of naïve proposals for regulating unions, based on false conceptions of labor markets and of labor organizations.

PRINCETON UNIVERSITY

---

[73] *Hearings on S. 55 and S.J. Res. 22*, Part IV, p. 1984.

[74] Space limitations necessitated the omission of a specific proposal outlined in the first draft of this paper.

THE CHANGING CHARACTER
OF AMERICAN INDUSTRIAL RELATIONS

By Sumner H. Slichter

I

Three times since the turn of the century a major effort has been made to induce American employers voluntarily to base their labor policy upon the recognition of trade unions and the acceptance of collective bargaining, and three times the attempt has failed.[1] The result has been the Wagner Act which not only prohibits employers from interfering with the organization of their workers but also imposes on employers the obligation to bargain with representatives of a proper bargaining unit. Thus the determination of the fundamental labor policy of American industry has been taken from employers and has been made a matter of public instead of private decision.[2] Although the Wagner Act may be amended in superficial respects, there are no signs that the country in the foreseeable future is likely to change the fundamental policy of the Act.[3]

The new public policy may be expected to have profound effects upon the labor movement, the operation of industry, the functioning of our econ-

[1] The first effort was made about 1898 to 1902 under the leadership of the National Civic Federation, Mark Hanna, and other business leaders. The second effort was made by President Wilson in the fall of 1919. His Industrial Conference endeavored to develop into a form acceptable to business and labor alike the principles of employer-employee relations temporarily accepted during the war. It failed because the representatives of business insisted upon the right of employers to start company unions. The third effort was represented by Section 7a of the National Recovery Act which sought to pledge employers to the principle of noninterference with the organization of their workers. Note that in 1926 the employers and unions in the railroad industry did succeed in agreeing upon the terms of a fundamental labor policy for the industry. The result was the Railway Labor Act of 1926.

[2] Small wonder that this attempt to change by act of Congress some of the most firmly established mores of American industry has been difficult to administer. The Wagner Act, however, has been enforced with surprising effectiveness.

[3] Underlying the change in public policy is the change in the composition of the working force of American industry. Immigration has virtually ceased. At the same time the number of high school graduates has increased twenty-five fold since 1890. Indeed, slightly more than half of the children in this country now complete a high school education and almost all of them have two or three years in high school. Such workers may or may not desire to form unions, but they are quite insistent that they may be permitted to have unions in case they wish them. It outrages their sense of justice when the employer discharges some one because he tries to form a union. Evidence of the change in community sentiment on this point is found in the statements of policy of many employers asserting that the management will not discriminate against any employee for joining a union. Such statements are found in many employee representation plans adopted in the period 1918 to 1920. It was the failure of business in general, however, to perceive the change in public opinion and its persistent effort to enforce a labor policy of which the public disapproved that eventually led the government to take the determination of the fundamental labor policy of American industry out of the hands of employers and to make it a matter of public policy.

omy, and even upon our political institutions.[4] It is not my purpose, however, to explore the probable consequences of collective bargaining, because these will depend upon the policies that are pursued by each side.
The immediate problem that confronts us is one of making collective bargaining work. Collective bargaining has two principal aspects. First, it is
a method of introducing civil rights into industry; that is, of requiring that
management be conducted by rule rather than by arbitrary decision. Second,
it is a method of price fixing—fixing the price of labor. The problem of
making it work, therefore, may be defined as the problem (1) of introducing civil rights into industry, and (2) of fixing the price of labor in such
a manner as to increase the national income—or at least so as not to retard
its increase. That is the problem to which I invite your attention.

II

The introduction of civil rights into industry raises two principal problems: (1) the preservation of a proper balance between the employer's freedom to manage his plant and the protection of workers from arbitrary
management; (2) the avoidance of rules which become obsolete. If the
management is given too much freedom, hostile employers may take advantage of it to destroy the union. If the management is too severely restricted in rewarding efficiency or in discarding old methods of production, collective bargaining becomes a method of protecting the old against
the new, of retarding technological change, and of protecting vested interests in obsolete methods. Thus it becomes a method of keeping down the
standard of living. Railroading is a conspicuous illustration of an industry
in which changes in the location of plant, the type of equipment, and
methods of operation have been substantially restricted by the terms of trade
agreements and union-sponsored statutes. Many of these restrictions are
easily defended, but let anyone who doubts the seriousness of some of them
note the obstacles (some imposed by statute and some by trade agreement)
which confront railroads which wish to combine terminals, to pool traffic,
or to meet truck competition by running shorter, faster, or lighter trains,
or by having road crews perform yard service. The history of collective
bargaining in this country is full of instances of unions, such as the old
window glass workers, the cigarmakers, or the upholstery weavers, which

[4] It may, for example, compel the labor movement to abandon its traditional policy of
awarding exclusive jurisdiction over particular groups of workers to a given union and to
adopt the policy of the British Trade Union Congress that no union has the exclusive right
to organize any class of workers. Depending upon the nature of the working rules adopted,
it may enhance or diminish the ability of industry to adapt itself to changes in conditions.
Depending upon whether a good or bad job is done in setting the price of labor, it may
either diminish or increase the volume of unemployment and, therefore, raise or lower
the standard of living. Finally, it may be either a bulwark or a threat to democratic institutions. By spreading democratic habits of thought into industry, it may broaden the
acceptance of the democratic way of life. On the other hand, by retarding the expansion of
industry, it may impair the very foundations upon which political democracy rests.

destroyed themselves or made themselves weak by imposing excessive restrictions upon employers.

There are several reasons why trade agreements in American industry have tended to develop into long and complicated documents which, in the course of time, were bound to contain many obsolete rules. The most important one has been the fear of the men that the employer would destroy their unions by discriminating against its most active members— a natural result of the great organizing difficulties experienced by unions in this country. Consequently, unions have felt it necessary to restrict the employer's discretion at every point where he might discriminate. A second reason for complicated agreements has been the lack of effective managerial control of department heads, with the result that favoritism rather than efficiency has determined many promotions and layoffs. A third reason has been the tendency of some employers to keep unions weak by making it difficult for them to get prompt and satisfactory adjustment of grievances. In some instances, this failure has led employers to deny redress where the agreement contained no specific rule governing the issue. A fourth reason for detailed and complicated agreements has been the attempt of unions to meet technological and market changes by sponsoring make-work rules rather than pursuing a policy of adjustment. The primary effect of a policy of restriction is to promote the security of the group, but the secondary effect is to undermine security of the group. Hence, in a rapidly changing world real security is only achieved by pursuing a policy of adjustment. Nevertheless, it is natural that some unions (particularly inexperienced ones) should base their policies upon the immediate rather than the long-run interests of their members.

There is danger that instead of profiting from the mistakes of the past we shall repeat these mistakes on a larger scale. Most of the new unions are deeply concerned over their existence and must fight hard for restrictions upon discrimination by employers. Furthermore, the new agreements are being developed rapidly and usually with little understanding by either side that in settling specific issues they are unwittingly settling matters of basic policy. Indeed, many new agreements are more complicated and elaborate than agreements (such as those in the glass bottle or the flint glass industry) which have been in existence for fifty years. The tendency toward elaborate agreements is well illustrated by the recent development of seniority rules. Among 387 predepression agreements, seniority rules were found in only 117; but among 300 agreements made since 1933, seniority rules were found in 171. Let me assure you that it is not an accident that strong unions such as the United Mine Workers, the flint glass workers, the molders, the glass bottle blowers, the potters, the women's garment workers, or the men's clothing workers, have made little or no use of seniority.[5]

[5] In these samples, agreements from the building trades were excluded because it was known that they almost never contained regulations of layoff procedure.

It is not an exaggeration, however, to say that at the present time virtually no one either inside the labor movement or out of it knows very much about seniority, particularly when applied to factory industries. The only safe procedure is to develop policies by the case method.[6]

A few unions, such as the Amalgamated Clothing Workers, the hosiery workers, and the Steel Workers' Organizing Committee, have made the maintenance of short, simple, and flexible agreements a matter of definite union policy. The leaders of these organizations understand that they can protect the security of their members in a rapidly changing world only by pursuing a policy of adjustment and that elaborate and detailed agreements hinder the pursuit of a policy of adjustment. Curiously enough, however, thinking on this matter seems to be much farther advanced among unions than among employers. Indeed, few employers seem to have made the promotion of simplicity and flexibility in trade agreements a definite objective.

What policies are indicated if trade agreements are to be kept short, simple, and flexible and if workers are to be protected against arbitrary management by the administrative method of settling individual cases as they arise in the light of particular facts rather than by the legislative method of spelling out rules in advance? First, let the employer eliminate the issue of union status, either by encouraging membership in the trade union or by granting the closed shop. To most American employers the "closed shop" is a symbol for union domination. As a matter of fact, the employer is likely to have more freedom in a closed shop or its equivalent than in one where the union is uncertain of its status.[7] Instructive on this point is an analysis of the restrictions on layoffs in 300 agreements of which 173 provided for a closed shop and 127 for the open shop. Among the open shop agreements 109, or 85.8 per cent, restricted the employer's freedom to make layoffs but only 93, or 53.7 per cent, of the closed shop agreements contained similar restrictions. Second, let the management develop effective control over the decisions of secondary executives for the purpose of assuring that these decisions are either based upon objective facts or, where judg-

---

[6] Most employers, for example, at present are strongly in favor of departmental seniority rules. The day will come when these employers will wish that they had never restricted the flexibility of their operations by surrounding each department with a seniority wall. Many unions, which think that they are protecting their existence by seniority rules, have adopted these rules in such unqualified form as to threaten the life of the union. Observe that where frequent violent fluctuations of employment occur, as in the highly seasonal garment industries, seniority has the effect of dividing the workers into two groups—those which bear the full burden of unemployment and those which have steady work at the expense of the others. This is one reason why unions in seasonal industries have found it necessary to avoid seniority rules except in a severely restricted form—as when dealing with the problem of overcrowded sections or considering permanent layoffs for other reasons.

[7] In the latter, the union must view with extreme suspicion every decision which favors a nonmember as against a member. When all employees are members, the union's interest in the employer's decisions becomes of substantially less importance.

ment is unavoidable, upon carefully reviewed judgment. This will require substantially better records of individual employee performance than have been customary under nonunion conditions. Third, let managements plan technological changes well in advance and introduce them gradually. Fourth, let both sides do a good job of setting the price of labor. One source of make-work and restrictive rules has been the attempt of unions to provide work for men who have lost their jobs because their labor has been improperly priced. Fifth, let both sides develop union-management co-operation for the purpose of keeping costs in union plants from becoming too high in relation to costs in nonunion plants. Excessive costs in union plants which produce unemployment among union members are another source of make-work and restrictive rules. Finally, let managements take particular care that unions are satisfied that the administrative method gives them an adequate opportunity to get their cases heard and to protect the interests of their members. Arrangements for adjusting differences are more important than the specific rules in trade agreements, and agreements cannot be kept simple unless the machinery for adjusting cases works smoothly.[8]

III

Collective bargaining is a form of price fixing—a way of fixing the price of labor. It introduces a revolutionary change in the relationship between employment and the price of labor. Employment must adjust itself to the price of labor rather than the price of labor to employment. With five or six million men in trade unions, collective bargaining represents price fixing on a scale large enough to have important repercussions upon our economy. By skillful pricing of labor we can add to employment and production; by unskillful pricing, we can substract from employment and production. It is probable that the pressure of unions for higher wages will accelerate technological change. It is probably inevitable that collective bargaining will produce some maldistribution of resources. It is probable, but not certain, that collective bargaining will limit investment opportunities. Whether collective bargaining at the end of a given period has raised or lowered the standard of living will depend upon whether its tendency to accelerate technological change has offset (1) its tendency to produce some maldistribution of resources and (2) its possible tendency to limit the volume of investment. The subsequent discussion will deal with these two topics.

I have said that collective bargaining may be expected to produce some

[8] Notice the bearing that all of this has upon the proposal, frequently made by employers' associations, that trade agreements be made enforcible by law. The step has already been taken in this country with respect to agreements on the railroads. It is, I believe, a backward step. It takes away from the parties the right to interpret their own agreement and places this responsibility in a court of law. Thus the parties are hampered in adjusting the interpretation of their agreements to changes in industrial conditions.

maldistribution of resources, but examination of the marketing policies of trade unions suggests that this maldistribution has been greater than it need be. There are three principal reasons for this belief: (1) the tendency of many trade unions to underestimate the elasticity in the demand for labor; (2) their failure to determine carefully the effect of wage differentials in union and nonunion plants upon the demand for union labor; and (3) the failure of some unions to adjust wages to changes in markets and technology.

Most unions assume that they can raise wages by moderate amounts with little or no effect upon employment. They are probably right, provided a short enough time is taken into consideration. There are several reasons, however, for concluding that the plant demand for labor is quite elastic when periods of several years are involved.[9] One is competition between the old and the new—the most pervasive form of competition in our economy and the one most completely neglected in economic treatises.[10] A second is the ever growing pervasiveness of product competition.[11] A third is the rise of large buyers among both retailers and manufacturers who purchase to their own specifications from the lowest bidder (often doing the development work on the product themselves). In competition for the business of such buyers small differences in costs are of decisive importance. A fourth is the rapid spread of organized industrial research with its tendency to increase the elasticity of substitution both between products and between factors of production.[12] As the technical schools turn out an increasing number of better trained men, the elasticity of substitution will continue to increase.

[9] As a matter of fact, there is undoubtedly a marked difference in the elasticity in the demand for most products with the lapse of relatively short periods of time. This fact has not been adequately recognized by business enterprises and, consequently, has not affected selling policies as much as it should.

[10] The competition between the old and the new is not confined to industrial equipment or other durable goods. The NRA discovered that old hair cuts were in competition with new hair cuts and that if the price was put above fifty cents, people let their hair grow longer. The NRA also discovered that a dirty suit competed with a clean suit and that if the price of cleaning were substantially raised, suits are cleaned much less frequently. Old cars compete with new cars, old furniture with new furniture, old houses with new houses, and an old coat of paint on a house with a new coat. If one is particular about the appearance of his house, he may have it painted every four years, but sufficient protection is usually achieved if it is painted about every six—a great difference in the demand for painting.

[11] Paper containers compete with wood, cotton, burlap, glass; aluminum competes with steel and copper; wood competes with concrete, brick, stone, and other materials; plaster competes with ply-wood and wallboard; letter press printing competes with other types of printing some of which are making heavy inroads upon it; coal competes with oil; trucks and buses with railroads. Numerous durable consumers goods compete with each other for the eight to twelve billion dollars a year that consumers spend on durable goods.

[12] Elasticity of substitution is usually defined in terms of constant technology and refers simply to the changes in the proportions with which factors of production are combined when their relative prices change. I am using the expression above in a very different sense to mean the capacity of industry to change the proportions in which products or factors are used by making technological changes in response to changes in price relationships.

When trade unions underestimate the elasticity in the demand for labor, the handicap imposed on union employers and hence the unemployment among union members are greater than they otherwise would be.[13] Ultimately the unemployment of men attached to union plants will cause some of them to drift into the nonunion part of the industry and unemployment will take the form of capital unemployment in union plants rather than labor unemployment. At any rate, the ultimate result of the union's mistake in judging the elasticity of the demand for labor will be to aggravate the tendency for collective bargaining to produce maldistribution of resources.

A special case of the general tendency of unions to underestimate the elasticity of the demand for labor is the failure of many unions to determine carefully the effect of wage differentials between union and nonunion plants upon the volume of employment in union plants.[14] The differentials in terms of labor cost are usually not as large as differentials in wages because the high union wage scales tend to attract superior workmen and union employers cannot afford to retain inferior men. Because the withdrawal of capital from an industry involves cost, one must distinguish between the rate that will attract new capital and the rate that will cause the indefinite maintenance and replacement of capital already invested. Most unions have failed to determine the critical differential in labor costs beyond which capital leaves the union part of the industry.[15]

Some large differentials between union and nonunion plants are the result, not of union policy, but of the efforts of employers to defeat union organizing campaigns. As a general rule, however, they are a result of the fact that the bargaining power of most unions is greater than their organiz-

[13] This raises the question of whose income collective bargaining is expected to maximize—the income of the entire union (or group of unions) or only the income of the working majority of the bargaining group. The question is discussed below.
[14] Two situations may be distinguished in the relation of union to nonunion wage scales. One is the case where the union scale governs the nonunion scale rather completely. The other is the case, and it has been the usual one, in which the union is so remote or so weak that nonunion wages are relatively independent of union ones.
[15] Between 1915 and 1920, the tapestry carpet weavers in Philadelphia acquired control of that market and pushed up their wages by about 165 per cent. At the height of its prosperity in 1920, the union had about 1,800 members. It was believed that the union mills could stand a differential of 10 or 15 per cent above the nonunion, but the differential grew until it became about 50 per cent. By 1926, the union had only 800 members working in Philadelphia and more than half the union mills had ceased operating. In 1920, the union part of the bituminous coal industry produced nearly 60 per cent of the bituminous output. The union endeavored to maintain a basic wage of $7.50 a day. Nonunion mines were paying from 30 to 50 per cent less. By 1927, the union mines were producing only 40 per cent of the output. In 1922, the hosiery workers' union controlled 90 per cent of the market. Union wages during the twenties rose to roughly double nonunion. By 1929, union control had shrunk to 30 per cent. Thanks to the NRA, the Wagner Act, and skillful organizing campaigns, the union control is now back to 70 per cent. During the last several years it has been threatened by the rapid growth of the industry in the South where wages have been about 30 per cent lower and where three-fourths of the new machines installed during the last seven or eight years have gone. The union has recently taken steps to meet southern competition by accepting wage reductions in return for an agreement by the employers to purchase up-to-date machinery.

ing power.[16] Many large differentials are the result of temporary bulges in demand. The union takes advantage of the bulge to push up its rates substantially. After the demand has subsided or after production facilities have caught up with the demand, the union is reluctant to cut its rates and the drop in nonunion rates creates a dangerously large differential. Some of the differentials which proved so disastrous to unions during the twenties were the result of high rates bargained during the War which the unions were unwilling to adjust to the lower level of prices and wages that followed the drop in War demand.[17] The large differentials in the hosiery industry were the result of style changes which almost overnight produced an enormous jump in the demand for full-fashioned hose. Excessive differentials may be the result of failure to adjust union piece rates to increases in productivity. If rates in nonunion plants are cut, the difference may become dangerously large. Examples of this kind of differential are found in the flint glass industry, shoe industry, and hosiery industry.[18]

The first remedy for excessive differentials always proposed by the unions is organization of the nonunion plants in the industry. When the plant demand schedule for labor is elastic, the differential may enable workers in nonunion plants to earn more than workers in union plants and thus may be a serious obstacle to union organization. The lamp chimney department of the flint glass workers union experienced this difficulty in acute form. The first remedy for excessive differentials which employers suggest is wage reductions in union plants. This procedure often fails because nonunion plants counter with offsetting cuts.[19] There are techniques, however, particularly in piece working industries, by which union rates can be reduced without provoking counter-reductions in nonunion plants. Differences in wages do not inevitably mean differences in labor costs. A few unions have attempted to reduce the disadvantages of union plants by helping management improve efficiency. The hosiery workers have employed this method in the seamless hosiery industry, the Amalgamated Clothing Workers have used it extensively, and now the Steel Workers' Organizing Committee is using it. In fact, the Steel Workers' Organizing Committee is helping some employers reduce costs who got themselves into competitive difficulties by raising wages in an attempt to keep out the union!

Once unions achieve a given wage rate, they have a strong tendency to cling to it however much markets and technology may change. The anthracite miners have maintained their 1923 scale while the sales of an-

[16] Note that excessive differentials are almost inevitable in case the union underestimates the elasticity of the demand for the labor of its members.

[17] The differentials between the union and nonunion parts of the bituminous coal industry are an example.

[18] In the hosiery industry most of the rates which had been rendered out of line by changes in conditions have been eliminated.

[19] The nonunion employer may use the fact that the union workers had consented to a cut as a reason why the nonunion workers must accept a corresponding cut.

thracite have dropped almost in half. The railroad unions have actually raised wage scales while railroad traffic was falling in half. Perhaps these unions were pursuing a sensible marketing policy from the standpoint of their members. Their officers might argue in each instance that the price of the product and *pro tanto* the price of labor had little to do with the decline of sales. These extreme cases of price rigidity in the face of violent market changes, however, raise two principal questions: (1) are the union members being guided by future as well as present considerations—in other words are they underestimating the long-run elasticity in the demand for labor; and (2) whose income is the union intended to maximize—the income of all members regarded as an entity or simply the incomes of a majority. Many cases of rigid wages simply reflect the fact that union members do not know that their long-run interests conflict with their short-run. Hence they do not attempt to determine whether wage cuts today might substantially retard the decline in employment. Of particular interest is the question of whose income the union is trying to maximize—the income of all the members or only the income of a majority. If the union is attempting to maximize the income of all its members, then wage reductions in the face of technological and market changes would often be indicated because men with specialized skill will earn more at reduced rates at their customary occupations than in new jobs. If, on the other hand, unions simply undertake to maximize the income of a controlling majority of their members, they become organizations by which some workers exploit other workers.

IV

Most momentous of all is the question of the effect of collective bargaining upon the demand for investment funds. I shall discuss this question under the heads of the effect of collective bargaining upon (1) technological change; (2) the propensity to consume; (3) the relations between costs and selling prices; (4) the relation between the prices of capital goods and other goods; and (5) the adjustment of the price of labor to cyclical changes in business. The discussion will necessarily be suggestive rather than exhaustive.

The great pressure which collective bargaining puts on wages will tend to accelerate technological change so long as collective bargaining does not extend to research workers and does not, therefore, tend to raise the cost of discovery. It is reasonable also to assume that pressure for higher wages will encourage laborsaving rather than capital saving inventions and thus will facilitate the absorption of savings by industry.[20] About 57 per cent

---

[20] Observe, however, that several special influences, such as the rapid rate of technological change itself and certain changes in markets (particularly the rise of large buyers who may switch large orders from one producer to another), are encouraging capital saving inventions. The possibility of losing the account of a mail order house or automobile company in a year or two compels producers to show a lively interest in ways of keeping down the capital required to produce a given article.

of the employment and half of the pay rolls in American industry outside of railroads and agriculture are in approximately 1,700,000 concerns employing less than 400 workers. Nearly all of these enterprises are too small to perform their own research, and outside facilities for giving them research service are far from adequate. Since the pressure which collective bargaining is bound to create for higher wages makes industrial research more imperative than ever, perhaps the state universities can make research available to the small concerns by offering it at cost.

Efforts to raise the propensity to consume by increasing the price of labor and encroaching upon profits seem to reduce the propensity to invest even more than the propensity to save. This is inevitable because otherwise the previous situation would not have been one of equilibrium. The best opportunity to raise the propensity to consume in such a manner as to increase the propensity to invest is by keeping the prices of personal services and of durable consumers goods relatively low.[21] The demand for these goods seems to be elastic and they are purchased in large measure with funds that would otherwise be saved. About 30 per cent of the saving in the community is done by persons with incomes of less than $10,000 a year and nearly half by persons with incomes of less than $25,000 a year.[22] It is impossible to predict whether collective bargaining will be conducted so as to keep the prices of personal services and of durable consumers goods relatively low. In an economy in which collective bargaining was quite prevalent, wages might be expected to vary with the bargaining power of the several groups of employers and the several groups of wage earners. Bargaining power may be defined as the cost to one party of imposing a loss on the other. Cost to the group of wage earners would include to a rather indefinite extent

---

[21] Mr. Keynes seems to think about reducing the propensity to consume simply in terms of taxing the very rich (*The General Theory of Employment, Interest, and Money*, pp. 372-74). He does not visualize the important competition between durable consumers goods and savings. Unless the taxes on very large incomes are very carefully devised, they have repercussions which Mr. Keynes has overlooked. Investment opportunities are created by pioneering—by men who put funds into new products and new processes and demonstrate their profitability. This actual demonstration that new products can be made at a profit or new processes are practical is necessary to attract more timid capital. Hence, the pioneering type of investment may be regarded as opening up investment opportunities. It is obviously of particular importance to encourage rather than discourage the pioneering type of investment. The persons who are best able to undertake the riskiest type of investment are the persons with very large incomes and it is from such incomes in the past that a large part of pioneering investment funds have come. Very heavy taxes, however, on high incomes are likely to cause the very persons who are best able to take risks to shift from risky to safe ventures. Thus the heavy taxes which Mr. Keynes advocates are likely to reduce, not merely the volume of savings, but, even more, the opportunities to invest. The oversight is a natural one for Mr. Keynes to make because his entire analysis is worked out in a framework that visualizes static technology—a convenient simplification, but, after all, a shocking limitation in a work that purports to offer a general theory of employment. When very high tax rates are imposed on incomes in the higher brackets, a differential should be made between income from interest and income from dividends with substantially lower tax rates upon income from dividends. Furthermore, pioneering capital should be encouraged by liberal loss carry-over provisions in the income tax law. A new venture is likely to be in the "red" for from two to five years after its beginning.

[22] See the estimates of M. Ezekiel, *Review of Economic Statistics*, Nov., 1937, pp. 178-91.

the unemployment that might follow an increase in wages. Hence when the product is elastic in demand (as in the case of durable consumers goods), the union might be restrained by the fear of unemployment from pushing up the price of labor very far. As I have indicated above, however, two difficulties stand in the way of accepting this conclusion. One is that trade unions seem to underestimate the elasticity of the demand for the services of their members—just as most employers under conditions of monopolistic competition put the price of their products too high. A second is that the majority of the union may not care whether a minority is unemployed, provided the minority is not dangerously large.

Will collective bargaining raise operating costs so high as to restrict the utilization of present equipment and to narrow the outlook for profits and restrict the demand for investment funds? So long as collective bargaining is far from covering all of industry and is growing slowly, union wage policy may open up large and attractive investment opportunities in the nonunion parts of industry. At the cost of considerable duplication of plant, therefore, collective bargaining may substantially increase investment and employment. Let us assume, however, that collective bargaining becomes so prevalent that union wage policy determines the general wage level. The productivity of a large proportion of the working population of the United States is substantially less than the present union wage scales in the several occupations. Indeed, precisely here we have a large part of the explanation of the somewhat surprising success of union plants in holding their own against nonunion plants—union plants, as pointed out above, can attract superior workmen and cannot afford to keep inferior men. Hence, unions tend to become devices by which superior workers enforce differentials for their efficiency.[23] Because of this very condition, however, an attempt to apply present union wage scales to a very large proportion of industry would have disastrous results.[24]

Mr. Keynes and his followers would disagree with this statement. They argue that MV may be depended upon to translate changes in the price of labor into changes in the prices of finished goods and to keep the volume of output unchanged subject only to the effect of changes in MV upon the rate of interest. I have tried without success to persuade myself to accept this comfortable conclusion. Suppose that there is a general increase in the price of labor. There is no reason to expect an instantaneous change in MV

[23] As a matter of fact, if the evidence of existing wage scales and profit statements mean anything, a surprisingly large proportion of the workers do not produce as much as fifty cents worth of goods per hour. This, of course, is not necessarily the fault of the employees. It represents in part the scarcity of managerial ability and in part the fact that the amount of capital per worker in American industry is still quite small—not much above $4,000 per worker in industry as a whole. The fact, nevertheless, remains that a very large part of the workers have a productivity of less than fifty cents an hour and many of them a productivity of considerably less.

[24] The case of piece work scales is somewhat different, provided these scales do not include a time rate guarantee.

sufficient to translate the higher price of labor into correspondingly higher prices of finished goods, because businessmen feel higher costs before they experience a higher demand for goods. Hence it is reasonable to expect businessmen to curtail production pending at least a test of the higher prices made necessary by higher costs.[25] The Keynesians may argue, however, that an ultimate increase in MV will occur because at any volume of output less than the original one, the community will attempt to invest more than it saves. If this were not so, the original position would not be one of equilibrium. It is true that if businessmen curtail production in response to the increase in the price of labor, incomes and, hence, the propensity to save would be reduced. But it does not follow (as the Keynesians assume) that investment opportunities would be reduced less than the propensity to save. Investment opportunities are partly determined by physical volume of production and this has been reduced. They are also determined by the relationship between cost schedules and income. Cost schedules have been raised, but incomes have been little changed.[26] Hence it is quite possible that investment opportunities may be reduced even more than the propensity to save and that still further contraction of production is necessary before equilibrium is reached. This is not inconsistent with the fact that the economy may have been in equilibrium before a general increase in wages occurred, because that equilibrium was predicated upon the (then) existing cost schedules, and labor cost schedules were raised by the general increase in the price of labor.

More important than these logical difficulties is the appeal to experience, because, after all, in discussing MV, we are dealing not merely with a quantity in an equation but with the behavior of human beings. Between 1929 and 1937, wage rates in the United States increased about 21 per cent in manufacturing and about 10 or 15 per cent in other branches of industry. In the same period the price level of finished goods dropped 10 per cent. The real change in the price of labor is uncertain because the change in labor efficiency is not known. That it was not sufficient to offset the changes in wages and prices is indicated by the state of profits. Even as late as 1936 scarcely two out of five of the 478,000 active corporations in the United States made any money. Indeed, corporate profits in 1936 were

[25] The businessman is not acting irrationally when he adopts a "wait-and-see" attitude because he knows that consumer resistance to higher prices even in the face of rising consumer incomes is a reality. Witness the experience of the United States in the latter part of 1936 and the early part of 1937. Between May, 1936, and April, 1937, the cost of living rose about 5.4 per cent, and nonagricultural labor income rose about 15 per cent. Despite the fact that labor incomes were outrunning the increase in prices, definite consumer resistance to the higher prices developed about the end of 1936. The New York Federal Reserve Bank's index of physical distribution to consumers reached its peak in December, 1936, and January, 1937. Thereafter, the index dropped. The event proved that any businessmen who may have accepted the Keynesian assumption that higher expenses are equivalent to a proportionate increase in demand were wrong.

[26] They may be slightly increased or even slightly decreased because a smaller volume of production is occurring at a higher price level.

substantially less than in 1924, a year of mild depression when the index of industrial production was 10 per cent below 1936. They were even lower than in 1922, another year of depression when the index of industrial production was 20 per cent below 1936.

Will collective bargaining seriously narrow the opportunities for investment by raising the prices of investment goods and thus reducing the marginal efficiency of capital? The danger of this does not appear serious in the case of industrial equipment. The demand for this seems to depend upon the businessman's judgment of the total business situation. Changes in his expectations cause violent shifts in his demand curve for capital goods but the curve at all times is pretty inelastic. Quite different, however, appears to be the case of residential building. There is a certain minimum demand for housing that is little affected by the prices of housing. After this minimum, the demand becomes increasingly sensitive to prices, and it is, of course, the elasticity of demand at the margin which counts. The building trades unions have seriously misjudged their market and are pursuing a price policy that is not only injuring their members but is substantially reducing the ability of private industry to absorb the savings of the community. Residential building is now at half the level of the twenties. The prices of building materials are 11 per cent below the levels of 1926, but union wage scales in the industry are nearly 5 per cent above 1926, the peak of the boom. In the face of this situation, union wage agreements in the building trades were raised 6 per cent in 1937, the largest annual increase since 1923. High labor costs have been only one of several obstacles to building, but the very existence of other obstacles is a reason why there should not be added to them the burden of a wage scale substantially above boom levels.[27] In 1937, residential building costs (according to the Boeckh index) were practically the same as in 1926. The prices of many durable goods, such as automobiles, refrigerators, and radios, were from 25 to 50 per cent below 1926. As a result, in 1926 the housing industry got about one out of every three dollars spent by consumers for durable goods, and in 1937, only one out of every seven dollars. Most important of all, however, the community was deprived of a major outlet for its savings.

Highly controversial is the question of the cyclical wage movements which will best maintain investment and employment. All economists probably would agree, however, that business stability is not promoted by a continued rise in wages after business has turned down. In the past, negotiators on both sides have often failed to take account promptly of the cyclical

[27] In the spring of 1937 the increases in union wage scales seem to have affected the wages actually paid residential building even though the union scale was often not paid. At the present time most of the building trades unions in most cities have priced themselves out of the private residential building market. In small housing operations, it is difficult for the employer-employee system to compete with the working contractor system.

movements of business. In 1930 union scales in the building industry rose 4.2 per cent above 1929. There was even a slight increase in building wages during 1931 over 1930! The experience in earlier depressions was similar. In 1908, for example, union wage scales in the building industry rose nearly 6 per cent above 1907. Union scales in book and job printing rose 12 per cent between 1920 and 1921. In the last depression they continued to rise until 1932, when they were 3.3 per cent above 1929. Union wage scales in general continued to rise well after the downturns of both 1920 and 1929. By June, 1937, the movement of raw material prices, demand deposits, and bond prices all indicated that a recession in business was at least probable. Wages, both union and nonunion, continued to rise throughout the summer and even well into the fall.

As a general rule, it may be assumed that unions discourage wage cuts in time of depression. The question of whether wage cuts aggravate or mitigate the severity of depressions breaks up into more parts than economists have been accustomed to assume.[28] At certain points where the demand for labor is instantaneously elastic, wage reductions are needed in times of depression in order to increase labor income and raise the propensity to consume. I have pointed out above that most forms of durable consumers goods seem to be elastic in demand and so also are many of the services which consumers are buying in rapidly growing quantities.[29] Expenditures for both durable consumers goods and services are, of course, competitive with savings. Here is a broad field, therefore, in which there is an opportunity to encroach upon savings and stabilize consumers' expenditures by making reductions in prices. Wage cuts to facilitate such price reductions would raise the propensity to consume and thus mitigate the severity of the depression. The case in favor of wage cuts may be broader than I have just indicated. Once a depression gets well started, the mere drop in incomes leads consumers to expect lower prices and to postpone buying until prices reach what the public regards as a proper level.[30] Under these circumstances, general cuts in wages may raise the propensity to consume.

When wage reductions are being made more or less simultaneously in a large number of plants, there is danger that they will produce a reaction

[28] To the makers of trade union policy the question of whether wage cuts aggravate or mitigate the severity of depressions may be of only academic interest. Only by accepting substantial wage cuts during the Great Depression was the Amalgamated Clothing Workers able to keep its employers in business and to obtain moderate employment for its members. Had the hosiery workers not accepted a 40 per cent wage cut in the fall of 1931, it is doubtful whether enough of the union would have survived to make the remarkable comeback that it achieved several years later.

[29] The expenditures of consumers on durable goods regularly run somewhat higher than the expenditures of all forms of industry on capital goods. Consumers' purchases of services are even larger. Expenditures on durable consumers goods and services together amount to more than 40 per cent of the total outlay by consumers.

[30] Note in this connection that inventory liquidation under pressure from maturing bank loans may have driven prices below reproduction costs but the public may strongly resist paying a higher price.

somewhat different from isolated cuts—that they will arouse an expectation of still further cuts and thus induce postponement of commitments. The effect of wage cuts upon the postponement of commitments depends upon how the cuts are made. Certainly there is more danger of a general postponement of commitments when sweeping cuts are announced by large corporations. Over two-thirds of the employment in American business, exclusive of railroading and agriculture, is in small concerns with less than 1,000 employees and more than half of it in concerns with less than 400 employees. Most of these enterprises can make cuts without producing general market effects. The timing of wage cuts is important. In seasonal industries it is possible to avoid a postponement of commitments by timing cuts to correspond with the seasonal upturns. Particularly important is the avoidance of general and sweeping wage changes. The system of payment by the piece lends itself to gradual but steady rate adjustments. Piece prices which are out of line may be changed and new lines and new operations may be priced on a somewhat lower level than the old, all with the result of appreciable reductions in labor costs without definite or sweeping decreases in rates. Finally, collective bargaining itself offer a way of making wages reductions without arousing expectations of an uncontrolled downward spiral.

Up to the present, there has been relatively little experimentation under collective bargaining with techniques for facilitating the adjustment of wages to changing conditions. Scattered efforts have been made to link wages to the cost of living or to the price of a commodity but none of these schemes, however satisfactory under the particular conditions of their operation, promises general usefulness. In 1921 a profit-sharing scheme was embodied in the collective agreement in the British bituminous coal industry. Though hailed by unions and employers alike as an epoch making achievement, one of its principal effects has been to breed friction as to the dividing line between profits and expenses. The growth of collective bargaining, however, is bound to compel the development of devices for introducing some element of contingency into wages and relating them to the ability of employers to pay. This might be achieved by making most wage changes take the form of temporary advances to or deductions from base rates. The addition or deduction would have a termination date before which continuation of the addition or deduction would be subject to negotiation. This procedure was followed in 1932 when temporary reductions were negotiated from base rates in the railroad industry. Certainly there is no reason in non-declining industries why the temporary necessity for lower labor costs should lead to changes in the base rates themselves. And since the average annual increase in per capita productivity is about 2 per cent, there is no reason why a temporary improvement in business should produce more than very small increases in base rates. Certainly there was no economic justification for permitting the temporary improvement in

1936 and 1937 to produce permanent increases of 10 to 15 per cent in the price of labor in many industries—increases which seem to have intensified the depression and impeded recovery.

V

What is the use of discussing the effect of collective bargaining upon the volume of employment? Are unions politically capable of considering the effect of their policies upon employment? Since they are democratic organizations, are they not bound to be devices by which the majority advances its interests quite regardless of the effect upon the minority and, above all, quite regardless of the effect upon the general economic situation?

I venture the opinion that considerable practical good may come of the exploration of the relationship of union policies to employment. In the first place, the fact that a given policy causes a minority to suffer does not necessarily mean that a majority is benefiting. The policy may reflect, not the exploitation of a minority by a majority, but simply the failure of the union leaders to formulate wise policies. Consider, for example, the efforts of some unions to protect their members against technological change by pursuing a policy of restriction rather than adjustment. When protection takes the form of permanent make-work rules, the ability of union employers to hold their own in competition with nonunion employers is impaired and a minority of the union members are thrown out of work without a corresponding gain to the majority. Indeed in the long run the majority itself is better protected by a policy of adjustment than by a policy of restriction. In the second place, whether the union is divided between a majority that is indifferent to the effects of union policies upon employment and a minority that bears the burden of unemployment depends upon how unemployment is distributed among the members. If it is concentrated by seniority rule among the junior members, the union may have little interest in employment problems. This goes far to explain the marketing policies of the railroad brotherhoods. On the other hand, if unemployment is spread thin among all members by limited equal-division-of-work, the union may be politically capable of interest in even a moderate degree of unemployment. In the third place, when the union members are keenly aware of their long-run as well as their short-run interests, the conflict between a majority not interested in unemployment and an exploited minority tends to disappear because in the long run the majority must consider the effect of union policies upon employment.

All in all one finds about the same differences in the marketing policies of trade unions as one does among corporations. At one extreme one finds the men's clothing workers and the hosiery workers with their sensitiveness to changes in markets and their willingness to adjust the price of labor to changes in demand. At the other extreme one finds the building trades and the railroad brotherhoods with little disposition to adjust the price of labor to conditions in the market—in fact with a tendency to buck the market and to put up the price of labor quite irrespective of demand. No one would assert that the first two unions do a poorer job of representing their members than the second group. In fact, most persons would probably agree that they do a better job. The difference simply is that the marketing policies of the first are more realistic and that in consequence they do a better job of selling labor. As trade unions gain more experience in selling labor, I venture the prediction that the successful marketing policies of the men's clothing workers and the hosiery workers will receive wider acceptance.

My discussion of our changing industrial relations has related solely to economic issues. In concluding, let me remind you that far more than economic issues are at stake. It is frequently said that political democracy cannot exist without industrial democracy. There is truth in the statement. It also is true that industrial democracy, if unwisely operated, may threaten the existence of political democracy. The basis for free institutions is economic opportunity, because it is opportunity that keeps social conflict mild, and only when social conflict is mild are men willing to settle their differences by voting, by negotiating, or by arbitrating rather than by fighting. The basis for opportunity is expansion. In the happy days of the nineteenth century one could rely upon the rapid expansion of industry to correct the mistakes of policy. Now we must rely upon wisdom in policy to encourage expansion. Whether the spread of collective bargaining helps or hinders the preservation of democratic institutions, will depend fundamentally upon whether it is so conducted as to encourage the expansion of industry.

ARE WE BECOMING A "LABORISTIC" STATE?

By Sumner H. Slichter

Few major transformations in the American community have occurred more rapidly than the rise of trade unions during the last fifteen years. The growth of unions means far more than the substitution of collective bargaining for individual bargaining. It means that the United States is gradually shifting from a capitalistic community to a laboristic one — that is, to a community in which employes rather than business men are the strongest single influence. A community in which employes are the principal influence will have its own ways of looking at things, its own scale of values, its own ideas on public policies, and, to some extent, its own jurisprudence. It will also have new and distinctive problems and its own ways of dealing with them. Hence, the rise of trade unions means that the United States stands on the threshold of major changes in its economic and political institutions.

I

Many people will deny that the United States is becoming a laboristic community. Trade union leaders in particular are inclined to question it. They are used to thinking of the country as the stronghold of capitalism and they point out that many persons who make policy today are not sympathetic with the aims of labor. It is true that on many matters of public policy employes have not developed a common and distinctive point of view. Perhaps on many matters they never will, because there are great differences in viewpoint among various groups of employes. There is no doubt, however, that on many issues employes are the most influential group in the community and that they are growing stronger. Today, the United States is virtually a nation of employes because three out of four persons who work for a living are on someone else's payroll. Employes outnumber stockholders about five to one.

The growing influence of employes is best shown by the steadily expanding labor legislation of the community. Some of this legislation, such as laws prescribing rules and standards to protect the safety and health of workers and workmen's compensation laws, has, of course, been in existence for over a generation.

With the rapid rise in union membership during the last fifteen years, the influence of employes has been increasing by leaps and bounds. It is manifested in the Social Security Act, in the Fair Labor Standards Act, and most conspicuously of all, in laws encouraging employes to organize to bargain over the price of labor. Any other sellers who combine to raise the price of their product commit a crime and are liable to fine or imprisonment.

The Taft-Hartley Act was in some respects a setback for labor but there is much evidence that on many points covered by this law the official position of unions did not represent the preferences of employes. At any rate, the act did not disturb the basic policy of encouraging employes to combine for the purpose of raising the price of their labor.

A recent development of great importance is the rise of community leaders from the ranks of labor. In the past the labor movement has produced only a few real community leaders — that is, men who have had influence far beyond the ranks of labor and whose ideas have pertained to matters other than questions of labor policy. Samuel Gompers, John Mitchell and Sidney Hillman are examples. Today, the participation of trade union officers in community affairs is spreading rapidly.

In scores of places, labor leaders are helping to direct Red Cross campaigns, Community Chest drives, Government savings bond drives. A few colleges and universities now have union officers among their regents or trustees. Some public corporations have directors who come from the labor movement.

Trade union leaders are contributing to the thinking of the community on a wide range of topics outside the field of trade unionism. In increasing numbers, for example, union speakers are found presenting papers on questions of business administration or public policy before meetings of business men, engineers and professional managers. Several colleges this spring will confer honorary degrees on trade union leaders — a new recognition of their services to the country.

The emergence of community leaders from the ranks of labor means that the country is better prepared to deal with its problems and to adjust itself to changing conditions. New problems are seen sooner and more clearly and policies, both in public affairs and business, are based upon more complete information and better understanding of conditions.

II

The shift of power from business to labor confronts the community with many new problems of great importance and difficulty. Five of these problems are of particular importance:

(1) *The right of individuals to belong to trade unions* — that is, the right to join a union and the right to remain in one. So long as trade unions included only a small part of the labor force, everyone conceded them the right to admit or exclude anyone that they saw fit. Today the livelihood of many workers depends upon their opportunity to belong to a union.

Most unions maintain an open door, but a few discriminate against certain racial groups and some charge high initiation fees. The constitutions of some unions permit members to be suspended or expelled for such vague offenses as "slandering an officer," "creating dissension," "undermining the union or working against its interests," or for "action which might injure the labor movement."

New York and Massachusetts have pioneered in protecting the right to belong to a union. Each state forbids unions from denying membership on the ground of race, color or creed. The Taft-Hartley Act attempts indirectly to deal with the problem by forbidding employers from discriminating in hiring against workers to whom membership in the union is not available. It also requires that unions which enter into union shop contracts shall not charge "excessive" initiation fees.

Little has been done to protect workers in their right to remain in a union, though the Taft-Hartley Act forbids employers from discharging workers who lose membership for any reason other than refusal to pay regular union dues and assessments.

Massachusetts has attempted to deal with the problem (a) by prohibiting unions from requiring the discharge of men who are appealing their cases through the regular machinery within the union, and (b) by giving workers the right to appeal from the highest tribunal within the union to the State Labor Relations Board.

If the worker wins his appeal before the Board, the union may still expel him from its ranks but it may not require the employer to discharge him.

(2) *The nature of the bargaining process.* Is collective bargaining to be a mere appeal to power in which the stronger party gets the better of the deal or is it to be an appeal to principle and reason, and an attempt to settle differences on the basis of what is fair? Merely settling wages on the basis of bargaining power would cause jobs requiring similar degrees of skill and responsibility and done under similar working conditions to be compensated at widely differing rates. Furthermore, if collective bargaining is merely an attempt to settle wages and other conditions on the basis of power, it can hardly produce good relations between employes and management and it can hardly command the respect and support of the community.

How can collective bargaining be made an appeal to principles and evidence? Obviously only by the development of a body of thought concerning how the fairness of wages shall be tested. This does not mean that solutions in particular cases can be reached by a mechanical procedure or that there will not be room for argument over principles as well as over facts in each case. It does mean, however, that collective bargaining must be guided by a well-developed body of thought about the economic consequences of different types of wage adjustment — a body of thought which carries weight with both sides and with the public and which, therefore, affects the outcome of negotiations and arbitrations.

(3) *The possibility of developing cooperation between managements and unions to deal with common interests.* Many union leaders and managers realize that it would be a calamity if unions were to do little more than represent workers in conflicts of interest between themselves and management. Formal cooperation between unions and management, however, is not easily accomplished.

Managers fear that it may become the beginning of interference by unions with routine administrative decisions; union leaders sometimes fear that cooperation with management will be interpreted by the rank and file as evidence that the officers are not vigilant in representing the members. Nevertheless, arrangements for cooperation between union representatives and management are slowly being developed. In the course of time, they promise greatly to improve the administration of business concerns and to make managers better aware of problems of employes, and employes better aware of problems of management.

(4) *The protection of the community against interruptions of production which jeopardize the health, safety, and economic welfare.* Several times during recent years strikes have deprived the community of essential services. This happened once in the case of railroads, once in the case of steel and several times in the case of coal. Indeed, never in the history of Western civilization have relatively small groups of men, such as coal miners, railroad workers or steel workers, been in a position to shut down the entire economic life of the country. It is plain that the community cannot tolerate extended stoppages or even threats of strikes or lockouts in vital industries. But it is not plain what the country should do about it.

The most sensible arrangement for dealing with disputes in vital industries would probably be one similar to the agreement between the unions and the employers in Great Britain to meet the emergency caused by the fall of France in 1940, but still in effect. Under this agreement, the unions and the employers refer to the Minister of Labor disputes which cannot be settled by collective bargaining or other processes. The Minister may refer the dispute to a national arbitration tribunal which makes a binding award. This does not mean universal compulsory arbitration, but it does mean that the unions and employers have given the Government an opportunity to protect the community against all stoppages which might create a national emergency.

It is not necessary, of course, that deadlocks be submitted to an arbitration tribunal through the Government — the parties might submit them directly. An arrangement by which the parties agree in advance to submit deadlocks to arbitration means that the unions, by agreeing not to use the right to strike, relieve the Government from the necessity of restricting this right.

(5) *The effect of collective bargaining upon the price level.* This is a matter of great importance which has been much neglected. During the last hundred years, technological progress has had the principal effect of raising wages rather than reducing prices. At any rate, hourly earnings rose about eight-fold between 1840 and 1940 but the price level changed little. Output per man-hour rose about 2 per cent a year. In view of the rapid rise of expenditures on industrial research, output per man-hour is likely to rise more rapidly in the future than in the past — perhaps as much as 3 percent or 4 percent a year. The unions, however, are likely to force up wages faster than the engineers and managers can raise output per man-hour.

If output rises by 3 percent a year and money wages by 5 percent, prices will need to rise by about 2 percent a year. Otherwise there will be a creeping increase in unemployment. If prices do not rise of their own accord, the Government will be compelled either to check the rise in money wages or to encourage a rise in prices. Of these two policies, the Government, it is safe to say, will adopt the latter because helping a rise in somebody's price is usually more popular (or less unpopular) than attempting to hold down a price.

The prospect that universal collective bargaining will lead to a slow rise in the price level raises questions of profound importance. Pensions or life insurance, which men started to buy on entering the labor force at about the age of 20 or 25, would have lost more than half their purchasing power by the time the workers had reached the age of 65 or 70. With prices rising 2 or 3 percent a year, who would wish to own savings accounts, Government bonds or other securities paying 2 or 3 percent a year?

All fixed-income securities would have to sell at yields which discounted the expected drop in the purchasing power of the principal. After ten or fifteen years millions of people would have noticed that collective bargaining was gradually reducing the purchasing power of their pensions, savings accounts, life insurance and bonds, and they would demand that something be done about it. Hence the Government might be faced with the widespread demand that it require that wage settlements made by collective bargaining conform to a national wage policy.

As a matter of fact, this question has already become important in other countries where collective bargaining has become fairly universal and where there has been danger that the wage policies of unions might conflict with the efforts of the Government to control prices. In Norway the wage policies of the unions have been subordinated to the interests of the community in stable prices. In England the reconciliation of national interests and the policies of the several unions has been more difficult because the traditions of the labor movement give much autonomy to the unions. The Labor Government, however, has discouraged unions from pressing wage demands. On February 4, 1948, the Government issued a "White Paper" entitled "Statement on Personal Incomes, Costs and Prices," in which it stated that: "It is essential * * * that there should be no further general increase in the level of personal incomes without at least a corresponding increase in the volume of production."

The United States is not yet prepared to recognize that there are likely to be important conflicts between the national interest in stable prices and free collective bargaining. Sooner or later, however, the community is bound to become aware of these conflicts. What changes in policies and institutions will follow is anyone's guess. If the decision is to accept rising prices in order to avoid interfering with collective bargaining, pensions and life insurance will have to be adapted to this fact and the Government and corporations will have to issue bonds payable in purchasing power rather than a fixed number of dollars. If the policy is to stabilize prices, the Government will have to develop ways and means of formulating a national wage policy to guide the operation of collective bargaining.

III

Many people view the shift of power from business to employes with much misgiving. Naturally one wonders what employes will do with their power and how the policies which they support will affect the operation of American industry. The American economy is the most productive and the most dynamic in the world. With about 6 percent of the world's population, it produces between one-third and two-fifths of the world's goods.

Two outstanding characteristics explain the great productivity of the American economy. One is the large number of business enterprises — about 3.5 million outside of agriculture and 6 million in agriculture. This means that there are millions of places where a new idea may be born and where an innovation or experiment may be authorized. Regimented economies with few centers of initiative can scarcely be expected to compete in dynamic drive with an economy which has millions of centers of initiative. The other characteristic which explains the high productivity of American industry is the opportunity to obtain immense rewards by pioneering. These rewards have supplied both incentives and capital for enterprises to grow from small beginnings to huge concerns within a generation.

Employes have fared exceedingly well under the American economy. Although the amount of capital per worker has been rapidly rising, the share of the national income going to property in the form of profits,

personal rents and interest has not been increasing. In 1940 capital per
worker was about three times as large (in dollars of constant purchasing
power) as in 1880. In each year, however, the share of the national income
going to property was only about one-fourth. In 1947, only about one-
sixth of the national income went to property owners. Most of the gains of
technological progress have gone to people in their capacity as employes
rather than in their capacity as consumers. For example, between 1840
and 1940 there was little change in the general price level but hourly
earnings of nonagricultural workers, as I have pointed out, increased
about eight-fold. It remains to be seen whether a nation of employes will
feel a sufficient stake in industrial progress to keep essentially unimpaired
the conditions which have made American industry highly dynamic or
whether they will follow some European countries in attempting to
introduce great centralization of decision-making with more or less drastic
control over the rewards of enterprise.

My guess is that the help which unions are likely to give the community
in solving its problems will be more important than the new problems which
unions create. The most important fact about the world today is the conflict between the philosophy of life represented by Russia and the philosophy which Western Europe and the United States have inherited from the
Greeks and the Anglo-Saxons. The Russian philosophy asserts that the
community has interests which are independent of and superior to those
of its members. Indeed, it recognizes no rights of the individual against
the Government. The philosophy of Western Europe asserts that the
supreme values are found in the interests of individuals and that institutions exist in order to serve individuals.

In this great conflict between two philosophies the trade unions are
an important ally of the West. In the first place, they are an effective
champion of the idea of the dignity of the individual. They have introduced the equivalent of civil rights into industry and have given workers
protection against arbitrary treatment by management. Thus they have
made a major contribution toward implementing the philosophy of the
West.

In the second place, the rise of trade unions and the gradual development of a laboristic community opens up to employes great opportunities
to participate in policy-making both in the plant and in the community.
Russia is gradually creating a community in which individuals are vassals
of the state — a new form of serfdom. Such an economy has little chance
of holding its own in competition with a laboristic economy in which
responsibility for decisions is widely dispersed and in which millions of
employes have a chance to feel that they have a stake in the community.

Union Wage Policies

The Theory of Union Wage Rigidity, by Joseph Shister, Quarterly Journal of Economics, Vol. LVII, August, 1943, pp. 522–542

The Responsibility of Organized Labor for Employment, by Sumner H. Slichter, American Economic Association, Papers and Proceedings, Vol. XXXV, No. 2, May, 1945, pp. 193–208

THE THEORY OF UNION WAGE RIGIDITY

SUMMARY

Scope of the paper: systematic analysis of the causes of rigid union wage policies, 522. — Union objectives: income, 523; philosophy, 524. — Demand schedules for union labor: oligopoly, 525; product price rigidity, 527; partial unionization, 528; relative importance of labor cost, 529. — Misinterpretation of the demand schedules: imperfect knowledge, 530; socio-economic structure of unionism, 531; method of negotiating wage agreements, 533.— Arbitrators' decisions, 536. — Employers' attitudes and policies, 539.

SCOPE OF THE PAPER

A perusal of the literature on labor costs and income variations will reveal that the following criticisms have been levelled at union wage policies:[1] (1) union wage scales are not flexible enough with respect to a deflationary price level; (2) union wage scales are frequently "too high" compared with non-union scales in the same industry;[2] (3) union wage scales are often "too high" for a declining industry.[3] At bottom these criticisms simply signify that union wage scales are "rigid" in a downward direction. The elimination of this rigidity would, according to the critics, lead to a greater national income and/or a greater income for the unions in question.

The writers making these criticisms generally support their assertions with more or less factual data, but few of them have inquired into the *raison-d'être* of the policies involved.[4] Furthermore, those who have investigated the causes have done so with respect to particular cases. As yet there exists no systematic analysis which can serve as a framework of reference in understanding these union wage policies.[5] The desirability of such a

1. For a discussion of the concept of "union wage policies," consult J. T. Dunlop, "Wage Policies of Trade Unions," American Economic Review, Supplement, March, 1942, p. 290.

2. Strictly speaking, the criticisms are levelled not so much against the union scales alone as against the unit labor costs in union shops. Thus restrictive working conditions are also brought into play.

3. Here, too, the emphasis is on unit labor costs, rather than on wage rates alone.

4. Professor Slichter is a notable exception. See, for example, his Union Policies and Industrial Management, Washington, 1941, passim.

5. Dr. Dunlop has done some work in this connection in the article quoted above.

339

framework is clear when one realizes that ". . . by the end of the
war, roughly one-third of the pay rolls of industry will be directly
determined by collective bargaining, [and] wage rates in many
non-union plants will be sensitive to changes in union scales. . . ."[6]
The purpose of this paper is not to condone or condemn the union
policies in the light of any given (social) criterion, but simply to
analyze the elements accounting for rigid union wage policies in
different circumstances.   These causal elements may be divided
into the following categories: union objectives; the structure of
the demand schedules for the various types of union labor; the
misinterpretation by the unions of the demand for their labor;
arbitrators' decisions; employers' attitudes; and governmental
policies. The last category, comprising such matters as unemployment insurance, minimum wage laws, and public works, has been
adequately treated elsewhere and needs no further comment here.[7]

UNION OBJECTIVES

Maximizing Income. It is not necessarily true, as some writers have assumed,[8] that every union is interested in maximizing
the income of its membership as a whole. It is quite possible for a
union to aim at the maximization of the income of only a given
group within the union. If the employed members in a given
organization constitute a majority, it can well happen that the
employed will pursue a wage policy which increases their income
at the expense of the unemployed in the union.[9] This might be
termed "intra-union exploitation." Although a wage reduction
would increase the employment opportunities of the furloughed
workers, as well as increase the income of the membership as a
whole, it would definitely reduce the income of those who had
been employed all along. It would thus be disadvantageous to the
majority to accept a wage reduction under these circumstances.

Examples of such an objective on the part of unions are not

6. S. H. Slichter, "The Conditions of Expansion," American Economic
Review, March, 1942, pp. 11–12.

7. On the question of Social Security, for example, see S. H. Slichter,
"The Impact of Social Security Legislation upon Mobility and Enterprise,"
American Economic Review, Supplement, March, 1940, p. 57.

8. Thus Bronfenbrenner writes: "A union may be expected generally to
depart from purely competitive practices, to attempt to alter the wage of
labor of the specified kind in the direction most favorable to the total income
of the members," this JOURNAL, August, 1939, p. 538.

9. This assumes, of course, that layoffs are based on seniority.

difficult to find. The employed members of the American Federation of Hosiery Workers refused to accept a six per cent wage reduction proposed by the employers in 1937, while simultaneously the many unemployed members were ready to do so.[1] The reluctance of the older men on some of the railroads to "share the work" with the younger men during the depression years following 1929[2] seems to point in the direction of "intra-union exploitation."[3] "Exploitation" of the unemployed also takes place, to a certain extent, in the printing crafts unions. Here the "regular" workers are not willing to decrease their scales for the purpose of providing more employment for the "substitutes."[4] John L. Lewis' policy of maintaining "high" wage rates in the bituminous coal mines was based, in part, on the belief that ". . . years of high wage rates were expected to force the highest-cost mines out of the market and to deprive their miners permanently of employment. . . ."[5]

Union Philosophy. A "revolutionary" union,[6] by its very nature, is meant to foster class consciousness among its members. Under these circumstances, concessions to employers, in any form whatever, are automatically ruled out. It is not surprising, therefore, that such labor groups resist wage cuts even though such cuts would lead to a greater income for the group. It is true that in recent years most, if not all, of the American trade unions have been of the "business"[7] rather than the "revolutionary" type. Still, there have been organizations which have been "radical" in their objectives, and their wage policies may be explained, in part at least, by this underlying philosophy. The Tapestry Carpet

1. Twentieth Century Fund, How Collective Bargaining Works, New York, 1942, p. 501.

2. Twentieth Century Fund, op. cit., p. 355.

3. Professor Slichter seems to corroborate this view when he states: "If [unemployment] is concentrated by seniority rule among the junior members, the union may have little interest in employment problems. This goes far to explain the marketing policies of the railroad brotherhoods." ("The Changing Character of American Industrial Relations," American Economic Review, Supplement, March, 1939, p. 136.)

4. This viewpoint was expressed by various printing crafts officials in interviews with the writer.

5. C. Edwards, in American Labor Dynamics (J. B. S. Hardman, editor), New York, 1928, p. 182.

6. The term is used here in Hoxie's sense, Trade Unionism in the United States, New York, pp. 48, 49.

7. Still following Hoxie's definitions. Op. cit., p. 45.

Workers' Union is a case in point.[8] Even in those unions which today are predominantly of the "business" type, there exist factions of the "revolutionary" kind whose opinion may well influence union policies to some extent.[9] Finally, it should be noted that in previous years "revolutionary unionism" was far more prevalent than it is today, and to explain wage policies in the past, as well as the present, the philosophical objectives of these unions must be invoked. The I.W.W. is a pertinent example; the Western Federation of Miners is another.[1] The needle trades unions were at one time "revolutionary" in function.[2]

DEMAND SCHEDULES FOR UNION LABOR

If a union is faced with an inelastic demand for the labor of its members (over the relevant range), it will actually decrease the income of the group as a whole by lowering its wage scale.[3] A policy of wage rigidity under these conditions is therefore directly attributable to the structure of the demand for the union labor. It is doubtless true that both the elasticity and the position of the demand curve for a given type of union labor may vary over time. This does not, however, alter the fact that so long as the demand is inelastic, a policy of wage rigidity is a "rational" pursuit for any union interested in maximizing the income of the group as a whole.[4] Such inelastic demand schedules can result from a variety of factors, of which the most important will be considered in this section.

Oligopoly. Where the product market is characterized by oligopoly with "little" (or no) product differentiation, where each

8. See G. Palmer, Union Tactics and Economic Change, pp. 46 et seq. Miss Palmer writes: "Although over a period of years, numerous occasions were offered when they (the tapestry carpet workers) might, by concessions in rates, have saved the union or salvaged some employment for their members while unemployment was steadily increasing in the trade, they steadfastly refused to do so. They 'went down fighting.'" (p. 48.)

9. See Palmer, op. cit., p. 73; Hoxie, op. cit., pp. 163–164; L. Levine, The Women's Garment Workers, New York, 1924, pp. 449–452.

1. See P. Brissenden, The I.W.W., New York, 1919, Chap. 1.

2. See Budish and Soule, The New Unionism, New York, 1920, pp. 168 et seq.

3. Aside from the effect of union wage rate reductions on the position of the various demand schedules for the different types of union labor. This problem lies beyond the scope of this paper.

4. It is assumed here that layoffs are based on the principle of equal division of work. If layoffs are based on seniority, and the union is trying to maximize its wage bill in the face of an inelastic demand for labor, the younger members will be out of employment.

firm takes into account both the direct and the indirect consequences of its price policy, and where each entrepreneur believes
that the aggregate demand for the product of the industry is
inelastic, each producer will visualize the demand schedule for his
product as having a kink in it at the prevailing price.[5] Under such
circumstances, the demand for the union labor by each of the
oligopolists is inelastic over a considerable range.[6] This applies
equally well whether all the firms in the industry are unionized or
not. The case of complete unionization is simple enough to visualize and needs no further elucidation here. If the industry is only
partially unionized, the non-union firms will (presumably) have
lower unit labor costs. Despite this, however, the non-union firms
will not charge lower prices than the union plants. Such a price
reduction might be misinterpreted by the union firms as a signal
for a price war, which would eventually drive the product price
down to the competitive level. Similarly, the union firms will not
raise their prices above those of the non-union firms, for since the
latter would not follow this price increase, the union firms would
lose sales.[7]

Without further investigation it is impossible to say which
industries fit the model developed above. It would seem, however,
that some of the mass production industries organized by the CIO
may be of this type.[8]

5. See P. M. Sweezy, "Demand Under Conditions of Oligopoly,"
Journal of Political Economy, August, 1939, passim.

6. This assumes, of course, that the elasticity of substitution between
capital and labor (in the market in question) is "low."

7. This statement does not hold true where (a) oligopoly is accompanied
by price leadership, and (b) where the price leader (assumed to be powerful)
is a unionized firm, while some (or all) of the others are not.

According to Professor Slichter ". . . differentials in labor costs above
the non-union plants are more disadvantageous to union plants (1) when the
proportion of labor cost to the total cost of production is large; (2) when the
differentiation between the products of the several plants is small; (3) when
costs other than labor costs are uniform between plants and not easily altered;
(4) when it is easy to start new plants in the industry; (5) when the capital
demands created by technological change are large; (6) when the industry is
contracting; and (7) during periods of severe depression," Union Policies, p.
367. While this thesis is correct as far as it goes, it is not complete. The
analysis in the text above shows that the structure of the product market of
the industry should also have been included in Slichter's classification, for
even if all of Slichter's conditions are fulfilled, the union firms may lose little
business if the market structure is of the type described in the text.

8. It should be noted that the preceding schema does not preclude the
possibility of a change in the product price as a result of changes in costs. It

Product Price Rigidity.[9] If the price of a given product is kept stable in the face of a declining market (cyclical or secular), the union involved does not stand to gain in employment or income by consenting to a lower wage scale. For the purposes of this analysis two types of "rigid" prices must be distinguished: (1) the stability of the individual price results from the existence of some form of monopoly in the product market, with "little" (or no) product differentiation involved; (2) there is a substantial degree of competition in the product market, but the competition is essentially on a product basis, with prices remaining more or less constant.

The rationale of the first type of price rigidity has been adequately treated elsewhere.[1] All that needs to be added here is that unions have gained a fairly strong position in many of the industries where so-called price rigidity is in force. Among these might be mentioned:[2] agricultural implements, certain steel products, and anthracite coal. In some other industries which are largely unionized, price rigidity is less marked, but it exists (or has existed), nevertheless, because of some form of collusion among the producers. Frequently, too, the unions are a party to this collusion. In this respect the building trades are the classical example,[3] but there are others.[4]

is, therefore, different from the case of so-called price "rigidity" to be discussed below. See L. G. Reynolds, "Relations Between Wage Rates, Costs and Prices," American Economic Review, Supplement, March, 1942, pp. 278-281.

9. For the various possible definitions of this term, see D. H. Wallace, "Monopoly Prices and Depression," in Explorations in Economics, New York, 1936.

1. See J. K. Galbraith, "Monopoly Power and Price Rigidities," this JOURNAL, May, 1936.

2. For a discussion of these industries, consult A. R. Burns, The Decline of Competition, New York, 1936, Chap. 5.

3. See Temporary National Economic Committee Hearings, The Construction Industry, p. 5150; C. Edwards, "Public Policy Toward Restraints of Trade by Labor Unions," American Economic Review, Supplement, March, 1942, pp. 445-448.

It might well be questioned whether the building crafts are acting wisely in facilitating monopolistic practices (and subsequent price rigidity). If, as some writers have maintained, the demand for building is elastic, the unions are perhaps pursuing a policy which is detrimental to their best interests.

4. The photo-engraving industry is another case in point. (See R. A. Lester, Economics of Labor, New York, 1941, pp. 147-150.) Similarly, the Seattle teamsters have encouraged price rigidity among the employers with whom they have contracts. (Lester, op. cit., pp. 150-155.) The pottery industry can serve as a final illustration: a special committee of the Brotherhood of Operative Potters agreed that if the committee of the East Liverpool manu-

Where price rigidity exists in conjunction with "intense" product competition, the situation faced by the union is, in one respect, different from that in the preceding type of price stability. Although here too there is no reduction in the price of the product following a unit labor cost reduction, the union can nevertheless benefit from the wage reduction, if the following conditions are met: (1) the decrease in labor costs is immediately siphoned off into increased advertising for the product;[5] (2) this increase in advertising shifts the demand function for the product to the right;[6] (3) the increased demand for the product results in a shift to the right of the demand schedule for labor. Industries characterized by the second type of price rigidity, where unions have gained a considerable stronghold, are, among others: ladies' dresses,[7] cigarettes, and newspapers.[8]

Partial Unionization. Given an industry which is only partially unionized, the demand for whose product is inelastic over

facturers "... would advise the employees of their different shops to join the National Brotherhood of Operative Potters so as to give us full control of said shops, we in return would do all we could to help the manufacturers to maintain a uniform selling price for their products, even to the calling out of the men of such manufacturers as tried to undersell." (Quoted by McCabe, National Collective Bargaining in the Pottery Industry, Philadelphia, 1932, p. 91.)

5. It should be remembered that the wage reduction can be siphoned off into improvements of the product instead of advertising. Nevertheless, these improvements cannot be made known to the public, in any substantial way, without some form of advertising.

6. The demand function for the "product" of the "industry" is in question here. It is assumed, also, that the industry is completely unionized. The quintessence of the conclusion would not be altered if it were assumed that the industry in question is only partially unionized.

7. It should be noted that, in the particular case of the dress industry, a union might be advised to take a wage cut during the course of a cyclical depression, even if the money is not siphoned off into advertising. This is due to the fact that during a depression many of the firms in this industry — especially the smaller ones — find themselves in a weak cash position, and a wage reduction may enable them to stay in business. It should also be noted that the volume of advertising in this industry is rather small.

8. A newspaper's revenue is derived from two sources, circulation and advertising. The prices of different newspapers in the city where they are published is usually the same, but each paper offers different features in the form of comics, editorials, etc. The price of newpapers does not decline during periods of cyclical depression. Advertising rates vary from newspaper to newspaper, according to the volume of circulation; the larger the circulation, the higher the rate charged. Advertising rates remain constant during periods of depression. (Consult the annual issues of Editor and Publisher for a verification of the above views.)

the relevant range,[9] whose product market is characterized by a substantial degree of price competition, where prices are based on average total unit costs,[1] where non-union wage rate changes follow union scale variations,[2] and where there *already* exists a differential between union and non-union unit labor costs, the union stands to gain little by consenting to a lower wage scale.[3] Under these conditions a lower wage scale will simply result in a lower price for the product with no increase in union employment or income.[4] It should be emphasized that in the model outlined here the differential in unit labor costs between union and non-union plants is assumed to be already well established in the industry.

Concrete instances of this situation are not difficult to find. The lamp chimney industry is a case in point; the full-fashioned hosiery industry is another.[5] The condition in many of the predominantly non-union book and job printing centers (Cincinnati, Boston, Baltimore, Los Angeles, Detroit and Philadelphia, for example) is somewhat analogous.[6]

Relative Importance of Labor Cost. In industries where the cost of labor is a small part of total costs of production and where, furthermore, the elasticity of substitution of capital (or a cheaper type of labor) for union labor is low, the demand for union labor

9. The conclusions will hold even if the demand is elastic, but not "very" elastic. It is also assumed in this model that the elasticity of substitution between capital and labor is "low."

1. This is a very realistic assumption. See R. L. Hall and C. J. Hitch, "Price Theory and Business Behavior," Oxford Economic Papers, No. 2; J. K. Galbraith, op. cit., p. 471.

2. It is assumed here that when union scale reductions do occur they are not "very large." If they are, the non-union plants will not necessarily cut their scales to the same extent. Thus, for example, the deflation of 30–45 per cent in wage rates accepted by the American Federation of Hosiery Workers in 1931 was not met by the non-union plants. (See Twentieth Century Fund, op. cit., p. 485.)

3. This case is different from the one discussed in the paragraph on "oligopoly," notably with respect to the structure of the product market.

4. This does not, of course, preclude the possibility of lowering unit labor costs in the union shops, relative to non-union shops, by an increase in the productivity of labor in the former. The removal of restrictive working conditions by the union is a case in point.

5. See Slichter, op. cit., pp. 350, 355.

6. It should be noted that the aggregate demand for letterpress printing may be elastic, as a result of the competition of such substitutes as lithography and gravure. But the demand will be inelastic if the reduction in the price of letterpress printing is followed by a similar reduction in the prices of the competing media.

would be highly inelastic (over the relevant range). Here again unions would derive little from lowering their wage scales. The baking industry is a case in point.[7] The newspaper industry is another.[8]

MISINTERPRETATION OF DEMAND

When a union is faced with an elastic demand for the labor of its members, a policy of wage rigidity will not maximize the income of the group. Yet we find numerous instances where unions, in such a situation, have pursued rigid wage policies. Sometimes the intensity of non-union competition is not sufficiently recognized. In other instances, the union members may not grasp the significance of technological change. Finally, the appearance of substitute products (or services) frequently goes unnoticed by the labor organizations affected. Three possible explanations for this misinterpretation of the demand will be suggested here: imperfection of knowledge arising from a condition of "uncertainty"; the structure of American trade unions; and the method of negotiating wage agreements.

Imperfect Knowledge. It sometimes happens that a union is confronted with a constellation of data which do not yield any definite answer with respect to the effect of wage changes on the employment and income patterns of the union members. Such a situation can well arise in the case where a unionized industry is faced with the competition of a substitute commodity (or service). Whether a wage reduction will increase the income of the union as a group, under the above conditions, will depend on (1) whether the employers will pass the savings in costs on to the consumer,

7. Labor costs in this industry constitute about 15 per cent of the total value of the product. (Census of Manufactures.) Furthermore, this industry is also characterized by a certain amount of price rigidity resulting from monopolistic practices. (See Temporary National Economic Committee, Competition and Monopoly in American Industry, Monograph No. 21, pp. 242–244.) A perusal of union wage rate data will show, however, that the bakery workers have pursued a less rigid wage policy than some unions less favorably situated. This can be explained only on the ground of weak bargaining power on the part of the union. "Bargaining power" may be divided into three elements: (*a*) the elasticity of demand for the union labor; (*b*) the quality of union representatives; (*c*) the ability to strike successfully. It would seem, therefore, that in the case of the bakery workers, their weakness lies in the second and third elements, although there has been a certain amount of technological change within the industry.

8. Aside from the condition discussed above in connection with price rigidity.

(2) whether the prices of the competing media will be lowered in
retaliation for the price reduction of the union product, and (3)
whether the aggregate demand for the union product and the "substitute" is elastic or inelastic. In the face of such uncertainty, only
the union is incurring a "risk" by agreeing to a wage reduction.
Should the lower wage rate lead to a larger union income (absolutely or relatively), the union members of course benefit, but so
do the employers in the form of a greater volume of business
(absolutely or relatively). If, on the other hand, the lower scale
does not result in any increase in employment (absolutely or relatively), the union will suffer an (absolute and relative) decrease in
its wage bill. In other words, the union runs the "risk," although
the employers share in any benefits which may follow.

The preceding discussion implies that unions would be ready,
in many cases, to pursue less rigid wage policies, if they were
assured of (relatively) more employment and income by so doing.
Such an implication is probably valid; the negotiation of employment guarantees in different industries seems to bear this out.[9]
Furthermore, sometimes the union may consent to a wage reduction without the guarantee of a given amount of employment, provided the employer promises to reduce the price of the product.
The case of the lamp chimney workers is pertinent in this respect.
This union accepted a wage reduction in 1924 but ". . . the concessions were made with the understanding that the union manufacturers would reduce their selling prices on all chimneys. . . ."[1]

The Socio-Economic Structure of Unionism. In any industry
characterized by craft unionism, conditions can easily arise which
may lead to a rigid wage policy. In the first place, the cost of each
craft is generally only a small part of total labor costs to the industry in question. American craft unions being highly individualistic
in their policies, each craft paying attention mainly to the effects
of its own policies on its own immediate interests,[2] it is quite likely
that each craft will concentrate solely on the fact that the cost to

9. See Dunlop, op. cit., p. 297.
1. Slichter, op. cit., p. 350.
2. This is not, of course, always true. Thus, for example, there sometimes occurs coöperation among local building crafts in negotiating wage
agreements. Furthermore, although crafts may not coöperate on matters of
wage policy, they may do so on other aspects of union policy. There is little
coöperation among the book and job printing crafts in negotiating wage
agreements, but they do coöperate on such matters as the issuance of the
union printing label.

the employer of *its* labor is relatively negligible. Since all the crafts may well reason in the same fashion, the result may be that the combined costs imposed on the employer are more than he is in a position to pay. Instances of such individualism among complementary crafts are not difficult to find. Miss Brown writes of the book and job printing crafts: "The . . . system of independent craft action is explained in part by the difficulty of getting unified action from a group of autonomous locals. . . . Each local tends to use every opportunity to promote its own position. Stronger unions hesitate to give up their special advantage in bargaining by coöperating with the weaker ones, while the weaker sometimes fear inadequate attention to their interests in joint action."[3] In speaking of the upholstery weavers in Philadelphia, Miss Palmer states: ". . . the upholstery weavers have always had to work with four other unions in the trade. The division of the workers in the industry into five separate craft unions has preserved wage scale differentials and uneconomical trade rules which would probably have disappeared in an industrial union."[4]

In the second place, even if each craft does take into account the total labor costs of production in framing its policies, rigidity may result for other reasons. Let us assume that there are seven crafts, each one dealing separately with an employer (or group of employers). If two of these crafts (which together we shall call group A) interpret correctly the elasticity of the demand for the combined union labor forces, while the other five (which together we shall call group B) underestimate this elasticity, group A may nevertheless pursue the same "erroneous" policies as group B. This may be so because the crafts which are correct in their interpretation fear that if they were to pursue a policy consistent with this interpretation (e.g. by accepting wage reductions), they might not benefit from it at all, since the failure of group B to pursue a similar policy might nullify the concessions which the employer gains from group A.[5] Furthermore, even if some benefit can be

3. Twentieth Century Fund, op. cit., p. 141.
4. Op cit., p. 61.
5. This assumes, in other words, that the percentage of total costs constituted by the combined wage bills of group A is not sufficiently high to affect the volume of employment in a "substantial" way.

It is assumed here that it is impossible to substitute capital or a "cheaper" type of labor for any of the crafts in question. If such substitution were possible in the case of group A, for example, and not in the case of the other group, then, of course, A would necessarily have to pursue a less rigid wage policy.

derived from concessions by group A alone, the other group will also share in it, although the former group (A) has borne the entire burden of the wage concession. This may well act as a deterrent to any concessions on A's part.

Even if collective bargaining were conducted by separate industrial unions on a national basis, each union would still be too small a part of the total labor supply to take into account the direct and indirect effects of its wage policies on the national income, and the consequences of variations in this income on its own members. In the United States, where many of the agreements are concluded on a local basis by craft organizations, this, of course, holds true, *a fortiori*. That such a condition can lead to rigid wage policies is obvious.

The Method of Negotiating Wage Agreements. Three basic types of alternatives are faced by a union in deciding on the procedure of negotiations. (1) Should the agreement be national or local?[6] (2) Should the union representatives be given full power to come to a settlement, or should the final decision rest with the rank and file?[7] (3) Should the personnel of the scale committee change frequently or not? These questions have been answered differently by different organizations, depending upon the structure of the industry, the past history of industrial relations, the government of the union, etc. Nevertheless, it can be argued with some degree of certainty that it is not indifferent for wage policy whether one or the other of these alternatives is adopted.

(1) Professor Slichter has attempted to show why national officers are less likely to misjudge market conditions and trends than local officers.[8] Even though his thesis is correct, it should not be inferred from it that wage agreements should necessarily be

6. There is also the possibility of regional agreements. It is assumed here that wherever a national agreement is concluded, the national officers of the union in question are in charge of negotiations. This is not, of course, always true. Similarly, it is assumed that local agreements are negotiated by local officers alone; this again is not always true.

7. Where the local membership has the final say on the agreement, further complications are involved in the case of some of the unions. For example, all locals of the International Typographical Union contain members of both branches of the printing industry. In such instances should all members of the union be allowed to vote on an agreement being negotiated in one of the branches of the industry, or should only the members working in the given branch be allowed to vote? Where both branches are allowed to vote, a possibility of intra-union exploitation exists.

8. *Op. cit.*, pp. 375–376.

concluded on a national basis. Although it is true that local agreements, in the making of which there has been no national supervision of any kind, are very likely to lead to wage rigidity, it is quite possible to combine local negotiations with sufficient national supervision. This supervision may take a variety of forms: national approval of local agreements, the counsel of national officers in local negotiations, the control of strikes by the national officers, etc. The question now arises, Why duplicate the work of local representatives by national officers? Why not sign national agreements? In the first place, national agreements are not economically feasible in many instances; the building construction industry is a case in point. In the second place, even in those industries where national agreements are feasible, it might still be desirable to conclude local agreements, *provided* there is sufficient national supervision. The reasons for this will appear in our analysis of the question of negotiators' powers.

(2) In attempting to show that the income of unions will be greater in the long run ". . . when agreements with employers are negotiated by officers of the union with full power to settle them than when the agreements are submitted to a referendum vote by the rank and file . . . ," Professor Slichter alludes to instances of national agreements.[9] The reason for the desirability of "full power to settle" under such circumstances is that it is often difficult to obtain ratification, because under a referendum (the "only" method available for approval by the rank and file in the case of national agreements)[1] it is hard to convince the rank and file of any errors in their "thinking" on wage policy, since there is no possibility of meeting with them and "talking things over." On the other hand, as Slichter himself admits, ". . . when a local agreement is negotiated, it is possible for officers to call a meeting of the rank and file and explain to them exactly what was done

9. Op. cit., pp. 374–383.
1. The other alternative would be a convention of delegates from the different locals to decide on the acceptance or rejection of the contract proposed by the national officers. In the first place, such a procedure would be impracticable in many instances, because of the costs involved. (It would be rather difficult to make the *general* convention of the union synchronize with the negotiation of wage agreements. What if conventions are biennial and contracts are only one year in duration — because of the desire for flexibility?) In the second place, even if such a convention were practicable, the rank and file would have a smaller say in the agreement than if it were signed on a local basis with the approval of the local membership.

and why and to answer objections from the floor. . . ."[2] Under
these circumstances, it is quite likely that the rank and file will
follow the advice of the local officers.[3] Since the rank and file
may have demands to make which are not at all inconsistent with
their desire and ability to maximize the income of the group in
question, it is essential that the officers be well informed on this.[4]
The best way of doing this is, of course, a meeting of the individuals whose income is affected directly by the union wage policy.
Furthermore, interest in union affairs will be greatly increased by
allowing the rank and file to discuss and vote on proposed wage
agreements. Finally, meetings to discuss wage agreements will
make for more democracy in the government of trade unions. All
this seems to point to the conclusion that local agreements, *coupled
with national supervision*, without full power to settle being vested
in the conferees,[5] may well be the most desirable method.[6]

(3) As a rule, employers favor the perpetuation of the personnel of a union scale committee. They believe that if committee
men serve long enough, they acquire a sound knowledge of the
industry in its various aspects and are less likely to misinterpret

2. Op. cit., p. 376.
3. It is assumed that the local officers do not misinterpret the demand for
the labor of the members, and/or there is a substantial amount of national
supervision over the negotiation of local agreements.
4. As Slichter himself writes: ". . . responsibility and authority within
the union (should) be distributed in such a way as to insure that all available
and relevant facts will receive consideration and that the short-run and
long-run effects of union policies will each be given a weight satisfactory to
the members." (Op. cit., p. 370.)
5. Unless, of course, the membership itself allows the scale committee
to sign the agreement on terms that it (the committee) deems desirable. This
sometimes occurs when negotiations have dragged for quite a long time with
little headway being made.
6. There is no contradiction between this conclusion and the one previously reached, namely, the bargaining unit in American trade unionism is
too small to take into account the effects of its policies on the national income.
This is so because the existence of local agreements, *under national supervision*,
does not preclude the possibility of coöperation among the officers of the
different national unions in framing "appropriate" wage policies in the light
of the operation of the entire economy. Thus, the national officers of each
of the unions could then influence the policy of their locals in accordance with
the national policy decided upon in coöperation with the officers of the other
national unions.
Even if agreements are signed on a national basis, there would still be
need for coöperation among the national unions, if one admits that (*a*) no
individual union is sufficiently large to take into account the effects of its
policies on the national income, and (*b*) it is impossible to set up "one big
union."

market conditions. Unions, however, take a different view. They believe that the personnel of a scale committee should change frequently,[7] because (*a*) it is "fair" to give everyone a chance to see what he (or she) can do, and (*b*) when the same members are on the committee too long they become "soft" and are likely to yield to the employers. This frequent changing of the personnel of the scale committees, especially if the scale committees are not comprised of union officers,[8] is a factor contributing to wage rigidity.

ARBITRATORS' DECISIONS

Arbitration of disputes arising in the negotiation of new wage agreements has become a widespread practice in American industry in recent years. Furthermore, contract clauses specifically prohibiting strikes and lockouts — so-called compulsory arbitration clauses — are not at all uncommon. It is, therefore, fairly safe to assume that the wage patterns of many unions throughout the country bear the imprint of the awards of one or more arbitrators.[9] And it is equally safe to assume that some of the wage rigidity has been caused by arbitrators' decisions. Before substantiating this thesis by factual data, it is pertinent to inquire into the rationale of arbitrators' awards.

An examination of such decisions[1] will show that arbiters are guided by some or all of the following factors: changes in the cost of living, "normal" standards of living, wages ruling in comparable industries, changes in the general wage level, the economic condition of the industry in question, and general economic conditions. Since no definite arbitration principles exist, the weight attached

7. Thus, for example, in speaking of the union conference committee in the pottery industry, McCabe states: "Of the 28 elected conferees of 1928, but five had served in 1926. Of these five, only two had served in 1924, and but one of these two in 1922 — and he did not serve in 1921." (Op. cit., p. 127.)

8. Or if the scale committee is elected by the rank and file, instead of being chosen by union officers, national or local. Thus, McCabe writes: "One would expect that election of the members of the conference committee by local unions would give less satisfactory results than appointment by national officers. . . . And it has worked out that way [in the pottery industry]." (Op. cit., p. 128.)

9. To illustrate: between 1920 and 1929 there occurred 23 arbitrations involving the negotiation of new wage scales in the New York book and job printing industry. (Twentieth Century Fund, op. cit., p. 153.)

1. Consult, for example, Soule, Wage Arbitration, New York. 1924; H. Feis, Principles of Wage Settlement, New York, 1924.

to each of the above factors will vary from arbitrator to arbitrator. It is possible, therefore, that the weighting process may be so combined in some cases as to yield an award which contributes to the establishment (or perpetuation) of wage rigidity.

It has been contended[2] that ". . . an arbitration award which is not accepted by one of the principal parties concerned is futile, and that . . . under the present conditions of society any effort to decide wages and conditions by other than a compromise method is . . . 'seeking the unattainable'. . ." If all arbitrators were to follow this principle, wage rigidity would be perpetuated, although its intensity might be mitigated over time. This necessarily follows from the assumption that the union in question would not accept a decision which, although perhaps beneficial to the industry and the union in the long run, would deprive the union of certain privileges — "make-work" rules, for example. The Landis arbitration award in the Chicago building trades is a case in point.[3] The refusal of the San Francisco building crafts to accept the decision of the 1921 Arbitration Board is another.[4]

A further complicating factor entering into the elaboration of an arbitration award is the question whether the arbitrator should take account of the consequences of his decision on wage policies elsewhere in the economy. This problem becomes particularly important where the arbitrator, or arbitration board, is officially representing the government, for in such cases the award is very likely to set a precedent for other disputes elsewhere.[5] The arbitrator may set a wage scale which does not entail rigidity in the industry with which he is concerned but which might well entail rigidity if established in some other industry. Similarly, the question frequently arises whether the arbitrator should take into account the effect of his decision on later arbitrations in the same industry.[6] The following cases may serve as concrete illustrations of wage rigidity entailed by arbiters' decisions.

2. R. H. Montgomery, Industrial Relations in the Chicago Building Trades, Chicago, 1927, p. 270.

3. Montgomery, op. cit., Chapters 12, 13.

4. F. L. Ryan, Industrial Relations in the San Francisco Building Trades, Norman, Oklahoma, 1935, pp. 153–154.

5. Thus, the Railroad Labor Board took into consideration the effect that its decision would have on the rest of the economy, in awarding the railroad crafts an increase in wages in 1920. H. Wolf, The Railroad Labor Board, Chicago, 1927, p. 128.

6. See Soule, op. cit., p. 51.

In the depth of the depression in 1932, the Cincinnati Typographical Union and the Cincinnati Newspaper Publishers' Association could not agree on the question of a new wage scale.[7] The dispute was taken to arbitration and the chairman of the local board, Judge Robert R. Nevin of the Federal District Court, ruled against a reduction in the scale, even though he admitted that ". . . there is . . . no doubt but what there is evidence tending to support the claims made on behalf of the Publishers to the effect that the Cincinnati newspapers have suffered tremendous decreases in advertising lineage and that . . . their principal source of revenue is from advertising. . . ."[8]

In November, 1921, two arbitrations of wage disputes occurred in the New York book and job printing industry. The first one was between the union employers and the New York Typographical Union No. 6, the second between the same employers and the New York Printing Press Assistants and Feeders' Union No. 23. Dr. John L. Elliot was the arbiter in the first case, while Dr. William M. Leiserson was in charge of the second one. The press assistants had accepted a reduction in March, 1921, while the typographical had not. Despite this, however, Elliot ruled against a reduction, while Leiserson ruled in favor of it.[9]

The United States Bituminous Coal Commission, in awarding the miners a "substantial" increase in wages in 1920, stated that in reaching its decision the majority of the commission was ". . . guided by the principle that every industry *must* support its workers in accordance with the American standard of living."[1]

The Anthracite Coal Commission of 1920 considered such data as the profits of the industry, freight rates, and the prices of anthracite coal as *irrelevant* to the question of whether wage rates

7. The union was willing to grant the employers "temporary relief" by accepting a slightly lower scale for a period of six months. This was not, however, acceptable to the publishers. (From the writer's field notes.)

8. The decision of the arbitrator. (From the writer's field notes.)

9. Soule, op. cit., pp. 65–94.

1. Quoted by A. E. Suffern, The Coal Miners' Struggle for Industrial Status, New York, 1926, p. 102. My italics. Compare this statement with the one made by the arbitration board in the dispute involving the Boston and Middlesex Street Railway Company in 1921. In the latter case the board contended that ". . . the living wage theory has attained a great popularity in this country. . . . The fundamental difficulty in its practical application, however, seems to lie in the fact that we cannot take from industry in the form of income a greater amount in the aggregate than has been put into it in the shape of productive effort." (Quoted by Feis, op. cit., p 157.)

of miners should remain constant, be decreased or increased. After ruling such evidence out, it granted the miners an increase in wage rates.

EMPLOYERS' ATTITUDES AND POLICIES

Whatever a given economist's opinion may be with respect to the usefulness of wage cuts during a depression as a means of stimulating recovery,[2] he will not deny that if a firm (or firms) is in a weak cash position during a depression, and cannot rely on the banks for financing,[3] a wage reduction in this establishment would decrease the (relative) volume of unemployment within the firm, especially if labor costs are an important part of total costs of production.[4] When a union is bargaining with an employer who is in a weak cash position, the former will doubtless attempt to convince the union officials of this point. Rarely, however, will the employer be willing to exhibit financial data to substantiate his viewpoint. Lacking adequate information, the union is uncertain whether the employer is sincere or not.[5] This doubt may be particularly great if the employer has not displayed good faith in the past. As a consequence, the union may misinterpret his financial position and refuse to grant a wage reduction. This may result in more unemployment in the union ranks, but it may then be too late for the union to revise its estimates.

This type of misinterpretation can be attributed to the employers' reluctance to exhibit financial records. Their reluctance is usually based on the assumption that if records become known in the industry, the competitive position of the business units in question may become endangered.[6] The unions feel, however, that if any employer (or employers) is really in need of a

2. This issue lies beyond the scope of this paper.
3. Such an assumption is very realistic indeed. See Hardy and Viner, The Availability of Bank Credit in the Seventh Federal Reserve District, Washington, 1935, passim.
4. In fact, even in such an industry as paper, where labor costs are proportionately small, some companies are forced to reduce wage scales when ". . . the cash position of the company becomes low . . ." (Temporary National Economic Committee, Monograph No. 5, p. 29.)
5. This would be particularly true if the firm in question did not make any of its financial statements available to the public. As a rule the "large" corporations publish their balance sheets and/or income statements in the press at least once a year.
6. Thus, in the arbitration in the book and job printing industry in New York in November, 1920, ". . . the employers stated that no publication of the affairs of individual firms was possible, as such information was kept confidential for business reasons." (G. Soule, Wage Arbitration, New York, 1928, p. 25.)

wage reduction, the burden of proof is upon him. The late President Howard of the International Typographical Union expressed this viewpoint thus: "If the situation cannot be met in any way other than by wage adjustment, certainly the worker is entitled to have the proof that it is necessary and unavoidable."[7] A similar viewpoint is expressed by another of the printing crafts: "Where we have established satisfactory collective bargaining relations with employers, so that records of operating expenses may be freely discussed in conference between management and union representatives, our members are in a position to coöperate to improve efficiency."[8] Furthermore, it should be noted that many arbitrators have taken the same stand as the unions.[9] It should be noted, however, that the mere display of financial records on the part of the employers will not automatically settle all differences of opinion with respect to wage changes. Issues can, and do, often arise in regard to the interpretation of the financial data.[1]

As a rule, employers are reluctant to grant unions an increase in scales to restore a previous cut, even when business conditions would permit it. The unions know, therefore, that they will have to "put up a fight" to restore a cut. It is quite likely, then, that they will be opposed to any reduction in the first place. As Dr. Dunlop so aptly puts it, "Better one fight than two."[2] Furthermore, some unions believe that even if a certain wage reduction is advisable at a given time, so far as business conditions go, it is still best to resist it. One reduction may well make the employers think that the union will consent to a further reduction, and they will press for it, whereas the union may be opposed to such a concession. Hence it seems wiser to resist even the first one. Thus, some of the tapestry carpet weavers of Philadelphia, in resisting a 15 per cent wage cut in 1926, expressed the view that ". . . the

7. Typographical Journal, April, 1932, p. 365.

8. International Bookbinder, January-February, 1938, p. 6. Quoted in Twentieth Century Fund, op. cit., p. 168. Solomon Barkin of the Textile Workers Union has put forward the same thesis: ". . . employers have been most reluctant to offer labor the facts necessary to guide them in the formulation of their policies. . . ." (American Economic Review, Supplement, March, 1942, p. 305.)

9. See, for example, the statement of the arbitrators in the 1920 wage dispute in the New York book and job printing industry, quoted in Soule, op. cit., pp. 41, 42.

1. In this respect consult Soule, pp. 135–138, 148–155; and A. G. Pool, Wage Policy and Industrial Fluctuations, London, 1938, pp. 235–243.

2. "The Movement of Real and Money Wage Rates," Economic Journal, September, 1938, p. 423.

manufacturers will not be satisfied with a fifteen per cent reduction. . . ."[3] Similarly, one of the principal reasons why the brotherhoods were opposed to the 1921 reduction imposed by the Railroad Labor Board, was the ". . . fact that certain carriers had notified the (labor) executives of their intention to apply to the Railroad Labor Board for further reductions in wages, additional to those ordered July 1, 1921."[4] Such viewpoints are quite typical of trade union philosophy.[5]

The policy of some employers of making promises to unions long before these promises are to be fulfilled is another influence making for union wage rigidity. Since socio-economic phenomena are continually changing over time, often at a very rapid pace, employers may find, when the time to fulfill the promise arrives, that conditions have changed to such an extent as to preclude the possibility of keeping the promise. Unions, especially the rank and file, frequently fail to understand this, and insist that all pledges be honored. For example, several employers' associations in the book and job printing industry promised the various printing crafts in 1919 that the forty-four hour working week would be established on the first of May, 1921.[6] When this date arrived, however, the industry found itself in the midst of a cyclical depression, and many of the employers refused to live up to their promises.[7] This led to numerous strikes, with the unions winning in some, and the employers successful in ousting the unions completely from their shops in others. Similarly, the railroad crafts insisted on a wage increase in 1935, partially because the reduction accepted in 1932 was, according to the employers' promises, to have been restored in 1933.[8]

3. Quoted by Palmer, op. cit., p. 43.
4. H. Wolf, The Railroad Labor Board, Chicago, 1927, p. 162.
5. Thus an editorial in Advance (the official newspaper of the Amalgamated Clothing Workers) states: "The employers are always pretty nearly the first to sense how the workers are likely to react to an effort to reduce wage levels, particularly when such an attempt is made by the employers during a period of industrial depression. If the employer has reason to believe that the workers will not readily offer resistance to such a move, they are likely to try their luck. . . ." (November 27, 1925, pp. 1–2.)
6. The hourly wage rate was to be increased.
7. The depression was not the only reason for the refusal of many employers to accept the shorter work week. For the other reasons, as well as further details on the whole problem, consult L. M. Powell, The History of the United Typothetæ of America, Chicago, 1926.
8. W. McCaleb, The Brotherhood of Railroad Trainmen, New York, 1936, p. 196.

The inability of many employers to forecast economic conditions exactly, and their desire to take advantage of any opportunity which may arise in the bargaining process, is another factor contributing to wage rigidity. Thus, since employers believe that unions are very unlikely to accept a wage reduction unless a severe depression occurs, they consider it advantageous to sign a relatively long-term contract at a constant wage scale. Even if the employers are successful in doing this, however, they may often find that it is detrimental to them if the contract thus signed has a considerable length of time to run during a period of cyclical depression. Examples of this can be found in the Cincinnati printing industry.[9]

The reluctance of large corporations to reduce high executive salaries[1] and/or dividends has been another reason for the opposition of many unions to wage reductions in a period of depression. The unions' thesis is that if labor is to take a cut in its scale, others should do likewise.[2] Some organizations have gone farther, claiming that labor has a preferred claim on income accruing to the firm, that returns to capital should be only in the form of a residual payment, and that, therefore, labor's wages should not be reduced before capital's remuneration is nil.[3] Finally, some unions may resist a wage cut because they feel that the profits of the firm or industry could be increased by an improvement in managerial efficiency. This was one of the main arguments used by the railroad unions against a scale reduction in the 1921 arbitration before the Railroad Board.[8]

J. SHISTER.

CORNELL UNIVERSITY

9. From the author's field notes.

1. See J. C. Baker, Executive Salaries and Bonus Plans, New York, 1938, p. 242. Baker adds, significantly, that "executives themselves many times have much to do with establishing the market rate [for their services]," (p. 253).

2. Some unions have agreements with employers whereby the unions will not accept a wage cut until others connected with the industry in question also accept a reduction in their remuneration. The case of the teamsters on the west coast is pertinent in this respect. None of these locals will consent to a scale reduction until ". . . those who receive significant shares of the employer's total costs — the landlord, the creditors, the raw material suppliers, etc. — meet in conference and each accept some cut in their incomes. . . ." (Lester, op. cit., p. 193.)

3. See Wolf, op. cit., p. 119; H. Feldman, Problems in Labor Relations, New York, 1937, pp. 7–9.

4. Wolf, op. cit., p. 151.

THE RESPONSIBILITY OF ORGANIZED LABOR
FOR EMPLOYMENT

By SUMNER SLICHTER

I

This discussion of the responsibility of organized labor for employment will fall into two broad parts. To begin with, I wish to discuss how collective bargaining affects the structure of wages and the behavior of wages and to deduce from these results some effects of collective bargaining upon employment. Then I wish to inquire to what extent and how trade unions and the labor movement might assume responsibility for the level of employment in the community.

II

How would the wage structure in a world of collective bargaining differ from the wage structure in a world of free markets? Under free markets wage rates for the same occupation or for different occupations which require men of similar degrees of skill or responsibility *tend* to equalize the attractiveness of jobs in different places, in different industries, and in different firms. The wide and persistent differences in the prices of given types of labor in different plants or different places, however, suggest that a variety of powerful and persistent influences are molding the wage structure. Consequently, even in free markets wage differences fail to equalize the attractiveness of the jobs in given occupations. The large spread in wages between large cities and rural regions, for example, appears to be greater than is needed to compensate for the lesser attractiveness of city life. There appears to be a pronounced tendency for wages to be higher in industries in which labor cost is low than in industries in which labor cost is high; to be higher in firms which are prosperous than in firms which are not; and to be low in industries in which a high proportion of the work force consists of women.[1] These differentials do not seem to be needed to equalize the attractiveness of jobs in these various types of enterprises and industries. Collective bargaining, therefore, must be regarded simply as an addition to many other influences which are determining the structure of wages.

Although collective bargaining does not obliterate the influences

[1] More precisely the wages of male workers in industries employing a high proportion of women are low in relation to the wages of male workers in the same occupations in other industries.

which have been making the pattern of wages in free markets, it does introduce a powerful new influence; namely, the relative "bargaining power" of unions and employers. In a world of collective bargaining the wage structure must be expected to reflect (a) the sacrifices which the workers would have to endure and their willingness to make those sacrifices in order to put the price of labor above the free market price (the workers' demand curve for a higher price of labor), and (b) the sacrifices which employers would have to endure and their willingness to make sacrifices to keep the price of labor from rising above a given point (the employers' resistence curve). In this paper I shall not attempt to explore the influences which determine the level and slope of workers' demand curves or of employers' resistence curves. The curves will have different slopes in different industries and for different occupations and the point of intersection will be at varying heights above the free market price.

The varying success of unions in bargaining wage increases may be expected to create "wage-distortion" unemployment in some industries, occupations, and places. Where the price of labor (and the working conditions) negotiated by a union is particularly favorable to labor, substantially more men than are needed will attach themselves to the industry, the occupation, or the place. The excessive number of men will remain indefinitely because they will prefer intermittent work at high wages and under attractive conditions for a limited proportion of the time to steadier jobs under less attractive wages and conditions. Hence, wage-distortion unemployment is a normal result of differences in the relative bargaining power of unions and employers.

It is easy to find examples of wage-distortion unemployment. In a world in which collective bargaining is limited to less than half of the work force, nearly every trade union attracts a surplus of labor to the industry, occupation, or place. Conspicuous examples of wage-distortion unemployment are found in the needle trades. The powerful and well-run unions in these industries have done much to increase the attractiveness of work in the several branches of the industry. They have raised hourly earnings, protected the employees against arbitrary treatment on the part of management, and, in many ways, made shop conditions more attractive. People are easily drawn into the needle trades by attractive working conditions. The work is light and clean; the factories are accessible. Much of the work can be done by women, who might not otherwise be in the labor market at all. The reduction in the length of the working week to forty hours and to thirty-five hours (the latter is the standard under many union agreements in the needle trades) has made the industries particularly attractive to women. As a result of the success of the unions in improving hourly earnings and working conditions, there has been an enormous increase of workers relative to jobs in all of the needle trades.[2] The dollar output of women's and children's apparel, for example, dropped from 1.4 billion dollars in 1923 to 1.3 billions in 1939; but the number of wage earners more than doubled, rising from 133,195 in 1923 to 279,402 in 1939.[3] In the men's and boys' clothing industry, dollar output dropped sharply from 1.0 billion dollars in 1923 to 681 millions in 1939, but the number of wage earners increased slightly from 158,173 in 1923 to 161,731 in 1939.[4] The increase in workers relative to jobs is reflected in the reduction in the average annual "take-home" compensation of the workers which in the production of women's and children's apparel dropped from $1,324 in 1923 to $920 in 1939 and in the production of men's and boys' clothing from $1,311 in 1923 to $971 in 1939.[5]

Union membership and collective bargaining are concentrated in the cities where the growth of jobs is greatest and where the natural increase in population is least. Indeed, if no one were allowed to enter or leave the large cities of America for the next twenty years, the population of these places would drop by about half a million.[6] Between 1920 and 1940 the population of the country increased by nearly 25.9 mil-

[2] In view of the fact that compensation per hour has gone up and in view of the additional fact that many of the women employees in the needle trades do not wish to work too steadily, the drop in the annual take-home is not necessarily to be interpreted as an unfavorable development.

[3] Joel Seidman, *The Needle Trades*, p. 335.

[4] *Ibid.*, p. 340.

[5] The experience in the needle trades raises interesting questions concerning the concept of unemployment. To what extent is the "excessive" labor supply in the needle trades to be regarded as unemployed? Present methods of measuring unemployment would cause a worker who wishes nine months' employment a year and who obtains only seven months' employment to be counted unemployed for five months of the year, not two months. The worker is always seeking more work. Consequently, he (or more likely she) is regarded as unemployed throughout the entire period of idleness.

It is interesting and important to explore how long and to what extent wage distortion unemployment remains unemployment. This depends upon one's definition of unemployment. The inquiry would lead one into further explorations of the nature and meaning of unemployment. In the course of time chronic unemployment in a community becomes a way of life and becomes leisure rather than unemployment. This does not mean that people do not work at all. Rather they work only six or eight or nine months of the year. They become adjusted to this and find ways of utilizing their idle time. That makes idle time become leisure. The shoe cities and textile cities of New England furnish examples of unemployment which contains important elements of leisure. The people would like more work, but they are strongly attached to the community and prefer intermittent employment where they are to following the textile industry or the shoe industry to other places.

[6] Thompson and Whelpton have projected the natural increase between 1920 and 1930 to 1960. With no rural-urban migration, the urban section would lose 500,000 workers or 0.8%; the rural section would gain 21.3 million or 3.9%. National Resources Board, *Report of the Land Planning Committee*, 1935, Pt. 2, p. 97, quoted by R. B. Vance, research memorandum on "Population Redistribution Within the United States" (S.S.R.C., Bulletin 42), p. 33.

The concentration of the increase in population in the rural regions is reflected in the ratio of persons below ten years of age to total population. In rural regions one out of four persons in 1940 were less than ten years of age; in the cities, less than one out of six.

lion. About 3.3 million of the increase was the result of net migration from abroad. Had there been no migration from abroad or from farms between 1920 and 1940, the nonfarm population would have increased only from 74.4 million to 84.2 million (instead of to 104.6 million); but the farm population would have increased from 31.4 million to 41.5 million (instead of dropping to 30.2 million). In the same period the number of jobs increased by over 5 million. The increase in jobs was entirely in nonfarm occupations. A large movement of population from country to city is needed in order to prevent a further accumulation of surplus population in the country and the development of acute labor shortages in the cities.

Does collective bargaining help or hinder the adjustment of the geographical distribution of population to jobs and of jobs to population? Since collective bargaining is mainly concentrated in the cities, it tends to increase the differences in compensation between city and farm employments. This encourages capital to move to nonurban regions where it is badly needed. It tends, however, to increase wage-distortion unemployment in the cities because (a) it increases the excessive labor supply which will remain attached to urban industries and (b) it retards the expansion of urban industries and of urban employment needed to absorb the influx of job seekers from the country.

Union membership and collective bargaining are also concentrated in the North and Far West where wages have always been high relative to the South. It is a reasonable presumption that collective bargaining has tended to increase wage differentials between northern and southern plants. As labor is abundant relative to capital in the South and capital is abundant relative to labor in the North, a differential between North and South wages is needed to improve the geographical distribution of both labor and capital.[7] Insofar as unions have accentuated this differential, they have tended to accelerate the movement of capital into the South and of labor into the North. Unions, of course, have not intended to produce this result. On the contrary, as fast as unions establish themselves in the South, they endeavor to reduce the differential. The miners' union, the steel workers, and, to a less extent, the textile workers have made considerable progress in organizing the South in recent years. From now on the effect of unions upon the differential between the North and South will probably be the opposite to what it has been. Whether one regards the influence of unions upon the distribution of labor between the North and the South as desirable or undesirable will depend upon whether one desires a faster or slower movement of labor and capital than would be induced by the differentials created in free markets.

[7] Although labor in general is abundant relative to capital in the South, some types of labor, particularly managerial labor, are very scarce in the South.

III

The structure of wages produced under collective bargaining may affect the volume of employment by modifying either the consumption function or the investment function. So far as I am aware, no attempts have yet been made to determine what patterns or uniformities may exist in the distribution of relative bargaining power among employers and unions. Possibly the distribution of bargaining power is a random one. In this event, it would have little effect upon either the investment function or the consumption function. It is possible, however, that bargaining power may be distributed so as materially to affect the volume of investment opportunities or the propensity to consume. This would be true if trade unions were particularly powerful among: (1) persons engaged in industrial research and in discovering new industrial processes; (2) management and persons charged with administering enterprises; (3) workers engaged in making capital goods and in doing construction; (4) workers engaged in transportation; (5) salesmen, advertising men, and others whose activities affect the propensity to consume; (6) workers engaged in the service industries who are producing goods which are elastic in demand; (7) workers engaged in making luxury goods which are bought in the main by the well-to-do and which are inelastic in demand; and (8) employees engaged in making consumption goods which are inelastic in demand.

A concentration of bargaining power among the first four groups of workers would tend to reduce investment opportunities and thus to limit the demand for labor; a concentration of bargaining power among the fifth and sixth groups would produce a consumption function that is less favorable to employment than would be produced by free markets. On the other hand, a concentration of bargaining power among the seventh and eighth groups would tend to produce a consumption function which would be more favorable to employment than would be produced by free markets. This would be particularly true of the concentration of bargaining power among the seventh group of workers.

These observations require little comment. Whatever raises the cost of discovery and of administration may be expected to diminish the flow of new investment opportunities. The cost of transportation has important effects upon investment opportunities because it determines the limits within which "deepening" of capital is advantageous.

How is bargaining power actually distributed among workers in different economic categories? No thorough statistical studies which might yield an answer to my question have been made. There has been little organization among the first two groups of workers. In the last several years, however, organization has started in both fields. Construction workers have been among the first to organize and are among the most strongly organized workers, at least in the commercial and industrial fields. In the early days of the country, the demand for most types of construction was probably quite inelastic. Hence, the strong bargaining position of some construction workers was not an important deterrent to expansion.[8] Indeed by forcing increases in expenditures on expansion it may have stimulated the entire economy. As the country grows older and as replacement demand increases in importance, the demand for construction will probably become more and more elastic. Consequently, increases in the cost of construction, whatever their cause, may limit the general level of employment in all industries.

Until recently there has been little trade unionism in the metal working industries which turn out industrial equipment. That situation has now been changed. One might expect a high degree of organization among the handicraftsmen who make luxury goods. Special investigations, however, would have to be made to determine whether or not there is a concentration of unionism among these workers. Luxury-goods industries in the United States are relatively unimportant. There is no evidence of concentration of organization in industries producing consumer goods that are inelastic in demand.

It is important that men who design machines and manage plants and, until recently, the men who build machines, have not been organized. This state of affairs may well have limited the results of the concentration of bargaining power at any point upon the structure of production costs. At any rate, if technology is sensitive to union pressure for higher wages, increases in rates may have little effect upon labor costs. This matter will be discussed in the next section. Now that organization is spreading into research and management and has become well established among the mechanics who build machines, collective bargaining may have greater effects upon costs.

IV

Does union pressure for higher wages increase investment opportunities by accelerating the rate of technological discovery and do union rules limit investment opportunities by retarding the rate at which discoveries are put into use? Lieutenant Gordon Bloom, who has been investigating these matters, has reached the tentative conclusion that the effect of union bargaining pressure upon technological discovery is slight.[9] So long as bargaining power is relatively weak among the de-

---

[8] The relatively high wages of the construction workers' unions attracted superior mechanics into the organizations. The fact that the workers engaged in producing machines have not been organized encouraged mechanization of parts of construction. All in all, it is doubtful whether unions in the construction industry have greatly increased costs.

[9] Further investigations by Lieutenant Bloom, of course, may lead him to modify his

signers of machines and among engineers and other research technicians, one might expect the pressure of unions for higher wages to stimulate the search for laborsaving inventions. Even if the relative bargaining power of unions and employers were the same in all industries and all occupations, the pressure of unions for higher wages would presumably increase the attractiveness of laborsaving inventions and, therefore, increase the efforts to make them. If one expects wages soon to be bargained upward, the greater would be the advantage of discovering laborsaving inventions today and putting them into effect.

Industrial research has been growing by leaps and bounds. This growth, however, has been mainly brought about by other conditions than the rise of unions. Consequently, one cannot easily identify the influence of unions upon research. One often finds a very conspicuous response of managerial practices to collective bargaining at the time when it is first introduced into a plant. The men's clothing industry furnishes many examples. Managements know that they are confronted with a more or less difficult problem of controlling labor costs, and they begin to devote a larger part of their time and attention to these matters. To some extent greater attention to labor costs may occur at the expense of other aspects of the business, but in the main it represents a general improvement in the quality of management. Do these initial effects of collective bargaining persist indefinitely or do they quickly peter out? Are managements in the railroad industry, the printing industry, or the clothing industry, which have been unionized for many years, conspicuously more alert, thorough, and farsighted than managements which do not operate under union pressure? The answer to this question seems to be "No."

Despite the absence of conspicuous differences between managements in union plants and managements in nonunion plants, it is difficult to reach the conclusion that union pressure on wages has no effect. The very fact that wage rates tend to be high in industries in which labor costs are a small proportion of sales suggests that the level of labor costs affects the attention which managements give to them. Furthermore, it should be noted that technological changes are often made outside the industries which use the changes: locomotives are developed by locomotive builders, not by railroads; printing presses by printing press manufacturers, not by printers; coal cutting machines by machine builders, not by coal operators. If labor costs in an industry are expected to rise, the equipment builders for the industry have an incentive to increase their efforts to develop laborsaving apparatus.

tentative conclusion. His investigation is the first attempt of which I am aware to obtain evidence of the effect of union bargaining pressures upon technological change by investigating specific situations and, in particular, the aftermath of specific wage changes.

Do unions retard the introduction of technological discoveries? If the coal miners keep the differential on coal cutting machines and hand mining small, the installation of coal cutting machines is presumably retarded—although the improvement of coal cutting machines is probably stimulated. When the locomotive firemen require an extra man on Diesel switch locomotives, the use of such locomotives may be limited, though this limitation may not be important until Diesels have been used in the situations where they can be most advantageously employed. The regulation of the size of crews on printing presses may diminish slightly the use of new presses designed to require smaller crews. Nevertheless, cases of this kind are scattered and are unimportant. Furthermore, savings in labor are only one of several considerations affecting the decision to adopt new machines and methods. One concludes that unions tend somewhat to retard the introduction of technological changes, but that their influence is not great.

Little is known of the process by which some industries slowly become tradition-bound and lose much of their capacity to adapt themselves to changing conditions. Until the aging of industries is better understood, one cannot satisfactorily discuss whether collective bargaining tends to retard or accelerate the process. Have the wage system, the seniority system, the full-crew laws on American railroads and the enforcement of sharp distinctions between road service and yard service materially affected the opportunities of managements to experiment with new operating methods? Light on how and why industries become tradition-bound, what role, if any, unions play in aiding or retarding the process might be gained by study of the Lancashire cotton textile industry which seems to be an extreme example.[10]

V

Collective bargaining may be expected to affect the behavior of wages as well as the structure of wages and through its influence upon wage movements to affect the volume of investment. Let us analyze briefly the effect of collective bargaining upon (1) the rewards of innovation; (2) the cost of expanion; (3) response of the supply price of labor to shifts in demand. This analysis will be followed by a brief inquiry into the effects of collective bargaining upon cyclical adjustments.

1. *The effect of collective bargaining upon the rewards of innovation.* A certain amount of imperfection in markets seems to be needed in order to provide a reward for innovation, experimentation, and discovery. The amount of monopoly (or imperfection) needed depends upon the

[10] A report of the mission, headed by the Cotton Controller, Sir Frank Platt, states that the United States cotton textile industry "is very far ahead of the Lancashire industry in production per man-hour." The mission found that with normal staffing British output per man-hour was less than American by 18 to 49% in spinning, 80 to 85% in winding, and 56 to 67% in weaving. *The Economist,* Oct. 28, 1944, pp. 581-582.

propensity to save. The larger the disposition to save, the more protection is needed for innovators. The patent system reflects the view that the ordinary frictions and imperfections in markets do not give innovators sufficient protection against imitators.

Collective bargaining must be expected to reduce somewhat the rewards of innovation and discovery because it provides another way in which innovators may lose the gains from their discoveries. In the ordinary course of events, competition forces innovators to pass on their savings to consumers. Unions, through collective bargaining, may appropriate part of these gains before they are passed on.[11] The spread of collective bargaining may increase the importance of revising the patent system so as to give more adequate protection to innovators.

2. *The effect of collective bargaining upon the costs of expansion.* Collective bargaining may limit the employment opportunities offered in expanding industries by raising the wage level at which the new industries start.[12] It would do this directly if unions grow up quite early in the new industry. It would do it indirectly if employers set wages at a higher level than they otherwise would choose in order to discourage unionism. It would do it indirectly also if collective bargaining, through seniority rules and other conditions attractive to workmen, reduce the willingness of men to leave established industries for new industries.

No comprehensive surveys have been made to determine how collective bargaining has influenced wages in new industries. As a general rule, trade unions are slow in developing in such industries. Consequently, the direct effects of collective bargaining upon the expansion of new industries have probably been small. This situation may change. Up to now, however, the conclusion seems to be that any effect of collective bargaining upon the expansion of new industries has been indirect rather than direct. The history of collective bargaining is, of course, full of cases where investment opportunities have been created for individual nonunion concerns in unionized industries by a union scale which is above the rate at which new nonunion concerns can easily procure labor.[13]

3. *The effect of collective bargaining upon the response of the supply*

[11] If an innovator expects to be compelled to pass on part of his gains to labor before the rise of new competition forces him to pass on the gains to consumers, will he not set his original price higher than he would in the absence of collective bargaining? If it does, the net effect of collective bargaining in reducing gains of innovation may be quite small.
[12] Sometimes new enterprises grow up in areas of surplus labor supply and are able to start out at even below prevailing wages. New concerns may seek cities or regions in which an important industry is declining and in which surplus labor is available at less than prevailing rates. Examples can be easily found in some cities of New England and in the anthracite coal region. Other new enterprises, while paying more than local prevailing rates, may seek places where rates are low. The movement of industries into the South is an illustration. On the other hand, the automobile industry and the rubber industry grew up where it was necessary for them to pay above prevailing rates in order to attract labor.
[13] The attractiveness of the investment opportunities depends, of course, upon the

price of labor to shifts in the demand for labor. Collective bargaining may affect employment opportunities by making the supply price of labor more responsive to shifts in the demand for labor. Under free markets the reservation prices of labor are assumed to be independent of the demand for labor. This assumption seems to be essentially accurate. With widespread collective bargaining, however, it is likely no longer to be accurate. When the demand for labor rises, trade unions are likely to raise the reservation price of labor. They are likely to decide that the time has come to press for wage increases. Consequently, an economy in which labor is extensively organized may be one in which increases in demand produce price effects to a greater extent and employment effects to a less extent than an economy of free markets.

Is there evidence to support or refute these deductions concerning the possible effects of collective bargaining upon investment opportunities? The evidence is meager and unsatisfactory, and it relates in the main to the period when trade unions were, on the whole, quite weak and their membership only a small proportion of the entire labor force. For this period there is no evidence that unions promptly pushed up wages to appropriate part of the gains of discovery or to take advantage of the expansion in the demand for certain products. Douglas, in his study of the earnings of factory workers, finds that "pay roll" hourly earnings increased 3.27 times between 1890 and 1926, and that the hourly earnings of union workers in manufacturing increased 3.11 times. Pay roll hourly earnings represent industries in which there were both union and nonunion workers. The nonunion workers, however, greatly predominated. The comparison is a crude one because union wage rates do not represent the same occupations or industries as do the pay roll data. Furthermore, the union wage rates apply to more skilled workers than do the pay roll. Nevertheless, the data show that the hourly earnings of union and nonunion workers rose at approximately the same rate between 1890 and 1926.

Of particular interest and significance are the cyclical movements of union and nonunion wages. In periods of expansion, union wages rise less and later than do nonunion wages. In periods of contraction, union wages fall less and later than do nonunion.[14] The slow response of

---

probability that the new concern will remain nonunion or will soon have to pay union rates in order to remain nonunion.

[14] This conclusion is confirmed by the various scattered data. The studies of Douglas (*Real Wages in the United States, 1890-1925*, pp. 96 and 101) show the following comparisons between union and "pay roll" hourly earnings:

	Union	Pay roll
	Periods of Contraction	
1893-94	—1.5%	—7.3%
1907-08	—2.0	—5.9
1920-22	—1.4	—21.1

union wages to changes in demand is to be expected. It results from the fact that union wages are governed by trade agreements which run for a year or more. Wage changes can ordinarily not be negotiated until the agreement expires or at least not oftener than once a year. If it turns out to be true that union wages respond more slowly to increases in demand than do nonunion wages, the spread of collective bargaining would help innovators reap the fruits of their inventions and would give new industries a more favorable opportunity to expand.

VI

Collective bargaining tends to prevent selective and piecemeal decreases of wages in times of depression. This effect is less pronounced in industries where payment is by the piece than in industries where time payment prevails. How useful are wage reductions in maintaining employment? This is another matter which has not been carefully investigated. No one knows what types of firms cut wages in times of depression or what is the effect of wage reductions upon the production and financial policies of these firms or of their competitors. Among the cuts which would be particularly advantageous are reductions in the wages of workers who make products which are elastic in demand. There is no reason, however, to expect that wage cutting is or will be concentrated in that part of industry. Wage cuts probably develop first and spread most rapidly in industries where competition is keen. Furthermore, weakest firms probably make the first cuts and the largest cuts. Wage cuts probably help these firms remain in business. To this extent wage reductions limit the distress dumping of inventories and help to keep secondhand machinery off the market. They may also be

Periods of Expansion		
1897-98	+20.0%	+31.8%
1908-13	+10.8	+20.6
1914-20	+101.8	+163.4
1922-26	+15.3	+10.2

Annual data are, of course, far less satisfactory for the above comparison than would be quarterly data. The union wage rates apply to more skilled workers than the pay roll data. The cyclical movement of the wages of skilled workers may well diverge from the cyclical movement of "unskilled" or "semiskilled" workers.

The hourly earnings of union workers and of all workers in the book and job printing industry moved as follows:

	Union	All Workers
1914-20	+88.0%	+110.1%
1920-22	+25.7	+1.1
1929-32	+1.4	−2.1
1933-39	+16.1	+21.4

Figures on union wages in the book and job printing industry from the U. S. Bureau of Labor Statistics, Bulletin No. 781, p. 3, and for all workers in the book and job printing industry from the National Industrial Conference Board, Study No. 229, "Wages, Hours, and Employment in the United States, 1914-1936," pp. 140-143; 1939 figures from *Economic Record*, Mar. 28, 1940, Vol. 2, No. 10, p. 129.

important in inducing banks to renew loans to some firms. In all of these respects wage cuts are likely to have favorable effects upon prices and the volume of spending. A few firms which make wage cuts may reduce the prices of their finished goods. A study of cases would probably show, however, that this usually does not happen. Rather, most of the firms which make wage cuts are probably having trouble in meeting competition at prevailing prices. Nor are firms which make wage cuts probably led to spend much of the saving upon new equipment. They may be led, however, to retain higher standards of maintenance and repair, which means more expenditures on certain types of labor and on repair parts, and they may spend their depreciation allowances more freely—which would mean some expenditures on replacements. To a considerable extent the savings of wage cuts are likely to be used to reduce accumulated debts. This may be important, however, (1) in preparing the foundations for ultimate revival and (2) in affecting the lending policies of banks. Business managements are likely to await correction of their financial condition to delay undertaking ambitious expenditures for expansion until they have reduced or funded short-term debts. There is general agreement that banks (and bank examiners) impose unduly strict credit standards in times of depression and refuse (or criticize) many good loans. Better experience on repayments would broaden the willingness of banks to extend credits. Since the spread of collective bargaining is virtually eliminating selective wage cuts as a method limiting the cumulative effects of contractions in spending, other methods, such as unemployment compensation, budget deficits, and more generous loan-carry overs in the tax laws, must be developed.

VII

The foregoing analysis shows that trade unions affect employment in many ways—some favorable, some unfavorable. Can they be held responsible for their effects upon employment? They can be expected to conform to such laws and such ethical rules as the community may seem fit to impose. Until the community outlaws by its ethical code or laws every action which is unfavorable to the general level of employment, trade unions cannot be expected to avoid certain types of behavior or certain types of policy simply because these policies are bad for employment or to pursue other policies simply because they are favorable to employment.

This point may be made plainer if put in terms of the behavior of individuals. A man might raise the general level of employment in the community by becoming an adventurer and starting a business of his own, rather than by getting on someone else's pay roll. No one would assert, however, that he is under any obligation to become a business starter rather than a job holder. He is entitled to pursue his self-interest, regardless of the effect upon employment, so long as he observes the laws and the ethical rules of the community. Informal rules of right and wrong are often somewhat vague in their application, and some people are more scrupulous than others in not taking advantage of this vagueness. Nevertheless, it is a basic principle of our economy that people may pursue their interests within the framework of the law and the community's ethical rules.

Let us apply this to trade unions. They are entitled, along with business concerns and individuals, to pursue their self-interest. No union is large enough to be able to take account of the effect of its actions and policies upon the community as a whole. It may be smart for a large and powerful union, such as the miners' union, the automobile workers, or the teamsters, to avoid arousing the indignation of the public. If the community, however, wishes protection against activities by unions which injure employment, it must provide laws or ethical rules against these activities. So long as the community fails to do this, the unions must be expected to take advantage of the community's inaction.

The view which union members and union leaders take of policies will depend upon their knowledge of the probable results of policies. Consequently, better and more complete market research may lead many unions to modify their policies. The long-term elasticity of demand for labor is considerably greater than the short-term. Many unions, however, assume that the demand for labor is inelastic in the long run simply because it is inelastic in the short run. Each organization must, of course, decide for itself to what extend it will achieve present gains at the expense of future income. Many labor organizations (or their officials) may attach little importance to the long-run results of their policies. It is probably true, however, that wage policies of unions are usually based upon an underestimate of the long-term elasticity of the demand for labor. In this respect there is similarity between the wage policies of unions and the price policies of employers —although employers probably underestimate the long-term elasticity of demand less than do unions.

Although unions are not big enough to avoid in their own interest policies which may injure the general level of employment, they are big enough effectively to pursue many policies which will assist the employment of their members. Occasionally they incorporate in their wage scales incentives for employers to stabilize employment—particularly to reduce seasonal unemployment. The most notable instance of this is the employment guarantee plan which existed in the Cleveland women's garment industry from 1921 to 1931. It seems to have the possibility of wide extension. The opportunity of the employer to re-capture his contributions by giving employment gives managements a strong incentive to explore the possibility of stabilization. In Cleveland about 85 per cent of the contributions of employers were recaptured. One of the best opportunities for unions to increase the employment of their members exists in the building trades, where the unions could play a leading role in increasing the demand for housing. This demand depends in part upon prospective taxes on real estate and upon the existence of well-conceived city plans. Expectations of reductions in local taxes are of first importance in determining the availability of mortgage money. This is especially true in old communities where the tax rates have climbed to high levels. City plans are necessary to assure investors of definite developments in transportation, schools, parks, and other public utilities. Up to the moment the unions in the building trades have done very little to increase the demand for housing. Indeed, in many communities the local leaders of building trades unions are accus-tomed to co-operating with stupid and corrupt municipal machines which derive considerable support from corrupt and unimaginative contractors. The national unions in the building trades have it within their power to bring about a revolution in local policy.

VIII

The position of the labor movement as a whole is very different from that of the constituent unions. The labor movement as a whole is large enough to be concerned with the interests of all groups of workers. It is large enough to consider the effects of the policies of any union upon the general level of employment and upon the general level of pay rolls in the country. In other words, the labor movement as a whole can afford to be interested in the total amount of employment and in the total size of pay rolls. It presumably has the responsibility of pro-tecting the interests of all workers against the excessive claims of any particular group. If a union pursues policies which limit total employ-ment and which limit pay rolls, the over-all organizations of labor (the American Federation of Labor and the Congress of Industrial Organi-zations) can afford to oppose such policies. If the building trades unions, for example, were to diminish employment by reducing one of the most important outlets for saving, the over-all organizations of labor would be appropriate bodies to protect the interests of the rest of labor against the policies of the building trades unions.

The labor movement in the United States is not yet well prepared to act where the interests of particular groups of workers conflict with the interests of the rest of labor. The same is true of the labor move-ment in Great Britain. The tradition of the labor movement in this country is one of autonomy. Indeed, the American Federation of Labor was founded, not to dominate its constituent unions, but to help them preserve their independence. Each national union in the United States makes its own policies quite independently of the American Federation of Labor or the Congress of Industrial Organizations. Neither federation would venture to oppose or criticize the wage policy of a national union, no matter how that policy might affect the rest of labor. Nor would either federation ordinarily think of opposing other policies of member unions, such as policies toward technological change. There is no immediate prospect of a shift in the centers of authority within the labor movement. Indeed, the men who compose the executive councils of each federation are the heads of powerful national unions who are interested, above everything else, in the problems of their own unions.[15]

All of this does not mean that the federations may not become effective representatives for labor as a whole on matters where there are no clashes between important groups and the rest of labor. Tax policy is an example. The labor movement has grown strong because it has had the opportunity to bargain over a rapidly expanding national product. Its rise is a part of the great burst of enterprise which characterized the nineteenth century and the early part of the twentieth century. The labor movement is simply one facet of this great expansion. Consequently, the trade unions have a strong interest in keeping the supply of enterprise in the community large and the spirit of enterprise vigorous. The tax system has gradually developed until it threatens to prevent an adequate supply of enterprise by placing drastic penalties upon any one who presumes to make a living by putting men and capital to work.

There will always be important problems with respect to which the labor movement and business have common interests. The scope of the common interests of labor and business and the ways of implementing them can best be determined by discussions between representatives of the two groups. Political processes, valuable as they are, tend to exaggerate areas of conflict and also the importance of conflicts. Furthermore, political processes increase the difficulties of broadening areas of agreement. Consequently, both the labor movement and business would serve themselves and also the community by establishing permanent arrangements for regularly exploring their mutual interests. Recommendations in the field of public policy made jointly by the A.F. of L.,

[15] The labor movement in the United States may never acquire a national point of view comparable to that which exists in the Swedish labor movement. In the field of government centuries were required for the transfer of authority from the nobles to the national governments, and the transfer was brought about only by severe struggles. If the transfer gradually occurs within the labor movement, it will not be as a result of struggle. Indeed, contests between the federations and the national unions would only impede the development of a national point of view in the labor movement.

the C.I.O., and the United States Chamber of Commerce, and possibly other organizations would, of course, carry great weight. Of great importance is the fact that each of the several organizations is large enough to share the concern of the entire community with the general level of employment and the size of national pay rolls.

IX

Does the spread of collective bargaining require that the community develop and enforce a national wage policy? Is it not inevitable that the country will have an employment policy—a policy designed to facilitate the maintenance of a high level of employment? If the country has an employment policy, will it also require a wage policy? In the absence of a national wage policy will the structure of wages fixed by bargains in different industries and plants inevitably produce a large amount of "wage-distortion" unemployment? Must the community take responsibility for seeing that increases in the demand for labor do not raise the supply price for labor rather than produce increases in employment?

The logic of collective bargaining seems to indicate a national wage policy. It would be a fortunate circumstance, however, if the country, in times of peace, could escape the necessity of formulating and enforcing a national wage policy. The traditions of the country are strongly against recommendations of conduct in this field, and a national wage policy would not be easily enforced. Furthermore, there is danger that an attempt to formulate a truly national wage policy would fail—that the making of the policy would be taken over by this, that, or the other special interest with results roughly comparable to those produced by tariff making. If the labor movement and business can work together effectively for national policies which encourage enterprise, as I have suggested in the previous section, the necessity of a national wage policy may be avoided. Vigorous enterprise would not avert all unemployment—in particular, it would not prevent the types of unemployment which are not sensitive to changes in the volume of spending, such as wage-distortion unemployment and other types of structural unemployment. It would, however, keep unemployment low enough to prevent an imperative demand that the employment policy of the country be supplemented by a national wage policy.

Wages Policy and Business Cycles

Wages Policy and Business Cycles, by E. Ronald Walker, International Labour Review, Vol. XXXVIII, No. 6, December, 1938, pp. 758–793

WAGES POLICY AND BUSINESS CYCLES

By E. Ronald Walker

Lecturer in Economics, University of Sydney

In the modern industrial community wages and employment are the basic realities of economic existence. If standards of living are to be improved substantially it is with these factors that public policy must primarily be concerned. Where wage rates are regulated by authority or can be influenced directly by public intervention, the question at once arises whether at any given time the interests of wage earners and of the community as a whole can best be served by action designed to raise, to maintain, or to reduce, the rates of wages fixed. If action is taken in any of these three directions, what will be its effect on employment, earnings, and business activity?

In the whole range of economic theory and practical policy there is no question more controversial than this, and none that calls more insistently for a clear answer. It is a question on which both theoretical analysis and statistical investigation may throw some light. At the present time, in view of the variety of theories put forward, one of the main needs is to take stock of the theoretical discussion and to distinguish clearly the salient points on which investigation must concentrate if any agreement is to be reached. The International Labour Office has therefore thought it useful to invite certain economists who have devoted particular attention to the subject to set out their views on what are at present the main unsettled points in the theories of wages and industrial fluctuations which are relevant to wage policy.

In the following article, which is the first of the series written in response to this request, Dr. E. R. Walker discusses the effects of wage policy on industrial fluctuations and sets out his conclusions as to the type of wage policy which is appropriate at different stages of the business cycle.

Introduction

IT will generally be admitted that the discussions of the last few years have done much to clarify some of the major issues regarding economic fluctuations. The framework of the theory is nearing maturity, and the disputed issues are now coming to be seen in something like their proper perspective. Concentration upon monetary policy and the related problems of interest rates, saving, and investment, has exposed certain fallacies to which economists had clung tenaciously for generations, and has thereby enabled us to gain a much clearer picture of the processes involved in fluctuations. The question of wages policy has been raised anew by some writers and more particularly by the persons responsible for American and French New Deals, but the literature still remains in a state of no little confusion. Indeed, a thorough study of the problem leads to a revision of traditional theory which is comparable in scope with that recently imposed upon monetary theory.

Our purpose is to study the effects of wages policy upon economic fluctuations, and this involves placing wages policy within the general framework of business cycle theory. Experience suggests that each separate cycle, from trough to trough, or from peak to peak, is a historical entity. Even apart from the efforts, well or ill judged, to control depressions through monetary, fiscal or other governmental measures, the influences which determine at any time the level of employment, the profitability of enterprise, and the degree of economic activity, are continually changing. There can be no simple theory of the business cycle because there is no such thing as a regular cycle in which successive stages repeat themselves with measured timing and intensity. For the purpose of description it is customary to distinguish four phases through which economic affairs may pass : the upswing, the upper turning point, the downswing, and the lower turning point of the cycle, and the most successful theoretical essays are those which set out to explain separately the forces which may operate in each phase, without presuming that the whole cycle can be explained as a symmetrical fluctuation. Both experience and theory suggest, moreover, that in different historical cycles the forces at work in the upswing, for instance, may be different. It is also essential to recognise the irregularity of the movement within each phase. The upswing may be interrupted, not by an upper turning point, but by a period of stability at a comparatively low level of activity, which may be a prelude not to a downswing but to a renewal of the upswing. A similar " plateau " may interrupt the downswing. Again the lower turning point is often preceded by a period of low-level stability—what American commentators call the U-shaped as contrasted with the V-shaped depression—and occasionally a period of high-level stability is interposed between the upswing and the upper turning point.

Among the dominant forces at work in the course of a cycle we may distinguish, therefore, " expansive " (conducive to an upswing), " depressive " (conducive to a downswing) and " neutral " forces. In a period of stability expansive and depressive forces are either absent or nicely balanced. It is obvious that the turning points are often due to the emergence of contrary forces which overbalance the previously dominant forces ; but the problem is complicated by the fact that an upswing and a downswing both tend, sooner or later, to generate forces which are depressive and expansive respectively. It is therefore necessary to take account of " self-reversing processes ".[1] And we must also grant that a force may operate as a brake upon either the upswing or the downswing, without earning recognition as a depressive or expansive force.

The influence of wages policy upon industrial fluctuations may be fitted into such a framework. A wages policy may turn out to be expansive, depressive, braking, neutral, or even self-reversing. And the further possibility suggests itself that the same policy may operate differently according to the conditions under which it is applied. For instance, in Australia the Commonwealth Arbitration Court reduced wage rates in 1931 in the hope that such a policy would be expansive, or at worst a brake upon existing depressive influences. In subsequent years it refused to restore wage rates to their former level on the ground that such a policy would exert a depressive force ; but in 1937 it raised wage rates in the belief that this policy would serve as a brake upon the boom, and prevent the growth of expansive but self-reversing forces.[2] It was not apparently considered likely that the wage increase would itself provoke a depression.

---

[1] This classification is applied to monetary policy in R. C. MILLS and E. R. WALKER : *Money*, Ch. VII. Sydney, 1935.

[2] For an examination of the 1931 Judgment see E. R. WALKER : *Unemployment Policy*. Sydney, 1936. Cf. also " Australian Wage Policy, 1929-1937 ", by W. B. REDDAWAY, in *International Labour Review*, Vol. XXXVII, No. 3, March 1938.

Each of these propositions was opposed, and the proceedings of the Court during these years illustrate abundantly the complicated nature of the problem of designing a wages policy to alleviate industrial fluctuations.

SIX TYPES OF WAGES POLICY

To speak of a wages policy implies a far greater degree of central control than exists in many countries. It is not proposed to consider here the machinery by which a consistent and planned policy may be developed. But it is important to set out clearly the adjustments which are implied in the term " wages policy ". The alternatives are often stated simply as wage rigidity and wage flexibility, but a wider range of possibilities must be recognised.

(*i*) Wages might be kept perfectly rigid at all phases of the cycle. In practice such a policy might be approached but not achieved in entirety. There are always methods of reducing wages below a legal minimum and of paying wages in excess of a legal maximum. For the latter purpose the collusion of employees in evading the letter of the law is easily obtained, and even for the former purpose if there is much unemployment. For this reason wage statistics based on collective contracts or legal awards usually understate the degree of fluctuation in the course of a cycle.

(*ii*) Wages might be allowed to rise under the influence of competition in good times, but prevented from falling during bad times. This is in fact the policy favoured by many trade union leaders. It seems probable that the acceptance of the view that wage cuts diminish consumers' demand would lead to such a policy rather than to one of complete rigidity of wages.

(*iii*) Wages may be varied generally on a sliding scale, according to movements in the cost of living. This was the general principle (subject to occasional aberrations) of Australian wages policy prior to 1931, so far as the legal minimum wage was concerned. The general object of such a policy may be referred to as " rigid real wage rates ", although the rigidity may only be opposed to downward movements.

(*iv*) Wages may be varied generally according to a definite plan for controlling or offsetting depressions, which may involve flexibility of real wage rates as well as of money wage rates. Mechanical methods have been suggested for linking wage rates (real or money) to some index of capacity to pay or prosperity. Or, as in Australia since 1931, minimum wage rates may be varied on occasion with a view to controlling tendencies towards expansion or contraction without recourse to any mechanical index.

(*v*) As distinguished from general wage movements, differential wage movements may be an essential part of wages policy. Indeed the concept of a general wage movement is somewhat arbitrary ; it might be applied either to the case in which all wage rates moved by the same percentage, or where they all moved by the same absolute amount. But the results would probably be different. For instance, in the Australian system the basic wage (for unskilled labour) is varied according to an index of the cost of living, and occasionally (since 1931) with a view to controlling fluctuations. Skilled trades have minimum " margins for skill "—absolute amounts which are added to the ruling basic wage. Consequently a change in the basic wage involves equal absolute changes in the wage rates of most trades, but unequal percentage changes. Such a policy may distribute a given increase in the total wages bill differently from a policy which maintained percentage margins for skill ; and the effects of the expenditure of the increased wages bill may be accordingly different. Of more importance for the course of a cycle might be the possibility of applying differential wage variations with a view to adjusting the activity of different branches of industry to each other. For instance, a wage reduction in the building trades might facilitate the growth of investment more than a reduction in the wages of retail shop assistants.

(*vi*) We might also consider the possibility of a wages policy amounting to laissez-faire. The consequence would be different degrees of wage flexibility according to the conditions of different trades and places. Apart from differences in bargaining strength based on organisation of employees and employers, the movement of wages would be influenced by the severity of the depression or the activity of business in the respective places of employment. Since, in the course of a cycle, different industries are affected differently, the result would be differential wage flexibility. The flexibility might be greatest in the industries most affected by the cycle, notably the industries depending directly upon investment, but so many other influences are at work that no general rule can be established.

It should also be noticed that although wages policy may be left to direct negotiations between employers and employees, the result of these negotiations may be influenced by other aspects of social policy. The outstanding example of this is the British unemployment insurance system, which is generally believed to have rendered wages less flexible (in a downward direction) by relieving the competitive pressure of the un-employed upon the price of labour.[1]

THREE ASPECTS OF WAGES

With these principal types of wages policy in mind we may now consider the various ways in which wages policy may influence the course of industrial fluctuations. Here, too, the issue is frequently over-simplified. It is important, therefore, to notice the different avenues through which wages policy impinges upon the existing expansive or depressive forces.

Wages as an Element in Cost.

One of the legacies of static analysis is the tendency to regard wages primarily as an element in cost of production, and wages policy as influencing fluctuations solely through move-ments or rigidity of costs. At this stage the term "wages" becomes insufficiently precise. Wage rates per unit of time, wages rates per unit of output (average wages cost), payroll or wages bill (total wages cost), and marginal wages cost, should be distinguished. Nevertheless a variation in time rates or piece rates involves a change in the same direction in both total wages cost and marginal wages cost, provided that other conditions remain constant.[2] Under given conditions it is profitable to carry the employment of labour up to the point where marginal cost is equal to the marginal revenue[3], or in other words where any further increase in output would add more to total costs than to total receipts. If such a state of equilibrium obtains, a decline in wage rates will, other things being equal, reduce

---

[1] In particular see the discussion by B. PFISTER : *Sozialpolitik als Krisen-politik*. Stuttgart, 1936.

[2] Marginal wages cost is the reduction in total wages cost which would be associated with the reduction of output by one unit ; it may or may not be equal to average wages cost. Even if the employer has never heard of marginal wages cost, he uses the figures from which marginal wages cost could be calculated, whenever he compares the total wages cost of different levels of output.

[3] Marginal revenue is the reduction in total sales receipts associated with the reduction of output by one unit.

marginal cost to below marginal revenue and make it possible to increase profits by expanding output and employment. On the basis of this analysis many economists are prepared to consider a wage reduction as an expansive force under all conditions. Conversely a wage increase is regarded as generally a depressive force. Such conclusions are not valid, however, unless it be shown that this change in profit conditions is effective at all stages of a cycle, and that the other conditions are not themselves altered by the movement in wage rates. At a later stage we shall consider the extent to which marginal analysis can be applied to the study of fluctuations.

Wages as a Form of Income.

In recent years the so-called " purchasing-power argument " against wage cuts has been prominent in popular discussion, and has even influenced wages policy in the United States. This argument rests upon the fact that wages are a form of income and the source of a portion at least of the effective demand for the products of industry. In this connection it is not time rates or piece rates which are relevant, but the total wages bill. Consequently this source of demand varies not only with wage rates, but also with the volume of employment. The relationship between wage rates and the total wages bill is sometimes expressed in terms of the elasticity of demand for labour. If the elasticity of demand is unity, then the wages bill remains constant whatever the changes in wage rates ; if the elasticity of demand exceeds unity, every fall in wage rates increases, and every rise in wage rates decreases, the total wages bill ; and conversely if the elasticity of demand is less than unity. This concept has unfortunate associations. It suggests immediately a mental picture of a demand curve, and some are ready to discuss the shape of the demand curve for labour in general. There is, however, no such thing as a demand curve for labour in general. Moreover if there be demand curves for particular types of labour, during a cycle the shifts in the curves are at least as important as their shapes. Indeed, the essential point of the purchasing power argument may be formulated as the affirmation that a wage reduction itself provokes a shift in the demand curves for particular types of labour. Discussion of the elasticity of demand for labour is permissible only if it be divorced from the concept of demand curves relating to constant conditions of demand, and be considered simply as a mathematical expression of the relationship between wage rates and wages bill in the circumstances which are under study.

If the discussion be carried on in terms of money, there are two conceivable rebuttals of the purchasing-power argument against wage cuts. One is to show that despite a fall in wage rates the wages bill actually expands, so that wage earners' purchasing power increases instead of declining. The other is to stress the existence of other forms of income, and to show that any fall in the wages bill is compensated for by a corresponding increase in profits, or in other incomes which may also serve as a source of demand. Moreover, if the wage reduction involves a fall in commodity prices, it is sufficient to show that total incomes fall by less than prices, so that the " real demand " for the products of industry expands. The simplest (and least convincing) reply to the purchasing-power argument, however, is arrived at by confining the discussion to " real terms ". Then, provided it can be shown that the fall in wage rates involves some net increase in employment, however small, it follows that the flow of real goods and services, and consequently the source of real demand, are strengthened. The first step in this argument is assumed to involve no difficulty, since a fall in wages reduces costs. But to affirm that this alone is sufficient to produce a growth of employment is to side-step the issue posed by the purchasing-power argument. To this point we shall return later.

At this stage it is worthy of notice that, whether or not movements in the wages bill affect the total level of money incomes, such movements may nevertheless be relevant to the fluctuations in demand associated with business cycles. The speed with which money disbursed in costs flows on to the market as purchasing power depends in part upon the form of income and method of payment which is involved. Assuming a constant propensity to consume in all classes of the community, a change in the wages bill is likely to react more quickly on wage earners' expenditure than a change in the profits bill will react upon profit earners' expenditure. The possibility of variations in propensity to consume is, of course, another subject for investigation.

It is also appropriate to observe that the redistribution of income due to a change in the wages bill may facilitate the introduction of new monetary resources into the system or the destruction of monetary resources—processes which in turn may modify the total level of incomes and the demand for labour. For instance, transfer of resources to the employers may cause them to reduce their indebtedness to the banks ; and, unless other bank advances are made, the level of money demand for the products of industry will consequently fall.

Wages and Interest Rates.

Despite the fact that a reduction in the total wages bill may involve redistribution of income in favour of other forms of income, including the yield on capital, it may nevertheless tend to reduce interest rates. A fall in the wages bill usually makes possible a decline in working capital, or in other words a fall in the demand for money on loan, which tends to reduce interest rates. On the other hand, if the demand for labour is elastic, so that a fall in wage rates leads to an expansion of the wages bill, this will tend to raise interest rates. On the latter assumption we may also expect some increase in the demand for loans for investment in fixed capital, since an expansion of the wages bill, despite lower wage rates, implies an optimistic view of the prospects of profit from enterprise. Consequently the tendency of interest rates to rise will be reinforced. To return to the other case, a fall in wage rates and in the wages bill may be consistent with some considerable expansion of employment, and consequently with improved prospects of profit. Accordingly the tendency of interest rates to fall on account of the diminished demand for working capital may be offset to a great or small degree by an increased demand for capital for fixed investment. If, as the purchasing-power argument suggests, there is no expansion of employment following the fall in wage rates, this offsetting factor will not operate.

These relationships do not exhaust the possible influence of wages policy upon interest rates. A change in the demand for loans may not produce the expected effect upon interest rates because of a simultaneous change in the supply of funds offered on loan. The latter factor is determined by the quantity of money in existence and the liquidity preferences of the owners of resources and of borrowers. The movement of wage rates may influence some of the motives to liquidity which Mr. Keynes has christened the transaction motive, the precautionary motive, and the speculative motive. Reactions upon the transaction motive are already assumed, to some extent, in the above references to the demand for working capital, but the other two motives require more detailed study. The problem cannot be dealt with satisfactorily at this stage, however, because our discussion of the effects of a wage change upon employment has been confined to a survey of the theoretical possibilities. In any case the effect of a change in interest rates due to wages policy upon the course of the cycle is likely to be experienced some time after the immediate and direct effect (if any) of wages policy upon the level of economic activity. We can safely postpone, therefore, any further reference to the indirect effects of wages policy through interest rates until we have dealt with the more direct effects.

FRAMEWORK OF THE THEORY OF FLUCTUATIONS

From the above discussion it is evident that the significance of wages policy in the course of a business cycle depends upon the part played by changes in cost, in the level and distribution of incomes, and in interest rates, within the sequence of events which constitutes the cycle in question. This can best be indicated in the course of a brief review of the framework of the theory of cyclical fluctuations.

The condition necessary for the maintenance of a stable level of economic activity is stability of profits at a level which does not encourage further expansion or contraction of enterprise, except compensatory movements in the different industries.[1]

This implies that the flow of purchasing power into the market must be maintained at a level equal to the total costs paid out plus the requisite amount of profits. And this in turn implies either that all money disbursed in costs or received in profits is spent by the recipients of these incomes, or that resources equivalent to any amount saved are placed at the disposal of people who proceed to spend them. The second alternative solution may be obtained either by the loan of saved income to those who will spend it or by the creation and expenditure of new money or credit. The latter is necessary in so far as saved income is added to the money balances of savers or borrowers, and is therefore not available for loan. It is fashionable to refer to this condition of stability as the " equality of saving and investment ", because the principal demand for loans or savings or other credit comes from those who wish to invest in new capi-

---

[1] This qualification introduces complicated problems which would require further study in any full length analysis of cyclical fluctuations.

tal equipment or in increased stocks. The condition might be satisfied, however, if savings were offset, at least in part, not by investment in the ordinary sense, but by subsidies or doles or payments for services, out of additional credit or new money.

Such a state of stability will be disturbed, and expansion or contraction of economic activity initiated, by an increase of profits above, or a decline in profits below, the level which is required for stability. If costs (excluding profits) can be reduced without reducing receipts to a corresponding degree, the result is an expansion of profits which may be sufficient to produce an increase in activity. Conversely, if costs are increased without a corresponding rise in receipts, this may exert a depressive influence. Here the first two of the three aspects of wages policy noticed above are both relevant, and the problem arises of discovering what connection, if any, exists between the movement of costs and the movement of receipts at different stages of the business cycle. This is greatly complicated by the fact that receipts may vary independently of an initial movement in costs, because expenditure can rise above or fall below the total amount previously disbursed through costs and profits. For instance, there may be a growth in investment or other expenditure from loans or new credit above the level of savings which were forthcoming at the previous level of incomes—that is, at the previous level of activity. So long as this excess of investment continues, entrepreneurs will receive excess profits, which encourage them to expand output and, if necessary, employment. Similarly a decline in activity may be traced to a deficiency of investment as compared with the level of savings appropriate to the previous level of incomes. In the former case the growth of economic activity tends to raise incomes to a level at which savings will be equal to investment; and in the latter case the decline in activity tends to reduce incomes to a level at which no more is saved than is required to maintain investment. If this tendency has full play, a period of expansion or contraction is followed by one of relatively high-level or low-level stability. But a further change in investment or other expenditure out of additional credit may prevent this stability from materialising. Thus, apart from the possibility of affecting profits through changes in costs which do not involve similar changes in receipts, expansion and contraction may be explained in terms of the reaction of the economy to a divergent movement of saving and investment (or other forms of expenditure out of supplementary credit). And, to return to our problem of the relationship between variations in costs and variations in receipts, it is evident that the solution depends upon the extent to which a movement in costs reacts upon the disposition of people to save, to invest, or to provide the loans or new credit which may finance additional investment.

There is one weakness in this analysis of which few writers seem to be conscious, namely the concept of a " requisite " level of profit—sometimes referred to as " normal " profit. The latter expression is positively misleading, whether " normal " be used in the sense of a standard to which profits should conform or in the statistical sense of an average or other measure of " central tendency ". Examination shows that the theory is tautological for, by definition, there will be stability if profits are such as to provide no incentive to expansion or contraction. Indeed, all formal analyses are tautological in this sense. The important point however is the assumption that the level of requisite profits has a certain degree of constancy, so that if profits increase above the level at which business was stable, they are *ipso facto* raised above the level necessary to keep business stable. If conditions change, so that now a higher level of profits than before is required to keep business stable, then the increase of profits which is actually registered may not lead to any expansion in economic activity. Similarly an increase in the necessary level of profits which is required to keep activity stable will provoke a decline in activity even if the previous level of profits is maintained by the equality of savings and investment. Again there is the problem of the *minimum sensibile*. Even assuming no alteration in entrepreneurs' dispositions, the change in profits must attain a certain magnitude before producing any expansion or decline in economic activity. There is no *a priori* reason for assuming the *minimum sensibile* to be large or small, or even constant over a period of time. Might it not vary with the stage of the cycle ? Admittedly it is easier to operate with simplified models, but if we are to consider policy in relation to actual economic fluctuations our theory cannot be confined to the analysis of simplified models, or of assumptions which are easy to handle. We shall see, when we deal more explicitly with wages policy, that the points raised here do not involve merely a minor correction in the theory, but that they are fundamental to the assessment of the effect of wages policy upon cyclical fluctuations. At this stage, however, we need only observe the qualifications of the general theory expounded above.

Subject to these qualifications we may class as expansive any forces calculated to encourage investment or to discourage saving, and as depressive any forces tending to discourage investment or to encourage saving. Similarly such forces may serve as a brake upon forces operating in the other direction. This opens up a series of further problems concerned with the causation of changes in saving and changes in investment.

As regards the former there is much to be said for Mr. Keynes's view that short-term changes are due chiefly to changes in incomes, saving varying directly with income. Then it is evident that each process of expansion, based on a growth of investment in excess of the previous rate of saving, sets up an increase in saving, which serves as a brake upon the expansive forces. Similarly a fall in saving, initiated by the process of contraction, tends to impose a brake upon depressive forces. Thus both the expansion and the contraction may " fade away " into a phase of relatively high-level stability or low-level stability. A sudden change in saving, independent of changes in income, which might either reinforce a dominant tendency towards expansion or contraction or provoke a reversal of the movement, would need to be explained in terms of changed opinions regarding the outlook for the future or changed evaluations of the comparative advantages of present and future consumption. Clearly, irrational factors may play an important part in producing such changes.

When we turn to the causation of changes in investment, the theoretical possibilities become embarrassingly numerous. An increase in investment may be due, in the first place, to a fall in the cost of investment in terms of the interest rate on borrowed funds, or to the adoption of a more liberal rationing policy on the part of the banks. Or it may be traced to a fall in the purchase cost of the investment—for example, a fall in building costs—which reduces the amount of money capital required. On the other hand the impulse to invest may come from the estimated yield of the investment. Again, investment may be undertaken with a view to displacing costly or unruly labour by machinery. Public expenditure financed either by floating loans or by specially-created central-bank credit may serve the same purpose as ordinary investment in offsetting the depressive effects of saving ; the cause of such expenditure may lie in any of a number of political situations ranging from an undesired deficiency of revenue to a deliberate policy of " reflation ", designed to stimulate industrial activity. The variety of these possible causes of variations in investment or other expenditure of additional credit presents an effective barrier to the establishment of any simple theory of business cycles.

It should be noted that a fall or rise in investment tends under certain conditions to operate for a time in a cumulative manner. A decline in profits due to a fall in demand for the products of industry is liable to discourage investment still further, and even to provoke disinvestment in the form of allowing stocks to decline and fixed capital to depreciate. This vicious circle is a recognised feature of major depressions. Conversely, once investment rises above the previous level of savings the profitable conditions thus initiated will usually stimulate a further expansion of investment. Moreover the " credit-worthiness " of prospective borrowers and investors will tend to vary with the prospects of profitable enterprise, and this tends to ensure that a movement of investment or other expenditure will feed on itself. The braking influence of variations in saving, consequent upon changes in incomes, may thus be offset for some time by a cumulative waxing or waning of investment. On the other hand a process of expansion or contraction is likely to reach, sooner or later, a self-reversing stage. This probability is stronger in the case of a contraction. In Mr. D. H. Robertson's picturesque terms, a boom, instead of fading away, may explode.[1] Several different self-reversing processes may be distinguished, each of which is theoretically possible, and some of which are sufficiently consistent to permit of their simultaneous operation.

A period of expansion normally requires the provision of additional quantities of working capital in the form of bank credit. Unless the cash resources of the banks are being strengthened, either by additional central-bank credit or by imports of gold or rights to foreign currency, sooner or later a stage will be reached in which the expansion of bank loans must be checked, either by raising interest rates or by refusing credit to certain borrowers. The result is the same—a decline in the profitability or possibility of investment, which may be sufficient to initiate a period of contraction. In a free economy,

---

[1] LLOYDS BANK LIMITED : *Monthly Review*, Sept. 1937.

reaction cannot be postponed indefinitely by creating additional central-bank credit, except at the risk of a collapse of the currency. And only exceptional circumstances would permit an uninterrupted importation of gold along with continued expansion of internal economic activity.

The process in question is more likely to be observed if the period of expansion carries the economy up to or near full employment of all resources except those which are stranded in permanently depressed areas. For the approach of full employment involves a tendency for prices and costs to rise, so that the growth of bank credit must be all the more rapid if the expansion of activity is to continue. Moreover, as full employment approaches, the process which Professor Hayek has advanced as the cause of the turning point becomes important.[1] This is the competition between investment trades and consumers' goods trades for the original factors of production, which, we may concede, serves to drive up costs still more violently.

Another self-reversing process may be traced to the operation of the " principle of acceleration ". An expansion of demand for consumers' goods (caused by a growth in investment, for instance) is liable to involve a more than proportionate growth in the demand for producers' equipment, unless industry is working far below capacity. The latter demand can only be met by increased investment. So far the acceleration principle tends to strengthen the process of expansion. But investment will fall again if the demand for consumers' goods is stabilised, since the demand for producers' equipment will fall to the level required for renewals and replacements. To prevent a fall in investment—that is, to keep investment constant—the demand for consumers' goods must expand at an ever-increasing rate ; but a constant level of investment will not yield such an increasing expansion in consumers' demand ; and the reaction is sooner or later inevitable, for this if for no other reason.

A third self-reversing process may be found in over-investment in the Hobsonian sense[2]— that is, relatively to the demand for the output of the capital equipment produced by the investments. According to Hobson, this process is due, above all to the large savings of the well-to-do, but it might follow just as well from a large expansion of bank credit in excess of the previous level of savings. Many critics have argued that entre-

---

[1] Friedrich A. HAYEK : *Prices and Production*. London, 1935.
[2] J. A. HOBSON : *The Industrial System*. London, 1910.

preneurs would not make investments in capital equipment unless there existed an adequate market for the produce, but this criticism implies a degree of foresight far beyond the capacity of most entrepreneurs. It should be noticed that this process is not altogether consistent with that described by Professor Hayek ; the latter would be checked by a fall in the wages bill, while the Hobsonian process would apparently be checked by a rise in the wages bill. Both theories are formally valid (assuming in neither case perfect foresight), and either process might bring to an end a particular historical period of expansion. But if both processes developed concurrently they might cancel each other out at the critical moment ; the flow of products from the equipment acquired by the new investments would reduce the demand for resources on the part of the consumers' goods industries and alleviate their competition with the capital goods trades.

A fourth example of a self-reversing process was mentioned earlier—namely, an investment boom based upon the acquisition of machines which are later to displace labour. Once the machines are installed there may be simultaneously a decline in investment and the discharge of the displaced employees.

A fifth self-reversing process was advanced by Marx—as the quantity of capital increases, the rate of profit which can be earned thereon tends to fall. A similar notion appears in Mr. Keynes's view that the marginal efficiency of capital falls as its quantity increases, although Mr. Keynes neither acknowledges Marx's priority nor attempts to elaborate a proof of his thesis as Marx did.

In the face of these different possible processes it is easy to accept the notion that economic fluctuations are inevitable, and especially that once a depression occurs it can be overcome only by developments which are themselves likely to produce subsequently a new decline in activity. Two corollaries may be added. The first is the supreme importance of checking any depression before it carries activity down to so low a level that a considerable investment boom is required to regain something like full employment again. The other corollary is the need for study of the question whether the upswing can be controlled in such a way as to reduce the violence of the subsequent recession. It is widely accepted that an " unduly " rapid upswing is likely to provide a more serious reaction ; but satisfactory criteria of whether a particular recovery is or is not " unduly " rapid are not available. Between the two extremes of fearing to get out of one depression because we shall then get into another, on the one hand, and subordinating everything to the speed of recovery, on the other, there must be a golden mean. It cannot be said, however, that economic theory gives clear instructions as to how to determine this golden mean, or even a certain measure of the dangers involved in the less cautious of the two policies just mentioned. This is highly relevant to the problem of wages policy, for an authority concerned with the control of cyclical fluctuations ought to know whether it desires " to stimulate recovery " or (as in Australia in 1937) to impose a brake upon the boom, as well as whether a particular wages policy would produce one effect or the other.

If the lower turning point of the cycle be considered, the self-reversing processes appear to be less in evidence ; the analysis of cyclical fluctuations is not symmetrical. For instance, the principle of acceleration serves to strengthen a decline in activity, but does not necessitate an ultimate reversal of the process. Again, whereas the approach of full employment tends to strengthen some of the forces making for higher interest rates or credit restriction, there is not, during the depression, a similar auxiliary to such forces as may be working for lower interest rates. Full employment imposes a ceiling to the upswing, if the latter be not otherwise checked ; but if a limit is imposed upon the downswing its explanation is not to be found in the approach of full unemployment. We can, however, distinguish two tendencies towards a self-reversing process which may end the downswing. One is the diminished demand for loan capital and the consequent tendency to lower rates of interest, which may lead in turn to a rise in investment. The other is disinvestment, which, by allowing equipment to deteriorate and stocks of goods and materials to run down, creates a situation in which new investment may be undertaken with some degree of suddenness. But experience and theory both suggest that a prolonged downswing is not likely to be followed by a sudden turning point unless there be some definite impulse to a growth of investment or other production, an impulse external to the processes we have been discussing.

Some economists are inclined to minimise the importance of so-called external impulses to expansion or contraction, and seek to develop a theory which makes no appeal at all to such forces. To succeed in such a task may be an intellectual *tour de force*, but it is no proof that the theory in question is an adequate explanation of fluctuations. Experience suggests that " psychological factors ", political action, natural phenomena, and other extraneous forces, can and do affect the course of particular historical fluctuations, and may operate at any or every phase of a particular cycle. Indeed, were it not so there would be no practical interest in the problem of wages policy in relation to economic fluctuations.

CRITICISM OF THE MARGINAL PRODUCTIVITY APPROACH

Before attempting to bring wages policy into the above framework of the theory of fluctuations, it is necessary to clear the ground by discussing the extent to which we can use the marginal productivity theory, which, stated with due qualification, has gained wide acceptance, not only as an explanation of the level to which wages tend under competition, but also of the volume of employment which will be offered by employers at any given wage. In the hands of Professor Pigou, for instance, it has provided some sort of answer to those who suggest that wage reductions will reduce purchasing power but not increase employment, and has been used as the basis for a rough estimate of the " elasticity of demand " for labour in Great Britain during a depression. Any differences of opinion on the former question would, of course, involve different conclusions on the latter ; the relation of wage movements to consumers' demand is one of the fundamental issues of modern wage theory. Professor Pigou's solution rests upon two foundations. First, a brief algebraical analysis serves to prove that, without any change in employment, a reduction in money wages must either reduce real wages or increase the value of non-wage goods relatively to wage goods. Into the significance of the latter possibility we need not go ; the important thing is the conclusion : " Hence the system is not in equilibrium. Additional labour *must* be employed, and additional output be forthcoming." [1] This is regarded as sufficient discussion on the point, because Professor Pigou has already laid the other foundation of his argument, namely that " the quantity of labour demanded ... at any given rate of real wage is such that the value in terms of wage-goods of its marginal net product ... approximates to that rate of wage ". Since the wage and the marginal net product are

---

[1] A. C. PIGOU : *The Theory of Unemployment*, p. 102. London, 1933.

approximately equal " in equilibrium ", a reduction in the real wage rate implies disequilibrium, and an extension of the demand for labour.   On this assumption Professor Pigou proceeds to determine what fall in money wage rates will be required, under various monetary conditions, to effect a given reduction in real wage rates. Professor Pigou stresses the fact that his analysis is concerned with a simplified model, from which some of the complications of the real world are omitted. It is permissible to criticise a theory not only on grounds of its internal consistency, but also on the extent to which it embodies the essential features of the problem as it appears in the real world. The major criticism which may be brought against Professor Pigou's work on unemployment is concerned with his assumption of the universal validity of the marginal productivity theory. There is in fact abundant reason to believe that an employer's demand for labour is not determined at all times by the factors advanced in the marginal productivity theory. Professor Pigou [1] himself has warned us that any study of elasticity of demand for labour which disregards the distinction between booms and depressions must be futile, because marginal productivity varies with the phase of the cycle, according to the extent of surplus capacity in industry. But it is equally important to distinguish between different phases of a cycle because the conditions which are taken as given in the theory of marginal productivity are not present in all phases.

Among the assumptions which are essential to the theory we may draw attention to the following : (*a*) the employer sets out to maximise the profits and to minimise the losses involved in the employment of labour ; (*b*) the employer knows the marginal productivity of labour over a sufficient range. In a stationary state, with self-interest the dominant motive, both assumptions are implicit ; but their approximation to the conditions of the real world varies considerably with the state of business activity. We shall consider these two assumptions in turn.

There are two cases in which the employer may not set out to maximise profits. In the first place, he may be so susceptible to the psychological influences of depression that he does not respond rationally to a wages reduction. The absence of confidence may well prevent him from engaging more workers even though it appears likely that their marginal productivity would exceed the reduced wage rate. This point is generally admitted ;

---

[1] *Op. cit.*, p. 89.

indeed it provides a convenient explanation of the failure of employment to respond to wage reductions in depression. On the other hand, it may be argued that knowledge of a general wage reduction may contribute to the restoration of confidence. In other words, the *minimum sensibile* of change in profit expectations which is required to stimulate an expansion of employment varies with the psychological situation.

In the second case, the employer may not be guided by marginal productivity because he has other purposes than the maximisation of profits. During a period of prosperity the desire to consolidate his position by meeting all orders and losing no trade to his competitors may lead him to pay wages in excess of the marginal product of labour, in the ordinary sense. It would require elastic definition to include the goodwill of customers in the marginal product of his otherwise " overpaid " employees. Again, during depression a stage may be reached in which survival of the firm depends upon maintaining prestige, and the employer may feel compelled to continue employing labour even at a wage in excess of its marginal productivity. To take another example, in the deflationary phase of a cycle, wage reductions may not lead to any expansion of employment, because the reduction of indebtedness is at the time a more important need than the maximisation of profits. It will be noticed that the examples of our second case do not involve irrational behaviour on the part of employers.

The second assumption of the marginal productivity theory the validity of which varies at different stages of the business cycle is that the employer knows the marginal net product of labour, and that in terms of money. We need not consider the doubt which may well arise whether any employer actually thinks in terms of marginal productivity ; the analysis is valid so long as the guides which influence his behaviour lead to the same results as would follow from calculation of the marginal productivity of labour in terms of money. The rational self-interested employer may be expected to balance total receipts against total costs, and to consider the movement in each which is occasioned by variation in the number of employees at a given rate of wages. Only when he believes that the employment of more men will add more to his receipts than to his costs will he take on additional workpeople. This type of calculation will lead to the same decision as calculation based upon the marginal product of labour in terms of money. In other words, the theory of marginal productivity assumes that the employer has such knowledge as would be needed for the construction of the marginal cost curve and the marginal revenue curve appropriate to his firm, over the relevant range of variation of output and employment. Given the money wage rate and other costs, it might be thought that the marginal cost curve need present no difficulty to an experienced producer. But at some stages of a cycle the movement of raw material costs and selling costs cannot be predicted. The curve of marginal revenue is still less easy to establish, because the experience which is necessary to supply the data embodied in the curve is so often lacking. Under stable conditions, with pure competition, marginal revenue is equal to price. And even under conditions of imperfect competition, if conditions of demand do not change, experiments with various outputs may provide the data necessary for determining the marginal revenue curve over a sufficient range of output. The scope for error is naturally greater than with pure competition, but reasonable accuracy of knowledge may be obtained, provided the factors affecting demand are stable.

This proviso is the crux of the matter. In a period of business contraction, for instance, when incomes are falling, the conditions of demand are liable to change rapidly, and with them the shape and position of the demand curve. The employer knows merely one point on the curve in its new position : that given by sales at the existing price. If incomes are falling he does not know whether a price reduction would yield a larger sale. Only experience can reveal the relationship between price changes and changes in demand, and each piece of experience is liable to be rendered immediately out of date. Consequently the entrepreneur cannot calculate the marginal revenue from various hypothetical outputs, nor can he estimate the relationship between marginal revenue and marginal costs. In such circumstances there is no reason for assuming that the employer's behaviour can be described in terms of the marginal productivity theory.

It is worth emphasising that this observation does not imply any lack of rationality on the part of the employer. We are not here concerned with the " results of neuroses or confused thinking " [1], but with the behaviour of " economic men "

---

[1] Cf. Joan ROBINSON : *The Economics of Imperfect Competition*, p. 16. London, 1933.

—psychologically normal and rational employers faced by market conditions which render the prediction of demand impossible.   Writing on a different point, Professor Pigou [1] reminds us that " the great complexity of modern economic structure makes it extremely difficult for any dealer to estimate correctly either the total final buyers' demand for any product a little while ahead or the extent of the preparations that other dealers are making to meet it ".   In view of what Professor Pigou calls the " lack of any real scientific ground for forecast ", it is somewhat surprising that the marginal productivity analysis should be used by him when discussing the relationship between wage rates and unemployment at all phases of the business cycle.   He stresses that it is essential to specify the sort of times to which any enquiry relates [2], because physical marginal productivity varies with the phase of the cycle ; our point is that the need to specify the sort of times to which the enquiry relates arises above all from the fact that there are times when it is not possible to discover the marginal productivity of labour in terms of money.

There may be scope for some difference of opinion regarding the duration of the periods in which uncertainty about demand renders the marginal productivity approach useless.   But it seems credible that during most of the period 1930-1936 there were few employers in any country whose behaviour followed the marginal principle.   Perhaps even this is an understatement.

In passing we may notice that the criticisms here advanced bear not only on the theory of fluctuations, but also on the theory of distribution.   Various objections to the marginal productivity theory of distribution have been offered in the past, such as the indivisibility of large units of resources, obstacles to transfer, and the difficulty of reorganising the constant factors when the variable factor alters.   Divergent movement of wages and marginal productivity is usually explained in terms of frictions and not attributed to any weakness of the principle itself.   But to the usual criticisms must now be added that developed in this section, which implies that for considerable periods at least the economic world is not even tending towards an equilibrium in which factor prices are proportional to their respective marginal productivities.   The trouble is, not merely that there are frictions, but also that the

---

[1] *Op. cit.*, p. 120.   [2] *Ibid.*, p. 89.

employer does not possess sufficient knowledge to discover this position of equilibrium. In other words, our argument implies that a new principle must be found to explain the distribution of the product between different factors in the periods to which the marginal principle cannot be applied. This fact alone is an obstacle to the acceptance of the criticisms advanced above, for the academic mind does not readily relinquish a theory on which so much has been built. But so long as such a foundation is retained nothing can be built on it but castles in the air. We need not pursue the problem of distribution theory here, however, for its solution is not essential to the theory of fluctuations.

BEHAVIOUR OF EMPLOYERS IN RESPONSE TO WAGE MOVEMENTS

We must now seek an alternative approach to replace the marginal productivity theory in those periods to which that theory cannot be applied. Our task amounts to an analysis of the assumption that the employer has records of past sales, but no confidence in them as a guide to the future relationship of price to sales. The implications of this assumption are altogether different from the conclusions of the marginal productivity theory, so far as wages policy is concerned.

Consider for example a period of contraction, in which sales have been declining for some time, despite price cuts, increased expenditure on advertising, and exceptional industry on the part of salesmen. Suppose, now, that wage rates are reduced. Would a rational employer immediately increase his staff and expand his output ? The obvious thing to do is to reduce selling price, if possible, and watch the effect of this on sales. An expansion of employment is not likely to precede an increase in sales unless the employer is convinced that better times are ahead or assumes that he can sell the increased output at a satisfactory price. In a period of contraction these conditions are not likely, and a wage reduction will not lead to an increase in employment immediately, even though the new wage rate is (unknown to the employer) lower than the marginal productivity of labour. The most it can achieve, in the first instance, is to check the fall in employment which might otherwise have taken place. An employer who is on the point of reducing his staff may be persuaded by a wage reduction to carry on a little longer, until he has seen the effect of the reduction on his sales.

In the meantime, the wages bill will undergo a general reduction, and, in so far as part of the market consists of wage earners, sales are likely to fall. The problem is whether the effects of a price reduction are such as to increase sales in other sections of the market, and whether on balance sales move up or down.

Some employers will not pass on the whole of the saving in wages cost in the form of lower prices, and to this extent the position is modified. We shall later consider the implications of price rigidity for this analysis.

Consider now the effect of a wage increase under similar depressing conditions. Such an event could only be the result of deliberate public policy, since the natural tendency is for wages to fall as unemployment grows. Nevertheless a policy of this type has its supporters, and it is sometimes suggested that those who oppose wage reductions in depression should " logically " advocate a wage increase instead. There is little doubt, however, that the effect of wage increases at such a time is to lead employers to reduce output and employment, and in some cases to close down their enterprises. We need not follow out in detail the effects of this upon sales!

A general wage increase is a common feature of most periods of expansion of any considerable duration, and its effects require study on the assumption underlying this section—namely, that the employer does not know, even approximately, what effect a price movement will have on his sales. In a period of expansion the conditions may be taken as the opposite of those associated with contraction. Sales are increasing, and even if a rise in other costs has necessitated increased prices the market is still absorbing readily an increasing flow of output.

One important element in this case is the provision of additional working capital to finance the increased wages bill if employment is to be maintained after the wage increase. Additional credit is more likely to be available at low interest rates if the period of expansion has not brought the economy near full employment, but banking policy may be influenced by other factors which cannot be dealt with here.

There is, however, another reason for taking into account the degree of employment. If the economy is already operating near full capacity of existing equipment, a wage increase is more likely to stimulate employers to replace labour by machinery than if there is still a great deal of idle capacity. For the moment the production of the new equipment may involve increased employment ; it is a form of investment and therefore exerts an expansive influence upon business activity. But, as we saw, this influence may later be reversed when the installation of the new equipment is complete.

If we consider a stage in which, although there has already been considerable improvement in the business situation, there is still considerable idle equipment in all industries, we may ignore the possibility of substitution of machinery for labour. The employer will attempt instead to pass on the rise in costs in the form of higher prices to the consumer. The problem then is to decide whether sales will alter as a result of the higher prices and the higher incomes of wage earners.

If a stage has been reached in which employers are very doubtful as to whether expansion or recovery can last much longer, then even though they cannot estimate the marginal product of labour they may alter their plans to the extent of taking on fewer new employees. This is particularly likely in the case of new enterprises, the establishment of which is a feature of most prolonged periods of expansion. Being in their early stages of development, these enterprises will not yet have begun to make large profits ; and it is possible that some of them may be killed altogether by an increase in wages cost. To the extent that this happens, we cannot assume that employment will be held constant while the employers are waiting to see the effect of price movements upon their sales. This assumption does seem appropriate, however, to an earlier stage of recovery, when, although expansion is definite enough to encourage employers to hope for its continuance, new enterprises have not yet got going.

To complete this picture of employers' responses to wage movements we must consider the unlikely case of a general wage reduction during a period of expansion. No doubt if such a policy were imposed by a wage-fixing authority it would stimulate many employers to expand output and employment rather more rapidly than if wages had not fallen. The rise in the total wages bill which might be expected in a period of expansion with stable wage rates would be checked, but this check might be inappreciable if the stimulating effect of the fall in costs were great. In particular this would be the case in those new enterprises which were just beginning to expand output when wages were reduced.

The importance of physical marginal productivity may, however, be stressed. Even though marginal productivity in terms of money cannot be estimated in advance, because of lack of knowledge of how demand will move, the employer will still be guided by the estimated movement of costs as output expands, and this depends in large measure upon the physical marginal productivity of labour. In all enterprises costs are likely to rise more rapidly as full capacity is approached. Consequently a given reduction in wages is likely to stimulate employment more in the earlier than in the later stages of a period of expansion.

On the other hand, at a later stage a wage reduction would do more to check substitution of machinery for labour, and to this extent would actually discourage investment.

In summary it may be said that the dominant response of employers to wage movements, when they cannot estimate marginal revenue, is to continue the policy which they were following previous to the wage movement, to pass on, as far as possible, any change in costs in the form of lower or higher prices, and to watch the effect of this upon their sales, before altering their policy to any considerable extent. But several qualifications to this generalisation have been noted, for a wage movement may serve as a brake upon an existing movement in either direction, and we have also seen that wage increases would aggravate contraction and wage reductions stimulate an existing expansion, although neither of these two movements is sufficiently likely to merit much attention.

The next step in our analysis is to see what does happen to sales, on the above assumptions, when wages are altered, for a subsequent movement in sales is likely to induce a similar movement in employment.

EFFECTS OF WAGE MOVEMENTS UPON SALES

We shall consider first the effect of a general wage reduction, and later the effect of a wage increase, building our analysis on the principles set out in the previous section. Account is to be taken, not only of the effect of the wage reduction upon wage earners' demand, but also of the response from other sections of the market. If the wage reduction is passed on in the form of lower prices, we may expect that those people whose incomes are not reduced by the wage movement will buy more, and this expansion of demand is to be balanced against the decline in wage earners' demand. The relative strength of these two opposed tendencies will determine whether there is any net movement in total sales.

This somewhat complicated problem is best approached by examining first a simplified case. We shall assume a closed economy, zero saving so far as received income is concerned, and complete sale of all output. Thus all incomes are spent. Unless profits are already so low as to induce contraction, or so high as to encourage expansion, the position is one of stability. Let us start from such a stable position, assuming still, however, that it has not lasted long enough for employers to learn the shape and position of the marginal revenue curves for their products.

Three sections of the market may be distinguished, composed respectively of wage earners, employers, and others. The " others " include landlords, rentiers, civil servants, and any other groups paid out of taxation—indeed all who are not directly affected by the general wage reduction in industry. We leave aside the complications involved in such institutions as banks, and in the possibility that wage reductions are applied also in public services. We may assume these " other " persons' incomes to be constant ; if they move, it is not due to the wage reduction. We may also make the heroic assumption that there is some unit of " produce in general " and an average " price per unit of output " of this produce—ignoring the difficulties involved in such concepts. Then the initial price per unit of output, which we may call y, may be divided into three components ; wages cost per unit (yw), profit per unit (yp), and other costs per unit (yo). Thus, w, p, and o, are fractions, and their sum is unity. The three sections of the market derive their incomes from these three components of price ; consequently the market is divided between the three sections according to the three fractions w, p, and o. Let x stand for total sales, or the number of units of output, before wages are reduced. The incomes of the three groups amount to xyw, xyp, and xyo, respectively ; and they buy xw, xp, and xo, respectively.

Let wages now be reduced by the fraction r, and the price per unit of output by the whole of the saving in wages cost per unit—that is, by ywr. The new price is therefore not y, but $y(1 - wr)$. Employers' incomes and those of the " other " persons are not altered ; at the new price they can buy, respectively,

$\dfrac{xyp}{y\,(1-wr)}$ and $\dfrac{xyo}{y\,(1-wr)}$. But wage earners' incomes have

fallen to $xyw\,(1-r)$, and can therefore buy only $\dfrac{xyw\,(1-r)}{y\,(1-wr)}$.

The new level of sales is found by summing the sales to the

three sections of the market : $\dfrac{xy\,(p+o+w-wr)}{y\,(1-wr)}$. Since

$p+o+w=1$, the expression reduces to x ; in other words, total sales are the same as before wages were reduced.

This result, it may be noticed, is independent of the magnitude of the wage reduction, and also of the proportion of wages cost to selling price. The larger the wage reduction, the greater the decline in sales to wage earners, but, at the lower price, the greater the increase in sales to the other two sections of the market. Again, the larger the element of wages cost in price before the wage reduction, the greater the absolute fall in sales to wage earners, but the greater the fall in price and the greater the expansion of demand in the other two sections of the market. Although the change in the distribution of demand is affected by the magnitude of the wage reduction and by the proportion of wages cost to selling price, the total demand is not.

It is conceivable, however, that not the whole of the saving in labour costs will be passed in lower prices, and our analysis will then require modification. To take the limiting case, assume that price is not reduced at all, but that the employer hopes to add the saving in labour cost to profit. The question then arises whether he will anticipate this increase in profit by increasing his expenditure in advance above his previous income. This implies negative saving, so far as his received income is concerned, even though he does not intend to save anything out of his expected increase in profit. The possibility of negative saving depends upon his liquidity and his credit-worthiness. If, adhering to our assumption of zero saving, the employer maintains his expenditure constant, there will be a fall in total sales, and his expected increase in profits will not materialise.

This can readily be seen from our earlier analysis. Since prices are not reduced, neither employers nor the " other " section of the market can buy any more than before, and wage earners, faced by constant prices, must restrict their purchases to

their new incomes. Total sales will be $\dfrac{xy\,(p+o+w-wr)}{y}$; that

is, $x\,(1-wr)$. In this case the influence of the wage reduction is clearly depressive. In order for it to be neutral, employers must dis-save—that is, spend in excess of their received income—a sum equal to the whole of the saving in labour cost, namely *xywr*. For any smaller increase in expenditure the wage reduction, with rigid prices, is depressive. If employers pass on a portion of the saving in wages cost in the form of lower prices, then in order that the effect of the wage cut shall be neutral or expansive they need only dis-save an accordingly smaller sum.

The analysis of the effects of a general wage increase, under these simplifying assumptions, is identical, except that for each minus sign we must now write a plus sign. If the rise in wages cost is all passed on in the form of higher prices, sales will remain constant ; the decreased demand of employers and " others " will be just offset by the increased demand of wage earners. With rigid prices—implying a fall in expected profit—the wage increase is neutral if employers reduce their expenditure, in anticipation of the fall in their incomes, by the whole amount of the increase in wages cost. This implies saving out of received income, although no saving is planned out of the profits expected in the next period. If prices are rigid, and employers continue to spend as much as before, sales will actually increase.

It may be as well to trace out what happens to profits in each of these cases. When the change in wages cost is passed on in lower or higher prices, and sales remain constant, total profits remain constant ; but the profit element in the price is increased in the case of a wage reduction, and decreased in the case of a wage increase. With rigid prices, if, owing to a variation in employers' expenditure, sales remain constant, both total profits and the profit element in the price vary inversely with wage rates. If, however, with rigid prices, employers' expenditure is constant, then total sales vary ; and, although the profit element in price varies inversely with wage rates, total profits remain constant. On our assumptions, then, a general wage movement will only alter total profits if prices are rigid, and employers adjust expenditure in anticipation of a rise or fall in profits. It is variations in total profits which are likely to induce expansion or contraction, if the *minimum sensibile* is attained or exceeded. We may conclude, therefore, that general wage movements are neutral unless they cause employers' spending to vary in anticipation of profit movements.

The assumptions made in these simplified cases apply only

to a fraction of the period of a business cycle, for they take as a starting point what we have called a plateau—although it might be a valley—of stability. If we assume that there is neither saving nor investment, but that the initial profit level is too high or too low to permit stability, the general trend of our analysis still seems applicable. A general wage movement will not modify the existing tendency for sales to expand or contract, if the change in cost is passed on in altered prices, or if with rigid prices the employers alter their expenditure appropriately. But with rigid prices and constant employers' expenditure expansion will be reinforced by a wage increase, and contraction reinforced by a wage reduction, provided that employers do not immediately alter employment in response to the wage movement. We saw in the last section that this proviso is not always fulfilled.

Our simplified case also assumed zero saving to start with, although we considered the possibility of saving or dis-saving by the employer in anticipation of changes in profits. We must now consider the implications of saving both before and after the wage movement. The first point to notice is that if a portion of income is saved we can no longer assume that the three sections of the market purchase goods in the same proportions as the three respective cost components bear to the total price before the wage movement. This condition would still hold, and our symbolic analysis would still be valid, if investment and other supplementary expenditure were equal to saving, and if all groups saved the same proportion of their incomes before the wage movement, and did not alter the absolute level of their saving after wage movement. Such a case may rarely occur, but its definition draws attention to the essential point of the problem—namely, the possibility that wage movements may evoke variations in saving and investment. This is regarded by Mr. Keynes and his followers as the central issue in the problem of wages policy, the effect of a wage movement being assessed wholly in terms of its influence upon thrift and upon investment.

From the side of saving, a wage reduction may lead to an increase in sales if wage earners' saving falls more than the saving of employers and other persons increases. The former movement is a natural response to a decline in real incomes, and the latter is a no less natural response to a reduction in the cost of living. *A priori* analysis cannot measure the force of these two tendencies. We can only notice that, operating in opposite directions, they offset each other to some extent. Many factors help to determine whether there is a net movement in any direction. We may notice in passing that if wages were close to the subsistence minimum before the reduction there would be little scope for saving to be affected. If wages were already high, the tenacity of the conventional standard of living would influence the result of the reduction. But such observations do not lead to a positive conclusion regarding the effect upon saving. A wage increase may be expected to affect saving in the opposite direction to a wage reduction, but again the dynamic aspects of conventional living standards may prove to be very important.

Investment, it will be remembered, is likely to vary inversely with the purchase cost of equipment, and directly with the estimated yield therefrom. It is not certain that at all stages of the cycle the purchase cost will move in the same direction as wages cost in the capital goods industries, since the employer may not attempt to pass on changes in cost in the form of changed prices. But where the change in cost is passed on, since the capital goods industries must be included in any general movement, we can say that a general movement of wages may affect the level of investment. But the latter result might be obtained by a wage movement confined to the capital goods trades. The expected yield of capital equipment depends largely upon the view which employers take of business prospects, and in so far as they believe that these vary inversely with the wage level wage movements will react upon their willingness to demand new capital equipment. But this influence is often swamped by such factors as the extent of idle capacity, the recorded movement of sales, and the political situation. Another way in which wage movements may affect investment has already been noted —namely, by encouraging or discouraging substitution of machinery for labour.

There is a further possibility to be considered. If, as a result of these repercussions of a general wage movement, employment and incomes begin to move, this in turn may induce a movement of saving in the same direction, which will tend to check the movement in employment. Or a movement in investment may be initiated which will reinforce the movement in employment. Mr. Keynes has attributed overwhelming importance to the former reaction, arguing that, even if a general

wage reduction led employers to expand employment immediately in expectation of increased sales, as the marginal productivity theory implies, this expectation would inevitably be
proved false, unless independent action were taken to encourage
investment. For, as employment expanded, the sum laid out
in additional costs would not all come back in sales receipts ;
a portion would be saved by its recipients, and this saving would
impose losses upon employers until they reduced employment
again to a level at which saving, too, would fall to its former
level. If we assume no functional relationship between wages
and the level of investment, and a constant functional relationship between income and saving, it follows that employment
must fall to its former level. Otherwise it is possible to say only
that the process envisaged would serve as a brake upon any
expansion which might be induced by a wage reduction.

The above discussion deals only with a closed economy, and
we now turn to the possibility of reactions through imports or
exports. Advocates of wage reductions usually make the most
of this possibility. There are two reactions to be considered.
In Great Britain, for instance, it was suggested that a wage
reduction would lead to the expansion of oversea demand for
exports. In Australia, on the other hand, during the depression,
it was commonly argued that export producers, whose incomes
would not be affected by the wage reduction, and little affected,
if at all, by the fall in wage earners' demand, could buy so
much more local produce at the lower prices which the wage
reduction would make possible that the fall in sales to wage
earners would be more than offset.

The possibility of increasing exports, in a period of depression,
by reducing wages and prices is severely limited by the pre-
disposition of other countries to impose trade restrictions. To
assume no retaliation of this kind is unduly optimistic.

The second possible reaction requires closer examination.
If wage earners buy less than usual of exportable produce,
more of the latter is offered abroad. If the country contributes
a large portion of the world supply, this may depress prices and
even reduce the incomes of export producers. But if the exports
are small, as compared with world production, no appreciable
fall in price would be caused, and export producers' incomes
would not be affected. This situation implies that the demand
of wage earners for products which cannot be exported falls
by less than the demand of employers and other sections of

the market, including export producers, rises. On balance total employment tends to increase. The essential point in this analysis is that the wage earners do not economise entirely on goods which cannot be exported. If they do, the reaction of the wage reduction is similar to that in a closed economy. It is worth noting that in Australia, for instance, where exportable produce consists chiefly of food and raw materials, wage earners are most likely to economise on their purchases of goods destined solely for the home market, and open economy considerations involve little modification of the conclusions reached in the study of a closed economy.

It must not be thought, however, that the effects of a general wage increase in an open economy are just the reverse of those of a wage reduction, but of similar strength. It may be possible to conceive of negative retaliation, or the relaxation of trade restrictions in response to wage increases. Indeed a somewhat similar suggestion has been made, that countries should agree to make tariff concessions to those countries which ratify International Labour Conventions. But if anything is achieved in this direction it will be by negotiation between Governments, while retaliation to wage cutting may be regarded as a natural response in any but a free-trade world. Consequently a rise in wages will generally lead to a decline in exports ; and unless imports consist solely of necessary foods, or other goods the demand for which is rigid, there will also be an increase in imports. This implies a movement of the balance of payments which may involve deflationary pressure within the economy. We may conclude, therefore, that in an open economy the depressive influence of a general wage increase is much more certain than the expansive influence of a general wage reduction.

Conclusions

We may now attempt a general view of wages policy in relation to economic fluctuations, drawing together the main points of the preceding discussion. A number of different reactions to wage movements have been exposed, and attention has been drawn to the importance of other contemporaneous conditions such as monetary policy and the political situation. It is therefore evident that no laws can be propounded to cover all historical circumstances. We can however note the probable effects of different wage policies at certain stages of a cycle.

From such a general statement many of the qualifications brought out in earlier pages may be omitted, but they should not be omitted when formulating an actual policy.

Considering first a period of contraction following a period of prosperity, there seems to be little scientific foundation for the widespread view that a general wage reduction will contribute considerably to the restoration of prosperity. It may exert some expansive influence through international trade, but apart from this the best one can hope for is that it will act as a brake upon the process of contraction, maintaining employment at a higher level than that to which it would have sunk with constant wages. But if monopolistic situations prevent price flexibility there is a distinct likelihood that a general wage reduction will intensify the forces making for depression.

Some expansive influence may be exerted indirectly through interest rates. In the above circumstances the wage reduction involves a reduced wages bill ; this implies a diminished demand for working capital, and a tendency for interest rates to fall. If this tendency is not offset by other factors, it facilitates the recovery of investment, which is an expansive force. To this influence is added the reduced cost of capital equipment. But if the contraction has already proceeded some distance there will be idle capacity, and little incentive to invest in new equipment.

A particular wage reduction, confined to capital goods trades, would also serve to stimulate investment, without risking the unfavourable repercussions which may follow a general wage reduction. Such a localised reduction is not always practicable.

At this stage of the cycle a general wage increase may be ruled out as definitely depressive. On the whole a strong case can be made for rigid wages at such a time. Firstly, there is no certainty that employment will be any worse than with lower wages, and it may be even better with rigid wages if prices too are rigid. Secondly, reduction during depression implies a moral case for restoration during prosperity, and, as we shall see, this is not always innocuous or advantageous from the standpoint of economic fluctuations.

The case for wage reduction is no stronger after a period of decline in activity which appears likely to continue still further. But if a phase of stability is reached, after a considerable decline, so that stocks of goods have run down, equipment has been allowed to depreciate, and unexploited inventions are

5

to hand, the case for a general wage reduction is strengthened. For in these circumstances there is more hope of stimulating an increase in investment by the wage reduction, and by the subsequent pressure for lower interest rates. There is still no case for a general wage increase.

Consider next the phase in which recovery has just started, but has not continued long enough to breed confidence in the breasts of business men. A general wage reduction now may supply just what is needed to stimulate a more rapid increase in investment. On the other hand, a general wage increase might kill the incipient recovery.

Proceeding a stage further, when expansion of activity is apparent on all sides, and prospects of further improvement are bright, a general wage reduction is highly improbable. What will be the effect of a general wage increase ? Provided employers are sufficiently confident to pass on the increased cost in higher prices, and to maintain their own expenditure constant, the expansive process will be strengthened. This is only true, however, if monetary conditions permit the employers to obtain additional working capital without an undue rise in interest rates, and in some cases of open economy this conclusion may require qualification.

As full employment approaches, however, the case for wage increases becomes weaker, despite the fact that wages tend to rise at such a time. Some economists advocate wage increases at this stage as a means of eating into profits, checking the boom in investment, and stimulating the growth of demand for consumers' goods, an increasing flow of which is supposed to result from earlier investment. The risks involved in such a policy are great, unless it is known for certain that a self-reversing process along " Hobsonian " lines is on the point of maturing, and that monetary conditions are such as to prevent any sharp rise in interest rates from following the rise in labour costs. Otherwise the rise in wages may not merely check the boom but actually precipitate the depression. We need only recall the operation of the acceleration principle to see that a sudden check to the growth of investment may involve a definite fall. Again, the monetary repercussions of the wage increase are liable to be depressive. Moreover, in an open economy there may be a movement in exports and imports which not only discourages investment but also creates credit stringency through gold movements or similar factors.

All these observations are based on the assumption that conditions are such as to prevent employers from behaving according to the principles assumed in the marginal productivity theory. It is not surprising that they should differ from the conclusions reached by those economists who insist on applying only that theory. Our conclusions must be modified, however, whenever a period of stability lasts long enough for employers to learn the shape and position of their marginal revenue curves over a sufficient range. For then, apart from opposed influences from the side of saving, which cannot, however, be ignored, a wage reduction tends to stimulate employment and a wage increase to have the reverse effect.

If wage-fixing authorities were seized with all these complexities they might despair of devising and operating a wages policy which could be expected to contribute substantially to the control of economic fluctuations, by raising or lowering wage rates at the moments when these movements would be effective in achieving the desired end. Modest men might disclaim the possession of the nice judgment involved, and most countries lag far behind in the provision of information upon which such judgment must be based. In a desire to adopt a simple clear-cut policy, wage-fixing authorities are tempted to work for wage reduction in depression and wage " restoration " in prosperity. There is always the danger that such a policy will make fluctuations more violent than they need have been, and on the whole a policy designed to stabilise wages throughout the cycle is to be preferred. This raises important social issues, however, for labour demands a rising trend in wage rates. Our analysis suggests that, if control of fluctuations is also desired, the best time for wage increases is when recovery has been well established, but has not yet brought the economy near to full employment. This assumes, however, that there will be considerable fluctuations, despite whatever steps are taken in an attempt to control them. If the other factors making for instability are all brought under control, and it is desired to raise wages, it will be necessary to study the question how to offset any depressive influence which the wage increase may have. At present it is more important that wider recognition should be obtained for the difficulties in the way of contributing to the control of fluctuations through wages policy, except by adopting a policy of stable wages during contraction and raising wages only at the appropriate stage in recovery.

Social Security

The Impact of Social Security Legislation upon Mobility and Enterprise, by Sumner H. Slichter, American Economic Review, Vol. XXX, No. 1, Supplement, March, 1940, pp. 44–60

Experience Rating in Unemployment Compensation, by Charles A. Myers, American Economic Review, Vol. XXXV, No. 3, June, 1945, pp. 337–354

Our Pension Madness — and Possible Cures, by John J. Corson, The New York Times Magazine, July 3, 1949

Social Insurance in Evolution, by Eveline M. Burns, American Economic Review, Vol. XXXIV, No. 1, Part 2, Supplement, March, 1944, pp. 199–211

Report to the President of the United States on the Labor Dispute in the Basic Steel Industry, General Summary, submitted September, 1949, by Samuel I. Rosenman, David L. Cole, and Carroll R. Daugherty.

THE IMPACT OF SOCIAL SECURITY LEGISLATION UPON MOBILITY AND ENTERPRISE

By SUMNER H. SLICHTER

I

By the mobility of labor I mean the willingness and the ability of labor to move from one employer to another, one place to another, or one occupation to another in response to changes in the demand for labor. Mobility must be distinguished from movement because much movement is initiated by the employer through layoffs.[1] Some movement is necessary in order to achieve an optimum distribution of resources, but movement in excess of this amount is wasteful.[2] When people wonder about the effects of social security legislation upon mobility of labor, they are usually fearful that social security will prevent the movement from reaching the optimum amount. The probable effects of the social security program upon mobility must be analyzed in the light of the amounts and kinds of mobility in the American labor market and of the conditions which determine mobility.

The American labor market is only beginning to be explored. Nevertheless, I feel safe in asserting six propositions concerning the mobility of labor: (1) the majority of the working population are relatively stable and do little moving either between employers or places and probably between occupations; (2) the amount of movement in the labor market is large, and, indeed, is much larger than is generally suspected; (3) the amount of movement from employer to employer and from place to place is declining; (4) the character of movement has been changing from a voluntary to a forced movement; (5) the obstacles to movement between employers are increasing; (6) changes in managerial policy and the spread of unionism are tending to increase the proportion of layoffs that are temporary rather than permanent, to reduce the proportion of casual work, and to sharpen the distinction between regular and temporary employers.

Twenty-five years ago, when labor turnover was first studied, most employers thought that it was of negligible importance, despite the fact that it turned out to be about 100 per cent a year. The employers were misled by the concentration of turnover among a small part of the force—usually one fourth or less. Although the number of separations might be as large as the force itself, from two thirds to three fourths of the names on the

---

[1] Hence increases and decreases in movement do not necessarily mean increases or decreases in willingness or ability to move.

[2] Movement of both capital and labor is, of course, necessary in amounts determined by the relative costs of moving each. Movement is to some extent necessary in order to develop men.

pay roll at the beginning of the year would be there at the end. Today the nation suffers from the same optical illusion. It still seems to be true that in any given plant from two thirds to three fourths of the employees do not move in the course of a year. The prevalence of geographical stability is suggested by the Michigan study of mobility which indicates that during the fifty-seven month period from April, 1930, to January, 1935, 87.1 per cent of the workers did not make the kind of geographical change defined as movement for purposes of the study.[3]

Despite the fact that the great majority of the workers do not move, the amount of movement is large—much larger than most people have supposed. Evidence is found in the figures on business births and deaths, in the labor turnover figures, in the large movement between agricultural and nonagricultural pursuits, and in the large number of account numbers issued by the social security administration. Business births and deaths run each about 400,000 a year. Many of them represent merely a change in ownership, but special studies indicate that there are about 200,000 births of new going concerns each year and almost the same number of deaths. The average number of employees in the 2,000,000 nonagricultural enterprises is between thirteen and fourteen. It is probable that the infant concerns and also the dying concerns have less than the average number of employees. If we assume that the average dying concern has less than half the average number of employees, say about five, 200,000 deaths would produce 1,000,000 terminations a year. If new concerns on the average have four employees at the end of the first year, they would represent the employment of about 800,000 persons.[4] The separation rate in manufacturing industries in 1936 was 40.35 per cent, in 1937, 53.11 per cent, and in 1938, 49.22 per cent. As temporary layoffs are not ordinarily included in separations, these figures represent terminations of employment with the enterprise. The movements of labor between agricultural and nonagricultural pursuits are not accurately known but appear to be large. Woytinsky estimates that the number of farmers working in nonagricultural pursuits reaches a peak of about a million and a half at the turn of the year and that the seasonal demand for hired help by farmers rises in July to nearly a mil-

---

[3] *Monthly Labor Review,* April, 1939, pp. 789-802.

A person was considered to have made a move whenever his work history showed a change between communities under one of the following circumstances: (1) between places of work, when the person was employed both before and after moving, (2) between places of residence, when the person was unemployed both before and after moving, or (3) between place of work and place of residence, when the person was employed at one end of the move and unemployed or not seeking work at the other, provided in this case that the move was longer than between adjoining counties. This restriction was adopted because short-distance moves between employment and unemployment were usually of the "commuting" type which did not involve a definite transfer of workers from one labor market to another.

[4] Concerns which die are likely to have a considerable shrinkage of employment for several years before their death. Likewise, some new enterprises grow rapidly for the first few years. Of course, a very large proportion of concerns have a life of less than a year.

lion and a half over the level of January and February.[5] The number of account numbers issued by the social security administration is about 60 per
cent greater than the number of persons employed in the covered industries.[6]
Allowance must be made for the fact that many account numbers have been
issued to unemployed persons, that many holders of account numbers have
retired or died, and that a few duplicate account numbers were issued.
Nevertheless, Woytinsky estimates that during 1937 and 1938, 9,600,000
persons who usually work in employment not covered by the old age pension tax were engaged at least part of the time in covered employments.[7]
This does not include the persons who receive temporary or intermittent
work entirely within covered employments. Probably one fourth of the
country's labor force in any one year works for more than one employer.
Many of these workers are employed in more than one industry. Lack of
definite information about who these workers are and what is the pattern
of their employment is a most serious gap in our information about the
labor market.

The amount of movement from employer to employer and probably from
place to place is declining. Before the war, separation rates of 100 per cent
were normal. In 1920, separations in manufacturing started to decline. By
1929, the rate was less than half the level of 1920.[8] During recent years the
changes in the total separation rate have been moderate, but the general
drift has been downward with the rate for 1937 definitely below 1930.
Evidence of changes in the amount of movement from place to place over
time is scanty. There are several types of geographical movement and they
may not be changing in the same direction. However, the estimates of the
Department of Agriculture show a decline in the farm-city movement from
10.8 millions in the five years ending in 1928 to 5.6 millions in the five
years ending in 1938, and in the city-farm movement from 7.7 millions in
the first period to 3.9 millions in the second.[9]

Not only is the amount of movement declining, but its character has
changed during the last ten years from predominantly voluntary to predominantly involuntary. This change does not go back beyond 1929, and
it remains to be seen whether it is the result of temporary conditions. Until
1929, the turnover reports of the Metropolitan Life Insurance Company
showed that over 70 per cent of the separations were resignations. Layoffs
constituted about 15 per cent, and discharges about 13 per cent. In 1936,

[5] W. S. Woytinsky, *Seasonal Variations in Employment in the United States*, p. 95.

[6] At the end of 1939, 47,500,000 account numbers had been issued. The number of persons whose usual employment is in the covered industries was about 27,500,000 at the end
of 1938, and about 28,500,000 at the end of 1939.

[7] W. S. Woytinsky, *Fluctuations in Employment Covered by the Federal Old-Age Insurance Program*, p. 75.

[8] *Monthly Labor Review*, July, 1929, pp. 64-65.

[9] These are movements of persons, not necessarily workers, but the movement of workers
may be expected to be roughly proportionate to the movement of persons.

61.2 per cent of the separations were layoffs, in 1937, 67.3 per cent, in 1938, 82.2 per cent. In 1937, scarcely one out of four of the quits was a resignation, and in 1938, scarcely one out of seven.[10] Layoff rates today appear to be higher than before the war or before the depression. The reason in the main is the drop in the resignation rate which prevents employers from letting resignations produce adjustments in the size of the force.

In some respects movement is easier today than ever before. The automobile and the greatly improved public employment offices facilitate movement both between employers and places. On balance, however, the obstacles to movement seem to be increasing. The greatest change in recent years has been the spread of union rules governing layoffs and to a less extent hiring. Equal-division-of-work rules discourage involuntary movement because they limit layoffs. But equal-division-of-work rules also reduce the number of hirings and this discourages resignations. Seniority rules discourage resignations because new employees in a plant must start at the bottom of the seniority list. Furthermore, when the seniority rule provides, as it often does, that workers with seniority status shall be given preference in hiring, it discourages the movement of workers who have been laid off. The depression has greatly stimulated the interest of workers in protecting themselves against layoffs. Among several hundred union agreements negotiated between 1923 and 1929 only about one out of three contained regulations of layoffs. Among another group of several hundred agreements negotiated since 1933, two out of three regulated layoffs.[11]

When a seniority rule provides that the workers laid off shall be rehired, if qualified, before other persons are engaged, it has the effect of converting permanent layoffs into temporary ones.[12] Whenever a union imposes an equal-division-of-work rule it is necessary to define clearly the persons who are entitled to share in the work. This brings about a sharp distinction between temporary and permanent workers. A seniority rule has the same effect because temporary workers are usually denied seniority status, especially with respect to rehiring. Sometimes a closed shop sharpens the dis-

---

[10] Deaths and retirements (the latter not always entirely voluntary) are included in resignations. The resignation rates in manufacturing are today only one fifth to one tenth of the prewar resignation rates.

[11] The experience of union officials confirms these statistics. An international officer in one of the paper unions says: "When we first began to sign agreements with paper manufacturers, seniority was not much of an issue. However, since the depression, this question of seniority seems to loom larger in the workers' minds than anything else. It is very difficult to write a satisfactory seniority clause in a trade agreement. As a matter of fact, if employers would agree to let us write our own seniority clause, I do not believe the union could write a clause that would be satisfactory to all our members."

A high official for many years in one of the unions of the glass industry says: "I have been in the glass industry for over a generation and never once had to work under the seniority rule. That came into the trade union movement after I had given up active work in the glass factory. When getting around the country I find that this is the paramount question in local meetings. It seems to overshadow all other questions before the group."

[12] Such a rule may attach a large number of persons to a plant in hope of sometime being rehired.

tinction between regular and temporary employees because the union may not require that temporary employees be members. The general tendency of trade agreements, therefore, seems to be (1) to reduce the proportion of permanent layoffs, (2) to reduce the amount of work done by temporary workers, and (3) to sharpen the distinction between regular and temporary workers. It is not clear, at this stage of development, that union layoff and hiring policies cause an excessive number of men to be attached to union plants or industries. Probably they do.

II

It is against this general setting that we must appraise the effect of the social security program upon the mobility of labor. We must consider separately the effects of (1) pensions, (2) unemployment compensation, and (3) relief.

1. The pension plan will tend to encourage mobility. In the first place, it will lead to retirements at an earlier age and the vacancies thus created stimulate movement.[13] In the second place, it will permit employees to move from one employer to another without losing pension rights. Practically all of the private pension plans which sprouted so luxuriantly during the twenties and in the early part of the depression were carefully designed to discourage movement. The man who left lost all of the employer's contribution and in some instances his own. Private pension plans will continue to supplement the public pension plans for some years to come and they will tend to discourage movement. Their effect, however, will be limited by the public pension plan.

2. The brief experience with state unemployment compensation schemes indicates that their effect upon mobility will be small. Experience rating will cause the conversion of some intermittent or casual employment into regular employment.[14] This will reduce the amount of movement but not the willingness to move. Some of the unemployment compensation acts give employers an incentive to spread work rather than to make layoffs. This will reduce involuntary movement and indirectly voluntary movement. There are two principal reasons for concluding that unemployment compensation will have little effect upon mobility. One is that most of the men who qualify for benefits are in the stable rather than the mobile group of employees. The provisions concerning qualifications vary. Of the states specifying definite minimum earnings during a specified base period (usually the preceding year), only seven put it below $200,[15] and of the

---

[13] In a majority of cases this movement is a forced rather than a voluntary one. The employer feels able to retire men earlier because the men are provided for by pensions. This, indeed, has always been one of the principal arguments used by insurance companies in selling pension plans to employers.

[14] This will not be true, however, if the layoff of workers who have not qualified for benefits is not counted in measuring experience.

[15] Rhode Island, $100; Delaware, $125; South Dakota, $126; North Carolina, $130; Idaho, $140; and Maine, $144.

states requiring earnings of a given multiple of weekly benefits only four-teen require earnings of less than twenty-four weeks' benefits.[16] A large part of the people who constitute the mobile part of the working force will not qualify for many weeks' benefits.[17] Sample studies of the people who are receiving unemployment benefits indicate that they do not ordinarily suffer long periods of unemployment and that few of them have ever been on relief. Many of them have only been temporarily laid off, they have not lost their check numbers, and they have not lost their jobs. They do not expect to move and they would not move even if they did not receive unemploy-ment benefits, because although they may not have work, they still have jobs. It is this fact rather than the receipt or nonreceipt of unemployment benefits which determines their willingness to move. As indicated above, union policy is increasing the number of persons in this class because unions endeavor to replace permanent layoffs with temporary ones and to give people who have been laid off a right to re-employment before outsiders are engaged.

Another reason why unemployment benefits are not likely to have great effect upon mobility is that they are paid for only a few weeks—fifteen or sixteen in most states. Even if they were paid for twenty-six weeks, the effect on mobility would be small.[18] With the end of his benefits never far

[16] Pennsylvania, thirteen; Arizona, fourteen; Iowa, fifteen; and Alabama, Arkansas, Georgia, Kansas, Louisiana, Mississippi, Missouri, Nevada, New Jersey, Oklahoma, Vir-ginia, sixteen.

Three jurisdictions require a specified number of weeks of employment: Wisconsin, over four; District of Columbia, thirteen out of the fifty-two ending with the last week of employment; and Ohio, twenty in the base year.

[17] Unfortunately there are no figures available on the number of persons laid off who lack sufficient employment or earnings to qualify for benefits. Indeed, the total number of layoffs in covered employments is not known because there are many layoffs for which claims are not presented. In manufacturing, the layoff rate during the first ten months of 1939 was running at the annual rate of 26.45 per hundred employees, a rate probably 20 per cent higher than in nonmanufacturing industries. If Massachusetts experience is repre-sentative, there were about 6.5 million (permanent) layoffs in covered employment during 1939. Temporary layoffs are not included in the turnover figures and are more difficult to estimate. The unemployment census of April, 1930, found one temporary layoff to every 3.2 permanent layoffs. This ratio may not be typical as the proportion is likely to vary with con-ditions in the labor market and even with the season of the year. I suspect that in April, 1930, the proportion of permanent layoffs was unusually high. If we assume, however, that the ratio 1 to 3.2 is fairly typical, the total number of layoffs, both temporary and permanent, in covered industries in 1939 was approximately 8.5 millions. Returns for three quar-ters of 1939 indicate that the number of layoffs in which unemployment compensation was paid would be about 5.7 millions for the entire year. Apparently, there were about 2.8 million layoffs in covered industries in which no unemployment benefits were paid. In some of these cases the workers had sufficient wage or employment credits, but failed to draw benefits because they obtained employment before the expiration of the waiting period. In other cases the workers failed to obtain benefits because they lacked sufficient wage or employment credits. It is unfortunate that we do not know the number of em-ployees who fall in each of these two classes. All that we know is that there was a number of claims disallowed because of insufficient wage credits. During the first three quarters of 1939, about 10 per cent of the claims from workers who had wage credits in covered employment was disallowed because of insufficient wage credits. In the first quarter the percentage was 12.2, in the second, 8.7, in the third, 9.4.

[18] In Great Britain, for example, where a twenty-six weeks' benefit is paid, it is the relief program rather than unemployment insurance which affects mobility. M. B. Gilson, *Unemployment Insurance in Great Britain*, p. 204.

away, a worker is not likely to neglect hunting for employment. It is significant that in England only about one out of four vacancies is filled by the public employment offices; most of the men get their own jobs.[19] Undoubtedly, unemployment benefits will cause the unemployed worker to be more particular about the job he accepts and thus may extend somewhat the average period of unemployment.[20] Unemployment benefits may discourage long-distance movement of workers in search of work. It is not likely, however, to discourage the kind of search which a man can now make in his car without failing to report at his local public employment office once a week. Furthermore, it should be observed that in the past there has been much aimless wandering by the unemployed and that this should be discouraged. The transfer of men over great distances should be made by the public employment offices in response to requisitions which cannot be filled in the local market.

3. The main impact of the social security program upon the mobility of labor will occur in connection with relief. Persons on relief seem to be more mobile than persons not on relief.[21] This does not mean that relief usually encourages mobility. Indeed, it probably does the opposite, but relief is most likely to affect the workers who do not belong to the regular working force and who do the most moving—not because of preference but because of necessity.[22] Up to the moment, the effect of relief upon the mobility of labor has not been tested. It can be tested only by a substantial increase in the number of jobs. The effect may be expected to vary with the type of labor. Among the 53,000,000 or 54,000,000 persons who constitute the would-be gainfully employed, there are great variations in employability. Perhaps 10 or 15 per cent have a very high degree of employability and another 10 to 15 per cent a very low degree of employability. Among the 5,000,000 persons of low employability, the effect of relief upon mobility will undoubtedly be great. Payments of $50 a month for twelve months in the year would give probably most of these persons more than they would earn in industry.

[19] The public offices have been endeavoring for some years to increase the proportion of vacancies which they fill and with moderate success. In 1926, the proportion filled by the public employment offices was about 18 per cent. In 1932, it was 21.2 per cent; in 1933, 26.6 per cent; in 1934, 24.8 per cent; and in 1935, 26.9 per cent. Cornelia M. Anderson, "British Employment Exchanges," *Harvard Business Review*, XVI, 96.

[20] Even in bad years, there is a considerable amount of hiring. In both 1931 and 1932, for example, the number of hirings by manufacturing establishments included in the sample of the Bureau of Labor Statistics, was over three fourths as large as the number of separations. In 1931, the monthly accession rate was 3.05 per 100 employees on the pay roll, and the separation rate, 4.03; in 1932, the monthly accession rate was 3.32 per 100 employees, and the separation rate, 4.33.

[21] The Michigan study of 149,379 workers showed that 13,621, or 10.9 per cent, of 131,532 not on relief made a geographical move during the period under study and that 4,226, or 17.2 per cent, of the 24,589 workers on relief made a move. (*Monthly Labor Review*, January, 1939, XLVIII, 16-24.) The same conclusion was reached by C. E. Lively and C. Taeuber in their study, *Rural Migration in the United States*, pp. 116-118.

[22] There are some cases in which relief definitely does encourage mobility, but the kind of mobility it fosters is not necessarily desirable. Relief is likely to encourage movement in the direction of relief opportunity rather than in the direction of employment opportunity.

Of course, the persons on relief, particularly work relief, do not necessarily consist of the least efficient 10 per cent of the would-be gainfully employed. The longer the relief program is in operation, however, the more completely its rolls will consist of persons of low employability. Even during the worst of the depression the re-employment rate among persons with a year or less of unemployment seems to have been about 40 per cent among males and even higher among females.[23] Each time someone leaves relief there is a chance that he will be replaced by a person of low employability. No one knows what the chance is. At any rate, if separations from the relief rolls frequently mean the addition of a person of low employability, the relief rolls will more and more consist of persons for whose services industry cannot hope to compete with relief.[24] In other words, precisely the reverse process goes on among the unemployed as goes on in industry. Just as employers by constantly sifting the employed gradually build up a better selected force, so the same process of selection and rejections gradually converts the unemployed more and more completely to a group of low employability. This is how the "hard core" of unemployment is created.[25]

Not only will relief compete effectively with industry for the services of several million of the least employables, but it will hold many thousands of persons in regions where employment opportunities are low, unless operated to encourage movement. The great migrations of human history have been a mixture of pushes and pulls. The strongest push areas in the United States seem to be the Southern Appalachians, the cutover lands, the cotton areas of the Southeast, the dust bowl. There are, however, many cities

---

[23] *See* forthcoming study by W. S. Woytinsky on this point.

[24] Among the unemployed in Philadelphia, according to the samples collected by the Industrial Research Department of the Wharton School and the Works Progress Administration, the percentages unemployed for three years or more increased as follows:

	Males	Females
1931	2.8	1.8
1932	3.3	2.2
1933	7.9	4.9
1935	34.9	19.6
1936	34.4	27.3
1937	37.7	26.1
1938	25.7	17.5

[25] A hard core of unemployment is bound to be created in any period of unemployment long enough to permit the segregation of the least employables among the unemployed. When the volume of employment fluctuates at only slightly below the labor supply (in other words when unemployment is low) the persons of low employability are not effectively segregated.

Congress has attempted to deal with the problem of the hard core of unemployment in so far as the WPA is concerned by requiring that persons employed continuously on WPA for eighteen months be dropped for at least a month. It is not clear that this is a wise approach to the problem. Possibly the objective of public policy should be, not to keep persons of low employability off WPA, but to take care of them there. That may be precisely the place for them. Certainly work relief is not a good device for taking care of persons whose employability is high and whose unemployment, therefore, is likely to be very short; it is a more appropriate device for taking care of those whose employability is so low that they have slight chance of getting work again in private industry.

which are push areas. Relief may be administered to offset the pushes of these unfavorable environments and to cause people to remain where employment opportunities are poorest. Or it may be used to create movement among those best fitted to move and to encourage the growth of a subsistence economy among the persons who are not fitted to move.

Will not the tendency of relief to keep persons of low employability out of industry and to hold present inhabitants in regions of meager employment opportunities be broken by the first pronounced boom in business? A substantial growth of employment would undoubtedly produce an appreciable reduction of even the long-term unemployed. I venture the prediction, however, that the percentage of the population between the ages of sixteen and forty-five actually at work in gainful nonagricultural employment may expand above the level of the twenties while leaving half or more of the 5,000,000 least employable on relief. The actual result will depend partly upon the wage policies of the country. The United States, however, has enormous reserves of labor not only among the unemployed, but also among the nonemployed; that is, women and young people who are not working and not seeking work. In addition, there are at least 2,000,000 persons attached to agriculture at a low intensity of employment who could easily be drawn into nonagricultural pursuits. Industry will draw heavily upon the nonemployed and upon agricultural workers before rehiring the least employable among the unemployed.

III

Who will bear the cost of the social security program and how will the program affect the wages, enterprise, and employment? As the cost for some years will be met by the pay roll tax, an inquiry into the incidence of the program requires an analysis of the incidence of the pay roll tax. The effects in the short-run (too short to permit the capital of industry to be adjusted to changes in the prospect for profits) must be distinguished from the long-run effects.

It is assumed that the price of labor is too sticky to be immediately affected by a tax on pay rolls. In that event the incidence of the tax in the short run is dispersed in several directions. Since the marginal costs of existing plants in the short run consist of labor and raw materials, an increase in the price of one causes the demand curve of the other to move to the left.[26] Hence, part of the pay roll tax in the short run falls on the suppliers of raw materials. The rise in marginal costs produces an advance in

[26] This point is important also in judging the consequences of wage cuts in times of depression. Even if the demand for labor in the short run is inelastic, wage reductions, by moving the demand curve for raw materials to the right, may cause an increase in disbursements by business enterprises. Since raw materials are largely produced by a group (farmers) who have even a lower income level than industrial workers, wage reductions may increase low-bracket consumer incomes even in those cases where the plant demand for labor is inelastic.

the prices of finished goods so that the cost falls partly on consumers. The rise in the price also limits the quantity sold which means that labor bears part of the cost in the form of less employment. The rise in labor costs and the limitation of the quantity sold means that profits are reduced and that capital bears part of the cost.

In the long run the effect of the pension and unemployment compensation schemes upon enterprise must be judged by the relationship between the benefit disbursements and the collections under the pay roll tax, because the noninsurance schemes (such as old age assistance, aid to dependent children and the blind) must be financed out of the general budget. But since the pay roll tax and the relief schemes were made effective by the same act of Congress, it is more realistic to appraise the immediate effects of the act by considering it as a whole. From the beginning of 1937 to the middle of 1939, tax collections and benefit payments under the Social Security Act were as follows:

	Collections[a] (millions)	Pension and unemployment benefit payments (millions)	Other[b] payments (millions)	Excess of receipts over payments (millions)
1937	$1,184	$ 3	$ 383	$ 798
1938	1,316	404	495	417
1939 (first half)	755	237	273	245
	$3,255	$644	$1,151	$1,460

[a] Includes collections under state unemployment insurance schemes of $586.5 million.
[b] Includes old age assistance, aid to dependent children, aid to the blind.

During 1937 collections exceeded disbursements by 798 million dollars. Perhaps not more than half of the excess of collections over payments, however, fell upon profits and of this perhaps between 300 and 350 million dollars fell upon corporate profits.[27] This was equivalent to an increase of one third of the federal corporate income tax. As corporate profits in 1937 were 3.9 billion dollars, the effect upon profits was moderate. The pay roll taxes had no direct relationship to the downturn in the spring of 1937, but they were an important factor in preventing profits in 1937 from rising above 1936 and so they must have materially restrained the vigor of the expansion.[28] In 1938, the excess of receipts over expenditures was only 417 million dollars, but the effect on enterprise may have been more serious than in 1937. Returns from 167 large companies indicate that profits were less than half the level of 1937. Thus they may have been about 1.8 bil-

[27] This guess may be too low as there was considerable resistance by consumers to higher prices. On this point see my paper, "Corporate Price Policies as a Factor in the Recent Business Recession," *Proceedings of the Academy of Political Science,* January, 1939.

[28] Even in 1937, the best year of the recovery, corporate profits were low—42.3 per cent below 1926, when gross corporate income was virtually the same as in 1937. In fact, only two out of five corporations made money in 1937 as against three out of five in 1926. Perhaps it is true that when profits are very low, the influence of any encroachment upon them is magnified.

lion dollars. If half of the excess of collections over receipts fell on profits, the net income of corporations would have been cut by 10 per cent. Such a cut may well have materially affected investment policy and substantially accentuated the depression.

More serious was the effect of social security taxes upon the railroads, because the roads cannot even temporarily pass on higher costs in the form of higher prices. During the year 1937, the net cost of social security to the roads was about 76 million dollars and their net profits were 98 millions. In 1937, therefore, social security cut the profits of the roads by nearly 44 per cent. In 1938, the roads had a deficit of 124 million dollars and the net cost of social security to them was 67 millions. In this year social security was responsible for 54 per cent of the deficit.[29] It is evident that social security taxes add greatly to the difficulties of this grievously depressed industry.

IV

Who will bear the pay roll taxes in the long run? Three principal theories have been suggested. One is that the tax will produce higher prices so that all nonrecipients of benefits, in their capacity of consumers, will bear it. A second is that the social security program, by producing forced saving, will reduce the rate of interest, especially during the next twenty years. To that extent the cost would fall on owners of capital. A third theory is that the tax will move the demand curve for labor to the left so that the burden will fall on labor.

What is the possibility that the tax on pay rolls will produce higher prices and thus fall largely upon consumers? Keynes and others have argued that, given proper monetary policies, a rise in marginal costs will raise prices rather than reduce output. Higher prices presuppose either an expansion of demand deposits or a rise in their velocity. The demand for demand deposits and the willingness to spend them depends upon the outlook for profits and the scale of operations that businessmen plan as a result. Until an increase in expenditures occurs to raise prices, the advance in marginal cost must be regarded as reducing the marginal efficiency of capital and causing the demand curve for short-term loans to move to the left. Because the demand for short-term loans is inelastic, it is not practical to reduce their supply price sufficiently to prevent the shift in the demand curve from reducing the volume of demand deposits. It is even more difficult by

---

[29] The Railway Pension Act of 1937 provided that persons on the pension rolls of the railroads should be transferred to the public pension scheme beginning July 1, 1937. As a result, the roads were relieved of pension payments to about 54,000 employees who had been receiving on the average slightly more than fifty dollars a month. The saving to the roads during the second half of 1937 was slightly more than 16.2 million dollars and during 1938 slightly more than 32.4 millions. In estimating the net cost of social security to the roads these amounts must be deducted from the 92.4 millions in social security taxes paid by the roads in 1937 and the 99.5 millions paid in 1938.

reducing the supply price of short-term loans to produce an increase in demand deposits sufficient to raise expenditures and prices in proportion to the rise in costs and thus to restore the marginal efficiency of capital to the level prevailing before the increase in costs. There is slight prospect, therefore, that banking policy will cause the pay roll tax to produce higher prices with no restriction on production and with the cost falling in the main upon consumers and to some extent upon capitalists. If the banking system were able to control the supply price of venture capital, this conclusion might have to be altered.

V

Will the pay roll taxes increase the amount of saving with the result that (1) the amount of capital per worker is increased; (2) the marginal worth of labor (and hence the price of labor) is raised; and (3) the return on capital is reduced? Were these results to follow, the cost of the social security program would fall in the main upon property owners in the form of lower interest rates but partly upon consumers in the form of higher prices.[30]

At one time it was estimated that a pension reserve fund of over 40 billion dollars would be accumulated by 1980. No guesses concerning the size of the reserve a few years hence can pretend to be accurate, but changes in the estimates of costs and changes in the law itself now indicate that the reserve will reach a maximum of roughly 7 billions about 1955. The accumulation of such a reserve will increase the volume of investment-seeking funds by less than 5 per cent a year. During prosperous times the unemployment insurance schemes will run a surplus. The amount will depend upon the terms of the laws, which are still in a state of flux. Perhaps it will be 300 million dollars a year. At any rate during the next fifteen years the social insurance schemes may increase the volume of investment seeking funds by about 8 per cent in good years and perhaps 1 to 2 per cent in bad years.[31] At most periods of the business cycle the demand for investment funds seems to be inelastic, although the demand for funds for housing at times seems to be elastic. If the demand is inelastic, the burden of the social security program for the next fifteen years may fall to an appreciable degree upon capital. After that period, the accumulation of the old age reserve will cease and the burden on capital from the shift in the supply curve of investment funds to the right will be negligible.[32]

---

[30] It would fall partly upon consumers because there is a connection between long-term and short-term interest rates. Hence the forced saving which reduced long-term interest rates would produce some increase in short-term funds and some increase in demand deposits and prices.

[31] During the next fifteen years the liquidation of the unemployment insurance funds in times of depression will not quite offset the accumulation of the old age reserve.

[32] The liquidation of the unemployment insurance funds during periods of depression will provide an outlet for savings and help support the rate of interest at such times. The

VI

If the pay roll tax does not produce an increase in incomes and prices, the demand curve for labor will shift to the left. At the wage rates prevailing before imposition of the pay roll tax, the quantity of labor employed will be reduced. Unemployment will retard the increase in wage rates as technological progress raises the marginal worth of labor. It might be supposed that the retarding of the increase in wage rates would continue until the unemployed displaced by the pay roll tax had all been absorbed. This presupposes, however, that the benefits paid have no effect upon the labor supply curve. Pensions, even though low, will undoubtedly produce a few retirements. Likewise, unemployment benefits will slightly raise the reservation prices of unemployed workers and make them less willing to accept the first job that comes along.[33] More important than either unemployment compensation or old age pensions upon the reservation prices of labor will be relief payments. The social security program by producing unemployment may cause an expansion of relief payments. To the extent that social security benefits and relief move the supply curve of labor to the left, they counteract the tendency of the pay roll tax to keep down the price of labor.

Even though the social security program (including relief) raises the reservation prices of labor, it is not likely to affect materially the number of workers available at prevailing wage rates to existing nonagricultural enterprises. In existing concerns the price of labor seems to be set during periods of contraction by the employed rather than the unemployed—by the resistance of the employed to cuts rather than the willingness of the unemployed to accept less than prevailing rates.[34] If the reservation prices created by social security affect the volume of employment, it will be through their effect upon wages in new concerns and, therefore, upon the number of business births. Even in periods of contraction the number of business births is close to 200,000 a year for new going concerns. The wage rates paid by new concerns in periods of great unemployment appear to be substantially below prevailing rates. Consequently, the reservation prices established by social security may substantially affect wages in new concerns

---

increase in consumer incomes made possible by the liquidation of the unemployment funds will also improve the general business situation. Consequently, during periods of depression, property owners will gain but not at the expense of other groups in the community.

[33] May not the payment of benefits reduce the reservation prices of labor? The workers in covered industries receive protection which workers in uncovered employments do not enjoy. Will not workers, therefore, be attracted to the covered industries? As between the covered and the uncovered industries, this is probably true at least to some extent. The fact remains, however, that reservation prices are to considerable extent determined by the amount of resources upon which unemployed workers may draw. Pensions and the unemployment compensation may reduce slightly the reservation prices of workers with respect to employment in the covered industries, but all payments in compensation of unemployment tend to raise the reservation prices of workers as a whole.

[34] In periods of expansion the effect of the unemployed upon wages in old concerns is probably greater than in periods of contraction.

and thereby reduce the business birth rate.[35] If so, social security legislation (and wage-hour legislation as well) may affect the resiliency of our economy—its capacity to spring back after a shrinkage in employment. This, however, is still an unexplored field. Little is known about the determinants of the birth rate of new enterprises. Until exploration has occurred, we remain very much in the field of conjecture and we must not be surprised if the unintended consequences of public policies are more important than the intended ones.

VII

Thus far we have discussed the incidence of a pay roll tax on the assumption that the price of labor is set by supply and demand. To an increasing extent, however, the price of labor is an administered one, fixed by bargaining between trade unions and employers. To explain the effect of social security in such a world, one must consider how it will affect the bargaining power of unions and employers. Bargaining power may be defined as the cost to A of imposing a loss upon B. Part of the cost to union members of raising wages beyond a given rate is unemployment. To the extent that unemployment is compensated by insurance or relief, unions will be willing to endure larger amounts of it in order to raise the wages of their members. Trade union wage policy has been influenced by the fear of nonunion competition. To the extent that social security and relief diminish the birth rate of new concerns they will limit the influence of nonunion competition upon union wage policy. Hence we may conclude that in a world of administered prices of labor, social security will tend both to raise the wages of the employed and to increase the number of the unemployed.

Will the increase in the bargaining power of labor be harmful to enterprise? Possibly, but not necessarily. The greater pressure on employers to raise the price of labor will (1) accelerate technological discovery, but (2) reduce the proportion of new ideas which are considered worth exploiting. It is sometimes said that wage increases will not increase the use of labor-saving inventions because (unless labor costs are less important in the capital goods industries than in other industries) the price of capital goods will be raised in the same proportion as wages.[36] But the expectation of wage increases will produce laborsaving inventions as a method of embodying today's labor costs into tomorrow's production costs. Likewise, the expectation that higher wages will raise the prices of capital goods will stimulate the making of capital-saving inventions. The proportion of laborsaving and

[35] However, the effect of the social security program upon the wages paid by new enterprises will be substantially less in most industries than the minima established under the Wage-Hour Act.

[36] See H. G. Hayes, "The Rate of Wages and the Use of Machinery," *American Economic Review*, XIII, 461-465, and P. H. Douglas, "The Effect of Wage Increases Upon Employment," *Proceedings of the American Economic Association*, 1939, pp. 138-157.

capital-saving inventions may not be changed, but the rise in the bargaining power of unions will increase the marginal efficiency of expenditures on discovery and thus will raise proportion of the community's resources devoted to discovery.

Although the rate of discovery will be raised, it is not certain that the volume of investment will expand. The volume of investment depends upon the prospects for profits over the long period. If employers expect wages to be promptly bargained upward whenever profits appear, their estimates of the marginal return on capital will be lowered and the proportion of the new discoveries which seem worth developing will be reduced. It is impossible to determine whether the net effect of a faster rate of discovery and a more selective exploitation of discoveries will be a larger or smaller volume of investment.

This analysis must be qualified by the observation that collective bargaining is still in a very rudimentary stage and that the policies of unions are likely to be influenced more by experience with collective bargaining than by the effect of the social security program upon their bargaining power. For example, experience in selling labor is likely to alter the tendency of unions to underestimate the elasticity of the demand for labor and to overlook the fact that the elasticity over a period of several years is much greater than the elasticity at a given moment. Nor must the present crude and simple wage structures necessarily be regarded as final in a rapidly changing world. Wage systems may develop which greatly increase the interest of the unions in the volume of employment.

VIII

The following general conclusions stand out from this analysis:

1. About one fifth of the labor supply is mobile and works for more than one employer in the course of the year.

2. Despite the fact that the amount of movement in the labor market is considerably less than in prewar times, it is probably excessive. It is excessive in the main because it is forced and represents organization of work to an uneconomical extent upon a casual basis, but partly because much of it is uninformed.

3. Little is known about the 10,000,000 or more persons who supply the demand for temporary workers. Many of them undoubtedly have a principal occupation which dovetails with temporary employment outside of it. Some of them are seeking only part-time employment either for a few months of the year or part-time throughout the year. Some are young workers who have not succeeded in obtaining the status of regular employees. Until more complete and definite information concerning the suppliers of temporary labor becomes available, we shall be in the dark in deciding many important questions of policy.

4. The excessive amount of intermittent employment creates a strong prima facie case in favor of experience rating. This does not mean that specific experience rating provisions in existing legislation are well conceived.

5. The old age provisions of the Social Security Act tend to break down barriers to movement—a desirable result. To some extent their effect will be counteracted by the old age assistance plans which are based upon residence requirements that should be altered.

6. Definite information is lacking on how many and what kinds of people fail to qualify for unemployment benefits because their earnings or employment is insufficient.

7. Unemployment insurance is not likely to affect the mobility of most of the covered workers because the great majority who qualify for benefits have attachments to particular employers which discourage them from moving and because the duration of benefit payments is short. To some extent, however, unemployment benefits may discourage movement by encouraging workers to remain on the chance that more or less indefinite reemployment opportunities may become realities. This is likely to be a good result in a majority of cases.

8. The present trend is to make eligibility requirements for unemployment compensation more strict. Perhaps the trend should be reversed as the present laws seem to give protection to the workers least in need of it and not to reach those workers most in need of protection. The problem of more liberal eligibility requirements is complicated by the fact that many short-term or intermittent workers are not seeking full-time employment. Until more is known concerning the persons who fail because of insufficient earnings or employment to qualify for unemployment compensation, we are not in a position to judge the desirability of changes in eligibility requirements.

9. Relief is likely to affect the mobility of many thousands of persons of low employability. However, the effect of relief upon mobility must not be exaggerated. The rise in hiring standards will probably cause industry to draw on the huge labor reserves among the nonemployed and in agriculture before engaging the persons of low employability on relief. Hence, an expansion of the proportion of the population at work in nonagricultural pursuits to substantially higher figures than prevailed in the twenties will probably not reduce unemployment (over and above seasonal unemployment) to below 2,500,000.

10. Social security taxes encroached upon profits to a moderate extent in 1937 and limited the expansion of business. The excess of collections over disbursements was less in 1938, but the proportionate reduction in profits was greater. Although the social security taxes were not an influence of first importance in intensifying the depression, the encroachment upon

profits must have restricted commitments. In both 1937 and 1938, the social security taxes substantially affected the profits of the railroads.

11. It is unlikely that the incidence of the pay roll tax in the long run will be broadly diffused throughout the economy by higher costs which will induce larger income flows and thereby higher prices. For a period of fifteen years interest rates may be moderately affected by the program. After that time its effect upon interest rates will be negligible. In the area of competitive wage determination, the pay roll tax will move the demand curve for labor to the left. To a small extent the payment of benefits will also move the supply curve of labor to the left. This will affect new enterprises far more than existing ones. It remains to be seen whether or not the program will materially affect the birth rate of new enterprises and the resiliency of our economy.

12. The social security program will increase the bargaining power of trade unions and tend to reduce the interest of unions in the effect of their wage policies upon the volume of employment. It will tend to increase the rate of discovery but to reduce the proportion of discoveries that are worth exploiting. Its effect upon the volume of investment, therefore, is uncertain. Trade union wage policies, however, are likely to be less affected by social security than by longer experience of unions with collective bargaining. But since the social security program tends to diminish the concern of trade unions with the volume of employment, it creates the need for developing wage structures and forms of wage payment which increase the interest of unions in employment.

EXPERIENCE RATING
IN UNEMPLOYMENT COMPENSATION

By Charles A. Myers

I

The importance of adequate provision for unemployed workers during the reconversion period has properly focused attention on some of the shortcomings of our present system of unemployment compensation.[1] But social security programs also need reëxamination in the light of their probable impact on the level of employment after the transition from war to peace. This long-run problem should not be disregarded simply because immediate demands are more pressing.

Unemployment compensation, and social security programs generally, are designed primarily to provide some protection for covered workers against certain unavoidable hazards. The possibility of using social security taxes and funds as a major weapon in governmental efforts to assure high-level employment has received only secondary attention in this country. Although it has been claimed that payment of unemployment benefits in depression periods would have a bolstering effect on consumer demand, and although experience-rating provisions in some 40 state laws have been designed to encourage individual firms to stabilize their employment, neither of these is tied in directly with a positive government fiscal policy as an instrument of economic stabilization.

II

A concrete and significant proposal in this direction is made in the recent British White Paper on *Employment Policy*.[2] This White Paper is notable in many respects, but principally because it commits the present British government to a far-reaching program for meeting

* The author is assistant professor of industrial relations at the Massachusetts Institute of Technology.

[1] Richard A. Lester, *Providing for Unemployed Workers during the Postwar Transition Period,* chap. iv, "Improvements in Unemployment Compensation" (New York, McGraw-Hill, 1945). Gladys R. Friedman and William H. Wandel, "Unemployment Compensation Goals in the Reconversion Period," *Social Security Bulletin,* Vol. 7 (Sept., 1944), pp. 6-10; and "Unemployment Compensation in the Reconversion Period: Recommendations by the Social Security Board," *Social Security Bulletin,* Vol. 7 (Oct., 1944), pp. 3-8.

[2] Cmd. 6527 (reissued in the United States by Macmillan Company, New York, 1944).

"those long-term problems connected with the maintenance of an adequate and steady volume of employment which eluded solution before the war."[3]

The Keynesian influence on British thinking in this instance is clear. One of the "essential conditions" of the program is that "total expenditure on goods and services must be prevented from falling to a level where general unemployment appears." In addition to "public investment" to maintain "capital expenditure," the White Paper recommends, "we must create another line of defence against this progressive degeneration of the state of trade by putting ourselves in a position to influence the community's expenditure on consumption."

The core of the proposal is stated as follows:[4]

For this purpose, the Government, after examining a number of methods, favour the adoption, when settled conditions return, of a scheme for varying, in sympathy with the state of employment, the weekly contribution to be paid by employers and employed under the proposed new system of social insurance. The standard rate of contribution would be assessed on the basis of a forecast of the average level of unemployment, in such a way as to keep the social insurance fund in balance over a number of years. But the rate of contribution actually levied would exceed the standard rate at times when unemployment fell below the estimated average level and would be less than the standard rate at times when unemployment exceeded this average. . . .

The effect of this scheme would be that, above a certain level of unemployment, a rise of two points in the unemployment percentage would decrease by an average of £500,000 a week the total of the social insurance contribution paid by workers in employment—apart from the corresponding reduction in the costs of employers. This would substantially augment the purchasing power in the hands of employed workers; and the additional money thus left in the hands of many millions of people would help to maintain demand for consumers' goods, thereby offsetting, at least in part, the decline in the expenditure of those who had lost their employment. This maintenance of purchasing power would reduce substantially the variations in total expenditure and employment.

Here, it must be admitted, is something new in social security policy, given influential support by the government of a nation which has pioneered in social security.[5] The sharp contrast with our own social

---

[3] *Ibid.*, p. 15.

[4] *Ibid.*, pp. 22-23. Fuller details of the plan are included in an appendix to the report.

[5] In his *Fiscal Policy and Business Cycles* (New York, Norton, 1941), Professor Alvin H. Hansen made a somewhat similar proposal, but it was not related directly to social insurance or unemployment compensation. He suggested that a payroll tax might be increased during the late upswing and boom, and dropped entirely after the turning point had been reached. Funds previously collected could then, he said, be "returned to aid employers to maintain current wage rates." And, "in so far as payroll taxes had been deducted from wages, they should be returned to the wage earners (employed as well as

security program is striking. During a period when employment and payrolls were expanding, Congress voted in 1943 and again in 1944 to postpone the scheduled increases in employer and employee contributions (payroll and earnings taxes) for federal old-age insurance. The scheduled increase to 2 per cent on January 1, 1945, would have doubled the annual revenue of $1,300,000,000 at 1 per cent. Contribution rates may later have to be raised at a time less favorable from the standpoint of consumer demand and employer costs. But it is with experience rating under state unemployment compensation laws that the contrast is sharpest. The remainder of this paper will be devoted to a reëxamination of our present experience-rating systems in the light of the British proposal and other considerations.

III

The primary and announced purpose of experience rating in unemployment compensation is to provide a financial incentive, in the form of a reduced contribution rate, for the individual employer to make a real effort to stabilize his employment. Britain experimented on a limited basis with this idea before 1920, but abandoned it.[6] Hence it is usually regarded as a peculiarly American invention. Three years before the Social Security act was passed in 1935 in this country, Wisconsin adopted an unemployment compensation law with definite provisions for "merit rating" (as it was then called).

The pressure for some form of merit or experience rating grew as other states adopted unemployment compensation laws after 1935. By the end of 1943, experience rating was effective in 40 states, and during 1944-45 it will go into operation in 5 more states.[7] In most of these states, the revenues used for payment of unemployment benefits come from a payroll tax ("contribution") levied on employers exclusively. Only three states require contributions from employees (1 per cent) based on their earnings. Reductions below the standard rate of 2.7 per

---

unemployed) to help maintain labor incomes in the depression" (pp. 293-94).

A brief suggestion along similar lines, in connection with experience rating under unemployment compensation, was made in the Unanimous Report of the Committee on Employer Experience Rating of the Interstate Conference of Employment Security Agencies (Washington, September, 1940), pp. 71-72.

[6] Mary B. Gilson, *Unemployment Insurance in Great Britain* (New York, 1931), p. 43. See also chap. vi.

[7] Many of the following data on experience rating were taken from "Experience Rating Operations in 1943," *Social Security Bulletin*, Vol. 7 (Sept., 1944), pp. 11-19. The only states or territories without provision for experience rating are Alaska, Mississippi, Montana, Rhode Island, Utah, and Washington. After this manuscript was prepared, New York adopted a type of "experience rating" different from existing provisions. It does not provide for direct variations in contribution rates, but allows rebates in the form of tax credits under certain conditions. It is too early to evaluate the probable effects of this plan.

cent may go as low as zero in some states, but in only 16 of the 40 states are higher-than-standard rates assessed against "unstable" firms.

Between January 1, 1941, and December 31, 1943, employment and payrolls increased substantially. Yet during these three years, as experience-rating provisions became effective in 40 states, the average employer contribution rate in these states dropped to 1.8 per cent, compared to the standard rate of 2.7 per cent. (See Table I.) The revenue collected, compared to what it would have been at the standard rate,

TABLE I.—REDUCTIONS IN CONTRIBUTION RATES AND REVENUES UNDER EXPERIENCE RATING

Year	Average Employer Contribution Rate (All States)	States with Experience Rating					Reduction in Revenue as % of Contributions at Standard Rate (All States)
		Number	Average Employer Contribution Rate	Reduction in Revenue from Standard Rate[a] (millions)	Reduction as % of Contributions at Standard Rate	
1941	2.58%	17	2.17%	$54	20%	5%
1942	2.18	34	1.81	269	34	20
1943	2.00[b]	40	1.80	416	36	26

Source: Condensed from Table 1, "Experience-Rating Operations in 1943," *Social Security Bulletin*, Vol. 7 (Sept., 1944), p. 11.

[a] Excluding special war risk contributions provided in 9 states, amounting on 1943 payrolls to 30 million dollars.

[b] An unofficial tabulation reported an average employer contribution rate for all states in 1944 of 1.8 per cent. (*Business Week*, Apr. 28, 1945, p. 34.)

also declined each year, until in 1943 it was more than a third lower than the probable revenue at the standard rate.[8] For all states, this represented a reduction in revenues of one-fourth from the potential revenue of 1.6 billion dollars.

The opposite result may be expected in a future period of falling employment and declining payrolls. Under present experience-rating provisions, the average employer contribution rate will have to be increased, and the revenue collected per payroll dollar will also increase.

[8] This possibility was foreseen in *Experience Rating under Unemployment Compensation Laws*, in the Unanimous Report of the Committee on Employer Experience Rating of the Interstate Conference of Employment Security Agencies (Washington, Sept., 1940): ". . . Even those States which already have accumulated rather substantial reserves might do well to 'make haste slowly' in using their present reserves as a basis for reducing contribution rates to a point where current collections would merely match current out-go" (p. 56).

To the extent that this loss of revenue through lower contribution rates is reflected in higher profits or lower prices, however, some of it will be recovered by the Treasury (though not for the Unemployment Compensation Fund), through excess profits taxes and lower costs of war goods.

Except for the fact that the variations apply to employer contributions alone in this country, these results are just the opposite of those recommended by the British White Paper in the interest of maintaining high-level employment. Total revenues collected will be greater in boom than in depression, because total payrolls are higher, but the *rate* of contribution will vary in the opposite direction.

IV

Why does experience rating bring these results? The answer is to be found in an examination of the mechanics of contribution rate reductions in our various state laws. The earliest form of experience rating, adopted in the Wisconsin law in 1932, was the "reserve-ratio" method. Under this plan an employer qualified for a lower-than-standard contribution rate if the ratio between his credited "reserve" (total contributions less benefits charged against his account) and his average annual payroll in preceding years was at specified percentage levels. Thus, if an employer succeeded in reducing benefit payments, either by employment stabilization or other devices, his reserve ratio might rise, provided his annual payroll remained about the same or at least increased less rapidly. He would, therefore, be qualified for a lower contribution rate the following year. In Wisconsin he might even qualify for a zero rate.[9]

The Wisconsin law was the pattern for many other states adopting experience rating. By the end of 1943, 24 of the other 39 states in this group had a reserve-ratio type of law, although most of these differed from the Wisconsin law in that employer contributions were largely pooled, rather than kept in separate "employer reserves." Seven states with experience rating had adopted a method known as the "Cliffe plan" (developed originally by an official of the General Electric Company); and 5 others followed a "benefit-ratio" plan. Two states used a combined reserve-ratio—benefit-ratio plan, and one state (Connecticut) used a "compensable separations" method, under which an employer's experience is measured by an index involving the number of separations resulting in benefits multiplied by the benefit rates.[10]

The "Cliffe plan" differs from the reserve-ratio method in several important respects. The intention of the former is to replenish the fund for the average annual amount of benefits paid during the preceding three years, and in effect to put operations on a "pay-as-you-go"

[9] For a fuller discussion of the Wisconsin act, see a study by the author, *Employment Stabilization and the Wisconsin Act* ([Employment Security Memorandum No. 10] Social Security Board, Washington, Sept., 1940). A condensed version appeared in the *Am. Econ. Rev.*, Vol. XXIX, No. 4 (Dec., 1939), pp. 708-23.

[10] "Experience-Rating Operations in 1943," *op. cit.*, Table 2, pp. 12-13.

basis rather than to accumulate a growing reserve. The employer's contribution rate is determined by his "experience factor" adjusted by the state "experience factor." His experience factor may be defined as follows: the base-period wages ("benefit wages") earned from him by employees who are laid off and subsequently draw benefits, in a three-year period, divided by his total annual payrolls for three years. The state experience factor is simply the total benefits paid, divided by the total of all "benefit wages" in the state over three years. Benefit wages are charged to previous employers after the first week of benefits, and are the same whether the employee draws one or 15 weeks of benefits.[11]

The "benefit-ratio" method of experience rating awards lower employer contribution rates on the basis of a low ratio between the total benefits paid to present or former employees over a three-year period and the employer's total payroll for the same period. The reserve-ratio plan, in contrast, measures the ratio between the net reserve (total contributions minus total benefits) and the average annual payroll in preceding years.

In both the Cliffe and benefit-ratio types of plans, falling benefit payments and rising payrolls, resulting from a continued general increase in employment rather than from individual employment stabilization efforts, can lead automatically to lower employer contribution rates. Under the reserve-ratio plans, on the other hand, an increasing reserve caused by a decline in benefits due to increased employment is likely to be offset somewhat by a higher payroll, and the ratio between the two remains the same if the two have risen in the same proportion. The fact that the reserve-ratio plans take account of the employer's benefit and contribution experience since the beginning, rather than only during the preceding three years as in the two other plans, also accounts for greater stability of rates in the face of a continued increase in employment.

This contrast is shown clearly in the proportion of employers receiving rate reductions under each type of experience rating. During 1943, 84.5 per cent of the eligible employers qualified for lower-than-standard contribution rates in the seven states with the Cliffe plan, and 80.6 per cent got lower rates in the five states with benefit-ratio plans. On the other hand, only 69 per cent of the eligible employers received lower rates in the twenty-five states with reserve-ratio plans.[12]

---

[11] This was one of the major defects pointed out by the Unanimous Report (*Experience Rating under Unemployment Compensation Laws*), *ibid.*, p. 37. For further analysis and criticism of the Cliffe plan, see Adolph Appleman, "Notes on the Cliffe Plan of Experience Rating," *Personnel*, Vol. 17 (Aug., 1940), pp. 67-74. Mr. Cliffe describes and defends the plan in "The Texas Plan of Experience Rating," *Personnel*, Vol. 17 (Nov., 1940), pp. 151-61.

[12] "Experience-Rating Operations in 1943," *op. cit.*, Table 4, p. 15.

With several exceptions,[13] however, the reserve-ratio plans do not appear to have been free from the influence of rising employment and payrolls. The over-all picture of states with experience rating shows that from 1941 to 1943 an increasing proportion of employers have qualified for reduced contribution rates. (Table II.) Surely few people would seriously contend that in 1943 three-fourths of all eligible employers in all types of industry in 40 states had succeeded in "stabilizing" employment by their own efforts! Of course, in the 16 states which provide for higher-than-standard rates, some employers in industries

TABLE II.—PERCENTAGE DISTRIBUTION OF ACTIVE ACCOUNTS ELIGIBLE FOR RATE MODIFICATION, BY EMPLOYER CONTRIBUTION RATE, IN STATES WITH EXPERIENCE RATING IN EFFECT

Year	Number of States	All Rates %	Below Standard	Standard[a]	Above Standard
1941	17	100.0	54.9	31.8	13.3 (5 states)
1942	34	100.0	67.4	24.1	8.5 (15 states)
1943	40	100.0	74.8	19.9	5.3 (15 states)

Source: Compiled from Tables 3 and 4, "Experience-Rating Operations in 1943," *op. cit.*, pp. 14–15, Table I, *Social Security Bulletin*, Vol. 5 (June, 1942), p. 12; *Social Security Bulletin* Vol. 6 (Feb., 1943), p. 9.

[a] Standard rate is 2.7 per cent in all states except Michigan, where it is 3 per cent.

such as bituminous coal mining and building construction had to pay rates above 2.7 per cent, but in Hawaii 98 per cent of building construction employers qualified for below-standard rates.[14] Did they all "stabilize" employment by their own individual efforts, or was the construction boom after Pearl Harbor responsible?

V

A few states have apparently recognized the potential danger in widespread reductions of employer contribution rates during periods of rising payrolls. In contrast to most states, average contribution rates in Nebraska and Wisconsin were higher during 1943 than during 1941. The reserve-ratio plans in effect in these states differed from the usual reserve-ratio laws. Thus, in Nebraska the greatest amount of benefits in any year, 1940-42, is subtracted from the employer's reserve balance at the beginning of 1943, and the remainder is then expressed as a ratio of either his average annual payroll for the three years or the 1942 payroll, whichever is higher. A somewhat similar method is used in

[13] Principally Wisconsin and Nebraska, where there has been an increase in average rates between 1941 and 1943 because of a special type of reserve ratio plan in effect in these states. This point is discussed in the following section.

[14] "Experience-Rating Operations in 1943," *op. cit.*, p. 19.

Wisconsin. The employer's reserve balance is expressed as a percentage of the highest of the following: (1) payroll for the year ending, (2) 3-year average annual payroll, or (3) 60 per cent of the highest annual payroll in any one of the three years. Under these methods, reserve ratios are lower and contribution rates higher, in periods of rising payrolls, than under the usual reserve-ratio plan or other experience-rating methods.

Nine other states, including Wisconsin but not Nebraska, collected additional contributions during 1943 under special "war risk" provisions added to their laws. Supplementary rates of varying amounts are assessed against employers with specified increases in their payrolls.[15] The statement of policy in the Wisconsin law expresses clearly the need for such provisions:[16]

Wartime expansion has increased the payrolls of some employers substantially over their 1940 payrolls, with a corresponding increase in the potential post-war benefit liabilities of their reserve accounts, but without a corresponding increase in the level of those accounts under this chapter. Unless corrected, this condition would endanger the post-war solvency of such accounts, and would require higher contribution rates to be collected from employers generally, during the post-war years. Therefore, such accounts should now be built up toward more nearly adequate post-war levels, to help avoid (or reduce) the post-war rate increases which would otherwise result, by collecting contributions from such employers at higher-war-time rates, based on their payroll increases and the relative adequacy of their accounts.

While these provisions were undoubtedly included in part because the states realized that the federal government would bear the added cost where war contractors were involved, they are a step in the direction of correcting the anomalous results which experience rating has brought under rising payrolls. Yet apparently only in three of these states was the operation of the war-risk provision sufficient in 1943 to reverse the increasing trend toward reduced revenues from employer contributions.[17]

These war-risk provisions are presumably temporary devices. But it is not inconceivable that they may develop into more permanent methods by which states, or the federal government, can counteract the tendency of experience rating to reduce over-all contribution rates, without regard to individual employer stabilization efforts, in good

---

[15] For a full discussion, see Gladys R. Friedman, "War-Risk Contribution Provisions in State Unemployment Compensation Laws," *Social Security Bulletin,* Vol. 7 (May, 1944), pp. 2-8. Also, *"Experience-Rating Operations in 1943," op. cit.,* pp. 11-12, and Table 3, p. 14.

[16] Sec. 108.18(7) of the Wisconsin law.

[17] "Experience-Rating Operations in 1943," *op. cit.,* Table 3, p. 14.

times, and to increase them in bad times. The changes adopted in the reserve-ratio plans of Nebraska and Wisconsin are also designed to counteract this tendency, and deserve serious consideration by other states. One of the most serious objections to present experience rating in operation is that the ability of state reserve funds to pay future adequate benefits is unnecessarily jeopardized by rate reductions.

If standard rates of contributions were raised in periods of high unemployment and reduced in periods of low unemployment, it would still be possible to retain the experience-rating feature. Reductions from the current standard rate could be granted to those firms which met the necessary qualifications, or each firm's rate might be based on its experience over the cycle period. But the stabilization incentive might be reduced, and with present experience rating formulas the variations in standard rates would have to be still wider to compensate for the perverse effects of these formulas.

VI

Without variations in average contribution rates as suggested by the British proposal, the effects of experience rating on aggregate demand and employment will certainly be injurious. In periods of rising payrolls, contribution rates and expected revenues will fall, and in periods of falling payrolls, rates and revenues will have to be increased.

An analysis of these effects requires consideration of the probable incidence of the tax on employers' payrolls, which finances unemployment compensation exclusively in nearly every state. Though some economists are more inclined than others to stress shifting in one direction, most would probably agree that the incidence of this tax is diffused.[18] In perfect labor and product markets, it would eventually rest on the wage earners, but because of imperfections, it is probable that consumers bear some of the burden, through higher prices, and employers through reduced profits in certain firms and industries.

If the tax is eventually borne by workers, as some economists have contended, the effect of a decrease in average contribution rates during

[18] Various theories on the incidence of the payroll tax are well summarized by C. Ward Macy, in "Social Security Taxes in the War Finance Program," *Jour. Pol. Econ.*, Vol. LI (April, 1943), pp. 135-40. The best and most extended discussion in the literature is found in Seymour Harris, *Economics of Social Security* (New York, 1941), Pt. III. Professor Harris concludes: "The more or less accepted theory that labor ultimately pays the cost either through a reduction of money wages or of employment is subject to *important reservations. A substantial part of the burden falls elsewhere.* The marginal productivity theory upon which the theory of incidence has been based is, itself, subject to reservations and amplifications. . . . Furthermore, the theory of monopolistic competition with its concentration on imperfect elasticity of supplies of factors and of demand for commodities also suggests to the student of social security the possibility of putting part of the burden on the consumer and factors of production other than labor" (pp. 440-41).

good times and an increase in bad times is to accentuate the swings in worker incomes and hence in aggregate demand.[19] This result, of course, assumes no considerable time lag in shifting, and therefore is probably unrealistic.

But suppose the changes in contribution rates are reflected in higher or lower profits, or in higher or lower prices. It is clear that an increase in costs which raises prices or lowers profits does not furnish a sound basis for recovery. Conversely, during the boom period, when full employment has been reached, lower prices and increased profits resulting from reduced contribution rates under experience rating may have adverse results in the opposite direction.

Furthermore, if the prospect of lower contribution rates under experience rating furnishes an inducement for employment stabilization, as proponents contend, will the increases in average rates occasioned by falling employment act as a "tax" on employment? For every man hired in a period of business depression, an additional cost equal to 2.7 per cent of his earnings (or more in states with above-standard rates) will have to be paid by most employers. Yet at a time when the only problem in the hiring of men was to find them (as during 1943), the tax on payrolls in 40 states averaged only 1.8 per cent. To be sure, the difference is not great in percentage terms, but to the extent that payroll taxes are regarded as variable costs, even small absolute differences may be important.[20] In addition, an increase in variable costs during a period of depression may have a depressing effect on employers' investment decisions, thus further reducing aggregate demand.

VII

The effects of experience rating on aggregate demand are not the only effects worthy of consideration, however. Experience rating was directed primarily toward individual employers, though most states have modified the full incentive value of tax reductions by pooling contributions to insure greater adequacy of the total fund. What is the incentive value of experience rating in encouraging employment stabilization efforts by individual firms? This question has been the subject of much controversy between partisans on both sides.

It is my belief, based on field studies several years ago in Wisconsin when this state pioneered in experience rating, that the prospect of a

---

[19] The effect on worker incomes is, of course, offset to some extent by opposite variations in benefit payments.

[20] An interesting and unexplored question here is whether employers *do* regard payroll taxes as variable costs, or whether, through questionable cost-accounting practices, they consider these taxes as part of fixed overhead for the year.

tax reduction can start employers thinking of ways to iron out day-to-day or intermittent irregularities in employment and to reduce seasonal unemployment.[21] The prospect of a reduced contribution rate is a tangible financial incentive for many firms which have overlooked the intangible costs of irregular employment.

This is a real gain, if the cost is not too great. But once attained, it may be questioned whether experience rating is necessary to encourage employers to *continue* these desirable employment practices. Firms which have discovered, after stabilizing employment under the impetus of experience rating, that irregular employment is costly *in itself* are not likely to go back to their old haphazard methods of hiring and firing, transfers, producing excessive amounts of standard products in peak seasons and curtailing operations afterward, etc.[22]

Only where a close balance is achieved between the costs of stabilization (such as storage costs of inventory manufactured in advance of orders) and the lower contribution rate would the modification or abandonment of experience rating in its present forms result in a slackening of stabilization efforts where they are practical. Even in this case a firm may decide that the newly-discovered advantages of more regular employment and steady production offset the costs of attaining them.

Some other effects of experience rating in practice must be weighed against any positive gains resulting from greater efforts by employers to stabilize employment. Six points stand out in a review of the results under experience rating.[23]

1. The experience-rating formulas in use make it possible for an employer in a naturally stable business to qualify for a lower contribution rate without much effort on his part, while an employer in an unstable industry may be unable to qualify for the lower rate even though he is doing a better job of stabilizing than most firms in his

---

[21] "Employment Stabilization and the Wisconsin Act," *Am. Econ. Rev.*, Vol. XXIX, No. 4 (Dec., 1939), pp. 712-13, and chap. 4 of *Employment Stabilization and the Wisconsin Act* ([Employment Security Memorandum No. 10], Social Security Board, Washington, September, 1940). See also Herman Feldman, *Stabilizing Jobs and Wages* (New York, 1940), chap. xvi; and *To Make Jobs More Steady and to Make More Steady Jobs* (Minnesota American Legion Foundation, St. Paul, 1944), a collection of 109 case studies of employment stabilization, largely in states with experience rating. These case studies were made under the direction of Dr. Emerson P. Schmidt, formerly of the University of Minnesota, and they constitute the most comprehensive collection available.

[22] In 1937-38 officials of a number of Wisconsin firms which also had plants in states without experience rating stated that stabilization devices adopted under stimulus of the Wisconsin act were applied in the other plants, or that there was no difference in stabilization efforts between the different plants of the same company.

[23] The following discussion of effects of experience rating is not meant to be exhaustive. For a suggestive analysis, see Karl Pribram, "Employment Stabilization through Pay Roll Taxation," *Quart. Jour. Econ.*, Vol. LVII (Nov., 1942), pp. 142-52.

industry.[24] There are notable exceptions, of course, and strong advocates of experience rating always cite the fact that some employers in nearly every line of business qualify for lower rates. For example, 35 per cent of the rated accounts in bituminous coal mining got lower rates in 1943, and the same was true of 43 per cent of those in building construction. Yet 87 per cent of the rated accounts in finance, insurance and real estate, and electric and gas utilities—which are all comparatively stable industries—received lower rates in 1943.[25]

The fact that as many as one-third of the eligible employers in bituminous coal got lower rates would seem to be as much the result of the present demand for coal as of any special efforts they made to stabilize their employment. Similarly, high rates in ordinarily stable industries might be found in firms hit by wartime priorities or other controls. Only a field study of the particular firms would show the extent to which this is or is not true, and one of the few that have been made indicated that special characteristics of the firm's business played a more important part in rate reductions or increases than did individual stabilization efforts.[26] Consequently, the stabilization incentive, through rate reductions, is somewhat dulled.

2. Payment of higher contribution rates by firms in unstable industries and lower contribution rates by firms in stable industries may not be the best way to allocate the "social costs" of irregular employ-

[24] The contrast with accident compensation in this respect is striking. The contribution rate that an employer pays is a composite of the accident experience of the industry in which he is classified, and his individual accident experience *within* that industry. Thus it is possible for an employer with a good safety program to qualify for a rate lower than the average for his industry, even though he is in an industry where the accident hazard is high.

Would it be possible to do this in unemployment compensation? A member of the Social Security Board, Mr. George E. Bigge, has commented on this aspect of the problem: "To reflect individual achievement in this field it would be necessary to relate a given employer's experience to a norm for his industry, but this has been too difficult and is not attempted. England tried it for a time but soon gave it up." ("Strength and Weakness of Our Unemployment Compensation Program," in *Social Security in America*, addresses at the National Conference on Social Security sponsored by the Chamber of Commerce of the United States, January, 1944, p. 31.)

[25] "Experience-Rating Operations in 1943," *Social Security Bulletin*, Vol. 7 (Sept., 1944), Table 6, p. 18.

[26] Myers, *Employment Stabilization and the Wisconsin Act* (Employment Security Memorandum No. 10): "Close examination of the characteristics of firms within the same industrial classification or subclassification indicated that very few were comparable; in a very real sense, almost each firm was unique. One firm's line of products might be slightly different from that of its competitors. This was reflected in different seasonality of demand, and varying ability to manufacture for stock or transfer between departments. . . . These factors, rather than the sincerity and thoroughness of stabilization efforts, appeared to be the more usual explanation of differences in benefit-contribution percentages between firms in the same group" (p. 107). The same point was made in the Majority Report of the Committee on Employer Experience Rating of the Interstate Conference of Employment Security Agencies (Washington, September, 1940), p. 36.

ment. When confronted with the fact that a greater proportion of firms in stable industries qualify for lower rates than do those in unstable industries, advocates of experience rating shift their argument to "social cost" grounds. They argue that unstable industries *should* pay for a larger share of the costs of unemployment compensation than should stable industries.[27]

But this assumes that the incidence of the payroll tax is clearly on consumers through higher prices. To the extent that the tax is shifted to workers, because it is an added labor cost, or to owners through reduced profits, the social cost argument appears in a different light. Why should workers who stay in unstable industries pay for the costs of unemployment inherent in their jobs? With a few exceptions, the rate of pay in seasonal industries is not generally sufficient to compensate for irregular employment. Furthermore, if the tax is partly borne by profits, is it sound public policy to raise taxes (and reduce profits) in unstable industries—such as the capital-goods industries—when unemployment increases during downturn and depression?

3. Under present experience-rating provisions, employers may be encouraged to reduce benefits by devices which do not stabilize employment but which count equally in determining contribution-rate reductions. These have been discussed in more detail elsewhere,[28] and include the following: (1) under-employment through excessive spreading of work down to the benefit-rate level, (2) hiring during peak seasons workers who are ineligible for benefits, (3) laying off unskilled workers before they acquire eligibility for benefits under the law, and (4) laying off workers with low benefit rights or low "benefit wages" chargeable to the employer.

4. Employment stabilization may mean more stable employment for a smaller number of workers. When seasonal unemployment is reduced

---

[27] Although he is critical of certain aspects of experience rating, Professor Edwin E. Witte has taken this position: "Honest cost accounting requires that all costs be ascertained and properly allocated to the commodities produced or services rendered. An industry which operates intermittently occasions great costs to its employees and to society through its methods of operation. Whether it can or cannot operate more regularly, the unemployment which arises by reason of its intermittent or irregular operation is a cost which should be charged to the establishment producing the goods or services and which gets the profits of the enterprise. Every reason which can be advanced for contributions from employers only—and in all but six states all contributions come from the employers —logically leads to variable contribution rates—rates adjusted to risk and costs." *Social Service Review*, Vol. XIV (Sept., 1940), p. 433.

[28] "Employment Stabilization and the Wisconsin Act," *Am. Econ. Rev.*, Vol. XXIX, No. 4 (Dec., 1939), pp. 714-16. Professor Witte has condemned this aspect of experience rating, because "it is possible to reduce compensable unemployment without reducing unemployment, through taking advantage of the qualifications and exclusions of these laws so as to throw most of the unemployment into these groups among the employees who have no benefit rights. So long as this loophole exists, experience rating is very defective." *Social Service Review*, Vol. XIV, p. 435.

by manufacturing for inventory during slack periods, for example, fewer additional workers are needed in rush times. This same tendency, incidentally, is found in "guaranteed employment" plans where one class of workers does not participate in the guarantee, or in schemes such as the "decasualization" of the longshore industry. More stable employment for a smaller number of workers, however, is not necessarily bad, unless everyone agrees that the way to "reduce" unemployment is to spread work.

5. The competition of the various state legislatures to provide generous experience-rating provisions for employers in their states is said to have been at the expense of adequate benefit provisions.[29] This appears to be particularly true of benefit "disqualification" provisions. Under these provisions, workers who leave their jobs voluntarily for legitimate personal reasons (such as illness in family, lack of transportation, etc.) lose their entire accumulated benefit rights, even though they later are unable to find work, simply because their separation is "without good cause attributable to the employer."[30] Provisions of this sort are difficult to defend but the number of beneficiaries affected by them is probably not very great.[31]

Minimum and maximum weekly benefit rates, maximum duration of benefits, and percentage of beneficiaries exhausting their benefit rights before reëmployment are other tests of benefit adequacy. Here the differences between states with experience rating and those without it are not great enough to be significant, as Table III shows. Since 1941 there has been a gradual liberalization of benefit amounts and duration, in experience-rating states as well as in others, and this may continue when state legislatures meet during 1945. There is still much room for

[29] Friedman and Wandel, *op. cit.*, p. 10.

[30] George E. Bigge cites some concrete examples of this tendency in "Strength and Weakness of Our Unemployment Compensation Program," *op. cit.*, pp. 24-34. In his opinion, "This general tendency to impose more numerous and more rigorous disqualifications is one of the most serious developments of recent years, and there seems to be little doubt that it is related to increasing emphasis on tax reduction in the form of experience rating. . . . It is very significant that of the states which do not have experience rating not one has this kind of disqualification, especially the mandatory cancellation of benefit rights, and the double penalties; whereas in the states which have reduced rates (under experience rating), there has been a rapid spread of such disqualifications" (pp. 30, 32). States which do not have disqualification in the form of cancellation of benefit rights usually provide for a penalty by postponing benefit payments for a number of weeks. See also Ewan Clague and Ruth Reticker, "Trends in Disqualification from Benefits under State Unemployment Compensation Laws," *Social Security Bulletin*, Vol. 7 (Jan., 1944), pp. 12-23.

[31] Conclusive data are lacking. Paul A. Raushenbush, Director of Unemployment Compensation in Wisconsin, in his testimony before the George Committee, quoted a figure of 1.4 per cent of all claimants disallowed benefits in 1942 for "other reasons." *Hearings before the Special Committee on Post-War Economic Policy and Planning*, United States Senate, Part 3, "The Problem of Unemployment and Reemployment after the War; Unemployment Compensation" (Washington, 1944), p. 866.

improvement, especially in extending the duration of benefits, raising maximum benefit rates because of higher weekly wages,[32] and ironing

TABLE III.—BENEFIT STANDARDS IN STATE UNEMPLOYMENT COMPENSATION LAWS
(as of January, 1944)

Type of Law	Minimum Weekly Benefit (average)	Maximum Weekly Benefit (average)	Maximum Duration of Benefits (aver. weeks)	Per Cent of Beneficiaries Exhausting Benefit Rights (1942)
Reserve ratio (25 states)	$5.50	$16.80	17.0	35.9%
Cliffe plan (7 states)	5.00	16.40	18.3	43.6%
Benefit ratio (5 states)	7.20	19.00	18.2	38.3%
Combined plans (2 states)	6.50	15.00	17.0	41.5%
Compensable separations (1 state)	6.00	22.00	18.0	22.5%
Total—all states with exp. rating (40 states)	5.70	17.10	17.4[a]	37.6%
Experience rating effective during (1944–45 (4 states)	5.25	16.50	17.5	47.8%
No experience rating (7 states)	5.96	16.70	17.5[b]	36.1%

Source: Minimum and maximum benefit rates from Helen Ward Tippy, "Comparison of Benefit Schedules, Unemployment Compensation, and Workmen's Compensation," *Social Security Bulletin*, Vol. 7 (Mar., 1944), Table 2, p. 8; data on maximum duration and per cent of beneficiaries exhausting benefit rights in 1942 from "Duration of Unemployment Benefits, Benefit Years Ended in 1942," *Social Security Bulletin*, April, 1944, pp. 16–23, Tables 1 and 2, and from state laws as subsequently amended during 1943.

[a] In 11 of the 40 states with experience rating in 1943, the duration of benefits was uniform for all eligible claimants, regardless of previous wage credits. Duration was variable in the other states.

[b] Four of the 7 states without experience rating had uniform duration provisions.

out inequalities between states. But this need for improvement is not confined to states with experience rating. Only if the pressure for con-

[32] There is a possible danger, however, that a high benefit rate based on wartime weekly wages with overtime would be too high a percentage of weekly earnings at a 40-hour week, and that "malingering" might be encouraged as a consequence.

tinued low payroll taxes prevents needed liberalization of the benefit structure in 1945, can experience rating be blamed.

6. It is clear from the earlier discussion of variations in contribution rates and revenues under experience rating that the ability of some state funds to provide for future large demands is being endangered, and in many other states this may be true if benefit standards are liberalized.[33] This possibility is less likely in the states with "war risk" provisions in their laws, but it should be remembered that during 1943 only 9 of the 40 states with experience rating had these provisions in effect. Furthermore, of the 40 states with experience rating in operation during 1943, only 16 provided for higher-than-standard rates as a partial offset to the loss of revenues through lower-than-standard rates, and two of these abandoned higher-than-standard rates during 1943.[34]

VIII

The conclusions reached in this brief reëxamination of experience rating in state unemployment compensation laws may be summarized as follows:

1. Variations in contribution rates and revenues for payment of benefits are exactly the opposite of the variations in social security contributions suggested as desirable over the cycle by the British White Paper on *Employment Policy*.

2. Experience rating was intended to encourage individual employers to stabilize employment. Yet the mechanics of experience-rating provisions make it possible for employers as a group to qualify for lower

---

[33] The desire to keep experience rating has also led many states to oppose any tendency toward a national system of unemployment compensation, and the existence of 51 separate accounting reserves in Washington means that a state faced with heavy post-war unemployment might exhaust its reserve while another state more fortunately situated for the post-war period would have ample funds. Yet the latter states will oppose any suggestion that some of their revenues ought to be used to pay benefits in other states. This is a little bit like a man's saying that the fire insurance company should not use *his* premiums to pay claims because *his* house has not yet burned down. It is also reminiscent of the "plant reserves" controversy in Wisconsin. A "balancing account" was eventually established in that state to take care of exhausted company reserves, and the "Federal unemployment account" established by Congress in the Social Security act amendments of October, 1944, is a step in the same direction.

[34] These were Cliffe-plan states, Delaware and Texas. "Experience-Rating Operations in 1943," *Social Security Bulletin*, Vol. 7 (Sept., 1944), Table 4, p. 15. Two additional states, Indiana and Oklahoma, will have a higher-than-standard rate beginning in 1945 (Table 2, p. 13).

The Unanimous Report of the Committee on Employer Experience Rating of the Interstate Conference of Employment Security Agencies (Washington, 1940), recommended that "it is essential to a sound experience-rating system that the maximum contribution rate should be higher than the general rate of 2.7 per cent which would presumably exist if there were no individual rate variations" (p. 45).

contribution rates when employment and payrolls are rising, largely regardless of their own individual employment stabilization efforts. Increases in contribution rates generally will be necessary, on the other hand, when employment and payrolls are declining.

3. The probable effect of these variations in contribution rates and revenues is to accentuate, rather than to counteract, the swings that ordinarily occur in aggregate demand. Thus, the effect may be unstabilizing on the economy, although the intended effect was to encourage stabilization of employment by individual firms. Furthermore, increases in average rates in depression may act as a tax on the giving of jobs.

4. Although experience rating can serve as an inducement to employers to reduce intermittent and seasonal employment irregularities, which are more within their control, the gains from such stabilization, once they are realized, may be sufficient in themselves to encourage continued efforts. After an initial period of several years, therefore, the novelty of the incentive may wear off.

5. A review of some of the other effects of experience rating in operation indicates that (a) rate reductions are related as much to the stability of the industry as they are to stabilization efforts of the firm, (b) such variations in rates between industries may not be a sound method of allocating the "social costs" of unemployment, (c) firms may increase their chances of qualifying for lower rates by using devices which avoid benefits but do not stabilize employment, (d) employment stabilization may result in more stable work for a smaller number of workers, although this is not necessarily bad, (e) competition between states to liberalize experience rating appears to have been at the expense of adequate benefit provisions so far as "disqualifications" are concerned, and (f) present variations in contribution rates and revenues under experience rating jeopardize the ability of states to meet large drains on their funds in the future, especially if benefits are liberalized.

6. The "war risk" provisions effective in 9 states during 1943 are a significant development because they are a recognition of the unwisdom of lowering contribution rates generally in periods of rising payrolls. Provisions of this type might well become a permanent part of state unemployment compensation laws.

So long as unemployment compensation is developed and administered in 51 different jurisdictions, however, it seems unlikely that the ingenious suggestion involved in the British proposal will receive much encouragement in this country. The only practical possibility in the immediate future is for the 44 states whose legislatures meet during 1945 to consider the strengthening of their unemployment compensation laws in terms of reserves and benefit standards. Continued concern about reducing payroll tax rates in a period of high payrolls can only lead to an accentuation of present undesirable results.

7. This reëxamination of experience rating suggests the general conclusion that, without proper safeguards in the form of war-risk provisions, or improvements in the experience-rating formula as in Nebraska and Wisconsin, the probable social gains from experience rating as it now exists are outweighed by its disadvantages. There is a strong movement in Washington to federalize unemployment compensation and eliminate experience rating, and there are equally strong efforts in the states to retain the present federal-state system with experience rating of each state's choice. Logically, there is no reason why some form of experience rating could not be continued under a federal system, or why certain safeguards and minimum standards could not be incorporated in the state systems. Unfortunately, the whole issue is tied in with a political controversy, and therefore it is not likely to be resolved solely upon its own merits.

OUR PENSION MADNESS — AND POSSIBLE CURES

By John J. Corson

This generation of Americans has no intention of ending its days in a poorhouse. Nor do Americans intend to spend old age as an unwanted burden on their children. Californians have just feathered their nests by voting to guarantee most oldsters $75 a month. In Louisiana, the new Long regime, with the aid of Federal funds, is now paying an average of $47 a month to eight of every ten persons over 65. Organized veterans are battling in Congress for pensions that would cost the Government $65 billions in the next fifty years. After having won three rounds of wage raises, organized labor is now concentrating on demands for employer-supported pension and welfare programs.

Indeed, Americans must appear pension mad to the world at large.

Four or five of every ten Americans over 65 already enjoy a pension of some sort. More than 10,000 employers provide pensions for their employes. Twoscore unions had established pensions for their members before the United Mine Workers won a fixed royalty on every ton of coal to pay for pensions of $100 a month to miners. Hundreds of pension systems have long existed for teachers, preachers, policemen, firemen, soldiers, sailors and civil servants. Under the Social Security Act there is old-age assistance for two and one half million needy oldsters and old-age insurance for 1,600,000 who have contributed through payroll taxes for their security.

But existing arrangements are not satisfactory. While a relative handful of workers get two or more pensions, many get nothing, and others receive pensions inadequate in amount or pensions based on a humiliating show of need. Thus, the demand for more pensions, bigger pensions and better pensions is insistent.

The problem of the aged is relentlessly growing. In 1900 only 4.1 per cent of the 76 million persons living in the United States were 65 years of age or older. In 1950, it is estimated, more than 11 million will be over 65, or 7.7 per cent of the total population. By 1980 — when you and I are old — there will be 22 million aged, and we will constitute 12 per cent of the population.

Better medical care, improved public health work and higher living standards have lengthened American lives dramatically. Only three-fourths of those born in 1899 could expect to live to reach 25 years of age.

Three-fourths of those born in 1949 will live to the age of 60. By 1980 there will be more people over 70 than are today over 60.

With more and more people in the older age groups, there is still little disposition among employers to hire older workers. At the peak of war time employment only one-third of the men and women 65 years of age and over were gainfully occupied. Today not more than one of every four aged persons (forty per cent of the men and nine per cent of the women) are working for a living. Why? Are they incompetent as workers? Well, yes, and then again, no. Many older workers are successfully holding down jobs. Studies of the Bureau of Labor Statistics show that they have less absenteeism than younger workers, that they have fewer accidents and that they make fewer visits to medical clinics in the plants where they are employed.

On the other hand, many older people are hanging onto jobs they can no longer do well in competition with younger workers. Many are maladjusted and unhappy in the face of their inadequacy; some are temperamental, inflexible, not too easy to manage. So when an employer has a job to fill, he may look for a younger man.

Moreover, there just are not as many job opportunities for older people in towns and cities as there were on the farm. The industrial world moves faster and faster. Every day brings new inventions, new products, new processes. Each new development makes hundreds of occupations obsolete and eliminates thousands of jobs. The older worker may lose out. Sometimes he does not get a chance to learn the new jobs; sometimes he can not learn them. Older workers are not able to adjust rapidly enough as industry changes.

Add these together. The sum constitutes a critical problem of old-age dependence. Two of every three aged are neither working for a living nor married to someone who is. Only one out of the three lives on returns from investments or income from public or private retirement systems. The remaining third are dependent on public relief or the bounty of friends and relatives.

The problem of old-age dependency is made up of millions of individual personal tragedies. There is tragedy for each aged person who has to admit to himself: "I am all washed up; from here on I have got to beg for my living, beg from my children or beg from the Government." There is tragedy, too, for every son and daughter who has to assume the support of aging parents, thereby curtailing opportunities for the oncoming generation.

There is tragedy for the aging man who stares ahead at the prospect of losing his job and no longer being able to maintain himself. Already a little more than one-fifth of the nation's labor force is over fifty years of age; by 1960 it will be one-fourth; by 1980, three-tenths. For each of these men and their dependents the problem of old-age dependency becomes more real every day.

Out of this growing interest in the fate of the individual in old age emerges a variety of proposals as to what should be done. Dr. Townsend is only the best publicized of a dozen messiahs who have capitalized on the dread in the hearts of the aged and "near-aged."

There was Upton Sinclair's EPIC (End Poverty in California), the Ham and Eggs Crusade, the Thirty Dollars Every Thursday bonanza, and the Every Man a King campaign. Each proposal promised a flat pension of thirty dollars a week, two hundred dollars a month, or the like.

No longer are such panaceas mere slogans or hopes. The Citizens Committee for Old Age Pensions provided a striking illustration of the political strength of the organized aged when it pushed over the present law in California which promises most of that state's oldsters seventy five dollars a month for life.

Technically, these pensions go only to California's "needy" aged; that requirement is essential so that the state may obtain Federal social-security funds. But according to California standards a couple can be "in need" and still own a home assessed at as much as $10,000, insurance policies worth up to $2,000, two automobiles, usual personal property and as much as $3,000 in stocks and bonds. The cost to state — and Federal — taxpayers approximates $125 million a year. If such a pension were in effect in all forty eight states, such pensions would cost eight billion dollars a year. By 1980 the annual cost would reach sixteen billion dollars.

Consider the veterans' proposals. To live up to commitments prescribed in the latest veterans' pension bill to emerge from the House would cost about $1,600,000,000 yearly, and over the next fifty years sixty five billion dollars. This measure was far more generous than the House Veterans Affairs Committee proposed. And yet the House overwhelmingly upped the committee's proposal by a vote which cut party lines.

Some unions long ago provided pensions or homes for their aged members. But during recent years they have sought larger pensions and other forms of protection through collective bargaining. Employers' objections that such topics were not logically within the scope of collective bargaining have been met by a Supreme Court decision (Inland Steel case) requiring employers to discuss proposals for retirement provisions with unions.

The United Mine Workers have led this new demand for pensions and other welfare provisions from their employers. A retiring miner of twenty years' union persuasion will get $100 a month at age 60. The garment workers, auto workers, musicians, steel workers, longshoremen and others have followed suit. The UAW at the moment is presenting to auto manufacturers a demand for pensions which would represent an increase in wages of almost thirty cents an hour. The goal of organized labor is 4,000,000 members under collectively bargained pension contracts by the close of 1949. This would cost employers and consumers about $70,000,000 in 1950, but at least $150,000,000 in 1980.

By and large, organized labor seeks, through collective bargaining, protection which is not now provided by the Social Security Act — employer-supported arrangements for medical care and benefits for workers who are sick, and similar benefits. Some unions are demanding pensions to supplement the meager benefits now paid as Federal old-age insurance. Their 1949 demands are founded realistically in the knowledge that a fourth round of wage raises will be hard to get.

Long before there was a Social Security Act in this country, some employers had voluntarily provided for the retirement of their employes. The war greatly encouraged employers to establish such pensions and to make them more generous. The Revenue Act of 1942 made clearer the employer's right to deduct the costs of such pensions as a business expense; hence, the employer took moneys which would otherwise have been paid, in large part, in taxes, and provided pensions as indirect compensation for employes whose wages and salaries were "frozen." All in all, more than 10,000 employers have established retirement plans.

Employers had their own reasons. Such pension systems aided in attracting the best employes. It built employe morale, tended to keep workers with an employer longer, reduced turnover. But, pension systems also enabled employers more easily to get rid of workers who had outlived their usefulness.

To offset pension pressures and the rigors of the 1929–33 depression, Congress enacted the Social Security Act of 1935. This act established two methods of providing security for the aged. Old-age insurance was established as the basic institution for caring for our aged. It was to be financed by contributions from employes and their employers, and it was to pay benefits to workers who retired after sixty five in relation to the earnings on which their tax contributions had been calculated.

But many aged were already out of work and in need during the Thirties. Hence, Congress created a Federal-state system of "Old Age Assistance," or old-age relief, to care for those aged already in need. Federal moneys were made available to the states which could be used for grants to those aged persons who applied and were determined to be in need. In the long run, it was expected that the need for "old-age assistance" would diminish. More and more workers would have contributed under old-age insurance, would be entitled to old-age insurance when they retired and fewer and fewer individuals would have to seek old-age assistance.

But old-age insurance benefits, inadequate when first conceived, have not been liberalized to keep up with rising prices. The present level for a retired man is about twenty five dollars a month. Coverage has not been extended to major groups. Only about three out of five workers are covered by the program. And the eligibility requirements for older workers have proved to be too strict in practice. Only one out of five persons over sixty five is either insured or receiving benefits.

In the absence of an adequate insurance plan, old-age assistance has boomed. Annual expenditures by Federal and state Governments for old-age assistance have increased eightfold since 1936. The number receiving old-age assistance has more than doubled. Politicians have been prone to press each year for larger and larger Federal and state appropriations for old-age assistance even when it meant less money for schools or highways.

In a few states, notably Colorado, Louisiana and Oklahoma, these forces have combined to put from fifty to eighty per cent of all aged persons on the assistance rolls. More than twice as many aged persons will receive assistance because they are in need than will be paid insurance benefits in 1949. As it looks today, our Social Security Act condemns half of all the aged persons to living on relief when they can no longer work.

And yet in 1949 the cost of pensions — veterans', labor's, employers', railroad workers', soldiers', sailors' — and social security for the aged will claim two to three billion dollars; by 1980 even the present level of pensions will cost five to seven billion dollars. Still many can look forward only to a meager existence on the bounty of their friends or the humiliation of old-age assistance or relief. Better provisions must be made if the aged are to be adequately cared for — and if we are to avoid social chaos when one of every eight persons is considered old.

If we are to provide security we must face three fundamental, controlling factors.

First, consider the number who are dependent (the aged, but the young and disabled as well) and the number of productive workers in our society who are left to maintain them. As the number of aged grows and the forces of industrialization tend to make it more difficult for them to continue at work, our culture simultaneously proposes that young men and women should remain in school longer. Hence, the number of productive workers in the society is whittled away at both its upper and lower limits.

Yet more production will be essential to create a national income sufficient steadily to raise the general standard of living and to provide adequate pensions. To keep the productive capacity up and the burden of dependency down requires that every aged person who can and wants to work shall work. This is simple economics which brands as unrealistic plans to pension everyone over sixty five, employers' practices in automatically firing all workers who reach sixty five, and union demands that older workers be retired "to make places for the young."

But uprooting these ideas will require the revision of employers' habits and union demands. It will require the imaginative revamping of our schools to equip many workers for two jobs, not one — one for the period up to forty or fifty and another for the second half of his working career. It will necessitate the creation of vocational schools for retraining workers in their forties. It will call for great improvement in our employment service facilities that they may find jobs for retrained mature workers. And it makes necessary the abandonment of some political notions which politicians have found are sure vote getters.

Second, we must consider what we mean by the "aged." Apart from the persistent demand to raise pensions, there is simultaneously a demand to lower the age at which pensions are paid. A pension of $100 a month to all over 65 would cost $13,000,000,000 in 1950. The same pension to all over 60 would cost over $20,000,000,000. The growth of the number of aged alone, whatever age limit we fix, will assure that we double the aggregate number of dollars required by 1960.

And is it not more important to provide for the "aged" under sixty five than the "young" who have passed their sixty-fifth birthday? For the birthdays do not really count. Those who are physically worn out, disabled and unable to work again are clearly more dependent than the hale and hearty fellow of seventy who wants nothing so much as the opportunity to continue in the job he holds. In determining who are aged we must assuredly include the disabled — and we cannot afford to include those who are still at work no matter what their age.

Third, we must choose that method which will truly provide the aged — and all who are looking ahead — with security. This is more than the promise of income; it includes peace of mind.

Most persons come to old age possessing something. To assure self-respecting security it is only necessary to use that method which enables the individual to contribute as he earns and which assures him, when he can no longer work, a benefit roughly related to his own productive effort. In this way he gains security and loses none of the incentives to build his own retirement income. And, of equal importance, this sort of system is the best-known antidote to the threat that the growing political power of the aged will be used to raid the public treasury.

The future age distribution of the voting population pragmatically assures that the aged will be taken care of by their Government. But how? Will the promises made to the aged be within the capacity of this nation's productive workers?

As yet there is little evidence that Congress proposes to adopt a rational system of public old-age security that will fit the needs of the aged as well as the bounds of our economy. A significant number of the state governments have demonstrated that they cannot forego the temptation to make political capital of assistance for the needy aged.

Essential steps have been prescribed by an advisory council headed by Edward R. Stettinius, Jr., ex-Secretary of State, and Sumner H. Slichter, Lamont Professor of Economics, Harvard University. This distinguished group of business men, labor leaders and civic figures advised the Senate Finance Committee to extend and improve the existing old-age and survivors' insurance provisions of the Social Security Act.

Specifically the advisers recommended that old-age and survivors' insurance be extended to cover farm workers, domestic servants, self-employed persons and many others not now included. This council recommended that the insurance benefits payable to retired workers or their widows and orphans be substantially raised. And they recommended that benefits be paid to totally and permanently disabled workers.

This prescription must be taken promptly if we are to meet rationally, and without tempting national bankruptcy, the unavoidable problem of old-age dependency. If the Congress fails to take this step, then it seems sure that, sooner or later: (a) The veterans and pension "panacears" will force through a pension for everyone at sixty five and a better one for veterans with staggering costs to the national economy; or (b) the stronger unions will win relatively high pensions for a favored group of employes, and more money will be poured into the relief methods of caring for the aged.

SOCIAL INSURANCE IN EVOLUTION

By Eveline M. Burns

National Planning Association

I

Few topics of economic study present a more perfect example than social insurance of the interrelationships between economics and the other social sciences: sociology, social psychology, political science and history, using the latter word in the sense of the study of institutional evolution. Few make greater demands on the ability of the student accurately to diagnose and specifically to state his premises concerning the prevailing temper and social psychology of the period to which his generalizations relate. Few illustrate better the need for a dynamic and evolutionary approach to the study of social institutions. Finally, few topics of study expose the economist to greater temptations to introduce implicit value judgments into his "purely theoretical" analyses.

It is part of my thesis that the institution of social insurance is a social invention which was brought into being to perform a specific function in a specific economic and social environment. As I have said elsewhere, "It was the ideal instrument for effecting a significant break in the deterrent treatment of insecure workers, because its apparent analogy with private insurance made the change acceptable to a society which was dominated by business ethics and which stressed individual economic responsibility."[1] Its forms were necessarily conditioned by the job to be done and by the social and economic environment. But, and this is the second part of my thesis, social insurance is a dynamic invention in the sense intended by Gunnar Myrdal, when in his recent book he urges social scientists to pay more attention to "those inventions which have the greatest promise of moving the society in a desired direction, and to seek *social* inventions which would modify economic organization and the effects of mechanical inventions."[2] For I believe it can be shown that the social invention of social insurance has modified the environmental factors that form part of the premises of the economist. In so doing it has not only broadened the prevailing concept of the job to be done, and made possible the use of new social techniques, but the institution itself has undergone significant changes of form. These changes within social insurance itself and in the environment in which it operates must be always held in mind if the analyses

[1] *British Unemployment Programs*, p. 316.
[2] *An American Dilemma*, p. 1053.

of economists are to be relevant and if their advice on policy is to be fruitful.

From this point of view I suggest that, up to and including the present, it is possible to distinguish at least three stages in the evolution of this important social invention. Stage I is characterized by the application of the social insurance principle to relatively few risks and only to selected groups. There is either no government contribution, or at most a nominal or token contribution.

These characteristics reflect the function which social insurance was brought into being to perform and the prevailing social and economic environment. It was a period of expanding capitalism in which great emphasis was placed upon individual responsibility, coupled with a firm belief in the wide range of economic opportunities open to the individual. Hence there was broad social acceptance of the theory that poverty was a disgrace or a sign of incompetence. It was thus to the interest of society as a whole that loss of income should be provided for on a deterrent basis, and this policy worked and was acceptable because it was not too sharply contradicted by the facts of everyday experience. It was a period, too, in which men were still apprehensive about the use of government as an instrument for effectuating desired income redistributions or other social policies.

At this stage it was important, in view of prevailing social attitudes, to stress the analogy of social, to private, insurance. Using this analogy, the concern of those who feared lest assurance of income would weaken the spur to participation in production, could in large measure be set at rest. No harm was done in paying assured benefits to selected and limited groups, it was argued, because (a) beneficiaries had contributed and were as much entitled to benefits as if they had contributed to a private insurance scheme; (b) the groups were carefully selected and long eligibility periods would ensure that beneficiaries were those and only those whose past behavior had demonstrated the earnestness of their determination to participate in productive work; (c) the short duration of benefit (in the case of unemployment insurance) and the low level of the benefit was a practical safeguard against the temptation to malinger.

This stage of social insurance may be said to have lasted in this country from the introduction of workmen's compensation legislation, up to, and including, the passage of the Social Security Act, and in Great Britain, from 1911 to 1920. During this stage the problems attracting attention are in the main narrowly technical or actuarial. Problems of administration and procedures, methods of investment and management of funds, analysis of experience records and refinement of controls assume prime importance. Discussion of the extension of social insurance to additional risks or groups is also found, but always from the same basic assumption of a program for those who might be described as good risks from the viewpoint of society and of the productive mechanism.

Stage II in the evolution of social insurance is marked by a growing but uneven extension of social insurance to cover not only new risks but more importantly, new population groups. Either explicitly or implicitly (as in our own old age and survivors insurance system) the systems begin to include a more substantial contribution from general tax revenues. The institution tends to be a hybrid, exhibiting some of the characteristics typically found earlier in stage I and later in stage III.

Stage II is, I suggest, the stage in which we now find ourselves in the United States. In Great Britain it has persisted from 1920 until the present time, although the appearance of the Beveridge Plan and the public reaction thereto indicates that Britain may be about to enter stage III.

Stage II is essentially a period of instability and transition and it has this character because social attitudes and prevailing opinions concerning the character of the economic environment are also in transition. The environmental change is in part due to closer familiarity with the prevalence of mass unemployment which, when millions of obviously self-reliant workers are unable to secure employment, challenges the assumption that those without income are by definition improvident. In part the change is due to a recognition of the fact that a rising general wage level does not automatically solve the problems associated with interruptions to income.

But in part the change is directly due to the influence of an operating social insurance program. Once such a program is in existence it exerts, as I have said, a dynamic influence. Workers come to realize that there is in existence a technique for assuring security which from their viewpoint is preferable to the older methods. There are demands for coverage from groups previously excluded. These demands are the harder to resist because there are no sharply defined categories in the population which precisely correspond to the groupings suggested by logical reasoning. In the last resort the drawing of the line must work with averages and give rise to individual anomalies, cases of apparent hardship, or charges of arbitrariness. The attempt to resist these demands for extensions of social insurance by modifications and liberalization of the alternative social security programs only increases the pressure to change the character of social insurance. Once public assistance payments become more adequate for maintenance, invidious comparisons are drawn between, e.g., benefits paid on a social insurance system toward the cost of which the worker directly contributes and public assistance which is financed out of general taxation. This kind of comparison is often made in this country in regard to old age assistance and old age insurance and in the thirties was frequently made in Great Britain in regard to unemployment insurance and unemployment assistance.

The dynamic influence exerted by social insurance as a going concern is evident in yet another direction. The discovery is made that the bases of an individualistic and capitalistic society are not utterly destroyed by such an institution. Even more important men become accustomed to the idea of using the instrument of government to carry out policies desired by a substantial segment of the population, and this willingness to countenance an extension of governmental activity in the realm of economic security is strengthened by other environmental influences which are accustoming the population to extensions of governmental activities and controls in other fields.

It is not surprising that in this period new problems begin to appear in contemporary technical discussion. There is a growing recognition of the interrelationships of the different types of public aid, and problems of over-all co-ordination assume importance. Increasing attention is given to anomalous situations created by the differing or inconsistent social insurance treatment of groups whose situations appear to be identical—situations inevitable because an increasingly comprehensive program has developed on a piecemeal basis. There is a growing recognition that social insurance is one of several available mechanisms for dealing with the problem of loss or inadequacy of income, which, among other consequences, adds new complexity to discussions of actuarial soundness. For it becomes evident that actuarial soundness for any one insurance program may be obtained at the expense of the residual programs for those who are excluded from a carefully circumscribed and selective social insurance measure.

In this period, too, theoretical discussions of "the banking versus the insurance principle," and of "private versus social insurance" assume increasing importance: They are the intellectual manifestation of a growing awareness of the changing character of the institution called "social insurance."

The third stage of social insurance for convenience may be indicated as that which now prevails in New Zealand and into which, as I have said, Great Britain appears to be moving. It is marked firstly by universal or practically universal coverage: social insurance now becomes a scheme for citizen protection and not only for industrial wage earners. Secondly it is marked by the inclusion of all the more common risks to continuity and adequacy of basic income. I use both concepts deliberately for it is evident that with the introduction of children's allowances, maternity payments, health insurance for medical care and even funeral benefits, the scope of social insurance has extended beyond that of income maintenance in the strict sense. Social insurance in this stage is characterized also by relatively heavy governmental contributions toward costs.

The accompanying social environment is one in which majority opinion holds the view that all citizens should be assured a certain minimum income so long as they are incapable of working through disability or economic dislocations or who should not work as a matter of social policy (e.g., mothers with young children). This prevailing acceptance of the doctrine of public assurance of minimum income is vital and is a necessary condition for the forms assumed by social insurance in stage III.

II

The differing stages in the evolution of social insurance and in their accompanying environmental context change the types of questions with which students of economics and social insurance policies are concerned—and also the answers to these questions. I have already indicated in discussing stages I and II that differing problems assumed importance in the two periods. I can most clearly illustrate my thesis in regard to stage III by considering three problems which in one way or another have attracted attention during the years in which social insurance has been in operation. They are the basic objectives of the benefits paid, the relation of social insurance financing to other fiscal policies of government, and the appropriateness of the pay roll tax as an earmarked source of funds.

1. *The Basic Objective of the Benefits.* In the first stage of social insurance it was theoretically and practically possible to disregard the question of whether or not benefits would or should guarantee a minimum standard of subsistence or maintenance. It was theoretically a dead issue because in the early stages the emphasis was upon the private insurance analogy of social insurance. The relationship between benefits and contributions being stressed, it was inevitable that the benefit should be a purely arithmetically or, if you will, an actuarially determined product. We can see this in the benefit provisions of the original Social Security Act of 1935. Even had there been no wide geographical variations in money or real wages and standards of living, I suspect our initial social security act would still have provided for differential benefits based upon differential earnings. It was, significantly, not only the federal old age insurance program that contained this provision but also the state unemployment compensation programs.

Neglect of the whole question as to the relationship of benefits to the costs of maintenance was also theoretically possible in the sense of being logically justifiable because in many cases the scope of the initial social insurance programs was restricted to certain carefully selected groups. These groups were in the main the higher paid or normally employed workers. Thus in Britain unemployment insurance was first restricted to trades which were relatively highly organized and which were, in the words of Mr. Churchill, "not decaying trades, they are not overstocked trades, they are not congested with a surplus or an insufficient supply of labour." Similarly in the United States the important old age and survivors' insurance and unemployment insurance programs exclude two typically low-paid groups who are characterized by a considerable amount of part-time work; namely, agricultural and domestic workers.

In these circumstances it was quite consistent to provide benefits which the authors of the British system described as "exiguous" and "narrowly cut" for it was reasonable to assume some prior savings on the part of the recipient which would serve to eke out his benefit. It could be held, in other words, that the function of the system was merely to supplement private savings for the contingency in question. The short period for which benefit was then payable served further to strengthen the consistency of the type of benefit provided, for it was reasonable to assume that the payment of a small sum supplementing private savings performed a real social function so long as the worker was not expected to possess savings on which he could draw indefinitely.

In the same way the limitation of social insurance under the Social Security Act to the relatively higher paid groups facilitated a quite logical retention of the doctrine of proportionality between benefits and wages with no questions asked as to adequacy for maintenance.

I said that the character of social insurance programs in their first period of development made it not only theoretically but also practically possible to avoid discussions of the adequacy of the benefits for maintenance. The importance of the practical considerations can be seen by observing the effects of changes in the coverage of social insurance programs, in the duration of unemployment insurance benefits, and in the historical situations which brought them about.

A general trend toward the expansion of coverage is evident in all countries which have embarked upon social insurance programs. In our own country the popularity of the social insurance type of protection has stimulated demands from groups still excluded for coverage under the plan. But the attempt to extend coverage to groups such as agricultural workers and domestic servants inevitably raises questions as to the adequacy of benefits payable. Retention of the automatic percentage-of-wages formula when applied to groups whose earnings are notoriously low raises doubts as to the net social advantage to the group to whom coverage is to be extended. The question may, for example, be raised whether it is any kindness to an agricultural worker to collect taxes from his admittedly meager current earnings, in order to pay him at age sixty-five a benefit which is likely to be far less than adequate to provide a minimum subsistence. The question is particularly relevant when it is recalled that the low-paid worker who gets the lowest benefit from a percentage formula is also the worker who is least likely to possess any significant volume of private savings, so that it cannot even be argued that the social insurance benefit, though small, will fill in the gap between independence and resort to public assistance.

It was for this reason that the National Resources Planning Board's Security Report, in discussing extension of old age insurance and unemployment insurance to agricultural and domestic workers stated:

> The inclusion of workers in domestic, agricultural and other low-paid employments should, therefore, be considered in relation to their patterns of employment and the character and amount of their earnings, and the feasibility of devising a benefit formula which will yield them significant payments. Additional groups of employees should be covered as rapidly as it can be demonstrated that they will receive adequate or significant benefits from the system.[3]

It is also significant that the Wagner-Murray-Dingell bill, which proposes immediate extension of coverage of old age and survivors' insurance to include agricultural and domestic workers and the self-employed (many of whom are members of the low income groups) simultaneously recommends an increase in the present minimum benefit from $10 to $20 a month.

The influence of the extension of scope of social insurance programs upon the character of the benefit structure is also evident in Great Britain. The influence can most clearly be seen in the unemployment insurance program, where extension of the scope of the program after the coverage expansion of 1920 took the form of extensions of duration of benefit. Once it was decided, for a variety of reasons into which we need not enter here, to extend duration of the now more comprehensive program to twenty-six weeks and later, almost indefinitely, it became increasingly difficult to divorce considerations of adequacy from the determination of benefit levels. For, given the general wage level and the low wages of many groups covered by the system, it was patently impossible to argue that the average worker would, even at the end of six months, let alone at the end of one year or eighteen months of unemployment, still possess savings which it was the function of the social insurance program merely to supplement. The ensuing development was logical and indeed inevitable. Over the next ten years de-

---

[3] *Security, Work, and Relief Policies*, p. 516.

pendents' benefits were introduced and the basic benefit was raised so that by 1931 benefits approximated a maintenance level. It is true that the British government (other than the Labor government) always firmly denied that maintenance was the standard; it denies it even today, as witness the most important reservation of the government in regard to the Beveridge proposals. But the fact remains that benefits were in fact raised to this level and in public discussion and in parliamentary debates it was the inadequacy of the benefit for maintenance which was the powerful argument in favor of benefit changes.

The point I am making is that the growth of consideration of the adequacy of benefits for maintenance is both a logical and a practically inevitable concomitant of extensions of the scope of social insurance programs. A problem that could be ignored in stage I becomes a central issue in stage III.

2. *The Fiscal Aspects of Social Insurance.* The economic repercussions of the timing and amount of insurance payments, and the methods whereby the funds are collected and the timing of collections become of tremendous significance for the economy as a whole once social insurance enters or approaches stage III. So long as social insurance payments were meager in amount, and confined to a small segment of the population, their effect upon the economy as a whole could be disregarded; at any rate they were not so noticeable as to compel attention.

Current proposals as in the United States, Great Britain, and Canada and the program in New Zealand envisage expenditures (and the corresponding necessity to raise funds) which may ultimately run as high as 10 per cent or 12 per cent of total national income payments. The fiscal implications of programs of this magnitude become of vital public interest, especially in view of the increasing recognition given to fiscal policy as an element in full employment policies—itself, note, an important and relevant environmental change.

In the United States we are today in the midst of a controversy as to whether or not the originally planned stepping-up of social security taxes should be postponed, and the same issue arose in 1939. Opponents and proponents alike center their arguments around the supposed inflationary or deflationary effects of imposition of new taxation at a specific time. Indeed, we even find in some cases that extension of social security coverage is urged today on the ground that it is an easy and acceptable method of increasing taxation as part of an anti-inflation policy.

Similar considerations appear in discussions of the benefit side of the picture. In 1938-40 increased payments to the aged (or even a universal pension) were urged in some quarters on the ground that such payments would be a politically acceptable and very effective method of increasing consumer spending. Today we find the case for extension and liberalization of unemployment insurance deriving considerable strength from the argument that assured payments to the unemployed in a period of serious economic readjustment will, by maintaining a minimum level of purchasing power, assist in stabilizing the economy as a whole.

Once stage III is fully entered into, these considerations are not difficult for the economist to handle. In a country which has accepted the idea of publicly-guaranteed minimum income for the entire population, when, if you like, this policy is regarded as a first charge upon annual appropriations, there is no risk to the objectives of the program in merging social insurance financing with the general budget. The question of borrowing or reserve accumulation versus pay-as-you-go policies can be subordinated to the broader economic and fiscal policies of government. There will be no fear that promised payments will not be honored even though the public household (including social insurance programs) may have operated at some time on a deficit.

But the situation is far otherwise in stages I and II. Earmarked funds and a close tie-up between taxes and benefits may then be psychologically necessary for two reasons: to afford what appears to be a guarantee of the rights of the contributors, and to serve as a continual reminder that those who benefit have "earned" their privilege by contributing. Furthermore, so long as the concept of the basic minimum guarantee is not generally accepted, a simultaneous extension of benefits and lowering of taxes, which purely fiscal considerations might at times suggest, weakens the *quid pro quo* status of a social insurance program, threatens its public acceptance, and hence the dynamic influence this social invention is likely to exert.

It is for this reason that I could conceive it would be quite consistent for an economist who took into account not only the purely economic repercussions of social insurance programs *but also the function these programs were brought into being to perform and the environment in which they were operating* to support a proposal to subordinate social insurance financing to general fiscal considerations in New Zealand or Great Britain, but oppose it in the United States at the present time.

3. *The Appropriateness of the Use of Pay Roll Taxes.* The emergence of stage III will also require a reconsideration of the particular types of taxes to be utilized for social insurance financing. This is especially true of the pay roll tax. One of the more evident stigmata of social insurance programs in the past has been the fact that the programs were financed in whole or in part by employer contributions or taxes.

The appropriateness of reliance on taxes of this type has always given rise to uneasy discussion. Economists who have explored problems of incidence have reached differing conclusions but appear to be in agreement on one point; namely, that the effect of the tax varies considerably as between different industries. The feasibility of shifting varies with the degree of monopolization of the industry, the elasticity of demand for the product, relative significance of labor costs in total expenses of production and the degree of labor organization. From the social point of view, the effect of these taxes has been deplored by those who have reached the conclusion that in general the pay roll tax is shifted to workers, whether it be via lower wages or unemployment or through elimination of wage increases that would otherwise have occurred or through increased prices. Again, those who believe that so far as possible tax policy should be neutral in regard to the process of production itself have criticized the pay roll tax because, being imposed upon an item of cost, it may cause otherwise uneconomic shifts in methods of production: a substitution of labor by capital equipment due solely to the "artificially" increased price of labor.

A survey of the literature on this point suggests that faced with these real disadvantages of the pay roll tax, its defenders have been forced to fall back upon the following justifications for its continuance:

1. The argument of fiscal expediency. The pay roll tax is fiscally a very convenient and richly yielding source of revenue for a social insurance program. It provides a relatively steady source of income, which, once earmarked for this specific purpose, may, like the gasoline taxes used for road construction, become identified in the public mind with a particular program and thus in a sense be secure from appropriation for other purposes. Fiscally, also, the pay roll tax was convenient for it facilitated the use of the employer as a tax-collecting agent; when he is paying taxes himself he can simultaneously collect the employees' contribution and his joint liability provides certain controls on the correctness of tax payments. Finally, so long as the fiscal incidence of the pay roll tax is not widely understood, the simultaneous imposition of a tax on employers renders more acceptable the new tax policy introduced by social insurance; namely, the imposition of an income tax on all wage earners which is at best proportional rather than progressive and which has no personal allowances. Workers "do not feel so badly" about the new tax when it is explained that their employers too are contributing to a fund that is, after all, to benefit workers alone.

2. The brake-upon-extravagance argument. A second defense of use and retention of the pay roll tax builds upon the desirability of enlisting the interest of employers in the effective and economical administration

of the program. If they contribute they have a financial interest in guarding against extravagance or excessive liberalization and because they contribute they may rightly claim to have some say in administrative and policy determinations. It is this last argument, incidentally, which Beveridge finally falls back upon after having built up what to most readers would seem to be a convincing case against retention of the pay roll tax.

3. The argument of incentive taxation. The third defense of retention of the pay roll tax appeals to the potentialities of incentive taxation. So long as there is a pay roll tax it can be varied upwards or downwards in such a way as to reward or penalize employers for action tending to reduce or increase the prevalence of the risk insured against.

I suggest that the validity of these theoretical justifications of the pay roll tax cannot be evaluated without reference to which stage of social insurance evolution is under discussion. Thus the fiscal justification is powerful and necessary in stage I and perhaps also in stage II. But in stage III I suggest it has little validity. Once social insurance programs have become almost universal in coverage, every voter has a stake in the continuity of appropriations to make good the payments guaranteed. Indeed the very fact of universality of coverage is an indication of a change in social attitudes. For it is a response to a widespread desire for minimum security; social insurance has become the device through which society ensures that this new demand can make itself felt. The need for earmarked taxes as a bulwark against failures to appropriate adequate funds is no longer so necessary in view of the changed attitude.

Nor are the other fiscal justifications very strong in stage III. By the time this stage is reached workers will necessarily have become accustomed to the payment of taxes. Furthermore, as knowledge of the incidence of the employers' contribution becomes more widespread the strength of the argument that "employers too are contributing" is less convincing.

The brake-upon-extravagance theory retains some validity in stage III in the sense that a powerful lobby against undue liberalization is more likely to appear if the earmarked taxpayers are also relatively small groups with a strongly developed group consciousness. But it is also possible that concentration of the immediate impact of social insurance taxes upon a relatively small group may give that group a disproportional power to block liberalizations that are desired by the majority of the citizens. This consideration is especially important in a program of universal coverage: a country dependent on export trade may find itself unable to afford a certain level of social insurance bene-

fits when the cost of these is assessed against an item in costs of production although with a different method of financing the desired degree
of income redistribution could have been attained.

Finally, retention of the pay roll tax for incentive taxation reasons
can be urged only in certain limited fields at any stage of social insurance development. It obviously has no application in an old age and
survivors' insurance program or in a general disability program. And
even in regard to unemployment insurance its sphere of application is
likely to be relatively restricted if it is to be limited to those types of
unemployment, and these alone, which are in any real sense within the
employer's control. It seems probable that the incentive tax theory
alone cannot justify retention of the pay roll tax as a major source
of revenue for a comprehensive social insurance program covering all
citizens and a wide variety of risks.

III

It is, I think, evident that in this country we are today in stage II.
Whether we shall ever emerge into stage III I do not know. Obviously
many of the developments which have carried other countries into stage
III are already present. The demand for broadened coverage is strong;
the extension of duration of unemployment insurance benefit is already
under way; we are already contemplating the introduction of new risks
such as disability; we have adopted dependents' benefits in our most
important program and minimum benefits are now accepted in principle in all programs. Above all, with each year of the operation of social
insurance programs, the country is becoming more familiar with the
activities of government in this field.

On the other hand, the country as a whole is, I suspect, far from
accepting the idea of public responsibility for assuring minimum income. Furthermore, the implementation of such a policy will meet tremendous technical difficulties in a country where standards of living
and real wages are still so far from homogeneous. And the influence of
the labor movement, which in other countries has been the dynamic
agent forcing social insurance in the direction of stage III, is likely to
be somewhat different. For organized labor in America holds a firm
belief in industrial action, with high wage rates as the goal. It is somewhat suspicious of dependents' benefits, and above all insists on the re-
flection of higher earnings in higher benefits. If the country has to face
a continuance of these differentials over and above any minimum maintenance benefit—more specifically if using a social insurance program
even to assure a minimum of $20 a month means also using government
programs to assure monthly benefits of $120 a month—the proposal to

raise minimums toward the maintenance level may meet strong resistance.

But so long as we are in stage II I believe that economists will have to recognize the impossibility of securing a neat and consistent social insurance program. Equally impossible will be a complete reconciliation of the objectives of our social insurance program with policies which are "economically desirable" in the sense of those contributing to a maximization of production. In these circumstances, therefore, while as economists we should at all times draw attention as honestly as possible to the economic implications of social insurance programs operating at any given moment, we must exercise restraint in inferring from this analysis that a specific course of action "ought" to be adopted.

In conclusion, I venture to suggest that in studying social inventions such as social insurance, we run the risk not only of spending our time on the discussion of irrelevant issues but also of drawing false conclusions as to what is desirable policy unless we recognize: (a) that the institution in question was brought into being—invented, if you will—to carry out a specific function; (b) that the operation of the institution can never be studied except in a specific social and economic environmental context, which must at all times be clearly stated as the premises from which the analysis proceeds; (c) that the prevailing relevant environment may change, and that the existence of the new institution itself may be instrumental in bringing about some of these changes; (d) that these environmental changes may change both the function to be performed and the techniques which are available for achieving the objective.

REPORT TO THE PRESIDENT OF THE UNITED STATES ON THE LABOR DISPUTE IN THE BASIC STEEL INDUSTRY

I. FINDINGS AND RECOMMENDATIONS; GENERAL SUMMARY

The following is a summary of the Board's findings on the chief matters in issue between the parties, and a statement of the Board's recommendations for a fair and equitable settlement of the dispute.

A. THE ISSUES BETWEEN THE PARTIES

The issues arise out of union demands based on reopening clauses executed in 1948, amending the 1947 collective-bargaining contracts between the companies in the basic steel industry and the union.

The main issues are—

1. *Wage-rate increases.*—The union requests a general wage-rate increase of 12½ cents per hour. This the companies refuse.

2. *Social insurance program.*—This is defined as insurance against death or total and permanent disability, benefit payments during temporary disability caused by sickness or accident occurring off the job, and hospital and surgical benefits. The union's estimate of the cost of providing the benefits which it requests is 6.27 cents per hour on the basis of a 2,000-hour workyear. It requests that the companies pay the full cost. As to the request for this program, some of the companies reject it entirely and some have indicated a willingness to bargain with respect to it.

3. *Pensions.*—The union requests a program paid for entirely by the companies providing a uniform pension of $125 per month for each worker retiring voluntarily at age 65 or later, and also a pension of $150 per month for a worker retired for permanent disability after 10 years of service, to be reduced to $125 per month at age 65. The union's estimate of the cost of this program is 11.23 cents per hour per worker on a basis of a 2,000-hour workyear. This demand the companies reject on the ground that the subject of pensions is not now bargainable under the reopening clauses.

B. THE ISSUE OF WAGE-RATE INCREASES; ECONOMIC ANALYSIS

Under this heading the Board has considered the economic arguments of both sides, not only as they relate to the steel industry but also as they relate to the economy as a whole. While these economic considerations have a more direct bearing on wage rates than on the other two issues of social insurance and pensions, they serve also in part as the economic justification for the recommendations made hereafter on such other issues.

1. *Criteria for conclusions on raising wage rates or labor costs*

There are no mathematical formulae by which to settle the question of whether wage rates or labor costs should be increased at any particular time in a particular industry or particular plant. The Board seeks to form its best judgment based upon two major inquiries:

a. The first major inquiry.—Is the present position of the steelworkers inequitable in earnings as compared with those of other groups in the economy? This involves the following three subsidiary considerations:

(1) Are the steelworkers in an inequitable position as compared with other industrial workers?

(2) Are they suffering any inequity as compared with certain other groups whose economic welfare depends substantially upon the steel industry, namely, the corporations themselves, their stockholders, and the consumers of steel?

(3) Are they suffering any inequity as compared with all other income-receiving groups in the general economy outside the steel industry?

The subsidiary criterion listed above as (2) includes a consideration of employers' "ability to pay" increased wage rates; and among the important factors to be considered in such determination are:

(*a*) The increased productivity (output per man-hour) of the industry;

(*b*) The level of profits earned over a period of years and currently;

(*c*) The percentage of plant capacity that must be utilized in order to "break even";

(*d*) The probable movement of raw materials, prices, and other costs.

b. The second major inquiry.—What would be the probable effects of granting the union's demands on the general level of economic activity in the country as a whole?

The argument advanced by the companies that, on a reopening dispute such as this, the only criterion to be considered is the change that has occurred since the contract was originally made, is not tenable here. The parties themselves did not ascribe this meaning to the reopening provision, as was evidenced by the facts and arguments they presented; they treated the merits of the dispute as though it was the negotiation of a new wage rate. Furthermore, the argument cannot apply to items like social insurance and pensions where neither was originally included in the contract.

2. Findings and conclusions relative to the above criteria

  a. Steelworkers in relation to workers in other industries.—

(1) The steelworkers' present average hourly earnings of about \$1.65 compare favorably with all other manufacturing workers. Their average hourly earnings have risen more in cents per hour since 1939 and 1941 than those of manufacturing workers as a whole, and more than those of the durable-goods workers; in very few industries, manufacturing or non-manufacturing, have hourly earnings risen more in cents.

(2) On balance the steelworkers are not suffering from a wage-rate inequity in terms of their relations to the workers of other industries.

  *b. Steelworkers in relation to other groups whose economic welfare depends on the steel industry.—*Of such groups those to be compared with the steelworkers are the corporations themselves, the stockholders, and consumers of steel.

This involves the subject of ability to pay increased wage rates as related to profits, dividends, and prices. Taking up the factors to be considered, as listed above, and other relevant considerations, the Board finds:

(1) Productivity: The union has not satisfied the Board that steelworkers do not share equitably in the increased productivity of the industry.

  (*a*) It has not succeeded in proving its contention that productivity has risen by 49.5 percent since 1939.

  (*b*) It is the belief of the Board that, as hereinafter explained, wage rates in a particular industry should not be tied directly to productivity in that industry but rather should be related to the general industrial rise in productivity, and that any excesses of productivity in any one industry over the general average should provide primarily the means of reducing the prices of the products of that industry. Therefore even if the union had succeeded in showing that the 1939–49 rise in labor productivity was 49.5 percent, it still would not establish an inequity by showing that the real average hourly earnings of steelworkers (present average hourly money earnings deflated by the general rise in the cost of living since 1939) had risen only 14 percent since 1939.

The evidence before us reveals that for our whole national economy output per man-hour increased from 1899 to 1939 at an annual rate of about 2 percent, but that, in the decade which followed, the general rise in productivity was at a lesser rate. Therefore, the steelworkers' rise of 14 percent in real average hourly earnings during this decade is fairly consonant with the apparent rise in labor productivity in the whole economy during the same period and reflects no inequity in that regard.

(*c*) The union compared the productivity of 1939, a year of low volume, with 1948, a year of practically maximum volume, which is an unsound comparison.

(*d*) In computing an index of productivity for the steel industry, the union used the assumption that the production mix of the industry after 1945 was substantially the same as during the war years. This assumption is open to serious question.

(*e*) Trustworthy productivity studies can be made only if the companies provide full and accurate data upon which such studies can be made. Such data were not offered in evidence.

(*f*) The companies also made invalid comparisons in their own productivity claims by insisting that an index of money rather than real average hourly earnings was the proper comparison with the productivity index.

(2) The level of profits of the steel industry, and labor's share therein:

(*a*) The Board has decided to accept as a basis for comparison the "reported" rather than the "adjusted" profit figures. Each party claimed these figures should be adjusted—upward by the union, downward by the companies—but the Board finds that it is impossible accurately to compute the amount of adjustments which each side has urged should be made.

(*b*) The reported profits after taxes of the steel industry in 1948 were substantial, and in the first half of 1949 they rose even higher. In 1948 profits after taxes were 511.9 million dollars as compared with an average of 271.3 million dollars in the period 1940–41, a rise of 89 percent; and in the first half of 1949, the annual rate of profit was 606.6 million dollars, or 124 percent above the 1940–41 average.

(*c*) The rates of profit—the dollar amounts of these profits figured as percentages of net worth—must be substantially discounted, however, for we are now considering 1948 and 1949 dollars which are considerably less valuable than those of 1939 or 1940 or 1941, whereas a large part of the capital assets in the net worth is in terms of dollars of higher value.

(*d*) The profits of the industry stated as a percentage of sales are also substantial for the year 1948 and the first quarter of 1949 (6.3 percent and 6.8 percent, respectively) ; but are not out of line with comparable prewar years like 1940 and 1941 when the percentages were 8.2 and 6.1.

(*e*) In evaluating the amount of profits in any given year like 1948 or 1949, to determine whether the workers have received a fair share thereof, it is necessary also to consider the low level of profits or lack of profits in other years of the business cycle. The prosperity of a volatile industry like steel and its ability to pay should be judged over a longer range.

(3) Break-even point: In considering the break-even point, which is the next factor in appraising the companies' ability to pay, the Board finds that it is unable to accept the union's estimate of the break-even point for the industry of 32 percent under present wage and cost levels. At the same time the Board doubts that the estimates made by some of the companies running as high as 65 or 70 percent reflect the actual break-even points for the larger tonnage producers. The Board's conclusion is that the present break-even point, for most of the large tonnage producers, is somewhere above the union's figure of 32 percent and below the companies' estimates of 55 to 70 percent. These conclusions are reached for the following reasons:

(*a*) Reliable supporting data are lacking for all the estimates made, and the union made certain assumptions which are unacceptable.

(*b*) Most of the companies failed to inform the Board of their break-even points; none of them provided the data needed to make a reliable estimate; and the Board believes each of the major companies could have indicated its own break-even point and the basis thereof.

(*c*) The union's testimony that the break-even point before the war was at 45 percent of capacity was not controverted.

(*d*) The favorable course of profits in 1949 as compared with 1948 indicates that the break-even point has become lower since 1948, because in the second quarter of 1949 when operations were at the average rate of 91 percent, profits before taxes were about $230,000,000 as compared with the same quarter in 1948 when operations were at 90 percent and the profit figure $170,000,000, a rise of $60,000,000, or about 35 percent, at approximately the same rate of operations. A comparison of the first half in 1948 with the second quarter of 1949 leads to similar conclusions.

(4) With respect to the factor of probable movement of raw materials prices and other costs, the Board has taken into consideration the large decline since 1948 in the prices of certain materials, notably scrap; but it has also noted the recent recovery in some of these prices. It has also noted rises since 1948 in the prices of certain other important materials, such as iron ore and coal. Experience shows that scrap prices quickly respond to increased demand, and that if rates of operation rise substantially, the price of scrap moves upward rapidly.

(5) When years of similar operation rates are compared, there is no substantiation of the union's claim that labor has been receiving a continually smaller share, or that ownership equity has been receiving an increasingly larger share of the industry's sales dollar. If the share of ownership be defined in terms of dividends, its rate of return becomes very low, for the total dollar amounts of dividends, when

paid, have consistently been only minor fractions of profits after taxes.

(6) The industry's recent policy of modernizing and expanding physical plant and facilities has absorbed most of its recent substantial profits. Given the country's peacetime and possible wartime needs for larger steel-making capacity, the program seems entirely desirable. But there is a question as to whether a larger part of the financing of such long-term assets should not have been through long-term debt instead of recent profits, thus leaving more of the current profits for dividends to stockholders and for social insurance and for setting up reserves for pensions.

(7) The plant modernization and expansion program should result in efficiencies which, other things being equal, will better enable the companies to meet the cost of the insurance and pension plans recommended, and also to look toward a lower level of prices for their products.

(8) There are no inequities of steelworkers at present which require redress through a general wage-rate increase; and the recommendation is that the union withdraw its request for a general wage-rate increase.

(9) However, with increased efficiency and lowered costs resulting from the plant-modernization program, and with no great decrease in the demand for steel, there should be continued and higher profits. If these profits do not result in benefit to the consumer in the form of lower prices, there would be justification for the union to renew its demand for increase of wage rates in order better to participate in the industry's prosperity.

c. *Steelworkers in relation to other income-receiving groups.*—The cost of living has remained stable within the last year; in fact it has slowly declined. The post-war race between rising wage rates and rising costs of living has been called off by the operation of economic forces. Therefore there is no inequity in respect to other income-receiving groups in the general economy.

d. *Findings and conclusions on increased wage rates in relation to economy as a whole.*—With respect to the second major criterion mentioned above—weighing the effect of granting the union's demands on the general levels of economic activity in the country as a whole—the Board finds:

(1) While the Board's findings and recommendations are based on the facts and figures of the steel industry alone, there is a probability that a wage-rate increase in steel would be urged as a pattern to be followed in other industries; this in turn might well cause price dislocations, with adverse effects on the general economy and on the steel industry itself.

(2) The course of the "recession" which started late in 1948 and manifested itself in increased unemployment and in a decline in gross national product seems to have flattened out or turned upward. In three of the four main components of the gross national product, slight increases were experienced in the second quarter of 1949. Since the low point of July 1949 there have been upward movements in production and employment, with declines in unemployment; this has been established by official Government publications. As late as the day before yesterday, September 8, 1949, these improvements were again reported by the Bureau of the Census and the Federal Reserve Board. Steel operations, which were at slightly over 70 percent of capacity in July 1949, have moved up steadily to a point more than 86 percent of capacity as of last week.

(3) While there may be conditions in particular industries which require correction through wage rate adjustments, in general it seems desirable at this time to stabilize the level of wage rates. In the steel industry we have not found such conditions or inequities and, for all the reasons stated, do not believe there should be a wage rate adjustment now. General stability is desirable now in order that consumers and dealers may have confidence in the price structure and resume less restricted buying habits.

3. Economic justification for social insurance and pensions

(a) The estimated net cost of these two programs, based upon the liberal assumption that labor costs average 50 percent of total production cost, would provide an increase of only 2½ percent of total costs on operations of 2,000 workhours per worker per year.

(b) The substantial profits of the steel industry in the past two years and the current reversal of the downward trend in production satisfy the Board that the net cost of the insurance and pension plans herein recommended can be absorbed without unduly narrowing the profit margins of the industry or its ability to hold or even lower its prices.

(c) Whereas increases in wage rates depend upon profits of companies under relatively current conditions and over relatively short periods of time, social insurance and pensions—especially pensions—involve long-range considerations because, once installed, they cannot well be discontinued.

(d) For that reason, although immediate and generally foreseeable ability to pay is very important in wage-rate determinations, it is not as important in the questions of social insurance and pensions. Here the more important consideration is the social obligation which the Board finds rests upon industry to provide insurance against the economic hazards of modern industrial life, including retirement allowances, in an adequate amount as supplementary to the amount of the security furnished by Government.

(*e*) The inauguration and operation of insurance and pension programs will make a considerable contribution to the attainment of the economic stability so necessary at this time.   With the knowledge that the economic hazards of life will be at least partially met, workers will be more apt to help sustain consumption spending at a high stable level.

(*f*) For these reasons and those elsewhere herein indicated, the Board believes that insurance and pension programs should have priority at this time.

C. SOCIAL INSURANCE AND PENSIONS

1. *Findings and conclusions as to both*

(*a*) Social insurance and pensions should be considered a part of normal business costs to take care of temporary and permanent depreciation in the human "machine," in much the same way as provision is made for depreciation and insurance of plant and machinery.   This obligation should be among the first charges on revenues.

(*b*) As indicated in the foregoing economic discussion, the net cost of the social insurance and pension plans herein recommended can be absorbed by the companies without unduly narrowing the profit margin of the industry or its ability to hold or even lower its prices.

(*c*) Although the steel industry has kept pace with other industries in wages and other industrial relations matters, it has lagged behind other leading basic industries in social insurance and pensions.

(*d*) The fully integrated companies before us now have social insurance and retirement plans for such of their employees as are in their railroad or coal-mining operations, and this further supports the Board's conclusion that the steelworkers are now entitled to these types of protection.

(*e*) Social insurance and pension programs with the types of coverage requested by the union in this dispute have become prevalent in American industry and have been inaugurated either by the unilateral action of employers or, to an increasing extent, through collective bargaining.

(*f*) The concept of providing social insurance and pensions for workers in industry has become an accepted part of modern American thinking.   Unless government provides such insurance in adequate amount, industry should step in to fill the gap.

(*g*) Government (except in four States) has failed to provide social insurance (as defined herein) for industrial workers generally, and has supplied old-age retirement benefits in amounts which are not adequate to provide an American minimum standard of living.

(*h*) The recent trend in programs resulting from collective bargaining is toward complete financing of the plan by the employer, or toward lowering the employees' cost in existing contributory plans.

2. Findings and conclusions on social insurance

(*a*) Social insurance plans are now included in some 380 existing collective-bargaining agreements between the United Steelworkers of America and firms both within and without the basic steel industry. Of these the Board had information on some 300 plans, of which over 80 percent were noncontributory. These plans, in which the cost is paid solely by the employer, almost invariably provide for a lower level of benefits than those requested by the union in the present case; and the costs of such plans are definitely lower, on the basis of a 2,000-hour workyear, than the cost of 6.27 cents per hour which the union is requesting here.

(*b*) It is recommended as fair and equitable under all the circumstances, that a social insurance plan be incorporated into the collective-bargaining agreements of the industry. The details and specific benefits of the plans should be determined through collective bargaining between each company and the union. The plans should be paid for by the employers without contribution by the employees; but should be limited in net cost to a maximum of about $80 per year per employee, or 4 cents per hour, on a basis of a 2,000-hour workyear.

(*c*) The recommended net cost is meant to be the total cost, not a cost in addition to what any company is now incurring under its existing insurance plan for employees within the bargaining unit; therefore any plan which may be agreed upon between a company and the union shall not be in addition to any existing plan which the company may have but in substitution therefor; nor should any company be expected to provide duplicating sickness benefits where provision therefor is made by State law, except to the extent that the amount agreed on exceeds the amount payable under such laws. This will result in a diminution of the cost of the new social insurance plan for all companies which are now paying all or any part of the cost of existing plans, to the extent of the amounts of such present costs.

3. Findings and conclusions on pensions

(*a*) The subject of pensions is not bargainable at this time under the terms of the reopening clause providing for the right in either party in 1949 to negotiate for a general and uniform change in rates of pay and/or for described social insurance.

(*b*) However, the subject of pensions is bargainable under the law as interpreted by the National Labor Relations Board as to all the companies. Pensions are not included in the written agreement and "with respect to unwritten terms dealing with 'wages, hours and other terms and conditions of employment,' the obligation remains on both parties to bargain continuously."

(*c*) Such pension plans as are now in effect in the basic steel industry were the result of unilateral action by employers and are generally inadequate even as a minimum supplement to the amounts payable as old-age pensions under the Social Security Act, when compared with recognized minimum requirements of elderly individuals or couples.

(*d*) The level of pensions requested by the union in this case, however, is higher than that prevailing or agreed on where such plans are in effect.

(*e*) It is recommended as fair and equitable under all the circumstances that pension plans be established in this industry, with the cost to be borne by the employers without contribution from the employees. The details of such plans should be determined through collective bargaining between each company and the union.

(1) Pensions should be limited in net cost to a maximum of about $120 per employee per year, or 6 cents per hour on a basis of a 2,000-hour work-year. Based on the union's cost estimates, this will provide, when added to average Social Security old-age benefits, about $100 per month on retirement at age 65 of the average employee.

(2) The recommended net cost is meant to be the total cost, not a cost in addition to what any company is now incurring under its own pension plan for employees within the bargaining unit. Therefore any plan agreed upon between a company and the union should not be in addition to any existing plan which the company may already have, but in substitution therefor.

(3) Since the problems involved in a pension program are more complicated than those faced in social insurance programs, and because the costs are greater and the program less susceptible to change from year to year, it is recommended that a joint study in the industry should be made on pensions. Such a study is necessary before intelligent bargaining over a pension program can be concluded.

(4) Among the matters which will have to be resolved in collective bargaining are these: Should the plan be handled through an insurance company or through a trust fund and how may the parties participate in the supervision; how shall the accrued liability for past service be treated; shall there be provision for employees retired through permanent disability below the age of 65; what shall be the minimum length of service to be eligible for pensions; shall the payments be proportioned to length of service or amount of income, or shall the pensions be at a flat amount; shall withdrawing employees have any rights if they leave the company's employ before

they are 65; shall retirement at 65 be compulsory or shall there be some means provided for making exceptions, whether by mutual agreement of the employer and employee, or otherwise; and, having agreed on other principles and details, how large should the benefits be in light of the maximum cost stipulated?

D. SCOPE OF BOARD FINDINGS AND RECOMMENDATIONS

1. The findings and recommendations herein contained are based largely on evidence relating to 19 leading steel-producing companies as a group, and do not necessarily reflect the circumstances of any individual company. Unlike the recommendations on wage rates and on bargainability, the recommendations on social insurance and pensions are not intended to apply automatically to individual companies.

2. With respect to those companies which are among the group of 19 leading steel-producing companies, however, there is a presumption that the above-mentioned recommendations of this Board should apply. In spite of this presumption, there should be a return to collective bargaining in order to provide an opportunity to each company to prove that the considerations, conclusions, and recommendations herein discussed are in fact not applicable to it.

3. With respect to companies which are not included in the group of 19 leading steel-producing companies, there should be bargaining between the union and each company to ascertain what deviations, if any, should be made from the general recommendations.

E. COLLECTIVE BARGAINING

1. In collective bargaining in the basic steel industry, the practice has developed by which almost the entire industry generally follows the pattern set by United States Steel Corporation and perhaps a few of the other large companies in their contracts with the union.

2. As a result there is frequently little or no serious bargaining or discussion between most of the individual employers and the union.

3. This practice is clearly a variation from the accepted concept of collective bargaining as defined in the statutes and interpretations; it tends to promote a feeling of dissatisfaction and disharmony between the parties which makes cooperation difficult.

4. Now that the organizational phase of union activities has been passed, the field ought to be reexamined to see whether the public interest requires any modification in the definition and theories of collective bargaining in accordance with the new situation faced not only in the steel industry but in other industries where varying kinds of industry-wide rather than individual collective bargaining have grown up.

INDEX

479